Computer Industry Almanac

Egil Juliussen
Portia Isaacson

Editors

Luanne Kruse

Managing Editor

A Gift from the Estate of
Michael Hart
www.gutenberg.org

Computer Industry Almanac
8111 LBJ Freeway
Dallas, Texas 75251-1313
214/231-8735
MCI Telex 650/319-5215

ACKNOWLEDGMENTS

The Editors wish to thank the many contributors to Computer Industry Almanac. Without the input, counsel, hard work and support of the individuals listed below, this book could not have been completed.

Dale N. Dukes
Contributing Editor

Production: Betty Thompson
                     Bette Hamm
                     Toril McGowan
                     Wendy Shaw

Editorial: Shirley Kout
                     Vanessa Evans
                     Tom Byrne

Research: Sylvia Oesterwinter
                     Joyce Boeke
                     Jack Ware

Technical Support: Art Davis
                     Allen Isaacson
                     Harry Littlejohn

Cover Design: David Fiegenschue, Fiegenschue Designs, Dallas, TX

COMPUTER INDUSTRY ALMANAC HIGHLIGHTS

DISCLAIMER

COMPUTER INDUSTRY ALMANAC makes no representation or warranties with respect to the accuracy or completeness of the contents hereof and SPECIFICALLY DISCLAIMS ANY IMPLIED WARRANTIES OF MERCHANTABILITY OR FITNESS FOR ANY PARTICULAR PURPOSE.

COMPUTER INDUSTRY ALMANAC does not decide wagers.

TRADEMARKS

Most computer hardware and software brand names have trademarks or registered trademarks. Since COMPUTER INDUSTRY ALMANAC lists numerous product names from multiple sources, the individual trademarks have not been listed.

DESKTOP PUBLISHING

COMPUTER INDUSTRY ALMANAC is composed in Microsoft Word and printed "camera-ready" on the Apple LaserWriter. Tabular data and directories were first entered in Paradox from Ansa.

COMMENTS AND SUGGESTIONS

Users of COMPUTER INDUSTRY ALMANAC are encouraged to submit comments and suggestions for inclusion in subsequent editions. Unfortunate omissions are inevitable due to the scope and dynamic nature of the computer industry and its boundaries and the thousands of decisions the editors had to make for inclusion or exclusion. We apologize in advance for our oversights and omissions.

The information and statistical data contained herein have been obtained from sources that we believe to be reliable, but no attempt has been made to verify data or reconcile discrepancies. The Editors believe that the eclectic nature of an almanac, with inevitable resulting conflicts and controversies, add to the reader's fun. We hope you enjoy finding the problems and will not hesitate to send us your comments and suggestions for improving the accuracy, consistency, and completeness of future editions.

FOREWORD

COMPUTER INDUSTRY ALMANAC is a convenient reference for anyone who wants to understand the fast-moving world of computers. Ideal for the industry newcomer and the interested observer, it's also an insider's handbook. In one compact volume, the ALMANAC brings into focus the influential people, products, and trends that make this industry endlessly fascinating.

The ALMANAC encompasses a remarkably varied realm, with facts and forecasts on systems ranging from small-scale personal computers to multimillion dollar mainframes and supercomputers. Comprehensive directories list corporate trend-setters, industry associations, user groups, and key publications. Thoughtful overviews and definitive rankings--published together for the first time--put it all in perspective.

With the ALMANAC on your reference shelf, you can identify award-winning advertisers or discover upcoming conferences. You can study employment statistics or examine salary surveys. You can pore over financial data or locate computer museums.

Whether your goal is amusement or advancement, you'll use COMPUTER INDUSTRY ALMANAC to keep pace with today's technologies and tomorrow's trends.

SOURCES

COMPUTER INDUSTRY ALMANAC gratefully acknowledges the following publications, companies, and agencies that allowed reprint permission for information included in this edition.

A. S. Hansen, Inc.
1417 Lake Cook Road
Deerfield, IL 60015
Phone: 312/948-7400

Addison-Wesley Publishing Company
Route 128
Reading, MA 01867
Phone: 617/944-3700

American Electronics Association
P.O. Box 10045
2670 Hanover Street
Palo Alto, CA 94303
Phone: 415/857-9300

American Marketing Association
Suite 1211
310 Madison Avenue
New York, NY 10017
Phone: 212/687-3280

Association for Computing Machinery
11 West 42nd Street
New York, NY 10036
Phone: 212/869-7440

Association of Business Publishers
205 E 42nd Street
New York, NY 10017
Phone: 212/661-6360

B. Dalton
BOOKSELLERS
One Corporate Center
7505 Metro Boulevard
Minneapolis, MN 55435
Phone: 612/893-7000

Billboard Publications, Inc
1515 Broadway
New York, NY 10036
Phone: 212/764-7300

Bureau of Labor Statistics
See: U.S. Bureau of Labor Statistics

Business Software Review
Suite 200
9100 Keystone Crossing
Indianapolis, IN 46240
Phone: 317/844-7461

C Systems, Ltd.
P.O. Box 639
590 Danbury Rd.
Ridgefield, CT 06877
Phone: 203/438-0652

CLIO Magazine
CLIO Enterprises, Inc.
336 East 59th Street
New York, NY 10022
Phone: 212/593-1900

College Placement Council
62 Highland Avenue
Bethlehem, PA 18017
Phone: 215/868-1421

Computer Intelligence
Suite 210
3344 North Torrey Pines Court
La Jolla, CA 92037
Phone: 619/450-1667

(Continued next page)

SOURCES (Continued)

Computer Museum
300 Congress Street
Boston, MA 02210
Phone: 617/426-2800

Computer Reseller News
600 Community Drive
Manhasset, NY 11030
Phone: 516/365-4600

Computer Retail News
600 Community Drive
Manhasset, NY 11030
Phone: 516/365-4600

Computing Sciences Accreditation Board, Inc.
345 East 47th Street
New York, NY 10017
Phone: 212/705-7314

Consumer Electronics Shows
2001 Eye Street N.W.
Washington, DC 20006
Phone: 202/457-8700

Datamation
875 Third Avenue
New York, NY 10022
Phone: 212/605-9400

Derby Information Systems Corporation
Suite 302
2610 Hillegass
Berkeley, CA 94704
Phone: 415/841-1234

Electronic Business
Cahners Building
275 Washington Street
Newton, MA 02158
Phone: 617/964-3030

Electronic Industries Association
2001 Eye Street N.W.
Washington, DC 20006
Phone: 202/457-4900

Electronic News
Fairchild Publications
7 East 12th Street
New York, NY 10003
Phone: 212/741-4230

Entrepreneur Magazine
2311 Pontius Avenue
Los Angeles, CA 90064
Phone: 213/477-1011

Forbes
Forbes Building
60 Fifth Avenue
New York, NY 10011
Phone: 212/620-2379

Fortune (Time Inc.)
Time & Life Building
Rockefeller Center
New York, NY 10020
Phone: 212/586-1212

Future Computing
Suite 1300
8111 LBJ Freeway
Dallas, TX 75251
Phone: 214/437-2400

Gartner Group, Inc.
P.O. Box 10212
72 Cummings Point Road
Stamford, CT 06904
Phone: 203/964-0096

(Continued next page)

SOURCES (Continued)

ICP (International Computer Programs, Inc.)
Suite 200
9100 Keystone Crossing
Indianapolis, IN 46240
Phone: 317/844-7461

Inc.
38 Commercial Wharf
Boston, MA 02110
Phone: 617/227-4700

Infomart
1950 Stemmons Freeway
Dallas, TX 75207
Phone: 214/746-3500

Information Industry Association
Suite 800
555 New Jersey Avenue N.W.
Washington, DC 20001
Phone: 202/639-8262

In-Stat Inc.
P.O. Box 8130
7320 E. 6th Avenue
Scottsdale, AZ 85252
Phone: 602/994-9560

Institute of Electrical & Electronics Engineers
345 E 47th Street
New York, NY 10017
Phone: 212/705-7555

Institute of Electrical & Electronics Engineers
Computer Society
1730 Massachusetts Avenue N.W.
Washington, DC 20036
Phone: 202/371-0101

Integrated Circuit Engineering
15022 North 75th Street
Scottsdale, AZ 85260
Phone: 602/998-9780

International Computer Chess Association
Department of Computing Science
Jonathon Schaeffer
University of Alberta
Edmonton, Alberta T6G 2H1
Phone: 403/432-5198

National Computer Graphics Association
Suite 200
2722 Merrilee Drive
Fairfax, VA 22031
Phone: 703/698-9600

National Science Foundation
See: U.S. National Science Foundation

National Society of Professional Engineers
1420 King Street
Alexandria, VA 22314
Phone: 703/684-2800

Newton-Evans Research Company, Inc.
Suite 204
10176 Baltimore National Pike
Ellicott City, MD 21043
Phone: 301/465-7316

Northern Business Information Inc.
157 Chambers Street
New York, NY 10007
Phone: 212/732-0775

(Continued next page)

SOURCES (Continued)

P.C. Letter
113 Somerset Street
Redwood City, CA 94062
Phone: 415/363-8080

PC Magazine
Ziff-Davis Publishing Company
One Park Avenue
New York, NY 10016
Phone: 212/503-5255

PC World
PC World Communications, Inc.
501 Second Street, Suite 600
San Francisco, CA 94107
Phone: 415/546-7722

Soft*letter
1679 Massachusetts Avenue
Cambridge, MA 02138
Phone: 617/868-0157

Softsel Computer Products, Inc.
P.O. Box 6080
546 N. Oak Street
Inglewood, CA 90312
Phone: 213/412-8296

Softsel Hot List
P.O. Box 6080
546 N. Oak Street
Inglewood, CA 90312
Phone: 213/412-8296

Software News
Sentry Publishing Company, Inc.
1900 West Park Drive
Westborough, MA 01581
Phone: 617/366-2031

Software Publishers Association
1111 19th Street N.W., Suite 1200
Washington, DC 20036
Phone: 202/452-1600

StoreBoard Inc.
8111 LBJ Freeway, 13th Floor
Dallas, TX 75251
Phone: 214/231-5964

U.S. Bureau of Labor Statistics
General Office Accounting Bldg Rm 1539
441 G Street N.W.
Washington, DC 20212
Phone: 202/523-1327

U.S. National Center for Education Statistics
200 Independence Avenue S.W.
Washington, DC 20202
Phone: 202/245-8430

U.S. National Science Foundation
1800 G. Street N.W.
Washington, DC 20550
Phone: 202/357-9859

Venture
521 Fifth Avenue
New York, NY 10175
Phone: 212/682-7373

Wall Street Journal
Dow Jones & Company, Inc.
P.O. Box 300
Princeton, NJ 08540
Phone: 609/452-2000

Workstation Laboratories
P.O. Box 368
Humboldt, AZ 86329
Phone:602/632-5322

COMPUTER INDUSTRY ALMANAC

TABLE OF CONTENTS

1 COMPUTER INDUSTRY OVERVIEW

The computer industry is not the largest industry--yet--but it will be number one by the turn of the century. The computer industry is already the most important industry. Computer technological prowess is now considered a most important resource (if not the most important) by many companies and by many countries. Most industrial countries, including the U.S., Japan, Brazil, and several European nations, are funding specific programs and using incentives to catch up or get ahead in computer technology.

The computer industry is also exciting and glamorous. There are many visionary and colorful people. Fortunes are made and fortunes are lost. Several people in the computer industry have even become centimillionaires before reaching the age of 30.

Explosive growth has been the norm of the computer industry. In fact, we have become so accustomed to spectacular growth that when the computer industry is settling down to growth rates that are normal for large industries, it is a major news story and is being called "the computer slump." The growth of the computer industry has slowed due to its sheer size. However, compared to other industries of similar size, the computer industry moves many times faster--no matter how the speed is measured: market growth rates, product life cycles, distribution channel changes, market segment evolution, or technological changes.

Fifteen years ago computers were normally hidden behind locked doors in specialized air conditioned rooms. Today computers are common on office desks and in homes. In 1978 there were 0.5 million computers in use in the U.S. Today there are 35 million computers in use. By 1995 over 100 million computers will be used in the U.S.

The improvement in computer technology has been phenomenal in the last 35 years. In this time span, the performance of the fastest computers has increased nearly a million times. At the same time, the price of entry-level computers has decreased by a factor of 1000. And, there is no end in sight. The performance and price/performance of computers will continue to improve at breakneck speeds.

The tremendous computer technological advances are impacting and overlapping other industries. For instance, microcomputer chips and boards have replaced electromechanical or other control systems in nearly all types of equipment ranging from microwave ovens, TVs, stereo systems, automobiles, cash registers, copiers, telephones, toys, oscilloscopes, and sewing machines to military weapon systems.

With such diversity and rapid changes it is helpful to have a common framework of what constitutes the computer industry. The next ten figures explain the structure of the computer industry--primarily from a product viewpoint. This product structure is then used throughout the COMPUTER INDUSTRY ALMANAC.

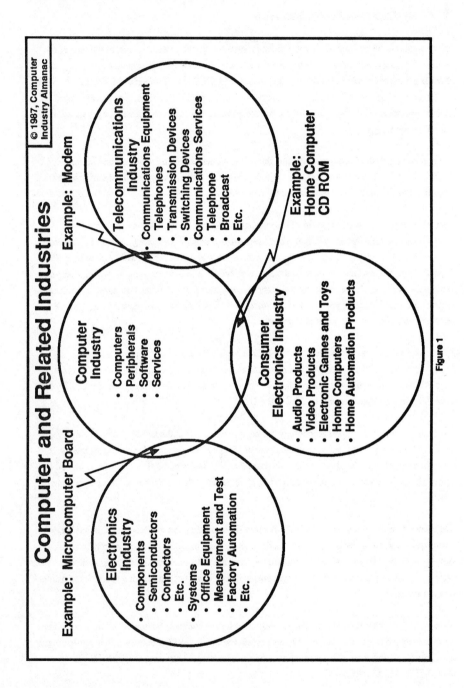

Figure 1

As seen in Figure 1, the computer industry overlaps considerably with three other industries. The biggest overlap is with the electronics industry which provides most of the components used to build computers and which also uses computers in many of its systems. Microcomputer boards are an example of products that are in both industries. The COMPUTER INDUSTRY ALMANAC has not included microcomputer boards as a product category or as a part of the sales forecasts.

The biggest overlap with the consumer electronics industry is home computers. Home computers or home PCs are included in the computer industry. CD ROM, based on the compact audio disk which can be a computer peripheral, is also an overlapping product. CD ROM will be an important computer peripherals product and is included in the computer industry.

The computer and telecommunications industries are also overlapping. Examples are modems, local networks, and micro/mainframe communications. These products are included in the COMPUTER INDUSTRY ALMANAC.

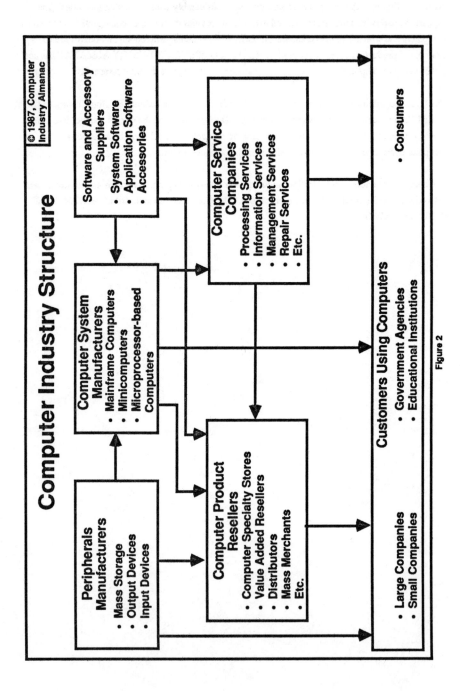

Figure 2

An overview of the computer industry structure is depicted in Figure 2. The three main product categories are shown at the top of the figure. There are basically three classes of computers. Mainframe computers are the fastest and largest computers and normally need special cooling equipment. Ten years ago there were clear distinctions between mainframe and minicomputers. Today the line is blurred. In general, a minicomputer is used in an office environment or industrial setting and is a cabinet-size computer. There are several types of microprocessor-based computers ranging from personal computers to supermicrocomputers. The line between minicomputers and microcomputers is also blurred.

There are three types of peripherals. Mass storage peripherals such as disks and tapes keep the data and programs that computers use. Output devices such as printers and displays show the results from the computers' calculations and information processing. Input devices such as keyboards and graphics tablets are used to enter data into the computer.

Software consists of two main types: system software and application software. System software manages the computer systems or provides tools for developing software. Application software accomplishes the users' tasks. Accessories range from computer paper and printer ribbons to surge protectors and diskette holders.

There are numerous computer services available. Examples are processing services which let users rent computer time, management services which will manage and run computer centers, and repair services which maintain and fix computers.

Product manufacturers and service providers sell their products directly to computer users or via a variety of computer product resellers. Computer specialty stores focus their energies on selling computers and related products and are the most important sales channel for small computers. Value added resellers (VARs) specialize in specific, narrow market segments (usually referred to as vertical markets). A distributor is primarily a middleman between the manufacturers and the resellers and usually does not sell to computer users. Mass merchants include stores such as consumer electronics stores, department stores, discount stores, and toy stores. All of these resellers, as well as many other resellers, are important sources of computer products.

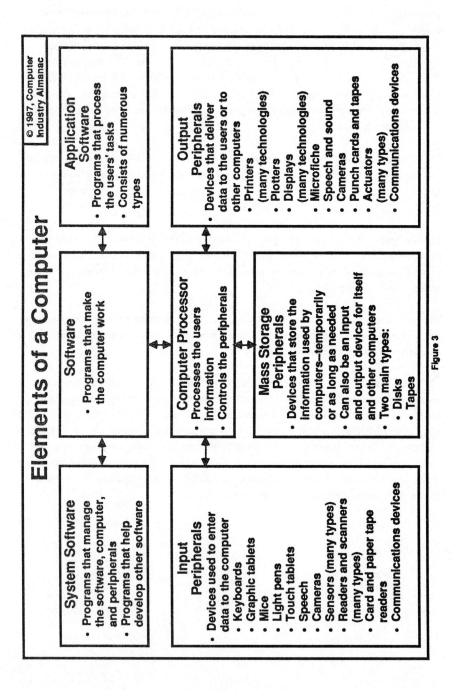

Elements of a Computer

© 1987, Computer Industry Almanac

System Software
- Programs that manage the software, computer, and peripherals
- Programs that help develop other software

Software
- Programs that make the computer work

Application Software
- Programs that process the users' tasks
- Consists of numerous types

Input Peripherals
- Devices used to enter data to the computer
  - Keyboards
  - Graphic tablets
  - Mice
  - Light pens
  - Touch tablets
  - Speech
  - Cameras
  - Sensors (many types)
  - Readers and scanners (many types)
  - Card and paper tape readers
  - Communications devices

Computer Processor
- Processes the users information
- Controls the peripherals

Mass Storage Peripherals
- Devices that store the information used by computers—temporarily or as long as needed
- Can also be an input and output device for itself and other computers
- Two main types:
  - Disks
  - Tapes

Output Peripherals
- Devices that deliver data to the users or to other computers
  - Printers (many technologies)
  - Plotters
  - Displays (many technologies)
  - Microfiche
  - Speech and sound
  - Cameras
  - Punch cards and tapes
  - Actuators (many types)
  - Communications devices

Figure 3

Figure 3 shows the various elements of a computer and gives a short explanation of each category. COMPUTER INDUSTRY ALMANAC has divided the computers into nine categories which are described in detail in the next section. The multitude of software categories are described in a separate section also. Mass storage devices store the programs and data used by computers. These devices may store the data temporarily or permanently. There are two types of output peripherals: hard-copy devices provide a permanent copy (i.e., printed paper) and soft-copy devices show the information only temporarily (i.e., display).

Input devices are used for two purposes: enter data and control the operation of the computer. Keyboards, graphics tablets, and readers are examples of data input devices. Mice, joysticks and light pens are input devices that control how the software and computer operate.

Computer Product Categories

© 1987, Computer Industry Almanac

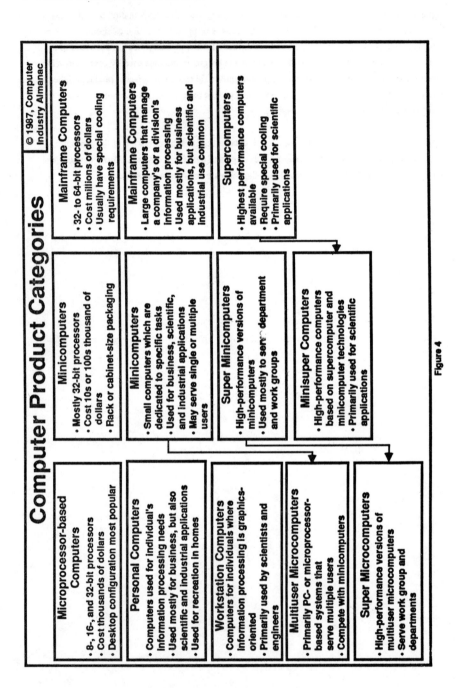

Microprocessor-based Computers
- 8-, 16-, and 32-bit processors
- Cost thousands of dollars
- Desktop configuration most popular

Personal Computers
- Computers used for individual's information processing needs
- Used mostly for business, but also scientific and industrial applications
- Used for recreation in homes

Workstation Computers
- Computers for individuals where information processing is graphics-oriented
- Primarily used by scientists and engineers

Multiuser Microcomputers
- Primarily PC- or microprocessor-based systems that serve multiple users
- Compete with minicomputers

Super Microcomputers
- High-performance versions of multiuser microcomputers
- Serve work group and departments

Minicomputers
- Mostly 32-bit processors
- Cost 10s or 100s thousand of dollars
- Rack or cabinet-size packaging

Minicomputers
- Small computers which are dedicated to specific tasks
- Used for business, scientific, and industrial applications
- May serve single or multiple users

Super Minicomputers
- High-performance versions of minicomputers
- Used mostly to serve department and work groups

Minisuper Computers
- High-performance computers based on supercomputer and minicomputer technologies
- Primarily used for scientific applications

Mainframe Computers
- 32- to 64-bit processors
- Cost millions of dollars
- Usually have special cooling requirements

Mainframe Computers
- Large computers that manage a company's or a division's information processing
- Used mostly for business applications, but scientific and industrial use common

Supercomputers
- Highest performance computers available
- Require special cooling
- Primarily used for scientific applications

Figure 4

Computer Categories

The three main types of computers and their subtypes are summarized in Figure 4. Microprocessor-based computers started out with 8-bit microprocessors in the 1970s but use primarily 16-bit microprocessors today. The emergence of 32-bit microprocessors is the lastest trend; these powerful microprocessors will be prevalent in the future. The use of 32-bit microprocessors will greatly narrow the performance gap between microprocessor-based systems and minicomputers. Microprocessor-based computers are the lowest priced computers. Prices start at $1,000 for personal computer systems and range up to $50,000 for workstations and super microcomputers. Microprocessor-based systems are normally configured as desktop computers but may also be packaged in a rack or cabinet. These products are also called microcomputers or micros.

Personal computers are the most popular computers. In the U.S. over 30 million PCs are in use, which is over 90% of all computers. At the low end are home PCs which have entry prices of a few hundred dollars. At the high end, PCs compete with workstations and multiuser microcomputers. Home PCs are used for recreational purposes and for homework--both office work and school work. Office PCs are used to improve productivity of individual tasks such as writing, calculating, filing, and drawing.

Workstations are also computers designed for use by individuals. Their strength is graphics capabilities and performance in scientific calculations. Workstations are used primarily by engineers and scientists and are therefore often called technical workstations. Workstations are becoming increasingly popular to any individual who does graphics design work.

Multiuser microcomputers use PC technology and add the capability of serving more than one user at a time. This requires more sophisticated software and a display terminal or PC for each user. Business operations such as accounting and data base management are the most common applications for multiuser microcomputers. Usually, these systems serve 8 to 16 users.

Super microcomputers are also multiuser computers. They can handle more users, 32 to 64, than multiuser microcomputers. Both product categories compete with minicomputers. A distinguishing factor that sets them apart from minicomputers is that multiuser micros and supermicros use "de facto" standard operating systems such as UNIX^R, while minicomputers use proprietary operating systems that are different for each minicomputer manufacturer.

UNIX is a Registered Trademark of AT&T.

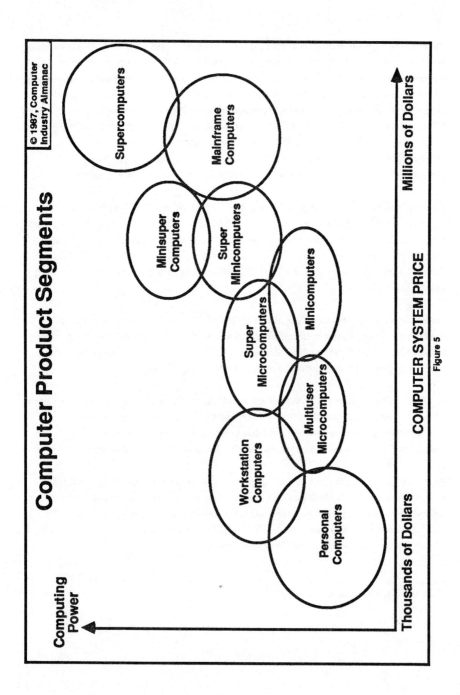

Minicomputers started out with 8-bit processors in the mid-1960s and went to 16-bit processors in the early 1970s. By the late 1970s, 32-bit processors started appearing and are now prevalent. Prices of low-end minicomputers start at $10,000 while superminis may cost several hundred thousand dollars. Minicomputers have traditionally been used for scientific and engineering applications and in industrial and automation tasks. Business applications such as accounting are also popular. Minicomputers may be single-user systems, but are normally multiuser computers. Minicomputers typically serve 16 to 64 users while superminis can handle over 100 users. High-end superminis have performance similar to mainframe computers and compete with such products.

Minisupercomputers are the newest computer category and are only a few years old. They are a mixture of minicomputer and supercomputer technology. Prices of a few hundred thousand dollars are common. Minisupers often use multiple processors to achieve their high performance. Minisupercomputers are sometimes called "Crayettes" after Cray, the leading manufacturer of supercompuers.

Mainframe computers were the first commercial computers that appeared in the 1950s. They are still room size, but today it is all the peripherals that require most of the room. Supercomputers, as a separate category, appeared in the mid-1960s.

Mainframe and supercomputers are the largest and most powerful computers. As a system, they cost millions of dollars and require special cooling, either air conditioning or liquid cooling (i.e., freon). Traditional mainframe computers are multiuser systems that can handle hundreds of users. They normally have an operational staff who run the system around the clock to get maximum use of such an expensive resource.

Supercomputers are used for large-scale scientific calculations. They have special purpose vector processors that can do certain calculations in parallel, and often consist of multiple processors.

Figure 5 shows the nine different computer product segments and how they overlap. The horizontal axis indicates the computer system price and the vertical axis shows relative computer performance. It is a qualitative picture and should not be used for quantitative comparisons. This picture is not static, and there are likely to be new categories. The most likely category to be added in the near term is so-called "personal supercomputers." Such computers are designed for individuals, but have much higher performance than PCs and workstations.

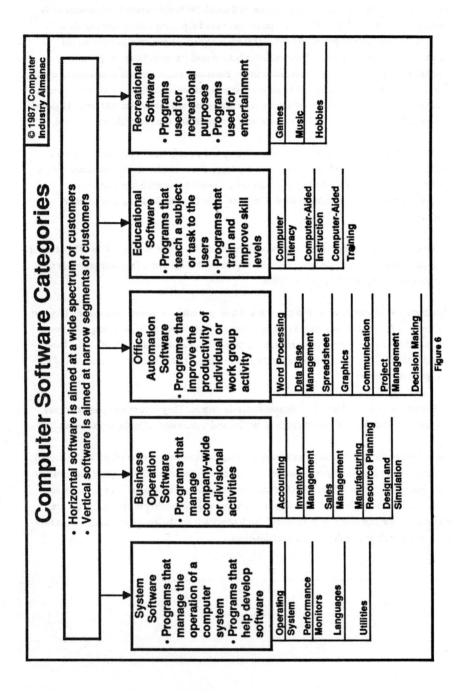

Computer Software Categories

- Horizontal software is aimed at a wide spectrum of customers
- Vertical software is aimed at narrow segments of customers

System Software
- Programs that manage the operation of a computer system
- Programs that help develop software

Operating System
Performance Monitors
Languages
Utilities

Business Operation Software
- Programs that manage company-wide or divisional activities

Accounting
Inventory Management
Sales Management
Manufacturing Resource Planning
Design and Simulation

Office Automation Software
- Programs that improve the productivity of individual or work group activity

Word Processing
Data Base Management
Spreadsheet
Graphics
Communication
Project Management
Decision Making

Educational Software
- Programs that teach a subject or task to the users
- Programs that train and improve skill levels

Computer Literacy
Computer-Aided Instruction
Computer-Aided Training

Recreational Software
- Programs used for recreational purposes
- Programs used for entertainment

Games
Music
Hobbies

Figure 6

Software Categories

There are numerous types of software. There are also several ways of categorizing software. COMPUTER INDUSTRY ALMANAC is using the categories and subcategories shown in Figure 6. In general, most categories have both vertical and horizontal software. Horizontal software can be used by a wide variety of people. Vertical software is used by narrow segments of customers. For instance, most word processing programs are horizontal and can be used across industries and job functions. However, a word processing program aimed toward scientists is a vertical program.

System software is required for every computer. There are two types of system software. The programs that manage the operation of a computer are called an operating system (OS). The operating system can be relatively simple, as it is for PCs, or very complex, as it is for mainframe computers. The operating system is probably the most important program of a computer because nearly all application programs use the capabilities of the operating system.

The other type of system software is software development tools that help construct new programs and maintain old programs. Examples are high-level languages such as Cobol, Fortran, and Pascal. Language compilers and interpreters translate the higher level languages into machine code that computers can understand. Utilities are various types of programs that simplify software development or computer operation.

Business operation software is a category of programs that manage company-wide activities. These applications usually have a centralized data base that is used by multiple divisions and by many people. Examples are accounting and inventory management. Most of the manufacturing process and product design activities also fall in this category. Most business programs are vertical software. Examples of vertical software are accounting for medical offices, sales management for home products dealers, design for mechanical engineers, and circuit design simulation for electronic engineers.

Office automation software became feasible as the price of computers could be justified for small groups and then for individuals. These programs can help with common tasks such as writing, calculating, filing, drawing, managing, decision making and communicating with others. Office automation software is primarily horizontal, but there are some vertical programs. The majority of this software is written for personal computers and, to a lesser degree, for workstations and multiuser micros.

Educational software teaches specific subjects or tasks to people. Such educational programs are called computer-aided instruction and computer-aided training. Educational programs that teach computer skills are often called computer literacy software. Nearly all educational programs are vertical software. Examples are mathematics for fifth grade, SAT training programs and high school physics.

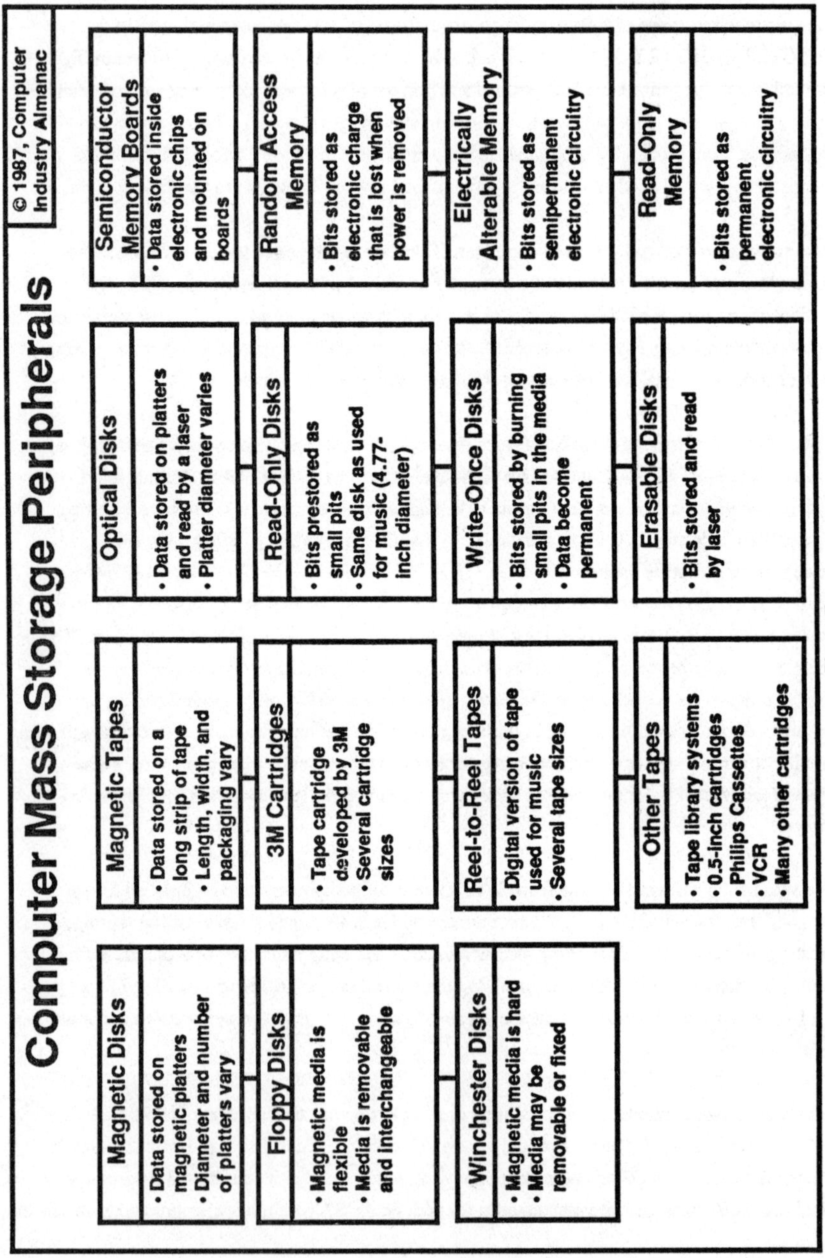

Computer Mass Storage Peripherals

© 1987, Computer Industry Almanac

Magnetic Disks
- Data stored on magnetic platters
- Diameter and number of platters vary

Floppy Disks
- Magnetic media is flexible
- Media is removable and interchangeable

Winchester Disks
- Magnetic media is hard
- Media may be removable or fixed

Magnetic Tapes
- Data stored on a long strip of tape
- Length, width, and packaging vary

3M Cartridges
- Tape cartridge developed by 3M
- Several cartridge sizes

Reel-to-Reel Tapes
- Digital version of tape used for music
- Several tape sizes

Other Tapes
- Tape library systems
- 0.5-inch cartridges
- Philips Cassettes
- VCR
- Many other cartridges

Optical Disks
- Data stored on platters and read by a laser
- Platter diameter varies

Read-Only Disks
- Bits prestored as small pits
- Same disk as used for music (4.77-inch diameter)

Write-Once Disks
- Bits stored by burning small pits in the media
- Data become permanent

Erasable Disks
- Bits stored and read by laser

Semiconductor Memory Boards
- Data stored inside electronic chips and mounted on boards

Random Access Memory
- Bits stored as electronic charge that is lost when power is removed

Electrically Alterable Memory
- Bits stored as semipermanent electronic circuitry

Read-Only Memory
- Bits stored as permanent electronic circuitry

Figure 7

Recreational software became popular when personal computers appeared. The large installed base of home PCs created a large market for recreational software such as games and music programs. There is now a large variety of computer games ranging from the classical board games such as chess and monopoly to card games and simulation games. A new category of games such as adventure games and flight simulators is not possible without computers.

Peripherals Categories

There are three main types of peripherals. Mass storage devices store the programs and data used by computers. Output peripherals provide the computer user with results from information processing. Output peripherals are also used for control purposes in computer automation applications. Input peripherals feed the computers with programs and data--either directly from computer users or from other computers and equipment. Input peripherals may also control the operation of a computer system. The next three sections explain the peripherals categories in more detail.

Mass Storage Peripherals. Mass storage capabilities are the most important peripherals in deciding the overall capabilities of computers. Figure 7 is an overview of most mass storage and memory devices. Mass storage technologies have more varieties in terms of capacity, performance, and price than any other peripherals device. The storage capacity may differ by a factor of more than 1000-- from a fraction of a megabyte for floppy disks to several gigabytes stored on large mainframe disks. The performance characteristics vary even more--by over a million times in access time between tapes and semiconductor memory boards, and by a factor of 1000 in data transfer between low-performance tapes and high-speed disks. Price variations are also substantial--a factor of over 100 between large mainframe disks and low-cost tape devices.

Magnetic disks are the most important and common mass storage devices. Each data bit is stored as individual magnets on magnetically coated platters. The platters spin under a movable read-write head (a magnetic coil). The operation is similar to a record player, except that there is no contact between the platter and the read-write head. The data organization is also different from the spiral traced by the pickup of a record player. The data on disks is stored along many concentric circles-- one inside the other (called tracks). The diameter of the disks varies; the most popular sizes are 3.5 inches, 5.25 inches, and 8 inches and 14 inches. The number of platters ranges from 1 to 10. Mainframe computers use disks with many large platters. Personal computers use disks with small size platters and just one or a few platters.

Floppy disks are the most common mass storage device for small computers. They are also used as the distribution media for software. Floppy disks store only up to a few megabytes or less.

Winchester disks have much higher performance than floppy disks. All computers larger than PCs have Winchester disks. An increasing portion of PCs are also using the smaller Winchester disks, which are fixed and do not have a removable media. Many of the medium and large size Winchester disks have a removable media called a disk pack.

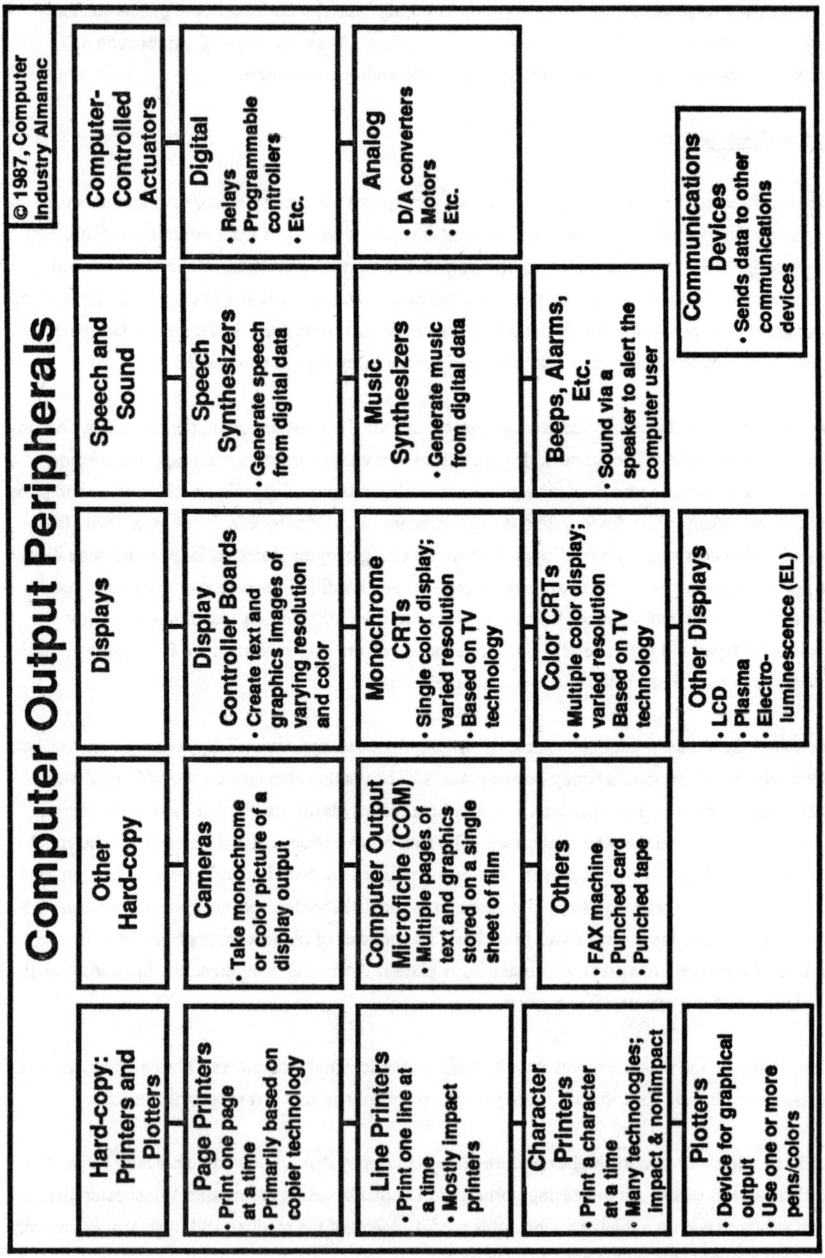

Computer Output Peripherals

© 1987, Computer Industry Almanac

Hard-copy: Printers and Plotters

- **Page Printers**
  - Print one page at a time
  - Primarily based on copier technology
- **Line Printers**
  - Print one line at a time
  - Mostly impact printers
- **Character Printers**
  - Print a character at a time
  - Many technologies; impact & nonimpact
- **Plotters**
  - Device for graphical output
  - Use one or more pens/colors

Other Hard-copy

- **Cameras**
  - Take monochrome or color picture of a display output
- **Computer Output Microfiche (COM)**
  - Multiple pages of text and graphics stored on a single sheet of film
- **Others**
  - FAX machine
  - Punched card
  - Punched tape

Displays

- **Display Controller Boards**
  - Create text and graphics images of varying resolution and color
- **Monochrome CRTs**
  - Single color display; varied resolution
  - Based on TV technology
- **Color CRTs**
  - Multiple color display; varied resolution
  - Based on TV technology
- **Other Displays**
  - LCD
  - Plasma
  - Electro-luminescence (EL)

Speech and Sound

- **Speech Synthesizers**
  - Generate speech from digital data
- **Music Synthesizers**
  - Generate music from digital data
- **Beeps, Alarms, Etc.**
  - Sound via a speaker to alert the computer user

Computer-Controlled Actuators

- **Digital**
  - Relays
  - Programmable controllers
  - Etc.
- **Analog**
  - D/A converters
  - Motors
  - Etc.

Communications Devices

- Sends data to other communications devices

Figure 8

Magnetic tapes store data on a long strip of magnetic media. Individual bits are reached by pulling the tape past a magnetic read-write head. The width and length of the tape and the number of tracks of data stored on the tape determine the storage capacity. Diverse methods are used to package the tape, ranging from reel-to-reel tapes, cartridges, and cassettes to automated cartridge library systems that use robot arms to retrieve any one of a large number of cartridges.

Optical storage is an emerging technology that shows great future promise. Optical disks are just now entering the marketplace in force. There are three types of optical disks, as shown in Figure 7.

Read-only disks have pre-recorded information, where the data is stored as individual microscopic pits in the disk surface. A laser detects the presence or absence of such pits. These disks are called CD ROMs because they are based on the compact digital audio disks used in the audio industry (4.77-inch diameter).

Write-once disks have no pre-recorded information. A laser can write information on the disk by burning small pits in the disk surface. Once written, these pits cannot be erased. Disk sizes of 5.25 inches, 8 inches, and 12 inches are used. Write-once optical disks are also called DRAW (Direct Read After Write) or WORM (Write Once, Read Mostly).

Erasable optical disks can both be written and erased. Drives using 12-inch diameter disks are available. The first smaller size disks (5.25 inches and 3.5 inches) will be available this year.

Semiconductor memory boards are used primarily as main memory. Main memory is the fastest memory available, and it stores the programs and data while the computer processes the users tasks. These memory boards can also be used as mass storage. When random access memory is used as a mass storage device, it is called an electronic disk because it simulates a very fast disk.

Output Peripherals. As shown in Figure 8, many different output peripherals exist. There are, however, two basic types of output devices. Hard-copy peripherals such as printers and plotters leave a permanent copy of the data. Soft-copy peripherals such as displays and sound devices leave only temporary images (unless they are recorded by some means).

Printers are the most important hard-copy output peripherals. There are three main printer categories. Page printers print one page a time and use nonimpact technology based primarily on copiers. The prices of page printers range from $2,000 for low-end products to $100,000 for high-speed mainframe laser printers. Page printers are used with all types of computers from PCs to supercomputers. The importance of page printers is rising rapidly.

Line printers print one line at a time. The technology is mostly impact printing (one line of characters strike the paper simultaneously). Line printers are the most popular printers used with mainframe and minicomputers but are rarely used with microcomputers. Line printers have peaked in importance and are losing market share to other printers.

Character printers print one character or a portion of a character at a time. Both impact and nonimpact printing technologies are used. There are two types of impact printers: fully formed character printers and dot matrix character printers. Fully formed characters mounted on a thimble or daisy wheel is a computer printer technology similar to that used in electronic typewriters. Sometimes these printers are called letter-quality printers. This technology has peaked in importance due to the growth and improvement in matrix impact printers. Dot matrix impact printers use a matrix of dots to form the characters. The trend is toward more and more dots, which improves the printing quality.

Nonimpact character printers may use regular paper or specially treated paper. Printers using special paper (such as thermal and electrostatic printers) are not very important. They are used only when low price is a main consideration. Nonimpact character printers using regular paper (such as thermal transfer and inkjet printers) are being used in increasing numbers.

Plotters are used when a hard copy of drawings and other graphics is needed. Plotter prices range from a few hundred dollars to tens of thousands of dollars. Plotters are used primarily in scientific and engineering applications.

There are numerous other hard-copy output devices. Cameras are used to record the image of displays. Slide cameras are increasing in importance due to the popularity of slide presentations and the ease of creating business graphics with PCs.

Computer output microfiche (COM) is used primarily with mainframe computers to store large amounts of data. A special viewer is needed to look at the pictures.

Other output devices which are rapidly increasing in popularity are fax machines, which may be connected to computers. Punched cards and punched tapes were important in the past, but are fading away except for special applications.

Displays are the most important soft-copy output devices. Monochrome and color CRTs (which are based on TV technology) are very important devices. The display controller boards that create the images are also crucial. A variety of new display technologies are being used (flat displays are desirable). Liquid crystal displays (LCD) are popular when low-power consumption is needed, such as in portable computers. The quality of LCD is still marginal but is improving rapidly. Plasma and electroluminescence (EL) are also flat displays but require much more power than LCD. They are also more expensive but have much better quality than LCD. Both have future potential and are used on portable computers.

Speech and sound synthesizers are also used as output peripherals. Speech synthesizers generate speech but have seen limited use. Speech quality is improving and prices are reasonable, but the technology will continue to be a niche market. Music synthesizers are used for recreational and entertainment purposes. The capability of computers as music synthesizers is improving rapidly. Beeps and alarms are used to alert computer users of specific conditions.

Computer-controlled actuators are used primarily in industrial automation applications. These output devices vary from relays and programmable controllers to motors and digital-to-analog (D/A) converters that control analog devices.

Finally, communications devices such as modems can be used as output peripherals and as input peripherals.

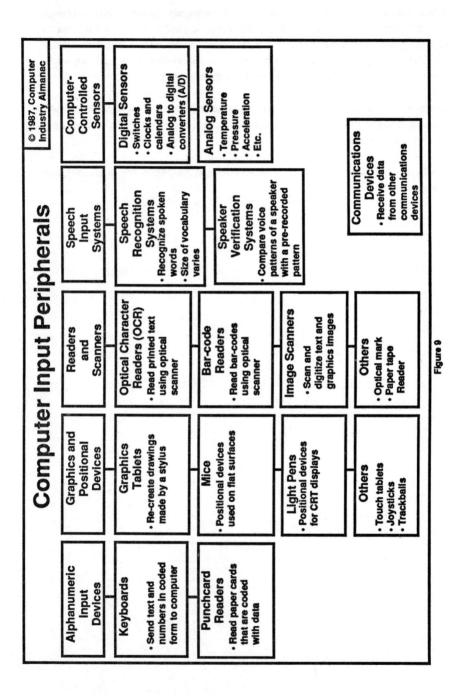

Figure 9

Input Peripherals. As depicted in Figure 9, there are numerous input peripherals. Input peripherals can be segmented into five categories plus communications devices. Alphanumeric input devices include keyboards and punched card readers. Keyboards are used with nearly all computers. Punched cards were very important in the past but are now used only with large computers.

Graphics and positional devices are increasing in importance. These devices are used for entering data but are even more important as control devices for selecting what is done when individuals use computers (sometimes called the user interface). The mouse is the most important input controller due to the popularity and ease of use of Apple's Macintosh computer, which uses a mouse.

There are several types of readers and scanners that provide information to computers. Optical character readers normally use a laser to read and recognize printed text. Special character fonts are used to minimize potential errors. Bar-code readers recognize bar-codes and are similar to the bar-code readers used in grocery stores. Image scanners digitize pictures regardless of whether the original is text and/or graphics. Image scanners are destined to increase in importance.

Speech input to computers has been a research goal for twenty years. The technology is improving fast but still has a long way to go. The size of the vocabulary that is recognized depends on the speech recognizer price. Products used with PCs recognize a few hundred words, and the system must be trained for each speaker (i.e., store the voice pattern of the words to be recognized). High-end systems are more capable but cost much more. Speaker verification systems are used to control the physical access to sensitive areas such as military installations or restricted laboratories.

There are numerous computer-controlled sensors that provide information to computers. Digital sensors range from switches to clock and calendar boards. Analog sensors include those for temperature, pressure, humidity, light, and acceleration. The data from analog sensors is normally translated to digital form by using an analog-to-digital (A/D) converter.

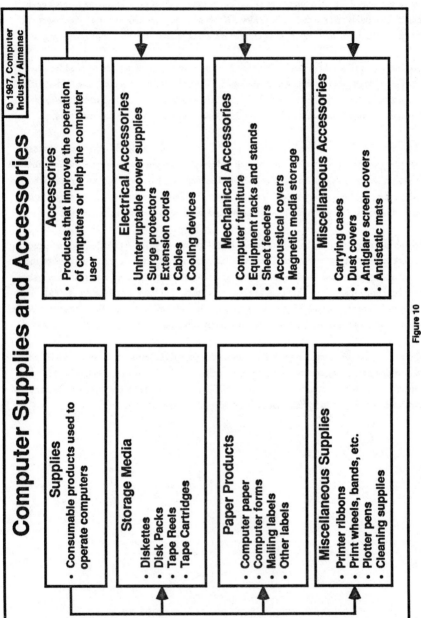

Computer Supplies and Accessories

© 1987, Computer Industry Almanac

Supplies

- Consumable products used to operate computers

Storage Media

- Diskettes
- Disk Packs
- Tape Reels
- Tape Cartridges

Paper Products

- Computer paper
- Computer forms
- Mailing labels
- Other labels

Miscellaneous Supplies

- Printer ribbons
- Print wheels, bands, etc.
- Plotter pens
- Cleaning supplies

Accessories

- Products that improve the operation of computers or help the computer user

Electrical Accessories

- Uninterruptable power supplies
- Surge protectors
- Extension cords
- Cables
- Cooling devices

Mechanical Accessories

- Computer furniture
- Equipment racks and stands
- Sheet feeders
- Accoustical covers
- Magnetic media storage

Miscellaneous Accessories

- Carrying cases
- Dust covers
- Antiglare screen covers
- Antistatic mats

Figure 10

Acessories and Supplies

The last computer product categories are shown in Figure 10. Supplies are all the consumables needed to operate computer systems. Supplies include all types of storage media, paper products, printer ribbons, and cleaning supplies.

Accessories are products that help make computer systems run smoother and products that lessen the users' efforts. Some accessories protect the computer against dust, static electricity, electrical surges, and even against power outages. Other products protect users against printer noise (accoustical covers) or help users avoid back pain (ergonomic furniture). Accessories may also help the user and the equipment by storing the supplies in an organized manner.

Supplies and accessories usually receive little attention, but having the right products will greatly improve the computer user's life.

2 COMPANIES

ENTREPRENEUR: FRANCHISE 500
January 1986

This ranking is the seventh annual statistical comparison of franchise operations in the U.S.--
COMPUTER INDUSTRY ALMANAC.
From this ranking COMPUTER INDUSTRY ALMANAC has selected only the hardware and
software industry franchises.
Reprinted with permission from ENTREPRENEUR, January 1986. Copyright 1986 by Entrepreneur
Group, Inc., Los Angeles, CA.

Franchise, City,State/Product or Service	Began Business/ Franchise	Number of Franchises	Range of Capital Needed*	Franchise Fee
ComputerLand, Hayward, CA Microcomputers & Accessories	1976/1977	806	$76K up	$15-75K
Entre' Computer Centers, Vienna, VA Microcomputers, Consulting, Training	1981/1982	261	$200-700K	$40K
Inacomp Computer Centers, Troy, MI Microcomputer Systems	1976/1980	32	$164-314K	$14-50K
Software Galeria, Sunnyvale, CA Personal Computers & Software	1982/1983	25	$200-250K	$30K
Personal Computer Rentals, Coral Gables, FL-- Microcomputer Rentals	1983/1984	8	$30-45K	$12-17.5K
MicroAge Computer Stores, Tempe, AZ Computer Store	1976/1980	151	$275-450K	$30K
Software City, Teaneck, NJ Computer Software & Accessories	1980/1982	105	$55-60K	$12.5K
Compucentre, Montreal, Que., Can. Microcomputers & Accessories (Continued next page)	1976/1981	53	$76K up	$25K

*Range of capital needed includes real estate, construction cost, location, type of business & other.

ENTREPRENEUR: FRANCHISE 500 (Continued)

Franchise, City,State/Product or Service	Began Business/ Franchise	Number of Franchises	Range of Capital Needed*	Franchise Fee
Micros, Etc., N. Miami Beach, FL Computers & Microwave Ovens	1975/1976	32	$70K	$10K
Data Terminal Mart, Mississauga, Ont., Can. Computers, Software, Terminals	1977/1977	11	$125-150K	$20K
Qualitech Computer Center, Memphis, TN Computer Hardware & Software	1983/1983	28	$10-75K	$45K
On-Line Computers Plus, Charlestown, MA Computer Specialty Store	1979/1980	12	$200-300K	$25K
Software Emporium, Cupertino, CA Software & Accessories	1981/1982	0	$60K	$15K
Computer Renaissance, Monroeville, PA Used-Computer Stores	1983/1984	1	$85-100K	$15K
National Computer Exchange, Overland Park, KS--Used-Computer Brokerage	1984/1984	3	$25K	$7.5K
AccuRent Computer Systems, Phoenix, AZ Computer Rental Store	1982/1985	0	$50.35K	$18.5K

*Range of capital needed includes real estate, construction cost, location, type of business & other.

FORBES 500: ANNUAL DIRECTORY
April 28, 1986

"One statistic alone is a poor measure of corporate size. That's why The Forbes 500s rank U.S.-based publicly held companies by four measures: sales, profits, assets and market value. This year, 255 companies make all four rosters. And 532 are on two or more Forbes 500s lists. Fiscal year-end results are used for companies with years ending in November, December or January. For all other firms, trailing 12 months are used for sales, profits and cash flow. Assets are for the most recently reported quarter. Market value is for December 31, 1985."--FORBES.

From this list COMPUTER INDUSTRY ALMANAC has selected only the industry-related companies and has shown only the sales and net profits figures. The ranking, however, has been given for all four categories: assets, sales, market value, and net profits.

Reprinted by permission of FORBES Magazine, April 28, 1986 issue. Copyright Forbes Inc., 1986.

| ---Where they rank:1985--- | | | | | Sales | Net profits | Number employed |
Assets	Sales	Market value	Net profits	Company	($mil)	($mil)	(thou)
*	*	274	*	Advanced Micro Devices	$624.0	$.5	14.2
23	9	4	8	American Tel & Tel	34,910.0	1,556.8	351.4
*	*	485	*	Analog Devices	320.0	26.4	4.8
*	392	317	412	Apple Computer	1,754.0	72.0	4.8
*	*	206	345	Automatic Data Processing	1,101.0	95.5	18.0
55	60	19	16	Bell Atlantic	9,084.0	1,092.9	79.4
42	48	8	10	BellSouth	10,664.0	1,417.8	94.1
136	34	38	41	Boeing	13,636.0	566.0	98.5
271	134	143	127	Burroughs	5,038.0	248.2	62.9
*	*	*	446	Comdisco	650.0	64.6	.7
146	140	486	*	Control Data	4,810.0	-567.5	49.2
*	*	228	398	Cray Research	380.0	75.6	2.7
*	*	356	*	Data General	1,199.0	2.4	17.1
181	87	39	80	Digital Equipment	7,029.0	400.6	87.3
100	49	16	97	Eastman Kodak	10,631.0	322.0	126.4
37	11	3	5	General Electric	28,285.0	2,336.0	304.0
11	1	5	3	General Motors	96,372.0	3,999.0	811.0
*	455	320	*	Gould	1,420.0	-175.7	19.1
*	302	376	460	Harris Corp	2,307.0	60.7	31.0
218	97	28	59	Hewlett-Packard	6,571.0	482.0	83.0
249	94	114	118	Honeywell	6,625.0	281.6	94.1
*	470	113	*	Intel	1,365.0	1.6	23.4
15	5	1	1	International Business Machines	50,056.0	6,555.0	400.2

(Continued next page)

* Figures not shown on 500 list.

FORBES 500: ANNUAL DIRECTORY (Continued)

---Where they rank:1985---						Net	Number
		Market	Net		Sales	profits	employed
Assets	Sales	value	profits	Company	($mil)	($mil)	(thou)
26	18	68	111	ITT**	$19,901.0	$293.5	233.5
*	157	227	124	Martin Marietta	4,410.0	249.4	46.1
170	45	138	94	McDonnell Douglas	11,478.0	345.7	92.7
272	278	161	247	MCI Communications	2,542.0	139.6	12.1
192	77	22	33	Minnesota Mining & Manufacturing	7,846.0	664.0	86.1
281	119	78	413	Motorola	5,443.0	72.0	95.1
*	421	367	*	National Semiconductor	1,606.0	-95.4	39.4
307	166	95	103	NCR	4,317.0	315.2	62.0
51	51	23	15	Nynex	10,314.0	1,095.3	92.3
*	485	315	390	Perkin-Elmer	1,310.0	79.5	15.5
*	378	243	226	Pitney Bowes	1,832.0	150.4	28.5
*	*	406	481	Prime Computer	770.0	57.8	7.7
188	63	65	91	RCA	8,972.0	369.1	96.5
477	487	319	287	Southern New England Telephone	1,304.0	119.9	13.8
59	75	32	22	Southwestern Bell	7,925.0	996.2	71.9
227	108	125	*	Sperry	5,736.0	37.4	75.6
*	*	448	*	Tandem Computers	635.0	32.0	5.4
*	234	104	155	Tandy	3,126.0	203.9	34.5
*	456	369	423	Tektronix	1,420.0	70.2	20.2
*	*	251	*	Tele-Communications	577.0	10.1	4.8
*	*	473	435	Telex	672.0	67.1	5.4
388	136	160	*	Texas Instruments	4,925.0	-118.7	82.2
326	104	170	*	TRW	5,917.0	-7.1	93.4
219	230	187	*	United Telecommunications	3,198.0	20.8	27.5
69	79	33	25	US West	7,813.0	925.6	70.5
449	289	149	*	Wang Laboratories	2,428.0	-63.3	31.7
73	44	61	60	Xerox**	11,526.0	475.3	111.9
*	419	*	*	Zenith Electronics	1,624.0	-7.7	31.0

* Figures not shown on 500 list.

** Figures include unconsolidated subsidiaries.

FORBES: 200 BEST SMALL COMPANIES IN AMERICA
November 3, 1986

"This is an annual ranking of the 200 Best Small Companies in America. Requirements for companies are a minimum five-year average return on equity of 10.9%, a profit of 10% or better for the latest twelve months, long-term debt must be less than equity, average annual gain in earnings per share of 9% over the past five years, and a five-year average annual sales growth of 8% or better."--FORBES.

From this list COMPUTER INDUSTRY ALMANAC has selected only the industry-related companies.

Excerpted by permission of FORBES magazine, November 3, 1986. Copyright Forbes Inc., 1986.

		Return on equity		5-year
			latest	EPS
		5-year	12	growth
Rank	Company/business	average	months	rate
19	Ultimate	35.1	29.5	60
	computer systems			
26	Telerate	33.1	25.2	43
	security price database			
30	Duquesne Systems	30.0	41.2	59
	computer software			
35	Interphase	29.5	22.5	33
	computer equipment			
40	MacNeal-Schwendler	27.5	29.2	22
	computer software			
52	Comarco	25.0	28.6	39
	defense engnrg, cmptr svcs			
56	Auxton Computer Eng	24.7	29.1	39
	computer services			
58	ACCO World	24.5	25.4	16
	computer supplies			
61	CCX Networks	22.8	19.5	36
	computer services			
70	QMS	21.7	16.8	40
	computer equipment			
71	Microsemi	21.6	29.5	62
	semiconductors			
81	BGS Systems	20.4	10.9	34
	software & computer services			
85	General Ceramics	20.2	31.1	36
	ceramics for electronics			

(Continued next page)

FORBES: 200 BEST SMALL COMPANIES IN AMERICA (Continued)

Rank	Company/business	Return on equity 5-year average	latest 12 months	5-year EPS growth rate
96	Distributed Logic computer equipment	19.3	13.9	10
101	Cybertek Computer Products software	18.7	21.3	43
113	AGS Computers computer software & services	17.6	15.4	28
114	Stanford Telecomm telecommunications equipment	17.5	15.4	34
118	American Software CI A software	17.1	15.2	55
119	Pansophic Systems software	17.0	16.3	27
131	Systematics bank computer services	16.4	17.3	31
135	First Financial Management bank computer services	16.2	13.1	36
140	Digital Comm Assoc telecomm equipment	16.0	17.3	113
141	Telxon computer equipment	16.0	16.9	30
146	Altos Computer Systems mini and micro computer	15.5	20.2	27
154	DBA Systems computer imaging tech	15.0	15.9	23
163	Scan-Tron optical reading equipment	14.2	17.8	24
169	Radiation Systems communications equipment	13.8	13.8	14
171	ISC Systems computer equipment	13.7	20.5	16
173	Syscon computer systems and services	13.7	13.6	10
186	Computer Assoc Intl software	12.8	11.1	45
189	KLA Instruments equip for semiconductor ind	12.8	13.0	62
197	Bolt Beranek & Newman consulting & research services	11.8	18.1	60

FORTUNE: THE 500 LARGEST U.S. CORPORATIONS RANKED BY SALES
April 28, 1986

"FORTUNE ranks the 500 Largest U.S. Industrial Corporations annually. All companies must have derived more than 50% of their sales from manufacturing/mining. Net income is shown after taxes and after extraordinary credit or charges. Employees figure is a year-end total except when it is followed by an *, in which case it is an average for the year."--FORTUNE.

From the list COMPUTER INDUSTRY ALMANAC has selected only industry-related companies and has shown only the rank, sales, net income and number of employees.

Copyright 1986 Time Inc. Reprinted from the FORTUNE Directory.

Rank 1985	Rank 1986	Company	Sales $ Thousands	Net Income $ Thousands	Employees Number
1	2	General Motors	$96,372	$3,999	*811,000
5	6	International Business Machines	50,056	6,555	405,535
8	8	American Telephone & Telegraph	34,910	1,557	337,600
10	9	General Electric	28,285	2,336	*304,000
21	29	Boeing	13,636	566	104,000
25	21	ITT	12,714	294	232,000
29	34	McDonnell Douglas	11,478	346	97,067
33	28	Eastman Kodak	10,631	332	128,950
40	38	Xerox	8,948	475	102,396
47	45	Minnesota Mining & Manufacturing	7,846	664	85,466
55	65	Digital Equipment	6,686	447	89,000
56	56	Honeywell	6,625	282	94,022
57	59	TRW	6,615	-7	93,186
58	60	Hewlett-Packard	6,505	489	84,000
63	69	Sperry	5,687	287	77,716
66	67	Motorola	5,443	72	90,200
72	76	Burroughs	5,038	248	60,519
75	63	Texas Instruments	4,925	-119	77,872
85	85	Martin Marietta	4,410	249	50,000
89	97	NCR	4,317	315	62,000
		(Continued next page)			

* Average total for the year.

FORTUNE: THE 500 LARGEST U.S. CORPORATIONS RANKED BY SALES (Continued)

Rank 1985	Rank 1986	Company	Sales $ Thousands	Net Income $ Thousands	Employees Number
106	71	Control Data	$3,680	-$568	38,856
149	274	BASF	2,568	39	20,781
161	165	Wang Laboratories	2,352	16	31,061
163	182	Harris	2,281	80	31,400
191	234	Apple Computer	1,918	61	4,300
204	217	Pitney Bowes	1,832	150	28,995
209	225	National Semiconductor	1,788	43	37,100
225	220	Zenith Electronics	1,624	-8	33,000
233	230	Gould	1,520	-176	18,605
245	252	Tektronix	1,438	90	20,525
251	226	Intel	1,365	2	21,300
256	275	Perkin-Elmer	1,305	82	15,515
269	279	Data General	1,239	24	16,535
308	327	General Instrument	994	-10	13,600
321	424	Advanced Micro Devices	931	135	15,299
341	366	Sanders Associates	886	37	11,413
348	357	Amdahl	862	29	7,000
350	363	M/A-Com	848	39	11,790
366	400	Prime Computer	770	58	8,115
373	395	Cincinnati Milacron	732	-45	9,197
396	349	Storage Technology	673	-57	8,540
409	445	Tandem Computers	624	34	5,494
410	421	Nashua	622	16	5,275
414	417	AM International	612	25	9,500
422	-	Telex	591	53	6,580
446	-	SCI Systems	538	14	4,290
458	416	Datapoint	520	-48	5,993
463	-	Compaq Computer	504	27	1,860
479	-	Dataproducts	472	28	5,300
494	436	Computervision	441	-81	4,770

INC.500: AMERICA'S FASTEST-GROWING PRIVATE COMPANIES
December 1986

"To qualify for the 1986 list, a company must be independent and privately held. The rankings are based on the percentage increase in sales during a five-year period."--INC.
From this list COMPUTER INDUSTRY ALMANAC has selected only the industry-related companies.
Reprinted with permission, INC. magazine, December 1986. Copyright 1986 by INC. Publishing Company, 38 Commercial Wharf, Boston, MA. 02110.

Rank	Company/Business Description	5-yr Sales Growth	1985 Sales ($000)	No. of 1985 Employees	Date Founded
4	Int'l Research & Evaluation Technology Transfer Database	$17,232%	$18,545	92	1972
9	Morris Decision Systems Computer sales & service	9,008%	21,131	90	1980
11	Zymark Automated lab instruments	7,555%	11,482	152	1981
16	Direct Marketing Technology Computer services to mktg ind	6,502%	8,120	139	1981
18	Information Systems & Networks Telecommunications engineering	6,410%	19,789	200	1980
19	May-Craft Information Systems Data Communications	6,169%	7,272	18	1978
20	Integrated Systems Analysts Defense systems engineering	6,005%	15,689	259	1980
21	Core International Computer mfr & retailer	5,940%	15,341	23	1973
23	Interactive Business Systems Data-processing software	5,622%	6,351	100	1981
25	Itron Hand-held computer systems	5,522%	27,999	280	1977
26	Richard Young Office Prods. Word/data-processing supplies	5,388%	9,988	30	1979
29	ADD Electronics Distr of electronic components	5,114%	10,220	58	1981
32	BMC Software Develops systems software	4,182%	9,335	60	1980
37	Lifetree Software Publisher of software	3,940%	4,121	30	1981

(Continued next page)

INC.500: AMERICA'S FASTEST-GROWING PRIVATE COMPANIES (Continued)

Rank	Company/Business Description	5-yr Sales Growth	1985 Sales ($000)	No. of 1985 Employees	Date Founded
38	General Computer Dvlps/mkts peripherals	3,908%	$20,441	113	1981
39	RJO Enterprises Info systems architecture	3,844%	4,970	116	1979
41	Tricom Group Computer distr & maintenance	3,717%	7,329	18	1981
42	F.A. Components Distr microcomputer hardware	3,699%	31,153	45	1980
45	Micro Center Computer department store	3,509%	25,988	120	1979
46	Teleconnect Telemktg & telecom syst dvlpmt	3,476%	72,306	700	1979
47	Alpharel Computerized mgmt systems	3,400%	7,596	80	1981
49	Mobile Imaging Computerized med-tech services	3,346%	4,480	11	1980
53	Broadway & Seymour Computer systems & services	3,096%	14,221	225	1981
54	DPCS Computer programming services	3,034%	8,807	36	1977
59	Computer Technology Associates Aerospace systs engineering	2,842%	22,389	324	1979
61	Sytek LAN data-communication systems	2,774%	70,422	475	1979
65	Broderbund Software Publ Software	2,682%	20,000	110	1980
68	Softsel Computer Products Distr microcomputer equipment	2,617%	206,790	450	1980
69	Summa Four Telecommunication peripherals	2,604%	12,170	135	1976
70	Abacus II Computers Computer retailer	2,577%	10,683	50	1980
75	Computer Specialists Computer programming services	2,473%	2,882	87	1980

(Continued next page)

INC.500: AMERICA'S FASTEST-GROWING PRIVATE COMPANIES (Continued)

Rank	Company/Business Description	5-yr Sales Growth	1985 Sales ($000)	No. of 1985 Employees	Date Founded
79	Strategic Management Group Bus simulations & mgmt trng	2,456%	$2,607	30	1981
82	Hartley Coursewares Educational computer software	2,369%	2,666	14	1981
83	Corporate Information Systems Data-processing consulting	2,317%	3,311	97	1981
88	Fusion Products International Utility SW for IBM minicomp	2,244%	4,642	31	1981
91	Execu-Flow Systems Turnkey computer sales	2,199%	2,368	15	1981
93	Datamatic Telecommunication systems	2,137%	8,277	40	1980
95	KOH Systems ADP, telecom & mgmt consult	2,098%	5,935	100	1980
97	Basic Computer Microcomputer sales	2,086%	42,062	170	1978
98	SRS Network Data processing	2,071%	5,407	68	1978
103	Computer Dynamics Computer engineering svcs	2,003%	11,148	435	1979
105	WRB Associates Computer SW dvlpmt & sales	1,987%	2,859	18	1969
106	Computer Components Int'l Distr abrasive materials	1,985%	2,523	4	1980
112	Integrated Systems Management Computer software & services	1,894%	2,034	20	1979
113	American Calculator & Computer Computer & calculator sales	1,853%	12,734	48	1980
115	Robec Distr microcomputer equip	1,828%	32,999	90	1978
120	OMNI Resources Manufacturer of floppy disks	1,777%	2,402	37	1980
121	Solution Systems Remote computer services	1,740%	2,061	8	1981

(Continued next page)

INC.500: AMERICA'S FASTEST-GROWING PRIVATE COMPANIES (Continued)

Rank	Company/Business Description	5-yr Sales Growth	1985 Sales ($000)	No. of 1985 Employees	Date Founded
122	Quality Systems	1,723%	$6,017	120	1981
	Computer systs engr & dvlpmt				
124	Tech Data	1,694%	37,652	63	1974
	Microcomputer peripherals				
125	Dynacom Telecommunications	1,673%	2,748	35	1980
	Business communication systems				
128	National Decision Systems	1,611%	6,416	116	1979
	Database applications				
131	Berger	1,594%	2,236	43	1981
	Information mgmt consultants				
132	Datatel	1,588%	5,604	67	1979
	Mfr data-communications equip				
135	Xscribe	1,577%	22,242	270	1978
	Comp-aided transcription syst				
136	Word & Data Processing Prods.	1,569%	4,758	35	1979
	Comp distr & software dvlpmt				
140	Parameter Driven Software	1,555%	4,021	20	1981
	Fourth-generation computer SW				
141	O/E Automation	1,543%	32,903	243	1979
	Office automation sales/cnsltg				
143	Dytronix	1,518%	2,815	53	1979
	Insurance software & cnsltg				
145	American Comp. Professionals	1,500%	3,776	72	1979
	Computer professional service				
170	Microdynamics	1,370%	8,613	59	1979
	CAD/CAM systems				
171	Walker Richer & Quinn	1,341%	1,971	6	1981
	Computer terminal emulation				
175	Interactive Networks	1,276%	1,981	13	1979
	Data & video communications				
177	Vista Technology	1,221%	12,548	35	1979
	Distr computer products				
180	Optim Electronics	1,216%	1,829	27	1980
	Data acquisition systems				

(Continued next page)

INC.500: AMERICA'S FASTEST-GROWING PRIVATE COMPANIES (Continued)

Rank	Company/Business Description	5-yr Sales Growth	1985 Sales ($000)	No. of 1985 Employees	Date Founded
185	Jacore Systems Supplies minicomputer systems	1,185%	$23,126	57	1979
187	Mantissa Develops/markets software	1,173%	1,719	7	1981
188	Innovative Computer Mgmt. Sys. Develops software	1,165%	1,430	17	1980
194	ComputerLand of Hawaii Computer sales & service	1,108%	16,095	69	1978
196	Micro Data Base Systems Software development tools	1,104%	13,003	166	1979
200	Spencer & Spencer Systems Computer software development	1,078%	4,510	60	1980
201	Dealer Information Systems Application software	1,072%	7,596	60	1980
202	Matrix Organization Data-pro professional services	1,069%	4,909	74	1980
211	Solectron Electronic mfr computer equip	1,017%	66,991	1500	1977
215	ParaData Computer Networks Computer hardware & software	997%	7,506	50	1979
216	Computer Comm. Specialists Computer software	996%	7,300	74	1977
218	ESCA Systems engineering	991%	12,844	128	1978
219	El Camino Resources Retail/lease computer equip	984%	36,944	33	1979
223	re: Member Data Processing Svcs Computer service bureau	969%	1,817	24	1981

(Continued next page)

INC.500: AMERICA'S FASTEST-GROWING PRIVATE COMPANIES (Continued)

Rank	Company/Business Description	5-yr Sales Growth	1985 Sales ($000)	No. of 1985 Employees	Date Founded
229	American Star Software	950%	$3,664	42	1980
	Publ small-business software				
233	MicroAge	937%	142,279	224	1976
	Computer-store franchisor				
234	Dataman Group	937%	3,640	32	1980
	Information management				
238	G.N.P. Loudspeakers	916%	3,383	13	1977
	Audio/video/computer retailer				
239	Phoenix Microsystems	914%	5,098	80	1977
	Telecommunications test equip				
242	Heurikon	906%	8,364	75	1972
	Microcomputer boards & systs				
247	Moss Telecommunications Svcs.	890%	1,376	30	1977
	Telephone & data cable systs				
248	Dexel Systems	889%	29,758	69	1972
	Small-business systems				
254	Computerized Lodging Systems	880%	8,655	27	1981
	Resells computer systems				
261	Metro Information Services	849%	5,038	125	1973
	Computer consulting				
264	ComputerLand of Phoenix	840%	28,024	110	1978
	Computer retailer				
271	Data Systems Computer Centre	818%	35,749	70	1973
	Microcomputer/peripheral sales				
275	Triangle Software	807%	2,894	17	1980
	Dvlps software systems				
292	Warwick Data Systems	754%	1,820	6	1981
	Data-communications equipment				
295	Mountain Computer	751%	28,973	205	1977
	Mfr/mkts peripherals				
296	Altex Electronics	749%	1,519	10	1981
	Electronics distribution				
300	National Instruments	733%	7,210	82	1976
	Computer interface equipment				
	(Continued next page)				

INC.500: AMERICA'S FASTEST-GROWING PRIVATE COMPANIES (Continued)

Rank	Company/Business Description	5-yr Sales Growth	1985 Sales ($000)	No. of 1985 Employees	Date Founded
303	Comfab	731%	$10,100	146	1974
	Telecom equip supplier				
304	T/Maker	728%	1,200	6	1980
	Publisher of software				
305	Systems Research & Application	724%	14,263	182	1978
	Computer professional services				
307	Money Market Services	719%	6,147	101	1974
	On-line market analysis				
318	Data Base Publications	697%	2,549	26	1980
	Publisher of computer magazine				
319	Software Clearing House	696%	3,146	45	1979
	Markets systems software				
336	World Leasing	652%	25,457	11	1976
	Computer-equipment leasing				
348	BATA Resources	640%	9,891	16	1979
	Remarkets used IBM computers				
360	Integrated Systems	626%	3,080	30	1980
	CAE & software development				
367	Granada Systems Design	617%	1,592	20	1979
	Communication software				
369	Administrative Inform. Systs.	617%	3,368	34	1977
	Medical soft/hardware systs				
383	Communications Packaging	596%	8,335	135	1980
	Pkg for software/cassettes				
387	Network Data Systems	589%	1,110	23	1980
	Develops software				
396	Information Builders	578%	72,374	325	1975
	Mfr computer software				
410	Infotec Development	549%	11,775	225	1978
	Computer systems engineering				
416	DSI Computer Services	543%	1,113	12	1980
	Installs/repairs comp equip				
418	University Computing Services	541%	1,512	10	1979
	Computing software & consltng				

(Continued next page)

INC.500: AMERICA'S FASTEST-GROWING PRIVATE COMPANIES (Continued)

Rank	Company/Business Description	5-yr Sales Growth	1985 Sales ($000)	No. of 1985 Employees	Date Founded
419	Engineered Data Environments	539%	$15,590	30	1980
	Mfr's rep/computer support				
420	DBMS	537%	18,671	270	1979
	Full-service software				
422	Publications & Communications	537%	3,083	43	1979
	Publishes computer magazine				
424	Avanti Communications	534%	17,251	220	1977
	Mfr telecommunication equip				
429	SAS Institute	531%	70,971	600	1976
	Fourth-generation software				
440	Motivational Marketing	525%	3,750	50	1978
	Software sales & consulting				
456	Kronos	511%	11,839	165	1977
	Computerized time-acctg systs				
459	Local Data	507%	8,472	104	1978
	Mfr protocol converters				
460	Management Dynamics	506%	981	14	1980
	Custom software dvlpmt				
462	Sage Federal Systems	504%	13,209	86	1974
	Computer programming svc				
464	Construction Systems Assocs.	500%	2,782	36	1976
	Computerized plant modeling				
465	NELCO	499%	9,656	6	1979
	Computer leasing				
474	WPDS	488%	7,121	25	1979
	Dvlps computer app systs				
478	Computer Methods	481%	7,443	170	1977
	Software sales & svc				
482	Cincinnati Electrosystems	473%	5,106	95	1975
	Peripheral equip./automation				
485	Micro Systems	472	1,351	20	1976
	Defense control systs				

INC. 100: FASTEST-GROWING SMALL PUBLIC COMPANIES
May 1986

The 1986 INC. 100 is the eighth annual ranking of the 100 fastest-growing publicly held smaller companies in the United States. Companies are ranked by the percentage increase in net sales over the five-year period 1981-1985."--INC.

From this list COMPUTER INDUSTRY ALMANAC has selected only the industry-related companies.

Reprinted with permission, INC. Magazine, May 1986. Copyright 1986 by INC. Publishing Company, 38 Commercial Wharf, Boston, MA 02110.

1986 Rank	Company/Business	81-85 % Sales Growth	1985 Sales ($000)	1985 Employees	Year Public
3	ALC Communications	24,327	$467,293	2290	1985
	Long-distance telephone svc				
4	Ashton-Tate	17,595	82,281	459	1983
	Microcomputer software prods				
5	Iomega	17,415	116,474	1154	1983
	Mfr disk drives				
6	American Businessphones	16,080	18,283	236	1984
	Distr/svc business phones				
9	VLSI Technology	14,126	78,671	820	1983
	Mfr integrated circuits				
13	3Com	9,050	46,300	274	1984
	Mfr LAN systems				
14	Apollo Computer	8,593	295,575	3200	1983
	Mfr computer systems				
17	Walker Telecommunications	6,867	33,718	100	1983
	Distr elec key tel sys				
22	V Band Systems	5,648	18,394	130	1984
	Mfr telecom terminal equip				
26	Archive	4,773	57,845	607	1983
	Mfr cartridge tape drives				
28	Fibronics International	4,512	25,460	425	1983
	Mfr fiber-optic comm sys				
30	Sterling Software	4,241	60,550	2950	1983
	Mfr computer SW prods & svc				
35	ORS Automation	3,153	4,750	100	1981
	Mfr CAD/CAM				

(Continued next page)

INC. 100: FASTEST-GROWING SMALL PUBLIC COMPANIES (Continued)

1986 Rank	Company/Business	81-85 % Sales Growth	1985 Sales ($000)	1985 Employees	Year Public
36	Electronic Tele-Comm. Mfr voice announcement systs	3,139	$4,696	54	1985
39	Convergent Technologies Mfr comps & computing systs	2,915	395,167	1994	1982
42	Artel Communications Mfr fiber-optic transm sys	2,791	6,013	80	1983
48	Comp-U-Card International Electronic shopping service	2,598	28,679	293	1983
53	Computer Telephone Telephone communication sys	2,383	7,100	122	1985
55	Ciprico Mfr disk controllers	2,310	8,171	76	1983
60	Computercraft Retailer/microcomputer sys	2,013	137,237	640	1983
66	Ungermann-Bass Mfr LAN	1,778	72,166	100	1983
67	DEST Mfr electronic document system	1,669	18,556	206	1985
68	Priam Mfr disk drives	1,651	105,025	898	1981
70	MBI Business Centers Sells microcomputer sys/prod	1,548	50,523	390	1984
81	Avant-Garde Computing Mfr integrated SW-based system	1,224	20,437	197	1983
83	Startel Microproc controlled telcom	1,202	10,823	90	1983
90	TeleByte Technology Mfr comp periph & data com	1,108	3,200	60	1983
92	Interand Mfr teleconferencing systems	1,096	6,926	92	1983
94	Applied Circuit Technology Mfr test sys/hard disk drive	1,053	18,520	237	1983
96	Idea Mfr integd circ't test equip	1,002	5,431	49	1983
97	Jack Henry & Associates Integrates bank SW/HW	996	12,452	42	1985
98	Reid-Ashman Mfr integd circ't test equip	990	7,457	81	1984

VENTURE: FAST-TRACK 100
May 1986

"The fifth annual Venture Fast-Track 100 is composed of 100 companies, ranked by revenues, that are 10 years old or younger, had at least one founder on the board during the fiscal year (Apple Computer still qualifies), and posted at least $42.06 million in revenues in their 1985 fiscal year."-- VENTURE MAGAZINE.

From this list COMPUTER INDUSTRY ALMANAC has selected only the industry-related companies.

Reprinted with permission from VENTURE Magazine, May 1986. Copyright 1986, Venture Magazine Inc., New York, NY.

1985 Rank	Company/City, State	Rank Last Year	1985 Rev. ($Mil.)/ % Change	Type of Business
1	Apple Computer Cupertino, CA	1	$1,918.28 26.55%	Microcomputers
8	Compaq Computer Corp. Houston, TX	11	503.88 53.15	Microcomputers
9	Convergent Technologies, Inc. San Jose, CA	10	395.17 9.23	Computer wrk-grp clusters for OEMs
11	Apollo Computer, Inc. Chelmsford, MA	15	295.58 36.89	Engineering workstations
14	Businessland, Inc. San Jose, CA	22	267.45 198.35	Business computer retailer
15	Lotus Development Cambridge, MA	23	225.50 43.65	Business software
16	Seagate Technology Scotts Valley, CA	12	214.65 -37.59	Winchester disk drives
18	Softsel Computer Products, Inc. Inglewood, CA	19	206.79 28.80	Microcomputer and software distributor
22	ISC Systems Corp. Spokane, WA	26	150.00 17.49	Financial hardware and software
26	LSI Logic Corp. Milpitas, CA	48	140.01 65.72	Custom semiconductors
27	AST Research Inc. Irvine, CA	--	138.58 117.16	Workstation enhancement products
28	Computer Craft, Inc. Houston, TX	59	137.24 94.77	Computer retailer
29	Mentor Graphics Beaverton, OR	46	136.75 55.56	Computer-aided engineering systems
30	LTX Corp. Westwood, MA	29	133.42 48.18	Semiconductor testing equipment

(Continued next page)

VENTURE: FAST-TRACK 100 (Continued)

1985 Rank	Company/City, State	Rank Last Year	1985 Rev. ($Mil.)/ % Change	Type of Business
32	First Software Corp. Lawrence, MA	69	$130.00 113.12%	Software and peripherals
33	Altos Computer Systems San Jose, CA	36	124.45 21.13	Microcomputers and software
34	Daisy Systems Mountain View, CA	63	122.55 77.23	Computer-aided engineering systems
35	Quantum Corp. Milpitas, CA	33	120.35 79.44	Disk drives
36	Iomega Corp. Stamford, CT	88	115.52 123.68	Disk drives
37	Sun Microsystems Mountain View, CA	60	115.25 196.58	Technical workstations
41	Computer Memories, Inc. Chatsworth, CA	45	108.71 129.21	Winchester disk drives
42	The Ultimate Corp. E. Hanover, NJ	24	107.31 51.69	Minicomputer systems
43	PRIAM Corp. San Jose, CA	49	105.03 2.92	Rigid high-capacity disk drives
44	Emulex Corp. Costa Mesa, CA	41	103.17 28.69	Computer storage and communications
45	TeleVideo Systems Sunnyvale, CA	20	103.09 -36.76	Video display terminals
47	Micropolis Corp. Chatsworth, CA	70	94.90 57.77	Disk drives
48	Lee Data Corp. Eden Prairie, MN	37	91.05 -7.77	On-line computer terminals
53	Stratus Computer Marlboro, MA	100	80.16 90.23	Fault-tolerant computer systems
54	Wyse Technology San Jose, CA	--	77.59 331.99	Microprocessor-based display products
56	Micron Technology, Inc. Boise, ID	47	75.88 -13.13	Components for microcomputers
59	SAS Institute Inc. Cary, NC	81	75.10 41.70	Software
60	Maxtor Corp. San Jose, CA	98	75.05 91.89	Winchester disk drives

(Continued next page)

VENTURE: FAST-TRACK 100 (Continued)

1985 Rank	Company/City, State	Rank Last Year	1985 Rev. ($Mil.)/ % Change	Type of Business
61	Ungermann-Bass Santa Clara, CA	85	$72.17 37.98%	Local-area networks
65	Sytek, Inc. Mountain View, CA	--	70.40 130.07	Local-area networks
66	Symbolics, Inc. Cambridge, MA	--	69.01 69.58	LISP-based computers
70	Solectron San Jose, CA	71	66.99 23.94	Printed circuit boards
77	ERC International Vienna, VA	--	62.79 62.56	Technological services
79	Tallgrass Technologies Overland Park, KS	72	60.00 0.00	Disk and tape drives
80	Archive Corp. Costa Mesa, CA	--	57.85 51.58	1/4-in. tape drives and controllers
83	Valid Logic Systems, Inc. San Jose, CA	93	56.06 16.09	Computer-aided engineering hw and sw
84	Microscience International Corp. Mountain View, CA	--	56.00 100.00	Winchester disk drives
85	Syntrex, Inc. Eatontown, NJ	89	55.73 5.99	Office automation equipment
86	Diceon Electronics, Inc. Irvine, CA	84	55.00 5.15	Multilayered circuit products
88	Corvus Systems San Jose, CA	87	53.22 5.30	Local-area networks
89	Alpha Microsystems Santa Ana, CA	78	51.74 -0.52	Computer products
95	Western Micro Technology, Inc. Cupertino, CA	92	46.23 25.17	Electronics distributor
97	MASSCOMP Westford, MA	--	45.20 106.02	Computer systems
98	Data Technology Santa Clara, CA	--	44.70 9.83	Controllers and disk drives
99	MicroPro International Corp. San Rafael, CA	66	42.65 -36.29	Business software
100	Zycon Corp. Santa Clara, CA	--	42.06 54.38	Circuit boards and laminates

VENTURE: THE FRANCHISOR 100
November 1986

"The Franchisor 100 is intended to offer U.S. franchisors a reference for evaluating their growth and to identify the fastest growing franchise system for potential franchisors. Drawn from a pool of 2,000 franchisors, the 600 companies surveyed have been franchising for at least two years and had at least 50 units operating in 1985."--VENTURE.

From this list COMPUTER INDUSTRY ALMANAC has selected only industry-related companies. Reprinted with permission from VENTURE, November, 1986. Copyright 1986 by Venture Magazine Inc., New York, NY.

ComputerLand Stores, Hayward, CA
Rank: 35   Parent company: ComputerLand Corp.
Two-yr. average annual growth in franchised units: 84
Founded/began franchising: 1976/1976
Company owned/Franchised units: 0/607
Franchisor revenues in thousands: $106,128
Franchisor net income in thousands: $2,028
Franchise fee: $5,000-75,000   Other startup costs: $39,800-842,800
Real Estate: Lease/buy
Royalty fee: 8%   Advertising and other ongoing fees: 1%
Term of agreement: 10 years   Initial training time: 15 days
Sub-franchising available: No   Financing available: Yes
Franchise must be owner's main job: Yes
Franchisee advisory council: Yes
Franchisee must do business with franchisor: Yes
Add-on or satellite franchises available: Yes
International franchisor: Yes

VENTURE: THE FRANCHISOR 100 (Continued)

MicroAge Computer Stores, Tempe, AZ
Rank: 60   Parent company: MicroAge Inc.
Two-yr. average annual growth in franchised units: 60
Founded/began franchising: 1976/1980
Company owned/Franchised units: 2/155
Franchisor revenues in thousands: $142,279
Franchisor net income in thousands: $3,824
Franchise fee: $30,000   Other startup costs: $190,000-470,000
Real Estate: Lease/buy/convert
Royalty fee: 6%   Advertising and other ongoing fees: 1%
Term of agreement: 10 years   Initial training time: 4 weeks
Sub-franchising available: No   Financing available: Yes
Franchise must be owner's main job: Yes
Franchisee advisory council: Yes
Franchisee must do business with franchisor: No
Add-on or satellite franchises available: No
International franchisor: Yes

ValCom, Omaha, NB
Rank: 99   Parent company: ValCom Inc.
Two-yr. average annual growth in franchised units: 30
Founded/began franchising: 1982/1982
Company owned/Franchised units: 20/155
Franchisor revenues in thousands: $86,330
Franchisor net income in thousands: $406
Franchise fee: $30,000   Other startup costs: $126,000-260,000
Real Estate: Lease/buy
Royalty fee: 8%   Advertising and other ongoing fees: none
Term of agreement: 10 years   Initial training time: 1 week
Sub-franchising available: No   Financing available: Yes
Franchise must be owner's main job: No
Franchisee advisory council: Yes
Franchisee must do business with franchisor: No
Add-on or satellite franchises available: No
International franchisor: No

WALL STREET JOURNAL: THE WORLD'S 100 LARGEST PUBLIC COMPANIES
(By market value on June 30, converted into U.S. dollars at the exchange rate for that date.)
September 29, 1986

This table of the world's largest public companies, ranked by market value, is based upon data from
Morgan Stanley Capital International Perspective. Employment figures are a 1986 Wall Street
Journal tabulation.--COMPUTER INDUSTRY ALMANAC.
From this list COMPUTER INDUSTRY ALMANAC has selected only the industry-related
companies.
Reprinted with permission from THE WALL STREET JOURNAL, Monday, September 29, 1986.
Copyright 1986 by Dow Jones & Company, Inc., Princeton, NJ.

Company Name	Headquarters	Market Value (In millions of U.S. dollars)	World-wide Employment (in thousands)	% Employed Outside Home Country
IBM	Armonk, N.Y.	$87,697	405	40
General Electric	Fairfield, Conn.	36,820	300	20
AT&T	New York	27,138	350	2
British Telecom	London	20,430	234	1
BellSouth	Atlanta	19,246	96	*
Hitachi	Tokyo	14,923	165	18
Bell Atlantic	Philadelphia	13,882	79	8
Nynex	New York	13,649	90	*
Siemens	Munich, W. Germany	13,469	357	32
Ameritech	Chicago	13,184	77	*
NEC	Tokyo	12,769	128	9
Pacific Telesis	San Francisco	12,050	75	*
GTE	Stamford, CT	11,466	183	23
Southwestern Bell	St. Louis	10,908	70	*
US West	Englewood, CO	10,620	67	0
Hewlett-Packard	Palo Alto, CA	10,501	84	33
Digital Equipment	Maynard, MA	10,162	95	37
Boeing	Seattle	9,777	112	1
Fujitsu	Tokyo	9,246	N/A	N/A
General Electric	London	9,102	165	21

*Less than 1%.

DATAMATION U.S. 100: THE LEADING U.S. DP COMPANIES
June 15, 1986

"Throughout the year, DATAMATION observes over 200 companies on a worldwide basis. The survey is meant to be used as a comparative analysis, and therefore all revenues and earnings figures have been adjusted to calendar-year calculations. Because over half the companies covered operate on a fiscal year that does not coincide with the calendar year, their revenues and earnings for purposes of this survey have been derived from quarterly reports and our best estimates."-- DATAMATION.

1985 Rank	Company	1985 DP Revenue ($M)
1	International Business Machines	$48,554.0
2	Digital Equipment Corp.	7,029.4
3	Sperry Corp.	4,755.1
4	Burroughs Corp.	4,685.3
5	NCR Corp.	3,885.5
6	Control Data Corp.	3,679.7
7	Hewlett-Packard Co.	3,675.0
8	Wang Laboratories Inc.	2,428.3
9	Xerox Corp.	1,959.0
10	Honeywell Inc.	1,951.9
11	Apple Computer Corp.	1,753.8
12	AT&T Co.	1,500.0
13	TRW Inc.	1,450.0
14	Tandy Corp.	1,200.0
15	Data General Corp.	1,199.7
16	General Electric Co.	1,130.0
17	McDonnell Douglas Corp.	1,104.5
18	Automatic Data Processing Inc.	1,102.1
19	General Motors Corp.	978.3
20	Amdahl Corp.	862.0
21	Harris Corp.	810.0
22	Computer Sciences Corp.	800.7
23	Prime Computer Inc.	769.7
24	ITT Corp.	756.0
25	Commodore International Ltd.	750.0
26	Texas Instruments	750.0

(Continued next page)

DATAMATION U.S. 100: THE LEADING U.S. DP COMPANIES (Continued)

1985 Rank	Company	1985 DP Revenue ($M)
27	Motorola Inc.	$704.0
28	Storage Technology Corp.	673.4
29	National Semiconductor Corp.	650.0
30	Tandem Computers Inc.	634.6
31	Telex Corp.	597.4
32	Intergraph Corp.	526.4
33	Compaq Computer Corp.	503.9
34	Comdisco Inc.	467.9
35	Computervision Corp.	441.1
36	Martin Marietta Corp.	429.9
37	Datapoint Corp.	404.2
38	Convergent Technologies	395.2
39	Cray Research Inc.	380.2
40	Dataproducts Corp.	378.4
41	Tektronix Inc.	366.9
42	Zenith Electronics Corp.	352.0
43	Arthur Anderson & Co.	343.6
44	Xidex Corp.	342.0
45	Diebold Inc.	324.2
46	Sanders Associates Inc.	323.4
47	Shared Medical Systems Corp.	312.2
48	M/A-COM Inc.	305.4
49	Apollo Computer Inc.	295.6
50	3M	295.4
51	Continental Telecom Inc.	277.8
52	Boeing Co.	270.0
53	Gould Inc.	269.4
54	Tandon Corp.	268.8
55	NBI Inc.	260.7
56	Perkin-Elmer Corp.	259.0
57	MAI Basic Four Inc.	252.8
58	Paradyne Corp.	252.5
59	Sterling Software Inc.	238.8
60	Lotus Development Corp.	225.5
61	Centronics Data Computer Corp.	216.2
62	Seagate Technologies	214.6

(Continued next page)

DATAMATION U.S. 100: THE LEADING U.S. DP COMPANIES (Continued)

1985 Rank	Company	1985 DP Revenue ($M)
63	General Instrument Corp.	$210.2
64	Eastman Kodak Co.	210.0
65	Gerber Scientific Inc.	207.2
66	Quotron Systems Inc.	205.7
67	UCCEL Corp.	204.8
68	Planning Research Corp.	203.0
69	Micom Systems Inc.	194.2
70	Intel Corp.	187.2
71	Cullinet Software Inc.	182.8
72	General DataComm Industries Inc.	179.4
73	Reynolds & Reynolds Co.	178.0
74	Decision Data Computer Corp.	176.4
75	ISC Systems Corp.	175.0
76	Computer Associates Int'l Inc.	170.4
77	Recognition Equipment Inc.	163.1
78	Microsoft Corp.	162.6
79	Mead Corp.	153.8
80	Cipher Data Products Inc.	152.5
81	Management Science America Inc.	151.7
82	Ameritech	150.0
82	Signal Cos.	150.0
84	CPT Corp.	149.3
85	National Data Corp.	149.1
86	Printronix Inc.	148.4
87	Telerate Inc.	148.0
88	Software AG Systems Inc.	143.0
89	Xebec	136.2
90	Daisy Systems Corp.	133.6
91	Lear Siegler Inc.	130.0
91	Schlumberger Ltd.	130.0
93	Floating Point Systems Inc.	128.3
94	Intelligent Systems Inc.	125.0
95	InteCom Inc.	123.6
96	Sun Micro Systems Inc.	115.0
97	American Management Systems Inc.	112.2
98	Commerce Clearing House Inc.	112.0
98	Computer Consoles Inc.	112.0
100	Ashton-Tate	110.4

DATAMATION 100: THE LEADING WORLDWIDE DP COMPANIES
June 15, 1986

"Throughout the year, DATAMATION observes over 200 companies on a worldwide basis. The survey is meant to be used as a comparative analysis, and therefore all revenues and earnings figures have been adjusted to calendar-year calculations. Because over half the companies covered operate on a fiscal year that does not coincide with the calendar year, their revenues and earnings for purposes of this survey have been derived from quarterly reports and our best estimates."-- DATAMATION.

Reprinted with permission of DATAMATION[R] Magazine. Copyright by Technical Publishing Company, A Dun & Bradstreet Company, 1986 - all rights reserved.

1985 Rank	1984 Rank	Company	1985 Total Revenue ($M)	1985 DP Revenue ($M)	DP Rev Change (%)
1	1	International Business Machines	$50,056.0	$48,554.0	9.6%
2	2	Digital Equipment Corp.	7,029.4	7,029.4	12.8
3	7	Sperry Corp.	5,526.8	4,755.1	18.4
4	3	Burroughs Corp.	5,037.7	4,685.3	4.1
5	6	Fujitsu Ltd.	6,563.0	4,309.5	12.3
6	5	NCR Corp.	4,317.2	3,885.5	5.9
7	9	NEC Corp.	9,899.4	3,761.8	14.1
8	4	Control Data Corp.	3,679.7	3,679.7	-0.3
9	8	Hewlett-Packard Co.	6,505.0	3,675.0	8.1
10	10	Siemens AG	18,574.9	3,265.0	17.0
11	12	Hitachi Ltd.	20,919.4	2,885.4	12.6
12	13	Ing. C. Olivetti & Co. S.P.A.	3,070.2	2,518.2	18.7
13	11	Wang Laboratories Inc.	2,428.3	2,428.3	0.3
14	17	Xerox Corp.	8,732.1	1,959.0	14.0
15	15	Honeywell Inc.	6,624.6	1,951.9	6.9
16	16	Groupe Bull	1,794.5	1,794.5	15.4
17	14	Apple Computer Corp.	1,753.8	1,753.8	-7.6
18	18	AT&T Co.	34,910.0	1,500.0	11.9
19	25	TRW Inc.	5,917.2	1,450.0	31.2
20	--	Matsushita Electric Indust. Co. Ltd.	21,221.4	1,447.6	30.0
21	22	Toshiba Corp.	14,377.9	1,409.0	30.1
22	26	N.V. Philips Gloeilampenfabrieken	18,085.6	1,365.6	9.6
23	21	Nixdorf Computer AG	1,339.9	1,339.9	16.8
24	20	STC plc	2,560.6	1,330.8	5.7
25	27	Northern Telecom Ltd.	4,246.9	1,240.8	6.1
26	24	LM Ericsson	3,779.3	1,232.8	9.8
27	38	Tandy Corp.	3,126.3	1,200.0	28.7

(Continued next page)

DATAMATION 100: THE LEADING WORLDWIDE DP COMPANIES (Continued)

1985 Rank	1984 Rank	Company	1985 Total Revenue ($M)	1985 DP Revenue ($M)	DP Rev Change (%)
28	19	Data General Corp.	$1,199.7	$1,199.7	-4.4
29	31	General Electric Co.	28,285.0	1,130.0	19.6
30	28	McDonnell Douglas Corp.	11,477.7	1,104.5	12.4
31	29	Automatic Data Processing Inc.	1,102.1	1,102.1	14.9
32	35	General Motors Corp.	96,371.7	978.3	24.4
33	33	Mitsubishi Electric Corp.	8,484.4	933.3	13.3
34	30	Oki Electric Industry Co. Ltd.	1,680.0	890.4	4.0
35	36	Amdahl Corp.	862.0	862.0	10.6
36	37	Harris Corp.	2,306.6	810.0	11.0
•37	39	Computer Sciences Corp.	800.7	800.7	12.8
38	40	Prime Computer Inc.	769.7	769.7	19.7
39	--	Nippon Telegraph and Telephone Corp.	20,651.4	764.1	20.8
40	41	ITT Corp.	20,007.0	756.0	18.1
41	23	Commodore International Ltd.	798.6	750.0	-34.8
41	32	Texas Instruments Inc.	4,924.5	750.0	-12.8
43	49	C. Itoh & Co. Ltd.	61,435.1	706.7	14.6
44	43	Motorola Inc.	5,443.0	704.0	13.9
45	34	Storage Technology Corp.	673.4	673.4	-16.7
46	47	National Semiconductor	1,605.9	650.0	18.2
47	65	Ricoh Co. Ltd.	2,441.2	634.7	35.3
48	45	Tandem Computers	634.6	634.6	12.1
49	50	Telex Corp.	683.1	597.4	34.9
50	--	Nippon Univac Kaisha Ltd.	552.9	552.9	11.5
51	52	Intergraph Corp.	526.4	526.4	30.4
52	61	Compaq Computer Corp.	503.9	503.9	53.2
53	--	Compagnie Generale d'Electricite	8,908.7	479.0	7.4
54	--	Comdisco Inc.	602.9	467.9	20.7
55	--	British Telecom pic	10,504.2	455.1	N/A
56	42	Volkswagen AG	17,855.2	452.9	16.0
57	46	Computervision Corp.	441.1	441.1	-20.7
58	58	Martin Marietta Corp.	4,410.1	429.9	18.9
59	44	Datapoint Corp.	404.2	404.2	-27.3
60	57	Convergent Technologies	395.2	395.2	9.3
61	51	Racal Elecronics plc	1,627.0	380.8	-17.7
62	77	Cray Research Inc.	380.2	380.2	66.2
63	48	Dataproducts Corp.	378.4	378.4	-13.8

(Continued next page)

NA: Not Available

DATAMATION 100: THE LEADING WORLDWIDE DP COMPANIES (Continued)

1985 Rank	1984 Rank	Company	1985 Total Revenue ($M)	1985 DP Revenue ($M)	DP Rev Change (%)
64	54	Tektronix Inc.	$1,434.5	$366.9	-5.1
65	63	BASF	15,092.6	357.1	19.7
66	60	Mannesmann Kienzle GmbH	448.1	355.7	3.7
67	75	Zenith Electronics Corp.	1,623.7	352.0	41.4
68	--	Arthur Andersen	1,573.9	343.6	22.0
69	--	Xidex Corp.	342.0	342.0	75.0
70	55	Diebold Inc.	410.9	324.2	-13.3
71	70	Sanders Associates Inc.	783.8	323.4	24.0
72	72	Shared Medical Systems Corp.	312.2	312.2	21.6
73	73	M/A-COM Inc.	855.2	305.4	22.2
74	80	Apollo Computer Inc.	295.6	295.6	36.9
75	67	3M	7,846.0	295.4	5.0
76	68	Mitel Corp.	294.8	294.8	1.9
77	69	Ferranti plc	737.2	282.1	6.1
78	76	Continental Telecom Inc.	2,557.0	277.8	14.6
79	71	Boeing Co.	13,636.0	270.0	3.8
80	79	Gould Inc.	1,420.1	269.4	20.0
81	53	Tandon Corp.	268.8	268.8	-32.5
82	84	NBI Inc.	260.7	260.7	36.4
83	74	Perkin-Elmer Corp.	1,310.0	259.0	11.2
84	--	MAI Basic Four Inc.	252.8	252.8	N/A
85	66	Paradyne Corp.	252.5	252.5	-12.9
86	64	Plessey Co. plc	1,862.0	250.0	-13.8
87	82	Cap Gemini Sogeti	245.1	245.1	19.0
88	--	Sterling Software Inc.	238.8	238.8	21.3
89	100	Lotus Development Corp.	225.5	225.5	43.7
90	--	Atlantic Computers plc	234.8	224.4	87.0
91	--	Sony Corp.	5,994.8	221.8	-10.3
92	96	Norsk Data AS	219.8	219.8	31.9
93	87	Nokia Corp.	1,777.5	217.6	20.2
94	92	Centronics Data Computer Corp.	216.2	216.2	26.1
95	62	Seagate Technology	214.6	214.6	-37.6
96	78	General Instrument Corp	848.0	210.2	-15.5
97	--	Eastman Kodak Co.	10,631.0	210.0	-4.1
98	86	Gerber Scientific	207.2	207.2	-2.8
99	85	Quotron Systems Inc.	205.7	205.7	8.4
100	59	Thorn EMI	4,108.4	205.0	-40.9

NA: Not Available

ELECTRONIC BUSINESS 200: THE LEADING U.S. ELECTRONICS CORPORATIONS
July 15, 1986

"The ELECTRONIC BUSINESS 200 is a cooperative effort between the magazine and Arthur D. Little, a Cambridge, Massachusetts-based consulting firm. For purposes of comparison, only companies whose electronics revenue constitutes over 70% of total revenue are included."-- ELECTRONIC BUSINESS.

From this list COMPUTER INDUSTRY ALMANAC has selected only 1985 figures.

Reprinted by permission from ELECTRONIC BUSINESS, July 15, 1986. Copyright 1986 by Reed Publishing USA, a division of Reed Holdings Inc., Newton, MA.

1985 Rank	Company	1985 Electronics Revenue ($)	1985 Company Revenue ($)	1985 Company Profits ($)
1	IBM	$50,056.0	$50,056.0	$6,555.0
2	AT&T	17,641.9	34,909.5	1,556.8
3	General Motors	9,503.8(1)	96,371.6(2)	3,999.0
4	General Electric	7,590.0	28,285.0	2,336.0
5	Xerox	7,545.0	8,732.1	380.5
6	DEC	7,029.4	7,029.4	400.6
7	ITT	7,010.0	11,871.2	286.4
8	Honeywell	6,624.6	6,624.6	281.6
9	Hewlett-Packard	6,571.0	6,571.0	482.0
10	Motorola	5,443.0	5,443.0	72.0
11	Burroughs	5,037.7	5,037.7	248.2
12	Sperry	5,000.0	5,717.6	37.4
13	Texas Instruments	4,924.5	4,924.5	-118.7
14	RCA	4,851.0	8,972.1	369.1
15	NCR	3,952.0	4,317.2	315.2
16	Raytheon	3,794.0	6,408.5	375.9
17	Control Data	3,679.7	4,679.7	-567.5
18	Rockwell	3,591.0	11,741.4	580.6
19	TRW	3,344.5	5,917.2	133.7
20	North American Philips	3,279.0	4,395.2	81.5
21	Tandy	3,137.6	3,137.6	203.9
22	Litton Industries	2,875.0	4,568.0	247.7

(Continued next page)

(1) GM Hughes Electronics Corp. (GMHE) electronics revenue
(2) Hughes 1985 revenue is not included in GM's revenue

ELECTRONIC BUSINESS 200: THE LEADING U.S. ELECTRONICS CORPORATIONS
(Continued)

1985 Rank	Company	1985 Electronics Revenue ($)	1985 Company Revenue ($)	1985 Company Profits ($)
23	Allied-Signal (3)	$2,850.0	$9,115.0	$-279.0
24	GTE	2,621.0	15,732.4	-161.1
25	Wang	2,428.3	2,428.3	-63.3
26	Westinghouse	2,350.0	10,700.2	605.3
27	Harris	2,306.6	2,306.6	60.7
28	3M	2,272.0	7,846.0	664.0
29	Ford	2,071.0	52,774.4	2,515.4
30	Martin Marietta	1,882.1	4,410.1	249.4
31	United Technologies	1,877.0	14,991.7	36.4
32	Boeing	1,850.0	13,636.0	566.0
33	Eaton	1,778.0	3,674.5	230.9
34	Apple	1,753.9	1,753.9	72.0
35	Lockheed	1,740.0	9,535.0	401.0
36	Zenith	1,623.7	1,623.7	-7.7
37	National Semiconductor	1,605.8	1,605.8	-89.5
38	Pitney Bowes	1,603.3	1,831.8	144.5
39	McDonnell Douglas	1,575.0	11,477.7	345.7
40	Gould	1,420.1	1,420.1	-100.8
41	Tektronix	1,419.8	1,419.8	70.2
42	DuPont	1,400.0	29,483.0	1,180.0
43	Intel	1,365.0	1,365.0	1.6
44	AMP	1,350.0	1,636.1	108.0
45	Singer	1,338.0	2,416.3	82.3
46	Perkin-Elmer	1,222.0	1,310.0	79.5
47	Emerson Electric	1,213.0	4,679.5	402.1
48	Avnet	1,201.0	1,384.8	31.3
49	Data General	1,199.0	1,199.0	2.4
50	Grumman	1,128.0	3,098.9	81.5

(Continued next page)

(3) Includes results of The Signal Companies Inc., which consolidated with Allied Corp. as of
October 1, 1985

ELECTRONIC BUSINESS 200: THE LEADING U.S. ELECTRONICS CORPORATIONS
(Continued)

1985 Rank	Company	1985 Electronics Revenue ($)	1985 Company Revenue ($)	1985 Company Profits ($)
51	Teledyne	$1,056.8	$3,256.2	$546.4
52	Varian Associates	962.9	962.9	15.3
53	Northrop	938.3	5,056.6	214.4
54	Sanders Associates	889.4	889.3	34.9
55	General Signal	867.5	1,800.9	49.3
56	Amdahl	862.0	862.0	24.4
57	M/A-COM	855.4	855.4	32.6
58	General Instrument	824.7	824.7	106.7
59	E-Systems	806.1	926.8	59.5
60	Prime	769.7	769.7	57.8
61	Chrysler	744.0	21,255.5	1,635.2
62	Lear Siegler	715.0	2,358.2	88.2
63	Penn Central	685.0	2,527.3	110.8
64	Telex	683.1	683.1	67.1
65	Continental Telecom	681.0	2,556.6	239.9
66	Storage Technology	673.4	673.4	-43.7
67	Johnson Controls	657.0	2,105.2	88.4
68	General Dynamics	640.0	8,163.8	372.5
69	Tandem	634.5	634.5	32.0
70	Advanced Micro Devices	623.8	623.8	0.5
71	SmithKline Beckman	619.0	3,256.6	514.4
72	Kodak	600.0	10,631.0	332.0
73	Loral	562.0	599.1	48.7
74	Corning Glass	534.8	1,690.5	107.6
75	SCI Systems	527.6	527.6	14.2

(Continued next page)

ELECTRONIC BUSINESS 200: THE LEADING U.S. ELECTRONICS CORPORATIONS
(Continued)

1985 Rank	Company	1985 Electronics Revenue ($)	1985 Company Revenue ($)	1985 Company Profits ($)
76	Integraph	$526.4	$526.4	$67.8
77	Monsanto	520.0	6,747.0	-128.0
78	COMPAQ	503.9	503.9	26.6
79	Emerson Radio	502.9	502.9	10.5
80	Arrow Electronics	500.0	534.1	-10.9
81	Tracor	498.0	546.5	18.9
82	United Telecommunications	475.0	3,198.4	20.8
83	Scientific-Atlanta	443.7	443.7	16.8
84	Computervision	441.1	441.1	-80.8
85	Compugraphic	400.8	400.8	21.8
86	Convergent	395.2	395.2	11.5
87	Medtronic	387.6	387.6	49.3
88	Cray Research	380.2	380.2	75.6
89	Dataproducts	370.6	370.6	-29.7
90	Ducommun	347.5	417.0	-3.3
91	EG&G	337.0	1,177.1	55.7
92	Teradyne	336.4	336.4	20.2
93	Datapoint	331.3	331.3	-68.7
94	Diebold	329.0	410.9	30.4
95	Tyler	325.3	912.4	15.4
96	TIE/communications	321.3	321.3	-75.0
97	Analog Devices	319.7	319.7	26.4
98	Savin	310.0	431.7	-52.8
99	Cubic	305.0	341.7	12.2
100	Seagate Technology	303.6	303.6	8.7

(Continued next page)

ELECTRONIC BUSINESS 200: THE LEADING U.S. ELECTRONICS CORPORATIONS
(Continued)

1985 Rank	Company	1985 Electronics Revenue ($)	1985 Company Revenue ($)	1985 Company Profits ($)
101	Apollo	$295.6	$295.6	$-1.5
102	DSC Communications	287.6	287.6	-63.3
103	Foxboro	286.0	572.2	-34.2
104	Mohawk Data Sciences	285.2	285.2	-79.2
105	Emhart	284.0	1,775.4	80.5
106	Kollmorgen	277.0	311.0	-6.4
107	Dover	276.0	1,439.5	100.0
108	Premier Industrial	269.0	433.7	39.3
109	CTS	261.6	261.6	7.9
110	Molex	255.4	255.4	28.2
111	Augat	255.0	255.0	12.1
112	Paradyne	252.5	252.5	-31.2
113	Exxon	250.0	92,869.0	4,870.0
114	Square D	246.0	1,348.1	102.4
115	Union Carbide	240.0	9,003.0	-599.0
116	Dynatech	238.1	238.1	22.0
117	Bally Manufacturing	238.0	1,344.8	25.6
118	Oak Industries	238.0	284.3	-37.6
119	Watkins-Johnson	232.6	232.5	18.4
120	Marshall Industries	231.6	231.6	1.5
121	NBI	230.0	260.7	7.8
122	Western Digital	227.6	227.6	-2.9
123	Tandon	225.9	225.9	-119.1
124	Xidex	225.0	342.1	25.6
125	Eli Lilly	222.0	3,260.6	517.6

(Continued next page)

ELECTRONIC BUSINESS 200: THE LEADING U.S. ELECTRONICS CORPORATIONS
(Continued)

1985 Rank	Company	1985 Electronics Revenue ($)	1985 Company Revenue ($)	1985 Company Profits ($)
126	Cooper Industries	$220.0	$3,067.2	$135.1
127	GenRad	218.3	218.3	-52.3
128	Bell & Howell	217.0	759.8	32.2
129	Centronics	216.3	216.3	0.2
130	Fluke	214.7	214.7	14.5
131	LTV	214.0	8,198.8	-771.5
132	Figgie International	208.0	803.4	29.2
133	Andrew	207.8	207.8	12.2
134	Gerber Scientific	207.3	207.3	19.7
135	Pioneer-Standard	207.2	207.2	0.2
136	Cincinnati Milacron	206.0	732.2	-44.8
137	Spectra-Physics	198.9	198.9	-1.7
138	Wyle Laboratories	195.4	260.8	1.5
139	Micom Systems	194.2	194.2	14.9
140	Avantek	190.3	190.3	17.7
141	Ball	188.5	1,106.2	51.2
142	Logicon	187.9	187.9	9.6
143	AM International	186.0	614.0	23.3
144	Bell Industries	185.0	295.8	4.5
145	Nashua	185.0	621.6	16.4
146	General DataComm	179.4	179.4	8.7
147	Recognition Equipment	179.4	179.4	3.6
148	AVX	178.7	178.7	-12.3
149	Hazeltine	177.7	177.7	10.1
150	Sundstrand	177.0	1,284.1	74.4

(Continued next page)

ELECTRONIC BUSINESS 200: THE LEADING U.S. ELECTRONICS CORPORATIONS
(Continued)

1985 Rank	Company	1985 Electronics Revenue ($)	1985 Company Revenue ($)	1985 Company Profits ($)
151	Measurex	$176.6	$176.6	$17.7
152	Decision Data	176.4	176.4	7.8
153	Pittway	175.0	548.5	31.1
154	Monolithic Memories	171.6	171.6	5.5
155	AST Research	171.0	171.0	29.2
156	Millipore	170.0	367.2	31.7
157	Unitrode	168.0	168.0	9.2
158	ISC Systems	161.5	161.5	11.5
159	Applied Materials	160.1	160.1	5.9
160	Polaroid	160.0	1,295.2	36.9
161	Allen Group	159.0	399.2	16.7
162	American District Telegraph	158.0	479.6	-56.6
163	Tyco Laboratories	158.0	646.2	31.1
164	Diasonics	157.9	157.9	3.5
165	GCA	156.5	156.5	-94.2
166	Kidde	155.0	2,164.8	47.6
167	Cipher Data Products	152.5	152.5	7.9
168	Computer Memories	151.2	151.2	16.4
169	Becton, Dickinson	151.0	1,156.1	92.4
170	Veeco Instruments	150.4	150.4	7.3
171	AccuRay	150.4	150.4	8.0
172	Rexnord	143.0	1,108.1	42.4
173	Esterline	142.0	246.1	0.0
174	International Rectifier	141.1	141.1	-0.8
175	Mark Controls	140.8	279.0	2.7

(Continued next page)

ELECTRONIC BUSINESS 200: THE LEADING U.S. ELECTRONICS CORPORATIONS
(Continued)

1985 Rank	Company	1985 Electronics Revenue ($)	1985 Company Revenue ($)	1985 Company Profits ($)
176	SI Logic	$140.0	$140.0	$10.1
177	Fairchild Industries	140.0	855.9	-194.5
178	CPT	139.3	139.3	0.0
179	Sun Electric	139.0	168.8	-7.8
180	Mentor	136.7	136.7	8.0
181	Coherent	136.6	136.6	5.9
182	Printronix	136.3	136.3	-12.4
183	Xebec	136.1	136.1	-22.7
184	Cordis	136.0	195.9	4.5
185	United Industrial	135.0	269.4	19.1
186	Daisy	133.6	133.6	22.6
187	Electrospace Systems	133.2	133.2	12.6
188	Aydin	133.0	133.0	3.8
189	Analogic	132.4	132.4	10.3
190	Altos Computer	132.2	132.2	9.9
191	Allegheny International	129.0	2,056.7	-57.5
192	Floating Point Systems	128.4	128.4	14.1
193	Dynascan	128.1	128.1	0.1
194	Gulton Industries	128.0	155.5	6.2
195	Burndy	127.0	219.0	-9.1
196	National Computer Systems	127.0	156.5	12.4
197	Quantum	126.6	126.6	21.4
198	Conrac	126.5	150.3	7.2
199	Insilco	124.0	811.8	26.1
200	InteCom	123.6	123.6	-6.6

ELECTRONIC BUSINESS: FASTEST GROWING ELECTRONICS COMPANIES
April 15, 1986

"To be represented on the ELECTRONIC BUSINESS list of fastest growing companies, a firm must be publically held, based in the U.S., achieve revenues of $80 million or more, derive 70% of its revenues from electronics or computers and have a five-year operating history. Excluded are software firms and companies that provide services such as R&D, engineering assistance, or data processing."--ELECTRONIC BUSINESS.

Reprinted with permission from ELECTRONIC BUSINESS, April 15, 1986. Copyright 1986 by Reed Publishing USA, a division of Reed Holdings Inc., Newton, MA.

1985 Rank	Company	Sales growth (5-yr comp. annual rate)	Fiscal 1985 sales ($ millions)	Fiscal 1985 net profit margin
1	Convergent Technologies	307.7%	$395.2	2.9%
2	Comdial	203.3	85.2	-35.8
3	Lee Data	170.3	91.1	0.5
4	Emulex	85.2	103.2	7.6
5	Apple	74.9	1,918.3	3.2
6	Xebec	66.7	149.2	-13.9
7	Tandon	63.8	268.8	-50.4
8	SCI Systems	63.0	538.1	2.6
9	Micom Systems	62.7	193.3	13.3
10	ISC Systems	59.7	150.0	5.5
11	Intergraph	56.3	526.4	12.9
12	Western Digital	53.8	177.4	-2.6
13	Intelligent Systems	53.6	123.9	1.4
14	Micropolis	52.6	94.9	2.9
15	NBI	52.5	216.7	6.1
16	TeleVideo	52.1	103.1	-18.6
17	Cipher Data Products	50.6	169.1	8.7
18	LTX	46.7	133.4	5.1
19	Cray Research	44.3	380.2	19.9
20	Tandem Computers	41.8	624.1	5.5
21	Timeplex	40.6	96.0	10.4
22	TIE/communications	40.0	321.3	-24.2
23	Xidex	34.7	259.5	9.4
24	Diasonics	34.7	157.9	4.6
25	Emerson	34.3	357.5	3.7
26	Wang Laboratories	34.1	2,351.7	0.7
27	Advanced Micro Devices	32.8	931.1	4.5
28	Decision Data Computer	32.2	176.4	4.4

(Continued next page)

ELECTRONIC BUSINESS: FASTEST GROWING ELECTRONICS COMPANIES (Continued)

1985 Rank	Company	Sales growth (5-yr comp. annual rate)	Fiscal 1985 sales ($ millions)	Fiscal 1985 net profit margin
29	Printronix	32.0%	$148.4	4.8%
30	Telex	29.4	601.6	8.9
31	General DataComm Industries	28.3	186.6	5.8
32	Anthem Electronics	28.2	119.6	5.1
33	Avantek	26.7	190.3	9.3
34	Paradyne	26.4	252.5	-12.3
35	Electrospace Systems	26.3	107.8	9.7
36	Marshall Industries	26.0	265.3	2.2
37	Sanders Associates	25.8	885.8	4.2
38	Burroughs	25.6	5,037.7	4.9
39	Computer Products	25.3	92.5	7.1
40	Key Tronic	25.0	122.7	2.3
41	AccuRay	25.0	150.4	5.3
42	Adams-Russell	24.8	129.0	7.3
43	Gerber Scientific	24.7	224.2	11.2
44	Floating Point Systems	24.4	126.6	11.4
45	Nicolet Instruments	23.8	112.6	4.3
46	Prime	23.5	769.7	7.5
47	DEC	23.1	6,686.3	6.7
48	California Microwave	22.6	105.4	4.4
49	Logicon	21.7	168.3	4.9
50	Pioneer-Standard Electronics	21.7	233.4	1.6
51	Systems Industries	21.1	98.6	-11.3
52	M/A-COM	21.0	884.1	4.5
53	Diplomat Electronics	20.7	104.4	5.7
54	Ducommun	20.6	419.6	-0.8
55	CPT	20.3	149.3	-2.0
56	Kulicke & Soffa Industries	20.2	125.1	-0.4
57	Dynascan	20.1	128.1	0.1
58	Loral	20.1	502.3	8.4
59	Dataproducts	20.0	471.8	5.9
60	Electro Scientific	19.9	84.1	10.2
61	Applied Materials	19.8	174.6	5.3
62	Unitrode	19.6	200.1	11.1
63	Dynatech	19.5	204.6	9.4
64	Andrew	19.3	215.5	6.5
65	Analog Devices	18.9	322.4	9.2

(Continued next page)

ELECTRONIC BUSINESS: FASTEST GROWING ELECTRONICS COMPANIES (Continued)

1985 Rank	Company	Sales growth (5-yr comp. annual rate)	Fiscal 1985 sales ($ millions)	Fiscal 1985 net profit margin
66	Sensormatic Electronics	18.3%	$91.3	8.2%
67	Computervision	18.2	441.1	-18.3
68	Monolithic Memories	18.2	177.7	5.9
69	Scientific-Atlanta	17.9	436.9	3.8
70	Computer Consoles	17.0	111.9	-37.5
71	Amdahl	16.9	862.0	3.3
72	Coherent	16.5	131.7	5.6
73	Hewlett-Packard	16.4	6,505.0	7.5
74	E-Systems	15.9	926.8	6.4
75	Molex	15.8	253.2	12.3
76	Tandy	15.6	2,853.0	6.6
77	Teradyne	15.3	336.4	6.0
78	N.A.Phillips	15.1	4,395.2	1.9
79	Regency Electronics	14.7	114.4	3.8
80	Hazeltine	14.7	177.7	5.7
81	Analogic	14.5	132.0	7.5
82	National Semiconductor	14.5	1,787.5	2.4
83	Harris	14.1	2,281.2	3.5
84	IBM	13.8	50,056.0	13.1
85	Triad Systems	13.7	107.3	-5.1
86	Data General	13.6	1,239.0	2.0
87	Applied Magnetics	12.2	120.8	2.6
88	Varian Associates	11.9	972.5	2.7
89	Watkins-Johnson	11.9	232.6	7.9
90	Tracor	11.7	546.5	2.4
91	Transitron Electronics	11.4	116.5	8.9
92	Cubic	11.1	331.7	4.4
93	Burr-Brown	11.0	94.5	6.0
94	Data Card	10.9	104.0	7.7
95	Wyle Laboratories	10.6	354.6	2.6
96	Motorola	10.6	5,443.0	1.3
97	Siliconix	10.3	108.0	8.4
98	Datapoint	10.3	520.2	-9.3
99	Kollmorgen	10.2	311.0	-2.0
100	John Fluke	10.1	216.6	7.0

FORBES

COMPUTERS AND ELECTRONICS: YARDSTICKS OF MANAGEMENT PERFORMANCE
January 13, 1986

"The computer slump spared almost no one: Virtually every computer company on the list showed earnings drops in 1985." The chart indicates profitability as Return On Equity and growth as Sales.-- FORBES

Reprinted by permission of FORBES Magazine, January 13, 1986. Copyright Forbes Inc., 1986.

| Company | Return On Equity: | | | Sales: | | |
	Rank	5-Year Average	Latest 12 Months	Rank	5-Year Average	Latest 12 Months
Computers						
Apple Computer	1	63.8%	12.9%	1	99.8%	26.6%
Tandy	2	40.1	19.3	12	18.7	5.3
Prime Computer	3	33.2	17.0	5	30.7	18.8
Telex	4	29.5	32.4	7	28.1	52.0
Wang Laboratories	5	29.0	*def	4	45.0	1.4
Computervision	6	28.0	*def	6	29.9	-3.2
IBM	7	24.7	22.8	14	15.1	6.9
Hewlett-Packard	8	20.4	13.8	11	19.1	7.6
Tandem Computers	9	19.3	8.9	3	56.7	17.2
SCI Systems	10	18.2	15.7	2	61.9	15.2
Harris Corp	11	15.2	8.0	17	11.9	12.3
NCR	12	14.7	14.6	22	5.6	5.4
Digital Equipment	13	14.3	8.5	8	24.3	12.8
General Instrument	14	13.9	*def	21	5.7	-8.0
Honeywell	15	13.0	.08	20	6.9	5.7
Datapoint	16	12.0	*def	10	20.7	-13.4
Data General	17	11.6	3.8	13	15.2	6.7
Sperry	18	9.4	1.1	23	1.3	13.6
Control Data	19	8.7	*def	18	8.3	1.8
Zenith Electronics	20	8.0	0.1	19	8.0	1.7
Gould	21	7.9	*def	24	-9.6	-11.3
Amdahl	22	7.8	7.4	9	21.7	7.1
Burroughs	23	7.1	9.9	15	12.6	4.3
Storage Technology	24	*def	*def	16	11.9	-25.7
Medians		14.5	8.0		17.0	6.2

*def: Deficit

NEWTON-EVANS RESEARCH COMPANY
BIG 12 COMPUTER MAKERS
1986

This list ranks the top computer companies by information processing revenue in billions for calendar years 1984 and 1985.--COMPUTER INDUSTRY ALMANAC.
Reprinted with permission from Newton-Evans Research Co., 1986. Copyright 1986 by Newton-Evans Research Co., Elliott City, MD.

Rank	Company	1985 IP Revenue	1984 IP Revenue	Percent Change
1	IBM	$45.10	$41.30	9.2%
2	Digital Equipment	7.02	6.23	12.7
3	Sperry	4.94	4.62	6.9
4	Burroughs	4.38	4.18	4.8
5	NCR	3.93	3.70	6.1
6	Control Data	3.68	3.69	-0.3
7	Hewlett-Packard	3.41	3.37	1.2
8	Wang	2.43	2.42	0.4
9	Honeywell	1.99	1.82	9.3
10	Apple	1.75	1.90	-7.9
11	Data General	1.20	1.25	-4.0
12	Xerox	1.13	1.10	2.7

WORKSTATION LABORATORIES
SUPERCOMPUTER COMPANIES RANKED BY PERCENT OF WORLDWIDE INSTALLED
BASE
1987

"For this data, supercomputers are defined to be those systems produced specifically for very computationally intensive applications with a performance level of at least 150 million floating point operations per second (MFLOPS). Excluded from this data are those products based on standard mainframes with hardware to accelerate floating point operations, such as the IBM mainframes with vector processors or the Unisys (Sperry) product. Also excluded from this data are the minisupercomputers ("Crayettes") such as those manufactured by Convex, Elexi, or Scientific Computer Systems. At this time, the performance levels of both excluded categories are lower than standard supercomputer levels."--Workstation Laboratories.

Reprinted with permission from Workstation Laboratories, 1987. Copyright 1987 by Workstation Laboratories, Humboldt, AZ.

Manufacturer	% of Worldwide Installed Base*
Cray	65
Control Data/ETA	17
Fujitsu	11
Hitachi	5
NEC	2

*These percentages are based on a worldwide installed base of 215 supercomputers in late 1986. Control Data and ETA are considered together because of the large percentage of ETA stock owned by Control Data Corporation.

COMPUTER INTELLIGENCE
TOP MAINFRAME MANUFACTURERS
BASED ON VALUE OF INSTALLED U.S. SYSTEMS
1986

"This ranking of mainframe computer manufacturers is based on the value of installed systems in the U.S."--Computer Intelligence.
Reprinted with permission from Computer Intelligence, July 1986. Copyright 1986 by Computer Intelligence, La Jolla, CA.

Rank	Manufacturer	Total Purchase $ Billions
1	IBM	$23.8
2	Sperry	3.1
3	Amdahl	1.5
4	Honeywell	1.3
5	NAS	1.2
6	Burroughs	1.1

DATAMATION
DATAMATION 100: THE TOP 15 COMPANIES IN MAINFRAMES
June 15, 1986

This ranking is derived from the "Datamation 100: The Leading Worldwide DP Companies,"
DATAMATION Magazine, June 15, 1986.-- COMPUTER INDUSTRY ALMANAC.
Reprinted with permission of DATAMATION^R Magazine. Copyright by Technical Publishing
Company, A Dun & Bradstreet Company, 1986 - all rights reserved.

Rank	Company	1985 ($ Mil.)	1984 ($Mil.)	Percent Change*
1	IBM	$14,010.0	$13,131.0	6.7
3	Sperry Corp.	1,890.8	1,451.1	30.3
5	Fujitsu Ltd.	1,618.6	1,535.5	5.4
7	NEC Corp.	1,216.6	1,076.6	13.0
8	Control Data Corp.	856.0	813.0	5.3
11	Hitachi Ltd.	836.8	745.3	12.3
15	Honeywell Inc.	775.0	665.0	16.5
4	Burroughs Corp.	747.3	747.3	NC
16	Groupe Bull	574.3	499.9	14.9
6	NCR Corp.	485.5	485.5	NC
35	Amdahl Corp.	434.0	400.0	8.5
10	Siemens Corp. AG	374.1	350.9	6.6
24	STC plc	370.0	362.9	2.0
62	Cray Research	332.6	200.0	66.3
46	National Semiconductor Corp.	300.0	250.0	20.0

*Percent change in dollars. In actual accounting currencies, Fujitsu's mainframe revenues were up
5.4% to ¥385.5 billion; NEC's were up 13% to ¥289.6 billion; Groupe Bull's were up 18% to FF5.1
billion; Siemen's were up 10% to DM1.1 billion; and STC plc's were up 6% to L288 million.

NC: no change.

DATAMATION
DATAMATION 100: THE TOP 15 COMPANIES IN MINICOMPUTERS
June 15, 1986

This ranking is derived from the "Datamation 100: The Leading Worldwide DP Companies," DATAMATION Magazine, June 15, 1986. It includes superminicomputers.--COMPUTER INDUSTRY ALMANAC.

Reprinted with permission of DATAMATION^R Magazine. Copyright by Technical Publishing Company, A Dun & Bradstreet Company, 1986 - all rights reserved.

Rank	Company	1985 ($ Mil.)	1984 ($ Mil.)	Percent Change*
1	IBM	$3,500.0	$3,500.0	NC
2	Digital Equipment Corp.	1,600.0	1,527.0	4.8
9	Hewlett-Packard Co.	1,050.0	950.0	10.5
13	Wang Laboratories Inc.	870.9	970.5	-10.3
28	Data General Corp.	799.7	840.0	- 4.8
38	Prime Computer Inc.	563.7	479.1	17.7
48	Tandem Computers Inc.	533.1	477.1	11.7
36	Harris Corp.	470.0	410.0	14.6
5	Fujitsu Ltd.	439.0	383.9	14.4
23	Nixdorf Computer AG	407.9	340.0	20.0
3	Sperry Corp.	400.5	409.5	- 2.2
4	Burroughs Corp.	400.0	400.0	NC
6	NCR Corp.	400.0	335.0	19.4
56	Volkswagen AG	366.7	314.0	16.8
12	Ing.C.Olivetti & Co. S.P.A.	348.6	394.9	-11.7

*Percent change in dollars. In actual accounting currencies, Fujitsu's mini revenues were up 14.3% to ¥104.5 billion; Nixdorf's were up 23.8% to DM1.1 billion; Volkswagen's were up 20.5% to DM1.0 billion and Olivetti's were up 5.9% to L697.1 billion.

NC: no change.

WORKSTATION LABORATORIES
INSTALLED BASE OF TECHNICAL WORKSTATION MANUFACTURERS
December 1986

"This data shows the worldwide installed base of technical workstations for the major workstation manufacturers as of December 1986. The percentage of installed base is based on a total of 81,100 system units."--Workstation Laboratories.

Reprinted with permission from Workstation Laboratories, December 1986. Copyright 1986 by Workstation Laboratories, Humboldt, AZ.

Company	Installed Workstations	% of Installed Base
Apollo Computer	25,500	31.4
Sun Microsystems	22,500	27.7
Digital Equipment	10,000	12.3
Hewlett-Packard	9,500	11.7
IBM	6,000	7.4
Masscomp	2,800	3.5
Silicon Graphics	1,600	2.0
Other Manufacturers	3,200	4.0

COMPUTER INTELLIGENCE
PERSONAL COMPUTER HARDWARE MARKET SHARE IN U.S. LARGE BUSINESS SITES
October 1, 1986

"The market share is represented from 14,000 sites. The survey is comprised of primary mainframes (which are the IBM/PCM and general-purpose computers) and DEC VAX sites. Market share information is comprised of the number of suppliers installed as opposed to the quantity of products. The chart shows the installed market share of personal computer hardware in large business sites in the U.S. as of October 1, 1986."--Computer Intelligence.

Reprinted with permission from Computer Intelligence, October 1, 1986. Copyright 1986 by Computer Intelligence, La Jolla, CA.

Rank	Manufacturer	% Sites
1	IBM	73
2	Apple	4
2	Compaq	4
2	DEC	4
5	Tandy	3
6	AT&T	2
6	Hewlett-Packard	2
6	Wang	2
9	Others	6

DATAMATION
DATAMATION 100: THE TOP 15 COMPANIES IN MICROS
June 15, 1986

This ranking is derived from the "Datamation 100: The Leading Worldwide DP Companies,"
DATAMATION Magazine, June 15, 1986.--COMPUTER INDUSTRY ALMANAC.
Reprinted with permission of DATAMATION^R Magazine. Copyright by Technical Publishing
Company, A Dun & Bradstreet Company, 1986 - all rights reserved.

Rank	Company	1985 ($ Mil.)	1984 ($ Mil.)	Percent Change*
1	IBM	$5,500.0	$5,500.0	NC
17	Apple Computer Corp.	1,603.0	1,747.0	- 8.2
12	Ing. C. Olivetti & Co. S.P.A.	884.5	496.9	78.0
27	Tandy Corp.	796.8	573.5	38.9
3	Sperry Corp.	742.8	503.4	47.6
41	Commodore International Ltd.	600.0	1,000.0	-40.0
52	Compaq Computer Corp.	503.9	329.0	53.2
9	Hewlett-Packard Corp.	400.0	500.0	-20.0
60	Convergent Technologies Inc	395.2	361.7	9.3
67	Zenith Electronics Corp.	352.0	249.0	41.4
7	NEC Corp.	338.6	305.1	11.0
74	Apollo Computer Corp	295.6	215.9	36.9
20	Matsushita Electronics Corp.	270.6	278.4	- 2.8
26	LM Ericsson	232.6	217.6	6.9
2	Digital Equipment Corp.	225.0	250.0	-10.0

*Percent change in dollars. In actual accounting currencies, Olivetti's micro revenues were up
113.6% to L1.7 trillion; NEC's were up 11% to ¥80.6 billion; Matsushita's were down 2.8% to
¥64.4 billion; and Ericsson's were up 11.1% to Skr2.0 billion.
NC: no change.

FUTURE COMPUTING INCORPORATED
LEADING PERSONAL COMPUTER HARDWARE COMPANIES
December 1986

This list ranks the leading personal computer hardware companies by estimated revenue.--
COMPUTER INDUSTRY ALMANAC.

Reprinted with permission from Future Computing Incorporated, December 1986. Copyright 1986
by Future Computing Incorporated, Dallas, TX.

Company	1986 Estimated Revenue ($M)
1. IBM	$4,105.*
2. Apple	1,567.
3. Tandy	650.**
4. Compaq	608.
5. AT&T	455.

*Worldwide company revenue personal computers only.
**Estimated, excluding printers, S/W, and other.

DATAMATION
DATAMATION 100: THE TOP 15 COMPANIES IN PERIPHERALS
June 15, 1986

This ranking is derived from the "Datamation 100: The Leading Worldwide DP Companies,"
DATAMATION Magazine, June 15, 1986.--COMPUTER INDUSTRY ALMANAC.
Reprinted with permission of DATAMATIONR Magazine. Copyright by Technical Publishing
Company, A Dun & Bradstreet Company, 1986 - all rights reserved.

Rank	Company	1985 ($ Mil.)	1984 ($ Mil.)	Percent Change*
1	IBM	$12,676.0	$11,652.0	8.8%
2	Digital Equipment Corp.	2,750.0	2,500.0	10.0
4	Burroughs Corp.	1,479.0	1,412.0	4.7
14	Xerox Corp.	1,430.0	1,180.0	21.2
11	Hitachi Ltd.	1,416.7	1,049.0	35.1
8	Control Data Corp.	1,270.0	1,314.5	-3.4
13	Wang Laboratories Inc.	1,229.5	1,100.6	11.7
9	Hewlett-Packard Corp.	1,100.0	900.0	22.2
5	Fujitsu Ltd.	1,064.3	932.1	14.2
7	NEC Corp.	1,053.3	882.3	19.4
6	NCR Corp.	1,000.0	950.0	5.3
10	Siemens AG	816.2	701.8	16.3
21	Toshiba Corp	759.5	521.7	45.6
16	Groupe Bull	699.1	605.9	15.4
15	Honeywell Inc.	656.0	600.0	9.3

*Percent change in dollars. In actual accounting currencies, Hitachi's peripherals revenues were up
35.1% to ¥337.3 billion; Fujitsu's were up 14.2% to ¥253.4 billion; NEC's were up 19.4% to
¥250.7 billion; Siemens' were up 20% to DM2.4 billion; Toshiba's were up 45.6% to ¥180.8
billion; and Groupe Bull's were up 18.5% to FF6.2 billion.

COMPUTER RETAIL NEWS (CRN)
TOP 10 PERIPHERAL DISTRIBUTORS: NATIONWIDE
August 11, 1986

"Based on information compiled for CRN's 'Preferred Distributor Study.' The study, conducted by the CRN Research staff under the direction of Lee Tunick, was designed to measure buying preferences of resellers purchasing software from distributors. Because the study was completed in April 1986, the results might include companies that are no longer major players."--COMPUTER RETAIL NEWS.
Reprinted with permission from COMPUTER RETAIL NEWS, August 11, 1986. Copyright 1986 by CMP Publications, Inc., Manhasset, NY.

Rank	Distributor	# of Mentions	% of Base
1	Microamerica	202	14.3
2	Softsel	120	8.5
3	Micro-D	99	7.0
4	Epson	86	6.1
5	FA Components	79	5.6
6	Arrow	63	4.5
7	Tech Data	54	3.8
8	Hall-Mark Electronics	38	2.7
9	Robec Dist.	36	2.6
10	Distribution Plus	32	2.3

Base = 1414

COMPUTER RETAIL NEWS (CRN)
TOP 10 SOFTWARE DISTRIBUTORS: NATIONWIDE
August 4, 1986

"Based on information compiled for CRN's 'Preferred Distributor Study.' The study, conducted by
the CRN Research staff under the direction of Lee Tunick, was designed to measure buying
preferences of resellers purchasing software from distributors. Because the study was completed in
April 1986, the results might include companies that are no longer major players."--COMPUTER
RETAIL NEWS.
Reprinted with permission from COMPUTER RETAIL NEWS, Monday, August 4, 1986.
Copyright 1986 by CMP Publications, Manhasset, NY.

Rank	Distributor	# of Mentions	% of Base
1	Softsel	536	37.9
2	First Software	378	26.7
3	Micro D	193	13.7
4	Softeam	158	11.2
5	Ingram	70	5.0
6	SoftKat	36	2.6
7	Microamerica	35	2.5
8	Software Resource	31	2.2
9	Fortune 1000 Dist.	27	1.9
10	Software America	20	1.4

Base = 1414

ELECTRONIC NEWS
TOP 25 DISTRIBUTORS OF INDUSTRIAL ELECTRONICS
December 1, 1986

This list ranks the top 25 distributors of industrial electronics. The 1986 sales figures are estimated by ELECTRONIC NEWS.--COMPUTER INDUSTRY ALMANAC.
Reprinted with permission from ELECTRONIC NEWS, December 1, 1986. Copyright 1986 by Fairchild Publications, New York, NY.

Rank	Distributor	1986 Sales ($ millions)
1	Avnet	$1,100
2	Lex	520
3	Arrow	520
4	Ducommun	400
5	Hall-Mark	385
6	Pioneer	290
7	Marshall	285
8	Premier	220
9	Future	217
10	Wyle	195
11	Anthem	170
12	Bell	160
13	Zeus	88
14	Milgray	65
15	TTI	59
16	Powell	57
17	SAI	55
18	Western Micro	52
19	Deanco	48
20	Diplomat	47
21	Shelley-Ragon	46
22	Sterling	44
23	IEC	40
24	Chelsea	38
25	Hammond	35

FORBES

COMPUTERS AND ELECTRONICS: YARDSTICKS OF MANAGEMENT PERFORMANCE
January 13, 1986

"The computer slump spared almost no one: Virtually every computer company on the list showed earnings drops in 1985." The chart indicates profitability as Return On Equity and growth as Sales.--FORBES.

Reprinted by permission of FORBES Magazine, January 13, 1986. Copyright Forbes Inc., 1986.

Company	Return On Equity (%):			Sales Growth (%):		
	Rank	5-Year Average	Latest 12 Months	Rank	5-Year Average	Latest 12 Months
Electronic Equipment						
EG&G	1	28.6	35.2	6	15.0	11.2
AMP	2	23.3	13.7	11	11.3	-9.0
Hewlett-Packard	3	20.4	13.8	4	19.1	7.6
Raytheon	4	20.3	18.8	15	8.5	1.0
Sanders Associates	5	18.2	11.6	2	33.2	18.7
Pitney Bowes	6	18.0	20.8	12	10.2	5.4
Tyler	7	16.5	10.8	7	14.1	-18.8
M/A-COM	8	16.4	9.3	1	38.1	9.9
Perkin-Elmer	9	15.9	13.2	16	7.0	7.8
Tektronix	10	15.4	9.3	13	10.1	4.5
General Signal	11	14.4	11.5	20	4.4	2.2
Baimco	12	14.3	15.2	3	32.6	10.1
General Instrument	13	13.9	*def	18	5.7	-8.0
Insilco	14	13.4	10.6	19	4.5	6.6
North Amer Philips	15	13.1	9.7	9	12.3	2.9
Honeywell	16	13.0	8.0	17	6.9	5.7
Sun Chemical	17	12.8	10.7	8	13.2	1.1
Xerox	18	12.2	4.3	22	3.4	.4
American District	19	11.7	6.5	14	9.3	7.8
Varian Associates	20	10.8	6.1	10	11.6	4.7
Penn Central	21	8.8	7.5	5	15.1	-1.1
Eaton	22	8.0	20.1	23	-1.6	9.0
Gould	23	7.9	*def	26	-9.6	-11.3
Nashua	24	4.0	11.9	24	-2.1	2.6
Oak Industrial	25	*def	*def	21	2.6	-30.6
AM International	26	**def	NE	25	-7.4	2.2
Medians		13.7	10.7		9.7	3.7

*def: Deficit   **def: Three-year average
NE: Negative Equity

COMPANIES - Copyright 1987 Computer Industry Almanac

ELECTRONIC NEWS
LOOKING AT THE LEADERS 1986
August 25, 1986

This list ranks the 50 leading manufacturers in the U.S. electronics industry by each company's
electronic sales.--COMPUTER INDUSTRY ALMANAC.
Reprinted with permission from ELECTRONIC NEWS, August 25, 1986. Copyright 1986 by
Fairchild Publications, New York, NY.

	U.S. Companies	Electronic Sales	Percent of Electronic Sales	Gross Sales in Latest Available Four Quarters
1	IBM Corp.	*$40,998,000,000	80.0%	$51,248,000,000
2	General Motors	9,954,700,000	9.8	101,578,400,000
3	AT&T	8,990,000,000	25.0	35,960,000,000
4	General Electric Co.	*7,227,750,000	25.0	28,911,000,000
5	Hewlett-Packard Co.	6,672,000,000	100.0	6,672,000,000
6	ITT Corp.	6,602,100,000	30.0	22,007,000,000
7	Sperry Corp.	5,762,800,000	100.0	5,762,800,000
8	Motorola, Inc.	5,587,000,000	100.0	5,587,000,000
9	Honeywell, Inc.	*5,187,000,000	76.0	6,825,000,000
10	Digital Equipment Corp.	5,161,443,000	68.0	7,570,357,000
11	RCA Corp.	*4,894,100,000	54.0	9,063,100,000
12	Xerox Corp.	4,606,500,000	50.0	9,213,500,000
13	N.A. Philips Corp.	4,517,155,000	95.0	4,754,923,000
14	NCR Corp.	4,183,807,000	91.5	4,572,467,000
16	Raytheon Co.	4,043,000,000	59.2	6,830,000,000
17	Texas Instruments, Inc.	*3,975,300,000	83.0	4,789,500,000
18	Westinghouse Electric Corp.	*3,668,300,000	33.0	11,116,000,000
19	Rockwell International	*3,646,000,000	30.0	12,154,000,000
20	Allied-Signal, Inc.	3,573,000,000	44.0	8,058,000,000
21	Control Data Corp.	3,500,500,000	100.0	3,500,500,000
22	TRW, Inc.	3,371,300,000	56.0	5,993,100,000
23	Burroughs Corp.	3,172,300,000	62.0	5,116,600,000
24	Tandy Corp.	3,035,969,000	100.0	3,035,969,000
25	Litton Industries, Inc.	2,965,023,000	66.0	4,494,263,000
26	Wang Laboratories, Inc.	2,642,500,000	100.0	2,642,500,000
27	GTE Corp.	2,449,299,000	15.0	16,326,660,000
28	Harris Corp.	2,216,636,000	100.0	2,216,636,000
29	Schlumberger Ltd.	2,084,400,000	36.0	5,790,000,000

*Estimated by Electronic News

ELECTRONIC NEWS: LOOKING AT THE LEADERS 1986 (Continued)

U.S. Companies		Electronic Sales	Percent of Electronic Sales	Gross Sales in Latest Available Four Quarters
30	Eaton Corp.	$1,951,900,000	53.0%	$3,682,900,000
31	Apple Computer, Inc.	1,800,721,000	100.0	1,800,721,000
32	Zenith Electronics Corp.	1,626,000,000	100.0	1,626,000,000
33	Amp, Inc.	1,492,959,000	85.0	1,758,422,000
34	National Semiconductor	1,478,116,000	100.0	1,478,116,000
35	Penn Central	*1,407,000,000	56.5	2,491,000,000
36	Teledyne, Inc.	1,382,992,000	42.5	3,254,100,000
37	Gould, Inc.	1,378,800,000	100.0	1,378,800,000
38	Intel Corp.	1,320,527,000	100.0	1,320,527,000
39	Singer Corp.	1,301,900,000	53.6	2,490,885,000
40	General Signal Corp.	1,280,284,500	75.0	1,707,046,000
41	E.I. du Pont de Nemours & Co.	1,247,000,000	4.3	29,003,000,000
42	Data General	1,237,388,000	100.0	1,237,388,000
43	Avnet	1,146,636,000	81.0	1,415,600,000
44	Ford Aerospace & Comm. Corp.	1,116,500,000	85.0	1,319,700,000
45	Perkin-Elmer Corp.	968,164,000	75.0	1,290,885,000
46	Varian Associates, Inc.	915,000,000	100.0	915,000,000
47	Amdahl Corp.	887,837,000	100.0	887,837,000
48	Sanders Associates, Inc.	861,169,000	100.0	861,189,000
49	M/A-Com, Inc.	835,846,000	100.0	835,846,000
50	E-Systems, Inc.	835,872,000	80.0	1,032,240,000

*Estimated by Electronic News

FORBES

COMPUTERS AND ELECTRONICS: YARDSTICKS OF MANAGEMENT PERFORMANCE
January 13, 1986

"The computer slump spared almost no one: Virtually every computer company on the list showed earnings drops in 1985." The chart indicates profitability as Return On Equity and growth as Sales.-- FORBES.

Reprinted by permission of FORBES Magazine, January 13, 1986. Copyright Forbes Inc., 1986.

| Company | Return On Equity (%): | | | Sales Growth(%): | | |
	Rank	5-Year Average	Latest 12 Months	Rank	5-Year Average	Latest 12 Months
Semiconductors						
Schumberger	1	30.6	15.1	7	9.0	6.2
Advanced Micro	2	25.1	8.5	1	30.2	-14.3
Avnet	3	16.7	5.8	9	5.5	-15.9
Motorola	4	15.8	6.8	5	14.4	3.1
Intel	5	15.3	2.9	3	16.8	-5.3
General Instrument	6	13.9	*def	8	5.7	-8.0
Natl Semiconductor	7	11.7	*def	4	14.7	-4.0
Texas Instruments	8	11.6	*def	6	9.8	-5.3
Arrow Electronics	9	9.1	*def	2	21.2	-22.3
Medians		15.3	2.9		14.4	-5.3

*def: Deficit

INTEGRATED CIRCUIT ENGINEERING (ICE)
TOP TEN SEMICONDUCTOR SUPPLIERS WORLDWIDE
1986

This list ranks the worldwide top 10 producers of semiconductors by production revenue.--
COMPUTER INDUSTRY ALMANAC.

Reprinted with permission from INTEGRATED CIRCUIT ENGINEERING CORP, 1986.
Copyright 1986 by Integrated Circuit Engineering Corp, Scottsdale, AZ.

1985 Rank	1986 (Est) Rank	Company	1985 Production ($M)	1986 Estimated Production ($M)
1	1	NEC	$2,070	$2,825
4	2	Hitachi	1,675	2,045
5	3	Toshiba	1,460	2,005
3	4	Motorola*	1,800	2,000
2	5	TI	1,830	1,830
6	6	Fujitsu	1,055	1,550
7	7	Philips**	1,010	1,215
10	8	Matsushita	855	1,165
9	9	National	950	970
-	10	Mitsubishi	660	910

*Includes $150M of non-Semiconductor Sector packaging (non-hybrid)
** Including Signetics

IN-STAT INC.
TOP 10 WORLDWIDE SEMICONDUCTOR MANUFACTURERS
January 1987

"This ranking shows the top worldwide semiconductor manufacturers ranked by estimated 1986 worldwide semiconductor revenues. In 1986 there are four U.S. companies in the top ten. Because of the fluctuating exchange rate between the dollar and the yen, the U.S. companies, when measured equally with the Japanese companies, are higher in the rankings than they were a year ago. For example, Texas Instruments ranked second in 1985 and now in 1986 ranks first. In unit sales the Japanese companies exceed the U.S. companies, but as shown here, the U.S. companies rank higher in revenues."--In-Stat Inc.

Reprinted with permission from In-Stat Inc., January 1987. Copyright 1987 by In-Stat Inc., Scottsdale, AZ.

Company	Est. 1986 Worldwide Semiconductor Revenues ($M)
1. Texas Instruments	$1,800
2. NEC	1,750
3. Hitachi	1,700
4. Motorola	1,700
5. Toshiba	1,400
6. Philips/Signetics	1,100
7. Fujitsu	1,000
8. Intel	900
9. National	890
10. Matsushita	800

COMPUTER INTELLIGENCE
TOP 10 LEADING INDEPENDENT COMPUTER LESSORS
January-August 1986

"This chart shows the top ten independent computer lessors in the U.S. by the percentage of total lease revenue. Estimates are based on the Uniform Commercial Code Initial Financial Filing data."-- Computer Intelligence.
Reprinted with permission from Computer Intelligence, 1986. Copyright 1986 by Computer Intelligence, La Jolla, CA.

Rank	Company	Percent of Market
1.	Comdisco, Inc.	45
2.	CMI Corp.	18
3.	Unilease Computers	7
4.	Computer Financial	6
5.	CIS Corp.	5
5.	Meridian Leasing	5
7.	Finalco, Inc.	4
7.	Capital Associates	4
9.	Lincoln Lease/Way	3
9.	Somerset Investment	3

DATAMATION
DATAMATION 100: THE TOP 15 COMPUTER SERVICES COMPANIES
June 15, 1986

This ranking is derived from the "Datamation 100: The Leading Worldwide DP Companies,"
DATAMATION Magazine, June 15, 1986.--COMPUTER INDUSTRY ALMANAC.
Reprinted with permission of DATAMATION[R] Magazine. Copyright by Technical Publishing
Company, A Dun & Bradstreet Company, 1986 - all rights reserved.

Rank	Company	1985 ($Mil.)	1984 ($Mil.)	Percent Change*
31	Automatic Data Processing Inc.	$1,102.1	$959.4	14.9%
8	Control Data Corp.	1,058.7	930.5	13.8
32	General Motors Corp.	978.3	786.1	24.4
29	General Electric Co.	950.0	825.0	15.2
37	Computer Sciences Corp.	800.7	709.6	12.8
30	McDonnell Douglas Corp.	650.0	608.0	6.9
58	Martin Marietta Corp.	429.9	361.5	18.9
39	Nippon Telegraph and Telephone Corp.	382.0	375.0	1.9
3	Sperry Corp.	302.5	288.6	4.8
6	NCR Corp.	300.0	285.0	5.3
1	IBM	300.0	200.0	50.0
79	Boeing Corp.	270.0	260.0	3.8
14	Xerox Corp.	200.0	180.0	11.1
96	General Instrument Corp.	190.2	193.4	-1.7
99	Quotron Systems Inc.	187.5	189.9	-1.3

*Percent change in dollars. In actual accounting currencies, Nippon Telegraph and Telephone's
computer services revenues were up 1.9% to ¥90.9 billion.

BUSINESS SOFTWARE REVIEW
ICP 200: AMERICA'S TOP 200 SOFTWARE PRODUCT AND SERVICE COMPANIES
June 1986

"This years's ICP 200 is the eighth report in a series of annual surveys of the top U.S. software products and services (SP&S) companies conducted by International Computer Programs (ICP), publisher of the BUSINESS SOFTWARE REVIEW, and Input, a Mountain View, California-based market research firm."--BUSINESS SOFTWARE REVIEW.
Reprinted with permission from BUSINESS SOFTWARE REVIEW, June 1986. Copyright 1986 by International Computer Programs Inc., Indianapolis, IN.

Rank	Company	Software Products and Services (SP&S) Offered	Years in SP&S Business	SP&S Revenue (Mil.)
1	International Business Machines (IBM)	abcdefghijklm	17	$5,045
2	Electronic Data Systems (EDS)	ehijkl	24	3,445
3	Control Data Corporation	abcdefghijklm	24	1,227
4	Automatic Data Processing	ghi	36	1,102
5	TRW	abkl	28	1,100
6	McDonnell Douglas Information Systems	abcdeghijk	2	842
7	Computer Sciences	behijkl	27	801
8	Hewlett-Packard	abce	19	633
9	General Electric Information Services	abceghiklm	22	589
10	Digital Equipment Corporation	abekl	28	562
11	Intergraph	el	17	526
12	Arthur Andersen	aklm	26	505
13	Burroughs	abceklm	29	450
14	Computervision	e	17	441
15	NCR	abcdefghijklm	33	431
16	Sperry	abcelm	45	358
17	Boeing Computer Services	abcghijklm	16	339
18	Shared Medical Systems	abeij	17	312
19	Concurrent Computer	abc	11	270
20	Equifax	aghi	20	250
*	Science Applications International	abcekl	17	250

(Continued next page)

Legend for SP&S business classes:

a-Applications Software Supplier f-Software Product Retailer j-On-Site Processing Firm
b-Systems Software Supplier g-Local Batch Processing Firm k-Custom Programming Firm
c-Utilities Software Supplier h-Remote Non-Interactive l-DP Consulting Supplier
d-OEM Distributor Processing Firm m-Education/Training Supplier
e-Turnkey Systems Supplier i-Interactive Processing Firm

*Companies with the same SP&S revenues are given the same rank and arranged alphabetically.

ICP 200: AMERICA'S TOP 200 SOFTWARE PRODUCT AND SERVICE COMPANIES
(Continued)

Rank	Company	Software Products and Services (SP&S) Offered	Years in SP&S Business	SP&S Revenue (Mil.)
22	Martin Marietta Data Systems	abcdefghijklm	16	249
23	CAP Gemini America	abek	12	245
24	Sterling Software	abceghijkl	5	$243
25	Grumman	abcklm	17	240
26	Lotus Development	a	4	226
27	Planning Research Corporation	eijk	32	224
28	Gerber Scientific	e	20	205
*	Uccel	abeh	23	205
30	First Data Resources	i	15	200
31	Quotron Systems	ei	23	195
32	Data General	abcdekm	18	192
33	HBO & Company	aeijl	12	189
34	Cullinet Software	ab	18	183
35	Computer Associates International	abc	10	170
36	McGraw Hill Financial & Economic Info.	ai	17	165
37	Telerate	i	17	164
38	Applicon	eg	17	160
*	MTech	abdhi	18	160
40	Management Science America (MSA)	a	23	152
41	National Data	aij	19	149
42	Applied Data Research	bk	21	143
43	Reynolds & Reynolds	eghi	23	142
44	Dun & Bradstreet	ahi	20	140
*	GTE	hk	11	140
*	Honeywell	abcef	30	140
*	Litton Industries	aeghijkl	17	140
*	Microsoft	abc	12	140
*	Price Waterhouse	akl	30	140
50	Bolt Beranek and Newman	akl	20	137
51	Daisy Systems	e	6	134
	(Continued next page)			

Legend for SP&S business classes:

a-Applications Software Supplier
b-Systems Software Supplier
c-Utilities Software Supplier
d-OEM Distributor
e-Turnkey Systems Supplier

f-Software Product Retailer
g-Local Batch Processing Firm
h-Remote Non-Interactive Processing Firm
i-Interactive Processing Firm

j-On-Site Processing Firm
k-Custom Programming Firm
l-DP Consulting Supplier
m-Education/Training Supplier

*Companies with the same SP&S revenues are given the same rank and arranged alphabetically.

ICP 200: AMERICA'S TOP 200 SOFTWARE PRODUCT AND SERVICE COMPANIES
(Continued)

Rank	Company	Software Products and Services (SP&S) Offered	Years in SP&S Business	SP&S Revenue (Mil.)
52	BankAmerica	ghi	25	131
53	Mead Data Central	i	16	128
54	CCH Computax	g	20	127
55	Bunker Ramo Information Systems	i	30	125
56	Batelle Memorial Institute	bl	22	120
57	AGS Computers	adk	19	117
58	Computer Task Group	gk	10	115
*	Fidata	ahil	18	115
60	Systematics	aj	18	113
61	American Management Systems	ahijkl	16	112
62	Tandy	ab	10	110
63	Anacomp	aeghijk	18	108
64	Policy Management Systems	adeijl	12	103
65	Baxter Travenol	acejkl	5	100
*	Citicorp Information Resources	aghij	7	100
*	Lockheed	abijklm	7	100
*	Sanders Associates	abcde	35	100
*	Wang Laboratories	abe	34	100
70	Cincom Systems	ab	18	95
71	Comdata Network	gh	17	92
72	Computer Language Research	agh	22	90
*	General Instrument	ej	11	90
*	Telecredit	i	25	90
75	Syscon	abeijkl	20	88
76	Prime Computer	abcklm	14	86
77	CACI	bcikl	24	85
*	Metier Management Systems	ae	9	85
79	Triad Systems	eh	14	84
80	Ashton-Tate	a	5	82

(Continued next page)

Legend for SP&S business classes:

a-Applications Software Supplier
b-Systems Software Supplier
c-Utilities Software Supplier
d-OEM Distributor
e-Turnkey Systems Supplier

f-Software Product Retailer
g-Local Batch Processing Firm
h-Remote Non-Interactive Processing Firm
i-Interactive Processing Firm

j-On-Site Processing Firm
k-Custom Programming Firm
l-DP Consulting Supplier
m-Education/Training Supplier

*Companies with the same SP&S revenues are given the same rank and arranged alphabetically.

ICP 200: AMERICA'S TOP 200 SOFTWARE PRODUCT AND SERVICE COMPANIES
(Continued)

Rank	Company	Software Products and Services (SP&S) Offered	Years in SP&S Business	SP&S Revenue (Mil.)
81	Xerox Computer Services	ak	16	81
82	Apple Computer	ab	7	80
83	Pansophic Systems	abc	17	78
*	SAS Institute	a	10	78
85	CompuServe	i	17	75
*	Tandem Computers	abcm	8	75
87	Ask Computer Systems	aeim	14	72
*	C3	e	18	72
89	Information Builders	blm	11	71
90	DST Systems	gh	17	68
91	Comshare	aik	3	66
92	Auto-Trol Technology	e	24	65
93	Computer Data Systems	ehl	18	61
*	Interactive Data	adghikl	18	61
95	Candle	b	9	60
*	Deltak	a	20	60
97	Software AG of North America	bc	14	59
*	Telos	akl	17	59
99	Continuum Company (The)	ahikl	18	58
100	SEI	aikl	18	55
*	SunData	ahij	11	55
102	American Telephone & Telegraph	bei	3	53
103	Endata	ablk	15	52
*	Kirchman Corporation (The)	ah	18	52
105	CGA Computer	abkl	18	50
*	Commodore International	a	9	50
*	Safeguard Business Systems	eg	6	50
108	Compuware	ckl	13	49
*	Cycare Systems	abdikm	18	49

(Continued next page)

Legend for SP&S business classes:

a-Applications Software Supplier
b-Systems Software Supplier
c-Utilities Software Supplier
d-OEM Distributor
e-Turnkey Systems Supplier

f-Software Product Retailer
g-Local Batch Processing Firm
h-Remote Non-Interactive Processing Firm
i-Interactive Processing Firm

j-On-Site Processing Firm
k-Custom Programming Firm
l-DP Consulting Supplier
m-Education/Training Supplier

*Companies with the same SP&S revenues are given the same rank and arranged alphabetically.

ICP 200: AMERICA'S TOP 200 SOFTWARE PRODUCT AND SERVICE COMPANIES
(Continued)

Rank	Company	Software Products and Services (SP&S) Offered	Years in SP&S Business	SP&S Revenue (Mil.)
110	Analysts International	akl	20	48
*	Technicon Data Systems	abcdhk	15	48
112	Computer Power	adiklm	24	45
*	Paychex	g	17	45
114	Computer Horizons	kim	17	44
*	Digital Research	abcd	10	44
*	STSC	abi	17	44
117	Computer Company (The)	agijkl	18	42
*	Systems & Computer Technology	aj	18	42
119	Cincinnati Bell Information Systems	aeghikl	3	41
*	MicroPro International	a	7	41
121	ISSCO (Integrated Software Systems Corp)	a	16	40
*	Keane	ajklm	21	40
*	Redshaw	e	9	40
124	Intermetrics	abcekl	17	39
125	Computer Corporation of America	akl	11	38
*	Epsilon Data Management	gi	11	38
127	Advanced Systems Applications	ai	8	35
*	American Software	a	16	35
*	Dyatron	aeghik	22	35
*	Four-Phase Systems	ab	20	35
131	International Computaprint	hijk	19	34
132	On-Line Software International	bcl	17	32
*	Oracle	bcdfkl	9	32
*	Pentamation Enterprises	aehij	16	32
*	Software Publishing	a	6	32
136	Autodesk	a	4	30
*	Borland International	ac	3	30
*	Computone Systems	aei	21	30

(Continued next page)

Legend for SP&S business classes:

a-Applications Software Supplier
b-Systems Software Supplier
c-Utilities Software Supplier
d-OEM Distributor
e-Turnkey Systems Supplier

f-Software Product Retailer
g-Local Batch Processing Firm
h-Remote Non-Interactive Processing Firm
i-Interactive Processing Firm

j-On-Site Processing Firm
k-Custom Programming Firm
l-DP Consulting Supplier
m-Education/Training Supplier

*Companies with the same SP&S revenues are given the same rank and arranged alphabetically.

ICP 200: AMERICA'S TOP 200 SOFTWARE PRODUCT AND SERVICE COMPANIES
(Continued)

Rank	Company	Software Products and Services (SP&S) Offered	Years in SP&S Business	SP&S Revenue (Mil.)
139	Comserv	aglm	17	29
*	Users Incorporated	ej	22	29
141	Barrister Information Systems	e	14	28
*	Genigraphics	j	11	28
*	Micro Data Base Systems	bk	7	28
144	Lomas & Nettleton Financial	ahi	11	27
145	Boole & Babbage	bclm	19	25
*	Computer Assistance	abcegkl	19	25
*	Hogan Systems	a	9	25
*	Syncsort	b	18	25
149	Applied Communications	abckl	11	24
*	NCA	agil	17	24
*	OAO Corporation	eghijk	13	24
*	Project Software & Development	ael	18	24
153	Morino Associates	bm	13	23
*	Scientific Software-Intercomp	ag	18	23
*	Sierra On-Line	ad	6	23
*	World Computer	abcek	7	23
157	Broderbund Software	a	6	22
*	Erisco	ag	18	22
*	Sage Systems	be	12	22
160	Cybertek	ahijkl	17	21
*	Data Architects	ak	6	21
*	Integral Systems	ak	14	21
*	MacNeal-Schwendler	a	15	21
164	Execucom Systems	jklm	12	20
*	ITT Dialcom	aikl	16	20

(Continued next page)

Legend for SP&S business classes:

a-Applications Software Supplier   f-Software Product Retailer   j-On-Site Processing Firm
b-Systems Software Supplier   g-Local Batch Processing Firm   k-Custom Programming Firm
c-Utilities Software Supplier   h-Remote Non-Interactive   l-DP Consulting Supplier
d-OEM Distributor   Processing Firm   m-Education/Training Supplier
e-Turnkey Systems Supplier   i-Interactive Processing Firm

*Companies with the same SP&S revenues are given the same rank and arranged alphabetically.

ICP 200: AMERICA'S TOP 200 SOFTWARE PRODUCT AND SERVICE COMPANIES
(Continued)

Rank	Company	Software Products and Services (SP&S) Offered	Years in SP&S Business	SP&S Revenue (Mil.)
*	Saddlebrook Corporation (The)	aeklm	12	20
*	SKK	bm	8	20
168	Computer Partners	akl	10	19
*	Manager Software Products	b	9	19
*	Science Management	abl	7	19
*	TSR	aghijkl	17	19
172	Baron Data	e	10	18
*	Goal Systems International	abl	11	18
*	Information Resources	ai	15	18
*	VM Software	b	5	18
176	Activision	a	7	17
*	Packaged Automated Life/Liability Mgmt.	ak	17	17
*	SPSS	a	11	17
179	Information Associates	a	18	16
*	Information Science	ai	21	16
*	Lawson Associates	ak	11	16
*	MCRB Software	abceghijkl	9	16
*	On-Line Business Systems	bfghik	10	16
184	Advanced Computer Techniques	abdeghijkl	24	15
*	Timberline Systems	ae	7	15
186	BGS Systems	bl	11	14
*	Data Design Associates	a	13	14
*	Vista Concepts	al	7	14
189	Collier-Jackson	ae	11	13
*	Group 1 Software	gij	19	13
*	Madic	e	12	13
*	Mom Corporation (The)	ack	3	13
*	Precision Visuals	a	7	13
*	Professional Computer Resources	al	11	13

(Continued next page)

Legend for SP&S business classes:

a-Applications Software Supplier   f-Software Product Retailer   j-On-Site Processing Firm
b-Systems Software Supplier   g-Local Batch Processing Firm   k-Custom Programming Firm
c-Utilities Software Supplier   h-Remote Non-Interactive   l-DP Consulting Supplier
d-OEM Distributor   Processing Firm   m-Education/Training Supplier
e-Turnkey Systems Supplier   i-Interactive Processing Firm

*Companies with the same SP&S revenues are given the same rank and arranged alphabetically.

ICP 200: AMERICA'S TOP 200 SOFTWARE PRODUCT AND SERVICE COMPANIES
(Continued)

Rank	Company	Software Products and Services (SP&S) Offered	Years in SP&S Business	SP&S Revenue (Mil.)
*	Stockholder Systems	a	15	13
*	Technalysis	ack	18	13
197	Bonner & Moore Associates	ajklm	20	12
*	System Software Associates	a	4	12
*	Thorn EMI Computer Software	alm	13	12
200	J.D. Edwards & Company	a	8	11

Legend for SP&S business classes:

a-Applications Software Supplier   f-Software Product Retailer   j-On-Site Processing Firm

b-Systems Software Supplier   g-Local Batch Processing Firm   k-Custom Programming Firm

c-Utilities Software Supplier   h-Remote Non-Interactive   l-DP Consulting Supplier

d-OEM Distributor   Processing Firm   m-Education/Training Supplier

e-Turnkey Systems Supplier   i-Interactive Processing Firm

*Companies with the same SP&S revenues are given the same rank and arranged alphabetically.

BUSINESS SOFTWARE REVIEW
TWENTY COMPANIES TO WATCH IN THE NEXT FIVE YEARS
July 1986

The following is a list of 20 companies which our editors and advisors suggest you keep an eye on. Some names you know already, some are low profile. But all have some combination of technical expertise, resources, superior management, market presence or strategic direction that makes them potential movers and shakers in the software business. Sometime within the next five years, one or more of these companies will probably have an impact on your organization, so be prepared."--
BUSINESS SOFTWARE REVIEW.

Reprinted with permission from BUSINESS SOFTWARE REVIEW, July 1986. Copyright 1986 by International Computer Programs, Inc., Indianapolis, IN.

Rank	Company
1	IBM Corporation
2	Arthur Andersen & Company
3	Language Technology, Inc.
4	Autodesk, Inc.
5	Sterling Software Marketing
6	Distribution Management Systems
7	Oracle Corporation
8	Boole & Babbage (B&B)
9	Uccel
10	Computer Associates
11	Applied Data Research (ADR)
12	Group 1 Software
13	AT&T
14	Pallm (Packaged Automated Life/Liability Management Inc.)
15	VM Software Inc.
16	Ashton-Tate
17	Cincom Systems, Inc.
18	Teknowledge
19	Microsoft Corporation
20	Systematics, Inc.

COMPUTER INTELLIGENCE
PERSONAL COMPUTER SOFTWARE MARKET SHARE IN U.S. LARGE BUSINESS SITES
October 1, 1986

"The market share is represented from 14,000 sites. The survey is comprised of primary mainframes (which are the IBM/PCM and general-purpose computers) and DEC VAX sites. Market share information is comprised of the number of suppliers installed as opposed to the quantity of products. The data lists the installed market share for three major personal computer software categories: database, financial analysis, and word processing. The financial analysis market consists of spreadsheet and integrated spreadsheet products."--Computer Intelligence.
Reprinted with permission from Computer Intelligence, October 1, 1986. Copyright 1986 by Computer Intelligence, La Jolla, CA.

Rank	Manufacturer	% Sites
Database		
1	Ashton-Tate	73
2	Microrim	7
3	Software Publishing	3
4	Condor	2
4	Information Builders	2
4	MDBS	2
7	Other	11
Financial Analysis		
1	Lotus	81
2	Microsoft	9
3	CAI-Micro	5
4	Access Technology	1
4	Ashton-Tate	1
4	Cullinet Software	1
7	Other	2
Word Processing		
1	Micropro	36
2	IBM	19
3	Ashton-Tate	14
4	WordPerfect	8
5	Microsoft	4
6	DEC	3
6	Lifetree	3
6	Software Publishing	3
9	Other	10

COMPUTER RETAIL NEWS
TOP TEN SOFTWARE COMPANIES 1986
February 10, 1986

"The list presented is based on a compilation of revenue estimates provided by the companies and analyzed by software industry experts. The list is confined to companies whose sales are principally derived from development or publishing microcomputer operating systems and applications software sold through computer dealers to the business/professional market."--CRN.
Reprinted with permission from COMPUTER RETAIL NEWS, February 10, 1986. Copyright 1986 by CMP Publications, Inc., Manhasset, NY.

Rank	Company	Actual 1985 Sales($M)	Projected 1986 Sales($M)
1	Lotus	220	270
2	Microsoft	170	209
3	Ashton-Tate/Multimate	141	180
4	MicroPro	41	45
5	Borland	34	50
6	Software Publishing	32	37
7	Computer Assoc. Micro Products	27	35
8	Autodesk	26	41
9	Broderbund	24	30
10	Satellite Software	20	40

SOFT*LETTER
THE 1986 SOFT*LETTER 100
April 3, 1986

"A ranking of the top 100 independent microcomputer software publishers and developers in the U.S., based on calendar 1985 revenues."--SOFT*LETTER.
Reprinted with permission from SOFT*LETTER, April 3, 1986. Copyright 1986 by Soft*letter, Cambridge, MA.

Rank	Company	1985 Revenue	Growth Rate (%)	Owner	Number of Employees
1	Lotus Development Corp. Cambridge, MA	$225,526,000	44	Pub	1075
2	Microsoft Corp. Redmond, WA	162,630,000	30	Pub	998
3	Ashton-Tate Torrance, CA	110,397,000	40	Pub	815
4	Digital Research Inc. Monterey, CA	45,179,000	0	Pvt	250
5	Micropro International San Rafael, CA	40,061,000	-27	Pub	289
6	Software Publishing Corp. Mt. View, CA	31,664,000	-3	Pub	179
7	Borland International Scotts Valley, CA	30,000,000	114	Pvt	150
8	Autodesk Inc. Sausalito, CA	28,425,000	286	Pub	165
9	Broderbund San Rafael, CA	25,000,000	102	Pvt	165
10	Satellite Software Int'l. Orem, UT	22,983,000	155	Pvt	210
11	Electronic Arts San Mateo, CA	20,000,000	33	Pvt	80
11	Epyx Inc. Sunnyvale, CA	20,000,000	82	Pvt	40
13	Spinnaker Software Cambridge, MA	18,000,000	13	Pvt	50
14	Activision Inc. Mt. View, CA	16,360,000	-63	Pub	110
15	Microrim Inc. Redmond, WA	16,000,000	100	Pvt	125

(Continued next page)

THE 1986 SOFT*LETTER 100 (Continued)

Rank	Company	1985 Revenue	Growth Rate (%)	Owner	Number of Employees
16	Micro Data Base Systems Lafayette, IN	$13,400,000	31	Pvt	230
17	Software Bottling Co. Maspeth, NY	$13,000,000	64900	Pvt	25
18	Accountants Microsystems Bellevue, WA	12,500,000	19	Pvt	145
19	Infocom Cambridge, MA	11,000,000	10	Pvt	60
20	BPI Systems Inc. Austin, TX	10,048,000	4	Pub	140
21	Realworld Corp. Chichester, NH	10,000,000	5	Pvt	144
22	Software Solutions Trumbull, CT	9,800,000	227	Pvt	50
22	Thoughtware Coconut Grove, FL	9,800,000	78	Pvt	55
24	Decision Resources Inc. Westport, CT	9,600,000	169	Pvt	80
25	Libra Programming Salt Lake City, UT	8,361,000	13	Pvt	69
26	Innovative Software Overland Park, KS	8,300,000	98	Pub	100
27	Lifeboat Associates Tarrytown, NY	7,234,000	-64	Pvt	40
28	State of the Art Inc. Costa Mesa, CA	6,950,000	10	Pvt	52
29	Samna Corp. Atlanta, GA	6,500,000	33	Pvt	100
30	Springboard Software Inc. Minneapolis, MN	6,478,000	536	Pub	30
31	Graphic Software Systems Beaverton, OR	6,150,000	146	Pvt	70
32	Sir-Tech Software Inc. Ogdensburg, NY	6,100,000	27	Pvt	15
33	Microprose Software Hunt Valley, MD	6,000,000	100	Pvt	35

(Continued next page)

THE 1986 SOFT*LETTER 100 (Continued)

Rank	Company	1985 Revenue	Growth Rate (%)	Owner	Number of Employees
33	T & W Systems Inc. Huntington Beach, CA	$6,000,000	173	Pvt	5
35	Central Point Software Inc. Portland, OR	5,180,000	178	Pvt	30
36	Alpha Software Corp. Burlington, MA	5,000,000	-28	Pvt	25
37	Chang Laboratories San Jose, CA	4,800,000	75	Pvt	28
37	IMSI San Rafael, CA	4,800,000	92	Pvt	20
39	Lifetree Software Monterey, CA	4,200,000	17	Pvt	40
39	TCS Software Houston, TX	4,200,000	-9	Pvt	31
41	Strategic Simulations Mt. View, CA	4,100,000	32	Pvt	28
42	Sublogic Corp. Champaign, IL	4,000,000	100	Pvt	21
43	Davidson & Associates Torrance, CA	3,925,000	60	Pvt	n/a
44	DAC Software Dallas, Tx	3,700,000	n/a	Pvt	39
45	Channelmark Corp. San Mateo, CA	3,679,000	n/a	Pvt	17
46	Peter Norton Computing Inc. Santa Monica, CA	3,550,000	255	Pvt	6
47	Human Edge Software Corp. Palo Alto, CA	3,500,000	40	Pvt	24
48	American Training Int'l. Los Angeles, CA	3,400,000	-32	Pvt	32
49	Data Access Corp. Miami, FL	3,300,000	65	Pvt	n/a
50	Arrays Inc. Van Nuys, CA	3,041,000	-46	Pub	n/a

(Continued next page)

THE 1986 SOFT*LETTER 100 (Continued)

Rank	Company	1985 Revenue	Growth Rate (%)	Owner	Number of Employees
51	Breakthrough Software Corp. Novato, CA	$3,000,000	500	Pvt	15
51	Communications Research Grp. Baton Rouge, LA	3,000,000	200	Pvt	35
51	Construction Data Control Norcross, GA	3,000,000	20	Pvt	32
51	Origin Systems Inc. Manchester, NH	3,000,000	100	Pvt	18
55	Softsync New York, NY	2,772,000	91	Pvt	23
56	Micrografx Richardson, TX	2,500,000	67	Pvt	25
56	Groundstar Software Inc. Capitola, CA	2,500,000	39	Pvt	15
58	Aldus Corp. Seattle, WA	2,400,000	n/a	Pvt	36
58	Fox & Geller Inc. Elmwood Park, NJ	2,400,000	0	Pvt	20
58	Oregon Software Inc. Portland, OR	2,400,000	0	Pvt	38
61	Champion Software Golden, CO	2,365,000	-17	Pvt	30
62	WordTech Systems Inc. Orinda, CA	2,300,000	156	Pvt	34
63	Office Solutions Madison, WI	2,239,000	69	Pvt	30
64	Persoft Inc. Madison, WI	2,228,000	35	Pvt	31
65	Kriya Systems Sterling, VA	2,200,000	10	Pvt	12
66	Queue Inc. Bridgeport, CT	2,100,000	24	Pvt	22

(Continued next page)

THE 1986 SOFT*LETTER 100 (Continued)

Rank	Company	1985 Revenue	Growth Rate (%)	Owner	Number of Employees
67	Associated Systems Inc. Wichita, KS	$2,000,000	25	Pvt	27
67	Bus. & Prof. Software Cambridge, MA	2,000,000	0	Pvt	18
67	Funk Software Cambridge, MA	2,000,000	33	Pvt	6
67	Megahaus La Jolla, CA	2,000,000	0	Pvt	20
67	Softa Group Inc. Northfield, IL	2,000,000	400	Pvt	22
67	Southwest Data Systems Burbank, CA	2,000,000	33	Pvt	30
67	Summa Technologies Beaverton, OR	2,000,000	-35	Pub	20
67	Xyquest Bedford, MA	2,000,000	100	Pvt	12
75	Traveling Software Seattle, WA	1,900,000	70	Pvt	n/a
76	Palantir Software Houston, TX	1,884,000	21	Pvt	25
77	Individual Software Foster City, CA	1,800,000	20	Pvt	16
78	Micro-Integration Inc. Friendsville, MD	1,760,000	68	Pvt	25
79	T-Maker Inc. Mt. View, CA	1,700,000	42	Pvt	7
80	Spectrum Holobyte Inc. Boulder, CO	1,649,000	475	Pvt	16
81	Artsci Inc. N. Hollywood, CA	1,600,000	-27	Pvt	n/a
81	Darien Microsystems Darien, CT	1,600,000	84	Pvt	33
83	Trinity Solutions San Jose, CA	1,566,000	29	Pvt	9

(Continued next page)

THE 1986 SOFT*LETTER 100 (Continued)

Rank	Company	1985 Revenue	Growth Rate (%)	Owner	Number of Employees
84	Buttonware, Inc. Bellevue, WA	$1,500,000	n/a	Pvt	13
84	Info Designs Bloomfield Hills, MI	1,500,000	-25	Pub	15
86	Consumers Software Inc. Gilroy, CA	1,458,000	220	Pvt	18
87	Symantec Cupertino, CA	1,439,000	n/a	Pvt	39
88	I.E. Systems Newmarket, NH	1,352,000	6	Pvt	12
89	S.S.R. Corp. Rochester, NY	1,313,000	4	Pvt	n/a
90	Sensible Software Birmingham, MI	1,280,000	-4	Pvt	n/a
91	Boston Software Publishers Co. Boston, MA	1,200,000	n/a	Pvt	n/a
91	Softronics Colorado Springs, CO	1,200,000	50	Pvt	n/a
91	Interface Technologies Corp. Houston, TX	1,200,000	n/a	Pvt	11
94	American Educational Computer Palo Alto, CA	1,130,000	-56	Pub	7
95	Cisco Computer Systems Crockett, TX	1,100,000	47	Pvt	7
96	Micro Associates Port Arthur, TX	1,030,000	14	Pvt	n/a
97	Enertec Inc. Lansdale, PA	1,000,000	25	Pvt	20
97	Hel Custom Software Mt. Laurel, NJ	1,000,000	-17	Pvt	n/a
97	Paperback Software Berkeley, CA	1,000,000	n/a	Pub	20
97	Tom Snyder Productions Cambridge, MA	1,000,000	-17	Pvt	16

SOFTWARE NEWS
TOP 50 INDEPENDENT SOFTWARE VENDORS
June 1986

"Here is the ranking of independent software companies. The ranking criteria were U.S. software products revenues (sales, maintenance, support) of independent companies, i.e. non-captive or non-proprietary products. Thus, there is no IBM (the biggest of the software companies), no ADP (a "carrier" of applications through its remote services)."--SOFTWARE NEWS.
Reprinted from SOFTWARE NEWS, June 1986. Copyright 1986, Sentry Publishing Company, Inc., Westborough, MA.

Rank	Company	City & State	U.S. Software Revenues	Worldwide Software Revenues
1	Lotus Development Corp.	Cambridge, MA	$195,809,000	$225,526,000
2	Cullinet Software	Westwood, MA	144,649,000	182,803,000
3	Management Science America (MSA)	Atlanta, GA	115,974,000	151,661,000
4	Microsoft Corp.	Redmond, WA	114,000,000	162,500.000
5	Computer Associates Int'l.	Garden City, NY	114,000,000	128,936,000
6	Uccel	Dallas, TX	110,000,000	123,200,000
7	The Dun & Bradstreet Corp.	New York, NY	101,800,000	127,700,000
8	Applied Data Research	Princeton, NJ	86,400.000	133,700,000
9	Ashton-Tate	Torrance, CA	82,300,000	110,400,000
10	Sterling Software, Inc.	Dallas, TX	69,900,000	81,900,000
11	Software AG	Reston, VA	68,600,000	143,000,000
12	SAS Institute, Inc.	Cary, NC	62,500,000	77,000,000
13	Information Builders, Inc.	New York, NY	58,000,000	72,000,000
14	Cincom Systems, Inc.	Cincinnati, OH	54,500,000	94,000,000
15	Pansophic Systems Inc.	Oak Brook, IL	53,526,000	67,325,000
16	Candle Corp.	Los Angeles, CA	52,000,000	61,000,000
17	Micropro International Corp.	San Rafael, CA	40,000,000	40,061,000
18	McDonnell Douglas	St. Louis, MO	37,800,000	42,000,000
19	Martin Marietta Corp.	Princeton, NJ	35,700,000	54,100,000
20	American Management Systems Inc.	Arlington, VA	35,114,000	35,114,000
21	Integrated Software Systems (ISSCO)	San Diego, CA	34,277,000	38,154,000
22	Cognos, Inc.	Peabody, MA	33,000,000	45,000,000
23	Software Publishing Corp.	Mountain View, CA	30,954,000	31,664,000
24	Borland International	Scotts Valley, CA	30,000,000	30,000,000
25	Software International	Andover, MA	26,000,000	40,000,000

(Continued next page)

SOFTWARE NEWS: TOP 50 INDEPENDENT SOFTWARE VENDORS (Continued)

Rank	Company	City & State	U.S. Software Revenues	Worldwide Software Revenues
26	Computer Corporation of America	Cambridge, MA	$26,000,000	$29,000,000
27	Compuware Corp.	Birmingham, MI	24,300,000	28,000,000
28	Information Science (InSci)	Montvale, NJ	24,000,000	24,500,000
29	Oracle Corp.	Belmont, CA	23,000,000	34,000,000
30	American Software, Inc.	Atlanta, GA	22,395,000	24,883,000
31	AGS Computers, Inc.	Mountainside, NJ	21,753,000	21,753,000
32	Autodesk, Inc.	Sausalito, CA	21,231,000	26,911,000
33	Boole & Babbage, Inc.	Sunnyvale, CA	20,648,000	28,485,000
34	Multimate International Corp.	E. Hartford, CT	20,000,000	25,000,000
35	Digital Research Inc.	Monterey, CA	20,000,000	40,000,000
36	Comserv Corp.	Eagan, MI	19,898,000	20,588,000
37	Morino Associates, Inc.	Vienna, VA	19,217,000	22,115,000
38	On-Line Software International	Ft. Lee, NJ	18,000,000	18,800,000
39	Relational Technology	Alameda, CA	17,730,847	18,616,620
40	Goal Systems Int'l.	Columbus, OH	16,300,000	17,900,000
41	Project Software & Development Inc.	Cambridge, MA	16,000,000	20,000,000
42	Integral Systems	Walnut Creek, CA	15,345,000	16,150,000
43	Duquesne Systems, Inc.	Pittsburgh, PA	14,090,000	20,095,000
44	Anacomp, Inc.	Indianapolis, IN	14,000,000	14,000,000
45	VM Software, Inc.	Vienna, VA	13,928,000	18,032,548
46	Execucom Systems Corp.	Austin, TX	13,350,000	16,250,000
47	The MacNeal-Schwendler Corp.	Los Angeles, CA	13,298,000	19,485,000
48	Lawson Associates	Minneapolis, MN	13,100,000	13,100,000
49	Micro Data Base Systems, Inc.	Lafayette, IN	13,000,000	N/A
50	Stockholder Systems, Inc.	Norcross, GA	12,555,000	12,555,000

FORBES

TELECOMMUNICATIONS: YARDSTICKS OF MANAGEMENT PERFORMANCE
January 13, 1986

Within the "$160 billion-a-year telecommunications industry" (FORBES), this list ranks companies
by return on equity as a measure of management performance. The chart shows profitability as
Return on Equity and growth as Sales.--COMPUTER INDUSTRY ALMANAC.
Reprinted by permission of FORBES Magazine, January 13, 1986. Copyright Forbes Inc., 1986.

Company	Rank	Return On Equity (%): 5-Year Average	Latest 12 Months	Rank	Sales Growth (%): 5-Year Average	Latest 12 Months
Carriers						
MCI Communications	1	32.1	9.8	1	75.5	16.5
Centel	2	17.6	16.2	3	12.7	-1.7
United Telecom	3	16.0	12.0	6	9.7	16.5
Continental Telecom	4	14.8	17.4	2	16.2	4.9
Alltel	5	14.5	15.4	4	11.9	7.6
GTE	6	14.4	14.2	8	8.2	8.2
So New England Tel	7	13.4	12.6	5	11.7	4.3
Western Union	8	0.7	def	7	9.6	-0.1
American Info Tech		NA	14.6		NA	NA
American Tel & Tel		NA	10.5		NA	NA
Bell Atlantic		NA	14.2		NA	NA
Bellsouth		NA	15.3		NA	NA
Nynex		NA	13.7		NA	NA
Pacific Telesis		NA	14.2		NA	NA
Southwestern Bell		NA	14.2		NA	NA
US West		NA	14.3		NA	NA
Medians - Carriers		14.7	14.2		11.8	6.3
Manufacturing						
TIE/Communications	1	30.3	def	1	71.0	29.9
Anixter Bros	2	19.0	9.1	3	16.9	8.9
M/A-Com	3	16.4	9.3	2	38.1	9.9
Motorola	4	15.8	6.8	4	14.4	3.1
ITT	5	10.6	6.9	5	-6.9	-14.2
Medians - Manufacturing		16.4	6.9		16.9	3.1
Industry Medians		15.8	13.7		12.7	4.9
All-industry medians		13.7	12.7		6.9	4.3

NA: Not Available

NORTHERN BUSINESS INFORMATION
MARKET SHARE OF WORLD TELECOM EQUIPMENT SUPPLIERS
1986

This chart shows the 1986 market share of the leading world telecom equipment suppliers based on the total revenue shown for each segment. The ranking is by total telecom market share.--
COMPUTER INDUSTRY ALMANAC.
Reprinted with permission from Northern Business Information, 1987. Copyright 1987 by Northern Business Information, New York, NY.

Market Shares in %

Rank	Supplier	Central Office	Transmission	Customer Premise Equipment (CPE)*	Other**	Total Telecom
1	AT&T/Philips	21.3%	16.6%	35.3%	71.1%	34.4%
2	Alcatel/ITT	22.7	15.5	13.1	6.1	14.8
3	Northern Telecom	14.1	4.7	8.0	3.1	8.1
4	NEC	7.3	8.1	8.3	3.5	7.0
5	Siemens	7.6	7.2	6.3	3.1	6.2
6	Ericsson	6.9	1.7	9.1	1.8	5.4
7	GTE	8.8	5.9	2.6	2.6	5.1
8	Other	11.3	40.3	17.3	8.7	19.0
	TOTAL REVENUE	$15.8M	$21.2M	$13.9M	$239.3M	$290.2M

*Includes related office systems
** Includes AT&T Customer Premise Equipment Rental Revenues

NORTHERN BUSINESS INFORMATION
WORLD TELECOM EQUIPMENT SALES BY SUPPLIER
1985

This chart ranks the top world telecom equipment suppliers by 1985 total telecom revenue.--
COMPUTER INDUSTRY ALMANAC.
Reprinted with permission from Northern Business Information, 1986. Copyright 1986 by Northern
Business Information, New York, NY.

Revenues in $M

Rank	Supplier	Central Office	Transmission	Customer Premise Equipment (CPE)*	Other**	Total Telecom
1	AT&T	$3090	$1750	$5341	$7274	$17,455
2	ITT	2302	921	921	460	4603
3	Northern Telecom	2092	528	1227	316	4163
4	NEC	1085	904	1266	362	3616
5	Siemens	1123	802	963	321	3210
6	Alcatel	1067	804	1089	90	3050
7	LM Ericsson	1015	195	1387	181	2778
8	GTE	1311	655	393	262	2621
9	Fujitsu	222	185	259	74	739
10	Hitachi	176	281	176	70	703
11	Plessey	150	240	150	60	600
12	GEC	130	208	130	52	520
13	Oki	120	192	120	48	480
14	Philips	65	104	65	26	260
15	Other Suppliers	874	3360	1814	672	6720
TOTAL		$14,820	$11,129	$15,300	$10,268	$51,517

*Includes related office systems
** Includes AT&T Customer Premise Equipment Rental Revenues

ADDISON-WESLEY
THE 100 BEST COMPANIES TO WORK FOR IN AMERICA

The list of 100 best companies was compiled with a journalistic rather than scientific methodology and with no preconceived set of standards. From a field of 350 companies, 135 were chosen and their personnel interviewed. Each company's attributes are rated using a five-point system in the categories of pay, benefits, job security, opportunity for advancement, and ambiance and are indicated with the code shown below.

***** means it ranks at the very top
**** means it's superior
*** means it's average (in this group)
** means it's below average (in this group)
* means it's at the bottom (of this group)

The top-rated 100 companies were then selected from the compiled material. The employment figures represent only U.S. totals and are compiled from the first and second editions of THE 100 BEST COMPANIES TO WORK FOR IN AMERICA. The rest of the company data is from the second edition.--COMPUTER INDUSTRY ALMANAC.

From this list COMPUTER INDUSTRY ALMANAC has selected only the industry-related companies.

Leavering, Moskowitz & Katz, THE 100 BEST COMPANIES TO WORK FOR IN AMERICA, copyright 1984, Addison-Wesley Publishing Company, Inc., Reading, MA. Reprinted with permission.

ADVANCED MICRO DEVICES, INC.
AMD is the fifth-largest maker of silicon chips in the United States. (Rated one of the 15 Best for Ambiance.)

	1984	1985
No. of employees	5,000	8,000

***	Pay	+ You won't be bored here.
***	Benefits	
*****	Job Security	
****	Chance to Move Up	− You have to like a little
****	Ambiance	bit of rah-rah.

ADDISON-WESLEY

THE 100 BEST COMPANIES TO WORK FOR IN AMERICA (Continued)

ANALOG DEVICES, INC.

Analog Devices makes components and systems that translate real-world signals (measurements of weight and temperature, for example) into the digital language of computers.

	1984	1985
No. of employees:	3,300	2,750

***	Pay	
***	Benefits	
**	Job Security	
*****	Chance to Move Up	
*****	Ambiance	

+ It's a young company where you can make your mark.

− Stress goes with the fast pace. A linear place in a digital world.

APPLE COMPUTER, INC.

Apple makes personal computers. (Rated one of the 10 Best for Benefits.)

	1984	1985
No. of employees:	4,700	5,600

****	Pay
*****	Benefits
***	Job Security
****	Chance to Move Up
*****	Ambiance

+ You feel like a trailblazer and there's a pot of gold at the end of the trail.

− Some find the trail leads to an early burnout.

AT&T BELL LABORATORIES

Bell Labs is the research-and-development arm of AT&T. (Rated one of the 10 Best Companies to Work for in America.)

	1984	1985
No. of employees:	18,000	19,000

****	Pay
****	Benefits
***	Job Security
***	Chance to Move Up
*****	Ambiance

+ Opportunity work at the frontiers of knowledge.

− The parent company, AT&T, is going through a "sea change."

ADDISON-WESLEY
THE 100 BEST COMPANIES TO WORK FOR IN AMERICA (Continued)

CONTROL DATA CORPORATION

Control Data makes mainframe and minicomputers, sells
computer services, and runs a financial credit company.

	1984	1985
No. of employees:	47,000	47,000

***	Pay	**+** It combines high-tech with a
***	Benefits	touch of social conscience.
***	Job Security	
***	Chance to Move Up	**−** Although young, it's set in
****	Ambiance	its ways.

DIGITAL EQUIPMENT CORPORATION

Digital is the nation's largest manufacturer of minicomputers. (Rated one of the 10 Best for Job
Security.)

	1984	1985
No. of employees:	50,000	60,000

***	Pay	**+** It has been described as an
****	Benefits	"Eden for engineers."
*****	Job Security	
***	Chance to Move Up	**−** For a big company, it lacks
****	Ambiance	structure.

EASTMAN KODAK COMPANY

Eastman Kodak is the world's largest photographic company with entry into telecommunications and
magnetic media segments.

	1984	1985
No. of employees:	87,000	86,000

***	Pay	**+** One of the premier companies
*****	Benefits	of the world.
**	Job Security	
**	Chance to Move Up	**−** It's not as secure a place to
***	Ambiance	work as it used to be.

ADDISON-WESLEY
THE 100 BEST COMPANIES TO WORK FOR IN AMERICA (Continued)

GENERAL ELECTRIC COMPANY

GE makes light bulbs, turbine generators, jet engines, TV sets (in America yet), robots, dishwashers, nuclear reactors--and thousands of other industrial and consumer products.

	1984	1985
No. of employees:	267,000	245,000

***	Pay
****	Benefits
**	Job Security
****	Chance to Move Up
***	Ambiance

+ From here you can go on to become President.

− Antinuclear activists need not apply.

HEWLETT-PACKARD COMPANY

A premier electronics company that makes computers, calculators, and various precision instruments for computation and for the measurement and analysis of various phenomena. (One of the 10 Best in three categories: Pay, Job Security, and Ambiance. Rated one of the 10 Best Companies to Work for in America.)

	1984	1985
No. of employees:	49,000	56,000

*****	Pay
****	Benefits
*****	Job Security
****	Chance to Move Up
*****	Ambiance

+ You get a chance to work with a lot of brainy people who are not stuck on themselves.

− You may be handicapped here if you don't have a degree in engineering--or if you're female.

INTEL CORPORATION

Intel is one of the leading developers and makers of the microelectronic products that are at the heart of the computer revolution: the microprocessor, memory chips, and computer systems.

	1984	1985
No. of employees:	12,700	16,000

***	Pay
****	Benefits
***	Job Security
****	Chance to Move Up
***	Ambiance

+ A chance to be one of the best and the brightest.

− They yell at each other a lot.

ADDISON-WESLEY
THE 100 BEST COMPANIES TO WORK FOR IN AMERICA (Continued)

INTERNATIONAL BUSINESS MACHINES CORPORATION

IBM is the world's largest computer and office equipment company. (Rated as one of the 10 Best for Job Security and overall as one of the 10 Best Companies to Work for in America.)

	1984	1985
No. of employees:	216,000	220,000

****	Pay
*****	Benefits
*****	Job Benefits
***	Chance to Move Up
****	Ambiance

+ They make you feel like a giant.

− It's a place for team players, not rugged individualists.

MINNESOTA MINING & MANUFACTURING COMPANY

3M makes 45,000 different products, from Scotch tape and video cassettes to orthopedic casts to reflective coatings for street signs.

	1984	1985
No of employees:	52,000	52,000

***	Pay
****	Benefits
****	Job Security
****	Chance to Move Up
****	Ambiance

+ It's a good place for people who like to tinker with ideas.

− You won't like it if you don't like small towns.

ROLM CORPORATION

The second-largest maker of computerized telephone exchanges (PBXs), ROLM also makes all-weather minicomputers.

	1984	1985
No of employees:	5,000	10,000

****	Pay
****	Benefits
****	Job Security
****	Chance to Move Up
****	Ambiance

+ It survived a CBS "60 Minutes" shot.

− How do you look in a bathing suit?

ADDISON-WESLEY
THE 100 BEST COMPANIES TO WORK FOR IN AMERICA (Continued)

TANDEM COMPUTER INC.
Tandem makes fail-safe computer systems.

	1984	1985
No. of employees:	4,000	4,000

****	Pay	+ Lots of freedom, few rules.
****	Benefits	
****	Job Security	
****	Chance to Move Up	− Hard to predict the future
*****	Ambiance	of this company.

TANDY CORPORATION
America's largest retailer of consumer electronics. (Rated one of the 10 Best for Chances to Move Up.)

	1984	1985
No. of employees:	27,000	27,000

**	Pay	+ The American dream is still
****	Benefits	true.
**	Job Security	
****	Chance to Move Up	− Street fighters get ahead best.
***	Ambiance	

TEKTRONIX, INC.
Tek (nobody calls the company by its full name) makes more than 700 electronic instruments for display measurement and control, including the CRT oscilloscope, of which it is the largest producer.

	1984	1985
No. of employees:	16,624	16,400

***	Pay	+ An egalitarian atmosphere in a
****	Benefits	high-tech setting.
**	Job Security	
***	Chance to Move Up	− The profit-sharing is great--but
****	Ambiance	it depends on profits being made.

ELECTRONIC BUSINESS
EXCELLENT COMPANIES
August 15, 1986

"ELECTRONIC BUSINESS recently surveyed 1,400 industry executives and 1,000 securities analysts, asking them to select excellent companies in 10 categories. The results contain both familiar names and newcomers, but all exemplify the qualities that make the electronics and computer industry one of the most vibrant forces in the U.S. economy."--ELECTRONIC BUSINESS.
Reprinted with permission from ELECTRONIC BUSINESS, August 15, 1986. Copyright 1986 by Reed Publishing USA, Newton, MA.

Computers: Commercial
  International Business Machines Corporation
Computers: Industrial
  Digital Equipment Corporation
Peripherals
  Seagate Technology
Semiconductors
  Intel Corporation
Passive Components
  AMP Incorporated
Production Equipment
  Applied Materials Incorporated
Instruments
  Hewlett-Packard
Communications
  American Telephone and Telegraph Company
Defense Electronics
  Loral Corporation
Distribution
  Avnet Incorporated

DIRECTORY OF COMPUTER INDUSTRY COMPANIES

The 400 companies listed in this section are leading companies in the industry selected from those ranked in the preceding three sections, provided that they had more than $5 million in annual revenues. Data was obtained from the latest available annual reports supplemented by direct telephone calls to the companies. Addresses, telephone, and telex numbers are for corporate offices, generally where the listed executives can be found.

Descriptions are from an industry perspective and industry segments are intended to label each company's primary industry role. Key subsidiaries are usually domestic companies in the computer industry with names other than the parent's. In other words, we have not listed incorporated divisions and foreign subsidiaries where the parentage is obvious in the name or where the product or service is not directly related to the industry.

Number of employees and sales (in thousands of dollars) show relative size at the end of the fiscal year indicated. Investors will, of course, want more current and complete data on publicly held companies traded on the indicated primary market. SOFT*LETTER sales estimates, when indicated, have been used for private software companies.

For foreign companies, the market indicated may be for ADRs (American Depository Receipts) or, in other cases, may be shown as FO to indicate that the company is foreign. The address shown for a foreign company may be that of an industry-related U.S. subsidiary. Sales and employees are for the bolded company.

Executives listed are, in general, the top two executives in the company. In some cases, they have been selected to reflect industry-related job functions.

The directory is incomplete and subject to constant revision due to merger and acquisition activity as well as management changes and restructuring. Please let the editors know about obvious oversights and errors for correction in the next edition.

3COM Corporation
1365 Shorebird Way
P.O. Box 7390
Mountain View, CA 94043
Telephone: 415/961-9602   Telex: 345546
Description: Manufactures personal computer network systems.
Founded: 1979   Traded: OTC
No. of Employees: 372
Sales($000): 63,992   Fiscal Year: 05/31/86
Industry Segment: Local Area Networks
Executive(s): Robert M. Metcalfe, Chairman and Sr VP; William L. Krause, President and CEO

3M Company
3M Center
St. Paul, MN 55144-1000
Telephone: 612/733-1110   Telex: 297023
Description: Produces electrical, electronics, and telecommunications connectors and devices.
Markets a line of supplies and accessories for the microfilm market, and sells printers and
teleprinters.
Founded: 1902   Traded: NYSE
No. of Employees: 85,500
Sales($000): 8,602,000   Fiscal Year: 12/31/86
Industry Segment: Media; Printers
Executive(s): Allen F. Jacobson, Chairman and CEO; James A. Thwaits, President Intl Operations
Key Subsidiaries: Media Services Inc.

AGS Computer Inc.
1139 Spruce Drive
Mountainside, NJ 07092
Telephone: 201/654-4321   Telex: 6549794
Description: Provides automation solutions to the telecommunications, finance and computer
industries. Offers commercial systems development services, software products and microcomputer
distribution.
Founded: 1967   Traded: NYSE
No. of Employees: 2,300
Sales($000): 381,497   Fiscal Year: 12/31/86
Industry Segment: Software; Distribution
Executive(s): Lawrence J. Schoenberg, Chairman and CEO; Joseph Abrams, President and COO
Key Subsidiaries: Microamerica, Compuserve.

APTOS Systems Corporation
Formerly Chancellor Computer Corp.
4113 Scotts Valley Drive, Suite A
Scotts Valley, CA 95066
Telephone: 408/438-2199   Telex: 3710387
Description: Markets computer aided software.
Founded: 1982   Traded: OTC
No. of Employees: 32
Sales($000): 3,000   Fiscal Year: 12/31/86
Industry Segment: Software
Executive(s): John Roth, President and CEO; Robert Brooks, Board Member

AST Research Inc.
2121 Alton Avenue
Irvine, CA 92714
Telephone: 714/863-1333   Telex: 753699
Description: Manufactures add-in boards (SixPakPlus), laser printers, personal computers for desktop publishing.
Founded: 1980   Traded: OTC
No. of Employees: 800
Sales($000): 172,299   Fiscal Year: 06/30/86
Industry Segment: Peripherals
Executive(s): Safi U. Qureshey, President; Albert C. Wong, Exec Vice President

AT&T
550 Madison Avenue
New York, NY 10022
Telephone: 212/605-5500   Telex: 316913
Description: Manufactures telecommunications networks; information systems, including computers, and networks for offices and factories; telephone products for homes and businesses.
Founded: 1885   Traded: NYSE
No. of Employees: 338,000
Sales($000): 34,087,000   Fiscal Year: 12/31/86
Industry Segment: Telecommunications
Executive(s): Charles L. Brown, Chairman; James E. Olson, President & COO
Key Subsidiaries: AT&T Communications Inc.,AT&T Information Systems Inc., AT&T Technologies Inc., Bell Telephone Laboratories Inc.

Accountants Microsystems, Inc.
3633 136th Place, SE
Bellevue, WA 98006
Telephone: 206/643-2050 Telex: None
Description: Develops accounting software.
Founded: 1980   Traded: PVT
No. of Employees: 145
Sales($000): 12,500   Fiscal Year: 12/31/85 (Soft*letter)
Industry Segment: Software
Executive(s): Richard LaPorte, Chief Executive Officer; Guy Callari, Vice President, Sales

Activision Inc.
2350 Bayshore Parkway
Mountain View, CA 94043
Telephone: 415/960-0410 Telex: 172758
Description: Manufactures entertainment software for home computers.
Founded: 1979   Traded: OTC
No. of Employees: 170
Sales($000): 16,895   Fiscal Year: 03/31/86
Industry Segment: Software
Executive(s): Bruce Davis, Sr Vice President
Key Subsidiaries: Infocom Inc.

Advanced Computer Techniques Corporation
16 East 32nd Street
New York, NY 10016
Telephone: 212/696-3600 Telex: 422928
Description: Develops and supports software-based solutions.
Founded: 1962   Traded: OTC
No. of Employees: 159
Sales($000): 15,000   Fiscal Year: 12/31/86
Industry Segment: Programming; Software; Services
Executive(s): John F. Phillips, Chairman; Oscar H. Schachter, President & CEO
Key Subsidiaries: Creative Socio-Medics Corp.

Advanced Input Devices
West 250 AID Drive
Coeur d'Alene, ID 83814
Telephone: 208/765-8000   Telex: 510776 0584
Description: Manufactures data entry input devices.
Founded: 1978   Traded: PVT
No. of Employees: 450
Fiscal Year: 10/31/86 (Sales confidential)
Industry Segment: Keyboards
Executive(s): John C. Overby, President and CEO; Gordon Scott, Chief Financial Officer

Advanced Micro Devices
901 Thompson Place
P.O. Box 3453
Sunnyvale, CA 94088
Telephone: 408/732-2400   Telex: 346306
Description: Manufactures complex monolithic integrated circuits.
Founded: 1969   Traded: NYSE
No. of Employees: 15299
Sales($000): 576,124 Fiscal Year: 03/30/86
Industry Segment: Semiconductors
Executive(s): W.J. (Jerry) Sanders III, Chairman and CEO; Anthony B. Holbrook, President and COO

Alamo Learning Systems
Suite 500
1850 MT. Diablo Boulevard
Walnut Creek, CA 94596
Telephone: 415/930-8520   Telex: 880751
Description: Focuses on management training.
Founded: 1979   Traded: PVT
No. of Employees: 36
Fiscal Year: 12/31/86 (Sales confidential)
Industry Segment: Services
Executive(s): G.A. Hale, President; Jeff Hill, Vice President

Aldus Corporation
411 First Avenue, Suite 200
Seattle, WA 98104
Telephone: 206/622-5500   Telex: 650210 6205
Description: Develops desktop publishing software, including PageMaker.
Founded: 1984   Traded: PVT
No. of Employees: 100
Fiscal Year: 12/31/86 (Sales confidential)
Industry Segment: Software
Executive(s): Paul Brainerd, President and CEO; Mike Solomon, Vice President, Sales

Alloy Computer Products, Inc.
100 Pennsylvania Avenue
Framingham, MA 01701
Telephone: 617/875-6100   Telex: 710346 0394
Description: Manufactures a broad range of innovative products and subsystems that expand and improve the performance of microcomputer systems.
Founded: 1979   Traded: OTC
No. of Employees: 237
Sales($000): 40,856   Fiscal Year: 12/31/86
Industry Segment: Peripherals; Software
Executive(s): Richard A. Gorgens, Chairman, President & CEO; Paul J. Pedevillano, Sr Vice President & CFO
Key Subsidiaries: Micro Systems International, Advanced Peripheral Technology Inc.

Alltel Corporation
100 Executive Parkway
Hudson, OH 44236
Telephone: 216/650-7000   Telex: 810437 2350
Description: Telecommunications company providing local telephone service, also manufactures telephone equipment.
Founded: 1960   Traded: NYSE
No. of Employees: 5,590
Sales($000): 697,103   Fiscal Year: 12/31/86
Industry Segment: Telecommunications
Executive(s): Weldon W. Case, Chairman and CEO; Joe T. Ford, President and COO
Key Subsidiaries: Alltel Systems Inc., Alltel Telecommunications Systems.

Alpha Microsystems
3501 Sunflower Avenue
Santa Ana, CA 92704
Telephone: 714/957-8500   Telex: 910595 2666
Description: Manufactures microcomputer systems and software for business, professional,
scientific, engineering and educational markets.
Founded: 1977   Traded: OTC
No. of Employees: 412
Sales($000): 48,139   Fiscal Year: 02/23/86
Industry Segment: Microcomputers; Peripherals; Software
Executive(s): Richard C. Wilcox, Chairman; Richard Cortese, President and CEO

Alpha Software Corporation
30 B Street
Burlington, MA 01803
Telephone: 617/229-2924   Telex: 466168
Description: Designs software products for corporate microcomputer users.
Founded: 1981   Traded: PVT
No. of Employees: 25
Fiscal Year: 03/31/87 (Sales confidential)
Industry Segment: Software
Executive(s): Richard Rabins, President & CEO; Robie White, Chief Financial Officer

Altos Computer Systems
2641 Orchard Parkway
San Jose, CA 95134
Telephone: 408/946-6700   Telex: 184815
Description: Produces 8- and 16-bit microcomputer systems.
Founded: 1977   Traded: OTC
No. of Employees: 718
Sales($000): 134,189 Fiscal Year: 06/29/86
Industry Segment: Systems; Peripherals; Software
Executive(s): David Jackson, Chairman, Pres. and CEO; David Zacarias, Chief Operating Officer

Amdahl Corporation
1250 East Arques Avenue
P.O. Box 3470
Sunnyvale, CA 94086
Telephone: 408/746-6000   Telex: 3716812
Description: Manufactures large-scale, high performance, general purpose computer systems and complementary software, storage, communication and education products.
Founded: 1970   Traded: AMX
No. of Employees: 6,910
Sales($000): 966,349   Fiscal Year: 12/26/86
Industry Segment: Mainframe computers; Peripherals
Executive(s): Eugene R. White, Chairman; John C. Lewis, President and CEO

American Magnetics Corporation
13535 Ventura Boulevard, Suite 205
Sherman Oaks, CA 91423
Telephone: 818/783-8900   Telex: 213872 2589
Description: Manufactures card reader products and high density heads for data cartridges and digital cassettes.
Founded: 1963   Traded: OTC
No. of Employees: 298
Sales($000): 16,084   Fiscal Year: 12/31/85
Industry Segment: Peripherals
Executive(s): Marion W. Haun, Chairman; Verney Brown, President and COO

American Management Systems, Inc.
1777 North Kent Street
Arlington, VA 22209
Telephone: 703/841-6000   Telex: 64638
Description: Applies computer and systems engineering to solve complex management problems for large organizations.
Founded: 1970   Traded: OTC
No. of Employees: 1500
Sales($000): 135,521   Fiscal Year: 12/31/86
Industry Segment: Services
Executive(s): Ivan Selin, Chairman; Charles Rossotti, President and CEO

American Software, Inc.
470 East Paces Ferry Road, N.E.
Atlanta, GA 30305
Telephone: 404/261-4381   Telex: 804442
Description: Develops integrated computer application software systems to be used in a variety of mainframe IBM and IBM plug-compatible computers.
Founded: 1971   Traded: OTC
No. of Employees: 289
Sales($000): 38,289   Fiscal Year: 04/30/86
Industry Segment: Software
Executive(s): Thomas L. Newberry, Chairman and Co-CEO; James C. Edenfield, President and Co-CEO

American Training International
12638 Beatrice St
Los Angeles, CA 90066
Telephone: 213/823-1129   Telex: none
Description: Develops training tutorials for application software programs
Founded: 1981   Traded: PVT
No. of Employees: 32
Sales($000): 3,400   Fiscal Year: 12/31/85   (Soft*letter)
Industry Segment: Services
Executive(s): Joel Rakow, Exec VP and CEO; Julius Dizon, Vice President and CFO

Ameritech
American Information Technologies
30 South Wacker Drive
Chicago, IL 60606
Telephone: 312/750-5000   Telex: 7262348
Description: A regional Bell holding company (RBOC) with five bell companies in Illinois, Indiana, Michigan, Ohio and Wisconsin.
Founded: 1980   Traded: NYSE
No. of Employees: 74,883
Sales($000): 9,362,100   Fiscal Year: 12/31/86
Industry Segment: Telecommunications
Executive(s): William L. Weiss, Chairman and CEO; James J. Howard, President and COO
Key Subsidiaries: 5 Bell Companies, 6 Ameritech Companies, and Applied Data Research Inc.

Ametek Inc.
Station Square
Paoli, PA 14301
Telephone: 215/647-2121 Telex: 834637
Description: Manufactures components and motors for computer and peripheral manufacturers.
Markets graphics plotters.
Founded: 1930   Traded: NYSE
No. of Employees: 6500
Sales($000): 568,493 Fiscal Year: 12/31/86
Industry Segment: Peripherals
Executive(s): John H. Lux, Chairman and CEO; Robert L. Noland, President
Key Subsidiaries: Houston Instruments

Anacomp, Inc.
11550 North Meridian Street
P.O. Box 40888
Indianapolis, IN 46240
Telephone: 317/844-9666 Telex: none
Description: Offers micrographics, commercial and government systems, and software services for
the banking industry.
Founded: 1968   Traded: NYSE
No. of Employees: 2,000
Sales($000): 108,920 Fiscal Year: 09/30/86
Industry Segment: Systems; Services; Software
Executive(s): Louis P. Ferrero, Chairman, President & CEO; J. Mark Woods, Exec Vice President &
COO
Key Subsidiaries: Electronic Data Preparation Corp.,Kalvar Microfilm Inc.

Analog Devices, Inc.
Two Technology Way
Norwood, MA 02062-9106
Telephone: 617/329-4700 Telex: 924491
Description: Manufactures high performance electronic components, subsystems and systems.
Founded: 1965   Traded: NYSE
No. of Employees: 4,789
Sales($000): 334,437 Fiscal Year: 11/01/86
Industry Segment: Semiconductors; Peripherals
Executive(s): Ray Stata, Chairman and President; Joseph M. Hinchey, Sr Vice President Finance

Analogic Corporation
8 Centennial Drive
Peabody, MA 01961
Telephone: 617/246-0300   Telex: 353899
Description: Manufactures standard and customized high-precision data conversion and signal processing equipment.
Founded: 1969   Traded: OTC
No. of Employees: 1800
Sales($000): 136,769   Fiscal Year: 07/31/86
Industry Segment: Peripherals
Executive(s): Bernard M. Gordon, Chairman and President; Bernard L. Friedman, Vice Chairman

Analysts International Corporation
7615 Metro Boulevard
Minneapolis, MN 55435
Telephone: 612/835-2330   Telex: None
Description: Offers a variety of software services to a wide range of industries, including consulting, project management, systems analysis and design, programming software maintenance, training, and software packages.
Founded: 1966   Traded: OTC
No. of Employees: 830
Sales($000): 46,732   Fiscal Year: 06/30/86
Industry Segment: Software, Services
Executive(s): Frederick W. Lang, President; Victor C. Benda, Exec Vice President

Anderson Jacobson Inc.
521 Charcot Avenue
San Jose, CA 95131
Telephone: 408/435-8520   Telex: 910338 0136
Description: Manufactures and leases data communications equipment.
Founded: 1967   Traded: AMX
No. of Employees: 375
Sales($000): 38,973   Fiscal Year: 03/31/86
Industry Segment: Peripherals
Executive(s): Raymond E. Jacobson, Chairman and President; Thomas B. Zmach, Vice President, Marketing

Anthem Electronics Inc.
1040 E. Brokaw Road
San Jose, CA 95131
Telephone: 408/295-4200   Telex: 756001
Description: Distributes semiconductors and subsystems to original equipment manufacturers throughout the Western United States.
Founded: 1968   Traded: NYSE
No. of Employees: 265
Sales($000): 104,544   Fiscal Year: 03/31/86
Industry Segment: Distributors
Executive(s): Robert S. Throop, Chairman and CEO; Peyton L. Gannaway, President and COO

Apollo Computer Inc.
300 Billerica Road
Chelmsford, MA 01824
Telephone: 617/256-6600   Telex: 710343 6803
Description: Manufactures computer systems primarily used in engineering, scientific and other technical applications.
Founded: 1980   Traded: OTC
No. of Employees: 3300
Sales($000): 391,685   Fiscal Year: 01/31/87
Industry Segment: Systems
Executive(s): Thomas A. Vanderslice, Chairman, President & CEO; Richard P. Bond, Sr Vice President & CFO

Apple Computer
20525 Mariani Avenue
Cupertino, CA 95014
Telephone: 408/996-1010   Telex: 171576
Description: Manufactures personal computers and related software and peripherals products.
Founded: 1977   Traded: OTC
No. of Employees: 5200
Sales($000): 1,902,000   Fiscal Year: 09/30/86
Industry Segment: Systems; Peripherals; Software
Executive(s): John Sculley, Chairman, President & CEO; Delbert W. Yocam, Exec Vice President & COO

Applied Communications, Inc.
Acquired by US WEST, Inc.
330 South 108th Avenue
Omaha, NE 68154
Telephone: 402/390-7600   Telex: 910622 0314
Description: Develops product software for electronic funds transfer systems.
Founded: 1975   Traded: OTC
No. of Employees: 285
Sales($000): 29,274   Fiscal Year: 09/30/85
Industry Segment: Software
Executive(s): George F. Haddix, Chairman; Neal C. Hansen, President and CEO
Key Subsidiaries: JBA, Transaction Systems Arch. BankPro Sys

Applied Magnetics Corporation
75 Robin Hill Road
Goleta, CA 93117
Telephone: 805/683-5353   Telex: 910334 1195
Description: Manufactures magnetic heads used in tape, rigid-disk, and floppy-disk drives.
Founded: 1957   Traded: NYSE
No. of Employees: 3898
Sales($000): 128,000   Fiscal Year: 09/30/86
Industry Segment: Mass storage
Executive(s): Harold R. Frank, Chairman; Ben J. Newitt, President and CEO

Archive Corporation
1650 Sunflower Avenue
Costa Mesa, CA 92626
Telephone: 714/641-0279   Telex: 4722063
Description: Manufactures a line of 1/4-inch streaming cartridge tape drives for incorporation by
OEMs in minicomputer, microcomputer and desktop computer systems and sub-systems.
Founded: 1980   Traded: OTC
No. of Employees: 607
Sales($000): 78,824   Fiscal Year: 09/26/86
Industry Segment: Mass storage
Executive(s): Howard D. Lewis, Chairman and CEO; J. Peter Wilson, President and COO

Arrow Electronics, Inc.
Div of Grumman Systems
767 Fifth Avenue
New York, NY 10153
Telephone: 212/935-6100   Telex: 617933 9365
Description: Distributes electronic components, computer products and related equipment
manufactured by others.
Founded: 1946   Traded: NYSE
No. of Employees: 2000
Sales($000): 529,621   Fiscal Year: 12/31/86
Industry Segment: Distributors
Executive(s): John C. Waddell, Chairman and CEO; Stephen P. Kaufman, President and COO
Key Subsidiaries: Axiom Electronics Ltd., Arrow Electronics Canada Ltd.

Arthur Andersen & Co.
69 West Washington Street
Chicago, IL 60602
Telephone: 312/580-0069   Telex: 254436
Description: Focuses on management information consulting worldwide. It is one of the big 8
accounting firms.
Founded: 1920   Traded: PVT
No. of Employees: 36000
Sales($000): 1,924,000   Fiscal Year: 08/31/86
Industry Segment: Services
Executive(s): Duane R. Kullberg, Chief Executive Officer; Randal B. McDonald, Chief Financial
Officer

Ashton-Tate
20101 Hamilton Avenue
Torrance, CA 90502
Telephone: 213/329-8000   Telex: 5387996
Description: Develops microcomputer software to meet the information management, productivity
and software development needs of businesses and professionals. Best known products are dBase III
and Multimate.
Founded: 1980   Traded: OTC
No. of Employees: 822
Sales($000): 121,571   Fiscal Year: 01/31/86
Industry Segment: Software
Executive(s): Edward M. Esber Jr., Chairman and CEO; Luther Nussbaum, President and COO

Ask Computer Systems, Inc.
730 Distel Drive
Los Altos, CA 94022
Telephone: 415/969-4442 Telex: 297341
Description: Produces turnkey computer systems, microcomputer systems, business and
manufacturing software and data processing networks.
Founded: 1974   Traded: OTC
No. of Employees: 470
Sales($000): 76,019   Fiscal Year: 06/30/86
Industry Segment: Systems; Software; Networks
Executive(s): Sandra L. Kurtzig, Chairman; Ronald W. Braniff, President and CEO

Atari Corporation
1196 Borregas
Sunnyvale, CA 94088
Telephone: 408/745-2000 Telex: 172508
Description: Manufactures microcomputer systems and software as well as videogame systems
designed to offer advanced technology and low prices.
Founded: 1984   Traded: AMX
Sales($000): 92,667   Fiscal Year: 12/31/86
Industry Segment: Systems
Executive(s): Jack Tramiel, Chairman; Sam Tramiel, President

Autodesk
2320 Marinship Way
Sausalito, CA 94965
Telephone: 415/332-2344 Telex: 275946
Description: Develops computer-aided design and drafting software for use on leading desktop
computers. Best known product is AutoCAD.
Founded: 1982   Traded: OTC
No. of Employees: 214
Sales($000): 52,382   Fiscal Year: 01/31/87
Industry Segment: Software
Executive(s): John Walker, Chairman; Alvar Green, President and CEO

Automatic Data Processing
One ADP Boulevard
Roseland, NJ 07068
Telephone: 201/994-5000   Telex: 201994 6493
Description: Engaged in the computer service business.
Founded: 1949   Traded: NYSE
No. of Employees: 20,000
Sales($000): 1,204,246   Fiscal Year: 06/30/86
Industry Segment: Services
Executive(s): Josh S. Weston, Chairman and CEO; William J. Turner, President

Auxton Computer Enterprises Inc.
851 Trafalgar Court
Maitland, FL 32751
Telephone: 305/660-8400   Telex: 6600085
Description: Provides data processing services which include consulting, information processing and
proprietary software applications for the telecommunications industry.
Founded: 1969   Traded: OTC
No. of Employees: 400
Sales($000): 30,330   Fiscal Year: 12/31/86
Industry Segment: Services
Executive(s): John P. Croxton, Chairman and CEO; Cheryl Galloway, President and COO

Avant-Garde Computing, Inc.
8000 Commerce Parkway
Mt. Laurel, NJ 08054-2227
Telephone: 609/778-7000   Telex: 710940 1569
Description: Assembles integrated software-based systems used to monitor, secure and help manage
the operation of large data communications networks.
Founded: 1978   Traded: OTC
No. of Employees: 181
Sales($000): 16,309   Fiscal Year: 04/30/86
Industry Segment: Systems
Executive(s): Timothy P. Ahlstrom, Chairman and CEO; Michael L. Sanyour, President and COO
Key Subsidiaries: Connecticut Business Computers Inc.

Avnet, Inc.
767 Fifth Avenue
New York, NY 10153
Telephone: 212/644-1050   Telex: 858230
Description: Distributes electronic components and computer products.
Founded: 1955   Traded: NYSE
No. of Employees: 9000
Sales($000): 1,542,441   Fiscal Year: 06/30/86
Industry Segment: Distributors
Executive(s): Anthony R. Hamilton, Chairman and CEO; Leon Machiz, President
Key Subsidiaries: Hamilton/Avnet, Time, Loonam Computer, Data Tron.

BASF Aktiengesellschaft
Carl-Bosch-Strasse 38, D 6700
Ludwigshafen, W Germ,
Telephone: 621-601   Telex:
Description: Manufactures magnetic recording media and chemicals.
Traded: FO
No. of Employees: 114128
Sales($000): 13,700,000
Industry Segment: Media
Executive(s): Matthias Seefelder, Chairman; Gerhard Blumenthal, Deputy Chairman
Key Subsidiaries: BASF America Corp., BASF Systems Corp.

BKW Systems, Inc.
One Tara Boulevard
Nashua, NH 03062
Telephone: 603/888-8400 Telex: None
Description: Develops software primarily for the banking industry and also markets, sells and installs computer software, related data processing services and hardware.
Founded: 1982   Traded: OTC
No. of Employees: 20
Sales($000): 7,042   Fiscal Year: 09/30/86
Industry Segment: Software
Executive(s): Al Fichera, Chairman and President; Tom Warren, Sr Vice President

BPI Systems, Inc.
3001 Bee Cave Road
Austin, TX 78746
Telephone: 512/328-5400   Telex: None
Description: Develops business accounting software systems for use on microcomputers.
Founded: 1979   Traded: OTC
No. of Employees: 110
Sales($000): 10,938   Fiscal Year: 03/31/86
Industry Segment: Software
Executive(s): Randy Ferguson, Chairman; David Femald, President and CEO

BaronData Systems
1700 Marina Boulevard
San Leandro, CA 94577
Telephone: 415/352-8101   Telex: 415352 8923
Description: Manufactures computer aided transcription systems.
Founded: 1976   Traded: OTC
No. of Employees: 212
Sales($000): 24,324   Fiscal Year: 03/31/86
Industry Segment: Systems
Executive(s): Charles G. Davis, Jr., Chairman and CEO; J. Garrett Fitzgibbons, President and COO

Bell Atlantic
1600 Market Street
Philadelphia, PA 19103
Telephone: 215/963-6000   Telex: 215963 6108
Description: A regional Bell holding company (RBOC) with seven Bell operating companies in New Jersey, Pennsylvania, Delaware, Washington, D.C., Maryland, Virginia and West Virginia.
Founded: 1983   Traded: NYSE
No. of Employees: 79285
Sales($000): 9,920,800   Fiscal Year: 12/31/86
Industry Segment: Telecommunications
Executive(s): Thomas E. Bolger, Chairman and CEO; Philip A. Campbell, President
Key Subsidiaries: CompuShop, Sorbus, MAI Canada,A Beeper Co.

Bell Industries Inc.
11812 San Vicente Blvd.
Los Angeles, CA 90049
Telephone: 213/826-6778   Telex: 213258 6932
Description: Distributes electronic components and manufactures uncoated aluminum memory discs and other computer and electronic components.
Founded: 1952   Traded: NYSE
No. of Employees: 1800
Sales($000): 300,176 Fiscal Year: 06/30/86
Industry Segment: Distributors
Executive(s): Theodore Williams, Chairman, President & CEO; Howard B. Franklin, Sr Vice President

BellSouth
675 West Peachtree Street NE
Atlanta, GA 30375
Telephone: 404/420-8600   Telex: 6883771
Description: A regional Bell holding company (RBOC) with two Bell companies covering Alabama, Kentucky, Louisiana, Mississippi, Tennessee, Florida, Georgia, North Carolina and South Carolina.
Founded: 1983   Traded: NYSE
No. of Employees: 92,500
Sales($000): 11,400,000   Fiscal Year: 12/31/86
Industry Segment: Telecommunications
Executive(s): John L. Clendenin, Chairman, Pres. & CEO; William O. McCoy, Vice Chairman
Key Subsidiaries: Southern Bell, South Central Bell, Sunlink Corp.

Boeing Company
7755 East Marginal Way South
Seattle, WA 98108
Telephone: 206/655-2121   Telex: 484520
Description: Provides computer services. Major aerospace firm.
Founded: 1916   Traded: NYSE
No. of Employees: 104,000
Sales($000): 16,341,000   Fiscal Year: 12/31/86
Industry Segment: Services
Executive(s): T.A. Wilson, Chairman and CEO; Frank Shrontz, President
Key Subsidiaries: Boeing Computer Services Co.

Boole & Babbage, Inc.
510 Oakmead Parkway
Sunnyvale, CA 94086
Telephone: 408/735-9550   Telex: 910339 9368
Description: Designs standard, modular software products.
Founded: 1967   Traded: OTC
No. of Employees: 298
Sales($000): 34,520   Fiscal Year: 09/30/86
Industry Segment: Software
Executive(s): Franklin P. Johnson, Chairman; Bruce T. Coleman, President and CEO
Key Subsidiaries: The European Software Company

Borland International
4585 Scotts Valley Dr
Scotts Valley, CA 95066
Telephone: 408/438-8400   Telex: 332795
Description: Publishes micro computer software.
Founded: 1983   Traded: FO
No. of Employees: 200
Sales($000): 30,000   Fiscal Year: 03/31/86 (Soft*letter)
Industry Segment: Software
Executive(s): Philippe Kahn, Chief Executive Officer; Marie Bourget, Vice President, Finance

Broderbund
17 Paul Drive
San Rafael, CA 94903
Telephone: 415/479-1700   Telex: 172029
Description: Develops home computer software, including entertainment, educational, graphics, productivity and business software. Best known for Print Shop.
Founded: 1980   Traded: PVT
No. of Employees: 140
Sales($000): 24,500   Fiscal Year: 08/31/85
Industry Segment: Software
Executive(s): Gary Carlston, Chairman and VP; Douglas Carlston, President

Burr-Brown Corporation
6730 South Tucson Blvd.
Tucson, AZ 85706
Telephone: 602/746-1111 Telex: 666491
Description: Manufactures precision microelectronic components, subassemblies, and microprocessor-based systems.
Founded: 1956   Traded: OTC
No. of Employees: 1,483
Sales($000): 112,788 Fiscal Year: 12/31/86
Industry Segment: Microprocessors; Electronics
Executive(s): Thomas R. Brown Jr., Chairman; James J. Burns, President and CEO

Burroughs Corporation
Changed name to Unisys 11/86
Burroughs Place
Detroit, MI 48232
Telephone: 313/972-7000 Telex: 224015
Description: Manufactures electronic-based information systems and related equipment, services, software, and supplies.
Founded: 1886   Traded: NYSE
No. of Employees: 60,500
Sales($000): 5,037,700   Fiscal Year: 12/31/85
Industry Segment: Systems; Peripherals; Software; Services
Executive(s): W. Michael Blumenthal, Chairman and CEO; Paul G. Stern, President and COO
Key Subsidiaries: Memorex

Businessland
3610 Stevens Creek Blvd.
San Jose, CA 95117
Telephone: 408/554-9300 Telex: 278808
Description: Owns and operates a nationwide chain of centers which sell and service microcomputer systems and related business automation equipment.
Founded: 1982   Traded: OTC
No. of Employees: 1501
Sales($000): 404,300 Fiscal Year: 06/30/86
Industry Segment: Computer stores
Executive(s): David A. Norman, President and CEO; Enzo N. Torresi, Sr Vice President

C 3 Inc.
460 Herndon Parkway
Herndon, VA 22070-5201
Telephone: 703/471-6000   Telex: 4378799
Description: Assembles and markets microcomputer, minicomputer and IBM plug-compatible computer systems.
Founded: 1968   Traded: NYSE
No. of Employees: 506
Sales($000): 65,252   Fiscal Year: 03/31/86
Industry Segment: Systems
Executive(s): John G. Ballenger, Chairman and President; Richard C. Litsinger, Exec Vice President
Key Subsidiaries: Tempest Technologies Inc.

C. Itoh & Co. Ltd.
68 Kitakyutaromachi, 4-chome, Higashi-Ku
Osaka, 541 Japan
Telephone: 03-497-2121   Telex: J63335
Description: Trading company with peripheral products including printers and monitors.
Founded: Traded: FO
No. of Employees: 10000
Sales($000): 90,000,000
Industry Segment: Peripherals
Executive(s): Seiki Tosaki, Chairman; Isao Yonekura, President
Key Subsidiaries: CIE Systems, CIE Terminals

CAP Gemini Sogeti
6 boulevard Jean Pain, B.P. 206 38005
Grenoble, France
Telephone: 33-76-448201
Description: Holding company engaged in professional computer services.
Traded: FO
No. of Employees: 3003
Sales($000): 245,000
Industry Segment: Services
Executive(s): Serge Kampf, Executive Chairman; Philippe Dreyfus, Vice Chairman
Key Subsidiaries: CAP Group plc, CAP Gemini Software

CCX Network Inc.
301 Industrial Boulevard
Conway, AR 72032
Telephone: 501/329-6836   Telex: 62195620
Description: Develops list databases and provides computer-based decision support and related data
processing services to direct marketing organizations. Also licenses proprietary software.
Founded: 1983   Traded: OTC
No. of Employees: 268
Sales($000): 19,286   Fiscal Year: 09/30/86
Industry Segment: Services; Software
Executive(s): Charles D. Morgan Jr., Chairman and President; Rodger S. Kline, Exec Vice President

COMPAQ Computer Corporation
20555 FM 149
Houston, TX 77070
Telephone: 713/370-0670   Telex: 383904
Description: Manufactures personal computers for business and professional users.
Founded: 1982   Traded: NYSE
No. of Employees: 1,860
Sales($000): 625,243 Fiscal Year: 12/31/86
Industry Segment: Microcomputers
Executive(s): Benjamin M. Rosen, Chairman; Joseph R. Canion, President and CEO
Key Subsidiaries: Compaq Telecommunications Corp.

CSP Inc.
40 Linnell Circle
Billerica, MA 01821
Telephone: 617/272-6020   Telex: 710347 0176
Description: Manufactures array processors and various software and hardware packages designed
for use with array processors.
Founded: 1968   Traded: OTC
No. of Employees: 151
Sales($000): 14,036   Fiscal Year: 08/31/86
Industry Segment: Systems; Software
Executive(s): Edmund U. Cohler, Chairman and CEO; Samuel Ochlis, President and COO

Cadec Systems, Inc.
Acquired by Cummins Engine 12/86
8 East Perimeter Road
Londonderry, NH 03053
Telephone: 603/668-1010   Telex: None
Description: Produces microprocessor based on-board computers and support systems for physical distribution industries.
Founded: 1976   Traded: PVT
No. of Employees: 63
Sales($000): 4,141   Fiscal Year: 06/30/86
Industry Segment: Microcomputers
Executive(s): Edwin W. Booth, President and CEO; ,

Canon Inc.
7-1 Nishi Shinjuku 2-chome, shinjuku-Ku
Tokyo, Japan 160,
Telephone: 03-758-2111   Telex:
Description: Manufactures laser printers and photographic products.
Founded: Traded: OTC
No. of Employees: 11774
Sales($000): 6,100,000   Fiscal Year: 12/31/86 (Estimated)
Industry Segment: Printers
Executive(s): Takeshi Mitarai, Chairman; Ryuzaburo Kaku, President

Centel Corporation
5725 North East River Road
Chicago, IL 60631
Telephone: 312/399-2500   Telex: 3992569
Description: Installs business communications systems and distributes communications products and services.
Founded: 1909   Traded: NYSE
No. of Employees: 12159
Sales($000): 1,369,912   Fiscal Year: 12/31/86
Industry Segment: Telecommunications
Executive(s): Robert P. Reuss, Chairman and CEO; William G. Mitchell, President
Key Subsidiaries: Central Telephone Co., Keycom Inc., Telecommunications Service Bureau Inc.

Central Data
1602 Newton Drive
Champaign, IL 61821
Telephone: 217/359-8010   Telex: 9102450787
Description: Manufactures printed circuit boards, input/output controllers and memory boards.
Founded: 1976   Traded: PVT
No. of Employees: 69
Sales($000): 6,600   Fiscal Year: 12/31/85
Industry Segment: Peripherals
Executive(s): Jeff Roloff, President; Earl Jacobsen, Exec Vice President

Central Point Software Inc.
Suite 100
9700 SW Capitol Highway
Portland, OR 97219
Telephone: 503/244-5782   Telex: 757710
Description: Publishes utility software for microcomputers.
Founded: 1981   Traded: PVT
No. of Employees: 45
Sales($000): 15,000   Fiscal Year: 12/31/86
Industry Segment: Software
Executive(s): Michael Brown, President and CEO; Linda Swanson-Davies, Manager, Sales

Centronics Data Computer Corporation
One Wall Street
Hudson, NH 03051
Telephone: 603/883-0111   Telex: 943404
Description: Manufactures a broad range of impact serial, line dot matrix, and line computer printers.
Founded: 1968   Traded: NYSE
No. of Employees: 1,756
Sales($000): 216,279 Fiscal Year: 12/29/85
Industry Segment: Printers
Executive(s): Thomas G. Kamp, Chairman; Robert Stein, President and CEO
Key Subsidiaries: Advanced Terminals Inc.

Chang Laboratories
5300 Stevens Creek Blvd
San Jose, CA 95129
Telephone: 408/246-8020   Telex: 296653RCA
Description: Develops application software for personal- and microcomputers.
Founded: 1981   Traded: PVT
No. of Employees: 22
Sales($000): 8,900   Fiscal Year: 12/31/86
Industry Segment: Software
Executive(s): Dash Chang, Chairman and President; Gary Chappell, Director of Marketing

Chelsea Industries Inc.
1360 Soldiers Field Road
Boston, MA 02135
Telephone: 617/787-9010   Telex: None
Description: Distributes electronics components to small and medium-size companies.
Founded: 1964   Traded: NYSE
No. of Employees: 1,700
Sales($000): 179,510 Fiscal Year: 09/27/86
Industry Segment: Distributors
Executive(s): Ronald G. Casty, Chairman and President; Norman S. Dunn, Exec Vice President
Key Subsidiaries: RS Electronics.

Cincinnati Bell
201 E. 4th Street
Cincinnati, OH 45202
Telephone: 513/397-9900   Telex: 214729
Description: Provides telecommunications services and products, data processing services and
computer software systems.
Founded: 1873   Traded: NYSE
No. of Employees: 5100
Sales($000): 492,632 Fiscal Year: 12/31/86
Industry Segment: Telecommunications
Executive(s): Dwight H. Hibbard, Chairman, President & CEO; Dennis J. Sullivan Jr., Exec Vice
President
Key Subsidiaries: Creative Management Systems Inc., COMMTRACK Services, Cincinnati Bell
Telephone, Cincinnati Information Systems Inc., Cincinnati Bell Enterprises.

Cincinnati Milacron Inc.
4701 Marburg Avenue
Cincinnati, OH 45209
Telephone: 513/841-8100 Telex: 214447
Description: Focuses on machines, systems, computer controls and software for the metalworking and plastics processing industries. Also produces silicon epitaxial wafers for the semiconductor industry.
Founded: 1983   Traded: NYSE
No. of Employees: 9,197
Sales($000): 849,994 Fiscal Year: 12/31/86
Industry Segment: Factory automation; Process control
Executive(s): James A. D. Geier, Chairman and CEO; Donald G. Shively, Exec VP, Operations

Cipher Data Products, Inc.
P.O. Box 85170
San Diego, CA 92138-9198
Telephone: 619/693-7200 Telex: 501668
Description: Manufactures a broad line of tape drives and related computer memory peripherals products.
Founded: 1968   Traded: OTC
No. of Employees: 2485
Sales($000): 163,005 Fiscal Year: 06/30/86
Industry Segment: Magnetic tape drives
Executive(s): Don M. Muller, Chairman and CEO; Gary E. Liebl, President and COO
Key Subsidiaries: Optimem and 4 Cipher Data Companies.

Ciprico Inc.
2955 Xenium Lane
Plymouth, MN 55441
Telephone: 612/559-2034 Telex: 910240 0585
Description: Manufactures direct access intelligent disk controllers and magnetic tape adapters for use with microcomputers.
Founded: 1978   Traded: OTC
No. of Employees: 79
Sales($000): 10,060   Fiscal Year: 09/30/86
Industry Segment: Mass storage
Executive(s): Ronald B. Thomas, Chairman, President & CEO; Michael L. Quealy, Vice President
Key Subsidiaries: Tech Source Laboratories Inc.

Commodore International Ltd.
Sassoon House
Shirley & Victoria Streets
Nassau, Bahamas
Telephone: 809/322-3807 Telex: None
Description: Manufactures microcomputer systems for the home, educational, personal and small business markets.
Traded: NYSE
Sales($000): 889,000 Fiscal Year: 06/30/86
Industry Segment: Personal computers
Executive(s): Irving Gould, Chairman; Marshall F. Smith, President and CEO
Key Subsidiaries: CEL Electronics N.V.

Compugraphic Corporation
200 Ballardvale Street
Wilmington, MA 01887
Telephone: 617/658-5600 Telex: 325322
Description: Supplies hardware and software for computerized systems, graphic arts and text management products, and equipment-operation tutorial packages.
Founded: 1960   Traded: NYSE
No. of Employees: 4,571
Sales($000): 341,082 Fiscal Year: 01/03/87
Industry Segment: Computerized typesetting equipment
Executive(s): Carl E. Dantas, President and CEO; Fred J. Butler, Sr Vice President
Key Subsidiaries: ONE Systems Inc.

Computer Associates International Inc.
711 Stewart Avenue
Garden City, NY 11530
Telephone: 516/227-3300 Telex: None
Description: Develops standardized computer software products for use primarily with IBM and IBM-compatible mainframe computers as well as for mini and microcomputers.
Founded: 1974   Traded: NYSE
No. of Employees: 1640
Sales($000): 191,032 Fiscal Year: 03/31/86
Industry Segment: Software
Executive(s): Charles B. Wang, Chairman and CEO; Anthony W. Wang, President and COO
Key Subsidiaries: Arkay Computer Inc., Discount Software Inc.

Computer Automation
2181 Dupont Drive
Irvine, CA 92715
Telephone: 714/833-8830   Telex: 910595 2543
Description: Manufactures high performance automatic test systems for testing electronic printed circuit boards, and minicomputers and microcomputers.
Founded: 1967   Traded: OTC
No. of Employees: 241
Sales($000): 20,416   Fiscal Year: 06/30/86
Industry Segment: Automatic testing systems
Executive(s): George Pratt, Chairman and CEO; Douglas L. Cutsforth, President and COO

Computer Consoles, Inc.
Watermill Center
800 South Street - 5th Floor
Waltham, MA 02154
Telephone: 617/893-3723   Telex: 920011
Description: Manufactures advanced systems that combine computing, communications and information processing technologies in innovative, practical ways.
Founded: 1971   Traded: AMX
No. of Employees: 1,421
Sales($000): 129,557 Fiscal Year: 12/31/86
Industry Segment: Systems; Software
Executive(s): John F. Cunningham, Chairman and CEO; Herman A. Affel Jr., Vice Chairman

Computer Data Systems Inc.
One Curie Court
Rockville, MD 20850
Telephone: 301/921-7000   Telex: None
Description: Provides professional services and data processing support services.
Founded: 1968   Traded: OTC
No. of Employees: 1103
Sales($000): 54,570   Fiscal Year: 06/30/86
Industry Segment: Services
Executive(s): Clifford Kendall, Chairman and President; Harold J. Johnson Jr., Exec Vice President, Operations

Computer Depot, Inc.
7450 Flying Cloud Drive
Eden Prairie, MN 55344
Telephone: 612/944-8780   Telex: None
Description: Sells personal computer systems, software, and related services through leased computer centers in major department stores.
Founded: 1977   Traded: OTC
Industry Segment: Computer stores
Executive(s): Stephen B. Parker, Chairman and CEO; Frederick S. Larson, President and COO

Computer Entry Systems Corporation
2141 Industrial Parkway
Silver Spring, MD 20904
Telephone: 301/622-3500   Telex: 898397
Description: Manufactures cash management and payment processing systems.
Founded: 1969   Traded: OTC
No. of Employees: 507
Sales($000): 72,635   Fiscal Year: 12/31/86
Industry Segment: Systems
Executive(s): Brian T. Cunningham, Chairman and CEO; Michael J. King, President and COO
Key Subsidiaries: Macroscan Systems Limited, AOM Corporation.

Computer Factory Inc.
399 A Executive Boulevard
Elmsford, NY 10523
Telephone: 914/347-5000   Telex: None
Description: Engages in sale and service of microprocessor-based personal computer systems. Develops and markets software.
Founded: 1977   Traded: AMX
No. of Employees: 450
Sales($000): 104,347 Fiscal Year: 09/30/86
Industry Segment: Computer stores
Executive(s): Jay Gottlieb, President; Ed Anderson, Vice President, Operations

Computer Horizons Corporation

747 Third Avenue

New York, NY 10017

Telephone: 212/371-9600   Telex: None

Description: Provides system analysis and programming services.

Founded: 1969   Traded: OTC

No. of Employees: 754

Sales($000): 50,892   Fiscal Year: 02/28/86

Industry Segment: Services

Executive(s): John Cassese, Chairman and President; Martin Pelcyger, Exec Vice President

Computer Language Research

2395 Midway Road

Carrollton, TX 75006

Telephone: 214/250-7000   Telex: 262985

Description: Markets mainframe tax processing services and microcomputer tax workstations under trade names "Fast-Tax," "Micro-Tax," and "Financial Sense".

Founded: 1964   Traded: OTC

No. of Employees: 1369

Sales($000): 93,392   Fiscal Year: 12/31/86

Industry Segment: Services

Executive(s): Francis Winn, Chairman; Steve Winn, President and CEO

Computer Network Technology Corporation

9440 Science Center Drive

New Hope, MN 55428

Telephone: 612/535-8111   Telex: None

Description: Manufactures high-speed mainframe computers and peripherals devices.

Founded: 1979   Traded: OTC

No. of Employees: 24

Sales($000): 37,000   Fiscal Year: 03/31/86

Industry Segment: Mainframe computers

Executive(s): C. McKenzie Lewis, President and CEO; Eugene D. Misukanis, Exec Vice President

Key Subsidiaries: CNT Inc.

Computer Products Inc.
2900 Gateway Drive
Pompano Beach, FL 33069-4804
Telephone: 305/974-5500 Telex: 592010
Description: Manufactures electronics products.
Founded: 1968   Traded: OTC
No. of Employees: 2,248
Sales($000): 111,416 Fiscal Year: 12/31/86
Industry Segment: Systems; Software
Executive(s): David C. Yoder, Chairman, Pres., & CEO; Edward J. Schneider, Vice President
Key Subsidiaries: Tecnetics Inc., Memodyne Corp., CPRC Inc., Grant Technology Systems Corp.,
Remote Systems Inc., Stevens-Arnold Inc., Boschert Inc., Power Products Ltd.

Computer Resources Inc.
4520 West 160th Street
Cleveland, OH 44135
Telephone: 216/362-1020 Telex: 980731
Description: Produces magnetic media used in disk memories including rigid disks, cartridges and
floppy disks.
Founded: 1967   Traded: OTC
No. of Employees: 145
Sales($000): 18,000   Fiscal Year: 09/30/86
Industry Segment: Media
Executive(s): Allan Schwartz, Chairman; Ramesh P. Shah, Vice Chairman and CEO

Computer Sciences Corporation
2100 East Grand Avenue
El Segundo, CA 90245
Telephone: 213/615-0311 Telex: 2153152 7267
Description: Provides hardware, software, software development, systems engineering, training,
computer management, consulting and installation services.
Founded: 1959   Traded: NYSE
No. of Employees: 15600
Sales($000): 838,587 Fiscal Year: 03/28/86
Industry Segment: Systems; Software
Executive(s): William R. Hoover, President; George Barratt, Vice president and CFO
Key Subsidiaries: Comtec Inc.

ComputerLand Corporation
2901 Peralta Oaks
Oakland, CA 94605
Telephone: 415/487-5000   Telex: 852922
Description: Markets personal computer hardware, software, and peripherals in its franchised
computer stores.
Founded: 1976   Traded: PVT
No. of Employees: 700
Sales($000): 1,400,000   Fiscal Year: 09/30/86
Industry Segment: Computer stores
Executive(s): Ed Faber, Chairman and CEO; Ken Waters, President and COO
Key Subsidiaries: GreatWest Technology Inc., Corporate Owned Stores Inc.

Computercraft, Inc.
Suite 900
1616 South Voss Road
Houston, TX 77057
Telephone: 713/977-8419   Telex: 466896
Description: Markets microcomputer systems for personal and business use in its computer stores.
Founded: 1977   Traded: OTC
No. of Employees: 350
Sales($000): 91,792   Fiscal Year: 05/03/86
Industry Segment: Computer stores
Executive(s): William Ladin, President and CEO; Avery More, Exec Vice President
Key Subsidiaries: ABC Computers and Telephones Inc.

Computer & Communications Technology Corp
9177 Skypark
San Diego, CA 92123
Telephone: 619/279-8973   Telex: 910334 1171
Description: Manufactures magnetic disc recording heads, plated disc media and disc drives.
Founded: 1969   Traded: OTC
No. of Employees: 2100
Sales($000): 62,000   Fiscal Year: 12/31/86
Industry Segment: Mass storage
Executive(s): Everett Bahre, Chairman, President & CEO; Robert McKay, Exec Vice President &
CFO
Key Subsidiaries: Disctron Inc., Information Magnetics Corp., Zeta Laboratories Inc., Ultra-Disc
Inc.

Computervision
100 Crosby Drive
Bedford, MA 01730
Telephone: 617/275-1800   Telex: 923345
Description: Manufactures computer-based interactive graphics systems which are used by its customers in computer-aided engineering, design, manufacturing and product data management applications.
Founded: 1969   Traded: NYSE
No. of Employees: 4400
Sales($000): 494,672   Fiscal Year: 12/31/86
Industry Segment: Systems; Software; Super minicomputers
Executive(s): Martin Allen, Chairman; Robert L. Gable, President and CEO
Key Subsidiaries: Grado Software, Computer Systeme GmbH., Cambridge Interactive Systems Ltd., Applied Graphics Systems, OIR Europe Inc., Designer Systems Insurance Ltd., CIS Inc., CIS Medusa Inc.

Computone Systems, Inc.
One Dunwoody Park, Suite 200
Atlanta, GA 30338
Telephone: 404/393-3010   Telex: 544016
Description: Provides computer products and services for a variety of business applications.
Founded: 1966   Traded: OTC
No. of Employees: 413
Sales($000): 83,340   Fiscal Year: 05/31/86
Industry Segment: Distributors; Software
Executive(s): William O. Robeson, President and CEO; Frank B.Thomason, Vice President, CFO and Accounting Officer
Key Subsidiaries: Future Information Systems, Infotecs Inc., Insurance Publishing & Computers Inc., Computer Room Inc., Logical Choice Inc., Gulf Coast Computer Shoppe Inc.

Comshare Inc.
3001 South State Street
Ann Arbor, MI 48104
Telephone: 313/994-4800   Telex: 810223 6014
Description: Provides computer software and services, principally data management, business planning, forecasting, analysis and business graphics products marketed as decision support systems.
Founded: 1966   Traded: OTC
No. of Employees: 935
Sales($000): 68,871   Fiscal Year: 06/30/86
Industry Segment: Services
Executive(s): Richard L. Crandall, President and CEO; Ian McNaught-Davis, Group Vice President

Concurrent Computer Corporation
15 Main Street
Holmdel, NJ 07733
Telephone: 201/946-8883   Telex: 710722 4903
Description: Manufactures high performance 32-bit digital super minicomputers designed to meet the requirements of time-critical applications.
Founded: 1985   Traded: OTC
No. of Employees: 2626
Sales($000): 244,794   Fiscal Year: 07/31/86
Industry Segment: Super minicomputers
Executive(s): Gaynor N. Kelley, Chairman; James K. Sims, President and CEO
Key Subsidiaries: 82% owned by Perkin-Elmer

Continental Telecom, Inc.
245 Perimeter Center Parkway
Atlanta, GA 30346
Telephone: 404/391-8000   Telex: 810757 0155
Description: An integrated telecommunications company providing a broad range of communications and information processing products and services.
Founded: 1960   Traded: NYSE
No. of Employees: 21926
Sales($000): 2,556,000   Fiscal Year: 12/31/86
Industry Segment: Telecommunications
Executive(s): Charles Wohlstetter, Chairman; John N. Lemasters, President and CEO
Key Subsidiaries: Continental Telephone Co., Cado Systems Corporation, Contel Business Networks Inc., Data Equipment Systems Inc., Execucom Systems Corp., Executone Inc., Northern Data Systems Inc., STSC Inc.

Continuum Company, Inc.
3429 Executive Center Drive
Austin, TX 78731
Telephone: 512/345-5700   Telex: 767175
Description: Develops proprietary computer software useful to life insurance companies and their agents, and other marketing people.
Founded: 1968   Traded: OTC
No. of Employees: 691
Sales($000): 52,674   Fiscal Year: 03/31/86
Industry Segment: Software
Executive(s): Ronald C. Carroll, Chairman, President & CEO; W. Michael Long, Exec Vice President
Key Subsidiaries: Continuum co. Ltd., Continuum Systems Research Inc.

Control Data Corporation
P.O. Box O
Minneapolis, MN 55440
Telephone: 612/853-8100 Telex: 759938
Description: Provides computer hardware and software and related services to worldwide markets.
Founded: 1957   Traded: NYSE
No. of Employees: 38856
Sales($000): 3,346,700   Fiscal Year: 12/31/86
Industry Segment: Systems; Software; Services
Executive(s): Robert M. Price, Chairman, President & CEO; Norbert R. Berg, Deputy Chairman
Key Subsidiaries: Autocon Industries Inc., Commercial Credit Co.

Convergent Technologies, Inc.
2700 North First Street
San Jose, CA 95150-6685
Telephone: 408/434-2848 Telex: 176825
Description: Manufactures microprocessor-based computers and computer systems used in a variety
of network computing applications.
Founded: 1979   Traded: OTC
No. of Employees: 1,994
Sales($000): 305,825 Fiscal Year: 12/31/86
Industry Segment: Systems
Executive(s): Paul C. Ely Jr., President and CEO; John M. Russell, Vice President and CFO

CONVEX Computer Corporation
701 N. Plano Road
Richardson, TX 75081
Telephone: 214/952-0200
Description: Manufactures high performance computer systems that bridge the gap between
supercomputers and superminicomputers.
Founded: 1982   Traded: OTC
No. of Employees: 400
Sales ($000): 40,200 Fiscal Year: 12/31/86
Industry Segment: Systems
Executive(s): Robert J. Paluck, President and CEO; Steven J. Wallach, VP Technology

Copytele Inc.
900 Walt Whitman Road
Huntington Station, NY 11746
Telephone: 516/549-5900   Telex: 516549 5974
Description: Develops a new type of display for the presentation of data and graphics systems.
Founded: 1982   Traded: OTC
No. of Employees: 15
Sales($000): 0   Fiscal Year: 10/31/85
Industry Segment: Displays
Executive(s): Denis Krusos, Chairman and CEO; Frank Disanto, President

Cordatum, Inc.
4720 Montgomery Lane
Bethesda, MD 20814
Telephone: 301/652-5424   Telex: None
Description: Develops and maintains software systems.
Founded: 1974   Traded: OTC
No. of Employees: 28
Sales($000): 2,047   Fiscal Year: 12/31/85
Industry Segment: Software; Services
Executive(s): Merle C. Garvis, President; Lawrence J. Fedewa, Vice President

Corvus Systems, Inc.
2100 Corvus Drive
San Jose, CA 95124
Telephone: 408/559-7000   Telex: 278976
Description: Manufactures a local area networking system called OMNINET and the necessary
network management software, file servers, mass storage systems and backup storage systems to
support its use with microcomputers.
Founded: 1979   Traded: OTC
No. of Employees: 378
Sales($000): 53,223   Fiscal Year: 05/31/86
Industry Segment: Network Products
Executive(s): James L. Siehl, President and CEO; Joseph W. Rooney, Exec Vice President
Key Subsidiaries: OemTek Inc., OYNX + IMI Inc., Applied Intelligence Inc.

Cray Research, Inc.
608 Second Avenue South
Minneapolis, MN 55402
Telephone: 612/333-5889 Telex: 290789
Description: Manufactures large-scale, high speed computing systems.
Founded: 1972   Traded: NYSE
No. of Employees: 3180
Sales($000): 596,685 Fiscal Year: 12/31/86
Industry Segment: Supercomputers; Peripherals
Executive(s): John A. Rollwagen, Chairman and CEO; John F. Carlson, Exec Vice President

Cullinet Software Inc.
400 Blue Hill Drive
Westwood, MA 02090
Telephone: 617/329-7700 Telex: 3291134
Description: Develops integrated computer software for IBM and IBM-compatible hardware users.
Founded: 1968   Traded: NYSE
No. of Employees: 1800
Sales($000): 184,296 Fiscal Year: 04/30/86
Industry Segment: Software
Executive(s): John Cullinane, Chairman; David Chapman, Vice Chairman & President

Cycare Systems
P.O. Box 1278
520 Dubuque Building
Dubuque, IA 52001
Telephone: 319/556-3131 Telex: None
Description: Provides computerized information processing services.
Founded: 1969   Traded: OTC
No. of Employees: 677
Sales($000): 57,186 Fiscal Year: 12/31/86
Industry Segment: Services
Executive(s): James Houtz, Chairman and President; James Dyer, Exec Vice President

DSC Communications Corporation
1000 Coit Road
Plano, TX 75075
Telephone: 214/519-3000   Telex: 8673105
Description: Manufactures telecommunications systems and products for domestic and international markets.
Founded: 1976   Traded: OTC
No. of Employees: 2450
Sales($000): 303,951   Fiscal Year: 12/31/86
Industry Segment: Telecommunications
Executive(s): James M. Nolan, Chairman; James L. Donald, President and CEO
Key Subsidiaries: Digital Switch Corp., Granger Associates Inc., DSC Technologies Corp.

DST Systems Inc.
1004 Baltimore Avenue
Kansas City, MO 64105
Telephone: 816/221-5545   Telex: 704837
Description: Develops proprietory software systems to provide accounting and record-keeping services to the mutual fund industry.
Founded: 1971   Traded: OTC
No. of Employees: 1220
Sales($000): 100,200   Fiscal Year: 12/31/86
Industry Segment: Software
Executive(s): Thomas A. McDonnell, Vice Chairman and CEO; Robert Gould, President and COO
Key Subsidiaries: Transaction Services Inc.

Daisy Systems Corporation
700 Middlefield Road
Mountain View, CA 94039-7006
Telephone: 415-960-0123   Telex: 858262
Description: Manufactures computer-aided engineering systems used in all segments of the electronics industry.
Founded: 1980   Traded: OTC
No. of Employees: 883
Sales($000): 107,149   Fiscal Year: 09/30/86
Industry Segment: Super minicomputers
Executive(s): Max Palevsky, Chairman and CEO; Harvey Jones, President and COO

Data 3 Systems Inc.
P.O. Box 441
2544 Cleveland Avenue
Santa Rosa, CA 95402
Telephone: 707/528-6560 Telex: 176058
Description: Provides software and support services for companies who are integrating their
manufacturing facilities. Known for the software package, MRPS 38-S, a manufacturing resource
planning system that includes integrated financial reporting.
Founded: 1980   Traded: PVT
No. of Employees: 100
Sales($000): 6,000   Fiscal Year: 6/30/86
Industry Segment: Software; Services
Executive(s): Richard C. Anderson, President; Jeffrey Lundeen, Vice President, Sales

Data Architects, Inc.
245 Winter Street
Waltham, MA 02154
Telephone: 617/890-7730 Telex: 6817234
Description: Develops proprietary software product licenses and provides customized computer
software systems design.
Founded: 1967   Traded: OTC
No. of Employees: 261
Sales($000): 27,085   Fiscal Year: 11/30/86
Industry Segment: Software
Executive(s): Martin Cooperstein, Chairman and CEO; Norman Zachary, President and COO
Key Subsidiaries: DAI Decision Systems Inc.

Data Card Corporation
11111 Bren Road West
P.O. Box 9355
Minneapolis, MN 55440
Telephone: 612/933-1223 Telex: 9337971
Description: Produces specialized business machine products and related supplies and services.
Founded: 1969   Traded: OTC
No. of Employees: 1,900
Sales($000): 153,554 Fiscal Year: 03/29/86
Industry Segment: Systems
Executive(s): D.J. Ekberg, Chairman and CEO; Gary R. Holland, President and COO
Key Subsidiaries: Laserdyne Corp., Laser Data Systems Inc., Toppan Moore Data Products Ltd.,
Security Imprinter Corp., Credit Card Sentinel Inc., CPE Data Card Ltd.

Data General
4400 Computer Drive
Westboro, MA 01580
Telephone: 617/366-8911   Telex: 920329
Description: Manufactures general purpose computer systems, including peripherals equipment and
software.
Founded: 1968   Traded: NYSE
No. of Employees: 16,535
Sales($000): 1,268,000   Fiscal Year: 09/26/86
Industry Segment: Systems; Peripherals; Software
Executive(s): Edson D. de Castro, President; Herbert J. Richman, Exec Vice President
Key Subsidiaries: Datagen Inc., Digital Computer Controls Inc., WSA Systems and Services Inc.

Data Switch Corporation
One Enterprise Drive
Shelton, CT 06484
Telephone: 203/926-1801   Telex: 9296408
Description: Manufactures electronic switching and control systems, collectively marketed as
configuration management systems.
Founded: 1977   Traded: OTC
No. of Employees: 331
Sales($000): 42,177   Fiscal Year: 12/31/86
Industry Segment: Network products
Executive(s): Richard E. Greene, Chairman; Robert G. Gilbertson, President and CEO
Key Subsidiaries: ChannelNet Corp., IntelliNet Corp

DataEase International Inc.
12 Cambridge Drive
Trumbull, CT 06611
Telephone: 203/374-8000   Telex: 703972
Description: Develops microcomputer software.
Founded: 1982   Traded: PVT
No. of Employees: 60
Fiscal Year: 06/30/87 (Sales confidential)
Industry Segment: Software
Executive(s): Arun Gupta, Chairman. President & CEO; Guy Scalzi, Vice President

Datacopy Corporation
1215 Terra Bella Avenue
Mountain View, CA 94043
Telephone: 415/965-7900 Telex: 701994
Description: Manufactures low cost, high resolution electronic digitizing scanners and image
processing systems.
Founded: 1973   Traded: OTC
No. of Employees: 74
Sales($000): 7,410   Fiscal Year: 12/31/86
Industry Segment: Input devices
Executive(s): Richard M. Drysdale, Chairman; Rolando C. Esteverena, President and CEO

Datapoint Corporation
8119 Datapoint Drive
San Antonio, TX 78229
Telephone: 512/699-7000 Telex: 512699 7171
Description: Manufactures a range of office and computer products and systems, including local area
networks, multifunction workstations, and dispersed computing systems.
Founded: 1969   Traded: NYSE
No. of Employees: 3,621
Sales($000): 325,227 Fiscal Year: 07/26/86
Industry Segment: Systems; LAN; Software
Executive(s): Asher B. Edelman, Chairman; Edward P. Gistaro, President and CEO

Dataproducts Corporation
6200 Canoga Avenue
Woodland Hills, CA 91365-0746
Telephone: 818/887-8000 Telex: 674734
Description: Manufactures a broad range of data handling and output equipment consisting of
printers and associated products, and digital communications equipment.
Founded: 1962   Traded: AMX
No. of Employees: 4200
Sales($000): 353,837 Fiscal Year: 03/29/86
Industry Segment: Printers
Executive(s): Jack C. Davis, Chairman and CEO; Graham Tyson, President
Key Subsidiaries: Integral Data Systems Inc.

Dataram Corporation

P.O. Box 7528

Princeton, NJ 08543-7528

Telephone: 609/799-0071   Telex: 6858012

Description: Manufactures computer memory and peripherals products.

Founded: 1967   Traded: AMX

No. of Employees: 110

Sales($000): 17,458   Fiscal Year: 04/30/86

Industry Segment: Peripherals

Executive(s): Raymond P. Von Culin, Chairman; Robert V. Tarantino, President and CEO

Datasouth Computer Corporation

4216 Stuart Andrew Boulevard

Charlotte, NC 28210

Telephone: 704/523-8500   Telex: 6843018

Description: Manufactures computer printers and related products.

Founded: 1977   Traded: OTC

No. of Employees: 178

Sales($000): 19,212   Fiscal Year: 12/31/86

Industry Segment: Printers

Executive(s): Carl Morath, Chairman; James W. Busby, President

Datatab Inc.

770 Broadway

New York, NY 10003

Telephone: 212/475-7800   Telex: 212475262

Description: Operates data-processing service centers, utilizing computer packages for processing of data for use in market research, file maintenance and commercial applications.

Founded: 1959   Traded: OTC

No. of Employees: 99

Sales($000): 4,183   Fiscal Year: 12/31/85

Industry Segment: Services

Executive(s): Ari Bachana, President; Herb Shaver, Vice President

Decision Industries Corporation
Formerly Decision Data Corp.
400 Horsham Road
Horsham, PA 19044-0996
Telephone: 215/674-3300 Telex: 831471
Description: Produces workstations and computer peripherals, primarily printers.
Founded: 1969   Traded: OTC
No. of Employees: 1,783
Sales($000): 195,083 Fiscal Year: 11/30/86
Industry Segment: Workstations; Printers
Executive(s): Carl W. Stursberg Jr., Chairman; Richard J. Schineller, President and CEO
Key Subsidiaries: Decision Data Service Inc.

Decision Systems Inc.
200 Route 17
Mahwah, NJ 07430
Telephone: 201/529-1440 Telex: 490000 4677
Description: Develops educational games for personal computers, word processing, and
micrographics and provides consulting services for proprietary financial software.
Founded: 1960   Traded: OTC
No. of Employees: 150
Sales($000): 13,796   Fiscal Year: 04/30/86
Industry Segment: Software
Executive(s): George Morgenstern, President; Robert Greenburg, Exec Vice President

Delta Data Systems Corporation
2595 Metropolitan Drive
Trevose, PA 19407
Telephone: 215/322-5400 Telex: None
Description: Manufactures personal computers and computer terminals.
Founded: 1968   Traded: OTC
No. of Employees: 271
Sales($000): 20,524   Fiscal Year: 03/31/86
Industry Segment: Personal computers
Executive(s): Robert W. Cross, Chairman and CEO; William I. Rolya, President and COO
Key Subsidiaries: Delta Data Systems Corp.

Dicomed Corporation
P O Box 246
12000 Portland Avenue South
Minneapolis, MN 55440
Telephone: 612/885-3000   Telex: 290837
Description: Manufactures high performance computer graphic products.
Founded: 1969   Traded: OTC
No. of Employees: 213
Sales($000): 22,337   Fiscal Year: 12/31/85
Industry Segment: Peripherals
Executive(s): Wayne Huelskoetter, President & CEO; Lee Runzheimer, Chief Financial Officer

Diebold, Inc.
P.O. Box 44711
818 Mulberry Road SE
Canton, OH 44711
Telephone: 216/489-4000   Telex: 983421
Description: Manufactures automated transaction systems and security equipment used in financial
service applications.
Founded: 1876   Traded: NYSE
No. of Employees: 5,229
Sales($000): 410,926 Fiscal Year: 12/31/85
Industry Segment: Systems
Executive(s): Raymond Koontz, Chairman; Robert W. Mahoney, President and CEO
Key Subsidiaries: Retail Terminal Systems Inc.

Digilog Inc.
1370 Welsh Road
Montgomeryville, PA 18936
Telephone: 215/628-4530   Telex: 6851019
Description: Manufactures digital data communications monitoring and testing equipment and
network management and control systems.
Founded: 1969   Traded: OTC
No. of Employees: 122
Sales($000): 15,718   Fiscal Year: 09/30/86
Industry Segment: Test equipment
Executive(s): Ronald G. Moyer, Chairman and President; Thomas M. Emory Jr., Vice President,
Tech.

Digital Equipment Corporation
111 Powdermill Road
Maynard, MA 01754-1418
Telephone: 617/897-5111   Telex: 948457
Description: Supplies network computer systems and associated peripherals, communications and software products.
Founded: 1957   Traded: NYSE
No. of Employees: 94700
Sales($000): 7,590,357   Fiscal Year: 06/28/86
Industry Segment: Systems; Peripherals; Software
Executive(s): Kenneth H. Olsen, President and CEO; James M. Osterhoff, Vice President and CFO

Digital Research Inc.
P.O. Box DRI
60 Garden Court
Monterey, CA 93940
Telephone: 408/649-3896   Telex: 910360 5001
Description: Develops operating systems, graphics products, and micro-to-mainframe connectivity products. Known for GEM-based presentation graphics applications.
Founded: 1976   Traded: PVT
No. of Employees: 200
Sales($000): 45,179   Fiscal Year: 08/31/85 (Soft*letter)
Industry Segment: Software
Executive(s): Gary Kildall, Chairman and CEO; Robert Obuch, Chief Operating Officer

Distributed Logic Corporation
1555 South Sinclair Street
Anaheim, CA 92806
Telephone: 714/937-5700 Telex: 6836051
Description: Manufactures intelligent disk and tape controllers.
Founded: 1977   Traded: OTC
No. of Employees: 82
Sales($000): 14,634   Fiscal Year: 12/31/86
Industry Segment: Mass storage
Executive(s): Glenn C. Salley, President and CEO; Dennis Edwards, Sr Vice President
Key Subsidiaries: Accord Computer Corporation.

Ducommun Inc.
10824 Hope Street
Cypress, CA 90630
Telephone: 714/952-9500   Telex: 277809
Description: Distributes computer systems, peripherals and software to resellers, distributes complete computer systems to commercial users, and manufactures molded external interconnect devices for the electronics industry.
Founded: 1849   Traded: AMX
No. of Employees: 1650
Sales($000): 417,034   Fiscal Year: 12/31/85
Industry Segment: Distributors
Executive(s): Wallace W. Booth, Chairman and CEO; W. Donald Bell, President and COO
Key Subsidiaries: Kierulff Electronics, Ducommun Data Systems, MTI Systems, Tri-Tec Engineering.

Dyatron Corporation
210 Automation Way
P.O. Box 235
Birmingham, AL 35201
Telephone: 205/956-7500   Telex: 205956 7834
Description: Provides applications software systems, hardware, and systems support for the automotive, medical, banking, employee benefits, computerized billing and mass mailing industries.
Founded: 1981   Traded: OTC
No. of Employees: 375
Sales($000): 40,102   Fiscal Year: 12/31/85
Industry Segment: Software
Executive(s): James R. Forman Jr., Chairman; Charles E. Rueve, President and CEO
Key Subsidiaries: Compu Service Ltd., Action Computer Technology, Business Communications Sciences Inc., General Computer Services Inc., Computech Financial Services Inc.

ELXSI Ltd.
Formerly Trilogy Ltd.
2334 Lundy Place
San Jose, CA 95131
Telephone: 408/942-0900   Telex: 172320
Description: Manufactures high speed mainframe computers.
Founded: 1980   Traded: OTC
No. of Employees: 220
Sales($000): 18,000   Fiscal Year: 12/31/86
Industry Segment: Mainframe computers
Executive(s): Gene M. Amdahl, Chairman; Peter Appleton Jones, President and CEO

ESCA Corporation
13208 Northup Way
Bellevue, WA 98005
Telephone: 206/746-3000   Telex: 590155
Description: Develops software applications and systems for real time supervisory operations.
Founded: 1978   Traded: PVT
No. of Employees: 160
Fiscal Year: 10/31/86 (Sales confidential)
Industry Segment: Software
Executive(s): Parker Srouse, Chairman and CEO; Robin Podmore, Vice President

Eastman Kodak Company
343 State Street
Rochester, NY 14650
Telephone: 716/724-2241   Telex: 978481
Description: Manufactures imaging and chemical products including floppy diskettes.
Founded: 1880   Traded: NYSE
No. of Employees: 128,950
Sales($000): 11,550,000   Fiscal Year: 12/31/86
Industry Segment: Media
Executive(s): Colby H. Chandler, Chairman and CEO; Kay R. Whitmore, President
Key Subsidiaries: Atex Inc., Cyclotomics Inc., Datatape Inc., Diconix Inc., Eikonix Corp., Verbatim Corp.

Eaton Corp
Eaton Center
Cleveland, OH 44114
Telephone: 216/523-5000   Telex: 980352
Description: Manufactures advanced technology products for the automotive, electronics, defence and capital goods markets worldwide.
Founded: 1916   Traded: NYSE
No. of Employees: 41,134
Sales($000): 3,811,600   Fiscal Year: 12/31/86
Industry Segment: Electronic components
Executive(s): E.M. de Windt, Chairman and CEO; James R. Stover, President and COO
Key Subsidiaries: AIL International Inc., Cutler-Hammer, The Yale & Towne Co.

Electronic Arts
1820 Gateway Dr
San Mateo, CA 94404
Telephone: 415-571-7171   Telex: 709204
Description: Distributes educational software for personal computers.
Founded: 1982   Traded: PVT
No. of Employees: 120
Sales($000): 20,000   Fiscal Year: 03/31/86 (Soft*letter)
Industry Segment: Software
Executive(s): Trip Hawkins, Chief Executive Officer; Bing Gordon, Vice President

Electronic Associates Inc.
185 Monmouth Parkway
West Long Branch, NJ 07764
Telephone: 201/229-1100   Telex: 178131
Description: Manufactures computers for complex simulation applications.
Founded: 1946   Traded: NYSE
No. of Employees: 492
Sales($000): 28,130   Fiscal Year: 12/31/86
Industry Segment: Systems
Executive(s): William R. Smart, Chairman; Robert G. Finney, President and CEO

Emergency Power Engineering
1660 Scenic Avenue
Costa Mesa, CA 92626
Telephone: 714/557-1636   Telex: 183535
Description: Manufactures power conditioning equipment, including uninterruptible power systems.
Founded: 1971   Traded: PVT
No. of Employees: 800
Fiscal Year: 06/30/87 (Sales confidential)
Industry Segment: Peripherals
Executive(s): Hans Imhof, Chairman, President & CEO; ,

Emulex Corporation
3545 Harbor Blvd.
Costa Mesa, CA 92626
Telephone: 714/662-5600 Telex: 183627
Description: Manufactures mass storage peripherals controllers and communications multiplexer products for use with mini and microcomputers.
Founded: 1979 Traded: OTC
No. of Employees: 910
Sales($000): 104,949 Fiscal Year: 06/29/86
Industry Segment: Peripherals; Software
Executive(s): Fred B. Cox, Chairman and CEO; Stephen W. Frankel, President and COO
Key Subsidiaries: Digital House Ltd., Personal Systems Technology Inc., Computer Array Development Inc., Highspeed Communications Inc.

Endata Inc.
501 Great Circle Road
Nashville, TN 37228
Telephone: 615/244-0244 Telex: None
Description: Provides data imagery services and information systems and services.
Founded: 1969 Traded: OTC
No. of Employees: 565
Sales($000): 38,390 Fiscal Year: 12/31/86
Industry Segment: Output devices (COM)
Executive(s): Douglas C. Altenbern Sr., Chairman, President & CEO; Julius M. Dziak, Exec Vice President
Key Subsidiaries: DataFILM Corp., COM-Microfilm Systems of America.

Entre' Computer Centers, Inc.
1951 Kidwell Drive
Vienna, VA 22180
Telephone: 703/556-0800 Telex: 790152232
Description: Markets microcomputer systems and services to businesses and professionals. Largest publicly held franchisor of retail computer centers in the world.
Founded: 1981 Traded: OTC
No. of Employees: 629
Sales($000): 66,893 Fiscal Year: 08/31/86
Industry Segment: Distributors
Executive(s): Bert I. Helfinstein, President; Margaret Rodenburg, Vice President, Marketing

Epsilon Data Management, Inc.
50 Cambridge Street
Burlington, MA 01803
Telephone: 617/273-0250   Telex: 940886
Description: Provides computer-based marketing services to assist clients in the design and
implementation of direct response marketing programs.
Founded: 1970   Traded: OTC
No. of Employees: 761
Sales($000): 53,219   Fiscal Year: 05/31/86
Industry Segment: Services
Executive(s): Thomas O. Jones, President and Chairman; Robert J. Drummond, Senior Vice
President
Key Subsidiaries: Epsilon Securities Corp.

Epyx Inc.
600 Galveston Drive
Redwood City, CA 94063
Telephone: 415/366-0606   Telex: 295881
Description: Manufactures software and accessories for home computers.
Founded: 1978   Traded: PVT
No. of Employees: 50
Sales($000): 20,000   Fiscal Year: 12/31/86
Industry Segment: Software
Executive(s): Gilbert K. Freeman, President and CEO; John Brazier, Sr Vice President, Sales

Ericsson
100 Park Avenue
New York, NY 10017
Telephone: 212/685-4030   Telex: 758765
Description: Develops and manufactures telecommunications equipment.
Founded: 1874   Traded: OTC
No. of Employees: 78159
Sales($000): 4,300,000   Fiscal Year: 12/31/85
Industry Segment: Telecommunications
Executive(s): Bjorn Svedberg, President & CEO; Arne Mohlin, Executive Vice President
Key Subsidiaries: Facit Inc.

Esprit Systems, Inc.
100 Marcus Drive
Melville, NY 11747
Telephone: 516/293-5600 Telex: 221666ESPRI
Description: Develops video display computer terminals.
Founded: 1983   Traded: AMX
No. of Employees: 75
Sales($000): 23,222   Fiscal Year: 05/31/86
Industry Segment: Terminals
Executive(s): Anthony P. Palladino, Chairman and CFO; John A. Sasso, President, CEO and COO
Key Subsidiaries: Esprit Systems Ltd., Esprit Computer Products Inc.

F.A. Components
4700 76th Street
Elmhurst, NY 11373
Telephone: 718/507-1444 Telex: 645020
Description: Distributes computer peripherals.
Founded: 1980   Traded: PVT
No. of Employees: 100
Sales($000): 31   Fiscal Year: 09/31/85
Industry Segment: Distributors
Executive(s): Jay Freeman, President; Samuel D. Freeman, Vice President

FDP Corp.
2140 South Dixie Highway
Miami, FL 33133
Telephone: 305/858-8200 Telex: None
Description: Engaged in the development of computer applications software to meet the needs of the life insurance and employee benefit industry.
Founded: 1968   Traded: OTC
No. of Employees: 160
Sales($000): 16,039   Fiscal Year: 11/30/85
Industry Segment: Software
Executive(s): Michael C. Goldberg, Chairman, President & CEO; Douglas Kennedy, Executive Vice President
Key Subsidiaries: Financial Data Planning Corp., Actuarial Research & Development Corp., FDP Leasing Corp.

First Financial Management Corporation
Suite 700
3 Corporate Square
Atlanta, GA 30329
Telephone: 404/321-0120   Telex: 6347239
Description: Provides data processing services and related software services. Also sells and leases computer equipment and related products.
Founded: 1971   Traded: OTC
No. of Employees: 944
Sales($000): 69,694   Fiscal Year: 12/31/86
Industry Segment: Services; Software
Executive(s): Patrick H. Thomas, Chairman, President & CEO; Richard E. Martin, Exec Vice President & CFO

First Software
13 Branch Street
Methuen, MA 01844
Telephone: 617/689-0077   Telex: 595913
Description: Distributes software and accessories for the IBM, Apple and Macintosh personal computers to retail stores.
Founded: 1982   Traded: PVT
No. of Employees: 60
Sales($000): 120,000   Fiscal Year: 12/31/85
Industry Segment: Destributors
Executive(s): Rick Faulk, President and CEO; David Levenson, Controller

Flextronics Inc.
35325 Fircrest Street
Newark, CA 94560
Telephone: 415/794-3539   Telex: 910381 7016
Description: Manufactures printed circuit assemblies for computer-related industries.
Founded: 1980   Traded: PVT
No. of Employees: 1500
Sales($000): 50,000   Fiscal Year: 03/31/86
Industry Segment: Services
Executive(s): Robert Todd, President and CEO; David Craft, Sr Vice President

Floating Point Systems, Inc.
P.O. Box 23489
Portland, OR 97223
Telephone: 503/641-3151   Telex: 360470
Description: Manufactures computers used to perform complex mathematical calculations.
Founded: 1970   Traded: NYSE
No. of Employees: 1607
Sales($000): 88,579   Fiscal Year: 10/31/86
Industry Segment: Super computers
Executive(s): Milton R. Smith, Chairman and CEO; George P. O'Leary, President and COO

Fortune Systems Corporation
300 Harbor Boulevard
Belmont, CA 94002
Telephone: 415/593-9000   Telex: 176865
Description: Manufactures desk-top computer systems.
Founded: 1980   Traded: OTC
No. of Employees: 255
Sales($000): 38,340   Fiscal Year: 12/31/86
Industry Segment: Hardware
Executive(s): James S. Campbell, Chairman, President & CEO; Gregg A. Anderson, Vice President & CFO

Fujitsu Ltd.
6-1 1-chome, Marunochi, Chiyoda-Ku
Tokyo, Japan
Telephone: 03-216-3211
Description: Manufactures electronic computer equipment and peripherals. Focuses on telegraph and data communications and electronics components.
Traded: FO
No. of Employees: 52600
Sales($000): 6,600,000
Industry Segment: Systems; Telecommunications; Electronics
Executive(s): Taiyu Kobayashi, Chairman; Takuma Yamamoto, President

GTE Corporation
One Stamford Forum
Stamford, CT 06904
Telephone: 203/965-2000   Telex: 9641644
Description: Telecommunications, lighting products and precision materials.
Founded: 1935   Traded: NYSE
No. of Employees: 183,000
Sales($000): 15,111,528   Fiscal Year: 12/31/86
Industry Segment: Telecommunications
Executive(s): Theodore F. Brophy, Chairman and CEO; James L. Broadhead, Sr. Vice President
Key Subsidiaries: 15 General Telephone Companies.

GTECH Corporation
101 Dyer Street
Providence, RI 02903
Telephone: 401/273/7700   Telex: 710347 8795
Description: Engaged in the production, operation and sale of computer-based networks.
Founded: 1981   Traded: OTC
No. of Employees: 795
Sales($000): 81,281   Fiscal Year: 02/22/86
Industry Segment: Network products
Executive(s): Guy B. Snowden, President and CEO; Robert K. Stern, Chairman
Key Subsidiaries: Datamax Inc.

Gandalf Technologies Inc.
9 Slack Road
Nepean, ON K2G OB7
Telephone: 613/225-0565   Telex: 0534728
Description: Manufactures data communications and information network equipment.
Founded: 1971   Traded: OTC
No. of Employees: 1361
Sales($000): 77,600   Fiscal Year: 07/31/86
Industry Segment: Network products
Executive(s): Desmond Cunningham, Chairman and CEO; James M. Bailey, Exec Vice President & COO
Key Subsidiaries: Redifacts Advanced Manufacturing Aids Ltd., Computer Dispatch Systems.

Gateway Computer Systems
5142 Argosy Drive
Huntington Beach, CA 92649
Telephone: 714/898-0784   Telex: None
Description: Retail sales and services for microcomputers and minicomputers.
Founded: 1979   Traded: PVT
No. of Employees: 180
Fiscal Year: 01/31/87   (Sales confidential)
Industry Segment: Computer stores
Executive(s): Ron Siegel, President and CEO

General Datacomm Industries, Inc.
Rt. 63
Middlebury, CT 06762-1299
Telephone: 203/574-1118   Telex: 710474 0027
Description: Markets data communications equipment and networks that transmit data via telephone
lines, microwave, satellites, fiber optics, and other telecommunications media.
Founded: 1969   Traded: NYSE
No. of Employees: 2517
Sales($000): 178,024   Fiscal Year: 09/30/86
Industry Segment: Telecommunications
Executive(s): Charles P. Johnson, Chairman; Fredrick R. Cronin, Vice President, Tech.

General Electric Company
3135 Easton Turnpike
Fairfield, CT 06431
Telephone: 203/373-2431   Telex: 643893
Description: Manufactures a wide variety of products for the generation, transmission, distribution,
control and utilization of electricity. Finances computer purchases.
Founded: 1892   Traded: NYSE
No. of Employees: 304000
Sales($000): 35,210,000   Fiscal Year: 12/31/86
Industry Segment: Distributors; Services
Executive(s): John F. Welch Jr., Chairman and CEO; David C. Genever-Watling, Vice President
Key Subsidiaries: RCA, NBC, GE Financial Services Inc., GE Information Services Inc.

General Instrument Corporation
767 Fifth Avenue
New York, NY 10153-0082
Telephone: 212/207-6200   Telex: 510101 2910
Description: Manufactures electronics components, systems and services for communications and computer-related products.
Founded: 1923   Traded: NYSE
No. of Employees: 20500
Sales($000): 794,281   Fiscal Year: 02/28/86
Industry Segment: Electronic components
Executive(s): Frank G. Hickey, Chairman, President & CEO; John A. DeVries, Sr Vice President
Key Subsidiaries: American Totalisator Co., Century III Electronics, Northern Scientific Laboratories Inc., Sytek Inc. Taiwan Electronics Corp., Tocom Inc.,C.P. Clare Electronique.

General Motors Corporation
3044 West Grand Boulevard
Detroit, MI 48202
Telephone: 313/556-5000   Telex: 224081
Description: Participates in the computer industry though EDS, a subsidiary providing computer systems, software and communications, and the application of high technology electronics products for automotive, defense and space applications.
Founded: 1916   Traded: NYSE
No. of Employees: 811000
Sales($000): 102,814,000   Fiscal Year: 12/31/86
Industry Segment: Services
Executive(s): Roger B. Smith, Chairman and CEO; F. James McDonald, President and COO
Key Subsidiaries: Electronic Data Systems Corporation, GM Hughes Electronics Corp., Delco Electronics Corp.

General Signal Corporation
P.O. Box 10010
High Ridge Park
Stamford, CT 06904
Telephone: 203/357-8800   Telex: 965851
Description: Produces instrumentation and controls, and related systems and equipment for semiconductor production, telecommunications transmission, test and measurement.
Founded: 1904   Traded: NYSE
No. of Employees: 22,000
Sales($000): 1,800,878   Fiscal Year: 12/31/85
Industry Segment: Electronics; Telecomm; Factory Auto.
Executive(s): David T. Kimball, Chairman and CEO; Edward C. Prellwitz, Vice President, Planning
Key Subsidiaries: Axel Electronics Inc., General Railway Signal Co.

Genisco Technology Corporation
18435 Susana Road
Rancho Dominquez, CA 90221
Telephone: 213/537-4750   Telex: 910346 6773
Description: Provides computer graphics, peripherals and related electronic products.
Founded: 1950   Traded: AMX
No. of Employees: 390
Sales($000): 40,265   Fiscal Year: 09/30/86
Industry Segment: Peripherals; Systems; Services
Executive(s): Robert B. Phinizy, Chairman and CEO; Philip G. Halamandaris, President and COO

Gerber Scientific, Inc.
P.O. Box 305
Hartford, CT 06141
Telephone: 203/644-1551   Telex: 6972453
Description: Applies computer-aided design and manufacturing. Develops products in computer-controlled drafting and photoplotting, interactive design and computerized marker making.
Founded: 1948   Traded: NYSE
No. of Employees: 1600
Sales($000): 224,158   Fiscal Year: 04/30/86
Industry Segment: Systems
Executive(s): H. Joseph Gerber, President; Stanley Leven, Sr Vice President

Goal Systems International
5455 North High Street
Columbus, OH 43214
Telephone: 614/888-1775   Telex: 245337
Description: Develops software for IBM mainframes and microcomputers.
Founded: 1975   Traded: PVT
No. of Employees: 250
Sales($000): 17,500   Fiscal Year: 02/28/86
Industry Segment: Software
Executive(s): Jim Rutherford, President; Neal Ater, Vice President

Gould Inc.
10 Gould Center
Rolling Meadows, IL 60008
Telephone: 312/640-4000   Telex: 282473
Description: Manufactures electronic systems and components used in electronics, industrial,
medical, defense and research applications.
Founded: 1928   Traded: NYSE
No. of Employees: 18,476
Sales($000): 908,800   Fiscal Year: 12/31/86
Industry Segment: Microcomputers
Executive(s): William T. Ylvisaker, Chairman and CEO; James F. McDonald, President and COO
Key Subsidiaries: American Microsystems Inc.

Graphic Software Systems
9590 SW Gemini Drive
Beaverton, OR 97005
Telephone: 503/641-2200   Telex: 4994839
Description: Develops high performance graphics tools for desktop computers.
Founded: 1981   Traded: PVT
No. of Employees: 55
Fiscal Year: 10/31/87 (Sales confidential)
Industry Segment: Software
Executive(s): Tom Clarkson, Chairman; Peter Neupert, Vice President, Oper.

Haba Systems, Inc.
Formerly Arrays Inc.
6711 Valjean Avenue
Van Nuys, CA 91406
Telephone: 818/994-1899   Telex: None
Description: Publishes software and books for personal and small business computers.
Founded: 1981   Traded: OTC
No. of Employees: 30
Sales($000): 2,871   Fiscal Year: 11/30/85
Industry Segment: Software
Executive(s): Chaz Haba, Chairman and CEO; Ron Debry, Vice President, Oper.

Hadron, Inc.
9990 Lee Highway
Fairfax, VA 22030
Telephone: 703/359-6201   Telex: 248454
Description: Provides technical and consulting services in the fields of engineering and computer science.
Founded: 1964   Traded: OTC
No. of Employees: 500
Sales($000): 22,329   Fiscal Year: 03/31/86
Industry Segment: Services
Executive(s): Domonic A. Laiti, Chairman and CEO; L. Kenneth Johnson, President and COO
Key Subsidiaries: Acumenics Research & Technology Inc., Atlantic Contract Services Inc., G.E. Boggs & Associates Inc., Telcom International Inc., Compulaser Inc.

Harris Corporation
1025 West NASA Boulevard
Melbourne, FL 32919
Telephone: 305/727-9100   Telex: 514930
Description: Produces advanced information processing, communication and microelectronic products for the worldwide information technology market. Leases computer equipment.
Founded: 1926   Traded: NYSE
No. of Employees: 31,400
Sales($000): 2,216,600   Fiscal Year: 06/30/86
Industry Segment: Communications; Information processing
Executive(s): Joseph A. Boyd, Chairman and CEO; John T. Hartley, President and COO
Key Subsidiaries: Lanier Business Products Inc., Scientific Calculations Inc.

Health Information Systems Inc.
4522 Fort Hamilton Parkway
Brooklyn, NY 11219
Telephone: 718/435-6300   Telex: None
Description: Develops, sells and leases comprehensive computer information and financial management systems for use in the health care field.
Founded: 1978   Traded: OTC
No. of Employees: 38
Sales($000): 2,710   Fiscal Year: 06/30/86
Industry Segment: Distributors
Executive(s): George Weinberger, Chairman and President; Gershon Weintraub, Vice President

Hewlett-Packard Company
3000 Hanover Street
Palo Alto, CA 94304
Telephone: 415/857-1501   Telex: 348461
Description: Manufactures precision electronics instruments and systems for measurement, analysis and computation.
Founded: 1939   Traded: NYSE
No. of Employees: 84,000
Sales($000): 6,505,000   Fiscal Year: 10/31/85
Industry Segment: Systems; Printers; Software
Executive(s): David Packard, Chairman; John A. Young, President and CEO
Key Subsidiaries: Fleet Systems Inc.

Hitachi Ltd.
6 Kanda-Surugadai, 4-chome, Chiyoda-Ku
Tokyo, Japan, FF 00101
Telephone: 03-258-1111
Description: Manufactures information and communications systems and electronics equipment.
Founded: 1910   Traded: NYSE
No. of Employees: 164117
Sales($000): 28,000,000   Fiscal Year: 03/31/86
Industry Segment: Systems; Electronics
Executive(s): Hirokichi Yoshiyama, Chairman; Katsushige Mita, President
Key Subsidiaries: Hitachi America Ltd., Maxell Corp of America

Hogan Systems, Inc.
5080 Spectrum Drive Suite 400E
Dallas, TX 75248
Telephone: 214/386-0020   Telex: 214386 0315
Description: Develops a line of banking applications software packages.
Founded: 1977   Traded: OTC
No. of Employees: 300
Sales($000): 27,013   Fiscal Year: 03/31/86
Industry Segment: Software
Executive(s): Gregor G. Peterson, Chairman; George L. McTavish, President and CEO
Key Subsidiaries: Henco Research Inc.

Honeywell Inc.
Honeywell Plaza
P.O. Box 524
Minneapolis, MN 55048
Telephone: 612/870-5200   Telex: 8706703
Description: Manufactures computers and computer related products.
Founded: 1885   Traded: NYSE
No. of Employees: 94022
Sales($000): 5,378,200   Fiscal Year: 12/31/86
Industry Segment: Systems
Executive(s): Edson W. Spencer, Chairman and CEO; James J. Renier, Vice Chairman

IBM Corporation
Old Orchard Road
Armonk, NY 10504
Telephone: 914/765-1900   Telex: 137405
Description: Largest manufacturer of data processing equipment in the world.
Founded: 1914   Traded: NYSE
No. of Employees: 403,508
Sales($000): 51,250,000   Fiscal Year: 12/31/86
Industry Segment: Systems; Peripherals; Software; Commun.
Executive(s): John R. Opel, Chairman; John F. Akers, President and CEO
Key Subsidiaries: RealCom Communications Corp., IBM Credit, International Video Disk Corp.,
Rolm Corp., Science Research Associates Inc.

IPL Systems, Inc.
360 Second Avenue
Waltham, MA 02254
Telephone: 617/890-6620   Telex: 923412
Description: Manufactures mid-range general purpose computer systems designed to utilize the same
operating software and peripheral equipment as the IBM 360 and 370 and the IBM 4300 series
computer systems.
Founded: 1973   Traded: OTC
No. of Employees: 25
Sales($000): 2,527   Fiscal Year: 12/31/86
Industry Segment: Mainframe Computers
Executive(s): Stephen J. Ippolito, Chairman and CFO; Robert W. Norton, President and CEO

ISC Systems Corporation

East 901 Second Avenue
P.O. BOX TAF-C8
Spokane, WA 99220
Telephone: 509/927-5600   Telex: 152203
Description: Provides financial institutions with on-line data terminal systems and services. Also designs, develops, markets and implements turnkey systems.
Founded: 1977   Traded: OTC
No. of Employees: 1841
Sales($000): 166,086   Fiscal Year: 06/27/86
Industry Segment: Systems
Executive(s): Ted C. DeMerritt, Chairman and CEO; John Lindeblad, President and COO

ITT

320 Park Avenue
New York, NY 10022
Telephone: 212/752-6000   Telex: 126546
Description: Manufactures telecommunications equipment, electronics components, defense and space, automotive, fluid technology, and natural resources products.
Founded: 1920   Traded: NYSE
No. of Employees: 232,000
Sales($000): 7,600,000   Fiscal Year: 12/31/86
Industry Segment: Telecommunications
Executive(s): Rand V. Araskog, Chairman and CEO; Edmund M. Carpenter, President and COO

Inacomp Computer Centers, Inc.

1800 West Maple Road
Troy, MI 48084
Telephone: 313/649-5580   Telex: 313649 3289
Description: Operates company owned and franchised retail outlets for the sale of microcomputer systems, software and peripherals for business and personal use.
Founded: 1976   Traded: OTC
No. of Employees: 486
Sales($000): 158,410   Fiscal Year: 08/02/86
Industry Segment: Computer stores
Executive(s): Joseph T. Inatome, Chairman and Exec VP; Rick Inatome, President and CEO
Key Subsidiaries: Seven Inacomp Computer Centers.

Information Builders
1250 Broadway
New York, NY 10001
Telephone: 212/736-4433 Telex: 661558
Description: Publishes FOCUS, a fourth-generation language data base management system, which operates uniformly across all major operating environments.
Founded: 1974   Traded: PVT
No. of Employees: 600
Sales($000): 93,000   Fiscal Year: 12/31/86
Industry Segment: Software
Executive(s): Gerald Cohen, Chairman and President; Peter Mittleman, Vice President, Dev.

Innovative Software, Inc.
9875 Widmer Road
Lenexa, KS 66215
Telephone: 913/492-3800 Telex: 209542
Description: Develops microcomputer software for business applications.
Founded: 1979   Traded: OTC
No. of Employees: 63
Sales($000): 13,464   Fiscal Year: 06/30/86
Industry Segment: Software
Executive(s): Michael J. Brown, President; Mark R. Callegari, Exec Vice President

Integral Systems
2185 N California Boulevard
Walnut Creek, CA 94596
Telephone: 415/939-3900 Telex: 415944 1416
Description: Develops and markets software for IBM and mainframes.
Founded: 1972   Traded: PVT
No. of Employees: 200
Sales($000): 30,000   Fiscal Year: 12/31/85
Industry Segment: Software
Executive(s): David Duffield, Chairman; Bryan Aspland, President

Integrated Software Systems Corporation
10505 Sorrento Valley Road
San Diego, CA 92121
Telephone: 619/452-0170   Telex: 697810
Description: Develops software used on mainframe, mini and workstation computers to access and manipulate data.
Founded: 1970   Traded: OTC
No. of Employees: 344
Sales($000): 40,367   Fiscal Year: 12/31/85
Industry Segment: Software
Executive(s): Peter Preuss, Chairman and CEO; Meldon K. Gafner, President
Key Subsidiaries: AUI Data Graphocs Inc., and 7 ISSCO companies.

Intel Corporation
3065 Bowers Avenue
Santa Clara, CA 95051
Telephone: 408/496-8935   Telex: 4943604
Description: Manufactures electronic "building blocks" used by OEMs to construct their systems. Intel is the world's largest manufacturer of microprocessors.
Founded: 1968   Traded: OTC
No. of Employees: 21,300
Sales($000): 1,265,011   Fiscal Year: 12/27/86
Industry Segment: Microprocessors
Executive(s): Gordon E. Moore, Chairman and CEO; Andrew S. Grove, President and COO

Intellicorp
1975 El Camino Real West
Mountain View, CA 94040-2216
Telephone: 415/965-5500   Telex: 171596
Description: Develops software based on artificial intelligence technology.
Founded: 1980   Traded: OTC
No. of Employees: 190
Sales($000): 18,597   Fiscal Year: 06/30/86
Industry Segment: Software
Executive(s): Thomas P. Kehler, Chairman and CEO; Ralph E. Kromer, President, COO and CFO

Intelligent Systems Corporation
4355 Shackleford Road
Norcross, GA 30093
Telephone: 404/381-2900   Telex: 810766 4915
Description: Manufactures enhancement products for personal computers, color graphics display
terminals, and microcomputers.
Founded: 1973   Traded: OTC
No. of Employees: 645
Sales($000): 125,541   Fiscal Year: 03/31/86
Industry Segment: Peripherals
Executive(s): J. Leland Strange, Chairman, President & CEO; Francis A. Marks, Vice President
Key Subsidiaries: Quadram, Princeton Graphics,Intecolor Corp., Asher Technologies Inc., Peachtree
Software Inc.

InterTAN Inc.
2000 Two Tandy Center
Fort Worth, TX 76102
Telephone: 817/332-7181   Telex: 758253
Description: Operates approximately 2119 retail consumer electronics outlets in Canada, the United
Kingdom, France, Belgium, West Germany, The Netherlands and Australia.
Founded: 1986   Traded: OTC
No. of Employees: 5087
Sales($000): 410,310   Fiscal Year: 06/30/86
Industry Segment: Computer stores
Executive(s): John V. Roach, Chairman and CEO; Robert E. Keto, President and COO

Interface Systems Inc.
5855 Interface Drive
Ann Arbor, MI 48103
Telephone: 313/769-5900   Telex: None
Description: Manufactures and markets printers and interfaces which are plug-compatible with IBM
3270 product line and certain IBM mainframe computers.
Founded: 1966   Traded: OTC
No. of Employees: 70
Sales($000): 11,841   Fiscal Year: 09/30/85
Industry Segment: Printers
Executive(s): Carl L. Bixby, President; David O. Schupp, Vice President
Key Subsidiaries: I.G.K. Industries Inc.

Intergraph Corporation
One Madison Industrial Park
Huntsville, AL 35807-4201
Telephone: 205/772-2000   Telex: 706626
Description: Applies current computer graphics and data management technologies to a variety of
engineering and mapping applications.
Founded: 1969   Traded: OTC
No. of Employees: 5100
Sales($000): 605,737   Fiscal Year: 12/31/86
Industry Segment: Workstations
Executive(s): James W. Meadlock, Chairman and President; Roland E. Brown, Exec Vice President
Key Subsidiaries: M&S Computing International Inc., The Rand Group Inc.

Intermetrics, Inc.
733 Concord Avenue
Cambridge, MA 02138
Telephone: 617/661-1840   Telex: 710320 7523
Description: Markets computer software services and products.
Founded: 1969   Traded: OTC
No. of Employees: 640
Sales($000): 42,631   Fiscal Year: 02/28/86
Industry Segment: Software; Services
Executive(s): John E. Miller, President and CEO; Joseph A. Saponaro, Exec Vice President & COO

Iomega Corporation
1821 West 4000 South
Roy, UT 84067
Telephone: 801/778-1000   Telex: 295811
Description: Manufactures and markets disk drives and removable cartridges.
Founded: 1980   Traded: OTC
No. of Employees: 1,154
Sales($000): 125,906   Fiscal Year: 12/31/86
Industry Segment: Mass storage
Executive(s): David J. Dunn, Chairman; Gabriel P. Fusco, President

Kaypro Corporation
533 Stevens Avenue
Solana Beach, CA 92075
Telephone: 619/481-4300   Telex: 361128
Description: Designs, manufactures and markets portable and desktop microcomputer systems and electronic instruments.
Founded: 1953   Traded: OTC
No. of Employees: 576
Sales($000): 77,925   Fiscal Year: 08/29/86
Industry Segment: Personal computers
Executive(s): Andrew F. Kay, Chairman; David A. Kay, President

Keane Incorporated
Ten City Square
Boston, MA 02129
Telephone: 617/241-9200   Telex: None
Description: Engaged in the management, programming, and installation of computer-based information systems.
Founded: 1967   Traded: OTC
No. of Employees: 608
Sales($000): 39,701   Fiscal Year: 12/31/85
Industry Segment: Services
Executive(s): John F. Keane, President; Michael C. Ruettgers, Vice President

Key Tronic Corporation
P.O. Box 14687
Spokane, WA 99214
Telephone: 509/928-8000   Telex: 509927 5248
Description: Manufactures input devices, primarily keyboards, for computers, word processors and terminals.
Founded: 1969   Traded: OTC
No. of Employees: 2,100
Sales($000): 111,655   Fiscal Year: 06/30/86
Industry Segment: Keyboards
Executive(s): Lewis G. Zirkle, Chairman, President & CEO; Randall M. Pierson, Sr Vice President, Mktg
Key Subsidiaries: Key Tronic Taiwan and Key Tronic Europe Ltd.

Kronos Inc.
62 4th Avenue
Waltham, MA 02154
Telephone: 617/890-3232   Telex: 951591
Description: Manufactures computerized time and attendance systems.
Founded: 1979   Traded: PVT
No. of Employees: 280
Fiscal Year: 10/31/86 (Sales confidential)
Industry Segment: Peripherals
Executive(s): Mark Aim, President; Yazir Kadar, Chief Operating Officer

Kyocera Corporation
5-22 Kitainoue-cho, Higashino
Yamashina-ku,
Kyoto 607, Japan
Telephone: 075-592-3851
Description: Focuses on ceramic products for electronics and other industries. Manufactures
modems, and makes laptop computers for Tandy.
Founded: 1959   Traded: NYSE
Sales($000): 1,550,572   Fiscal Year: 03/31/86
Industry Segment: Peripherals; Personal Computers
Executive(s): Kazuo Inamori, Chairman and President; Shingo Moriyama, Vice Chairman
Key Subsidiaries: Kyocera International Inc.

Lawson Associates
2021 E Hennepin Avenue
Minneapolis, MN 55413
Telephone: 612/379-2634   Telex: 3709000
Description: Develops application software packages for accounting, human resources, and
distribution.
Founded: 1975   Traded: PVT
No. of Employees: 200
Sales($000): 14,000   Fiscal Year: 05/31/86
Industry Segment: Software
Executive(s): Richard Lawson, Chairman; Ken Holec, President and CEO

Lee Data Corporation
7075 Flying Cloud Drive
Minneapolis, MN 55344
Telephone: 612/828-0300   Telex: 910576 1690
Description: Manufactures multifunction interactive terminal systems and personal computer attachments.
Founded: 1979   Traded: OTC
No. of Employees: 1,133
Sales($000): 93,068   Fiscal Year: 03/31/86
Industry Segment: Peripherals
Executive(s): John M. Lee, Chairman and CEO; Charles Askanas, President and COO
Key Subsidiaries: Phaze Information Machines Corp., Datastream Communications Inc.

Lex Electronics Inc.
Bldg 5 High Ridge Park
Stamford, CT 06905
Telephone: 203/968-1900   Telex: None
Description: Distributes electronics products.
Founded: 1982   Traded: PVT
No. of Employees: 1860
Sales($000): 520,000
Industry Segment: Distributors
Executive(s): Anthony J. Whitton, President; Dave Peterschmidt, Vice President, Sales

Libra Programming
1954 E 7000 South
Salt Lake City, UT 84121
Telephone: 800/453-3827   Telex: None
Description: Focuses on software for construction, distribution, public accounting and property management industries.
Founded: 1976   Traded: PVT
No. of Employees: 69
Sales($000): 8,361   Fiscal Year: 12/31/85   (Soft*letter)
Industry Segment: Software
Executive(s): Michael C. Saylor, Vice President, Sales; William A. Maasberg Jr., Chief Executive Officer

Lifeboat Associates
55 S Broadway
Tarrytown, NY 10591
Telephone: 914/332-1875   Telex: 510610 7602
Description: Develops software development tools for programming professionals.
Founded: 1976   Traded: PVT
No. of Employees: 40
Sales($000): 7,234   Fiscal Year: 12/31/85   (Soft*letter)
Industry Segment: Software
Executive(s): Dr. Edward Currie, Chairman; Francis Pandolfi, Chief Executive Officer

Litton Industries, Inc.
360 North Crescent Drive
Beverly Hills, CA 90210-4867
Telephone: 213/859-5000   Telex: 674991
Description: Manufactures computer-integrated machine tools and components for computer equipment and peripherals.
Founded: 1953   Traded: NYSE
No. of Employees: 55,500
Sales($000): 4,521,005   Fiscal Year: 07/31/86
Industry Segment: Systems
Executive(s): Fred W. O'Green, Chairman; Orion L. Hoch, President, CEO and COO
Key Subsidiaries: Western Geophysical Company of America

Local Data, Inc.
2771 Toledo STreet
Torrance, CA 90503
Telephone: 213/320-7126   Telex: 182518
Description: Manufactures communications products including protocol converters.
Founded: 1977   Traded: PVT
No. of Employees: 150
Sales($000): 13,000   Fiscal Year: 10/31/86
Industry Segment: Network products
Executive(s): Robert E. Lee, Chairman, President & CEO; Gordon M. Watson, Sr Vice President, Sales

Lockheed Corporation
4500 Park Granada Boulevard
Calabasas, CA 91399
Telephone: 818/712-2000 Telex: 797847
Description: Produces aerospace products and systems. Has subsidiaries in computer services.
Founded: 1932 Traded: NYSE
No. of Employees: 87,800
Sales($000): 9,535,000 Fiscal Year: 12/29/85
Industry Segment: Services
Executive(s): Lawrence O. Kitchen, Chairman and CEO; Robert A. Fuhrman, President and COO
Key Subsidiaries: Cadam Inc., Metier Mgmnt., Lockheed Dataplan, Datacom Systems, Dialog
Information Services Inc.

Lodgistix, Inc.
1938 North Woodlawn, Suite 1
Wichita, KS 67208
Telephone: 316/685-2216 Telex: 437108IHSWIC
Description: Develops automated property management systems, and designs computer software.
Founded: 1978 Traded: OTC
No. of Employees: 255
Sales($000): 24,834 Fiscal Year: 06/30/86
Industry Segment: Software
Executive(s): George A. Zugmier, Chairman and President; Paul E. Hammar, Exec Vice President

Logicon Inc.
3701 Skypark Drive
Torrance, CA 90505
Telephone: 213/373-0220 Telex: 9521822
Description: Provides professional services, including scientific research and the application of
computer and systems technology.
Founded: 1961 Traded: NYSE
No. of Employees: 2456
Sales($000): 200,474 Fiscal Year: 03/31/86
Industry Segment: Services
Executive(s): John R. Woodhull, President and CEO; Robert G. Walden, Sr Vice President and CFO
Key Subsidiaries: Chase, Rosen and Wallace Inc., Control Dynamics Co., R&D Associates.

Lotus Development Corporation
55 Cambridge Parkway
Cambridge, MA 02142
Telephone: 617/577-8500   Telex: 948107
Description: Produces business productivity software for personal computers, including 1-2-3,
Symphony, and Jazz.
Founded: 1981   Traded: OTC
No. of Employees: 1000
Sales($000): 282,864   Fiscal Year: 12/31/86
Industry Segment: Software
Executive(s): Jim P. Manzi, Chairman, President & CEO

M/A-Com, Inc.
7 New England Executive Park
Burlington, MA 01803
Telephone: 617/272-9600   Telex: 949464
Description: Manufactures electronic telecommunications products. Provides systems integration of
information systems to both commercial and government customers.
Founded: 1950   Traded: NYSE
No. of Employees: 11,790
Sales($000): 577,469   Fiscal Year: 09/27/86
Industry Segment: Telecommunications
Executive(s): Richard T. DiBona, Chairman, President & CEO; Dr. Frank A. Brand, Exec Vice
President & COO
Key Subsidiaries: Omni Spectra Ltd., Sigma Data Services Corp.

MAI Basic Four, Inc.
14101 Myford Road
Tustin, CA 92680
Telephone: 714/731-5100   Telex: 429566
Description: Manufactures business computers and information processing systems for multi-user
applications by small and medium-sized businesses.
Founded: 1984   Traded: NYSE
No. of Employees: 2,900
Sales($000): 281,013   Fiscal Year: 09/30/86
Industry Segment: Systems; Software; Services
Executive(s): Bennett S. LeBow, Chairman; William B. Patton Jr., President and CEO

MBI Business Centers (The Math Box, Inc.)
1201 Seven Locks Road
Rockville, MD 20854
Telephone: 301/279-0551   Telex: None
Description: The largest publicly held chain of company-owned computer centers on the East Coast.
Founded: 1974   Traded: OTC
No. of Employees: 236
Sales($000): 117,932   Fiscal Year: 01/31/86
Industry Segment: Computer stores
Executive(s): Cyrus A. Ansary, Chairman; Ronald R. Watkins, President

MCI Communications Corp.
1133 19th Street NW
Washington, DC 20036
Telephone: 202/872-1600   Telex: 64613
Description: Provides domestic and international voice and data communications services.
Founded: 1968   Traded: OTC
No. of Employees: 12,445
Sales($000): 2,542,271   Fiscal Year: 12/31/85
Industry Segment: Telecommunications
Executive(s): William G. McGowen, Chairman and CEO; Bert C. Roberts Jr., President and COO
Key Subsidiaries: Western Union International Inc.

MPSI Systems Inc.
8282 South Memorial Drive
Tulsa, OK 74133
Telephone: 918/250-9611   Telex: 4996640
Description: Develops proprietary computer applications software and related data bases.
Founded: 1970   Traded: OTC
No. of Employees: 428
Sales($000): 23,421   Fiscal Year: 09/30/86
Industry Segment: Software
Executive(s): Ronald G. Harper, Chairman, President & CEO; C. Robert Coulter, Senior Vice President

MacNeal-Schwendler Corporation
815 Colorado Boulevard
Los Angeles, CA 90041
Telephone: 213/258-9111 Telex: 852130
Description: Develops applications software for use by engineers and designers in industry, research laboratories and universities.
Founded: 1963   Traded: AMX
No. of Employees: 130
Sales($000): 21,101   Fiscal Year: 01/31/86
Industry Segment: Software
Executive(s): Richard H. MacNeal, Chairman; Joseph F. Gloudeman, President and CEO

Management Science America Inc.
3445 Peachtree Road, N.E.
Atlanta, GA 30326-1276
Telephone: 404/239-2000 Telex: 549638
Description: Develops standard computer applications software packages for mainframe computers.
Founded: 1963   Traded: OTC
No. of Employees: 2500
Sales($000): 193,449 Fiscal Year: 12/31/86
Industry Segment: Software
Executive(s): John Imlay Jr., Chairman and CEO; William M. Graves, President and COO

Marshall Industries
9674 Telstar Avenue
El Monte, CA 91731-3004
Telephone: 818/459-5500 Telex: None
Description: Distributes semiconductors, connectors, passive components, subsystems and peripherals, production supplies and workstations.
Founded: 1954   Traded: NYSE
No. of Employees: 1,083
Sales($000): 244,777 Fiscal Year: 05/31/86
Industry Segment: Distributors
Executive(s): Gordon S. Marshall, Chm., Pres., CEO and COO; David O. Zertuche, VP Finance and CFO

Martin Marietta Corporation
6801 Rockledge Drive
Bethesda, MD 20817
Telephone: 301/897-6000   Telex: 898437
Description: Manufactures systems and products in the fields of space, defense, electronics, communications, information management, energy, and materials.
Founded: 1961   Traded: NYSE
No. of Employees: 67,000
Sales($000): 4,752,537   Fiscal Year: 12/31/86
Industry Segment: Systems; Services
Executive(s): Thomas G. Pownall, Chairman and CEO; Norman R. Augustine, Exec Vice President & COO
Key Subsidiaries: Mathematica Products Group Inc., Oxford Software Corporation.

Masstor Systems Corporation
5200 Great America Parkway
P.O. Box 58017
Santa Clara, CA 95052-8017
Telephone: 408/988-1008   Telex: 910339 9310
Description: Manufactures data storage management systems and communications systems.
Founded: 1976   Traded: OTC
No. of Employees: 151
Sales($000): 24,867   Fiscal Year: 12/31/85
Industry Segment: Systems
Executive(s): David R. Addison, Chairman, President & CEO; Richard P. Beck, Exec Vice President & CFO

Matsushita Electric Industrial Co. Ltd.
1006 Oaza Kadoma, Kadoma City
Osaka Japan, FF,
Telephone: 06-908-1121
Description: Manufactures consumer electronic equipment and components, including video and audio equipment; sold under Panasonic and other trade names.
Traded: NYSE
No. of Employees: 134000
Sales($000): 29,794,200   Fiscal Year: 11/20/86
Industry Segment: Personal computers
Executive(s): Masaharu Matsushita, Chairman; Akio Tanii, President
Key Subsidiaries: Matsushita Electric Corp. of America

McDonnell Douglas Corporation
P.O. Box 516
St. Louis, MO 63166
Telephone: 314/232-0232 Telex: 44857
Description: A world leader in aerospace technology emerging as a supplier of information-related products and services.
Founded: 1921   Traded: NYSE
No. of Employees: 97,067
Sales($000): 11,477,700   Fiscal Year: 12/31/85
Industry Segment: Systems; Software; Services
Executive(s): Sanford N. McDonnell, Chairman and CEO; John F. McDonnell, President
Key Subsidiaries: McAuto

Measurex Corporation
One Results Way
Cupertino, CA 95014-5991
Telephone: 408/255-1500 Telex: 278871
Description: Manufactures sensor-based computer process control systems for continuous and batch manufacturing applications.
Founded: 1968   Traded: NYSE
No. of Employees: 2,360
Sales($000): 192,707 Fiscal Year: 11/30/86
Industry Segment: Systems
Executive(s): David A. Bossen, President and CEO; Larry Mueller, Exec Vice President, Operations

Mentor Graphics Corporation
8500 SW Creekside Place
Beaverton, OR 97005-7191
Telephone: 503/626-7000 Telex: 160577
Description: Manufactures CAE systems for use in the design, analysis, physical layout and testing of complex integrated circuits.
Founded: 1981   Traded: OTC
No. of Employees: 777
Sales($000): 173,545 Fiscal Year: 12/31/86
Industry Segment: Software; Systems
Executive(s): Thomas H. Bruggere, Chairman, President & CEO; Gerard H. Langeler, Exec Vice President & COO

Micom Systems, Inc.
4100 Los Angeles Avenue
P.O. Box 8100
Simi Valley, CA 93062-8100
Telephone: 805/583-8600 Telex: 687497
Description: Produces data communications products including remote communications products, local area network systems, and mail-order catalog sales of data communications devices and accessories.
Founded: 1973   Traded: OTC
No. of Employees: 2,032
Sales($000): 189,538 Fiscal Year: 03/31/86
Industry Segment: Network products
Executive(s): William A. Norred, Chairman; Roger L. Evans, President and CEO
Key Subsidiaries: Black Box Corp.

Micro D, Inc.
2801 South Yale Street
Santa Ana, CA 92704
Telephone: 714/540-4781 Telex: 182274
Description: Distributes microcomputer software, hardware, peripherals and accessories.
Founded: 1979   Traded: OTC
No. of Employees: 171
Sales($000): 221,418 Fiscal Year: 12/31/86
Industry Segment: Distributors
Executive(s): Linwood A. Lacy Jr., Chairman and CEO; Harold L. Clark, President and COO

Micro Data Base Systems
Box 248
Lafayette, IN 47902
Telephone: 317/463-4561 Telex: 209147ISEUR
Description: Develops and markets professional data base management systems with key analytic and presentation tools.
Founded: 1979   Traded: PVT
No. of Employees: 250
Sales($000): 13,400 Fiscal Year: 12/31/85 (Soft*letter)
Industry Segment: Software
Executive(s): Gary Koehler, Chief Executive Officer; Joyce Field, Director Human Res.
Key Subsidiaries: London MDBS Ltd.

MicroPro International Corporation
33 San Pablo Avenue
San Rafael, CA 94903
Telephone: 415/499-1200 Telex: 278947
Description: Develops applications software for microcomputers. Well known for the original WordStar and WordStar 2000.
Founded: 1978   Traded: NYSE
No. of Employees: 238
Sales($000): 38,230   Fiscal Year: 08/31/86
Industry Segment: Software
Executive(s): Leon Williams, President and CEO; Doug St. John, Sr Vice Pres., Prod Dev.

Micropolis Corporation
21123 Nordhoff Street
Chatsworth, CA 91311
Telephone: 818/709-3300 Telex: 651486
Description: Manufactures high performance disk drives for original equipment manufacturers.
Founded: 1976   Traded: OTC
No. of Employees: 1500
Sales($000): 213,135 Fiscal Year: 12/26/86
Industry Segment: Hard drives
Executive(s): Stuart P. Mabon, Chairman and President; Ericson M. Dunstan, Sr Vice President

Microprose Software
120 Lake Front Dr
Hunt Valley, MD 21030
Telephone: 301/771-1151 Telex: 759209
Description: Makes flight and battle simulations for home computers.
Founded: 1982   Traded: PVT
No. of Employees: 35
Sales($000): 6,000   Fiscal Year: 11/31/85 (Soft*letter)
Industry Segment: Software
Executive(s): Bill Stealey, Chief Executive Officer; Richard Todd, Vice President, Finance

Microrim Inc.
3925-159th Avenue NE
Redmond, WA 98073
Telephone: 206/885-2000   Telex: 8817723
Description: Focuses on data base management software for microcomputers.
Founded: 1981   Traded: PVT
No. of Employees: 120
Sales($000): 16,000   Fiscal Year: 04/30/86   (Soft*letter)
Industry Segment: Software
Executive(s): Kent L. Johnson, Chief Executive Officer; Frank Slouvenec, Vice President, Sales

Micros Systems, Inc.
12000 Baltimore Avenue
Beltsville, MD 20705-1384
Telephone: 301/490-2000   Telex: 440547
Description: Manufactures electronic terminals and computer software which provide target retail environments with transaction processing, in-store controls and management information.
Founded: 1977   Traded: OTC
No. of Employees: 226
Sales($000): 21,020   Fiscal Year: 06/30/86
Industry Segment: Terminals
Executive(s): Edward T. Wilson, Chairman; Louis M. Brown Jr., President and CEO
Key Subsidiaries: Control Systems Inc.

Microsoft Corporation
16011 NE 36th Way
Box 97017
Redmond, WA 98073-9717
Telephone: 206/882-8080   Telex: 160520
Description: Develops microcomputer software and related books and hardware peripheral devices.
Founded: 1975   Traded: OTC
No. of Employees: 998
Sales($000): 197,514   Fiscal Year: 06/30/86
Industry Segment: Software
Executive(s): William H. Gates III, Chairman and CEO; Jon A. Shirley, President and COO
Key Subsidiaries: Microsoft Press

Miniscribe Corporation
1871 Lefthand Circle
Longmont, CO 80501-6798
Telephone: 303/651-6000 Telex: 216101
Description: Manufactures micro-Winchester technology disk drives for incorporation by original
equipment manufactures into microcomputer systems.
Founded: 1980   Traded: OTC
No. of Employees: 1903
Sales($000): 184,861 Fiscal Year: 12/28/86
Industry Segment: Disk drives
Executive(s): Q.T. Wiles, Chairman and CEO; Gerald W. Goodman, President and COO

Mitel Corporation
P O Box 13089
350 Legget Drive
Kanata, ON K2k 1x3 FF
Telephone: 613/592-2122 Telex:
Description: Manufactures telecommunications equipment, principally microprocessor controlled
switching equipment.
Founded: 1971   Traded: NYSE
No. of Employees: 4655
Sales($000): 413,154 Fiscal Year: 03/28/86
Industry Segment: Telecommunications
Executive(s): Deryk Vander Weyer, Chairman; Anthony F. Griffiths, President and CEO

Mitsubishi Electric Corporation
2-3 Marunouchi 2-chome, Chiyoda-Ku
Tokyo, 100 Japan
Description: Manufactures computer systems, peripherals and semiconductors including logic
devices and microprocessor-related products, color printers and monitors, and disk drives.
Traded: FO
No. of Employees: 49000
Sales($000): 8,500,000
Industry Segment: Systems; Peripherals; Semiconductors
Executive(s): S. Shindo, Chairman; N. Katayama, President

Mohawk Data Sciences Corporation
Seven Century Drive
Parsippany, NJ 07054
Telephone: 201/299-8240 Telex: 201299 8353
Description: Manufactures mini-processor based business computers.
Founded: 1964   Traded: NYSE
No. of Employees: 550
Sales($000): 236,720 Fiscal Year: 04/30/86
Industry Segment: Minicomputers
Executive(s): Mathew E. Tutino, President and CEO; Karl H. Niemuller, Exec Vice President
Key Subsidiaries: MDS-Qantel Inc.

Motorola Inc.
1303 East Algonoquin Road
Schaumburg, IL 60196
Telephone: 312/397-5000 Telex: 282562
Description: One of the world's leading manufacturers of electronic equipment, systems and
components produced for both United States and international markets.
Founded: 1928   Traded: NYSE
No. of Employees: 90,200
Sales($000): 5,888,000   Fiscal Year: 12/31/86
Industry Segment: Microprocessors; Telecommunications
Executive(s): Robert W. Galvin, Chairman and CEO; William J. Weisz, Vice Chairman and COO
Key Subsidiaries: Codex Corp., Computer X Inc., Tegal Corp., Universal Data Systems Inc., Four-
Phase Systems Inc.

NBI, Inc.
3450 Mitchell Lane
P.O. Box 9001
Boulder, CO 80301
Telephone: 303/444-5710 Telex: 216159
Description: Manufacturer of workstations, applications processors, and data communications
equipment.
Founded: 1973   Traded: NYSE
No. of Employees: 3193
Sales($000): 282,354 Fiscal Year: 06/30/86
Industry Segment: Workstations
Executive(s): Thomas S. Kavanagh, President; David Klein, Executive Vice President

NCA Corporation
3250 Jay Street
Santa Clara, CA 95054
Telephone: 408/986-1800   Telex: 710339 9258
Description: Develops software products and services for engineering, manufacturing and financial uses.
Founded: 1970   Traded: OTC
No. of Employees: 163
Sales($000): 21,744   Fiscal Year: 12/31/85
Industry Segment: Software
Executive(s): Mark W. Ciotek, Chairman; John C. Cavalier, President and CEO
Key Subsidiaries: Avera Corporation

NCR Corporation
1700 South Patterson Blvd.
Dayton, OH 45479
Telephone: 513/445-5000   Telex: 513445 1238
Description: Manufactures business information processing systems for worldwide markets.
Founded: 1884   Traded: NYSE
No. of Employees: 62,000
Sales($000): 4,881,641   Fiscal Year: 12/31/86
Industry Segment: Systems
Executive(s): Charles E. Exley Jr., Chairman and President; William F. Buster, Vice President
Key Subsidiaries: NCR Comten Inc., Applied Digital Data Systems Inc.

NEC Corporation
33-1, Shiba Gochome, Minato-Ku
Tokyo, Japan 108
Telephone: 03-454-1111   Telex: None
Description: Manufactures communications systems, equipment computers, industrial electronic systems and home electronic products.
Founded: 1900   Traded: OTC
No. of Employees: 89000
Sales($000): 13,000,000   Fiscal Year: 03/31/86
Industry Segment: Telecommunications; Systems
Executive(s): Koji Kobayashi, Chairman; Tadahiro Sekimoto, President
Key Subsidiaries: NEC America Inc.

NYNEX Corporation
335 Madison Avenue
New York, NY 10017
Telephone: 212/370-7400   Telex: 212370 7615
Description: A regional Bell holding company (RBOC) with two Bell companies covering Maine,
New Hampshire, Vermont, Massachusetts, Rhode Island, Connecticut and New York.
Founded: 1983   Traded: NYSE
No. of Employees: 89600
Sales($000): 11,341,500   Fiscal Year: 12/31/86
Industry Segment: Telecommunications
Executive(s): Delbert C. Staley, Chairman and CEO; William G. Burns, Vice Chairman and CFO
Key Subsidiaries: Datago, Computer Solutions, New England Telephone, New York Telephone.

Nashua Corporation
44 Franklin Street
Nashua, NH 03061
Telephone: 603/880-2323   Telex: 943438
Description: Manufactures rigid memory discs, disc packs, cartridges and flexible discs.
Founded: 1904   Traded: NYSE
No. of Employees: 5275
Sales($000): 621,555   Fiscal Year: 12/31/85
Industry Segment: Media
Executive(s): Charles E. Clough, President and CEO; Eric N. Birch, Vice President

National Computer Systems, Inc.
11000 Prairie Lakes Drive
Eden Prairie, MN 55344
Telephone: 612/829-3000   Telex: 192126
Description: Manufactures computer-based optical mark reading systems and associated products
and services.
Founded: 1962   Traded: OTC
No. of Employees: 1859
Sales($000): 215,803   Fiscal Year: 01/31/86
Industry Segment: Input devices
Executive(s): Charles W. Oswald, Chairman and CEO; David C. Malmberg, President and COO
Key Subsidiaries: NCS Learning Corp., NCS Financial Systems Inc., NSC Data Forms Inc.

National Data Corporation
National Data Plaza
Corporate Square
Atlanta, GA 30329
Telephone: 404/329-8500   Telex: 542785
Description: Provides on-line processing of credit card, cash management, health care data and telemarketing transactions.
Founded: 1967   Traded: OTC
No. of Employees: 2,800
Sales($000): 142,823   Fiscal Year: 05/31/86
Industry Segment: Services
Executive(s): L.C. Whitney, Chairman, President & CEO; Rowland H. Thomas Jr., Sr Exec Vice President
Key Subsidiaries: National Billing Systems Inc., Communication Response Service Inc., Rapidata International Ltd., Technology Sales and Leasing Co. Inc.

National Micronetics, Inc.
5630 Kearny Mesa Road
San Diego, CA 92111
Telephone: 619/279-7500   Telex: 697932
Description: Manufactures magnetic recording heads for computer disc drives using Winchester Technology.
Founded: 1969   Traded: OTC
No. of Employees: 600
Sales($000): 42,897   Fiscal Year: 06/28/86
Industry Segment: Hard disks
Executive(s): Charles J. Lawson Jr., Chairman and CEO; Eric W. Markrud, Sr Vice President

National Semiconductor
2900 Semiconductor Drive
P.O. Box 58090
Santa Clara, CA 95052-8090
Telephone: 408/721-5000   Telex: 346353
Description: Manufactures electronic products including semiconductor components and information systems that utilize semiconductor components.
Founded: 1968   Traded: NYSE
No. of Employees: 30,800
Sales($000): 1,478,100   Fiscal Year: 05/31/86
Industry Segment: Semiconductor products; Systems
Executive(s): Peter J. Sprague, Chairman; Charles E. Sporck, President and CEO
Key Subsidiaries: Data Terminal Systems Pty. Ltd., National Semiconductor Datachecker/DTS, Dyna-Craft Inc., National Advanced Systems Corp.

Network Systems Corporation
7600 Boone Avenue North
Minneapolis, MN 55428
Telephone: 612/424-4888 Telex: 201678
Description: Manufactures data communications systems.
Founded: 1974   Traded: OTC
No. of Employees: 908
Sales($000): 108,792 Fiscal Year: 12/31/86
Industry Segment: Network products
Executive(s): James E. Thornton, Chairman and CEO; Lyle D. Altman, President and COO
Key Subsidiaries: NSC Limited, Hypernet Network Systems Ag.

Nippon Telegraph and Telephone Corporation
1-6 Uchisaiwai-cho I-chome
Tokyo, Japan 100
Telephone: 03-509-5111
Description: Engaged in data communications and telecommunications.
Traded: FO
No. of Employees: 327000
Sales($000): 20,700,000   Fiscal Year: 12/31/85
Industry Segment: Telecommunications
Executive(s): Hisashi Shinto, President; Yasusada Kitahara, Vice President

Nippon Univac Kaisha Ltd.
17-51 Akasaka 2-chome, Minato-Ku
Tokyo, 107 Japan
Telephone: 03-589-9550   Telex: J 24536
Description: Develops software for computer-aided design applications and value added networks.
Traded: FO
No. of Employees: 4250
Sales($000): 750,000
Industry Segment: Systems
Executive(s): Teruo Sawachi, President
Key Subsidiaries: Unisys and Mitsui each own 34.2%

Nixdorf Computer, A.G.
Furstenallee 7
4790 Paderbom, West Germany
Telephone: 05251-300780
Description: A leading computer manufacturer in West Germany and Europe.
Traded: FO
No. of Employees: 14760
Sales($000): 1,300,000
Industry Segment: Systems
Executive(s): Klaus Luft, Chairman
Key Subsidiaries: Nixdorf Computer Corp., Nixdorf Computer Software Co.

Norsk Data A.S.
c/o Norsk Data North America, Inc.
55 William Street
Wellesley, MA 02181
Telephone: 617/366-4662   Telex: 921740
Description: Norwegian-based company in the information technology industry which manufactures a compatible line of general purpose minicomputers.
Founded: 1978   Traded: FO
No. of Employees: 2,799
Sales($000): 250,000   Fiscal Year: 12/31/85 (Appx. U.S.$ equiv.)
Industry Segment: Minicomputers
Executive(s): Terje Mikalsen, Chairman; Rolf Skar, President

North American Philips Corporation
100 East 42nd Street
New York, NY 10017
Telephone: 212/697-3600   Telex: 127381
Description: Manufactures electronic home entertainment products, lighting and personal care products, home appliances, furnishings and musical instruments.
Founded: 1937   Traded: NYSE
No. of Employees: 51800
Sales($000): 4,531,600   Fiscal Year: 12/31/86
Industry Segment: Personal computers
Executive(s): Cees Bruynes, Chairman and President; Richard A. Daunoras, Exec Vice President & CFO
Key Subsidiaries: Airpax Corp., Amperex Electronics Corp., Dialight Corp., Genie Home Products, Magnavox, Mepco/Centralab Inc., Ohmite.

Northern Telecom Ltd.
33 City Centre Drive
Mississauga, ON L5B 3A2
Telephone: 416/275-0960   Telex: 06960348
Description: Manufactures telephones and terminals, wire and cable switching systems, transmission
systems, and operational and maintenance systems.
Founded: 1884   Traded: NYSE
No. of Employees: 46549
Sales($000): 4,384,000   Fiscal Year: 12/31/86
Industry Segment: Telecommunications
Executive(s): Edmund B. Fitzgerald, Chairman and CEO; D.G. Vice, President
Key Subsidiaries: Northern Telecom Inc., BNR Inc., Bell Northern Research Inc.

Novell, Inc.
1170 North Industrial Park Drive
Orem, UT 84057
Telephone: 801/226-8202   Telex: 3879541
Description: Manufactures a family of local area network (LAN) and communications products
which allow personal computers to share files, data and resources.
Founded: 1983   Traded: OTC
No. of Employees: 292
Sales($000): 81,531   Fiscal Year: 10/25/86
Industry Segment: Local area networks
Executive(s): Raymond J. Noorda, Chairman, President & CEO; Harry J. Armstrong, Vice President,
Sales

Numerix Corporation
20 Ossipee
Newton, MA 02164
Telephone: 617/964-2500   Telex: 948032
Description: Manufactures high speed array processors.
Founded: 1982   Traded: PVT
No. of Employees: 140
Fiscal Year: 04/30/87 (Sales confidential)
Industry Segment: Peripherals
Executive(s): Lawrence T. Sullivan, Chairman; Peter Alexander, President and CEO
Key Subsidiaries: 50% owned by Analog Devices Inc.

Oki Electric Industry Co. Ltd.
7-12 Toranomon 1-chome, Minato-Ku
Tokyo, 105 Japan
Telephone: 03-501-3111   Telex: 02226324
Description: Manufactures telecommunications, data processing and electric devices.
Traded: FO
No. of Employees: 1250
Sales($000): 2,300,000
Industry Segment: Printers
Executive(s): Namio Hashimoto, President and CEO; Zobumitsu Kosugi, Vice President
Key Subsidiaries: Okidata Corp., Oki America Inc.

Ing. C. Olivetti & Co. S.P.A.
Via Jervis, 77
Iveria, Italy 10010
Telephone: 514-282-1880
Description: Manufactures accounting systems, terminals, data processing systems,
telecommunications equipment and microcomputers.
Traded: FO
No. of Employees: 19849
Sales($000): 3,100,000
Industry Segment: Systems
Executive(s): Bruno Visentini, Chairman; Carlo DeBenedetti, Vice Chairman and CEO

On-Line Software International, Inc.
Two Executive Drive
Fort Lee, NJ 07024
Telephone: 201/592-0009   Telex: 135586
Description: Develops standardized computer software products.
Founded: 1969   Traded: OTC
No. of Employees: 318
Sales($000): 36,465   Fiscal Year: 05/31/86
Industry Segment: Software
Executive(s): Jack M. Berdy, Chairman, President & CEO; Edward J. Siegel, CFO & Exec Vice
President
Key Subsidiaries: Datascan America Inc.

Oracle Systems
20 Davis Drive
Belmont, CA 94002
Telephone: 415/598-8000 Telex: 171437
Description: Develops computer software products used for database management, applications
development, decision support and network communications.
Founded: 1977   Traded: OTC
No. of Employees: 820
Sales($000): 55,383   Fiscal Year: 05/30/86
Industry Segment: Software
Executive(s): Lawrence Ellison, President & CEO; Jeffrey L. Walker, Chief Financial Officer

Pacific Telesis Group
140 New Montgomery Street
San Francisco, CA 94105
Telephone: 415/882-8000 Telex: None
Description: A regional Bell holding company (RBOC) with two Bell companies in California and
Nevada.
Founded: 1983   Traded: NYSE
No. of Employees: 71,500
Sales($000): 8,977,300   Fiscal Year: 12/31/86
Industry Segment: Telecommunications
Executive(s): Donald E. Guinn, Chairman, President & CEO; John E. Hulse, Vice Chairman & CFO
Key Subsidiaries: Nevada Bell, PacTel Companies.

Pansophic Systems, Inc.
709 Enterprise
Oak Brook, IL 60521
Telephone: 312/572-6000 Telex: 3575920
Description: Develops systems and utility software products for large computers.
Founded: 1969   Traded: NYSE
No. of Employees: 1050
Sales($000): 81,433   Fiscal Year: 04/30/86
Industry Segment: Software
Executive(s): Joseph A. Piscopo, Chairman; Dr. William G. Nelson IV, President and COO

Par Technology Corporation
Par Technology Park
220 Seneca Turnpike
New Hartford, NY 13413
Telephone: 315/738-0600   Telex: 510100 6133
Description: Manufactures microprocessor based point-of-sale terminal systems for the restaurant industry.
Founded: 1970   Traded: OTC
No. of Employees: 1019
Sales($000): 70,759   Fiscal Year: 12/31/85
Industry Segment: Terminals
Executive(s): Dr. John W. Sammon Jr., Chairman and President; Charles A. Constantino, Exec Vice President
Key Subsidiaries: PAR Microsystems, PAR Business Systems, Transaction Control Industries Inc., PAR Government Systems, Rome Research Corp.

Paradyne Corporation
P.O. Box 2826
8550 Ulmerton Road
Largo, FL 34294-2826
Telephone: 813/530-2000   Telex: None
Description: Manufactures data communications equipment and systems for data processing networks.
Founded: 1969   Traded: NYSE
No. of Employees: 3,749
Sales($000): 261,109   Fiscal Year: 12/31/86
Industry Segment: Data communications
Executive(s): Robert S. Wiggins, Chairman, President & CEO; Jerry T. Kendall, Exec Vice President & COO
Key Subsidiaries: Ark Electronics, Solid State Circuits.

Perkin-Elmer Corporation
761 Main Avenue
Norwalk, CT 06859-0001
Telephone: 203/762-1000   Telex: 965954
Description: Manufactures diverse high technology products which serve broad industrial, business, scientific, engineering,education and government markets.
Founded: 1939   Traded: NYSE
No. of Employees: 15515
Sales($000): 1,304,612   Fiscal Year: 07/31/85
Industry Segment: Minicomputers
Executive(s): Horace G. McDonell, Chairman and CEO; Gaynor N. Kelley, President and COO
Key Subsidiaries: Concurrent Computer Corporation, Metco Inc., MRJ Inc.

Personal Computer Products, Inc.
11590 West Bernardo Court
San Diego, CA 92127
Telephone: 619/485-8411   Telex: 4992939
Description: Markets microcomputer accessory products and technology and microcomputers.
Founded: 1982   Traded: OTC
No. of Employees: 29
Sales($000): 2,312   Fiscal Year: 06/30/86
Industry Segment: Peripherals
Executive(s): Edward W. Savarese, Chairman and CEO; Daniel W. Zipkin, President and COO

Philips N V
Groenewoudseweg 1
5621 Eindohoven, Netherlands
Description: The largest European manufacturer of consumer electronics products. Also produces a variety of computer systems.
Traded: FO
No. of Employees: 352000
Sales($000): 18,100,000
Industry Segment: Electronics; Minicomputers
Executive(s): H. Van Riemsdijk, Chairman

Pioneer Electronic Corporation
4-1 Meguro 1-chome, Meguro-Ku
Tokyo, 153 Japan
Telephone: 03-494-1111
Description: Manufactures a variety of audiovideo, and other electronic products.
Traded: NYSE
No. of Employees: 14708
Sales($000): 1,900,000   Fiscal Year: 12/31/85
Industry Segment: Consumer electronics
Executive(s): Nozomu Matsumoto, Chairman; Seyia Matsumoto, President

Pioneer Standard Electronics, Inc.
4800 East 131st Street
Cleveland, OH 44105
Telephone: 216/587-3600   Telex: 216663 1004
Description: Distributes industrial and consumer electronic products.
Founded: 1963   Traded: OTC
No. of Employees: 936
Sales($000): 265,788 Fiscal Year: 03/31/86
Industry Segment: Distributors
Executive(s): Preston B. Heller Jr., Chairman and CEO; James L. Bayman, President and COO
Key Subsidiaries: Pioneer, Technologies Group Inc.

Plessey Company plc
Plessey North America Corporation
925 Westchester Ave
White Plains, NY 10604
Telephone: 914/328-6990   Telex: 710568 1348
Description: Designs and builds advanced electronic and communications equipment and systems,
including software.
Founded: 1956   Traded: NYSE
No. of Employees: 2200
Sales($000): 2,100,000   Fiscal Year: 03/28/86
Industry Segment: Systems; Software
Executive(s): Sir John Clark, Chm & CEO, Plessey Co; Warren J. Sinsheimer, Chm. of Plessey No.
Amer.

Policy Management Systems Corporation
PO Box Ten
One PMS Center
Blythewood, SC 29016
Telephone: 803/735-4000   Telex: 7354217
Description: Develops standardized software systems designed specifically for companies in
property and casualty insurance industries.
Founded: 1972   Traded: OTC
No. of Employees: 1999
Sales($000): 150,555 Fiscal Year: 12/31/86
Industry Segment: Software
Executive(s): G. Larry Wilson, Chairman and President; David T. Bailey, Sr Vice President
Key Subsidiaries: Seibels Bruce Policy Management Systems Ltd., Business Computer Systems
Corp., PMS Compuclaim Corp., Commercial Services, Inc., Underwriting Services of America
Corp., Insurance Companies Inspection Bureau Inc.

Premier Industrial Corporation
4500 Euclid Avenue
Cleveland, OH 44103
Telephone: 216/391-8300 Telex: 6873015
Description: Broad line distributor of electronic components used in the production and maintenance of equipment.
Founded: 1946   Traded: NYSE
No. of Employees: 3500
Sales($000): 435,040 Fiscal Year: 05/31/86
Industry Segment: Distribution
Executive(s): Morton L. Mandel, Chairman; Robert Warren, President
Key Subsidiaries: Car-Lac Electronics, Hoffman Products, MCM Electronics, Newark Electronics, Trexon Electronics.

Priam Corporation
20 West Montague Expressway
San Jose, CA 95134
Telephone: 408/946-4600 Telex: 910338 0293
Description: Manufactures disk drives.
Founded: 1978   Traded: OTC
No. of Employees: 900
Sales($000): 128,756 Fiscal Year: 06/30/86
Industry Segment: Mass storage
Executive(s): Donald Massaro, Chairman; Joseph T. Booker, President and COO
Key Subsidiaries: Vertex Peripherals.

Prime Computer, Inc.
Prime Park
Natick, MA 01760
Telephone: 617/655-8000 Telex: 951571
Description: Manufactures a compatible family of small-and medium-size computer systems primarely for the end user market.
Founded: 1972   Traded: NYSE
No. of Employees: 1,112
Sales($000): 860,173 Fiscal Year: 12/31/86
Industry Segment: Minicomputers
Executive(s): David J. Dunn, Chairman; Joe M. Henson, President and CEO

Printronix, Inc.
17500 Cartwright Road
P.O. Box 19559
Irvine, CA 92713
Telephone: 714/863-1900   Telex: 910595 2535
Description: Manufactures a broad line of business printers for use with microcomputers,
minicomputers and mainframe computers.
Founded: 1974   Traded: OTC
No. of Employees: 1,624
Sales($000): 131,892 Fiscal Year: 03/28/86
Industry Segment: Printers
Executive(s): Robert A. Kleist, President and CEO; Jack A. Anderson, Sr Vice President, Mktg.
Key Subsidiaries: Anadex Inc.

QMS Inc. (Quality Micro Systems)
One Magnum Pass
Mobile, AL 36618
Telephone: 205/633-4300   Telex: RCA 266013
Description: Manufactures products that enhance the intelligence of computer printers, enabling
them to be used in a wide variety of applications by expanding their graphic and other printing
capabilities.
Founded: 1977   Traded: NYSE
No. of Employees: 721
Sales($000): 73,633   Fiscal Year: 10/03/86
Industry Segment: Output devices
Executive(s): James L. Busby, Chairman, President & CEO; Jack R. Altherr, Exec VP, COO & CFO

Quality Systems, Inc.
17822 East 17th Street
Tustin, CA 92680
Telephone: 714/731-7171   Telex: None
Description: Markets computerized information systems for the health care industry.
Founded: 1974   Traded: OTC
No. of Employees: 123
Sales($000): 10,859   Fiscal Year: 03/31/86
Industry Segment: Software; Services
Executive(s): Sheldon Razin, Chairman and President; Glenn Hetzel, Vice President and CFO

Quantum Corporation
1804 McCarthy Boulevard
Milpitas, CA 95035
Telephone: 408/262-1100   Telex: 910338 2203
Description: Manufactures rigid disk drives and subsystems for computer systems.
Founded: 1980   Traded: OTC
No. of Employees: 696
Sales($000): 121,244   Fiscal Year: 03/31/86
Industry Segment: Subsystems; Disk Drives
Executive(s): James L. Patterson, President and CEO; David B. Pratt, Sr Vice President and COO
Key Subsidiaries: Plus Development Corporation.

Quotron Systems, Inc.
5454 Beethoven Street
Los Angeles, CA 90066
Telephone: 213/827-4600   Telex: 652455
Description: Supplies on-line, real-time financial information services to the financial industries in the U.S.
Founded: 1957   Traded: OTC
No. of Employees: 1671
Sales($000): 205,686   Fiscal Year: 12/31/85
Industry Segment: Services
Executive(s): Milton E. Mohr, Chairman, President & CEO; Bruce B. Jackson, Exec Vice President

RCA Corporation
Acquired by General Electric 1986
30 Rockefeller Plaza
New York, NY 10020
Telephone: 212/621-6000   Telex: None
Description: Manufactures electronic products.
Founded: 1919   Traded: NYSE
No. of Employees: 87000
Sales($000): 8,972,100   Fiscal Year: 12/31/85
Industry Segment: Electronics
Executive(s): Thornton F. Bradshaw, Chairman; Robert R. Frederick, President and CEO
Key Subsidiaries: NBC

Racal Electronics plc
Western Road
Bracknell, Berkshire
England
Telephone: 0344-481222
Description: Manufactures modems, data communications equipment, graphics equipment and other electronic products.
Traded: FO
No. of Employees: 33000
Sales($000): 1,600,000
Industry Segment: Electronics
Executive(s): Ernest T. Harrison, Chairman and CEO; David C. Elsbury, Deputy CEO
Key Subsidiaries: Racal-Milgo, Racal-Redac, Racal-Vadic

Raytheon
141 Spring Street
Lexington, MA 02173
Telephone: 617/862-6600   Telex: 8602172
Description: Manufactures electronic systems and subsystems, equipment and components for government and commercial use. Publishes reference books and educational software.
Founded: 1922   Traded: NYSE
No. of Employees: 73,000
Sales($000): 6,408,500   Fiscal Year: 12/31/85
Industry Segment: Electronics
Executive(s): Thomas L. Phillips, Chairman and CEO; D. Brainerd Holmes, President
Key Subsidiaries: Badger Company Inc., Beech Aircraft Corp., Sedco Systems Inc., Switchcraft Inc.

Realworld Corporation
P.O.Box 2051
282 London Rd
Concord, NH 03302-2051
Telephone: 603/798-5700   Telex: None
Description: Develops and manufactures accounting software for microcomputers.
Founded: 1980   Traded: PVT
No. of Employees: 144
Sales($000): 10,000   Fiscal Year: 06/30/86 (Soft*letter)
Industry Segment: Software
Executive(s): David Gale, Chief Executive Officer; Larry Byrnes, President

Recognition Equipment, Inc.
P.O. Box 660204
2701 East Grauwyler Road
Irving, TX 75061
Telephone: 214/579-6000 Telex: 730653
Description: Manufactures information processing systems which are used for data capture, document processing and the management of information.
Founded: 1962   Traded: NYSE
No. of Employees: 2900
Sales($000): 241,795 Fiscal Year: 10/31/86
Industry Segment: Systems; Services
Executive(s): William G. Moore Jr., Chairman, President & CEO; Israel Sheinberg, Exec Vice President
Key Subsidiaries: REI, Inforex Inc.

Rexon Incorporated
5800 Uplander Way
Culver City, CA 90230
Telephone: 213/641-7110 Telex: 673112
Description: Manufactures microcomputer-based small business computer systems for use in a variety of data processing, word processing and management applications.
Founded: 1978   Traded: OTC
No. of Employees: 299
Sales($000): 33,498   Fiscal Year: 09/30/85
Industry Segment: Multiuser microcomputers
Executive(s): Q.T. Wiles, Chairman and CEO; Michael Preletz, President and COO
Key Subsidiaries: Wangtek

Ricoh Co. Ltd.
15-5 1-chome, Tokyo
Japan 107
Description: Markets photographic products and laser printers.
Founded: 1936   Traded: FO
Sales($000): 3,300,000
Industry Segment: Printers
Executive(s): Duye Takeshi, President; Hisashi Kubo, President, Ricoh US

Rockwell International Corporation
600 Grant Street
Pittsburgh, PA 15219
Telephone: 412/565-2000   Telex: 866213
Description: Applies advanced technology to a wide range of products in its aerospace, electronics, automotive and general industries businesses.
Founded: 1928   Traded: NYSE
No. of Employees: 123,266
Sales($000): 11,337,600   Fiscal Year: 09/30/85
Industry Segment: Electronics
Executive(s): Robert Anderson, Chairman and CEO; Donald R. Beall, President and COO
Key Subsidiaries: Allen-Bradley Company

Rodime plc
Rothesay House
Rothesay Place, Glenrothes Fife
KY7 5PN Scotland
Telephone: 0592-757441   Telex: 728239
Description: Manufactures hard disk drives for micro and minicomputer applications.
Founded: 1980   Traded: FO
No. of Employees: 750
Sales($000): 110,000 Fiscal Year: 09/30/85
Industry Segment: Hard disks
Executive(s): Leonard Brownlow, Chairman and President; Mervyn Brown, Vice President and CEO
Key Subsidiaries: Rodime Inc, USA

SAS Institute
Box 8000
SAS Circle
Cary, NC 27511-8000
Telephone: 919/467-8000   Telex: 802505
Description: Markets SAS system software and system 2000 Data Base Management Systems.
Founded: 1976   Traded: PVT
No. of Employees: 800
Fiscal Year: 11/30/86 (Sales confidential)
Industry Segment: Software
Executive(s): James N. Goodnight, President; John P. Fall, Vice President

SCI Systems, Inc.
5000 Technology Drive
Huntsville, AL 35805
Telephone: 205/882-4800 Telex: 782421
Description: Manufactures computers, computer-related products and computer based systems
Founded: 1961   Traded: OTC
No. of Employees: 5,185
Sales($000): 470,224 Fiscal Year: 06/30/86
Industry Segment: Systems
Executive(s): Olin B. King, Chairman and CEO; A. Eugene Sapp Jr., President and COO
Key Subsidiaries: SCI Technology Inc., SCI Manufacturing Inc.

SEI Corporation
680 East Swedesford Road
Wayne, PA 19087
Telephone: 215/254-1000 Telex: 951258
Description: Provides information processing services to financial institutions.
Founded: 1968   Traded: OTC
No. of Employees: 1144
Sales($000): 118,540 Fiscal Year: 12/31/86
Industry Segment: Services
Executive(s): Alfred P. West Jr., Chairman, President & CEO; Carmen V. Romeo, Exec Vice President

Sage Software, Inc.
Formerly Sage Systems
3200 Monroe Street
Rockville, MD 20852
Telephone: 301/230-3200 Telex: 248813
Description: Develops computer software and specializes in Aps, a productivety software application package for IBM computers.
Founded: 1978   Traded: PVT
No. of Employees: 120
Fiscal Year: 04/30/87 (Sales confidential)
Industry Segment: Software
Executive(s): Kevin Burns, President and CEO; Peter Gorahan, Vice President and CFO

Samna Corporation
2700 NE Expressway
Atlanta, GA 30345
Telephone: 404/321-5006   Telex: 543226
Description: Manufactures office automation software for personal computers.
Founded: 1983   Traded: PVT
No. of Employees: 95
Sales($000): 6,500   Fiscal Year: 12/31/85 (Soft*letter)
Industry Segment: Software
Executive(s): Said Mohammadioun, Chief Executive Officer; Thomas Anderson, Vice President, Sales

Samsung Electron Devices Co., Ltd.
7 Soonwha-Dong, Chung-Ku
Seoul, Korea
Description: Manufactures color and monocrome computer monitors and cathode-ray picture tubes. Also personal computers.
Traded: FO
No. of Employees: 3300
Sales($000): 178,000
Industry Segment: Personal computers; Displays
Executive(s): Jung Jae-Dun, President
Key Subsidiaries: Samsung Electronics America Inc.

Sanders Associates, Inc.
Acquired by Lockheed Corp. 7/86
Daniel Webster Highway South
Nashua, NH 03061-0868
Telephone: 603/885-4321   Telex: 943430
Description: Manufactures advanced technology electronic systems and products in two principal industry segments: government systems and products; and graphic systems and products.
Founded: 1951   Traded: NYSE
No. of Employees: 11,413
Sales($000): 885,790 Fiscal Year: 07/27/85
Industry Segment: Electronics
Executive(s): Roy A. Anderson, Pres, Lockheed Elec Grp; Albert B. Wight, President and COO
Key Subsidiaries: Analytyx Electronic Systems Inc., California Computer Products Inc., Image Resource Corporation.

Sanyo Electric Co., Ltd.
18 Keihan-Hondori 2-chome, Moriguchi City
Osaka, Japan
Description: Manufactures consumer electronics including personal computers, disk drives and
monitors.
Founded: 1950   Traded: FO
No. of Employees: 22860
Sales($000): 5,800,000
Industry Segment: Personal computers; Peripherals
Executive(s): Kaoru Iue, President; Jinzo Otsuka, Exec Vice President
Key Subsidiaries: Sanyo Mfg. Corp., Sanyo Business Systems, Sanyo E & E Corp., Sanyo Electric
Inc.

Schlumberger Ltd.
277 Park Avenue
New York, NY 10172
Telephone: 212/350-9400   Telex: 516324
Description: Manufactures control products and components. Provides oilfield services to the
petroleum industry.
Founded: 1927   Traded: NYSE
No. of Employees: 73000
Sales($000): 4,938,420   Fiscal Year: 12/31/86
Industry Segment: Electronics
Executive(s): D. Euan Baird, Chairman; Michal Gouilloud, Exec Vice President
Key Subsidiaries: Fairchild Semiconductor Corp., Analysts Inc., Sangamo Weston Inc.

Scientific Computers Inc.
10101 Bren Road East
Minnetonka, MN 55343
Telephone: 612/933-4200   Telex: 229836
Description: Provides business services, including on-line data processing and data entry, data base
typesetting, personalized direct mail systems and laser printing.
Founded: 1959   Traded: OTC
No. of Employees: 190
Sales($000): 13,608   Fiscal Year: 06/30/86
Industry Segment: Services
Executive(s): Richard A. Walter, Chairman and CEO; Steven Dille, Exec VP and COO
Key Subsidiaries: Workman Service Inc.

Scientific Micro Systems, Inc.
339 North Bernardo Avenue
Mountain View, CA 94043
Telephone: 415/964-5700   Telex: 184160
Description: Manufactures data controllers, mass storage subsystems and multi-user microcomputer
systems.
Founded: 1969   Traded: OTC
No. of Employees: 303
Sales($000): 65,273   Fiscal Year: 12/31/86
Industry Segment: Mass storage; Multiuser microcomputers
Executive(s): Charles A. Mathews, President and CEO; John R. Henry, Sr. VP, Advanced Dev.
Key Subsidiaries: OMT Inc.

Scientific Software Intercomp, Inc.
3rd Floor
1801 California Street
Denver, CO 80202
Telephone: 303/292-1111   Telex: 4322061
Description: Develops proprietary computer applications software and related services to the oil and
natural gas industries in areas of exploration, production, pipeline simulation, land management,
accounting and economics/planning.
Founded: 1968   Traded: OTC
No. of Employees: 241
Sales($000): 26,099   Fiscal Year: 12/31/86
Industry Segment: Software
Executive(s): Dr. E. Allen Breitenbach, Chairman and CEO; Dr. Robert C. McFarlane, President and
COO

Seagate Technology
920 Disc Drive
Scotts Valley, CA 95066
Telephone: 408/438-6550   Telex: 176455
Description: Manufactures rigid Winchester disk drives.
Founded: 1978   Traded: OTC
No. of Employees: 8,900
Sales($000): 459,836   Fiscal Year: 06/30/86
Industry Segment: Disk drives
Executive(s): Alan F. Shugart, Chairman and CEO; David T. Mitchell, President and COO

Selecterm, Inc.
153 Andover Street
Danvers, MA 01923
Telephone: 617/246-1300   Telex: None
Description: Engaged in the configuration, assembly, servicing and distribution through lease and sale of general purpose computer terminals and related equipment.
Founded: 1968   Traded: OTC
No. of Employees: 226
Sales($000): 27,098   Fiscal Year: 12/31/85
Industry Segment: Distributors
Executive(s): Arthur D. Little, Chairman; Phillip K. Ciolfi, President

Setpoint
950 Threadneedle
Houston, TX 77079
Telephone: 713/496-3220   Telex: 4963232
Description: Engineering and consulting service dealing in software applications.
Founded: 1977   Traded: PVT
No. of Employees: 125
Fiscal Year: 06/30/87 (Sales confidential)
Industry Segment: Services
Executive(s): Wyman Titwell, President; Lloyd Van Horn, Vice President

Shared Medical Systems Corporation
51 Valley Stream Parkway
Malvern, PA 19355
Telephone: 215/296-6300   Telex: 244934RCA
Description: Provides hospitals and physicians with patient-related financial and administrative data processing services.
Founded: 1969   Traded: OTC
No. of Employees: 3383
Sales($000): 374,880   Fiscal Year: 12/31/86
Industry Segment: Services
Executive(s): R. James Macaleer, Chairman and CEO; James C. Kelly, Exec Vice President

Sharp Corporation
22-22 Nagaike-cho, Abeno-Ku
Osaka, Japan 545
Telephone: 06-621-1221
Description: Manufactures personal computers, printers, scanners and other electronic products.
Traded: FO
Sales($000): 6,800,000
Industry Segment: Personal computers; Printers
Executive(s): Akira Saeki, President; Yoshihide Fukao, Sr Exec Vice President

Siemens AG, Munich, West Germany
Siemens Information Systems, Inc.
5500 Broken Sound Boulevard
Boca Raton, FL 33431
Telephone: 305/994-8800
Description: The world's sixth largest electronics/electrical engineering company and third largest manufacturer of telecommunications equipment.
Founded: 1847   Traded: FO
No. of Employees: 350000
Sales($000): 26,000,000   Fiscal Year: 09/30/85
Industry Segment: Systems; Peripherals; Telecommunications
Executive(s): H. Werner Krause, Pres. & CEO of SIS Inc.; David R. Kinley, VP, Eng/Mfg of SIS Inc.
Key Subsidiaries: Hell Graphics Systems Inc., OSRAM Corp., Potter & Brumfield.

Sir-Tech Software Inc.
Charlestown/Ogdensburg Mall
Ogdensburg, NY 13669
Telephone: 315/393-6633   Telex: None
Description: Manufactures recreational software and home productivity software.
Founded: 1981   Traded: PVT
No. of Employees: 15
Sales($000): 6,100   Fiscal Year: 04/30/86 (Soft*letter)
Industry Segment: Software
Executive(s): F.B. Sirotek, Chief Executive Officer; Robert Sirotek, Vice President

SofTech, Inc.
460 Totten Pond Road
Waltham, MA 02254
Telephone: 617/890-6900   Telex: 710324 6401
Description: Develops custom software and provides systems engineering and integration services.
Founded: 1969   Traded: OTC
No. of Employees: 519
Sales($000): 45,148   Fiscal Year: 05/31/86
Industry Segment: Services
Executive(s): Douglas T. Ross, Chairman; Justus F. Lowe Jr., President and CEO
Key Subsidiaries: AMG Associates Inc., SofTech Microsystems Inc., SofTech Investments Inc.

Softsel Computer Products, Inc.
546 North Oak Street
Inglewood, CA 90312
Telephone: 213/412-1700   Telex: 664484
Description: Distributes computer products world wide.
Founded: 1980   Traded: PVT
No. of Employees: 340
Sales($000): 225,000   Fiscal Year: 01/03/86
Industry Segment: Distributors
Executive(s): David S. Wagman, Co Chairman; Michael Pickett, President and COO

Software AG Systems Inc.
11800 Sunrise Valley Drive
Reston, VA 22091
Telephone: 703/860-5050   Telex: 899122
Description: Develops an integrated line of "off the shelf" computer systems software packages.
Founded: 1971   Traded: OTC
No. of Employees: 382
Sales($000): 65,759   Fiscal Year: 05/31/86
Industry Segment: Software
Executive(s): John N. Maguire, Chairman; Stuart J. Miller, President and CEO

Software Publishing Corporation
1901 Landings Drive
Mountain View, CA 94043
Telephone: 415/962-8910   Telex: 709591
Description: Develops packaged applications software to increase the productivity of business professionals who are users of personal computers. Best known for PFS family of productivity software.
Founded: 1980   Traded: OTC
No. of Employees: 176
Sales($000): 37,181   Fiscal Year: 09/30/85
Industry Segment: Software
Executive(s): Fred M. Gibbons, President and CEO; Janelle Bedke, Sr Vice President and COO
Key Subsidiaries: Harvard Software Inc.

Solectron Corporation
2001 Fortune Drive
San Jose, CA 95131
Telephone: 408/942-1943   Telex: 910338 3237
Description: Manufactures printed circuit boards, disk drives, cable and harness assemblies.
Founded: 1977   Traded: PVT
No. of Employees: 1200
Sales($000): 60,000   Fiscal Year: 08/31/86
Industry Segment: Disk drives
Executive(s): Charles Dickenson, Chairman; Winston Chen, President and CEO

Sony Corporation
7-35 Kitashinagawa
6-chome, Shinagawa-Ku
Tokyo, 141 Japan
Telephone: 03-448-2111
Description: Manufactures various kinds of electronics equipment, instruments and devices including disk drives and media.
Traded: NYSE
No. of Employees: 45000
Sales($000): 8,131,800   Fiscal Year: 10/31/86
Industry Segment: Electronics; Mass storage
Executive(s): Akio Morita, Chairman; Norio Ohga, President
Key Subsidiaries: Sony Corporation of America

Southern New England Telephone Company
227 Church Street
New Haven, CT 06506
Telephone: 203/771-5200   Telex: None
Description: Independent telecommunications company supplying network servives, information management systems, and communications equipment.
Founded: 1878   Traded: NYSE
No. of Employees: 13567
Sales($000): 1,433,100   Fiscal Year: 12/31/86
Industry Segment: Telecommunications
Executive(s): Walter H. Monteith Jr., Chairman, President & CEO; Richard M. Donofrio, Sr Vice President
Key Subsidiaries: SONECOR Systems, SoneTran Inc.

Southwestern Bell Corporation
One Bell Center   39th Floor
St. Louis, MO 63101
Telephone: 314/235-9800   Telex: 324212
Description: A regional Bell holding company (RBOC) with four Bell companies covering Arkansas, Kansas, Missouri, Oklahoma and Texas.
Founded: 1983   Traded: NYSE
No. of Employees: 71,400
Sales($000): 7,902,400   Fiscal Year: 12/31/86
Industry Segment: Telecommunications
Executive(s): Zane E. Barnes, Chairman, President & CEO; Louis C. Bailey, Exec Vice President & CFO

Sperry Corporation
Acquired by Burroughs 9/86
1290 Avenue of the Americas
New York, NY 10104
Telephone: 212/484-4444   Telex: 126233
Description: Manufactures commercial computer systems and equipment, and defense and aerospace systems and equipment.
Founded: 1910   Traded: NYSE
No. of Employees: 65932
Sales($000): 5,740,800   Fiscal Year: 03/31/86
Industry Segment: Systems
Executive(s): Gerald G. Probst, Chairman and CEO; Joseph J. Kroger, President and COO

Spinnaker Software Corporation
One Kendall Square
Cambridge, MA 02139
Telephone: 617/494-1200   Telex: 466244
Description: One of the nation's largest independent publishers of home computer software.
Founded: 1982   Traded: PVT
No. of Employees: 50
Sales($000): 18,000   Fiscal Year: 02/28/86 (Soft*letter)
Industry Segment: Software
Executive(s): William Bowman, Chairman and CEO; David Seuss, President

Springboard Software Inc.
7808 Creekridge Circle
Minneapolis, MN 55435
Telephone: 612/944-3915   Telex: None
Description: Creates productivity and educational software for home, school and business use.
Products are compatible with Apple II, IBM PC, Commodore-64 & 128, and Macintosh.
Founded: 1982   Traded: OTC
No. of Employees: 41
Sales($000): 9,069   Fiscal Year: 12/31/86
Industry Segment: Software
Executive(s): John Paulson, President and CEO; Don Giacchetti, Exec Vice President, Operations

State of the Art Inc.
3191-C Airport Loop
Costa Mesa, CA 92626
Telephone: 714/850-0111   Telex: None
Description: Manufactures accounting software for microcomputers.
Founded: 1981   Traded: PVT
No. of Employees: 52
Sales($000): 8,200   Fiscal Year: 12/31/86
Industry Segment: Software
Executive(s): David S. Samuels, President and CEO; George Riviere, Vice President, Dev.

Sterling Software, Inc.
Suite 1140
8080 North Central Expressway
Dallas, TX 75206
Telephone: 214/891-8600 Telex: None
Description: Develops and markets computer software products.
Founded: 1983   Traded: AMX
No. of Employees: 2950
Sales($000): 60,550   Fiscal Year: 09/30/85
Industry Segment: Software
Executive(s): Sam Wyly, Chairman; Sterling William, President and CEO
Key Subsidiaries: Informatics General Corp., Directions Inc., Software Laboratories Inc., Dylakor Inc.

Stockholder Systems Inc.
4411 East Jones Bridge Road
Norcross, GA 30092
Telephone: 404/441-3387 Telex: None
Description: Develops standardized financial applications software packages which are used for transfer agent and security holder record keeping, electronic funds transfers, telephone bill paying and home banking.
Founded: 1971   Traded: OTC
No. of Employees: 95
Sales($000): 12,661   Fiscal Year: 03/31/86
Industry Segment: Software
Executive(s): Larry A. Dean, Chairman,President & CEO; John Stephens, Sr Vice President

Storage Technology Corporation
2270 South 88th Street
Louisville, CO 80028-0001
Telephone: 303/673-5151 Telex: 6735006
Description: Manufactures computer peripheral subsystems for the electronic data processing industry. Principal products are high-performance tape and disk subsystems and impact and non-impact printer subsystems.
Founded: 1969   Traded: NYSE
No. of Employees: 8,540
Sales($000): 696,009 Fiscal Year: 12/26/86
Industry Segment: Peripherals
Executive(s): Ryal R. Poppa, Chairman and CEO; Stephen G. Jerritts, President and COO
Key Subsidiaries: United Data Corp., Media Technology Corp., Documation Inc., CMOS Technologies Inc.

Stratus Computer, Inc.
55 Fairbanks Blvd.
Marlborough, MA 01752
Telephone: 617/460-2000   Telex: 294112
Description: Manufactures fault tolerant continuous processing systems for on-line transaction processing and communications control.
Founded: 1980   Traded: OTC
No. of Employees: 775
Sales($000): 124,559 Fiscal Year: 12/28/86
Industry Segment: Systems
Executive(s): William E. Foster, President and CEO; John H. Curtis, Exec Vice President & COO

Sun Microsystems, Inc.
2550 Garcia Avenue
Mountain View, CA 94043
Telephone: 415/960-1300   Telex: 287815
Description: Supplies distributed computing systems, including technical workstations, UNIX system software, data communications, and networking systems.
Founded: 1982   Traded: OTC
No. of Employees: 2700
Sales($000): 210,000 Fiscal Year: 6/27/86
Industry Segment: Systems
Executive(s): Scott McNealy, Chairman, President, & CEO; Bernard Lacroute, Exec Vice President

Syscon Corporation
1000 Thomas Jefferson Street, N.W.
Washington, DC 20007
Telephone: 202/342-4000   Telex: 3424792
Description: Provides systems engineering, computer systems, technical services and hardware/software products for projects of the U.S. government. Also develops, markets and supports certain computer hardware and application software products.
Founded: 1967   Traded: PVT
No. of Employees: 1600
Sales($000): 117,286 Fiscal Year: 11/30/85
Industry Segment: Services
Executive(s): Jose Yglesias, Chairman and CEO; Nils Ericson, President
Key Subsidiaries: Harnischfeger Industries Inc.

System Industries Inc.
560 Cottonwood Drive
Milpitas, CA 95035
Telephone: 408/942-1212   Telex: 6839138
Description: Manufactures high-performance disk and tape storage systems for use with minicomputers.
Founded: 1968   Traded: OTC
No. of Employees: 722
Sales($000): 103,290 Fiscal Year: 07/27/86
Industry Segment: Mass storage
Executive(s): Eugene R. White, Chairman; James K. Dutton, President and CEO

Systems Associates Inc.
Acquired by First Data Res. 12/86
412 East Boulevard
Charlotte, NC 28203
Telephone: 704/333-1276   Telex: None
Description: Designs, installs and supports integrated computer systems for acute care hospitals.
Founded: 1966   Traded: PVT
No. of Employees: 320
Sales($000): 32,885   Fiscal Year: 01/31/86
Industry Segment: Services
Executive(s): Larry R. Ferguson, President and COO; Darryl Bowles, Exec Vice President

Systems Management American Corporation
254 Monticello Avenue
Norfolk, VA 23510
Telephone: 804/627-9331   Telex: 6235548
Description: Computer systems integration firm.
Founded: 1970   Traded: PVT
No. of Employees: 750
Sales($000): 65,000   Fiscal Year: 12/31/85
Industry Segment: Services
Executive(s): Herman E. Valentine, President and CEO; Alton L. Skeeter, Exec Vice President

TDK Corporation
13-1 Nihonbashi
1-chome, Chuo-Ku
Tokyo, 103 Japan
Telephone: 03-278-5111   Telex: J 24270
Description: Manufactures magnetic recording tapes, and coil and ceramic electronic components.
Traded: NYSE
No. of Employees: 17800
Sales($000): 2,400,000   Fiscal Year: 11/30/85
Industry Segment: Media
Executive(s): Fukujiro Sono, Chairman; Yutaka Otoshi, President
Key Subsidiaries: TDK Electronics Corp.

TEC Inc.
2727 North Fairview Avenue
Tucson, AZ 85703
Telephone: 602/792-2230 Telex: None
Description: Manufactures computer peripheral products and electronic component products.
Founded: 1958   Traded: AMX
No. of Employees: 343
Sales($000): 12,814   Fiscal Year: 06/30/86
Industry Segment: Peripherals
Executive(s): Byron Hamilton, Chairman and President; Bruce Hamilton, Vice President

TIE/Communications, Inc.
5 Research Drive
Shelton, CT 06484
Telephone: 203/926-2000 Telex: 179051
Description: Manufactures telecommunications products including digitally controlled telephone systems, primarily for business use.
Founded: 1971   Traded: AMX
No. of Employees: 1,960
Sales($000): 321,263 Fiscal Year: 12/31/85
Industry Segment: Telecommunications
Executive(s): Thomas L. Kelly Jr., Chairman and President; William A. Merritt Jr., Exec Vice President
Key Subsidiaries: Technicom Systems Inc., Turret Equip. Corp.

TRW Inc.
1900 Richmond Road
Cleveland, OH 44124
Telephone: 216/291-7000   Telex: ITT 4332051
Description: Manufactures automotive equipment, electronic components, electronic systems and computer-based and analytical services.
Founded: 1916   Traded: NYSE
No. of Employees: 82491
Sales($000): 6,035,900   Fiscal Year: 12/31/86
Industry Segment: Electronics
Executive(s): Ruben F. Mettler, Chairman and CEO; Joseph T. Gorman, President and COO

Tab Products Co.
1400 Page Mill Road
Palo Alto, CA 94304
Telephone: 415/852-2400   Telex: 288086
Description: Manufactures filing systems for office documents and computer data media and video display terminals, desktop computers and data entry equipment.
Founded: 1949   Traded: AMX
No. of Employees: 975
Sales($000): 121,429   Fiscal Year: 05/31/86
Industry Segment: Systems
Executive(s): Harry W. Le Claire, Chairman and CEO; Dennis R. Searles, President and COO

Tandem Computers, Inc.
19333 Vallco Parkway
Cupertino, CA 95014-2599
Telephone: 408/725-6000   Telex: 171648
Description: Manufactures computer systems for on-line transaction processing. Leader in fault-tolerant computer systems.
Founded: 1974   Traded: OTC
No. of Employees: 5,719
Sales($000): 767,793   Fiscal Year: 09/30/86
Industry Segment: Systems
Executive(s): Thomas J. Perkins, Chairman; James G. Treybig, President and CEO

Tandon Corporation
20320 Prairie Street
Chatsworth, CA 91311
Telephone: 818/993-6644 Telex: 194794
Description: Manufactures personal computers and disk drive products for microcomputer-based
systems.
Founded: 1976   Traded: OTC
No. of Employees: 2,994
Sales($000): 214,080 Fiscal Year: 09/28/86
Industry Segment: Personal computers; Disk drives
Executive(s): Sirjang Lal Tandon, Chairman and CEO; Dan H. Wilkie, President and COO
Key Subsidiaries: Microtek Storage Corp., Triatek Media Corp.

Tandy Corporation
1800 One Tandy Center
Ft. Worth, TX 76102
Telephone: 817/390-3700 Telex: 203934
Description: Manufactures and distributes electronic products, including microcomputers,
peripherals and accessories through its retail stores.
Founded: 1921   Traded: NYSE
No. of Employees: 32000
Sales($000): 3,035,969   Fiscal Year: 06/30/86
Industry Segment: Personal computers
Executive(s): John V. Roach, Chairman, President & CEO; John H. McDaniel, Sr. VP and
Controller
Key Subsidiaries: Radio Shack, Tandy Electronics Inc., O'Sullivan Industries Inc., Memtek
Products.

Technalysis Corporation
6700 France Avenue South
Minneapolis, MN 55435
Telephone: 612/925-5900 Telex: None
Description: Provides computer system design and programming services to users and computer
manufacturers.
Founded: 1967   Traded: OTC
No. of Employees: 188
Sales($000): 13,526   Fiscal Year: 12/31/86
Industry Segment: Services
Executive(s): Victor A. Rocchio, President; Milan L. Elton, Vice President

Tektronix, Inc.
14150 S.W. Karl Braun Drive
Beaverton, OR 97077
Telephone: 503/627-7111   Telex: 151754
Description: Manufactures oscilloscopes, computer engineering workstations, television test equipment, computer graphic terminals , OEM displays, copiers, plotters, logic analyzers and image forming devices.
Founded: 1946   Traded: NYSE
No. of Employees: 20,525
Sales($000): 1,352,212   Fiscal Year: 05/31/86
Industry Segment: Electronics; Displays
Executive(s): John D. Gray, Chairman; Earl Wantland, President and CEO
Key Subsidiaries: CAE Systems Inc., Dubner Computer Systems Inc., The Grass Valley Group Inc., V-R Information Systems Inc.

TeleVideo Systems, Inc.
P.O. Box 3568
1170 Morse Avenue
Sunnyvale, CA 94088-3568
Telephone: 408/745-7760   Telex: 408734 5758
Description: Manufactures video display terminals, local area networks and PC-compatible business systems designed for office automation and data processing applications, and letter quality daisywheel printers.
Founded: 1976   Traded: OTC
No. of Employees: 751
Sales($000): 91,462. Fiscal Year: 10/31/85
Industry Segment: Multiuser microcomputers
Executive(s): Dr. K. Philip Hwang, Chairman and CEO; Howard Oringer, Exec Vice President & CFO

Teleconnect
500 2nd Avenue
Cedar Rapids, IA 52401
Telephone: 319/366-6600   Telex: 319366 0417
Description: Focuses on business telephone systems and communication products.
Founded: 1979   Traded: PVT
No. of Employees: 1100
Sales($000): 130,000 Fiscal Year: 12/31/85
Industry Segment: Telecommunications
Executive(s): Clark McLeod, President; Frank Yanda, Regional President

Teledyne, Inc.
1901 Avenue of the Stars
Los Angeles, CA 90067
Telephone: 213/277-3311   Telex: 314873
Description: Supplies engineering design, materials, parts, systems, instruments and services to the
U.S. space programs.
Founded: 1960   Traded: NYSE
No. of Employees: 47200
Sales($000): 3,256,200   Fiscal Year: 12/31/85
Industry Segment: Electronics
Executive(s): Henry E. Singleton, Chairman and CEO; George A. Roberts, President

Telex Corporation
6422 E. 41st Street
P.O. Box 1526
Tulsa, OK 74135
Telephone: 918/627-2333   Telex: 4947259
Description: Through one of its subsidiaries, Telex Computer Products, Inc., the company designs,
manufactures, markets and services a diverse group of computer terminal and peripheral equipment.
Founded: 1936   Traded: NYSE
No. of Employees: 7,384
Sales($000): 709,220   Fiscal Year: 03/31/86
Industry Segment: Peripherals
Executive(s): Stephen J. Jatras, Chairman; George L. Bragg, President
Key Subsidiaries: Telexcom International Inc., United Digital Networks Inc.

Telxon Corporation
3330 West Market Street
Akron, OH 44313
Telephone: 216/867-3700   Telex: 810431 2180
Description: Manufactures hand-held, portable and interactive microcomputer systems used to
gather, process, store and communicate data.
Founded: 1969   Traded: OTC
No. of Employees: 680
Sales($000): 82,095   Fiscal Year: 03/31/86
Industry Segment: Microcomputers
Executive(s): Robert Meyerson, Chairman; Raymond Meyo, President and CEO
Key Subsidiaries: Micro Office Systems Technology Inc.

Tera Corporation
2150 Shattuck Avenue
Berkeley, CA 94704
Telephone: 415/845-5200 Telex: 338592
Description: Provides computer-aided services in the engineering/environmental areas and software products.
Founded: 1974   Traded: OTC
No. of Employees: 155
Sales($000): 25,357   Fiscal Year: 12/31/85
Industry Segment: Services
Executive(s): R. Stephen Heinrichs, Chairman and CEO; Donald K. Davis, President and COO
Key Subsidiaries: Tenera Corp., Tera Systems Corp.

Teradyne, Inc.
321 Harrison Avenue
Boston, MA 02118
Telephone: 617/482-2700 Telex: 174112
Description: Supplies automatic test systems to the electronics industry.
Founded: 1960   Traded: NYSE
No. of Employees: 4300
Sales($000): 306,112 Fiscal Year: 12/31/86
Industry Segment: Electronics
Executive(s): Alexander V. d'Arbeloff, Chairman, President & CEO; Owen W. Robbins, Vice President & CFO

Terminal Data Corporation
2800 North Madera Road
Simi Valley, CA 93065
Telephone: 805/584-0500 Telex: 674049
Description: Manufactures automated document image processing systems and components. Provides engineering services and designs and manufactures products for incorporation into large automated document processing systems.
Founded: 1968   Traded: OTC
No. of Employees: 345
Sales($000): 31,010   Fiscal Year: 09/30/86
Industry Segment: Input devices
Executive(s): Michael Rothbart, Chairman and CEO; James R. Schwartz, President

Texas Instruments Incorporated
13500 North Central Expressway
P.O. Box 225474
Dallas, TX 75265
Telephone: 214/995-4855   Telex: 9953511
Description: Manufactures a variety of products in the electronics industry for industrial, consumer
and government markets, including semiconductors, digital systems and government products.
Founded: 1938   Traded: NYSE
No. of Employees: 77,872
Sales($000): 4,974,000   Fiscal Year: 12/31/86
Industry Segment: Systems; Semiconductor products
Executive(s): Mark Shepherd Jr., Chairman; Jerry R. Junkins, President and CEO
Key Subsidiaries: Geophysical Service Inc.

Thomson S.A.
173 Boulevard Haussmann
75379 Paris Cedex 08, France
Telephone: 1-561-9600   Telex: TCSF 204780F
Description: Holding company for consumer products, engineering and other industrial products,
detection systems, communications, electronic components and medical equipment.
Traded: FO
No. of Employees: 129000
Sales($000): 7,500,000
Industry Segment: Electronics
Executive(s): Jean-Pierre Bouyssonnie, President; Jean-Marie Fouries, Deputy General Manager
Key Subsidiaries: Thomson Components-Mostek Corp., Burtek Inc., Thomson CSI, Thomson CSF.

Thorn-EMI plc
Thorn EMI House
Upper Saint Martin's
La London WC2H 9 ED, UK
Telephone: 01-836-2444   Telex: 24184/5
Description: Manufactures home entertainment electronics. Develops information technologies.
Traded: FO
No. of Employees: 26615
Sales($000): 4,900,000
Industry Segment: Electronics
Executive(s): Sir Graham Wilkins, Chairman and CEO; G. Mourgue, Vice Chairman
Key Subsidiaries: Thorn EMI Computer Software, Thorn EMI USA Inc., Modutec Inc., Thorn EMI
Technology Inc.

Thoughtware
2699 South Bayshore Drive
Coconut Grove, FL 33133
Telephone: 800/THT-WARE   Telex: 6712408IMICO
Description: Focuses on software development and publishing in areas of management training.
Founded: 1984   Traded: PVT
No. of Employees: 40
Sales($000): 9,800   Fiscal Year: 12/31/85 (Soft*letter)
Industry Segment: Software
Executive(s): Jack Levine, Chief Executive Officer; Henry Kaplan, Exec Vice President

Toshiba Corporation
1-6 Uchisaiwei-cho, Chiyoda-Ku
Tokyo, Japan
Description: Manufactures electronic products including personal computers, dot matrix printers and laser printers.
Traded: FO
No. of Employees: 99,000
Sales($000): 20,000,000
Industry Segment: Personal computers; Printers
Executive(s): Kazuo Iwata, Chairman; Shoichi Saba, President
Key Subsidiaries: Toshiba America Inc.

Tyler Corporation
3200 San Jacinto Tower
Dallas, TX 75201
Telephone: 214/754-7800   Telex: None
Description: Distributes, through its subsidiary Hall-Mark Electronics, electronic components supplied by many of the major manufacturers of electronic components.
Founded: 1966   Traded: NYSE
No. of Employees: 7470
Sales($000): 912,415 Fiscal Year: 12/31/85
Industry Segment: Distributors
Executive(s): J. F. McKinney, Chairman and CEO; F. R. Meyer, President and COO
Key Subsidiaries: Hall-Mark Electronics

U.S. Robotics
8100 N McCormick
Skokie, IL 60076
Telephone: 800/342-5877   Telex: 6501317398
Description: Manufactures modems.
Founded: 1976   Traded: PVT
No. of Employees: 150
Sales($000): 25,000   Fiscal Year: 09/30/85
Industry Segment: Peripherals
Executive(s): Casey Cowell, President; John McCartney, Administrator

UCCEL Corporation
UCCEL Tower P O Box 660054
6303 Forest Park Road
Dallas, TX 75235
Telephone: 214/353-7100   Telex: 794417
Description: Engages in the data processing services industry, providing software products,
computing services, and turnkey minicomputer systems sales.
Founded: 1963   Traded: NYSE
No. of Employees: 1500
Sales($000): 141,592 Fiscal Year: 12/31/86
Industry Segment: Software; Services
Executive(s): Gregory J. Liemandt, Chairman and CEO; B. Tom Carter Jr., Exec Vice President

US Design Corporation
4311 Forbes Boulevard
Lanham, MD 20706
Telephone: 301/577-2880   Telex: 710826 0417
Description: Manufactures desk-top or rack-mountable disk and tape storage systems with integrated
microprocessor disk and tape controllers.
Founded: 1978   Traded: OTC
No. of Employees: 70
Sales($000): 8,066   Fiscal Year: 06/30/86
Industry Segment: Mass storage
Executive(s): William R. Anderson Jr., Chairman and CEO; John Tincler, President and COO

US West, Inc.
7800 East Orchard Road
Englewood, CO 80111
Telephone: 303/793-6500 Telex: 510601 1224
Description: A regional Bell holding company (RBOC) with three Bell companies covering Arizona, Colorado, Idaho, Iowa, Minnesota, Montana, Nebraska, New Mexico, North Dakota, South Dakota, Oregon, Utah, Washington and Wyoming.
Founded: 1983   Traded: NYSE
No. of Employees: 70,202
Sales($000): 8,308,400   Fiscal Year: 12/31/86
Industry Segment: Telecommunications
Executive(s): Jack A. MacAllister, President and CEO; Howard P. Doerr, Exec Vice President & CFO

Ungermann-Bass, Inc.
3990 Freedom Circle
Santa Clara, CA 95052
Telephone: 408/496-0111 Telex: None
Description: Supplies general purpose local area networking (LAN) systems capable of interconnecting information processing devices from different manufacturers.
Founded: 1979   Traded: OTC
No. of Employees: 811
Sales($000): 110,908 Fiscal Year: 12/31/86
Industry Segment: Local area networks
Executive(s): Ralph K. Ungermann, Chairman, President & CEO; Robert D. Krause, Vice President & CFO
Key Subsidiaries: Industrial Networking Inc., Linkware Corp., Software Decision.

Unisys
P.O. Box 418
Detroit, MI 48232
Telephone: 313/972-7000 Telex: 224015
Description: Manufactures electronic-based information systems and related equipment, services, software and supplies.
Founded: 1886   Traded: NYSE
No. of Employees: 100,000
Sales($000): 7,432,400   Fiscal Year: 12/31/86
Industry Segment: Systems; Peripherals; Software; Services
Executive(s): W. Michael Blumenthal, Chairman and CEO; Joseph J. Kroger, Vice Chairman
Key Subsidiaries: Memorex

United Telecommunications, Inc.
P.O. Box 11315
Kansas City, MO 64112
Telephone: 913/676-3000 Telex: 42224
Description: Holding company for computer and telecommunications companies.
Founded: 1938   Traded: NYSE
No. of Employees: 27,415
Sales($000): 3,058,783   Fiscal Year: 12/31/86
Industry Segment: Telecommunications
Executive(s): Paul H. Henson, Chairman; William T. Esrey, President and CEO
Key Subsidiaries: US Telecom Inc., United Telephone Systems Inc.

Valid Logic Systems, Inc.
2820 Orchard Parkway
San Jose, CA 95134
Telephone: 408/945-9400 Telex: 408371 9004
Description: Manufactures customer solutions for computer-aided engineering (CAE) and computer-aided design (CAD) applications.
Founded: 1981   Traded: OTC
No. of Employees: 447
Sales($000): 60,907   Fiscal Year: 12/31/86
Industry Segment: Systems
Executive(s): Dr. Jared A. Anderson, Chairman; Dr. Kenneth B. Fine, President

Valmont Industries, Inc.
Valley, NB 68064
Telephone: 402/359-2201 Telex: 484462
Description: Markets IBM, Compaq and AT&T personal computers, related peripherals and software through its subsidiary ValCom, Inc., a retail computer chain.
Founded: 1978   Traded: OTC
No. of Employees: 1,960
Sales($000): 313,500 Fiscal Year: 12/27/86
Industry Segment: Computer stores
Executive(s): Robert B. Daugherty, Chairman and CEO; William F. Welsh II, President and COO
Key Subsidiaries: Good-All Electric Inc., Gate City Steel Corp., ValCom Inc.

Vanguard Technologies International, Inc.
One Flint Hill Suite 300
10530 Rosehaven Street
Fairfax, VA 22030
Telephone: 703/273-0500 Telex: 3590456
Description: Provides highly skilled automatic data processing services to government agencies and government prime contractors, including development, installation and maintenance of custom application software.
Founded: 1979   Traded: AMX
No. of Employees: 866
Sales($000): 26,012   Fiscal Year: 1/31/86
Industry Segment: Services
Executive(s): Dean W. Crawford, Chairman and President; Gordon H. Clow, Sr Vice President

Verdix Corporation
14130-A Sullyfield Circle
Chantilly, VA 22021
Telephone: 703/378-7600 Telex: None
Description: Develops Ada-based software products and multi-level secure computer systems.
Founded: 1982   Traded: OTC
No. of Employees: 87
Sales($000): 3,818   Fiscal Year: 03/31/86
Industry Segment: Software; Systems
Executive(s): George Cowan, Ph.D., Chairman, President & CEO; Donn R. Milton, Ph.D., Exec Vice President

Vermont Research Corporation
Precision Park
North Springfield, VT 05150
Telephone: 802/886-2256 Telex: 710363 6533
Description: Manufactures rotating magnetic memory devices for electronic computers and data processing systems.
Founded: 1960   Traded: AMX
No. of Employees: 138
Sales($000): 4,638   Fiscal Year: 09/30/86
Industry Segment: Mass storage
Executive(s): Hugh M. Taft, Chairman and President; Robert Kaseta, Vice President

Versacad Corporation
Formerly T&W Systems, Inc.
7372 Prince Drive
Huntington Beach, CA 92647
Telephone: 714/847-9960   Telex: 5101011759
Description: Manufactures drafting software for personal computers and engineering work stations.
Founded: 1977   Traded: PVT
No. of Employees: 65
Sales($000): 6,000   Fiscal Year: 07/31/86 (Soft*letter)
Industry Segment: Software
Executive(s): Thomas Lazear, President and CEO; Bruce Anderson, Director Communications

Volkswagen AG
3180 Wolfsburg 1
West Germany
Telephone: 0536190   Telex: 095860VWWD
Description: Automobile manufacturer, involved in office automation through subsidiaries Adler,
Adler-Royal and Pertec Computer.
Founded: 1937   Traded: OTC
No. of Employees: 115874
Sales($000): 18,000,000 (Estimated)
Industry Segment: Multiuser Microcomputers; Disk drives
Executive(s): Carl H. Hahn, Chairman; Horst Muenzner, Deputy Chairman
Key Subsidiaries: Adler Business Machines, Adler-Royal Business Machines, Pertec Computer
Corp.

WICAT Systems, Inc.
1875 South State Street
Orem, UT 84058
Telephone: 801/224-6400   Telex: 2267367
Description: Manufactures microcomputer systems for business, education and training.
Founded: 1977   Traded: OTC
No. of Employees: 597
Sales($000): 39,405   Fiscal Year: 03/30/86
Industry Segment: Multiuser microcomputers
Executive(s): Dustin H. Heuston, Chairman and CEO; Robert C. Mendenhall, President and COO
Key Subsidiaries: PLATO/WICAT Systems.

Wang Laboratories, Inc.
One Industrial Avenue
Lowell, MA 01851
Telephone: 617/459-5000   Telex: 947421
Description: Manufactures computer systems and provides related products and services for the
worldwide automation marketplace.
Founded: 1951   Traded: AMX
No. of Employees: 31,000
Sales($000): 2,642,500   Fiscal Year: 06/30/86
Industry Segment: Systems; Peripherals; Software
Executive(s): An Wang, Chairman and CEO; Fredrick A. Wang, President
Key Subsidiaries: InteCom Inc.

Wespercorp
1821 E. Dyer Road
Santa Ana, CA 92705
Telephone: 714/261-0606   Telex: 4720629
Description: Manufactures peripherals including disks, tapes and printer controllers, and provides
consulting services.
Founded: 1981   Traded: AMX
No. of Employees: 98
Sales($000): 14,365   Fiscal Year: 06/30/86
Industry Segment: Peripherals; Services
Executive(s): George Dasheill, President and CEO

Western Digital Corporation
2445 McCabe Way
Irvine, CA 92714
Telephone: 714/863-0102   Telex: 706928
Description: Manufactures proprietary integrated circuits and board-level products based on those
circuits.
Founded: 1970   Traded: AMX
No. of Employees: 2468
Sales($000): 279,406   Fiscal Year: 06/30/86
Industry Segment: Semiconductor products; Peripherals
Executive(s): Roger W. Johnson, Chairman, President & CEO; Joseph Baia, Vice Chairman
Key Subsidiaries: Adaptive Data Systems Inc.

Western Union Corporation
One Lake Street
Upper Saddle River, NJ 07458
Telephone: 201/825-5000   Telex: 642490
Description: Provides telecommunications systems and services. Manufactures telecommunications and electronic equipment.
Founded: 1851   Traded: NYSE
No. of Employees: 9040
Sales($000): 889,192 Fiscal Year: 12/31/86
Industry Segment: Telecommunications
Executive(s): Robert Leventhal, Chairman, President & CEO; S.E. Smiszko, Vice President

Westinghouse Electric Corporation
Westinghouse Building
Gateway Center
Pittsburgh, PA 15222
Telephone: 412/244-2000   Telex: 866194
Description: Provides electrical and electronic products and services for industrial, construction and electric utility applications, and nuclear and fossil fueled equipment for power generation. Supplies defense electronic equipment.
Founded: 1886   Traded: NYSE
No. of Employees: 125,000
Sales($000): 10,700,200   Fiscal Year: 12/31/85
Industry Segment: Electronics
Executive(s): Douglas D. Danforth, Chairman and CEO; Leo W. Yochum, Sr Vice President, Fin.

Word Perfect Corporation
Formerly Satellite Software Int'l
288 West Center Street
Orem, UT 84057
Telephone: 801/227-4010   Telex: 820618
Description: Focuses on software for IBM personal computers and compatibles and microcomputers.
Founded: 1979   Traded: PVT
No. of Employees: 300
Sales($000): 22,983   Fiscal Year: 12/31/85 (Soft*letter)
Industry Segment: Software
Executive(s): Bruce Bastian, Chairman; Alan Ashton, President

WordTech Systems Inc.
P.O. Box 1747
21 Altarinda Road
Orinda, CA 94563
Telephone: 415/254-0900 Telex: 503599
Description: Develops data base management software.
Founded: 1982   Traded: PVT
No. of Employees: 42
Sales($000): 2,200   Fiscal Year: 12/31/86
Industry Segment: Software
Executive(s): David Miller, President and CEO; Bart Van Voorhis, Exec Vice President

Wyle Laboratories
128 Maryland Street
El Segundo, CA 90245
Telephone: 213/678-4251 Telex: 3223603
Description: Markets high-technology electronic components and systems, and is a major supplier of research, engineering, and testing services to the aerospace/defense and energy industries.
Founded: 1949   Traded: NYSE
No. of Employees: 1,755
Sales($000): 307,000 Fiscal Year: 01/31/87
Industry Segment: Electronics
Executive(s): Stanley A. Wainer, Chairman and CEO; Charles M. Clough, President and COO
Key Subsidiaries: Elmar Electronics Inc., Applied Research Inc.

Wyse Technology
3571 North First Street
San Jose, CA 95134
Telephone: 408/433-1000 Telex: 408946 3496
Description: Manufactures video display terminals, workstations which range from alpha-numeric monochrome terminals to high performance color graphics workstations with substantial standalone processing capability.
Founded: 1981   Traded: OTC
No. of Employees: 1519
Sales($000): 166,395 Fiscal Year: 03/31/86
Industry Segment: Terminals
Executive(s): Bernard K. Tse, Chairman and CEO; Philip E. White, President and COO
Key Subsidiaries: Amdek Corp.

Xebec

3579 Highway 50 East

Carson City, NV 89701

Telephone: 702/883-4000   Telex: 821460

Description: Manufactures disk drive controllers and disk storage products.

Founded: 1974   Traded: OTC

No. of Employees: 960

Sales($000): 149,246   Fiscal Year: 09/30/85

Industry Segment: Mass storage

Executive(s): James S. Toreson, Chairman, President & CEO; Christian C.E. Hoebich, Chief Financial Officer

Key Subsidiaries: United Peripherals, Information Memories Corp., Epelo Corp., First Class Peripherals, Disk Drive Systems Inc.

Xerox Corporation

P.O. Box 1600

Stamford, CT 06904

Telephone: 203/329-8700   Telex: 221981

Description: Manufactures copiers and duplicators, electronic typewriters, professional workstations, word processors, personal computers, magnetic storage devices, network products, programming products and facsimile products.

Founded: 1906   Traded: NYSE

No. of Employees: 102396

Sales($000): 9,781,000   Fiscal Year: 12/31/86

Industry Segment: Systems

Executive(s): David T. Kearns, Chairman and CEO; Melvin Howard, Exec Vice President

Key Subsidiaries: Century Data Systems Inc., Versatec Inc., Kurzweil Computer Products Inc., Rank Xerox Limited.

Xidex Corporation

2141 Landings Drive

Mountain View, CA 94043

Telephone: 408/988-3472   Telex: 408970 6531

Description: Manufactures data storage products and related hardware for all segments of the computer industry.

Founded: 1969   Traded: OTC

No. of Employees: 6400

Sales($000): 432,300   Fiscal Year: 06/30/86

Industry Segment: Mass Storage; Media

Executive(s): Lester L. Colbert Jr., Chairman, President & CEO; Gary B. Filler, Exec Vice President & CFO

Key Subsidiaries: Dysan Corporation

Xscribe Corporation
6160 Cornerstone Court
San Diego, CA 92121
Telephone: 619/457-5091   Telex: None
Description: Manufactures computer-aided transcription equipment.
Founded: 1978   Traded: PVT
No. of Employees: 300
Fiscal Year: 03/31/87 (Sales confidential)
Industry Segment: Systems
Executive(s): Robert Mawhinney, Chairman; Tom Delahanty, President

Zenith Electronics Corporation
1000 Milwaukee Avenue
Glenview, IL 60025
Telephone: 312/391-7000   Telex: 254396
Description: Manufactures consumer electronics products and personal computers.
Founded: 1918   Traded: NYSE
No. of Employees: 33,000
Sales($000): 1,892,100   Fiscal Year: 12/31/86
Industry Segment: Displays; Personal computers; Terminals
Executive(s): Jerry K. Pearlman, Chairman, President & CEO; Robert B. Hansen, Executive VP & Group Exec
Key Subsidiaries: Heath Company, Zenith Data Systems Corporation

Zentec Corporation
2400 Walsh Avenue
Santa Clara, CA 95051-1374
Telephone: 408/727-7662   Telex: 910338 0572
Description: Manufactures customized intelligent terminal systems for use with information processing computer systems.
Founded: 1973   Traded: OTC
No. of Employees: 105
Sales($000): 17,390   Fiscal Year: 12/31/85
Industry Segment: Terminals
Executive(s): Richard W. Calfee, Chairman; William D. Parker, President and CEO
Key Subsidiaries: Shasta General Systems.

Zitel Corporation
630 Alder Drive
Milpitas, CA 95035
Telephone: 408/946-9600   Telex: 171607
Description: Manufactures semiconductor memory systems and board level microcomputer systems.
Founded: 1979   Traded: OTC
No. of Employees: 130
Sales($000): 18,820   Fiscal Year: 09/30/86
Industry Segment: Semiconductor products; Boards
Executive(s): Jack King, President and CEO; Hank Harris, Chief Financial Officer

Ziyad Inc.
100 Ford Road
Denville, NJ 07834
Telephone: 201/627-7600   Telex: 136024
Description: Manufactures microprocessor based intelligent paper processors which automatically feed cut paper and envelopes into letter quality and near letter quality electronic printers.
Founded: 1979   Traded: OTC
No. of Employees: 150
Sales($000): 29,025   Fiscal Year: 02/28/86
Industry Segment: Output devices
Executive(s): Edward Rosen, President and CEO; Douglas Sims, Vice President, Mktg
Key Subsidiaries: Gradco Systems

3 PRODUCTS

COMPUTER INTELLIGENCE
TOP 50 GENERAL PURPOSE COMPUTER SYSTEMS
BASED ON VALUE OF INSTALLED U.S. SYSTEMS--JULY 1986

"This ranking of general purpose computer systems based on the value of installed systems is released twice annually (January and July). The 50 systems included constitute the principal market for the majority of the products and services in the DP industry. Ranking is based upon the Total Purchase, which is calculated by multiplying the number of systems times the purchase price of a 'typical' system."--Computer Intelligence.

Reprinted with permission from Computer Intelligence, July 1986. Copyright 1986 by Computer Intelligence, La Jolla, CA.

7/86 Rank	1/86 Rank	Manufacturer	System	Total Purchase $ Millions	Avg. Price $ (000)	# Systems
1	5	IBM	3090-200	$5,288	$7,800	678
2	1	IBM	3081	4,505	2,800	1,609
3	3	IBM	4381	4,159	960	4,332
4	7	IBM	System 36	4,139	80	51,735
5	2	IBM	3084	3.478	5,400	644
6	6	DEC	VAX11/78X	3,411	200	17,056
7	4	IBM	3083	2,587	1,600	1,617
8	8	IBM	System 38	2,347	240	9,781
9	13	DEC	VAX86X0	1,848	700	2,640
10	12	Sperry	1100/90	1,837	6,400	287
11	10	HP	3000	1,527	100	15,265
12	9	IBM	4341	1,291	260	4,964
13	11	DEC	VAX11/750	1,125	80	14,061
14	17	Wang	VS	790	100	7,903
15	16	NAS	AS/9000	774	3,000	258
16	16	IBM	System 34	679	20	33,948
17	27	Data-General	MV10000	622	420	1,480
18	14	IBM	3033	606	700	865
19	20	Amdahl	5860	603	3,000	201
20	15	IBM	4361	588	180	3,264
21	24	Prime	9950	564	400	1,410
22	19	IBM	8100	547	80	6,840
23	23	Data-General	MV6000/8000	446	180	2,477

(Continued next page)

COMPUTER INTELLIGENCE: TOP 50 GENERAL PURPOSE COMPUTER SYSTEMS
(Continued)

7/86 Rank	1/86 Rank	Manufacturer	System	Total Purchase $ Millions	Avg. Price $ (000)	# Systems
24	*	IBM	3090-1X0	425	4,780	89
25	22	Sperry	1100/80	393	800	491
26	21	Honeywell	DPS 8/50-70	$386	$4,800	483
27	30	Sperry	1100/70	378	540	700
28	29	Burroughs	4900	376	800	470
29	39	Cray	Cray X-MP	361	8,600	42
30	25	Prime	750	357	180	1,985
31	28	Cray	Cray I	336	4,540	74
32	26	Sperry	1100/60	324	520	623
33	31	Perkin-Elmer	Series 3200	323	120	2,690
34	36	Data-General	MV4000	316	80	3,947
35	*	Honeywell	DPS 6/9X	287	260	1,103
36	34	NCR	90X0	283	100	2,827
37	40	Amdahl	5870	274	5,600	49
38	32	Tandem	T16	264	160	1,650
39	*	Honeywell	DPS 88/8X	258	3,800	68
40	*	Amdahl	5880	250	6,400	39
41	41	DAS	AS/8000	227	1,600	142
42	42	Burroughs	7900	206	2,000	103
43	37	AT&T	3B20	192	300	640
44	45	DEC	VAX11/730	189	40	4,719
45	47	Tandem	TXP	188	240	780
46	*	Honeywell	DPS 6/7X	167	160	1,042
47	38	Burroughs	1900	163	80	2,032
48	33	Amdahl	470V/8	162	800	202
49	*	Burroughs	A9	154	600	257
50	43	DEC	System-20	137	200	686

*Not ranked in Top 50

COMPUTER INTELLIGENCE
SUPERCOMPUTERS IN THE TOP 50 GENERAL PURPOSE COMPUTER SYSTEMS
BASED ON VALUE OF INSTALLED U.S. SYSTEMS--JULY 86

"This ranking of general purpose computer systems based on the value of installed systems is
released twice annually (January and July). The 50 systems included constitute the principal market
for the majority of the products and services in the DP industry. Ranking is based upon the Total
Purchase, which is calculated by multiplying the number of systems times the purchase price of a
'typical' system."--Computer Intelligence.
Reprinted with permission from Computer Intelligence, July 1986. Copyright 1986 by Computer
Intelligence, La Jolla, CA.

7/86 Rank	1/86 Rank	Manufacturer	System	Total Purchase $ Millions	Avg. Price $ (000)	# Systems
29	39	Cray	Cray X-MP	$361	$8,600	42
31	28	Cray	Cray 1	336	4,540	74

WORKSTATION LABORATORIES
TYPICAL SUPERCOMPUTER PERFORMANCE LEVELS
1987

"For this data, supercomputers are defined to be those systems produced specifically for very computationally intensive applications with a performance level of at least 150 million floating point operations per second (MFLOPS). Excluded from this data are those products based on standard mainframes with hardware to accelerate floating point operations, such as the IBM mainframes with vector processors or the Unisys (Sperry) product. Also excluded from this data are the minisupercomputers ("Crayettes") such as those manufactured by Convex, Elexi, or Scientific Computer Systems. At this time, the performance levels of both excluded categories are lower than standard supercomputer levels."--Workstation Laboratories.

Reprinted with permission from Workstation Laboratories, 1987. Copyright 1987 by Workstation Laboratories, Humboldt, AZ.

Machine Name	Date Introduced	Processor Performance
Cray 1	1976	100 Million FLOPS
Cray XMP	1981	350 Million FLOPS
Cray 2	1983	1 Billion FLOPS
Cray YMP	(expected 1987)	est. 4 Billion FLOPS
Cray 3	(expected 1989)	est. 10 Billion FLOPS
Cray Chen MP	(expected 1991)	est. 40 Billion FLOPS

COMPUTER INTELLIGENCE
MAINFRAMES IN THE TOP 50 GENERAL PURPOSE COMPUTER SYSTEMS
BASED ON VALUE OF INSTALLED U.S. SYSTEMS--JULY 1986

"This ranking of general purpose computer systems based on the value of installed systems is
released twice annually (January and July). The 50 systems included constitute the principal market
for the majority of the products and services in the DP industry. Ranking is based upon the Total
Purchase, which is calculated by multiplying the number of systems times the purchase price of a
'typical' system."--Computer Intelligence.

Reprinted with permission from Computer Intelligence, July 1986. Copyright 1986 by Computer
Intelligence, La Jolla, CA.

7/86 Rank	1/86 Rank	Manufacturer	System	Total Purchase $ Millions	Avg. Price $ (000)	# Systems
1	5	IBM	3090-200	$5,288	$7,800	678
2	1	IBM	3081	4,505	2,800	1,609
5	2	IBM	3084	3,478	5,400	644
7	4	IBM	3083	2,587	1,600	1,617
10	12	Sperry	1100/90	1,837	6,400	287
15	18	NAS	AS/9000	774	3,000	258
18	14	IBM	3033	606	700	865
19	20	Amdahl	5860	603	3,000	201
24	*	IBM	3090-1X0	425	4,780	89
25	22	Sperry	1100/80	393	800	491
26	21	Honeywell	DPS 8/50-70	386	800	483
27	30	Sperry	1100/70	378	540	700
28	29	Burroughs	4900	376	800	470
32	26	Sperry	1100/60	324	520	623
37	40	Amdahl	5870	274	5,600	49
39	*	Honeywell	DPS 88/8X	258	3,800	68
40	*	Amdahl	5880	250	6,400	39
41	41	NAS	AS/8000	227	1,600	142
42	42	Burroughs	7900	206	2,000	103
48	33	Amdahl	470V/8	162	800	202
49	*	Burroughs	A9	154	600	257

*Not ranked in Top 50

COMPUTER INTELLIGENCE
MINICOMPUTERS IN THE TOP 50 GENERAL PURPOSE COMPUTER SYSTEMS
BASED ON VALUE OF INSTALLED U.S. SYSTEMS--JULY 1986

"This ranking of general purpose computer systems based on the value of installed systems is
released twice annually (January and July). The 50 systems included constitute the principal market
for the majority of the products and services in the DP industry. Ranking is based upon the Total
Purchase, which is calculated by multiplying the number of systems times the purchase price of a
'typical' system."--Computer Intelligence.
Reprinted with permission from Computer Intelligence, July 1986. Copyright 1986 by Computer
Intelligence, La Jolla, CA.

7/86 Rank	1/86 Rank	Manufacturer	System	Total Purchase $ Millions	Avg. Price $ (000)	# Systems
3	3	IBM	4381	$4,159	$960	4,332
4	7	IBM	SYSTEM 36	4,139	80	51,735
6	6	DEC	VAX11/78X	3,411	200	17,056
8	8	IBM	System 38	2,347	240	9,781
9	13	DEC	VAX86X0	1,848	700	2,640
11	10	HP	3000	1,527	100	15,265
12	9	IBM	4341	1,291	260	4,964
13	11	DEC	VAX11/750	1,125	80	14,061
14	17	Wang	VS	790	100	7,903
16	16	IBM	System 34	679	20	33,948
17	27	Data-General	MV10000	622	420	1,480
20	15	IBM	4361	588	180	3,264
21	24	Prime	9950	564	400	1,410
22	19	IBM	8100	547	80	6,840
23	23	Data-General	MV6000/8000	446	180	2,477
30	25	Prime	750	357	180	1,985
33	31	Perkin-Elmer	Series 3200	323	120	2,690
34	36	Data-General	MV4000	316	80	3,947
35	*	Honeywell	DPS 6/9X	287	260	1,103
36	34	NCR	90X0	283	100	2,827
38	32	Tandem	T16	264	160	1,650
43	37	AT&T	3B20	192	300	640
44	45	DEC	VAX11/730	189	40	4,719
45	47	Tandem	TXP	188	240	780
46	*	Honeywell	DPS 6/7X	167	160	1,042
47	38	Burroughs	1900	163	80	2,032
50	43	DEC	System-20	137	200	686

*Not ranked in Top 50

WORKSTATION LABORATORIES
RELATIVE PERFORMANCE FIGURES FOR COMMON TECHNICAL WORKSTATIONS
January 1987

"This data indicates the relative processor performance of a variety of technical workstations based on several processor-intensive benchmarks. Graphics information is based on a series of graphics benchmarks on the highest performance graphics unit available for the product. The price range starts at entry level pricing and extends to typical high-end systems."--Workstation Laboratories. Reprinted with permission from Workstation Laboratories, January 1987. Copyright 1987 by Workstation Laboratories, Humboldt, AZ.

Manufacturer	Model Number	Relative Performance	Graphics Performance	Price Range
Apollo Computer	DN3000	1.47	1.00	$10K-25K
	DN570	1.73	2.00	$30K-60K
	DN580	2.82	6.00	$45K-90K
COMPAQ	386	2.67	---	$7K-12K
Digital Equip	VAXStation	1.40	1.75	$15K-55K
	VAX 11/780	1.00	---	$50K-up
Hewlett-Packard	320	2.00	1.50	$12K-25K
	350	3.33	1.85	$15K-30K
IBM	RT PC	1.26	0.85	$10K-30K
	PC AT	.56	---	$3K-9K
Masscomp	5000	2.00	2.50	$15K-40K
Silicon Graphics	IRIS	2.67	8.00	$50K-90K
Sun Microsystems	Sun 3/50	1.60	0.50	$8K-13K
	Sun 3/160	2.22	0.90	$30K-50K
	Sun 3/260	4.06	1.20	$45K-70K

IBM PC AT, COMPAQ 386, and VAX 11/780 shown for comparison purposes.
Processor performance normalized to DEC VAX 11/780. Higher performance processors have values above 1.0.
Graphics performance normalized to Apollo DN3000. Higher performance graphics have values above 1.0.

STOREBOARD INC.
TOP 10 PERSONAL COMPUTER MODELS IN 1986
January 1987

"In this data, StoreBoard Inc. lists the best selling personal computer products. The best seller lists represent personal computer products sold in computer specialty stores such as ComputerLand, Businessland, Entre', Sears Business Systems Centers, MicroAge, Inacomp, MBI, etc. Computer stores sell primarily to businesses; these lists indicate the most popular products in the business marketplace. The IBM PC/XT sold over 300,000 units in 1986 in computer stores. The IBM PC/XT sales are used as the base (100) of the relative sales numbers given for each product."--StoreBoard Inc.

Reprinted with permission from StoreBoard Inc., January 1987. Copyright 1987 by StoreBoard Inc., Dallas, TX.

Rank	Product	Relative Sales*
1.	IBM PC/XT	100
2.	IBM PC AT	76
3.	Apple IIc	46
4.	IBM PC	42
5.	Apple Macintosh Plus	38
6.	Apple IIe	36
7.	Apple Macintosh 512	22
8.	COMPAQ Deskpro	19
9.	AT&T PC 6300	17
10.	COMPAQ Deskpro 286	14
10.	COMPAQ Portable	14

* Sold in computer stores and based on StoreBoard Inc.'s monthly surveys.

SOFTSEL HOT LIST
ACCESSORIES
Week of October 13, 1986

"The HOT LIST is compiled from Softsel sales to over 15,000 dealers in 50 states and 45 countries. Sales may vary regionally. The names of the products and companies appearing may be trademarks or registered trademarks."--SOFTSEL HOT LIST.
Reprinted with permission from SOFTSEL HOT LIST, October 13, 1986. Copyright 1986 by Softsel Computer Products, Inc., Inglewood, CA.

This Week	Last Week	Weeks on Chart	Accessories	Producer	Machine
1	1	89	Microsoft Mouse	Microsoft	IBM
2	2	106	Mach III	CH Products	AP, IBM
3	3	24	Safe Strip	Curtis Manufacturing	
4	7	34	PC Mouse/PC Paint Bundle Plus	Mouse Systems	IBM
5	5	168	Joystick	Kraft Systems	AP, IBM
6	4	212	System Saver	Kensington	AP, MAC
7	6	89	MasterPiece	Kensington	IBM
8	8	12	Intel 8087 Coprocessor	Intel	IBM
9	9	21	SS-II System Stand	Curtis Manufacturing	IBM
10	10	32	Mach II	CH Products	AP

SOFTSEL HOT LIST
BOARDS, MODEMS & INTERFACES
Week of October 13, 1986

"The HOT LIST is compiled from Softsel sales to over 15,000 dealers in 50 states and 45 countries. Sales may vary regionally. The names of the products and companies appearing may be trademarks or registered trademarks."--SOFTSEL HOT LIST.

Reprinted with permission from SOFTSEL HOT LIST, October 13, 1986. Copyright 1986 by Softsel Computer Products, Inc., Inglewood, CA.

This Week	Last Week	Weeks on Chart	Boards, Modems & Interfaces	Publisher	Machine
1	4	155	Hercules Graphics Card Plus	Hercules	IBM
2	1	145	SixPakPlus	AST Research	IBM
3	2	160	Smartmodem 1200B	Hayes	IBM
4	3	178	Smartmodem 1200	Hayes	AP
5	5	103	Hercules Color Card	Hercules	IBM
6	7	33	Above Board/AT	Intel	IBM
7	9	103	Grappler	Orange Micro	AP, COM
8	6	28	Advantage! AT	AST Research	IBM
9	8	58	Smartmodem 2400	Hayes	
10	12	25	Smartmodem 2400B	Hayes	IBM
11	11	27	Practical Modem 1200	Practical Peripherals	IBM
12	10	10	Rampage! AT	AST REsearch	IBM
13	15	4	Above Board PS/AT	Intel	IBM
14	13	7	Autoswitch EGA	Paradise Systems	IBM
15	--	24	Captain Multifunction Board	Tecmar	IBM
16	--	4	Above Board/PC	Intel	IBM
17	16	10	PC Host Adapter Card for QIC-60H	Tecmar	IBM
18	17	3	Bernoulli Box Adapter Card	Iomega	IBM
19	14	27	Gamecard III	CH Products	IBM
20	--	17	I/O Mini	AST Research	IBM

SOFTSEL HOT LIST
DISK DRIVES & STORAGE DEVICES
Week of October 13, 1986

"The HOT LIST is compiled from Softsel sales to over 15,000 dealers in 50 states and 45 countries. Sales may vary regionally. The names of the products and companies appearing may be trademarks or registered trademarks."--SOFTSEL HOT LIST.
Reprinted with permission from SOFTSEL HOT LIST, October 13, 1986. Copyright 1986 by Softsel Computer Products, Inc., Inglewood, CA.

This Week	Last Week	Weeks on Chart	Disk Drives & Storage Devices	Producer	Machine
1	2	17	**Laser FD100 Apple Drives**	Video Technology	AP
2	1	7	**Bernoulli Box Dual 20MB**	Iomega	IBM, MAC
3	4	13	**Bernoulli Box Dual 10MB**	Iomega	IBM, MAC
4	3	26	**QIC-60H External Tape Backup**	Tecmar	IBM
5	5	27	**On Board 20MB Hard Disk on a Card**	Maynard	IBM
6	6	16	**FileCard 20MB Hard Disk/Card**	Western Digital	IBM
7	7	18	**QIC-60AT Internal Tape Backup**	Tecmar	IBM
8	8	14	**Maynstream 60MB Portable Backup**	Maynard	IBM

SOFTSEL HOT LIST
MONITORS
Week of October 13, 1986

"The HOT LIST is compiled from Softsel sales to over 15,000 dealers in 50 states and 45 countries. Sales may vary regionally. The names of the products and companies appearing may be trademarks or registered trademarks."--SOFTSEL HOT LIST.
Reprinted with permission from SOFTSEL HOT LIST, October 13, 1986. Copyright 1986 by Softsel Computer Products, Inc., Inglewood, CA.

This Week	Last Week	Weeks on Chart	Monitors	Producer
1	1	30	JC 1401 Multisync	NEC Home Electronics
2	2	88	Video 310A Hi-Res Amber TTL	Amdek
3	5	23	JB 1285 Amber TTL	NEC Home Electronics
4	7	69	Color 600 Hi-Res RGB	Amdek
5	4	29	Color 722 CGA/EGA	Amdek
6	3	73	121 Green TTL	Taxan
7	8	44	Color 640 Ultra Hi-Res	Taxan
8	6	31	Color 620 Hi-Res RGB	Taxan
9	9	45	122 Hi-Res Amber TTL	Taxan
10	--	15	Color 630 Super Hi-Res	Taxan

SOFTSEL HOT LIST
PRINTERS
Week of October 13, 1986

"The HOT LIST is compiled from Softsel sales to over 15,000 dealers in 50 states and 45 countries. Sales may vary regionally. The names of the products and companies appearing may be trademarks or registered trademarks."--SOFTSEL HOT LIST.

Reprinted with permission from SOFTSEL HOT LIST, October 13, 1986. Copyright 1986 by Softsel Computer Products, Inc., Inglewood, CA.

This Week	Last Week	Weeks on Chart	Printers	Producer
1	1	33	120D Dot Matrix	Citizen America
2	2	90	MSP-10 Dot Matrix	Citizen America
3	3	24	Premiere 35 Daiseywheel	Citizen America
4	7	20	P7 Pinwriter	NEC Information Systems
5	4	76	MSP-15 Dot Matrix	Citizen America
6	6	27	MSP-20 Dot Matrix	Citizen America
7	5	11	P6 Pinwriter	NEC Information Systems
8	8	27	MSP-25 Dot Matrix	Citizen America
9	10	23	P5 Pinwriter	NEC Information Systems
10	9	37	3550 Spinwriter	NEC Information Systems

STOREBOARD INC.
TOP PERSONAL COMPUTER PERIPHERALS IN 1986
January 1987

"In this data, StoreBoard Inc. lists the best selling personal computer products. The best seller lists represent personal computer products sold in computer specialty stores such as ComputerLand, Businessland, Entre', Sears Business Systems Centers, MicroAge, Inacomp, MBI, etc. Computer stores sell primarily to businesses; these lists indicate the most popular products in the business marketplace. The IBM PC/XT sold over 300,000 units in 1986 in computer stores. The IBM PC/XT sales are used as a base (100) of the relative sale numbers given for each product."--StoreBoard, Inc.

Reprinted with permission from StoreBoard Inc., January 1987. Copyright 1987 by StoreBoard Inc., Dallas, TX.

Top 10 Personal Computer Add-In Boards in 1986*

Rank	Product	Relative Sales
1.	AST SixPakPlus	42
2.	Apple Super Serial Card	37
3.	IBM Color Graphics Card	35
4.	Hercules Color Card	26
5.	Hercules Graphics Card	21
6.	IBM Enhanced Graphics Card	20
7.	AST Advantage!	16
8.	Intel AboveBoard	11
9.	DCA IRMA Board	9
10.	Quadram Quadboard	8

Top 5 Personal Computer Modems in 1986*

Rank	Product	Relative Sales
1.	Hayes Smartmodem 1200B	34
2.	Hayes Smartmodem 1200	19
3.	Apple Personal Modem	15
4.	Hayes Smartmodem 2400	8
5.	Ven-Tel Half Card	4
	(Continued next page)	

* Sold in computer stores and based on StoreBoard Inc.'s monthly surveys.

STOREBOARD INC.
TOP PERSONAL COMPUTER PERIPHERALS IN 1986 (Continued)

Top 5 Monochrome Monitors for Personal Computers in 1986*

Rank	Product	Relative Sales
1.	IBM Monochrome Display	75
2.	Apple Monitor II/IIc	34
3.	Amdek 300 Series	26
4.	COMPAQ Monochrome Monitor	24
5.	AT&T Monochrome Monitor	11

Top 5 Color Monitors for Personal Computers in 1986*

Rank	Product	Relative Sales
1.	IBM Color Display	58
2.	Apple Color IIe/IIc	36
3.	IBM Enhanced Color Display	28
4.	Amdek Color 600/700	14
5.	Taxan 600 Series	10

Top 10 Personal Computer Printer Models in 1986*

Rank	Product	Relative Sales
1.	Apple Imagewriter II	83
2.	Epson FX-185/286	41
3.	IBM Proprinter	41
4.	Epson LX-80/86	29
5.	Epson FX-85	25
6.	Okidata ML 192/292	19
7.	Okidata ML 193/293	18
8.	Hewlett-Packard Laserjet	13
9.	IBM Quietwriter II	12
10.	IBM Proprinter XL	12

* Sold in computer stores and based on StoreBoard Inc.'s monthly surveys.

COMPUTER INTELLIGENCE
TOP MAINFRAME SOFTWARE
July 1986

This ranking of leading mainframe software is listed within four major categories: data base management software (DBMS), security software, report generator/query language software, and disk and tape management software. Within each category the leading players are ranked by marketshare among IBM/PCM mainframe sites in the U.S. as of July 1986.--COMPUTER INDUSTRY ALMANAC.

Reprinted with permission from Computer Intelligence, July 1986. Copyright 1986 by Computer Intelligence, La Jolla, CA.

Rank	Manufacturer	% Sites
Data Base Management Software (DBMS)		
1	IBM	46
2	Cullinet Software	15
3	Information Builders	10
4	Syncom	7
5	Applied Data Research	6
5	Software AG	6
7	Martin Marietta	4
8	CCA	2
9	SAS Institute	1
10	Other	3
Security Software		
1	Cambridge Systems Group	33
2	IBM	29
3	Computer Associates	19
4	On-Line Software Intl	10
5	VM Software	3
6	Other	6

(Continued next page)

COMPUTER INTELLIGENCE
TOP MAINFRAME SOFTWARE (Continued)

Rank	Manufacturer	% Sites
Report Generator/Query Language Software		
1	Pansophic Systems	28
2	IBM	23
3	Sterling Software	18
4	Cullinet Software	13
5	Goal Software	6
6	Applied Data Research	4
7	Other	8
Disk & Tape Management Software		
1	Computer Associates	34
2	UCCEL Corporation	27
3	IBM	14
4	Innovation	6
5	Tower Systems	4
6	Sterling Software	3
6	VM Software	3
8	Other	9

266 - SOFTWARE PRODUCTS: How They Rank

BILLBOARD
TOP COMPUTER SOFTWARE: EDUCATION
For week ending September 20, 1986

The information on this chart is compiled from selected samplings from retail software sales outlets. Numbers listed are actual sales from various unspecified areas of the United States.--COMPUTER INDUSTRY ALMANAC.

Copyright 1986 by Billboard Publications, Inc. Compiled by the Billboard Research Dept. and reprinted with permission.

This Week	Weeks on Chart	Title/Remarks	Publisher	Systems*
1	9	**Bingo Bugglebee Presents: Home Alone** Teaches childhood safety.	Quest Learning Systems	Ap,Com
2	31	**I Am The C-64** Introduction to C-64; basic programming.	Creative/Activision	Com
3	31	**Homework Helper Math Word Problems** Understand & solve math word problems.	Spinnaker	Ap,At,Com,IBM
4	103	**Typing Tutor III** Develops typing speed and accuracy.	Simon & Schuster	Ap,Com,IBM,Mac
5	138	**Math Blaster!** Over 600 math problems with game at end.	Davidson & Associates	Ap,Com,IBM
6	22	**Reader Rabbit and the Fabulous Word Factory.** Basic reading.	The Learning Company	Ap,Com,IBM
7	15	**Rocky's Boots** Teaches logic & circuitry (Ages 9 & up).	The Learning Company	Ap,Com,IBM
8	3	**States and Traits** Geography & state facts in game format.	DesignWare	Ap,Com,IBM
9	155	**New Improved Master Type** Teaches touch typing in game format.	Scarborough	Ap,At,Com,IBM,Mac
10	37	**Spanish** For use with any Spanish I course.	Amer.Educ.Computer	Ap

*Systems code: Apple (Ap); Atari (At); Commodore (Com); IBM; Macintosh (Mac); TRS; CP/M; Other (O).

BILLBOARD
TOP COMPUTER SOFTWARE: ENTERTAINMENT
For week ending September 27, 1986

The information on this chart is compiled from selected samplings from retail software sales outlets.
Numbers listed are actual sales from various unspecified areas of the United States.--COMPUTER
INDUSTRY ALMANAC.

Copyright 1986 by Billboard Publications, Inc. Compiled by the Billboard Research Dept. and
reprinted with permission.

This Week	Weeks on Chart	Title/Remarks	Publisher	Systems*
1	7	**World Karate Championship** Action Adventure Game	Epyx	At,Com
2	47	**Silent Service** Submarine Simulation Game	MicroProse	Ap,At,Com,IBM,TRS
3	13	**King's Quest II** Adventure Game	Sierra On-Line	Ap,IBM
4	11	**Infiltrator** Helicopter Flight Simulator	Mindscape	Com
5	New	**Bop'N Wrestle** Sports Simulation	Mindscape	Com
6	1	**World Greatest Baseball Game** Baseball Simulation Game	Epyx	Com
7	144	**Flight Simulator** Simulation Package	Microsoft	IBM
8	23	**Wizards Crown** Action Adventure Game	SSI	Ap,Com
9	17	**Leader Board** Pro Golf Simulation Game	Access	Com
10	31	**The Bard's Tale** Fantasy Role-Playing Game	Electronic Arts	Ap,Com
11	7	**Super Cycle** Motorcycle Simulation Game	Epyx	Com
12	5	**The Chessmaster 2000** Chess Program (Continued on next page)	Software Toolworks	Ap,At,Com,IBM,Mac

*Systems code: Apple (Ap); Atari (At); Commodore (Com); IBM; Macintosh (Mac); TRS; CP/M;
Other (O).

BILLBOARD TOP COMPUTER SOFTWARE: ENTERTAINMENT (Continued)

This Week	Weeks on Chart	Title/Remarks	Publisher	Systems*
13	21	**Elite**	Firebird	Ap,Com
		Space Trading and Combat Adventure Game		
14	29	**Hardball**	Accolade	Ap,Com
		Baseball Game		
15	55	**Jet**	Sublogic	Ap,At,Com
		Flight Simulation		
16	13	**U.S.A.A.F.**	SSI	Ap,At,Com
		Simulation Game		
17	RE**	**Kung Fu Master**	Data East	Ap,Com
		Action Arcade Game		
18	5	**Hacker II:**		
		The Doomsday Papers	Activision	Ap,At,Com,IBM,Mac
		Strategy Adventure Simulation		
19	47	**Ultima IV Quest of the Avatar**	Origins Systems Inc.	Ap,At,Com,IBM,Mac
		Fantasy Role-Playing Game		
20	New	**Gettysburg:**		
		The Turning Point	SSI	Ap,At,Com
		Simulation Game		

*Systems code: Apple (Ap); Atari (At); Commodore (Com); IBM; Macintosh (Mac); TRS; CP/M; Other (O).
**Re-entry.

BILLBOARD
TOP COMPUTER SOFTWARE: HOME MANAGEMENT
For week ending September 20, 1986

The information on this chart is compiled from selected samplings from retail software sales outlets. Numbers listed are actual sales from various unspecified areas of the United States.--COMPUTER INDUSTRY ALMANAC.

Copyright 1986 by Billboard Publications, Inc. Compiled by the Billboard Research Dept. and reprinted with permission.

This Week	Weeks on Chart	Title/Remarks	Publisher	Systems*
1	17	**Print Shop Companion** 16 new drawing tools; 50 new borders.	Broderbund	Ap,At,Com,IBM
2	19	**The Newsroom: Clip Art Collection Vol.1** 600 new graphics.	Springboard	Ap,Com,IBM
3	3	**Cardware** Animated greeting card maker.	Hi-Tech Expressions	Ap,At,Com,IBM
4	74	**The Newsroom** Newspaper program with word processor.	Springboard	Ap,Com,IBM
5	56	**3 In 1 Bundle** WP,DB,Spread sheet program.	Timeworks	Com
6	113	**Print Shop** At home print shop.	Broderbund	Ap,At,Com,IBM
7	19	**Better Working Spreadsheet** Spreadsheet with wp, dbase, & graphics.	Spinnaker	Ap,Com,IBM
8	15	**Word Perfect** Word processor.	Satelite SW Solutions	IBM
9	75	**Paperclip** Word processing package.	Batteries Included	At,Com
10	58	**Printmaster** At home print shop.	Unison World	Ap,At,Com,IBM,CP/M

*Systems code: Apple (Ap); Atari (At); Commodore (Com); IBM; Macintosh (Mac); TRS; CP/M; Other (O).

SOFTSEL HOT LIST
BUSINESS SOFTWARE
Week of October 13, 1986

"The HOT LIST is compiled from Softsel sales to over 15,000 dealers in 50 states and 45 countries. Sales may vary regionally. The names of the products and companies appearing may be trademarks or registered trademarks."--SOFTSEL HOT LIST.

Reprinted with permission from SOFTSEL HOT LIST, October 13, 1986. Copyright 1986 by Softsel Computer Products, Inc., Inglewood, CA.

This Week	Last Week	Weeks on Chart	Business Software	Publisher	Machine
1	1	39	dBase III Plus	Ashton-Tate/Multimate	IBM
2	3	128	WordPerfect	WordPerfect Corp.	AP, IBM
3	4	47	Q & A	Symantec	IBM
4	2	192	1-2-3	Lotus	IBM
5	5	151	Microsoft Word	Microsoft	IBM, MAC
6	7	21	SQZ!	Turner Hall (Symantec)	IBM
7	14	17	DAC Easy Accounting	DAC	IBM
8	6	103	Sidekick	Borland Int'l.	IBM
9	13	46	Paradox	Ansa Software	IBM
10	8	5	PFS:First Choice	Software Publishing	IBM
11	10	170	Multimate	Ashton-Tate/Multimate	IBM
12	9	169	PFS:Write	Software Publishing	AP, IBM
13	11	2	FastPak Mail	DHA Systems	IBM
14	12	210	Wordstar	Micropro Int'l.	IBM
15	17	45	Reflex	Borland Int'l.	IBM, MAC
16	24	47	VP Planner	Paperback Software	IBM
17	21	18	ProDesign II	American Small Bus. Comp.	IBM
18	15	42	Microsoft Windows	Microsoft	IBM
19	16	27	Multimate Advantage	Ashton-Tate/Multimate	IBM
20	18	11	Smart Notes	Personics	IBM

(Continued on next page)

SOFTSEL HOT LIST
BUSINESS SOFTWARE
Week of October 13, 1986 (Continued)

This Week	Last Week	Weeks on Chart	Business Software	Publisher	Machine
21	20	44	**Turbo Lightning**	Borland Int'l.	IBM
22	19	7	**MORE**	Living Videotext	MAC
23	25	87	**Wordstar 2000**	Micropro Int'l.	IBM
24	22	12	**Chart-Master**	Decision Resources	IBM
25	--	197	**Microsoft Multiplan**	Microsoft	IBM
26	--	19	**ClickArt Personal Publisher**	Software Publishing	IBM
27	--	3	**Clipper**	Nantucket	IBM
28	23	52	**Microsoft Excel**	Microsoft	MAC
29	--	1	**PFS:Professional Write**	Software Publishing	IBM
30	--	1	**Quicken**	Intuit	IBM

SOFTSEL HOT LIST
HOME & EDUCATION SOFTWARE
Week of October 13, 1986

"The HOT LIST is compiled from Softsel sales to over 15,000 dealers in 50 states and 45 countries. Sales may vary regionally. The names of the products and companies appearing may be trademarks or registered trademarks."--SOFTSEL HOT LIST.
Reprinted with permission from SOFTSEL HOT LIST, October 13, 1986. Copyright 1986 by Softsel Computer Products, Inc., Inglewood, CA.

This Week	Last Week	Weeks on Chart	Home & Education Software	Publisher	Machine
1	1	118	**Print Shop**	Broderbund	AP, IBM, MAC, COM, AT
2	2	85	**The Newsroom**	Springboard	AP, IBM, COM
3	4	153	**Math Blaster!**	Davidson & Assoc.	AP, IBM, MAC, COM, AT
4	3	11	**Certificate Maker**	Springboard	AP, IBM, COM
5	5	112	**Typing Tutor III**	Simon & Shuster	AP, IBM, MAC, COM
6	6	45	**Print Shop Companion**	Broderbund	AP, COM`
7	7	95	**Print Shop Graphics Library 1**	Broderbund	AP, IBM, COM
8	8	51	**Print Shop Graphics Library 2**	Broderbund	AP, IBM, COM
9		205	**Mastertype**	Scarborough	AP, IBM
10	10	2	**Fontasy 2**	Unison (Brown-Wagh)	IBM

SOFTSEL HOT LIST
RECREATION SOFTWARE
Week of October 13, 1986

"The HOT LIST is compiled from Softsel sales to over 15,000 dealers in 50 states and 45 countries. Sales may vary regionally. The names of the products and companies appearing may be trademarks or registered trademarks."--SOFTSEL HOT LIST.

Reprinted with permission from SOFTSEL HOT LIST, October 13, 1986. Copyright 1986 by Softsel Computer Products, Inc., Inglewood, CA.

This Week	Last Week	Weeks on Chart	Recreation Software	Publisher	Machine
1	1	193	Microsoft Flight Simulator	Microsoft	IBM, MAC
2	2	146	Sargon III	Hayden Software	AP, IBM, MAC, AT
3	3	81	F-15 Strike Eagle	Microprose	AP, IBM, COM, AT
4	4	3	Orbiter	Spectrum Holobyte	IBM, MAC
5	7	61	Jet	SubLogic	AP, IBM, COM
6	6	101	Gato	Spectrum Holobyte	AP, IBM, MAC, COM
7	8	194	Flight Simulator II	SubLogic	AP, COM, AT
8	10	2	Professional Blackjack	Screenplay	IBM, COM
9	5	193	Zork I	Activision/Infocom	AP, IBM, MAC, AT, ST
10	--	2	Toy Shop	Broderbund	AP, IBM, MAC

SOFTSEL HOT LIST
SYSTEMS & UTILITIES SOFTWARE
Week of October 13, 1986

"The HOT LIST is compiled from Softsel sales to over 15,000 dealers in 50 states and 45 countries.
Sales may vary regionally. The names of the products and companies appearing may be trademarks
or registered trademarks."--SOFTSEL HOT LIST.
Reprinted with permission from SOFTSEL HOT LIST, October 13, 1986. Copyright 1986 by
Softsel Computer Products, Inc., Inglewood, CA.

This Week	Last Week	Weeks on Chart	Systems & Utilities Software	Publisher	Machine
1	1	106	Norton Utilities	Norton Computing	IBM
2	2	157	Crosstalk XVI	Microstuf	AP, IBM
3	4	29	Fastback	Fifth Generation	IBM
4	3	130	Sideways	Funk Software	AP, IBM
5	5	99	Turbo Pascal	Borland Int'l.	AP, IBM, MAC
6	7	89	Smartcom II	Hayes	IBM, MAC
7	6	32	Microsoft Quick Basic	Microsoft	IBM
8	8	7	Carbon Copy	Meridian Technology	IBM
9	9	16	XTREE	Executive Systems	IBM
10	--	3	Microsoft C Compiler	Microsoft	IBM

STOREBOARD INC.
TOP PERSONAL COMPUTER SOFTWARE TITLES IN 1986
January 1987

"In this data StoreBoard Inc. lists the best selling personal computer products. The best seller lists represent personal computer products sold in computer specialty stores such as ComputerLand, Businessland, Entre', Sears Business Systems Centers, MicroAge, Inacomp, MBI, etc. Computer stores sell primarily to businesses; these lists indicate the most popular products in the business marketplace. The IBM PC/XT sold over 300,000 units in 1986 in computer stores. The IBM PC/XT sales are used as the base (100) of the relative sale numbers given for each product."--StoreBoard Inc.

Reprinted with permission from StoreBoard Inc., January 1987. Copyright 1987 by StoreBoard Inc., Dallas, TX.

Top 10 IBM PC-Compatible Software Titles in 1986*

Rank	Product	Relative Sales
1.	1-2-3 (Lotus)	70
2.	WordPerfect (WordPerfect)	27
3.	dBase III (Ashton-Tate)	25
4.	DisplayWrite 3 (IBM)	21
5.	WordStar (MicroPro)	19
6.	Print Shop (Broderbund)	15
7.	Sidekick (Borland)	14
8.	Writing Assistant (IBM)	12
8.	Word (Microsoft)	12
10.	MultiMate (Ashton-Tate)	11

Top 5 Macintosh Software Titles in 1986*

Rank	Product	Relative Sales
1.	Word (Microsoft)	27
2.	MacDraw (Apple)	24
3.	Excel (Microsoft)	23
4.	PageMaker (Aldus)	16
5.	MacWrite (Apple)	15
	(Continued next page)	

* Sold in computer stores and based on StoreBoard Inc.'s monthly surveys.

STOREBOARD INC.
TOP PERSONAL COMPUTER SOFTWARE TITLES IN 1986 (Continued)

Top 5 Apple II Software Titles in 1986*

Rank	Product	Relative Sales
1.	AppleWorks (Apple)	60
2.	Print Shop (Broderbund)	44
3.	Bank Street Writer (Broderbund)	16
4.	Mastertype (Scarborough)	9
5.	PFS:Write (Software Publishing)	9

* Sold in computer stores and based on StoreBoard Inc.'s monthly surveys.

COMPUTER INDUSTRY ALMANAC
CRYSTAL BALL: PREDICTED NEW PRODUCTS FOR 1987
December 1986

1987 will be a year noted for its new product introductions. IBM, Apple and many other companies have indicated that an unusually large number of products will be introduced. The emergence of the 80386 microprocessor and a projected new operating system will make the PC industry exceptionally busy. Optical disk technology is also poised for numerous product introductions. This table lists COMPUTER INDUSTRY ALMANAC's projected product introductions for 1987.

Product	Company
1. More Sierra Mainframes	IBM
2. More IBM 9370 Computers	IBM
3. More Spectrum Minicomputers	Hewlett-Packard
4. More VAX Computers	DEC
5. More RISC Workstations	Apollo, Sun & many others
6. Macintosh Workstation (Open Mac)	Apple
7. Desktop Publishing Systems	IBM & many others
8. 80386-based Personal Computers	IBM & many others
9. Laser Printers	IBM, Xerox, and many others
10. Read-Write Optical Disks	Kodak & many others
11. Write Once Optical Disks	Many companies
12. Read Only Optical Disks (CD ROM)	Many companies
13. Operating System for 80286 & 80386	Microsoft & IBM
14. Expert System Software	Many companies
15. Connectivity Application Software	Many companies
16. SQL-compatible Software for PCs	Many companies
17. 80286/80386 Software	Many companies

COMPUTER INDUSTRY ALMANAC
COMPUTER TRENDS OVER THE NEXT FIVE YEARS
1986

The technologies used for computers are continuing to evolve at a rapid pace. These technological advances will greatly improve the capabilities of computers in the next five years. Semiconductor (or integrated circuits) technology is the key to computer technological advances. Improvements in microprocessor and memory chips will be rapid and spectacular. Advancements in peripherals, especially in mass storage and printers, will also be extremely significant.

To give an idea of computer technological advances over the next five years, the following data compares today's capabilities with 1991 expected capabilities. Three price points are compared: the typical $3000 office personal computer, the $1000 personal computer used by students and consumers, and finally the typical $100 wristwatch computer.

A TYPICAL $3000 PERSONAL COMPUTER

Today, the typical $3000 personal computer has a 16-bit microprocessor and has the computing capabilities of a 1965 vintage computer that cost over a half million dollars. By 1991, such a personal computer will use a 32-bit microprocessor and will have ten times the computing power of today. It will also have 12 times as much main memory and will have nearly 100 times the mass storage capability due to the addition of a fixed (nonremovable media) hard disk drive, instead of one floppy disk drive.

All peripherals will also have significant improvements. The floppy disk will be smaller (3.5 inches in diameter versus 5.25 inches), but it will still store 4 times as much data. The display monitor will have twice as high resolution and will have color. The modem will be 8 times faster. The printer will have higher print quality and will have twice the printing speed. For an additional $1000, a page printer (laser technology) with significant higher quality and speed will be available. Finally, the 1991 personal computer will come with a built-in local area network (LAN) interface, which opens a vast area of communication with co-workers and outside information services.

A Typical $3000 Personal Computer in 1986

- 16-bit microprocessor
- Performance of 0.3 million instructions per second (MIPS)
- 640 kilobytes of main memory
- Two 5.25-inch floppy disk drives
- Monochrome CRT display
- Impact character printer with draft and near-letter-quality printing
- 1200-baud modem

A Typical $3000 Personal Computer in 1991

- 32-bit microprocessor
- Performance of 2 to 3 million instructions per second (MIPS)
- 8 megabytes of main memory
- One 3.5-inch floppy disk drive
- One hard disk drive with 80 megabytes of storage
- High-resolution color graphics CRT display or monochrome flat display
- Built-in 9600-baud modem
- Built-in local area network interface
- Multifunction printer: graphics, letter quality, and high-speed draft printing

A TYPICAL $1000 PERSONAL COMPUTER

The next data shows similar technological advances for a $1000 personal computer. Such a product will be common in homes in 1991. It is a scaled down version of the office personal computer. However, the addition of a CD ROM (similar to current compact disks for audio) will add a new dimension to recreation and entertainment. Tremendous opportunities open up due to the large storage capacity (about 550 million bytes) of one CD ROM even though this information is fixed (read-only memory) and cannot be changed.

A Typical $1000 Personal Computer in 1986

- 16-bit microprocessor
- Performance of 0.15 million instructions per second (MIPS)
- 128 kilobytes of main memory
- One 5.25-inch floppy disk drive
- Monochrome CRT display
- Low-speed matrix impact printer

A Typical $1000 Personal Computer in 1991

- 32-bit microprocessor
- Performance of 1 to 1.5 million instructions per second (MIPS)
- 4 megabytes of main memory
- One 3.5-inch floppy disk drive
- One CD ROM drive
- Color CRT display
- Letter-quality or near-letter-quality printer

A TYPICAL $100 WRISTWATCH COMPUTER

This data shows the capabilities of a $100 wristwatch computer. Today, it has limited capabilities and is primarily a calculator with information storage. In 1991, the functionality will be vastly improved. The storage capacity will have increased more than 100-fold. Due to physical size limitations, it is difficult to improve its peripherals. Therefore, there will be a computer interface for loading information from a desktop computer or via a communications link.

A Typical $100 Wristwatch Computer in 1986

- Standard calculator functions
- Standard watch functions
- Multiple alarm and reminder settings
- Information storage of 1000 characters
- 32-character display (LCD)

A Typical $100 Wristwatch Computer in 1991

- Built-in computer interface to transmit information from desktop computer
- Business and/or scientific-engineering calculator functions
- Advanced watch and alarm functions
- Information storage of 128,000 characters
- Built-in software to manage and record information:
  - Appointments
  - Names and addresses
  - Telephone numbers
  - Business expenses
- 100-character display

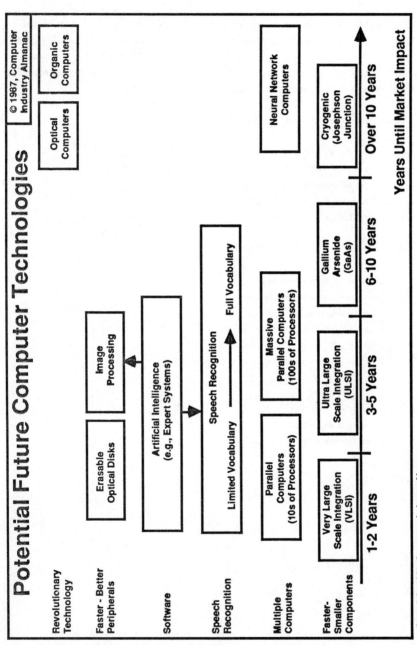

Potential Future Computer Technologies

© 1987, Computer Industry Almanac

	1-2 Years	3-5 Years	6-10 Years	Over 10 Years
Revolutionary Technology				Optical Computers / Organic Computers
Faster - Better Peripherals		Erasable Optical Disks		
Software		Artificial Intelligence (e.g., Expert Systems) / Image Processing		
Speech Recognition		Limited Vocabulary → Full Vocabulary / Speech Recognition		
Multiple Computers	Parallel Computers (10s of Processors)	Massive Parallel Computers (100s of Processors)		Neural Network Computers
Faster-Smaller Components	Very Large Scale Integration (VLSI)	Ultra Large Scale Integration (ULSI)	Gallium Arsenide (GaAs)	Cryogenic (Josephson Junction)

Years Until Market Impact

Copyright 1987, Computer Industry Almanac

COMPUTER INDUSTRY ALMANAC
POTENTIAL FUTURE COMPUTER TECHNOLOGIES
January 1987

The computer industry has seen phenomenal technological advances since its inception. There is still more to come. Current computer technologies are continuing to improve, and there are new technologies that have future potential at least as great as existing technologies. The accompanying chart shows the advances that COMPUTER INDUSTRY ALMANAC believes will have an impact. Both near-term and long-term technologies have been included.

There are many ways of advancing computers. By using faster and/or smaller components, the performance increases and price declines. Current integrated circuit technology will continue to improve for at least another 10 years. Additionally, two new technologies--gallium arsenide components and cryogenic components--are likely to be used for high-speed computers in the 1990s and beyond.

Another method of advancing computer speed is by using multiple computers. Research in multiple computer systems has been intense for 20 years, but it is only now that the technology has advanced far enough to have real commercial impact. In the next couple of years parallel computers using tens of computers will have a notable impact. Later, hundreds and even thousands of computers, usually called massive parallel computers, will have success for special applications. Another technology called neural network computers is showing some intriguing potential. Neural network computers are organized in a manner similar to brain cells and are objects of much research.

Computers can also be improved by having better user interfaces. Speech recognition continues to improve. Today only a limited vocabulary--a few hundred words--can be recognized by commercial systems. But each year the size of the vocabulary will increase, and in 10 years speech recognition will be very important.

Software technology must improve in order to take advantage of all the hardware improvements. Artificial intelligence (AI) is the technology that has the potential to revolutionize software. AI is not an application, but is a technology that will have tremendous impact on nearly all types of programs. AI is also needed to realize the potential of speech recognition and image processing.

Magnetic disk technology will continue as the main mass storage technology, but optical disk technology will gain in importance in the next decade.

Finally, there are a few potential technologies that could have a revolutionary impact. Optical computing has been a research topic for 20 years, but only limited advances have taken place. In 10 or more years, optical computers may be commercially available.

Organic computers are even further away. It may be possible to make computers in the 21st century by using technology that stems from gene-splitting bio-technology.

COMPUTER INDUSTRY ALMANAC
1986 PRODUCTS OF THE YEAR
January 1987

Every year there are several thousand computer products introduced in the computer industry. Only a fraction of these products are successful. They become influential, start trends, and even set standards for a market segment. Others are notable for their innovative characteristics which may or may not translate to commercial success. For products of the year COMPUTER INDUSTRY ALMANAC has selected three product classes: computers, software, and peripherals. Categories of influence are best sellers, influential new products, and innovative new products.

COMPUTERS

The list below is COMPUTER INDUSTRY ALMANAC's choices for computers of the year. These products were either introduced in 1986, sold in 1986, or shipped in 1986. Some products (e.g., IBM 9370) were introduced and sold in 1986 but will not be shipped until 1987. There are, of course, successful products introduced in 1986 that are not on this list.

Manufacturer & Product	Best Sellers	Influ- ential	Inno- vative
Product Type: Supercomputers			
Cray X-MP/44	x		
Floating Point Systems' Hypercube			x
Product Type: Mainframes			
IBM 3090 Model 150, 180, 400 (Sierra)	x	x	
NAS AS/XL Vector Series	x		
NCR 9800	x		
Product Type: Minicomputers			
IBM 4381 Models 11, 12, 13, 14	x		
DEC VAX 8300, 8500, 8550,8700	x	x	
IBM 9370	x	x	
HP Spectrum (RISC architecture)			x
Product Type: Minisupercomputers			
Convex Computer C1XL & C1XP			x
Sequent Balance 2100			x
(Continued next page)			

COMPUTER INDUSTRY ALMANAC: 1986 PRODUCTS OF THE YEAR (Continued)

Manufacturer & Product	Best Sellers	Influ- ential	Inno- vative
Product Type: Workstations			
IBM RT PC (RISC architecture)			x
Apollo DN 580	x		
Sun 3/110 LC	x		
Product Type: Personal Computers			
COMPAQ DeskPro 386	x	x	
Toshiba T3100	x	x	
COMPAQ II	x		
IBM PC Convertible		x	
Macintosh Plus	x		
Tandy 1000 EX and SX	x		
Apple IIGS	x		
DEC VAXmate			x
Product Type: Special Purpose Computers			
Thinking Machine Corp. Connection Machine			x
Pixar Image Computer			x

COMPUTER INDUSTRY ALMANAC: 1986 PRODUCTS OF THE YEAR (Continued)

SOFTWARE

There are over 1000 software products--either new titles or upgraded programs--introduced yearly in the computer industry. The majority of these products are introduced for the personal computer industry. A small percentage of these products achieve success. COMPUTER INDUSTRY ALMANAC has chosen 20 software titles as the 1986 products of the year. The criteria for being on this list are to be a bestseller (but not all best sellers are included), be an influential product or have an innovative program. The first item on the list is not a single product, but is a collection of IBM products. The reason for the inclusion is a significant and influential pricing change. IBM's graduated pricing means that the price depends on the power of the computer. The program will cost more for a high-performance (i.e. 3090) 370-family computer than on a low-performance (i.e. 4300) 370-family computer.

Software Title and Publisher	Best Sellers	Influ-ential	Inno-vative
Computer Target: **Mainframes** (IBM 370)			
Graduated Pricing; IBM (nearly 100 programs)	x	x	
DB2 Release 2; IBM	x	x	
SQL Star; Oracle	x		
Ingres/Star; Relational Technology, Inc.	x	x	
VM/IS; IBM	x		
C Compiler; IBM		x	
Computer Target: **Minicomputers**			
VAX OSI Transport Service; DEC VAX		x	
All Base/XL; HP 930/950			x
UNIX System V Release 3; AT&T (Minis & Micros)	x	x	
Computer Target: **Microcomputers** (IBM PC)			
Personal Consultant Easy; TI			x
Windows; Microsoft		x	
Paradox; Ansa	x		
Q+A; Symantec	x		
Javelin; Javelin			x
For Comment; Broderbund			x
SQZ; Turner Hall Publishing	x		x
HAL; Lotus			x
Turbo Prolog; Borland		x	
Advanced Program to Program Communication; IBM			x
Computer Target: **Microcomputers** (Apple Macintosh)			
Pagemaker; Aldus	x	x	x
Excel; Microsoft	x		x
MacWorks; Microsoft	x		
(Continued next page)			

COMPUTER INDUSTRY ALMANAC: 1986 PRODUCTS OF THE YEAR (Continued)

PERIPHERALS

Hundreds of new computer peripherals are introduced each year. There is such a variety of peripherals that it is difficult to compare the significance among the different types of peripherals. Below is a list of the peripherals that COMPUTER INDUSTRY ALMANAC believes warrants the status of 1986 products of the year.

A large variety of peripherals has been selected. The award winners range from a billion dollar success story (the IBM 3380) to a product with a hundred thousand units sold (the Apple Imagewriter II) to numerous innovative products with low sales but up-side potential.

Product	Best Sellers	Influ- ential	Inno- vative
Apple LaserWriter Plus	x	x	x
Apple Imagewriter II	x		
IBM Quietwriter II	x		
Kodak Ektaprint 1392 Page Printer			x
IBM 3380 Extended Disk Drive	x		
IBM 3.5-inch Diskette Drive		x	
Plus Development Hardcard	x		x
NEC MultiSync Monitor	x		x
Kurzweil Voice Terminal			x
IBM 3117 Optical Scanner			x
IBM 3720 Communications Controller	x		
IBM Token-Ring Local Area Network		x	
AppleTalk Network	x		
Virtual Microsystems Network Coprocessor			x
Intel/Flexlink IBM-VAX Channel-speed Link			x
Data Switch Corp. Channel Extender 9055			x

COMPUTER MUSEUM
EARLY MODEL PERSONAL COMPUTER CONTEST

The Early Model Personal Computer Contest was sponsored by The Computer Museum of Boston, ComputerLand, and CW Communications of Framingham, MA. For this contest people were invited to send in early-model personal computers. From over 300 entries from 13 countries, 137 early computers were chosen during final judging in April 1986 to remain as part of The Computer Museum's permanent collection. The purpose of the contest was to select the earliest personal computers as well as those that were historically important. Factors considered in judging each model were the interest, significance, and date of each model; its impact on the computer world; and its present condition. The winner and runners-up were presented awards in June 1986.--
COMPUTER INDUSTRY ALMANAC.
Reprinted with permission from The Computer Museum, 1986. Copyright 1986 by the Computer Museum, Boston, MA.

WINNER:

The Kenbak - 1PC
Inventor: John V. Blankenbaker
Date: 1971
Selling Price: $750
Features: It has 256 bytes. Its processor is built-up from small-scale and medium-scale integrated circuits; it contains no actual microprocessor. About 40 were sold.

RUNNERS UP:

Micral
Inventor: Thi T. Truong
Date: 1973
Selling Price: $1950
Features: It was a commercial PC built in France. It features a Pluribus (60-bit data bus) and has 256 bytes of RAM, expandable to 2 kilobytes. It is based on an 8008 Intel microprocessor.

TVT-1 Prototype
Inventor: Don Lancaster
Date: 1973
Selling Price: Prototype--not commercially sold; it was issued as a kit containing $120 worth of components.
Features: It is the first video terminal that displayed text on a screen. It is known as the "TV Typewriter." It is capable of storing 2 pages of text and can also use a cassette recorder that can hold up to 100 pages.
(Continued next page)

COMPUTER MUSEUM
EARLY MODEL PERSONAL COMPUTER CONTEST (Continued)

RUNNERS UP:

VDM-1 Video Display Terminal
Inventor: Lee Felsenstein
Date: 1974
Selling Price: Prototype only
Features: This model represents the first time that video terminals could be used interactively with personal computers. It was designed for use with S-100 bus systems.

MITS Altair 8800
Inventor: Ed Roberts & Bill Yates
Date: 1975
Selling Price: $297 or $395 with case
Features: This is the first commercially successful PC in the U.S. It has an 8080 Intel microprocessor. It originally came with 256 bytes of memory, expandable to 64 kilobytes.

CONSUMER ELECTRONICS SHOW
INNOVATIONS '86
Summer 1986

The CONSUMER ELECTRONICS SHOW "Innovations '86" awards are divided into three categories: Design and Engineering Exhibition, Software Showcase, and Packaging Design Exposition. These awards give formal recognition to the designers, engineers, producers, and marketers whose efforts during the past year have been of particular significance in the growth of the consumer electronics industry. The "Innovations '86" award winners were announced at the 1986 International Summer Consumer Electronics Show held in Chicago, IL.--COMPUTER INDUSTRY ALMANAC.

DESIGN AND ENGINEERING EXHIBITION

These awards recognize over 100 hardware products singled out for special achievement in design and/or engineering. From the award winners, COMPUTER INDUSTRY ALMANAC has selected only the computer-related winners.

ATARI U.S. CORPORATION

520ST COMPUTER: Power/performance are matched by this system's price and ease of use. 16 bit microprocessor complete with a two button mouse, 3.5 inch disk drive and high resolution monochrome or RGB color monitor.

BODYLOG, INC.

BODYLINK^{TM}: Bodylink is a revolutionary microcomputer peripheral that allows you to monitor physiological changes inside your body.

CATEO TELECOM INC.

TIU 2000 TELEX^{TM} INTERFACE: Telex board brings telex and TWX communications systems into the computer age of the 80's. You can use the power of a computer to handle all your telecommunications needs.

COMMODORE INTERNATIONAL LTD.

AMIGA 1000 PERSONAL COMPUTER: A low cost, high performance desk system with advanced graphics and sound features. It could be called the world's first personal supercomputer, a strong statement justified by the Amiga's performance. It uses a 16/32 bit 68000 main processor and three special purpose chips to deliver an unprecedented cost effective combination of computing power and graphics capability via a multi-tasking Operating System and a high speed windowing user interface.

DENON AMERICA, INC.

DRD-550 CD-ROM DRIVE: Utilizes the Compact Disc medium to offer fast access, economical 600 Megabyte data storage. Its intelligent controller allows one host computer to use up to four drives as well as interface with various host computers.

(Continued next page)

CONSUMER ELECTRONICS SHOW INNOVATIONS '86 (Continued)

HITACHI SALES CORP OF AMERICA

VY-50 COLOR PRINTER: Model VY-50, video printer produces a high resolution full color hard copy in 80 seconds from any video equipment and also from a personal computer.

OKIDATA

OKIMATE 20 COLOR PRINTER: The OKIMATE 20 prints dazzling shades of color for Apple, IBM, Commodore, Amiga and Atari ST users. Pictures, graphics, overhead transparencies and text.

PHIS/MAGNAVOX

VIDEOWRITER: Complete writing system for the home as easy to use as a typewriter with full word processing capabilities. All in one unit, built in video screen, desk memory, printer, software.

SATELLITE BROADCADST NETWORK

DMM-1000 DATA DEMODULATOR: Allows data to be down-loaded from a home satellite earth station to an IBM compatible computer and stored or printed, by-passing telephone costs.

SOFTWARE SHOWCASE

These awards recognize the most innovative, original computer, videocassette, and videodisk programs. At CES the computer programs were actually running on various microcomputers. From the more than 65 winners in this category, COMPUTER INDUSTRY ALMANAC has selected only the computer software winners.

ACTIVISION, INC.

ALTER EGO: In a category by itself, it provides consumers with the ultimate adventure--LIFE. From birth to the golden years consumers can relive realistic and complete life-stages without having to pay the consequences of real life decisions. Shown on Apple Macintosh. Other.

ACTIVISION, INC.

BORROWED TIME: Borrowed Time introduces an expanded parser, increased animation and an ease of use that sheds new light on the category of illustrated text adventures, thus allowing consumers to enjoy the adventures of private-eye Sam Harlow without having to worry about game-play technicalities. Shown on Amiga. Adventure.

(Continued next page)

CONSUMER ELECTRONICS SHOW INNOVATIONS '86 (Continued)

ACTIVISION, INC.

CHAMPIONSHIP GOLF: GREAT COURSES OF THE WORLD VOLUME I--PEBBLE BEACH: Championship Golf is one of the most realistic golf simulations on the market today. Designed from actual topographical maps of the Pebble Beach course, the consumer plays an 18-hole game of golf as realistic as possible without having to be at the actual course. Shown on IBM PC. Sports.

ACTIVISION, INC.

MURDER ON THE MISSISSIPPI: Introduces the consumer to a new way to play illustrated action/adventure games. Since the interface is completely joystick driven a knowledge of keyboards and parser phrases is unnecessary. Shown on Commodore 128. Action.

ACTIVISION, INC.

THE MUSIC STUDIO: The Music Studio is a comprehensive and complete musical composition tool with MIDI interface that provides a musical operating system easily accessible to both professional and beginning musicians. Shown on Amiga. Personal Productivity.

AEGIS DEVELOPMENT, INC.

AEGIS ANIMATORtm: Brings professional animation to personal computing. 3-D metamorphic and cell animation, the use of 'Tweens' for movement, pictures and backgrounds from AEGIS images and a nine-script storyboard. Shown on Amiga. Other.

AVALON HILL GAME COMPANY (THE)

SUPER SUNDAY: With all plays re-enacted by all 22 players, and their actual slats makes this football game real. Shown on Commodore 128. Sports.

BERKELEY SOFTWORKS

GEOS FOR C64/128: GEOS is a menu, icon, and windowing operating system that revolutionizes how people will use their Commodore 64/128 Computers. Package includes: desktop, geowrite, geopaint, diskturbo, and several desk accessories. Shown on Commodore 128. Personal Productivity.

BRODERBUND SOFTWARE INC.

BRIMSTONE: Blazes new territory in the test adventure field with a critically acclaimed parser for easy interaction and lifelike character dialogue, real-time game play, and excellent writing. Shown on Apple II. Adventure.

BRODERBUND SOFTWARE INC.

CAPTAIN GOODNIGHT: An arcade game with the depth and character of a movie thriller puts players in a 'movie length' secret agent mission, on land, sea and air. Uses 'secret decoder' and includes numerous surprises. Shown on Apple II. Action.

(Continued next page)

PRODUCTS - Copyright 1987 Computer Industry Almanac

CONSUMER ELECTRONICS SHOW INNOVATIONS '86 (Continued)

BRODERBUND SOFTWARE INC.

>FANTAVISION: Technological computer graphics breakthrough makes creating sophisticated special effects and disk 'movies' easy, automatic and virtually instantaneous. Creates special effects never before possible in a microcomputer software program. Shown on Apple II. Personal Productivity.

COMPU-JOB SOFTWARE, INC.

>JOBFINDER 1: Program for personal computers that assists an individual in finding a job. It writes resumes, creates cover letters, picks the best job offer and prints a personal history report for job applications. Shown on IBM PC. Personal Productivity.

ELECTRONIC ARTS

>ARCTICFOX: 3-D tank simulation on a personal computer. Adds strategic depth to classic arcade values. Shown on Amiga. Action.

ELECTRONIC ARTS

>DELUXE MUSIC CONSTRUCTION SET: Deluxe Music Construction Set combines the educational value of a 'word processor' for music, with the power to print professional quality sheet music. Shown on Apple Macintosh. Education.

ELECTRONIC ARTS

>DELUXE PAINT: Deluxe Paint has features and ease of use never before available on any personal computer. Shown on Amiga. Other.

ELECTRONIC ARTS

>DELUXE PRINT: Full-color home printing software for greeting cards, banners and rainy day activities. Shown on Amiga. Children/Kiddeo.

ELECTRONIC ARTS

>LORDS OF CONQUEST: Combines the family appeal of classic board games like RISK with the added computer features of solitaire play and infinite game board. Shown on Commodore 128. Strategy.

ELECTRONIC ARTS

>THE BARD'S TALE: The Dungeon fantasy game with detailed point-of view graphics. Shown on Apple II. Adventure.

ELECTRONIC ARTS

>TOUCHDOWN FOOTBALL: Football game with sophisticated pass plays and pass defense. Shown on Commodore 128. Business.

EPYX, INC.

>TEMPLE OF APSHAI TRILOGY: An all time adventure game classic--now with faster action and three classic adventures rolled into one. Includes the Temple of Apshai, Upper Reaches of Apshai, and the Curse of Ra. Mazes and monsters and evil potions. Shown on Commodore 128. Adventure.

(Continued next page)

CONSUMER ELECTRONICS SHOW INNOVATIONS '86 (Continued)

EPYX, INC.

> MULTIPLAN: Has powerful and versatile spreadsheets available. It has virtually unlimited business applications. Shown on Commodore 128. Business.

EPYX, INC.

> PROGRAMMERS' BASIC TOOLKIT: The Toolkit adds over 100 BASIC commands allowing users to develop games, animation, custom fonts, and special print drivers. Shown on Commodore 128. Personal Productivity.

EPYX, INC.

> VORPAL UTILITY KIT: Vorpal contains the most powerful collection of utilities for Commodore 64-128 computers, including a utility that allows programs to load up to 25 times faster than normally possible. Shown on Commodore 128. Other.

EPYX, INC.

> WINTER GAMES: Allows the player to experience the challenge of 7 sporting events: Bobsled, Ski Jump, Figure Skating, Speed Skating, Free Style Skating, Hot Dog Aerials, and Biathlon. There's also an opening ceremony complete with national anthems. Shown on Commodore 128. Sports.

EPYX, INC.

> WORLD KARATE CHAMPIONSHIP: This realistic karate action game includes more than 14 different moves: front punch, back spin kick, etc. Animation includes different ways to fall, different facial expressions. Eight international settings. Shown on Commodore 128. Action.

FIREBIRD LICENSEES INC.

> ADVANCED MUSIC SYSTEM: Is a compendium of integrated and interactive editor, keyboard, synthesizer, linker, printer and M.I.D.I. modules which permit full composition, editing and playback of polyphonic music through the host computer or optional M.I.D.I. devices. Shown on Commodore 128. Other.

FIREBIRD LICENSEES, INC.

> ELITE: Elite is an intense game which combines strategic space trading and combat adventure with flight simulation. Superb vector graphics, demanding play-action and virtually unlimited play scenarios combine to make Elite an international computer gaming favorite. Shown on Commodore 128. Strategy.

(Continued next page)

CONSUMER ELECTRONICS SHOW INNOVATIONS '86 (Continued)

FIREBIRD LICENSEES, INC.

THE PAWN: The Pawn is an illustrated text adventure which features stunning graphics demanding strategy and the most advanced language parser found on any microcomputer adventure game to date; it is destined to become a recreational software classic. Shown on Atari ST. Adventure.

FIRST STAR SOFTWARE, INC.

THE WORKS! A COMPLETE COLLECTION OF HOME SOFTWARE: Provides new and experienced computer users of all ages with 13 different programs on 1 side of 1 disk: illustrates many different uses. All modules share common commands, help screens always available, windowing, colorful graphics. Shown on Apple II. Personal Productivity.

FIRST STAR SOFTWARE, INC.

SPY VS SPY II: THE ISLAND CAPER: Action strategy sequel to game based on characters from MAD Magazine. Simulvision and Simulplay, split-screen. Natural and man-made booby traps including sharks, quicksand, coconut bombs, snares and jungle pits in a graphically unique tropical setting. Salsa soundtrack. Shown on Commodore 128. Action.

GESSLER EDUCATIONAL SOFTWARE

PASSPORT: THE COURSEWARE CREATOR: An authoring program for schools or businesses that allows you to customize individual lessons. Its capabilities include character sets of 19 languages, simultaneous use of 2 languages, branching and animation. Shown on Apple II. Education.

GESSLER EDUCATIONAL SOFTWARE/LEISURE GENIUS

MICRO SCRABBLE: This computer edition of the board game now enables students and adults to refresh or review French vocabulary. Contains a 20,000 word dictionary and can be played against the computer or by up to 4 players. Shown on Apple II. Other.

GREAT GAME PRODUCTS

TOM THROP'S BRIDGE BARON: Play bridge with the most advanced computer bridge program in the country, winner of the first computer bridge tournament. There are over one million random, but recreatable, deals. Shown on Apple II. Strategy.

JHM SOFTWARE OF MINNESOTA, INC.

THE TALKING COLORING BOOK: Youngsters now have a colorful friend to play with. Amiga talks to your child and tracks color recognition. Enhance creativity with draw, color, and print options. Shown on Amiga. Education.

(Continued next page)

CONSUMER ELECTRONICS SHOW INNOVATIONS '86 (Continued)

LEARNING WELL

> SAFETY FIRST: Youngsters develop safety sense of the home and outdoors as they work through three games. Parents can enter personal rules to keep children safe between school and home. Shown on Apple II. Other.

LEARNING WELL

> TYPING WELL: Five games introduce and hone touch-typing skills. Words-per-minute speeds can be adjusted to challenge both novice and expert typists. User may toggle between QWERTY and DVORAK keyboards. Shown on Apple II. Personal Productivity.

MASTERTRONIC INTERNATIONAL INC.

> KIKSTARD 128: Exceptional product value that appeals to all walks of life. Shown on Commodore 128. Other.

MASTERTRONIC INTERNATIONAL INC.

> MASTER OF MAGIC: Exceptional product value that appeals to all walks of life. Shown on Commodore 128. Adventure.

MASTERTRONIC INTERNATIONAL INC.

> SKIWRITER: Exceptional product that is very easy to use. Shown on Commodore 128. Personal Productivity.

MICROPROSE SOFTWARE, INC.

> DECISION IN THE DESERT: This is a fun and challenging new way to learn history (North African campaign of World War II) by using the interactive capabilities of a computer. Player is in command, making continuous real-time decisions. Shown on Apple II. Education.

MICROPROSE SOFTWARE, INC.

> SILENT SERVICE: Includes all the danger and thrill of captaining your own U.S. submarine in WWII South Pacific. Superb graphics. Multi-sub locations, maps, charts, armament. Constant action. Detailed and realistic. Shown on Commodore 128. Action.

MINDSCAPE, INC.

> BALANCE OF POWER: Artificial intelligence creates realistic simulation of world arena. Accurate background & historical information provide useful tool for learning and creating strategies. Develops strategic alternatives for peace in nuclear age. Shown on Apple Macintosh. Strategy.

MINDSCAPE, INC.

> BOP'N WRESTLE: Three-dimensional graphics and animation provide characters with realistic wrestling fun. Wrestling moves take full advantage of joystick potential. Lively rock soundtrack completes entertaining simulation. Shown on Commodore 128. Sports.

(Continued next page)

CONSUMER ELECTRONICS SHOW INNOVATIONS '86 (Continued)

MINDSCAPE, INC.

DEJA VU: A NIGHTMARE COMES TRUE: State-of-the-art interface eliminates need to type commands and allows complete exploration of environment. Digitized sound breaks new ground. Detailed graphics draw you into Deja Vu's world. Shown on Apple Macintosh. Adventure.

MINDSCAPE, INC.

INFILTRATOR: Combines a realistic helicopter simulation with exciting military ground action. Graphic and sound capability are state-of-the-art for Commodore. Ability to communicate with other pilots is another plus. Shown on Commodore 128. Action.

MINDSCAPE, INC.

THE HALLY PROJECT: A Mission in our Solar System, realistic simulation conveys vastness of solar system as well as teaching about constellations, planets, orbiting, eclipses and more. Star pilots have fun navigating through the universe as they learn. Shown on Commodore 128. Education.

PRACTICORP INTERNATIONAL

EXECUTIVE TRAINING WHEELS: The first software product that teaches productivity & leaves the user with usable software after learning to use an IBM PC. Shown on IBM PC. Personal Productivity.

PROGRESSIVE PERIPHERALS & SOFTWARE, INC.

BOBSTERM PRO 128: Supports all major telecommunication protocols, as well as allowing the user to redefine all parameters for complete operator control. Shown on Commodore 128. Personal Productivity.

RANDOM HOUSE ELECTRONIC PUBLISHERS

MR. & MRS. POTATO HEAD: Mr. & Mrs. Potato Head illustrates that pre-school children can have a fun program with exceptional graphics and versatility while being extremely easy to operate. Shown on Apple II. Children/Kiddeo.

RANDOM HOUSE ELECTRONIC PUBLISHING

TOURNAMENT BRIDGE: Geared to the adult entertainment market, engages the intermediate bridge player in a tournament setting using the computer's ability to analyze information in becoming a formidable opponent. Shown on IBM PC. Personal Productivity.

STRATEGIC SIMULATIONS, INC.

WIZARD'S CROWN: A multiple character role playing game that combines the mystery of a fantasy quest with the detailed tactical battles of wargaming. When fighting begins, you can choose to have the computer quickly resolve the battle or personally direct combat. Shown on Apple II. Adventure.

(Continued next page)

CONSUMER ELECTRONICS SHOW INNOVATIONS '86 (Continued)

STRATEGIC SIMULATIONS, INC.

> BATTLE OF ANTIETAM: Is a detailed and historically accurate simulation of the September 17, 1862 battle between the Union and Confederate armies on the outskirts of Sharpsburg, MD. Shown on Apple II. Education.

STRATEGIC SIMULATIONS, INC.

> BATTLEGROUP: A detailed tactical combat strategy game set on the western front 1943-45. The computers resolve combat down to each gun, tank and infantry man. Shown on Apple II. Strategy.

SUBLOGIC CORPORATION

> JET (SIMULATION): Combines state-of-the-art 3D graphics with an accurate simulation of the flight characteristics of two modern combat jet fighters: a land-based F-16 or a carrier-based F-18. Shown on IBM PC. Other.

WEEKLY READER FAMILY SOFTWARE/FIELD PUBLICATIONS

> CAR BUILDER: As a design engineer, the user selects the chassis, engine, suspension system, and all the other mechanical components. A custom body is then created and the car is run through a full testing procedure. Shown on Apple II. Other.

PACKAGING DESIGN EXPOSITION

These awards recognize the best in computer and video software packaging. From the award winners, COMPUTER INDUSTRY ALMANAC has selected only the computer software winners.

ACTIVISION, INC.

> MURDER ON THE MISSISSIPPI: Murder on the Mississippi appeals to a younger target audience with its violent and bold color combinations. Visuals depict an aura of mystery but with a touch of humor, and teaser photos on the back side aid in pulling consumers into the plot.

BATTERIES INCLUDED

> KEYS TO TYPING: Eyecatching, crisp and colorful blends.

BRODERBUND SOFTWARE, INC.

> FANTAVISION: How to visually illustrate the feelings of magic-motion and special effects in a static package cover environment. This cover says I'm high tech fun and fantasy for anyone with imagination!

BRODERBUND SOFTWARE, INC.

> GEOMETRY: Shelf impact and suitability for easy adaptation to a series of learning programs were key to Geometry's design. These programs are far afield from standard drill and practice and the design reflects it.

(Continued next page)

CONSUMER ELECTRONICS SHOW INNOVATIONS '86 (Continued)

BRODERBUND SOFTWARE, INC.

WIZARD OF WALL STREET: How better to give a potential user the feeling of big-board success than to depict someone who's already done it. Black and white financial page format stands out in a sea of color.

FIREBIRD LICENSEES INC.

THE PAWN: The sturdy box which houses The Pawn program disk, novella and related materials is finished in a high-gloss lacquer laminate coating which endows the process-color lithography with the appearance of being 'under glass' and further augments the package's 'eye appeal.'

MINDSCAPE, INC.

STEPHEN KING: THE MIST: Package prominently displays, 'Stephen King' in bold type which matches King's book cover format. The artwork conveys the terror and uncertainty associated with the unrecognizable creatures hidden in the mist.

MINDSCAPE, INC.

THE DOLPHIN'S RUNE: Serene blue colors convey the quiet beauty of the depths. The dolphin emphasizes the title and theme of the program. Dark depths foreshadow the poetic odyssey on which you'll travel.

MINDSCAPE, INC.

THE LUSCHER PROFILE: The repeating profiles emphasize the title and dramatize the changing moods and feelings people experience. Both male & female are represented. Clean, white border makes package stand out on shelf.

RANDOM HOUSE ELECTRONIC PUBLISHING

PATCHWORKS: Patchworks' packaging is basically 'an open book,' browsable to let people read and get an idea of the program before they buy. Color quilt photos enhance the presentation.

SUBLOGIC CORPORATION

JET: Continues the Flight Simulator II theme (floating pilot), with subdued border colors to emphasize screen photos. Easily-identifiable Scenery Disk compatibility symbol emphasizes product versatility.

SUBLOGIC CORPORATION

SCENERY DISK: Visually promotes the 'world-covering' aspects of these Flight Simulator program enhancement disk. Maintains the rich look of the product line yet attracts attention at the retail level.

DERBY INFORMATION SYSTEMS CORPORATION
THE DATABASE DERBY II
August 28, 1986

"The Database Derby II, a second annual contest sponsored by Derby Information Systems Corporation, Berkeley, CA, was held August 28, 1986 in San Francisco, CA. The purpose of the contest is to measure the productivity of the application development tools of database in the micro, mini, and mainframe markets. Ninety companies worldwide participated. Listed below in alphabetical order are the 16 companies who were able to complete the solution to the contest case study and publish their product for inspection by the public."--Derby Information Systems Corporation.

Reprinted with permission from Derby Information Systems Corporation, 1986. Copyright 1986 by Derby Information Systems Corporation, Berkeley, CA.

Company/Location	Product
1. Borland International Scotts Valley, CA	Reflex for the Mac
2. Data Equipment Sales West Allis, WI	Arrow
3. Data Language Corporation Billerica, MA	Progress
4. Information Dimensions Columbus, OH	DM
5. Mitrol, Incorporated Woburn, MA	Mitrol
6. Oracle Corporation Belmont, CA	Oracle
7. PC Manager, Incorporated Arlington, VA	PC Manager
8. Qint Database Systems, Inc. Waltham, MA	Qint-SQL
9. Relational Technology, Inc. Alameda, CA	Ingres
10. Software House Cambridge, MA	System 1032

(Continued next page)

DERBY INFORMATION SYSTEMS CORPORATION
THE DATABASE DERBY II (Continued)

Company/Location	Product
11. Software Merchants Unlimited San Francisco, CA	SIMPLE
12. Software Solutions Trumbull, CT	Dataease
13. Software Systems Technology College Park, MD	XDB
14. Texas Instruments Dallas, Texas	Info Engr Facility
15. WordTech Systems Orinda, CA	dBSQL
16. Unify Corporation Lake Oswego, OR	UNIFY

FORTUNE/AFIPS
PRODUCT OF THE YEAR AWARDS
1986

The American Federation of Information Processing Societies (AFIPS) Product of the Year Awards
sponsored by FORTUNE magazine have been created to recognize outstanding products in the
computer industry. The awards are presented in three categories: computer hardware, computer
software, and computer systems. Awards are limited to products, introduced in the U.S. within the
past two years, which have demonstrated exemplary innovation in design and structure. In addition,
Meritorious Product awards in each category may be presented. The awards are presented during une
annual AFIPS National Computer Conference. The 1986 award-winning products were chosen out
of a field of 72 entries from 58 U.S. companies.--COMPUTER INDUSTRY ALMANAC.

Reprinted with permission from AFIPS and FORTUNE magazine, 1986. Copyright 1986.

Category	Company	Product
Hardware	Plus Development Corp	Hardcard
Software	Telos Software Products	Business Filevision
Systems	Teradata Corporation	DBC/1012

NATIONAL COMPUTER GRAPHICS ASSOCIATION
INTERNATIONAL COMPUTER ANIMATION COMPETITION
January 1987

"The International Computer Animation Competition brings to the public an increased awareness of the potential of computer graphics for education, communication, entertainment, and personal use. The competition, sponsored annually by the National Computer Graphics Association, honors outstanding professional and non-professional uses of computer graphics in animation in 10 broad categories. Judges evaluate the quality and degree of innovation, uniqueness of presentation, and originality of composition."--National Computer Graphics Association.

1987 WINNERS

Best of Show - Non-Commercial Films

Pixar, San Rafael, CA
"Luxo Jr."

Broadcast Computer Graphics

First Place	**Robert Abel & Associates, an Omnibus Co.**, Los Angeles, CA "ABC National"
Second Place	**Pacific Data Images**, Sunnyvale, CA "CBS Dramatic Special"
Third Place	**Imagica Acme**, Tokyo, Japan "Oretachi Hyokin Zoku"

Television Commercials

First Place	**Robert Abel & Associates, an Omnibus Co.**, Los Angeles, CA "Hawaiian Punch 'Chain Reaction'"
Second Place	**Robert Abel & Associates, an Omnibus Co.**, Los Angeles, CA "Sam Sung"
Third Place	**Toyo Links Corp.**, Tokyo, Japan "Tokyo Gas: Liquefied Natural Gas"

NATIONAL COMPUTER GRAPHICS ASSOCIATION
INTERNATIONAL COMPUTER ANIMATION COMPETITION (Continued)

Corporate Communication Computer Graphics

First Place   **Sogitec Paris**, Paris, France
                     "Peugeot Promixa

Second Place   **The Post Group**, Hollywood, CA
                     "The Big Picture-Time Journey"

Third Place   **Post Perfect**, New York, NY
                     "Celerity"

Music Visualization with Computer Graphics

First Place   **Ohio State University**, Columbus, OH
                     "Vision Obious"

Second Place   **Steve Segal**, W. Hollywood, CA
                     "Dance of the Tumblers"

Third Place   **Peter Becker, Joanne Tolkoff**, North Salem, NY
                     "Eighth Wave"

Research Computer Graphics

First Place   **Lawrence Livermore National Laboratory**, Livermore, CA
                     "Light Beams"

Second Place   **Pacific Data Images**, Sunnyvale, CA
                     "Opera Industriel"

Third Place   **IBM T.J. Watson Research**, Yorktown Heights, NY
                     "Dynamics of $e^{10} \times (1-x)$"

Science and Industry Computer Graphics

First Place   **Synthetic Video**, San Francisco, CA
                     "UARS: Beyond the Clouds--Selections"

Second Place   **Thomson Digital Image**, Paris, France
                     "Stade"

Third Place   **Omnibus Simulation Inc.**, Los Angeles, CA
                     "Computer Simulations of Relativistic Star Clusters"

NATIONAL COMPUTER GRAPHICS ASSOCIATION INTERNATIONAL COMPUTER
ANIMATION COMPETITION (Continued)

Theatrical Motion Picture Graphics

First Place | **Robert Abel & Associates, an Omnibus Co.,** Los Angeles, CA
"Labyrinth"

Second Place | **Robert Abel & Associates, an Omnibus Co.,** Los Angeles, CA
"Flight of the Navigator"

Third Place | **Thomson Digital Image,** Paris, France
"Terminus"

Non-Commercial Films

First Place | **Pixar,** San Rafael, CA
"Luxo Jr."

Secondary and Undergraduate Students

First Place | **Art Center College of Design,** Pasadena, CA
"Speeder"

Second Place | **Adrian S. Iler,** Chatsworth, CA
"Squaredance"

Third Place | **Rochester Institute of Technology,** Rochester, NY
"Conscience of the King"

Graduate Students and Faculty

First Place | **Tokyo Kogakuin College of Arts,** Tokyo, Japan
"Dogumaster"

Second Place | **Ruedy W. Leeman, Michael Czeiszperger,** Columbus, OH
"Vision Obious"

Third Place | **Computer Graphics Research Group,** Ohio State University
Columbus, OH
"Metafable"

PC MAGAZINE
AWARDS FOR TECHNICAL EXCELLENCE
Fall 1986

"PC Magazine sponsors annual Awards for Technical Excellence to recognize the individuals who have advanced the state-of-the-art and who have expanded the horizons of personal computing. The PC Magazine Labs researchers tested and reviewed all products nominated. A committee of six editorial staff from PC Magazine selects the award winning products. Much in the computer industry has changed since PC Magazine instituted these awards three years ago. One thing remains, real progress is the product of genius, intuition, and hard work."--PC MAGAZINE.

Reprinted with permission from PC MAGAZINE, August 1986. Copyright 1986 by Ziff-Davis Publishing Co., New York, NY.

1986 THIRD ANNUAL AWARDS FOR TECHNICAL EXCELLENCE

Category	Winner	Products
Desktop Computers	Gary Stimac	Compaq Deskpro 386 Compaq Computer Corporation
Portable Computers	Tetsuya Mizoguchi Haruhiko Banno Yasuo Suzuki --and-- Robert Dilworth	T3100/Toshiba America,Inc. Z-181/Zenith Data Systems
Graphics Hardware	T. Nishimata T. Inoue	MultiSync NEC Home Electronics, Inc.
Programming Languages	Steve Rowe	QuickBASIC 2 Microsoft Corporation
Software Add-Ons	Sam L. Savage William J. Arendt Linus Schrage Kevin Cunningham --and-- Bill Gross	What's Best General Optimization Corp. HAL/Lotus Development Corp.

(Continued next page)

PC MAGAZINE AWARDS FOR TECHNICAL EXCELLENCE (Continued)

Application Software	Phil Quackenbush Ronald Benn Paul Salsbury	NewViews/QW Page, Inc.
Networking	R. Drew Major Dale R. Neibaur Kyle E. Powell	Advanced NetWare 286 Novell, Inc.
Operating System/ Environment	Bob Matthews	Windows, Version 1.03 Microsoft Corp.
Graphics Software	The Engineers and Designers of Island Graphics --and-- Martin Schmitt Kai Krause	TIPS Island Graphics Corp. Perspective Three/D/Graphics
Special Category	Bill Gates	Microsoft Corp.

1985 AWARDS FOR TECHNICAL EXCELLENCE

Winner	Product/Manufacturer
Joel Harrison	Hard Card/Plus Development
Edward P. Hutchins Shyam K. Nagrani Yi-Hsien Hao	EGA Chip Set/Chips & Technologies, Inc.
Paul Baran Bahman Zargham Gen. H.R. Johnson	10,000 BPS "TrailBlazer" Modem/Telebit Corporation
Charley Rogers John Newman Jerry Robinson	Proprinter/IBM Corporation
Rod Roark	LANLink/The Software Link, Inc.

(Continued next page)

PC MAGAZINE AWARDS FOR TECHNICAL EXCELLENCE (Continued)

Robert Firmin Stanley Kugell Christopher Herot	Javelin/Javelin Software Corp.
Dave Paterson Bayles Holt Gursharan Sidhu Alan Oppenheimer	LaserWriter/Apple Computer, Inc.
Reed Sturtevant	Freelance/Graphic Communications, Inc.
Mike Brown	Central Point Software

1984 AWARDS FOR TECHNICAL EXCELLENCE

Winner	Product/Manufacturer
Robert Carr	Framework/Ashton-Tate
Philippe Kahn	Turbo Pascal/Borland Intl
Henry Kee	The PC Blue Series
Jeff Garbers	Infoscope/Microstuf
Robert Hamilton	Enable/The Software Group
Eugene Hill Jim Slagery	Intel 80286/Intel Corporation

PC WORLD
WORLD CLASS PC CONTEST
October 1986

PC WORLD solicited the opinion of readers on their favorite hardware and software products in 39 categories. The results produced the winners in the World Class PC Contest based upon percentage of votes in each subcategory. "The tables list the winning products plus those receiving a significant percentage of the votes cast in each category. The 'Others' entry represents the combined percentages for all remaining products, so a large number here indicates that many products are competing for readers' piggy banks."--PC WORLD.

Reprinted by permission of PC WORLD from Volume 4, Issue 10 (October 1986) published at 501 2nd Street, San Francisco, CA 94107.

Hardware

Desktop Computer*

% of Votes	Product/Manufacturer	List Price
31	IBM PC AT, IBM	$3995
18	Compaq Deskpro 286, Compaq Computer Corp.	
13	IBM PC XT, IBM	
9	IBM PC, IBM	
6	AT&T 6300, AT&T	
23	Others	

*86% of respondents voted in this category

Transportable Computer*

% of Votes	Product/Manufacturer	List Price
34	Compaq Portable 286 (Model 2), Compaq Computer Corp.	$5499
22	Compaq Portable Computer, Compaq Computer Corp.	
15	Compaq Portable II, Compaq Computer Corp.	
9	Compaq Portable Plus Computer, Compaq Computer Corp.	
3	IBM Portable PC, IBM	
3	Executive Partner, Panasonic	
14	Others	

*52% of respondents voted in this category

(Continued next page)

WORLD CLASS PC CONTEST (Continued)

Lap-Size Computer*
% of

Votes	Product/Manufacturer	List Price
21	Data General/One, Data General Corp.	$2095
13	Executive Partner, Panasonic	
10	Zenith Z-171 Portable, Zenith Data Systems	
10	Toshiba T1100, Toshiba America, Inc.	
5	GridCase, Grid Systems Corp.	
5	Kaypro 2000, Kaypro Corp.	
36	Others	

*29% of respondents voted in this category

Printer-Dot Matrix/Near Letter Quality*
% of

Votes	Product/Manufacturer	List Price
9	LQ-1500, Epson America, Inc.	$1495
8	IBM Proprinter, IBM	
6	P351, Toshiba America, Inc.	
6	FX-286, Epson America, Inc.	
5	FX-185, Epson America, Inc.	
5	FX-85, Epson America, Inc.	
61	Others	

*70% of respondents voted in this category

Color Monitor*
% of

Votes	Product/Manufacturer	List Price
14	HX-12, Princeton Graphic Systems	$695
14	IBM Enhanced Color Display, IBM	$849
9	HX-12E, Princeton Graphic Systems	
8	IBM Color Display, IBM	
7	JC1401P3A MultiSync, NEC Home Electronics	
7	SR-12, Princeton Graphic Systems	
6	SR-12P, Princeton Graphic Systems	
35	Others	

*51% of respondents voted in this category

(Continued next page)

WORLD CLASS PC CONTEST (Continued)

Modem*
% of

Votes	Product/Manufacturer	List Price
26	Smartmodem 1200, Hayes Microcomputer Products, Inc.	$849
23	Smartmodem 1200B, Hayes Microcomputer Products, Inc.	
18	Smartmodem 2400, Hayes Microcomputer Products, Inc.	
5	Smartmodem 2400B, Hayes Microcomputer Products, Inc.	
4	Courier 2400, U.S. Robotics, Inc.	
24	Others	

*50% of respondents voted in this category

Memory Expansion Board*
% of

Votes	Product/Manufacturer	List Price
34	SixPakPlus, AST Research, Inc.	$395 (384K)
15	AboveBoard, Personal Computer Enhancement Operation, Intel Corp.	
9	Advantage, AST Research, Inc.	
9	RAMpage, AST Research, Inc.	
4	Expanded Quadboard, Quadram	
3	JRAM-3, Tall Tree Systems	
26	Others	

*46% of respondents voted in this category

Printer*
% of

Votes	Product/Manufacturer	List Price
19	LaserJet Plus, Hewlett-Packard	$3995
17	LaserJet, Hewlett-Packard	
6	LaserWriter, Apple Computer, Inc.	
4	Spinwriter Model 3550, NEC Information Systems, Inc.	
4	Quietwriter, IBM	
50	Others	

*41% of respondents voted in this category

(Continued next page)

WORLD CLASS PC CONTEST (Continued)

Graphics Board*

% of

Votes	Product/Manufacturer	List Price
19	IBM Enhanced Graphics Adapter, IBM	$524
18	Hercules Graphics Card, Hercules Computer Technology, Inc.	
9	Quadram QuadEGA+, Quadram Corp.	
9	Hercules Color Card, Hercules Computer Technology, Inc.	
5	Paradise Systems Modular Graphics Card, Paradise Systems	
5	IBM Color/Graphics Adapter, IBM	
35	Others	

*38% of respondents voted in this category

Hard Disk Drive*

% of

Votes	Product/Manufacturer	List Price
15	ST 225 (20MB), Seagate	$400
9	Bernoulli Box, Iomega Corp.	
8	Hardcard, Plus Development Corp.	
5	DriveCard, Mountain Computer, Inc.	
5	PC20, Qubie Distributing	
58	Others	

*35% of respondents voted in this category

Alternative Mass Storage*

% of

Votes	Product/Manufacturer	List Price
58	Bernoulli Box, Iomega Corp.	$3695
3	Core Tape, Core International	
3	Q60H, Tecmar, Inc.	
2	Everex Stream 60, Everex	
2	Sysgen XL, Sysgen, Inc.	
2	Masterflight 60, Kamerman Labs	
30	Others	

*25% of respondents voted in this category

(Continued next page)

WORLD CLASS PC CONTEST (Continued)

Plotter*

% of Votes	Product/Manufacturer	List Price
45	HP 7475A Plotter, Hewlett-Packard	$1895
10	HP 7550A Plotter, Hewlett-Packard	
9	HP 7470A Plotter, Hewlett-Packard	
4	HIPLOT DMP-40 Plotter, Houston Instrument	
3	1043 GT, California Computer Products, Inc.	
29	Others	

*22% of respondents voted in this category

Input Device*

% of Votes	Product/Manufacturer	List Price
36	Microsoft Mouse, Microsoft Corp.	$195
22	PC Mouse, Mouse Systems Corp.	
12	KB5151 Deluxe IBM PC Keyboard, Key Tronic Corp.	
4	The Mouse, Maynard Electronics	
3	Softstrip System Reader, Cauzin Systems, Inc.	
2	IBM PC Keyboard, IBM	
21	Others	

*20% of respondents voted in this category

Local Area Network*

% of Votes	Product/Manufacturer	List Price
12	EtherSeries, 3Com Corp.	$3565
11	Token-Ring, IBM	
10	PC Network, IBM	
9	Netware 4.61, Novell, Inc.	
8	Advanced Netware 1.01, Novell, Inc.	
50	Others	

*12% of respondents voted in this category

(Continued next page)

WORLD CLASS PC CONTEST (Continued)

Most Promising Newcomer - Hardware*
% of

Votes	Product/Manufacturer	List Price
9	Hardcard (10MB), Plus Development Corp.	$695
6	Softstrip System Reader, Cauzin Systems Inc.	
6	Compaq Portable II, Compaq Computer Corp.	
5	Leading Edge Model D, Leading Edge Products, Inc.	
4	AboveBoard, Personal Computer Enhancement Operations, Intel Corp.	
3	DriveCard, Mountain Computer, Inc.	
3	Tandy 3000, Tandy	
64	Others	

*23% of respondents voted in this category

Software

Word Processing*
% of

Votes	Product/Manufacturer	List Price
22	WordPerfect, WordPerfect Corp.	$495
14	Microsoft Word, Microsoft Corp.	
12	WordStar, MicroPro International Corp.	
7	Textra, Ann Arbor Software	
5	Wordstar 2000, MicroPro International Corp.	
5	MultiMate, Multimate Corp.	
35	Others	

*83% of respondents voted in this category

Spreadsheet*
% of

Votes	Product/Manufacturer	List Price
69	1-2-3, Lotus Development Corp.	$495
7	SuperCalc 3, Computer Associates	
6	Symphony, Lotus Development Corp.	
5	Multiplan, Microsoft Corp.	
3	VP-Planner, Paperback Software International	
10	Others	

*74% of respondents voted in this category
(Continued next page)

WORLD CLASS PC CONTEST (Continued)

Data Management*

% of Votes	Product/Manufacturer	List Price
45	dBase III Plus, Ashton-Tate	$695
12	R:base 5000, Microrim	
8	Reflex: The Analyst, Borland International Inc.	
5	Paradox, Ansa Software	
30	Others	

*60% of respondents voted in this category

Utilities*

% of Votes	Product/Manufacturer	List Price
60	Norton Utilities, Peter Norton Computing, Inc.	$99.95
4	SuperKey, Borland International, Inc.	
4	SideKick, Borland International, Inc.	
3	Copy II PC, Central Point Software, Inc.	
3	Direct Access, Delta Technologies	
26	Others	

*50% of respondents voted in this category

Communications*

% of Votes	Product/Manufacturer	List Price
39	Crosstalk XVI, Microstuf, Inc.	$195
22	Smartcom II, Hayes Microcomputer Products, Inc.	
11	PC-Talk III, Headlands Communications Corp.	
5	Qmodem, The Forbin Project	
3	Microsoft Access, Microsoft Corp.	
20	Others	

*41% of respondents voted in this category.

(Continued next page)

WORLD CLASS PC CONTEST (Continued)

Desktop Management*
% of

Votes	Product/Manufacturer	List Price
67	Sidekick, Borland International, Inc.	
	Not Copy Protected	$84.95
	Copy Protected	$54.95
8	The Desk Organizer, Warner Software, Inc.	
4	Microsoft Windows, Microsoft Corp.	
4	PolyWindows Desk, Polytron Corp.	
3	Pop-Up DeskSet Plus, Popular Programs	
14	Others	

*39% of respondents voted in this category

Programming Language*
% of

Votes	Product/Manufacturer	List Price
45	Turbo Pascal, Borland International, Inc.	$69.95
9	C Compiler, Microsoft Corp.	
5	BASIC Compiler, Microsoft Corp.	
5	Lattice C Compiler, Lifeboat Associates	
4	IBM BASIC, IBM	
32	Others	

*37% of respondents voted in this category

Integrated*
% of

Votes	Product/Manufacturer	List Price
34	Framework II, Ashton-Tate	$695
30	Symphony, Lotus Development Corp.	
9	1-2-3, Lotus Development Corp.	
8	Enable, The Software Group	
6	The Smart System, Innovative Software	
3	Ability, Migent, Inc.	
10	Others	

*32% of respondents voted in this category
(Continued next page)

WORLD CLASS PC CONTEST (Continued)

Games*

% of Votes	Product/Manufacturer	List Price
26	Microsoft Flight Simulator, Microsoft Corp.	$49.95
19	Jet, SubLogic Communications Corp.	
11	NFL Challenge, Xor Corp.	
5	Sargon III, Hayden Software	
5	Zork I, II, and III, Infocom, Inc.	
34	Others	

*31% of respondents voted in this category

Graphics--Business*

% of Votes	Product/Manufacturer	List Price
15	Chart-Master, Decision Resources, Inc.	$375
15	Microsoft Chart, Microsoft Corp.	$295
12	1-2-3, Lotus Development Corp.	
6	Energraphics, Enertronics Research, Inc.	
4	Graphwriter Combination Set, Graphic Communications, Inc.	
4	PC Storyboard, IBM	
3	Freelance, Graphic Communications, Inc.	
41	Others	

*25% of respondents voted in this category

File Management*

% of Votes	Product/Manufacturer	List Price
19	pfs:file, Software Publishing Corp.	$140
18	PC-File III, Buttonware, Inc.	
10	Reflex: The Analyst, Borland International, Inc.	
4	dBASE III, Ashton-Tate	
4	Nutshell, Leading Edge Products, Inc.	
45	Others	

*23% of respondents voted in this category

(Continued next page)

WORLD CLASS PC CONTEST (Continued)

Accounting*

% of

Votes	Product/Manufacturer	List Price
32	Dac-Easy Accounting, Dac Software, Inc.	$69.95
6	Accounting software, BPI Systems	
5	EasyBusiness Accounting Series, Computer Associates	
4	Solomon III, TLB Inc.	
4	Accounting software, Open Systems	
4	Peachtree's Business Accounting System, Peachtree Software, Inc.	
45	Others	

*22% of respondents voted in this category

Outline Processing*

% of

Votes	Product/Manufacturer	List Price
31	ThinkTank, Living Videotext, Inc.	$195
16	Ready, Living Videotext, Inc.	
16	Framework II, Ashton-Tate	
14	MaxThink, MaxThink, Inc.	
23	Others	

*19% of respondents voted in this category

Project Management*

% of

Votes	Product/Manufacturer	List Price
33	Harvard Total Project Manager, Software Publishing Corporation	$495
19	Microsoft Project, Microsoft Corp.	
11	Time Line, Breakthrough Software	
7	SuperProject, Computer Associates	
5	Primavera Project Planner, Primavera Systems, Inc.	
5	Project Manager Workbench, Applied Business Technology Corp.	
20	Others	

*18% of respondents voted in this category

(Continued next page)

WORLD CLASS PC CONTEST (Continued)

Tax Planning or Preparation*

% of

Votes	Product/Manufacturer	List Price
22	TurboTax, ChipSoft, Inc.	$65
20	Tax Preparer, HowardSoft	
16	PC/TaxCut, Best Programs Inc.	
12	Andrew Tobias' Managing Your Money, MECA	
2	1-2-3, Lotus Development Corp.	
28	Others	

*16% of respondents voted in this category

Graphics--CAD*

% of

Votes	Product/Manufacturer	List Price
65	AutoCAD, Autodesk, Inc.	$2500
9	ProDesignII, American Small Business Computers, Inc.	
2	In-a-Vision, Micrografx, Inc.	
2	Generic CAD, Generic Software, Inc.	
2	PC-Draw, Micrografx, Inc.	
20	Others	

*16% of respondents voted in this category

Applications Integrator*

% of

Votes	Product/Manufacturer	List Price
56	Microsoft Windows, Microsoft Corp.	$149
16	Desqview, Quarterdeck Office Systems	
6	TopView, IBM	
22	Others	

*15% of respondents voted in this category

(Continued next page)

WORLD CLASS PC CONTEST (Continued)

Personal Management*
% of

Votes	Product/Manufacturer	List Price
55	Andrew Tobias' Managing Your Money, MECA	$199.95
12	Dollars and Sense, Monogram	
4	PC Professional Finance Program II, Best Programs, Inc.	
4	Traveling SideKick, Borland International, Inc.	
3	Sylvia Porter's Personal Finance, Timeworks	
3	Continental Home Accountant Plus, Arrays, Inc./Continental Software	
19	Others	

*14% of respondents voted in this category

Micro-to-Mainframe Communications*
% of

Votes	Product/Manufacturer	List Price
13	IRMA, Digital Communications Associates, Inc	$1195
9	Crosstalk XVI, Microstuf, Inc.	
4	Kermit, The Columbia University Center for Computing Activities	
4	Barr HASP, Barr Systems, Inc.	
4	IBM 3101 Emulation, IBM	
3	SmarTerm 220, Persoft, Inc.	
3	Blast, Communications Research Group	
60	Others	

*13% of respondents voted in this category

Financial Modeling*
% of

Votes	Product/Manufacturer	List Price
39	1-2-3, Lotus Development Corp.	$495
14	Javelin, Javelin Software	
9	Andrew Tobias' Managing your Money, MECA	
6	Symphony, Lotus Development Corp.	
5	IFPS--Personal, Execucom Systems Corp.	
27	Others	

*12% of respondents voted in this category

(Continued next page)

WORLD CLASS PC CONTEST (Continued)

Investment*

% of Votes	Product/Manufacturer	List Price
40	Andrew Tobias' Managing Your Money, MECA	$199
6	Dow Jones Market Manager Plus, Dow Jones & Co., Inc.	
5	Dow Jones Market Analyzer, Dow Jones & Co., Inc.	
4	1-2-3, Lotus Development Corp.	
4	Value Screen, Value Line	
3	Dow Jones Market Analyzer Plus, Dow Jones & Co., Inc.	
3	Signal, Lotus Development Corp.	
35	Others	

*10% of respondents voted in this category

Training*

% of Votes	Product/Manufacturer	List Price
22	Training Power Series, American Training Intl	$75
8	Typing Tutor III, Simon & Schuster	
5	Cdex Corporation Series, Cdex Corporation	
5	Professor DOS, Individual Software, Inc.	
4	Teach Yourself dBASE III, American Training Intl	
56	Other	

*8% of respondents voted in this category

Education*

% of Votes	Product/Manufacturer	List Price
7	Study Program for the SAT, Barron's Educational Series	$49.95
6	Math Blaster, Davidson & Associates	
6	Spinnaker Early Learning Series, Spinnaker Software Corp.	
4	Mastering the SAT, CBS Software	
4	Newsroom, Springboard Software, Inc.	
4	Typing Tutor, Simon & Schuster, Inc.	
3	Master Type, Scarborough Systems. Inc	
66	Others	

*6% of respondents voted in this category

(Continued next page)

WORLD CLASS PC CONTEST (Continued)

Most Promising Newcomer--Software*

% of

Votes	Product/Manufacturer	List Price
21	Turbo Lightning, Borland International, Inc.	99.95
9	Javelin, Javelin Software	
8	Microsoft Windows, Microsoft Corp.	
7	Paradox, Ansa Software	
4	Reflex: The Analyst, Borland International, Inc.	
2	Q&A, Symantec Corp.	
49	Others	

*31% of respondents voted in this category

SOFTSEL COMPUTER PRODUCTS, INC.
SOFTSEL HOT LIST AWARDS
November 11, 1986

"Hot List Awards are presented yearly to hardware and software vendors whose products have achieved consistently high sales during the preceding year at Softsel. Softsel's Hot List is calculated from Softsel sales to resellers and has become an industry standard for measuring hardware and software sales success."--Softsel Computer Products, Inc.

Reprinted with permission from Softsel Computer Products, Inc., November 11, 1986. Copyright 1986, Softsel Computer Products, Inc., Inglewood, CA.

BEST-SELLING PRODUCTS 1986

Software

Business: Lotus 1-2-3
Home & Education: Broderbund's Print Shop
Recreation: Microsoft Flight Simulator
Systems & Utilities: Norton Computing's Norton Utilities

Hardware

Accessories: CH Products' Mach III
Boards, Modems, & Interfaces: Hayes' Smartmodem 1200
Disk Drives & Storage Devices: Tecmar's QIC-60H Tape Backup
Monitors: Amdek's Video 310A
Printers: Citizen's MSP-10 Dot Matrix

BEST-SELLING NEW PRODUCTS 1986

Software

Business: Ashton-Tate's dBase III Plus
Home & Education: Springboard's Certificate Maker
Recreation: Epyx's Winter Games
Systems & Utilities: Fifth Generation's Fastback

Hardware

Accessories: Curtis' Safe Strip
Boards, Modems, & Interfaces: Intel's Above Board/AT
Disk Drives & Storage Devices: Maynard's OnBoard 20 MB
Monitors: NEC Home Electronic's JC 1401 Multisync
Printers: Citizen's 120D Dot Matrix

SOFTWARE PUBLISHERS ASSOCIATION
EXCELLENCE IN SOFTWARE AWARDS
April 18, 1986

The two-year old Software Publishers Association presents annual awards to the "best" software programs in 16 categories. The winning products were selected by the 150 members in a mail vote managed by an accounting firm. All nominees are listed for each category and winners are noted with an *.--COMPUTER INDUSTRY ALMANAC.

From this list COMPUTER INDUSTRY ALMANAC has selected only the industry-related companies.

Reprinted with permission from SOFTWARE PUBLISHERS ASSOCIATION, April 18, 1986. Copyright 1986 by Software Publishers Association, Washington, DC.

BEST SOFTWARE PRODUCT

Fantavision	Broderbund Software
Deluxe Paint	Electronic Arts
Blueprint for Decision Making	MCE
*Windows	Microsoft Corporation
Newsroom	Springboard Software
Business Filevision	Telos Software Products

BEST BUSINESS PRODUCT

D Base III+	Ashton-Tate
*Excel	Microsoft Corporation
Windows	Microsoft Corporation
MacOneWrite	Sierra On-Line
Business Filevision	Telos Software Products

BEST PRODUCTIVITY PRODUCT

Pagemaker	Aldus Corporation
Macdraw	Apple Computer
*Excel	Microsoft Corporation
HomeWord Plus	Sierra On-Line
Newsroom	Springboard Software
Sylvia Porter's Financial Planner	Timeworks

(Continued next page)

SOFTWARE PUBLISHERS ASSOCIATION
EXCELLENCE IN SOFTWARE AWARDS (Continued)

BEST LEARNING PRODUCT

*Where in the World is Carmen...	Broderbund
Blueprint for Decision Making	MCE
Balance of Power	Mindscape
Homework Helper Math	Spinnaker Software

BEST CREATIVITY PRODUCT

Gamemaker	Activision
Fantavision	Broderbund Software
*Deluxe Paint	Electronic Arts
Videoworks	Hayden Software
*Newsroom	Springboard Software
Stickybear Printer	Weekly Reader

BEST SIMULATION PRODUCT

Kennedy Approach	MicroProse
Silent Service	MicroProse
Balance of Power	Mindscape
*Jet	Sublogic
NFL Challenge	Xor Corporation

BEST ENTERTAINMENT PRODUCT

Hacker	Activision
*Deja Vu	Mindscape
Ultima IV	Origin Systems
King's Quest II	Sierra On-Line
Airborne	Silicon Beach
NFL Challenge	Xor Corporation

BEST NEW USE OF A COMPUTER

Little Computer People	Activision
*Pagemaker	Aldus Corporation
Blueprint for Decision Making	MCE
Dinner at Eight	Rubicon Publishing
Business Filevision	Telos Software

(Continued next page)

SOFTWARE PUBLISHERS ASSOCIATION
EXCELLENCE IN SOFTWARE AWARDS (Continued)

BEST NEW WORLD

Hacker	Activision
Little Computer People	Activision
A Mind Forever Voyaging	Infocom
*Deja Vu	Mindscape
Ultima IV	Origin Systems

BEST SOUND (EFFECTS, MUSIC)

*Deluxe Music Constr. Set	Elec. Arts: Mac
One-on-One	Electronic Arts: Amiga
Kennedy Approach	Microprose: C-64
Black Cauldron	Sierra On-Line: Apple II
Airborne	Silicon Beach: Macintosh

BEST USER INTERFACE

Deluxe Paint	Electronic Arts: Amiga
*Window	Microsoft: IBM
Deja Vu	Mindscape: Macintosh
HomeWord Plus	Sierra On-Line: Apple II

BEST GRAPHICS

Hardball	Accolade: C-64
Fantavision	Broderbund Software: Apple II
*Deluxe Paint	Electronic Arts: Amiga
VideoWorks	Hayden Software: Macintosh
Perry Mason	Spinnaker Software: C-64

BEST TECHNICAL ACHIEVEMENT

Fantavision	Broderbund: Apple II
Deluxe Paint	Electronic Arts: Amiga
Skyfox	Electronic Arts: C-64
*Windows	Microsoft: IBM
Jet	Sublogic: IBM

(Continued next page)

SOFTWARE PUBLISHERS ASSOCIATION
EXCELLENCE IN SOFTWARE AWARDS (Continued)

BEST SOFTWARE PACKAGING

FightNight	Accolade
Cornerstone	Infocom
*Jazz	Lotus Development Corporation
Halley Project	Mindscape
MacOneWrite	Sierra On-Line
Gato	Spectrum Holobyte
Perry Mason	Spinnaker Software

4 PEOPLE

AMERICAN ELECTRONICS ASSOCIATION (AEA)
MEDALS OF ACHIEVEMENT

These awards, presented annually since 1959 by the American Electronics Association, are given for contributions to the advancement of electronics.--COMPUTER INDUSTRY ALMANAC.

Reprinted with permission from the American Electronics Association, 1986. Copyright 1986 by American Electronics Association, Palo Alto, CA.

1985 Ed E. Ferrey, American Electronics Association
1984 An Wang, Wang Laboratories
1983 John G. Linville, Stanford University
1982 Frank T. Cary, IBM
1981 Kenneth H. Olsen, Digital Equipment
1980 William J. Perry, U.S. Department of Defense
1979 William C. Norris, Control Data

ASSOCIATION FOR COMPUTING MACHINERY (ACM)
AWARDS PROGRAM

"The Association for Computing Machinery conducts an awards program to recognize excellence and to honor those individuals who have made exceptional contributions to the advancement of computing and the computing profession. Recipients may or may not be members of the Association."--Association for Computing Machinery.

Reprinted with permission from the Association for Computing Machinery, 1986. Copyright 1986 by Association for Computing Machinery, New York, NY.

A.M. TURING AWARD

"The A.M. Turing Award is presented 'to an individual selected for contributions of a technical nature to the computing community.' This award is presented in commemoration of Dr. A.M. Turing, an English mathematician who made many important contributions to the field of computing. It has been presented annually since 1966."--Association for Computing Machinery.

1986   John E. Hopcroft, Cornell University, Ithaca, NY and Robert E. Tarjan, Princeton Univ., Princeton, NJ
"For fundamental achievements in the design and analysis of algorithms and data structures."--Association for Computing Machinery.

1985   Richard Karp, University of California, Berkeley
"For his continuing contributions to the theory of algorithms including the development of efficient algorithms for network flow and other combinatorial optimization problems, the identification of polynomial-time computability with the intuitive notion of algorithmic efficiency, and, most notably, contributions to the theory of NP-completeness. Karp introduced the now standard methodology for proving problems to be NP-complete which has led to the identification of many theoretical and practical problems as being computationally difficult."--Association for Computing Machinery.

1984   Nicklaus Wirth
1983   Dennis M. Ritchie and Ken Thompson
1982   Stephen A. Cook
1981   Edgar F. Codd
1980   C. Anthony R. Hoare

ASSOCIATION FOR COMPUTING MACHINERY (ACM)
AWARDS PROGRAM (Continued)

SOFTWARE SYSTEM AWARD

"The Software System Award has been presented since 1983 'for a software system that has had a lasting influence.' The award is made either to an institution or to individuals responsible for developing and introducing the software system."--Association for Computing Machinery.

1986 Donald E. Knuth, Stanford University, Stanford, CA
"For the design and implementation of TEX, an innovative tool for the computer composition of documents of high typographical quality."--Association for Computing Machinery.

1985 Daniel Bricklin and Robert Frankston, Lotus Development Corporation, Cambridge, MA
"For the invention of VisiCalc, a new metaphor for data manipulation that galvanized personal computing in industry."--Association for Computing Machinery.

1984 Charles P. Thacker, Robert W. Taylor, and Butler W. Lampson

1983 Dennis M. Ritchie and Ken Thompson

ASSOCIATION FOR COMPUTING MACHINERY (ACM)
AWARDS PROGRAM (Continued)

DISTINGUISHED SERVICE AWARD

"The Distinguished Service Award is presented 'on the basis of value and degree of service to the computing community.' This award has been presented since, 1970."--Association for Computing Machinery.

1986 Clair G. Maple (Posthumous)
"For a lifetime of innovative contributions and distinguished leadership in the use of computers in higher education."--Association for Computing Machinery.

1985 Jean Sammet, IBM Corporation, Bethesda, MD
"For dedicated, tireless and dynamic leadership in service to ACM and the computing community; For advancing the art and science of computer programming languages and recording its history."--Association for Computing Machinery.

1984 Saul Rosen
1983 Grace Murray Hopper
1982 Anthony Ralston
1981 Aaron Finerman
1980 Bernard Galler

ASSOCIATION FOR COMPUTING MACHINERY (ACM)
AWARDS PROGRAM (Continued)

GRACE MURRAY HOPPER AWARD

"The Grace Murray Hopper Award is presented to 'the outstanding young computer professional of the year...selected on the basis of a single recent major technical or service contribution.' The prize is supplied by the Univac Division of Sperry Corporation and has been presented since 1971."--Association for Computing Machinery.

1986   William N. Joy, Sun Microsystems, Inc., Mountain View, CA
"For his work on the Berkeley UNIX Operating System as a designer, integrator, and implementor of many of its advanced features including virtual memory networking, the C-shell, and the VI screen editor."--Association for Computing Machinery.

1985   Cordell Green, Kestrel Institute, Palo Alto, CA
"For establishing several key aspects of the theoretical basis for logic programming and providing a resolution theorem prover to carry out a programming task by constructing the result which the computer program is to compute. For proving the constructive technique correct and for presenting an effective method for constructing the answer; these contributions providing an early theoretical basis for Prolog and logic programming."--Association for Computing Machinery.

1984   Daniel H. H. Ingalls, Jr.
1982   Brian K. Reid
1981   Daniel S. Bricklin
1980   Robert M. Metcalfe

ASSOCIATION FOR COMPUTING MACHINERY (ACM)
AWARDS PROGRAM (Continued)

ECKERT-MAUCHLY AWARD

"The Eckert-Mauchly Award is a joint ACM-IEEE Computer Society award 'presented for
technical contributions to computer and digital systems architecture.' This award has been
presented since 1979."--Association for Computing Machinery.

1986 Harvey G. Cragon, University of Texas at Austin
   "For major contributions to computer and digital systems architecture, especially for work
   performed during 25 years of service at Texas Instruments, Inc. Cragon designed and
   constructed the first integrated-circuit computer and the first TTL computer. He worked
   on the design of the TI advanced scientific computer and served as principal architect of
   the TMS 320 signal processing microcomputer."--Association for Computing Machinery.

1985 Dr. John Cocke, IBM Corp, Yorktown Heights, NY
   "For contributions to high performance computer architecture through lookahead,
   parallelism and pipeline utilization, and to reduced instruction set computer architecture
   through the exploitation of hardware-software tradeoffs and computer utilization."--
   Association for Computing Machinery.

1984 Jack B. Dennis
1983 Tom Kilburn
1982 C. Gordon Bell
1981 Wesley A. Clark
1980 Maurice V. Wilkes

ASSOCIATION FOR COMPUTING MACHINERY (ACM)
AWARDS PROGRAM (Continued)

PRESIDENT'S AWARD FOR CONTRIBUTIONS TO COMPUTER SCIENCE

"The President's Award for Contributions to Computer Science is presented for 'outstanding leadership and contributions that have provided major advances in the computing field.'"--Association for Computing Machinery.

1985 Dr. Robert E. Kahn, Director, Information Techniques Office, Defense Advanced Research Projects Agency

"During his tenure at the Defense Advanced Research Projects Agency of the Department of Defense, Dr. Kahn provided strong and imaginative leadership for one of the most wide-ranging and important research programs in computer science, computer-communications, and artificial intelligence. In the past two years, Dr. Kahn was instrumental in the establishment of the Strategic Computing Initiative, a DoD program that has far-reaching implications in the development of future generations of information technology."--Association for Computing Machinery.

ACM SIGCSE AWARD

"The ACM SIGCSE Award is presented for 'outstanding contributions to computer science education.' The award has been presented annually since 1982."--Association for Computing Machinery.

1986 Donald Knuth, Professor of Computer Science, Stanford University, Palo Alto, CA
"Donald Knuth is developer of the TEX Typesetting System and is author of the three volume series on THE ART OF COMPUTER PROGRAMMING."--Association for Computing Machinery.

COMPUTER RESELLER NEWS
LIFE AT THE TOP: THE INDUSTRY POWER BROKERS
November 10, 1986

Each year COMPUTER RESELLER NEWS ranks the 25 most influential executives in the personal computer industry. This year's list contains the names considered by COMPUTER RESELLER NEWS to merit this recognition.--COMPUTER INDUSTRY ALMANAC.

Reprinted with permission from COMPUTER RESELLER NEWS, November 10, 1986. Copyright 1986 by CMP Publications, Inc., Manhasset, NY.

1- Bill Gates, Microsoft
2- Ed Faber, ComputerLand
3- Dave Norman, Businessland
4- Bill Lowe, IBM
5- Rick Inatome, Inacomp
6- Jeff McKeever, MicroAge
7- Bill Campbell, Apple
8- Michael Shane, Leading Edge
9- Harvey Flam, FHP
10- John Martin-Musumeci, Solitaire
11- Ray Noorda, Novell
12- Jay Gottlieb, Computer Factory
13- Rod Canion, Compaq
14- Ed Esber, Ashton-Tate
15- Victor Alhadeff, Egghead
16- John Roach, Tandy
17- Avner Parnes, MBI
18- Alan Hald, MicroAge
19- Bert Helfinstein, Entre
20- Frank Barry, Ingram
21- Norm Dinnsen, ComputerLand of Los Angeles
22- Will Luden, PacTel
23- Paul Brainerd, Aldus
24- Mike Jackson, Qualitech
25- Mickey Dude, Microvision

COMPUTER RETAIL NEWS
THE INDUSTRY'S 25 MOST INFLUENTIAL EXECUTIVES
November 18, 1985

Each year COMPUTER RETAIL NEWS ranks the 25 most influential executives in the personal computer industry. This year's list contains the names of COMPUTER RETAIL NEWS' choices for this recognition.--COMPUTER INDUSTRY ALMANAC.

Reprinted with permission from COMPUTER RETAIL NEWS, November 18, 1986. Copyright by CMP Publications, Inc., Manhasset, NY.

1- Dave Norman, Businessland
2- Bill Millard, ComputerLand
3- Victor Goldberg, IBM
4- Avner Parnes, MBI
5- John Sculley, Apple
6- John Martin-Musumeci, Micro/Vest
7- Rod Canion, Compaq
8- Ken Carpenter, First Software
9- Alan Hald, MicroAge
10- Ben Rosen, Sevin Rosen
11- Mitch Kapor, Lotus
12- Ed Esber, Ashton-Tate
13- Rick Inatome, Inacomp
14- John Dobson, ITT Finance
15- Ed Ramos, Computone/FIS
16- Will Luden, PacTel
17- Jay Gottlieb, Computer Factory
18- Gordon Hoffstein, Microamerica
19- Bruce Burdick, ComputerLand/Kansas
20- Egil Juliussen, Future Computing
21- Ron Siegel, Gateway
22- Dave Wagman, Softsel
23- Michele Preston, L.F. Rothschild
24- Safi Qureshey, AST Research
25- Sheldon Adelson, Interface Group

ELECTRONIC BUSINESS
EXCELLENT EXECUTIVES 1986
April 1, 1986

"Electronic Business recognizes a group of excellent executives selected by surveying 2500 industry analysts, consultants, and managers drawn from the magazine's subscribers. Those polled were asked to select their choice for the best executives in each of 10 categories based on marketing, financial, organizational and motivational skills."--ELECTRONIC BUSINESS.

Reprinted with permission from ELECTRONIC BUSINESS, April 1, 1986. Copyright 1986 by Reed Publishing USA, a division of Reed Holdings Inc., Newton, MA.

Edward Botwinick
Timeplex Inc.
Communication Equipment

John H. Krehbiel
Molex Inc.
Components

Joseph R. Canion
COMPAQ Computer Corp.
Computers/Commercial

Kenneth Levy
KLA Instruments Corp.
Production Equipment

Wilfred J. Corrigan
LSI Logic Corp.
Semiconductors

Kenneth H. Olsen
Digital Equipment Corp.
Computers/Industrial

Alexander V. d'Arbeloff
Teradyne Inc.
Test and Measurement

James L. Patterson
Quantum Corp.
Computer Peripherals

Anthony R. Hamilton
Hamilton/Avnet Electronics
Distributors

Bernard L. Schwartz
Loral Corp.
Military Electronics

ELECTRONIC INDUSTRIES ASSOCIATION
MEDAL OF HONOR

The Electronic Industries Association (EIA) Medal of Honor awards are presented "to an indivdidual who has made outstanding contributions to the advancement of the electronic industries." This award has been presented annually since 1952.--COMPUTER INDUSTRY ALMANAC.

Reprinted with permission from Electronic Industries Association, 1986. Copyright 1986 by Electronic Industries Association, Washington, D.C.

1986   Sanford McDonnell, McDonnell Douglas Corporation
1985   Dr. Simon Ramo, TRW Incorporated
1984   Allen E. Puckett, Hughes Aircraft Corporation
1983   Charles L. Brown, American Telephone & Telegraph
1982   William C. Norris, Control Data Corporation
1981   William J. Weisz, Motorola Inc.
1980   Arthur A. Collins, Arthur A. Collins, Inc.

GARTNER GROUP INC.
EXCELLENCE IN TECHNOLOGY AWARD

"Starting in 1985, this award has been given annually to a CEO in recognition of outstanding leadership of his firm in the application of information technology. Among the criteria of the selection committee, a candidate needed to demonstrate support of advanced information technology which contributed to (1) his company's leadership in its industry; (2) increased internal productivity within the last 3 years. The selection committee is comprised of prominent professionals in the areas of aerospace, finance, government, manufacturing, petroleum, telecommunications, transportation, and utilities."--Gartner Group Inc.

Reprinted with permission from Gartner Group Inc., 1986. Copyright 1986 by Gartner Group Inc. Stamford, CT.

1986 Frederick W. Smith, President, CEO, Chairman and Founder of Federal Express

1985 Robert L. Crandall, Chairman & CEO of AMR Corporation and American Airlines Inc.

INFOMART
HALL OF FAME

"Infomart's Information Processing Hall of Fame, formed in 1985, recognizes individuals who have made significant scientific, technological and business contributions to the information processing industry."--Infomart.

1986 Hall of Fame Inductees

Philip D. Estridge, IBM vice president whose division fostered the IBM-PC.

H. Ross Perot, chairman of EDS Corp., who pioneered yesterday's and today's state-of-the-art data processing techniques.

1985 Hall of Fame Inductees

Dr. Gene Amdahl, considered the father of high-end, plug-compatible computers.

Jack St. Clair Kilby, inventor of the integrated circuit.

Sen. Frank Lautenberg, founder of the first major, worldwide computer service company.

Dr. John von Neumann, innovative mathematician who promoted the advantages of binary numbers in computer construction.

Drs. John Mauchly and J. Presper Eckert, co-developers of the ENIAC system that incorporated many of the components of modern computers.

Commodore Grace Hopper, developer of COBOL computer language and leading technological exponent.

INSTITUTE OF ELECTRICAL AND ELECTRONICS ENGINEERS (IEEE)
AWARDS PROGRAM

Each year the IEEE selects winners for its awards program to recognize individuals who have made outstanding contributions in the various areas in which it issues awards.--COMPUTER INDUSTRY ALMANAC.

MEDAL OF HONOR (IEEE's HIGHEST TRIBUTE)

1986   Jack St. Clair Kilby

"For his pioneering contributions to semi-conductor integrated circuit technology." Kilby left Texas Instruments, where he had worked since 1958, to become an independent consultant in 1970. Upon receiving a BSEE degree from the University of Illinois in 1947, Kilby joined the Centralab Division of Globe Union Inc., where he aided in the design and development of semiconductor devices with ceramic-based silk-screened circuits. Kirby holds more than 50 U.S. patents and the rank of distinguished professor of electrical engineering at Texas A&M University."--Institute of Electrical and Electronics Engineers.

ALEXANDER GRAHAM BELL MEDAL

1986   Bernard Widrow

"For fundamental contributions to adaptive filtering, adaptive noise and echo cancellation, and adaptive antennas." Widrow has been an electrical engineering professor at Stanford University since 1959. Upon completing his doctorate at MIT in 1956, he joined the MIT faculty as an assistant professor and researched adaptive filters and adaptive pattern-recognition systems, which led to the development of the Least Mean Square algorithm. He also co-authored a textbook on adaptive signal processing." --Institute of Electrical and Electronics Engineers.

INSTITUTE OF ELECTRICAL AND ELECTRONICS ENGINEERS (IEEE)
AWARDS PROGRAM (Continued)

EDISON MEDAL

1986 James L. Flanagan
"For a career of innovation and leadership in speech communication science and
technology." Flanagan is director of the Information Principles Research Laboratory at
AT&T Bell Laboratories. Flanagan joined AT&T in 1957, supervising speech, auditory,
and acoustics research. He has written over 140 technical papers and holds 45 U.S.
patents."--Institute of Electrical and Electronics Engineers.

FOUNDERS MEDAL

1986 George H. Heilmeier
"For outstanding leadership in the planning and management of semiconductor and
electronics research and development." Heilmeier has been a senior vice president and
chief technical officer of Texas Instruments since 1983. He holds 15 U.S. patents and is a
member of the National Academy of Engineering and the Defense Science Board."--
Institute of Electrical and Electronics Engineers.

THE MORRIS N. LIEBMAN MEMORIAL AWARD

1986 Bishnu S. Atal and Fumitada Itakura
"For pioneering contributions to linear predictive coding for speech processing."--
Institute of Electrical and Electronics Engineers.
Atal, a researcher at Bell Telephone Laboratories in Murray Hill, NJ, has worked in many
areas of acoustics, including speech coding and computer simulation of sound
transmission in rooms. He also served as a lecturer in acoustics at the Indian Institute of
Science in Bangalore. Atal is a past winner of the IEEE Centennial Medal.

Itakura, an electrical engineering professor at Nagoya University, Japan, was formerly a
researcher in speech analysis and synthesis at Nippon Telegraph & Telephone Corp. In
1969, he originated an application of partial correlation analysis, and developed the
Parcor vocoding system for narrowband speech coding and voice response. He was also
a resident visitor at Bell Telephone Laboratories in Murray Hill, NJ.

INSTITUTE OF ELECTRICAL AND ELECTRONICS ENGINEERS (IEEE)
AWARDS PROGRAM (Continued)

EMANUEL R. PIORE AWARD

1986 David C. Evans and Ivan E. Sutherland
"For pioneering work in the development of interactive computer graphics systems and contributions to computer science education."--Institute of Electrical and Electronics Engineers.

Evans, cofounder of Evans & Sutherland Computer Corp. and now its chairman and chief executive officer, did early work in incremental computers and in numerical controls for machine tools. He also contributed to the development of time-shared systems for interactive use and continuous-tone real-time graphics systems. Prior to forming his company, Evans was director of engineering in the Bendix Computer Division, and a professor of electrical engineering and computer science at the University of Utah.

Sutherland, cofounder and director of Evans & Sutherland and now vice president and technical director of Sutherland, Sproull and Associates Inc., is a general partner in Advanced Technology Ventures and a director of several private corporations. He has taught at Harvard College, the University of Utah, and the California Institute of Technology, and was also a senior scientist for the Rand Corp.

THE CHARLES PROTEUS STEINMETZ AWARD

1986 Chester H. Page
"For outstanding contributions to terminology, quantities, and units in national and international standards."--Institute of Electrical and Electronics Engineers.

Page, a retired coordinator of international standards activities at the National Bureau of Standards, joined the NBS in 1941. He was involved in designing proximity fuses, and later headed early computer projects. In 1960, Page became chief of the electricity division and later served as the coordinator of international standards activities of the NBS Institute for Basic Standards. Page was also active in the standards activities of the IRE, one of the IEEE's predecessors.

INSTITUTE OF ELECTRICAL AND ELECTRONICS ENGINEERS (IEEE)
COMPUTER SOCIETY
AWARDS PROGRAM

The Computer Society of the Institute of Electrical and Electronics Engineers annually issues technical awards in several categories to individuals in recognition of their contributions.-- COMPUER INDUSTRY ALMANAC.

W. WALLACE McDOWELL AWARD

The W. Wallace McDowell Award is established through a grant from IBM. Prior winners include Seymour Cray, C. Gordon Bell, Gene Amdahl, and Donald Knuth.

1985   William D. Stecker, Digital Equipment Corporation
"For his contributions as principal designer of the VAX architecture."

COMPUTER PIONEER AWARDS FOR 1985

John G. Kemeny, for the development of BASIC.

John McCarthy, director of the Artificial Intelligence Laboratory at Stanford University, for the development of LISP.

Alan Perlis, for work in computer language translation.

Ivan Sutherland, for the development of Sketchpad.

David Wheeler, professor of computer science at Cambridge University, for developing the first assembly language system with library subroutine capability.

Heinz Zemanek, for building MAILUEFTERL (May breeze) in 1959 in Vienna, the first Austrian electronic computer.

COMPUTER ENTREPRENEUR AWARDS FOR 1985

William Norris, founder and chairman emeritus of Control Data Corporation.

Kenneth H. Olsen, founder and president of Digital Equipment Corporation.

INSTITUTE OF ELECTRICAL AND ELECTRONICS ENGINEERS (IEEE)
COMPUTER SOCIETY
AWARDS PROGRAM Continued)

ECKERT-MAUCHLY AWARD FOR 1985

John Cocke, for contributions to high performance architecture through look-ahead, parallelism, and pipeline utilization, and for contributions to reduced instruction set computer architecture through the exploitation of hardware-software trade-offs and compiler optimization.

TECHNICAL ACHIEVEMENT AWARD FOR 1985

Algirdas Avizienis, for sustained contributions to the area of fault tolerant computing.

INSTITUTE OF ELECTRICAL AND ELECTRONIC ENGINEERS (IEEE)
COMPUTER SOCIETY
FELLOWS

In 1986 the IEEE Fellows Committee conferred the title of Fellow on 49 Computer Society members. The title recognizes the outstanding contributions made by senior IEEE members in one or more of the following fields: electrical engineering, electronics, computer engineering and computer science, and the allied branches of engineering and related arts and sciences. The listing follows in alphabetical order.--COMPUTER INDUSTRY ALMANAC.

Tilak K. Agerwala, Yorktown Heights, New York, for leadership in the development of very high performance computers.

Vishwani D. Agrawal, New Providence, New Jersey, for contributions to probalistic testing techniques for large integrated cuicuits.

Robert R. Boorstyn, Brooklyn, New York, for contributions to the theory and development of multihop packet radio networks.

Balakrishnan Chandrasekaran, Columbus, Ohio, for contributions to statistical pattern recognition and artificial intelligence.

Shi-Kuo Chang, Glencoe, Illinois, for contributions to pictorial information processing techniques, and leadership in computer engineering research and education.

Arthur C. M. Chen, Schenectady, New York, for contrbutions to the application of computer technology in medical electronics and to the automation of electric power distribution systems.

Maurizio Decina, Milan, Italy, for contributions to digital communications and to voice/data packet switching.

Hugo J. DeMan, Leuven, Belgium, for contributions to simulation, analysis, and optimization of devices, MOS circuits, and sampled data systems.

Bruce A. Eisenstein, Philadelphia, Pennsylvania, for contributions to signal processing.

Robert E. Fenton, Columbus, Ohio, for contributions to control systems for automatic control of high-speed highway vehicles.

David K. Ferry, Tempe, Arizona, for contributions to the study of carrier transport in semiconductors and the physics of submicron semiconductor devices.

INSTITUTE OF ELECTRICAL AND ELECTRONICS ENGINEERS (IEEE)
COMPUTER SOCIETY
FELLOWS (Continued)

James D. Foley, Washington, DC, for contributions to computer graphics.

Kenneth F. Galloway, Washington, DC, for contributions to the study of radiation effects in microelectronics.

Erol Gelenbe, Orsay, France, for leadership in the development of computer system performance evaluation.

Richard D. Gitlin, Holmdel, New Jersey, for contributions to data communication techniques.

Jacob Goldberg, Menlo Park, California, for contributions to fault-tolerant computer systems.

Claude J. Gueguen, Paris, France, for contributions to multivariable system theory and parametric systems modeling.

Ernest L. Hall, Cincinnati, Ohio, for contributions to computer image processing and recognition.

Carl Hammer, Washington, DC, for contributions to computer sciences and to the design of decision-sequential algorithms.

Gene H. Hostetter, Huntington Beach, California, for contributions to the theory and algorithms for observers of complex control systems, and to engineering education.

Kai Hwang, Los Angeles, California, for contributions to the theory, design, and applications of digital computers, particularly in the areas of digital arithmetic, systems architecture, and parallel processing.

Richard C. Jaeger, Auburn, Alabama, for contributions to device technology for high-performance analog and digital computer systems.

Yukio Kagawa, Toyama, Japan, for the development of the finite and boundary element methods and their applications to acoustic and electroacoustic simulation.

Gideon Kantor, Garrett Park, Maryland, for leadership and contributions to microwave and radio frequency diathermy and hyperthermia.

Murat Kunt, Lausanne, Switzerland, for contributions to research and educational programs for signal and image processing in Europe.

INSTITUTE OF ELECTRICAL AND ELECTRONICS ENGINEERS (IEEE)
COMPUTER SOCIETY
FELLOWS (Continued)

Glen G. Langdon, Jr., San Jose, California, for contributions to the Brazillian computer industry, computer design education, and data compression coding algorithms.

Alan J. Laub, Santa Barbara, California, for contributions to algorithms, numerical analysis, and mathematical software for control and systems theory.

Meir M. Lehman, London, England, for leadership in computer design, programming process analysis, development and measurement, study of large software systems, software technology, and computing science education.

Steven E. Levinson, Westfield, New Jersey, for contributions to the theory and application of statistical pattern recognition to automatic speech recognition.

James Chih-I. Lin, Chicago, Illinois, for contributions to understanding the biological effects of pulsed microwaves in the inner ear of humans.

Chung Laung Liu, Urbana, Illinois, for contributions to logical design, the theoretical foundations of computing, and engineering education.

Daniel J. Love, Hacienda Heights, California, for contributions to ground and phase fault protection for industrial and utility distribution systems.

Raman K. Mehra, Cambridge, Massachusetts, for contributions to development of theories of identification, estimation, and optimal control and their applications in aerospace and industrial systems.

Heinrich Meyr, Aachen, West Germany, for contributions to the theory of tracking loops and synchronization.

Leopold Neumann, Peabody, Massachusetts, for contributions to the field of medical electronics.

Jurg Nievergelt, Chapel Hill, North Carolina, for contributions to the field of data and file structures.

William H. Oldendorf, Los Angeles, California, for contributions to physiological scanning and the development of computerized axial tomography and magnetic resonance scanners.

INSTITUTE OF ELECTRICAL AND ELECTRONICS ENGINEERS (IEEE)
COMPUTER SOCIETY
FELLOWS (Continued)

Edward S. Parrish, Jr., Charlottesville, Virginia, for leadership in engineering education and contributions to microprocessor-based pictorial pattern recognition.

Barry S. Perlman, Cranbury, New Jersey, for contributions to microwave solid-state device and circuit design, and leadership in computer-aided methods for microwave engineering.

J. William Poduska, Belmont, Massachusetts, for leadership in the establishment of the first large virtual address minicomputers and distributed, cooperating workstations.

Louis L. Scharf, Boulder, Colorado, for contributions to the theory and practice of statistical signal processing.

H. Gene Slottow, Urbana, Illinois, for contributions to the electronic device field in the invention and development of plasma display panels.

Odo J. Struger, Cleveland, Ohio, for leadership and contributions to the development of programmable controllers.

Ching Y. Suen, Montreal, Canada, for contributions to research and development in optical character recognition and language processing by computer.

Samuel Chin-Chong Tseng, Tokyo, Japan, for innovative research and development of advanced workstations with multilingual capabilities.

Rein Turn, Pacific Palisades, California, for contributions to providing privacy protection and security in computer systems.

Tibor Vamos, Budapest, Hungary, for contributions to power system control, industrial robot vision systems, artificial intelligence for flexible manufacturing, and for leadership in international technical affairs.

Makoto Watanabe, Kanagawa, Japan, for contributions and leadership in microelectronics research and development in the fields of LSI and VLSI.

Hwa-Nien Yu, Yorktown Heights, New York, for leadership and contributions to advanced technology for VLSI circuits.

NATIONAL COMPUTER GRAPHICS ASSOCIATION (NCGA)
THE NCGA AWARD
January 17, 1987

"This annual award honors outstanding contributions to the field of computer graphics. Nominations for the award are based on the following criteria: innovation, impact, value, vision, and significance of the contribution. The NCGA Award is presented at the VideoGala dinner held during the annual NCGA Conference."--National Computer Graphics Association.

Reprinted with permission from the National Computer Graphics Association, 1986. Copyright 1986 by National Computer Graphics Association, Fairfax, VA.

1986

David C. Evans
Chairman & CEO
Evans and Sutherland
Salt Lake City, UT

1985

Harry E. Richter
Consultant
IBM Corporation
Milford, CT

Patrick J. Hanratty
President
Manufacturing and Consulting Services Inc.
Irvine, CA

1984

John S. Reed
Vice President and General Manager
Information Display Group
Tektronics
Wilsonville, OR

1983

William D. Beeby
President
William Beeby Associates
Kent, WA

DIRECTORY OF COMPUTER INDUSTRY PEOPLE

In this section COMPUTER INDUSTRY ALMANAC lists in alphabetical order over 1000 computer industry movers and shakers. Included are company founders, chairmen, presidents, and CEOs as well as analysts, gurus, inventors, venture capitalists and others. No such list can ever be current or complete. We anticipate and welcome your suggested additions and corrections.

Joseph **Abrams**
President and COO, AGS Computer Inc.

David R. **Addison**
Chairman, President & CEO, Masstor Systems Corporation

Sheldon **Adelson**
In 1973 founded The Interface Group, Inc., which created the first COMDEX Show held in December 1979 and has produced all COMDEX Shows since. It also sponsors Byte Computer Shows and several others.

Frederick R. **Adler**
Partner in the New York venture capital firm Adler & Co., backer of Data General Corp. Known for hands-on management of his investments, i.e., as chairman of MicroPro's executive committee and chairman of Daisy Systems' board.

Herman A. **Affel** Jr.
Vice Chairman, Computer Consoles, Inc.

Timothy P. **Ahlstrom**
Chairman and CEO, Avant-Garde Computing, Inc.

Mark **Aim**
President, Kronos Inc.

John F. **Akers**
Since February 1985, president & CEO of IBM, the largest computer company in the world. Chairman of IBM since June 1986.

Peter **Alexander**
President and CEO, Numerix Corporation

Victor **Alhadeff**
President of Egghead Discount Software Inc. with 33 company-owned outlets.

Pauline Alker
Founder, president and CEO of Counterpoint Computers Inc.

Martin Allen
Chairman, Computervision

Paul Allen
Founded Microsoft in 1975 with Bill Gates after adapting the computer language BASIC (Beginners' All-Purpose Symbolic Instruction Code) for use on microcomputers.

Marty Alpert
Founded Tecmar Inc. in 1974 to produce IBM-compatible add-on products. Tecmar was acquired in 1986 by Rexon Inc.

Stewart Alsop III
Editor and publisher of P.C. LETTER: The Insider's Guide to the Personal Computer Industry.

Douglas C. Altenbern Sr.
Chairman, President & CEO, Endata Inc.

Jack R. Altherr
Exec VP, COO & CFO, QMS Inc. (Quality Micro Systems)

Lyle D. Altman
President and COO, Network Systems Corporation

Gene M. Amdahl
Left IBM after 14 years to found Amdahl Corporation in 1970. Founded Trilogy Ltd. in 1979, now ELXSI Ltd. chairman.

Bruce Anderson
Director Communications, Versacad Corporation

Dr. Jared A. Anderson
Chairman, Valid Logic Systems, Inc.

Ed Anderson
Vice President, Operations, Computer Factory Inc.

Gregg A. Anderson
Vice President & CFO, Fortune Systems Corporation

Howard Anderson
Founded Yankee Group, a high-technology industry analysis firm.

Jack A. Anderson
Senior Vice President, Marketing, Printronix, Inc.

Reid Anderson
Started Anderson-Jacobson in 1967 with Ray Jacobson to make acoustic data couplers. In 1969 founded Verbatim Corporation, which became the largest maker of floppy disks before going public in 1979.

Richard C. Anderson
President, Data 3 Systems Inc.

Robert Anderson
Chairman, Rockwell International Corp.

Roy A. Anderson
President, Lockheed Elec Group, Sanders Associates, Inc.

Thomas Anderson
Vice President, Sales, Samna Corporation

William R. Anderson Jr.
Chairman and CEO, US Design Corporation

Peter Appleton Jones
President and CEO, ELXSI Ltd.

Rand V. Araskog
Chairman of ITT since 1980 and credited with moving it from a conglomerate back toward a technology and insurance concern.

Harry J. Armstrong
Vice President, Sales, Novell, Inc.

Alan Ashton
President, Word Perfect Corporation

Charles Askanas
President and COO, Lee Data Corporation

Bryan **Aspland**
President, Integral Systems

John Vincent **Atanasoff**
Won a U.S. District Court decision in 1973 recognizing him as the official inventor of the computer after a lengthy patent trial involving Honeywell and Sperry-Rand.

Neal **Ater**
Vice President, Goal Systems International

Norman R. **Augustine**
Exec Vice President & COO, Martin Marietta Corporation

Jessie **Aweida**
Left IBM after 13 years to found Storage Technology Corp. in 1969. Left STC to found Aweida Systems Corp., which markets peripherals.

Ari **Bachana**
President, Datatab Inc.

John **Backus**
Proposed and led the Fortran (Formula Translator) project at IBM in 1954 in New York City. IBM Fellow.

Everett **Bahre**
Chairman, President & CEO, Computer & Communications Technology Corp

Joseph **Baia**
Vice Chairman, Western Digital Corporation

David T. **Bailey**
Sr Vice President, Policy Management Systems Corporation

James M. **Bailey**
Exec Vice President & COO, Gandalf Technologies Inc.

Louis C. **Bailey**
Exec Vice President & CFO, Southwestern Bell Corporation

D. Euan **Baird**
Chairman, Schlumberger Ltd.

John G. Ballenger
Chairman and President, C 3 Inc.

Zane E. Barnes
Chairman, President & CEO, Southwestern Bell Corporation

George Barratt
Vice president and CFO, Computer Sciences Corporation

Franklyn S. (Frank) Barry
 President of Ingram Software Inc., the merger of the former Ingram Software, Software Distribution
Services Inc., Softeam Inc., and Aviva Software Distributors of Canada.

Bruce Bastian
Chairman, Word Perfect Corporation

Walter Bauer
 A 30-year industry veteran, was chairman & CEO of Informatics General before it was acquired by
Sterling Software in 1985.

James L. Bayman
President and COO, Pioneer Standard Electronics, Inc.

Donald R. Beall
President and COO, Rockwell International Corporation

Andreas Bechtolsheim
 Co-founder, VP Technology, and computer designer for Sun Microsystems Inc.

Richard P. Beck
Exec Vice President & CFO, Masstor Systems Corporation

Janelle Bedke
Sr Vice President and COO, Software Publishing Corporation

C. Gordon Bell
 Founded Encore Computer Corp. in 1983 with Kenneth Fisher and Henry Burkhardt. At DEC
engineered the PDP-5, 8, and 11 and helped design the first VAX. Founded the Computer Museum
in Boston. Assistant director of computing, National Science Foundation.

W. Donald Bell
President and COO, Ducommun Inc.

Victor C. Benda
Exec Vice President, Analysts International Corporation

Jack M. Berdy
Chairman, President & CEO, On-Line Software International, Inc.

Norbert R. Berg
Deputy Chairman, Control Data Corporation

Alfred R. Berkeley
Software analyst with Alex Brown.

Eric N. Birch
Vice President, Nashua Corporation

Carl L. Bixby
President, Interface Systems Inc.

John Blankenbaker
Designed Kenbak-1 in 1971 as a low-cost hands-on tool for the classroom. Kenbak-1 was certified by the Computer Museum of Boston to be the first personal computer.

Gerhard Blumenthal
Deputy Chairman, BASF Aktiengesellschaft

W. Michael "Mike" Blumenthal
CEO of Unisys by virtue of acquiring Sperry while president of Burroughs.

Thomas E. Bolger
Chairman and CEO, Bell Atlantic

Richard P. Bond
Sr Vice President & CFO, Apollo Computer Inc.

Joseph T. Booker
President and COO, Priam Corporation

Edwin W. Booth
President and CEO, Cadec Systems, Inc.

Wallace W. Booth
Chairman and CEO, Ducommun Inc.

R. Barry Borden
Co-founder of Franklin Computer.

Kenneth Bosomworth
Founder and president of Norwalk, CT-based International Resource Development, Inc., a high-tech information provider.

David A. Bossen
Founder, president, and CEO of Measurex Corp. since 1968. Measurex is a manufacturer of supervisory control systems and CIM (Computer Integrated Manufacturing)-based systems.

Dr. James Botkin
Author of two books on high technology--GLOBAL STAKES: The future of high technology in America and THE INNOVATORS: Rediscovering America's creative energy.

Edward Botwinick
Founder, chairman, president and chief executive of Timeplex Inc., leading supplier of private integrated services digital networks.

Marie Bourget
Vice President, Finance, Borland International

Jean-Pierre Bouyssonnie
President, Thomson S.A.

Darryl Bowles
Exec Vice President, Systems Associates Inc.

William Bowman
Chairman and CEO, Spinnaker Software Corporation

Joseph A. Boyd
Chairman and CEO, Harris Corporation

Otis T. Bradley
Computer industry analyst with Alex Brown.

Thornton F. Bradshaw
Chairman, RCA Corporation

George L. Bragg
President, Telex Corporation

Paul **Brainerd**
Formed Aldus Corporation in 1984 and coined the name desktop publishing.

Dr. Frank A. **Brand**
Exec Vice President & COO, M/A-Com, Inc.

Ronald W. **Braniff**
President and CEO, Ask Computer Systems, Inc.

John **Brazier**
Sr Vice President, Sales, Epyx Inc.

Dr. E. Allen **Breitenbach**
Chairman and CEO, Scientific Software Intercomp, Inc.

Dan **Bricklin**
In 1979 with Bob Frankston created VisiCalc, the first electronic spreadsheet, and founded Software Arts. Founded Software Garden in 1985.

James L. **Broadhead**
Sr. Vice President, GTE Corporation

Fred **Brooks**
Author of classic book on software development called "The Mythical Man-Month" based on his experience leading the team that developed the operating system for the IBM 360 family.

Paula **Brooks**
Founder and President of Unitech Software.

Rep. Jack **Brooks**
Author of 1965 Brooks Act, establishing DP procurement policy, and chairman of House Government Operations Committee, which manages government computing.

Robert **Brooks**
Board Member, APTOS Systems Corporation

Theodore F. **Brophy**
Chairman and CEO, GTE Corporation

Charles L. **Brown**
Chairman, AT&T

Dave **Brown**
Credited with developing the Hardcard product as executive VP of Plus Development Corp., division of Quantum Corp.

Mervyn **Brown**
Vice President and CEO, Rodime plc

Michael **Brown**
President and CEO, Central Point Software Inc.

Michael J. **Brown**
President, Innovative Software, Inc.

Roland E. **Brown**
Exec Vice President, Intergraph Corporation

Verney **Brown**
President and COO, American Magnetics Corporation

Louis M. **Brown Jr.**
President and CEO, Micros Systems, Inc.

Thomas R. **Brown Jr.**
Founder and Chairman, Burr-Brown Corporation.

Leonard **Brownlow**
Chairman and President, Rodime plc

Thomas H. **Bruggere**
Chairman, President & CEO, Mentor Graphics Corporation

Cees **Bruynes**
Chairman and President, North American Philips Corporation

David **Bunnell**
Started PC MAGAZINE and later PC WORLD, magazines focusing on IBM PCs and PC-compatible computers.

Bruce **Burdick**
Operates the 12-store ComputerLand/Kansas.

James J. **Burns**
President and CEO, Burr-Brown Corporation

Kevin **Burns**
President and CEO, Sage Software, Inc.

William G. **Burns**
Vice Chairman and CFO, NYNEX Corporation

Craig **Burr**
Venture capitalist with Burr, Egan, Deleage & Co.

James L. **Busby**
Chairman, President & CEO, QMS Inc. (Quality Micro Systems)

James W. **Busby**
President, Datasouth Computer Corporation

Nolan **Bushnell**
Inventor of the Pong video game. Founder of Atari, Pizza Time Theater, Catalyst Technologies, and Axlon Inc., a maker of talking teddy bears.

William F. **Buster**
Vice President, NCR Corporation

Fred J. **Butler**
Sr Vice President, Compugraphic Corporation

Brook H. **Byers**
Partner in venture capital firm Kleiner, Perkins, Caufield & Byers.

Larry **Byrnes**
President, Realworld Corporation

Richard W. **Calfee**
Chairman, Zentec Corporation

Guy **Callari**
Vice President, Sales, Accountants Microsystems, Inc.

Mark R. **Callegari**
Exec Vice President, Innovative Software, Inc.

James S. **Campbell**
Chairman, President & CEO, Fortune Systems Corporation

Philip A. Campbell
President, Bell Atlantic

William (Bill) Campbell
Vice President of sales and marketing for Apple Computer. Formerly with Eastman Kodak Company.

Joseph R. (Rod) Canion
Left Texas Instruments in 1981 with Jim Harris and Bill Murto to found Compaq Computer Corp. Compaq's 1983 sales of $111 million was the largest first full year sales of any company in the history of America. President and CEO of Compaq.

John F. Carlson
Exec Vice President, Cray Research, Inc.

Douglas "Doug" Carlston
Founded Broderbund Software, a leading recreational software company, with his brother Gary in 1980.

Gary Carlston
Chairman and VP, Broderbund

Edmund M. Carpenter
President and COO, ITT

Gale Carr
Founder and president of Rising Star.

Robert Carr
Designer and principal developer of Framework and Framework II. Co-founded Forefront Corp., which was acquired by Ashton-Tate in 1985. Chief scientist at Ashton-Tate.

Ronald C. Carroll
Chairman, President & CEO, Continuum Company, Inc.

B. Tom Carter Jr.
Exec Vice President, UCCEL Corporation

Weldon W. Case
Chairman and CEO, Alltel Corporation

John **Cassese**
Chairman and President, Computer Horizons Corporation

Ronald G. **Casty**
Chairman and President, Chelsea Industries Inc.

Frank J. **Caufield**
Partner in San Francisco-based venture capital firm of Kleiner, Perkins, Caufield & Byers.

John C. **Cavalier**
President and CEO, NCA Corporation

Doug **Cayne**
Computer industry analyst at Gartner Group.

Colby H. **Chandler**
Chairman and CEO, Eastman Kodak Company

Dash **Chang**
Chairman and President, Chang Laboratories

David **Chapman**
Vice Chairman & President, Cullinet Software Inc.

Gary **Chappell**
Director of Marketing, Chang Laboratories

Pallab K. **Chatterjee**
Texas Instruments Senior Fellow.

Winston **Chen**
President and CEO, Solectron Corporation

Jay **Chiat**
Founder, chairman and CEO of Chiat/Day advertising agency.

Phillip K. **Ciolfi**
President, Selecterm, Inc.

Mark W. **Ciotek**
Chairman, NCA Corporation

Harold L. **Clark**
President and COO, Micro D, Inc.

Sir John **Clark**
Chm & CEO, Plessey Company plc

Tom **Clarkson**
Chairman, Graphic Software Systems

John L. **Clendenin**
Chairman, Pres. & CEO, BellSouth

Charles E. **Clough**
President and CEO, Nashua Corporation

Charles M. **Clough**
President and COO, Wyle Laboratories

Gordon H. **Clow**
Sr Vice President, Vanguard Technologies International, Inc.

John **Cocke**
 An IBM Fellow who decided in 1975 that a simple architecture and a simple instruction set offered efficiencies. UC-Berkeley gave it the name RISC for reduced instruction set computing.

Edgar F. (Ted) **Codd**
 A 31-year IBM veteran who introduced the first multi-programming operating system, but is best known for development of the relational data base management concept.

William **Coggshall**
 A Stanford Research Institute alumnus who co-founded Dataquest Inc., Creative Strategies International, Software Access International, and Market Access.

Gerald **Cohen**
Chairman and President, Information Builders

Edmund U. **Cohler**
Chairman and CEO, CSP Inc.

Lester L. **Colbert** Jr.
Chairman, President & CEO, Xidex Corporation

Bruce T. **Coleman**
President and CEO, Boole & Babbage, Inc.

George **Colony**
Principal in Forrester Research and often-quoted computer guru.

Finnis **Conner**
Co-founded Seagate Technology with Alan Shugart. Founded Conner Peripherals Inc. in 1986.

Charles A. **Constantino**
Exec Vice President, Par Technology Corporation

Martin **Cooperstein**
Chairman and CEO, Data Architects, Inc.

Wilfred J. **Corrigan**
Founder and president of LSI Logic Corp., the leading U.S. manufacturer of gate arrays. President and chief executive of Fairchild Camera & Instrument Corporation in the late 1970s.

Richard **Cortese**
President and CEO, Alpha Microsystems

C. Robert **Coulter**
Senior Vice President, MPSI Systems Inc.

George **Cowan**, Ph.D.
Chairman, President & CEO, Verdix Corporation

Casey **Cowell**
President, U.S. Robotics

Fred B. **Cox**
Chairman and CEO, Emulex Corporation

Marshall **Cox**
Founded Intersil in 1970 and retired a millionaire in 1976 at age 40. Founded Western Micro Technology Inc. in 1977 with Bernard Marren.

David **Craft**
Sr Vice President, Flextronics Inc.

Richard L. **Crandall**
President and CEO, Comshare Inc.

Dean W. **Crawford**
Chairman and President, Vanguard Technologies International, Inc.

Seymour **Cray**
In 1972 organized Cray Research, Inc., the acknowledged leading designer of supercomputers.

Peter **Crisp**
Venture capitalist with Venrock Associates.

Fredrick R. **Cronin**
Vice President, Technology, General Datacomm Industries, Inc.

Robert W. **Cross**
Chairman and CEO, Delta Data Systems Corporation

Thomas J. **Crotty**
Computer industry analyst with Gartner Securities Corp.

John P. **Croxton**
Chairman and CEO, Auxton Computer Enterprises Inc.

John **Cullinane**
Founder of Cullinet, a leading vendor of data base software.

Brian T. **Cunningham**
Chairman and CEO, Computer Entry Systems Corporation

Desmond **Cunningham**
Chairman and CEO, Gandalf Technologies Inc.

John F. **Cunningham**
Chairman and CEO, Computer Consoles, Inc.

Dr. Edward **Currie**
Chairman, Lifeboat Associates

John H. **Curtis**
Exec Vice President & COO, Stratus Computer, Inc.

Douglas L. **Cutsforth**
President and COO, Computer Automation

Alexander V. **d'Arbeloff**
 Co-founder (1960) and president of Teradyne Inc., Boston-based manufacturer of automatic test equipment for electronic components and circuit boards.

Douglas D. **Danforth**
Chairman and CEO, Westinghouse Electric Corporation

Carl E. **Dantas**
President and CEO, Compugraphic Corporation

George **Dasheill**
President and CEO, Wespercorp

Robert B. **Daugherty**
Chairman and CEO, Valmont Industries, Inc.

Richard A. **Daunoras**
Exec Vice President & CFO, North American Philips Corporation

William H. (Bill) **Davidow**
 After 11 years at Intel, Davidow formed Mohr, Davidow Ventures with Larry Mohr. Investments include Tandem, Businessland, and Valid Logic.

Bruce **Davis**
Sr Vice President, Activision Inc.

Donald K. **Davis**
President and COO, Tera Corporation

Jack C. **Davis**
Chairman and CEO, Dataproducts Corporation

Charles G. **Davis**, Jr.
Chairman and CEO, BaronData Systems

Larry A. **Dean**
Chairman,President & CEO, Stockholder Systems Inc.

Carlos **De Benedetti**
 Transformed Olivetti into one of Europe's most profitable companies.

Ron Debry
Vice President, Operations, Haba Systems, Inc.

Edson D. de Castro
 Founder and president of Data General.

Tom Delahanty
President, Xscribe Corporation

Jean Deleage
 Partner in venture capital firm Burr, Egan, Deleage & Co.

Michael Dell
 Dropped out of college to form PC's Limited in Austin, Texas and sell $80 million of clones in 1986 at age 21.

Ted C. DeMerritt
Chairman and CEO, ISC Systems Corporation

John A. DeVries
Sr Vice President, General Instrument Corporation

E.M. de Windt
Chairman and CEO, Eaton Corp

Richard T. DiBona
Chairman, President & CEO, M/A-Com, Inc.

Charles Dickenson
Chairman, Solectron Corporation

John Diebold
 Founder and chairman of The Diebold Group, Inc., management consultants, and author of AUTOMATION, MAKING THE FUTURE WORK, and BUSINESS IN THE AGE OF INFORMATION.

Steven Dille
Exec VP and COO, Scientific Computers Inc.

Robert Dilworth
 President of Zenith Data Systems since 1985. Formerly president of Morrow Designs.

Norm Dinnsen
 Co-owner with Dave McDonough of ComputerLand of San Diego/Los Angeles.

Frank Disanto
President, Copytele Inc.

Julius Dizon
Vice President and CFO, American Training International

John W. Dobson
 Executive vice president and director of marketing services for ITT Commercial Credit, which has floor-planning agreements with 3000 computer retailers.

Howard P. Doerr
Exec Vice President & CFO, US West, Inc.

James L. Donald
President and CEO, DSC Communications Corporation

Richard M. Donofrio
Sr Vice President, Southern New England Telephone Company

Georges Doriot
 Founded American Research and Development after WWII. Provided seed money for Digital Equipment.

Stephen Dow
 President & CEO of Ansa Software, a startup publisher with $10 million sales in its first full year, 1986. Primary product is Paradox database software.

Daniel L. Drake
 With John Walker co-founded Autodesk, Inc., a leading supplier of CAD/CAM software for personal computers.

John Draper
 Alias "Captain Crunch," the hacker who pioneered tapping into telephone circuitry. Author of the first Easywriter word processing program.

Philippe Dreyfus
Vice Chairman, CAP Gemini Sogeti

Robert J. **Drummond**
Senior Vice President, Epsilon Data Management, Inc.

Richard M. **Drysdale**
Chairman, Datacopy Corporation

Stephen C. **Dube**
 Covers the computer industry for Shearson Lehman Brothers Inc.

Mickey **Dude**
 President of Microvision Inc.

David **Duffield**
Chairman, Integral Systems

David J. **Dunn**
Chairman, Iomega Corporation and Prime Computer, Inc.

Norman S. **Dunn**
Exec Vice President, Chelsea Industries Inc.

Ericson M. **Dunstan**
Sr Vice President, Micropolis Corporation

James K. **Dutton**
President and CEO, System Industries Inc.

John C. **Dvorak**
 Longest-running personal computer columnist.

James **Dyer**
Exec Vice President, Cycare Systems

Esther **Dyson**
 Acquired Rosen Letter (1983) from Ben Rosen, changed its name to Release 1.0, sold it to Ziff-Davis in 1985, continuing as Editor. A personal computer industry observer who also hosts an annual PC Forum.

Julius M. **Dziak**
Exec Vice President, Endata Inc.

J. Presper **Eckert**
Developed ENIAC with John Mauchly at U. of Pennsylvania and delivered it to the U.S. Army in 1946 as the first electronic mainframe computer to leave the laboratory. Founded the company that became Univac.

Asher B. **Edelman**
Chairman, Datapoint Corporation

James C. **Edenfield**
President and Co-CEO, American Software, Inc.

James J. **Edgette**
With Steve Heller in 1981, founded Entre' Computer Centers Inc., an international franchise with 250 stores. Resigned in June 1986.

Dennis **Edwards**
Sr Vice President, Distributed Logic Corporation

James D. **Edwards**
Left IBM in 1980 after 15 years to join Xerox. Later held top positions at Bausch & Lomb and AT&T. Now president of the AT&T computer business.

William P. **Egan**
Partner in venture capital firm Burr, Egan, Deleage & Co.

D.J. **Ekberg**
Chairman and CEO, Data Card Corporation

John **Ellenby**
Founded GRiD Systems Corp. in 1979 to design and build the Compass laptop computer.

Lawrence **Ellison**
President & CEO, Oracle Systems

David C. **Elsbury**
Deputy CEO, Racal Electronics plc

Milan L. **Elton**
Vice President, Technalysis Corporation

Paul C. Ely, Jr.
Replaced Allen Michels as president & CEO of Convergent Technologies after rising to VP at Hewlett-Packard.

Thomas M. Emory Jr.
Vice President, Technology, Digilog Inc.

Joe Engelberger
Called the "father of robotics." With Peter Scott founded Technology Transitions Inc., a venture capital firm.

Nils Ericson
President, Syscon Corporation

Edward M. Esber, Jr.
After four years with VisiCorp, became CEO of Ashton-Tate in 1984.

William T. Esrey
President and CEO, United Telecommunications, Inc.

Rolando C. Esteverena
President and CEO, Datacopy Corporation

Gordon Eubanks
Chairman of Symantec. Founded Compiler Systems Inc. and sold it to Digital Research Inc.

Paul A.D. Evans
Computer industry analyst with S.G. Warburg.

Roger L. Evans
President and CEO, Micom Systems, Inc.

Charles E. Exley, Jr.
Chairman and President, NCR Corporation

Ed Faber
Chairman and CEO of ComputerLand since 1985. Was the key person who built ComputerLand in the late 1970s and 1980s.

Deborah Fain
President of MSR and founder of Samna Software.

Bill Fairfield
President of ValCom since 1982. Built chain of 180 franchised computer centers.

John P. Fall
Vice President, SAS Institute

Rick Faulk
President and CEO, First Software

Lincoln Faurer
President of the Corporation for Open Systems (COS), an organization of computer vendors and users created to test and certify products to international standards. Retired Lt. General, USAF.

Lawrence J. Fedewa
Vice President, Cordatum, Inc.

Lee Felsenstein
Designer of the Osborne 1 portable computer. Led Homebrew Computer Club in Menlo Park from 1975 to 1986.

Larry R. Ferguson
President and COO, Systems Associates Inc.

Randy Ferguson
Chairman, BPI Systems, Inc.

David Fernald
President and CEO, BPI Systems, Inc.

Louis P. Ferrero
Chairman, President & CEO, Anacomp, Inc.

Al Fichera
Chairman and President, BKW Systems, Inc.

Joyce Field
Director Human Resources, Micro Data Base Systems

Gary B. Filler
Exec Vice President & CFO, Xidex Corporation

Dr. Kenneth B. **Fine**
President, Valid Logic Systems, Inc.

Aryeh **Finegold**
With David Stamm founded Daisy Systems Corp. in 1980 to make computer-aided engineering (CAE) work modules.

Robert G. **Finney**
President and CEO, Electronic Associates Inc.

George **Fisher**
Senior executive VP and deputy to the CEO of Motorola, Inc.

Edmund B. **Fitzgerald**
Chairman and CEO, Northern Telecom Ltd.

J. Garrett **Fitzgibbons**
President and COO, BaronData Systems

Harvey **Flam**
Founder of FHP, a microcomputer broker/gray-market reseller of IBM, Compaq, and other equipment.

Joe T. **Ford**
President and COO, Alltel Corporation

James R. **Forman** Jr.
Chairman, Dyatron Corporation

J. W. (Jay) **Forrester**
At MIT, headed Project Whirlwind. Pioneered ferrite core memories. Sold his patent to IBM for $13M in 1964. Developed industrial dynamics concepts.

William E. **Foster**
Founded Stratus Computer Inc. in 1980 to build fault tolerant computers.

Jean-Marie **Fouries**
Deputy General Manager, Thomson S.A.

Harold R. **Frank**
Chairman, Applied Magnetics Corporation

Stephen W. **Frankel**
President and COO, Emulex Corporation

Howard B. **Franklin**
Sr Vice President, Bell Industries Inc.

Bob **Frankston**
 With Dan Bricklin wrote VisiCalc and co-founded Software Arts in 1979. Chief scientist of
information services division of Lotus Development since 1985.

Robert R. **Frederick**
President and CEO, RCA Corporation

Gilbert K. **Freeman**
President and CEO, Epyx Inc.

Jay **Freeman**
President, F.A. Components

Samuel D. **Freeman**
Vice President, F.A. Components

Bernard L. **Friedman**
Vice Chairman, Analogic Corporation

Gary **Friedman**
 Founded Fortune Systems Corp. in 1980 and Communications Funding Corp. in 1986.

Robert A. **Fuhrman**
President and COO, Lockheed Corporation

Yoshihide **Fukao**
Sr Exec Vice President, Sharp Corporation

Gabriel P. **Fusco**
President, Iomega Corporation

Dan **Fylstra**
 With Peter Jennings founded Personal Software, later called VisiCorp, to market VisiCalc.

Robert L. **Gable**
President and CEO, Computervision

Mats Gabrielsson
 Acquired Datatronic AB in Sweden in 1978 for one Swedish krona (about 22 cents) and distributed Commodore computers before acquiring Victor Technologies in 1985 for $21 million.

Meldon K. **Gafner**
President, Integrated Software Systems Corporation

David **Gale**
Chief Executive Officer, Realworld Corporation

Cheryl **Galloway**
President and COO, Auxton Computer Enterprises Inc.

Robert W. **Galvin**
 Chairman of Motorola, Inc. and CEO from 1964-1986.

Peyton L. **Gannaway**
President and COO, Anthem Electronics Inc.

John **Gantz**
 Editor of TECH STREET JOURNAL, a newsletter on high-tech stock market and business performance.

Harry **Garland**
 PhD co-founder of Cromemco Inc. in 1975 with Roger Melen. An early pioneer in personal computers.

Gideon **Gartner**
 Founded the Gartner Group, a market research firm best known as IBM watchers. Founded Gartner Securities Corp., a Wall Street firm.

Merle C. **Garvis**
President, Cordatum, Inc.

William H. (Bill) **Gates** III
 Chairman of Microsoft Corp., which was co-founded with Paul Allen in 1975. Creator of MS-DOS operating system. Co-developer with Allen of first BASIC for microcomputers.

James A. D. **Geier**
Chairman and CEO, Cincinnati Milacron Inc.

Harold **Geneen**
Retired ITT chairman. During the 1960s and 1970s acquired unrelated firms transforming ITT into a conglomerate.

David C. **Genever-Watling**
Vice President, General Electric Company

H. Joseph **Gerber**
President, Gerber Scientific, Inc.

Don **Giacchetti**
Exec Vice President, Operations, Springboard Software Inc.

Fred M. **Gibbons**
In 1981 with Janelle Bedke and John Page, co-founded Software Publishing Corp., best known for its "pfs" products.

Robert G. **Gilbertson**
President and CEO, Data Switch Corporation

Edward P. **Gistaro**
President and CEO, Datapoint Corporation

Eugene **Glazer**
Computer industry analyst with Dean Witter Reynolds.

Joseph F. **Gloudeman**
President and CEO, MacNeal-Schwendler Corporation

William **Godbout**
In 1973 founded CompuPro, an early entrant in the personal computer market.

Martin **Goetz**
Received first software patent in 1968 for a sorting system. President of Applied Data Research, Inc. (ADR), which marketed the first commercial software product (Autoflow) in 1965.

Michael C. **Goldberg**
Chairman, President & CEO, FDP Corp.

Victor **Goldberg**
IBM executive. President of National Distribution Division from 1983 to 1986.

Gerald W. **Goodman**
President and COO, Miniscribe Corporation

James N. **Goodnight**
President, SAS Institute

Peter **Gorahan**
Vice President and CFO, Sage Software, Inc.

Bernard M. **Gordon**
Chairman and President, Analogic Corporation

Bing **Gordon**
Vice President, Electronic Arts

Richard A. **Gorgens**
Chairman, President & CEO, Alloy Computer Products, Inc.

Joseph T. **Gorman**
President and COO, TRW Inc.

Jay **Gottlieb**
President and CEO of The Computer Factory Inc., with 36 retail stores in northeastern U.S.

Michal **Gouilloud**
Exec Vice President, Schlumberger Ltd.

Irving **Gould**
Chairman, Commodore International Ltd.

Robert **Gould**
President and COO, DST Systems Inc.

Gordon **Graves**
Chairman, Syntech International Inc.

William M. **Graves**
President and COO, Management Science America Inc.

John D. **Gray**
Chairman, Tektronix, Inc.

Alvar **Green**
President and CEO, Autodesk

Robert **Greenburg**
Exec Vice President, Decision Systems Inc.

Richard E. **Greene**
Chairman, Data Switch Corporation

Anthony F. **Griffiths**
President and CEO, Mitel Corporation

Carl **Gritzmaker**
Chairman of Migent Corp. and formerly a vice president of Ashton-Tate.

Herbert **Grosch**
Grosch's Law defined in the early 1950s a relationship between computer speed and cost. Held jobs with IBM, GE, and the U.S. government. Now a consultant living in Europe.

Andrew S. **Grove**
President and COO, Intel Corporation

Paolo **Guidi**
President, Telenet Communications Corp.

Donald E. **Guinn**
Chairman, President & CEO, Pacific Telesis Group

Arun **Gupta**
Chairman. President & CEO, DataEase International Inc.

Chaz **Haba**
Chairman and CEO, Haba Systems, Inc.

George F. **Haddix**
Chairman, Applied Communications, Inc.

Walter **Haefner**
Reclusive Swiss multimillionaire who backed Sam Wyly in the 1960s and 1970s and now owns some 60% of Uccel through Careal Holding AG.

Carl H. Hahn
Chairman, Volkswagen AG, which owns Pertec Computer Corporation.

Philip G. Halamandaris
President and COO, Genisco Technology Corporation

G.A. Hale
President, Alamo Learning Systems

William **Hambrecht**
President and co-founder of Hambrecht & Quist, a San Francisco investment bank credited with
bankrolling Silicon Valley.

Anthony R. **Hamilton**
President of Avnet Inc.'s Hamilton Avnet Electronics subsidiary with 53 stocking outlets in the U.S.
and Canada. Chairman & CEO of Avnet, Inc.

Bruce Hamilton
Vice President, TEC Inc.

Byron **Hamilton**
Chairman and President, TEC Inc.

Paul E. **Hammar**
Exec Vice President, Lodgistix, Inc.

Earl J. **Hansen**
Vice President, Astrocom Corporation

Neal C. **Hansen**
President and CEO, Applied Communications, Inc.

Robert B. **Hansen**
Executive VP & Group Executive, Zenith Electronics Corporation

Bob Harp
Co-founder of Vector Graphic in 1976 and in 1981 of Corona, now called Cordata.

Lore **Harp**
Founded Vector Graphic in 1976 with Carole Ely and Bob Harp. Founded Aplex Corp. in 1985.
Runs Pacific Technology Venture Fund with husband Patrick J. McGovern.

Ronald G. **Harper**
Chairman, President & CEO, MPSI Systems Inc.

Hank **Harris**
Chief Financial Officer, Zitel Corporation

Ernest T. **Harrison**
Chairman and CEO, Racal Electronics plc

John T. **Hartley**
President and COO, Harris Corporation

Namio **Hashimoto**
President and CEO, Oki Electric Industry Co. Ltd.

Marion W. **Haun**
Chairman, American Magnetics Corporation

Trip **Hawkins**
Founder and president of Electronic Arts, a leading entertainment software company.

Zuo **Hayashi**
With Morton Panish at Bell Labs, built in 1970 the world's first reliable and practical semiconductor laser. Has since become technical director of MITI-backed research lab in Japan.

Dennis **Hayes**
Founded Hayes Microcomputer Products Inc. in 1977 to become the dominant supplier and "de facto" standard in microcomputer modems.

Jeffrey **Heimbuck**
Founder, president and CEO of Koala Technologies.

R. Stephen **Heinrichs**
Chairman and CEO, Tera Corporation

E.F. **Heizer, Jr.**
Chairman & president of Heizer Corp., a venture capital firm.

Bert I. **Helfinstein**
President and CEO of Entre' Computer Centers, Inc.

Steve Heller
Co-founder with James Edgette of Entre' Computer Centers Inc. in 1981. Resigned 1986.

Preston B. Heller Jr.
Chairman and CEO, Pioneer Standard Electronics, Inc.

John R. **Henry**
Sr. VP, Advanced Development, Scientific Micro Systems, Inc.

Joe M. **Henson**
President of Prime Computer since 1981. Previously at IBM for 27 years.

Paul H. **Henson**
Chairman, United Telecommunications, Inc.

Glenn **Hetzel**
Vice President and CFO, Quality Systems, Inc.

Dustin H. **Heuston**
Founded Wicat Systems in 1980.

William R. **Hewlett**
Co-founded Hewlett-Packard in 1939 (incorporated 1947) with David Packard. Vice chairman.

Dwight H. **Hibbard**
Chairman, President & CEO, Cincinnati Bell

Frank G. **Hickey**
Chairman, President & CEO, General Instrument Corporation

Jeff **Hill**
Vice President, Alamo Learning Systems

Daniel **Hillis**
Created the Connection Machine and helped found Thinking Machine Corp. to build and sell this parallel processing computer.

Joseph M. **Hinchey**
Sr Vice President Finance, Analog Devices, Inc.

Orion L. **Hoch**
President, CEO and COO, Litton Industries, Inc.

Christian C.E. Hoebich
Chief Financial Officer, Xebec

Gordon Hoffstein
Founder, president and CEO of Microamerica, a computer distribution company founded in 1979 and acquired in 1983 by AGS Computing, Inc.

Anthony B. Holbrook
President and COO, Advanced Micro Devices

Ken Holec
President and CEO, Lawson Associates

Gary R. Holland
President and COO, Data Card Corporation

D. Brainerd Holmes
President, Raytheon

William R. Hoover
President of Computer Sciences Corp. since 1969.

Grace Murray Hopper
Instigated development of Cobol (Common Business-Oriented Language) for the Univac I at Eckert-Mauchly (Sperry). Also worked on Mark I in 1940s. Retired (1986) Rear Admiral, USNR.

James Houtz
Chairman and President, Cycare Systems

James J. Howard
President and COO, Ameritech

Melvin Howard
Exec Vice President, Xerox Corporation

Wayne Huelskoetter
President & CEO, Dicomed Corporation

John E. Hulse
Vice Chairman & CFO, Pacific Telesis Group

Dr. K. Philip **Hwang**
Founder and majority stockholder of TeleVideo Systems Inc.

Hans **Imhof**
Chairman, President & CEO, Emergency Power Engineering

John P. **Imlay**, Jr.
Chairman and chief executive of Management Science America Inc. since 1972.

Kazuo **Inamori**
Founded Kyocera Corp. in 1959 in Kyoto, Japan. Sales were $1.55 billion for the fiscal year ending March 31, 1986.

Joseph T. **Inatome**
Chairman and Exec VP, Inacomp Computer Centers, Inc.

Rick **Inatome**
President and CEO, Inacomp Computer Centers, Inc.

B.R. (Bobby) **Inman**
Headed research consortium MCC (Microelectronics and Computer Technology Corp.) from its start in January 1983 until 1986. Resigned to form Westmark Systems Inc., a defense industry holding company.

Stephen J. **Ippolito**
Chairman and CFO, IPL Systems, Inc.

Portia **Isaacson**
Opened early computer store (1976). Chaired the first National Computer Conference that featured personal computers (NCC 1977). Co-founded Future Computing (1980), Intellisys (1985) and Infotrek (1985).

Kaoru **Iue**
President, Sanyo Electric Co., Ltd.

Kazuo **Iwata**
Chairman, Toshiba Corporation

Bruce B. **Jackson**
Exec Vice President, Quotron Systems, Inc.

David (Dave) **Jackson**
Founder, president and CEO of Altos Computer Systems.

J. Michael (Mike) **Jackson**
President of Qualitech Computer Centers Inc. of Lenexa, Kansas with 50 franchise outlets.

Earl **Jacobsen**
Exec Vice President, Central Data

Allen F. **Jacobson**
Chairman and CEO, 3M Company

Raymond E. **Jacobson**
Chairman and President, Anderson Jacobson Inc.

Jung **Jae-Dun**
President, Samsung Electron Devices Co., Ltd.

Stephen J. **Jatras**
Chairman, Telex Corporation

Stephen G. **Jerritts**
President and COO, Storage Technology Corporation

Sidney N. **Jerson**
Chairman and President, Astrocom Corporation

Steve **Jobs**
With Steve Wozniak founded Apple Computer Inc. in 1977. Left Apple in 1985 and founded Next, Inc.. Acquired Pixar from George Lucas in 1986.

Charles P. **Johnson**
Chairman, General Datacomm Industries, Inc.

Franklin P. **Johnson**
Chairman, Boole & Babbage, Inc.

Kent L. **Johnson**
Chief Executive Officer, Microrim Inc.

L. Kenneth **Johnson**
President and COO, Hadron, Inc.

Roger W. **Johnson**
Chairman, President & CEO, Western Digital Corporation

Terry **Johnson**
After 7 years with IBM and stays with Memorex and Storage Technology, founded MiniScribe
Corp. in 1980 to make hard disk drives.

Harold J. **Johnson** Jr.
Exec Vice President, Operations, Computer Data Systems Inc.

Harvey **Jones**
Co-founder of Daisy Systems Corp.

Thomas O. **Jones**
President and Chairman, Epsilon Data Management, Inc.

William **Joy**
A co-founder and VP of research and development at Sun Microsystems Inc.

Egil **Juliussen**
Co-founder of Future Computing Inc. (1980). Chairman & CEO of Intellisys, Infotrek, and
StoreBoard Inc. Writes regular column for COMPUTER RESELLER NEWS.

Jerry R. **Junkins**
President of Texas Instruments since May 1985.

Yazir **Kadar**
Chief Operating Officer, Kronos Inc.

Philippe **Kahn**
Founded Borland International in May 1983 and shipped Turbo Pascal at $69.95 in November 1983
and Sidekick in June 1984.

Robert H. **Kahn**
Founded non-profit Corporation for National Research Initiatives in Washington, D.C. in 1985 after
13-years with Darpa, the Defense Department's Advanced Research Projects agency, where he
headed the information processing techniques office.

Stephen **Kahng**
Founded Up To Date Technology Inc. in 1985 to design computer products, i.e. clones and file-
servers, to be manufactured by Korean conglomerates (for example, Daewoo, Samsung, and
Goldstar) for U.S. sales companies such as Leading Edge and Novell.

Ryuzaburo **Kaku**
President, Canon Inc.

Thomas G. **Kamp**
Chairman, Centronics Data Computer Corporation

Serge **Kampf**
Executive Chairman, CAP Gemini Sogeti

Henry **Kaplan**
Exec Vice President, Thoughtware

Mitchell D. (Mitch) **Kapor**
Founded Lotus Development Corp. in 1982 to market 1-2-3 which had been co-developed with Jonathan Sachs.

Narendra **Karmarkar**
At Bell Laboratories developed an algorithm for linear programming to make computers speedier.

Robert **Kaseta**
Vice President, Vermont Research Corporation

N. **Katayama**
President, Mitsubishi Electric Corporation

Stephen P. **Kaufman**
President and COO, Arrow Electronics, Inc.

Thomas S. **Kavanagh**
President, NBI, Inc.

Alan **Kay**
Apple Computer Fellow at MIT. A computer scientist whose pioneering work inspired Apple's Macintosh.

Andrew F. **Kay**
In 1953 founded Non-Linear Systems, which introduced the Kaycomp II in 1982 and became Kaypro in 1983.

David A. **Kay**
President of Kaypro following his father, Andrew.

John F. **Keane**
President, Keane Incorporated

David **Kearns**
 Chairman, Xerox Corp.

David T. **Kearns**
Chairman and CEO, Xerox Corporation

Thomas P. **Kehler**
Chairman and CEO, Intellicorp

Gaynor N. **Kelley**
Chairman, Concurrent Computer Corporation

Gaynor N. **Kelley**
President and COO, Perkin-Elmer Corporation

James C. **Kelly**
Exec Vice President, Shared Medical Systems Corporation

Thomas L. **Kelly** Jr.
Chairman and President, TIE/Communications, Inc.

Clifford **Kendall**
Chairman and President, Computer Data Systems Inc.

Jerry T. **Kendall**
Exec Vice President & COO, Paradyne Corporation

Douglas **Kennedy**
Executive Vice President, FDP Corp.

Brian W. **Kernighan**
 With Dennis Ritchie at Bell Laboratories, developed the UNIX operating system and the C
programming language, published in 1978.

Robert E. **Keto**
President and COO, InterTAN Inc.

Sat Tara Singh **Khalsa**
 In 1982 founded Kriya Systems, best known for Typing Tutor II and III.

Gary Kildall
Developed CP/M in 1973. Designed Dr. Logo and developed PL/1 programming languages. Chairman of Digital Research Inc. Founded Activenture (now KnowledgeSet) in 1984 to develop software for CD ROMs.

David T. Kimball
Chairman and CEO, General Signal Corporation

Jack King
President and CEO, Zitel Corporation

Michael J. King
President and COO, Computer Entry Systems Corporation

Olin B. King
Chairman and CEO, SCI Systems, Inc.

David R. Kinley
VP, Eng/Mfg of SIS Inc., Siemens AG, Munich, West Germany

Yasusada Kitahara
Vice President, Nippon Telegraph and Telephone Corporation

Lawrence O. Kitchen
Chairman and CEO, Lockheed Corporation

August Klein
President, Masscomp Co.

David Klein
Executive Vice President, NBI, Inc.

Robert A. Kleist
President and CEO, Printronix, Inc.

Rodger S. Kline
Exec Vice President, CCX Network Inc.

Donald E. Knuth
Designer of typographical composition software and professor of computer science at Stanford University.

Koji Kobayashi
Chairman, NEC Corporation

Taiyu Kobayashi
Chairman, Fujitsu Ltd.

Gary Koehler
Chief Executive Officer, Micro Data Base Systems

James G. Kolleger
In 1970 founded Environmental Information Center Inc., which later became EIC Intelligence Inc., a clearinghouse for information on telecommunications, robotics, and artificial intelligence.

Raymond Koontz
Chairman, Diebold, Inc.

Zobumitsu Kosugi
Vice President, Oki Electric Industry Co. Ltd.

George Kozmetsky
Co-founded Teledyne in 1960 with Henry Singleton. Dean of IC2 (Institute for Constructive Capitalism) at U. of Texas in Austin.

H. Werner Krause
Pres. & CEO of SIS Inc., Siemens AG, Munich, West Germany

Robert D. Krause
Vice President & CFO, Ungermann-Bass, Inc.

William L. Krause
President of 3Com Corp. since 1981 after 14 years at Hewlett-Packard Co.

John H. Krehbiel Sr.
Chairman of Molex Inc., supplier of electronic interconnection products.

Joseph J. Kroger
Vice Chairman of Unisys Corporation. Formerly President and COO of Sperry Corporation.

Ralph E. Kromer
President, COO and CFO, Intellicorp

Denis **Krusos**
Chairman and CEO, Copytele Inc.

Hisashi **Kubo**
President, Ricoh US, Ricoh Co. Ltd.

Duane R. **Kullberg**
Chief Executive Officer, Arthur Andersen & Co.

Sandra L. (Sandy) **Kurtzig**
Founded Ask Computer Systems in 1972.

Raymond **Kurtzweil**
Chairman, Kurtzweil Applied Intelligence, Inc.

Richard **LaPorte**
Chief Executive Officer, Accountants Microsystems, Inc.

Linwood A. **Lacy** Jr.
Chairman and CEO, Micro D, Inc.

William (Billy) **Ladin**
Founder, president, and CEO of Computercraft, a Houston-based computer retail chain.

Domonic A. **Laiti**
Chairman and CEO, Hadron, Inc.

Frederick W. **Lang**
President, Analysts International Corporation

Gerard H. **Langeler**
Exec Vice President & COO, Mentor Graphics Corporation

Frederick S. **Larson**
President and COO, Computer Depot, Inc.

Ed **Lauing**
President and CEO, Channelmark Corporation

Frank R. **Lautenberg**
Senator (D-NJ) and co-author of Senate bill S.786 (March 1985) to establish an Information Age Commission.

Richard Lawson
Chairman, Lawson Associates

Charles J. Lawson Jr.
Chairman and CEO, National Micronetics, Inc.

Thomas Lazear
President and CEO, Versacad Corporation

Bennett S. LeBow
Chairman, MAI Basic Four, Inc.

Harry W. Le Claire
Chairman and CEO, Tab Products Co.

Douglas R. LeGrande
IBM Vice President. In 1985-86 in charge of personal computer dealer operations at the National
Distribution Division (NDD).

Joshua Lederberg
Nobel prize-winning geneticist who, with Edward Feigenbaum, developed the expert system
Dendral at Stanford University.

John M. Lee
Chairman and CEO, Lee Data Corporation

Robert E. Lee
Chairman, President & CEO, Local Data, Inc.

Robert Leff
Co-founded Softsel Computer Products Inc. in 1980 with Dave Wagman.

John N. Lemasters
President and CEO, Continental Telecom, Inc.

Stanley Leven
Sr Vice President, Gerber Scientific, Inc.

David Levenson
Controller, First Software

Robert Leventhal
Chairman, President & CEO, Western Union Corporation

Jack Levine
Chief Executive Officer, Thoughtware

Kenneth Levy
Co-founder and president of KLA Instruments Corp., maker of image-processing equipment to inspect photomasks, reticles, wafers, and circuit boards.

C. McKenzie Lewis
President and CEO, Computer Network Techhnology Corporation

Howard D. Lewis
Chairman and CEO, Archive Corporation

John C. Lewis
President and CEO, Amdahl Corporation

Gary E. Liebl
President and COO, Cipher Data Products, Inc.

Gregory J. Liemandt
CEO of Uccel Corp. since April 1983. Formerly chairman of General Electric Information Services Co.

John Lindeblad
President and COO, ISC Systems Corporation

Richard C. Litsinger
Exec Vice President, C 3 Inc.

Arthur D. Little
Chairman, Selecterm, Inc.

William Lohse
Publishes PC MAGAZINE, which focuses on providing information to users of personal computers.

W. Michael Long
Exec Vice President, Continuum Company, Inc.

William C. (Bill) Lowe
President of IBM Entry Systems Division since 1985.

Justus F. Lowe Jr.
President and CEO, SofTech, Inc.

William H. (Will) Luden III
Former president and CEO of PacTel Information Systems. Previously marketing director at MicroPro and head of computer retail division at Macy's.

Klaus Luft
Chairman of Nixdorf Computer AG since the death of founder Heinz Nixdorf in March 1986.

Jeffrey Lundeen
Vice President, Sales, Data 3 Systems Inc.

John H. Lux
Chairman and CEO, Ametek Inc.

Lillian Lyles
President, Data Compression, Inc., an applications, engineering and consulting firm.

William A. Maasberg Jr.
Chief Executive Officer, Libra Programming

Stuart P. Mabon
Chairman and President, Micropolis Corporation

Jack A. MacAllister
President and CEO, US West, Inc.

Richard H. MacNeal
Chairman, MacNeal-Schwendler Corporation

R. James Macaleer
Chairman and CEO, Shared Medical Systems Corporation

Leon Machiz
President, Avnet, Inc.

John N. Maguire
Chairman, Software AG Systems Inc.

Robert W. **Mahoney**
President and CEO, Diebold, Inc.

David C. **Malmberg**
President and COO, National Computer Systems, Inc.

Morton L. **Mandel**
Chairman, Premier Industrial Corporation

Armen A. **Manoogian**
President and COO, MBI Business Centers (The Math Box, Inc.)

Jim P. **Manzi**
Joined Lotus Development Corp. as president in October 1984 from McKinsey & Co. Named CEO at Lotus in April 1986 and chairman in July 1986.

A.C. (Mike) **Markkula**
Veteran of Fairchild Semiconductor and Intel. First backer of Apple Computer and CEO from 1981 to 1983.

Eric W. **Markrud**
Sr Vice President, National Micronetics, Inc.

Francis A. **Marks**
Vice President, Intelligent Systems Corporation

Dave **Marquart**
Venture capitalist with Technology Venture Investors.

Bob **Marsh**
Sometimes regarded as the "father of supermicro technology." Co-founded Onyx Systems and introduced first supermicro, the C-8000, at NCC 1980. Chairman of Plexus Computers Inc.

Gordon S. **Marshall**
Chm., Pres., CEO and COO, Marshall Industries

James **Martin**
Founder of Knowledgeware, Inc. Author and lecturer on computer technology.

Richard E. **Martin**
Exec Vice President & CFO, First Financial Management Corporation

John Martin-Musumeci
Heads Micro/Vest Corp., an investor group that in a March 1985 court verdict was awarded 20% of ComputerLand plus $126 million in damages. President of Solitaire Corp.

Donald Massaro
Chairman of Priam Corporation. Previously with Xerox and Shugart Associates.

Charles A. Mathews
President and CEO, Scientific Micro Systems, Inc.

Richard Matlack
Founded InfoCorp, a computer industry information firm.

Nozomu Matsumoto
Chairman, Pioneer Electronic Corporation

Seyia Matsumoto
President, Pioneer Electronic Corporation

Masaharu Matsushita
Chairman, Matsushita Electric Industrial Co. Ltd.

John Mauchly
Developed ENIAC in 1946 with J. Presper Eckert Jr. and co-founded Eckert-Mauchly Computer Corp., which became the Univac division of Sperry Corp.

Robert Mawhinney
Chairman, Xscribe Corporation

John McCarthy
Director of the Artificial Intelligence Laboratory at Stanford. Coined the term "artificial intelligence" in 1956 and proposed the concept of time-sharing in 1957.

John McCartney
Administrator, U.S. Robotics

Tom McChristy
President, Syntech International Inc.

Stephen T. McClellan
Vice President and computer analyst at Merrill Lynch, Pierce, Fenner & Smith.

William O. **McCoy**
Vice Chairman, BellSouth

John H. **McDaniel**
Sr. VP and Controller, Tandy Corporation

F. James **McDonald**
President and COO, General Motors Corporation

James F. **McDonald**
President and COO, Gould Inc.

Randal B. **McDonald**
Chief Financial Officer, Arthur Andersen & Co.

Horace G. **McDonell**
Chairman and CEO, Perkin-Elmer Corporation

John F. **McDonnell**
President, McDonnell Douglas Corporation

Sanford N. **McDonnell**
Chairman and CEO, McDonnell Douglas Corporation

Thomas A. **McDonnell**
Vice Chairman and CEO, DST Systems Inc.

Dr. Robert C. **McFarlane**
President and COO, Scientific Software Intercomp, Inc.

Pat **McGovern**
In 1964 founded International Data Group, largest publisher of computer magazines including COMPUTERWORLD, INFOWORLD, PC WORLD, MACWORLD and others. Also owner of International Data Corp. (IDC), largest market research company in the computer industry.

William G. (Bill) **McGowen**
Founder and chairman of MCI Communications Corp. since 1968.

Robert **McKay**
Exec Vice President & CFO, Computer & Communications Technology Corp

Regis McKenna
In 1970 founded Regis McKenna Public Relations Inc., whose major clients include Apple, Intel & Businessland. Director of Convex, Digital Research, Genentech, and Linear Technology. General partner of Kleiner, Perkins, Caufield, Byers.

J. F. McKinney
Chairman and CEO, Tyler Corporation

Clark McLeod
President, Teleconnect

Ian McNaught-Davis
Group Vice President, Comshare Inc.

Scott McNealy
A co-founder and chairman of Sun Microsystems Inc.

George L. McTavish
President and CEO, Hogan Systems, Inc.

James W. Meadlock
Chairman and President, Intergraph Corporation

Lorraine Mecca
Founded Micro D. Sold her majority interest to Ingram Distribution in December 1985.

Jack L. Melchor
Venture capitalist with Melchor Venture Management Co.

Roger Melen
Co-founder with Harry Garland of Cromemco in 1975.

Robert C. Mendenhall
President and COO, WICAT Systems, Inc.

William A. Merritt Jr.
Exec Vice President, TIE/Communications, Inc.

Robert M.(Bob) Metcalfe
One of the original designers of Ethernet at Xerox. Founded 3Com Corp. in 1979.

Ruben F. **Mettler**
Chairman and CEO, TRW Inc.

F. R. **Meyer**
President and COO, Tyler Corporation

Robert **Meyerson**
Chairman, Telxon Corporation

Raymond **Meyo**
President and CEO, Telxon Corporation

Allen **Michels**
Former DEC and Intel manager who founded Convergent Technologies and Dana Group.

Terje **Mikalsen**
Chairman, Norsk Data A.S.

William (Bill) **Millard**
Founded Systems Dynamics Inc. in 1969. In 1972 founded IMS Associates Inc., which introduced the IMSAI 8080 microcomputer in 1975. Founded Computer Shack, later renamed ComputerLand. Moved to Saipan in 1986.

David **Miller**
President and CEO, WordTech Systems Inc.

Edward **Miller**
Principal of Software Research Associates.

John E. **Miller**
President and CEO, Intermetrics, Inc.

Stuart J. **Miller**
President and CEO, Software AG Systems Inc.

Donn R. **Milton**, Ph.D.
Exec Vice President, Verdix Corporation

Marvin **Minsky**
MIT Professor and Artificial Intelligence expert since mid-1950s. In 1960 founded the AI Project at MIT with John McCarthy.

Eugene D. Misukanis
Exec Vice President, Computer Network Techhnology Corporation

Katsushige Mita
President, Hitachi Ltd.

Takeshi Mitarai
Chairman, Canon Inc.

David T. Mitchell
President and COO, Seagate Technology

William G. Mitchell
President, Centel Corporation

Peter Mittleman
Vice President, Development, Information Builders

Said Mohammadioun
Chief Executive Officer, Samna Corporation

Arne Mohlin
Executive Vice President, Ericsson

Milton E. Mohr
Chairman, President & CEO, Quotron Systems, Inc.

Curt A. Monash
Computer analyst with Paine Webber.

Walter H. Monteith Jr.
Chairman, President & CEO, Southern New England Telephone Company

Gordon E. Moore
Founder, chairman, and CEO of Intel.

William G. Moore Jr.
Chairman, President & CEO, Recognition Equipment, Inc.

Carl Morath
Chairman, Datasouth Computer Corporation

Jacqueline **Morby**
 Venture capitalist with TA Associates.

Avery **More**
 Exec Vice President, Computercraft, Inc.

Charles D. **Morgan Jr.**
 Chairman and President, CCX Network Inc.

George **Morgenstern**
 President, Decision Systems Inc.

Akio **Morito**
 Founded Sony after WWII with Masaru Ibuka.

Shingo **Moriyama**
 Vice Chairman, Kyocera Corporation

George **Morrow**
 Founded Morrow Designs Inc. in 1979 and Intelligent Access Inc. in 1986.

G. **Mourgue**
 Vice Chairman, Thorn-EMI plc

Ronald G. **Moyer**
 Chairman and President, Digilog Inc.

Larry **Mueller**
 Exec Vice President, Operations, Measurex Corporation

Horst **Muenzner**
 Deputy Chairman, Volkswagen AG, which owns Pertec Computer Corporation.

Don M. **Muller**
 Chairman and CEO, Cipher Data Products, Inc.

Michael **Murphy**
 Editor of the CALIFORNIA TECHNOLOGY STOCK LETTER.

Leroy **Nelman**
 Computer artist who generated pictures for CBS during the 1978 Superbowl in New Orleans.

Dr. William G. Nelson IV
President and COO, Pansophic Systems, Inc.

Peter Neupert
Vice President, Operations, Graphic Software Systems

Thomas L. Newberry
Chairman and Co-CEO, American Software, Inc.

Ben J. Newitt
President and CEO, Applied Magnetics Corporation

Karl H. Niemuller
Exec Vice President, Mohawk Data Sciences Corporation

Kazuhiko (Kay) Nishi
Founder of Ascii K.K. Former partner of Bill Gates.

Jacques Noels
President of Thomson SA's electronic division. Led purchase of Mostek Corp from United
Technologies in 1985.

James M. Nolan
Chairman, DSC Communications Corporation

Robert L. Noland
President, Ametek Inc.

Raymond J. (Ray) Noorda
After 20 years at GE, revitalized General Automation Inc. from 1970 to 1975, then System
Industries Inc., Boschert Inc., and since 1982, Novell Data Systems Inc.

David A. Norman
Founded Creative Strategies Inc., co-founded Dataquest Inc., and started Businessland Inc., which
he heads.

William A. Norred
Chairman, Micom Systems, Inc.

William Norris
In 1946 founded Engineering Research Associates, which merged into Sperry Rand. Left Sperry in
1957 to form Control Data Corp., which he managed until retirement as Chairman Emeritus in 1986.

Peter **Norton**
 Author of The Norton Utilities file-recovery programs. Writer of books and columns.

Robert W. **Norton**
President and CEO, IPL Systems, Inc.

Robert **Noyce**
 Co-founded Fairchild Semiconductor in 1957 with seven others and, with Gordon Moore, co-founded Intel. Provided venture backing to Software Publishing.

Sam **Nunn**
 Senator (D-GA) and co-author of Senate bill S. 786 (March 1985) to establish an Information Age Commission.

Luther **Nussbaum**
President and COO, Ashton-Tate

Susan **Nycum**
 Foremost authority on computer law. Partner in Chickering & Gregory law firm.

Fred W. **O'Green**
Chairman, Litton Industries, Inc.

George P. **O'Leary**
President and COO, Floating Point Systems, Inc.

Robert **Obuch**
Chief Operating Officer, Digital Research Inc.

Samuel **Ochlis**
President and COO, CSP Inc.

Norio **Ohga**
President, Sony Corporation

Kenneth H. **Olsen**
 Founded Digital Equipment Corp. in 1957 with $70,000 in capital and continues as President of this top 3 computer maker.

James E. **Olson**
President & COO, AT&T

John R. **Opel**
Chairman, IBM Corporation

Howard **Oringer**
Exec Vice President & CFO, TeleVideo Systems, Inc.

Adam **Osborne**
Founded Osborne Computer Corp. in 1981 and Paperback Software International in 1984.

M. Kenneth (Ken) **Oshman**
Founder and former president of Rolm.

James M. **Osterhoff**
Vice President and CFO, Digital Equipment Corporation

Charles W. **Oswald**
Chairman and CEO, National Computer Systems, Inc.

Yutaka **Otoshi**
President, TDK Corporation

Jinzo **Otsuka**
Exec Vice President, Sanyo Electric Co., Ltd.

John C. **Overby**
President and CEO, Advanced Input Devices

David **Packard**
Chairman, Hewlett-Packard Company

John **Page**
Co-founder of Software Publishing and author of pfs:file.

Max **Palevsky**
Chairman and CEO, Daisy Systems Corporation

Anthony P. **Palladino**
Chairman and CFO, Esprit Systems, Inc.

Robert J. Paluck
In 1982 co-founded, with Steve Wallach, Convex Computer Corporation, a manufacturer of minisupercomputers. Previously, 11 years at Mostek Corporation as vice president of product development and marketing.

Francis Pandolfi
Chief Executive Officer, Lifeboat Associates

Stephen B. Parker
Chairman and CEO, Computer Depot, Inc.

William D. Parker
President and CEO, Zentec Corporation

Avner Parnes
In 1981 acquired The Math Box, Inc., making it the largest chain of company-owned computer centers on the East coast; and changed its name to MBI Business Centers, Inc. in 1985.

James L. Patterson
In 1980 founded Quantum Corporation, a manufacturer of hard disk drives.

Tim Patterson
Author of the operating system that served as the basis for MS-DOS. Left Microsoft in 1983 to found Falcon Technology Inc. Rejoined Microsoft in 1986.

William B. Patton Jr.
President and CEO, MAI Basic Four, Inc.

John Paulson
President and CEO, Springboard Software Inc.

Jerry K. Pearlman
Chairman, President & CEO, Zenith Electronics Corporation

Laura J. Peck
Computer and communications industries analyst with L.F. Rothschild, Unterberg, Towbin.

Chuck Peddle
Founded Intelligent Terminal Systems in 1970 and Sirius Systems Technology in 1980, which became Victor Technologies Inc. Designed 6800 chip at Motorola, 6502 chip at MOS Technology, and PET computer for Commodore.

Paul J. Pedevillano
Sr Vice President & CFO, Alloy Computer Products, Inc.

Martin Pelcyger
Exec Vice President, Computer Horizons Corporation

Arno Penzias
 Vice President of Research at Bell Laboratories and Nobel Prize-winner in Physics.

Thomas J. Perkins
 Founded University Laboratories and merged it into Spectra-Physics in 1970. Co-founded Kleiner, Perkins, Caufield & Byers in 1972 providing venture capital to Tandem Computer (Chairman), Sun Microsystems, Electronic Arts, Quantum, & Plexus.

H. Ross Perot
 In 1962 founded Electronic Data Systems Corp., which was acquired by General Motors in 1984 for $2.5 billion. Largest stockholder and director of GM (GM stocks were purchased for $700M). Investor with Steve Jobs in Next, Inc.

Dave Peterschmidt
Vice President, Sales, Lex Electronics Inc.

Gregor G. Peterson
Chairman, Hogan Systems, Inc.

John F. Phillips
Chairman, Advanced Computer Techniques Corporation

Thomas L. Phillips
Chairman and CEO, Raytheon

Robert B. Phinizy
Chairman and CEO, Genisco Technology Corporation

Richard A. (Dick) Pick
 President of Pick Systems, which markets the latest version of the Pick operating system. Since 1972, Pick operating systems have been implemented on 30 different hardware systems from PCs to mainframes.

Michael Pickett
President and COO, Softsel Computer Products, Inc.

Randall M. **Pierson**
Sr Vice President, Marketing, Key Tronic Corporation

Joseph A. **Piscopo**
Chairman, Pansophic Systems, Inc.

Robin **Podmore**
Vice President, ESCA Corporation

J. William **Poduska**
Founded Prime Computer Inc. in 1972 with Robert Baron. Founded Apollo Computer Inc. and Stellar Computer Corp.

Ryal R. **Poppa**
Revitalized Pertec Corp. from 1973 to 1979, then BMC Industries, and since 1985, Storage Technology Corp.

Jerry **Pournelle**
Science fiction writer and computer columnist for INFOWORLD.

Karl C. (Casey) **Powell**
Co-founder, with 16 other ex-Intel employees, of Sequent Computer Systems Inc. Chief executive since 1983.

Thomas G. **Pownall**
Chairman and CEO, Martin Marietta Corporation

David B. **Pratt**
Sr Vice President and COO, Quantum Corporation

George **Pratt**
Chairman and CEO, Computer Automation

Michael **Preletz**
President and COO, Rexon Incorporated

Edward C. **Prellwitz**
Vice President, Planning, General Signal Corporation

Michele Preston
 A PC analyst on Wall Street. Joined Salomon Brothers in 1986 after four years with L.F. Rothschild, Unterberg, Tobin, which arranged initial public offerings for Compaq, Businessland, Lotus and others.

Peter Preuss
Chairman and CEO, Integrated Software Systems Corporation

Robert M. Price
 Succeeded Bill Norris as chairman and CEO of Control Data in 1986.

Gerald G. Probst
 Chairman of Sperry Corp. prior to acquisition by Burroughs in 1986.

Michael L. Quealy
Vice President, Ciprico Inc.

Safi U. Qureshey
 Co-founder of and the "S" in AST Research.

Richard Rabins
President & CEO, Alpha Software Corporation

Joel Rakow
Exec VP and CEO, American Training International

Ed Ramos
 Ex-president of Future Information Systems, originally a Wall Street office machine retailer that added personal computers in 1977; sold to Computone Systems Inc. in 1985.

Andrew Rappaport
 Former editor of EDN. Now president of Technology Research Group consulting on electronic design automation product strategy.

C. Wayne Ratliff
 Developed Vulcan in 1978, a microcomputer database program renamed dBASE II and sold to Ashton-Tate for $6 million in 1983. Joined Migent Inc. in 1986.

Sheldon Razin
Chairman and President, Quality Systems, Inc.

James J. Renier
Vice Chairman, Honeywell Inc.

Robert P. Reuss
Chairman and CEO, Centel Corporation

Walden C. Rhines
President of the Data Systems Group at Texas Instruments.

Mary Rich
Chairwoman of NCC'86 and principal in consulting firm PFS which advises end users on data base management systems.

Herbert J. Richman
Exec Vice President, Data General

Dennis M. Ritchie
With Brian Kernighan at Bell Laboratories, developed the UNIX operating system and the C programming language, published in 1978.

George Riviere
Vice President, Development, State of the Art Inc.

John V. Roach
President, CEO and chairman of Tandy Corporation.

Owen W. Robbins
Vice President & CFO, Teradyne, Inc.

Dr. H. Edward (Ed) Roberts
Father of the personal computer. Founder of MITS Inc., which introduced the Altair PC in 1974; sold MITS to Pertec in 1977. Earned MD degree. Founded DataBlocks Inc. in 1986.

George A. Roberts
President, Teledyne, Inc.

Bert C. Roberts Jr.
President and COO, MCI Communications Corp.

Sandy Robertson
General partner at Robertson, Colman & Stephens.

William O. **Robeson**
President and CEO, Computone Systems, Inc.

Victor A. **Rocchio**
President, Technalysis Corporation

Arthur **Rock**
 Founded Arthur Rock & Co. and helped fund Intel Corp., Apple Computer and many others.

Margaret **Rodenburg**
Vice President, Marketing, Entre' Computer Centers, Inc.

John A. **Rollwagen**
Chairman and CEO, Cray Research, Inc.

Jeff **Roloff**
President, Central Data

William I. **Rolya**
President and COO, Delta Data Systems Corporation

Carmen V. **Romeo**
Exec Vice President, SEI Corporation

Joseph W. **Rooney**
Exec Vice President, Corvus Systems, Inc.

Benjamin M. (Ben) **Rosen**
 In 1981 with L.J. Sevin founded Sevin Rosen Management, which provided venture capital to Lotus
and to the following companies (which he also chairs): Compaq, Ansa, Quarterdeck & Expertel.
Analyst with Morgan Stanley for 15 years. Edited ROSEN LETTER.

Edward **Rosen**
President and CEO, Ziyad Inc.

Douglas T. (Doug) **Ross**
 Created APT (Automatically Programmed Tools), a standard programming language for machine
tools in 1959, and founded SofTech, Inc. in 1969.

Charles **Rossotti**
President and CEO, American Management Systems, Inc.

Jonathan **Rotenberg**
Founder at the age of 15 and president of The Boston Computer Society, the world's largest association of personal computer users.

John **Roth**
President and CEO, APTOS Systems Corporation

Michael **Rothbart**
Chairman and CEO, Terminal Data Corporation

Seymour **Rubinstein**
Founder and chairman emeritus of MicroPro, which developed WordStar, an early successful word processing program for personal computers.

Michael C. **Ruettgers**
Vice President, Keane Incorporated

Charles E. **Rueve**
President and CEO, Dyatron Corporation

Lee **Runzheimer**
Chief Financial Officer, Dicomed Corporation

John M. **Russell**
Vice President and CFO, Convergent Technologies, Inc.

Jim **Rutherford**
President, Goal Systems International

Harry J. **Saal**
Co-founded with Leonard Shustek first Nestar Systems Inc. in 1978 and then Network General Corp. in 1986.

Shoichi **Saba**
President, Toshiba Corporation

Jonathon **Sachs**
Single-handedly wrote 1-2-3, the Lotus Development hit conceived by Mitch Kapor.

Akira **Saeki**
President, Sharp Corporation

Glenn C. Salley
President and CEO, Distributed Logic Corporation

Jean Sammet
IBM authority on programming languages.

Dr. John W. Sammon Jr.
Chairman and President, Par Technology Corporation

David S. Samuels
President and CEO, State of the Art Inc.

Eric Sandberg-Diment
Syndicated writer for INFOWORLD.

W.J. (Jerry) Sanders III
Founder in 1969 and CEO of Advanced Micro Devices Inc.

Michael L. Sanyour
President and COO, Avant-Garde Computing, Inc.

Joseph A. Saponaro
Exec Vice President & COO, Intermetrics, Inc.

A. Eugene Sapp Jr.
President and COO, SCI Systems, Inc.

John A. Sasso
President, CEO and COO, Esprit Systems, Inc.

Edward W. Savarese
Chairman and CEO, Personal Computer Products, Inc.

Teruo Sawachi
President, Nippon Univac Kaisha Ltd.

Michael C. Saylor
Vice President, Sales, Libra Programming

Guy Scalzi
Vice President, DataEase International Inc.

Oscar H. **Schachter**
President & CEO, Advanced Computer Techniques Corporation

Richard J. **Schineller**
President and CEO, Decision Industries Corporation

Edward J. **Schneider**
Vice President, Computer Products Inc.

Lawrence J. **Schoenberg**
Chairman and CEO, AGS Computer Inc.

David O. **Schupp**
Vice President, Interface Systems Inc.

Allan **Schwartz**
Chairman, Computer Resources Inc.

Bernard L. **Schwartz**
Chairman and chief executive of Loral Corp., the defense electronics company acquired in 1986 by Lockeed Corp.

James R. **Schwartz**
President, Terminal Data Corporation

Gordon **Scott**
Chief Financial Officer, Advanced Input Devices

Michael (Mike) **Scott**
President of Apple Computer until 1981.

John **Sculley**
President of Apple Computer since 1983. Former president of PepsiCo Inc.'s Pepsi Cola subsidiary.

Dennis R. **Searles**
President and COO, Tab Products Co.

Matthias **Seefelder**
Chairman, BASF Aktiengesellschaft

Tadahiro **Sekimoto**
President, NEC Corporation

Ivan Selin
Chairman, American Management Systems, Inc.

David Seuss
President, Spinnaker Software Corporation

L.J. Sevin
Founded Mostek in 1965 and in 1981 with Ben Rosen co-founded Sevin Rosen Management, which provided venture capital to Lotus Development, Compaq, and some 25 others.

Michael Shabazian
President of ComputerLand from 1984 to 1986; then president & CEO of Abaton Technology Corp., a desktop publishing and peripherals firm.

Ramesh P. Shah
Vice Chairman and CEO, Computer Resources Inc.

Michael Shane
Founder and chairman of Leading Edge Products Inc. and Leading Edge World Trade.

Herb Shaver
Vice President, Datatab Inc.

Israel Sheinberg
Exec Vice President, Recognition Equipment, Inc.

Mark Shepherd, Jr.
Joined Texas Instruments in 1948; named president in 1967 and chairman in 1976.

Rick Sherlund
Computer industry analyst with Goldman Sachs.

Takayoshi Shiina
Founded Sord Computer Company in Tokyo in 1970 after seven years selling Digital Equipment Corp. minicomputers for Rikei Industries.

S. Shindo
Chairman, Mitsubishi Electric Corporation

Hisashi Shinto
President, Nippon Telegraph and Telephone Corporation

Dale L. Shipley
Co-founder and VP of engineering for Tolerant Systems Inc.

Jon A. Shirley
President & COO of Microsoft Corporation. Formerly VP at Tandy.

Donald G. Shively
Exec VP, Operations, Cincinnati Milacron Inc.

Frank Shrontz
President, Boeing Company

Alan F. Shugart
After 18 years at IBM, left for Memorex in 1969. Left Memorex in 1973 to start Shugart & Associates. Founded Seagate Technology.

Edward J. Siegel
CFO & Exec Vice President, On-Line Software International, Inc.

Ronald (Ron) Siegel
Founded Gateway Computer Systems in 1979 and built a regional chain of 11 computer stores before it was acquired by Boardroom Business Products in 1986.

James L. Siehl
President and CEO, Corvus Systems, Inc.

A. David Silver
Managing General Partner of the Santa Fe Private Equity Fund investing venture capital in some 140 companies. Also author of several books on venture financing.

Douglas Sims
Vice President, Marketing, Ziyad Inc.

James K. Sims
President and CEO, Concurrent Computer Corporation

Sir Clive Sinclair
British inventor who founded Sinclair Research Ltd., which develops products ranging from calculators to electric cars to low cost PCs. All product rights were acquired in 1986 by Amstrad Consumer Electronics plc.

Henry E. Singleton
Chairman and CEO, Teledyne, Inc.

Don F. Sinsabaugh
Computer industry analyst with Swergold Chefitz.

Warren J. Sinsheimer
Chm. of Plessey No. America, Plessey Company plc

F.B. Sirotek
Chief Executive Officer, Sir-Tech Software Inc.

Robert Sirotek
Vice President, Sir-Tech Software Inc.

Rolf Skar
President, Norsk Data A.S.

Alton L. Skeeter
Exec Vice President, Systems Management American Corporation

Frank Slouvenec
Vice President, Sales, Microrim Inc.

William R. Smart
Chairman, Electronic Associates Inc.

S.E. Smiszko
Vice President, Western Union Corporation

Marshall F. Smith
President and CEO Commodore International Ltd.

Milton R. Smith
Chairman and CEO, Floating Point Systems, Inc.

Roger B. Smith
Chairman and CEO, General Motors Corporation

Guy B. Snowden
President and CEO, GTECH Corporation

Mike Solomon
Vice President, Sales, Aldus Corporation

Fukujiro **Sono**
Chairman, TDK Corporation

Edson W. **Spencer**
Chairman and CEO, Honeywell Inc.

Charles E. **Sporck**
President and CEO, National Semiconductor

Peter J. **Sprague**
Chairman, National Semiconductor

Parker **Srouse**
Chairman and CEO, ESCA Corporation

Doug **St. John**
Sr Vice Pres., Product Development, MicroPro International Corporation

Delbert C. **Staley**
Chairman and CEO, NYNEX Corporation

David **Stamm**
Co-founder and director of Daisy Systems Corp.

Ray **Stata**
Chairman and President, Analog Devices, Inc.

Bill **Stealey**
Chief Executive Officer, Microprose Software

Robert **Stein**
President and CEO, Centronics Data Computer Corporation

John **Stephens**
Sr Vice President, Stockholder Systems Inc.

Paul G. **Stern**
President and COO, Burroughs Corporation

Robert K. Stern
Chairman, GTECH Corporation

James R. Stover
President and COO, Eaton Corp

J. Leland Strange
Chairman, President & CEO, Intelligent Systems Corporation

William D. Strecker
 At Digital Equipment Corp. principal designer of VAX-11 architecture, and interconnect and communications for VAX clusters.

Gary Streuter
 Former president of Computer Memories Inc. Founded ProAPP in 1986 to make add-on hard disk-drives for Apple computers.

Carl W. Stursberg Jr.
Chairman, Decision Industries Corporation

Go Sugiura
 Founded Amdek Corp. in 1977 to import monitors. Amdek was acquired in 1986 by Wyse Technology.

Lawrence T. Sullivan
Chairman, Numerix Corporation

Dennis J. Sullivan Jr.
Exec Vice President, Cincinnati Bell

Ivan E. Sutherland
 Co-founder and director of Evans & Sutherland. Also designer, professor, venture partner, and pioneer.

Bjom Svedberg
President & CEO, Ericsson

Linda Swanson-Davies
Manager, Sales, Central Point Software Inc.

Hugh M. Taft
Chairman and President, Vermont Research Corporation

Duye **Takeshi**
President, Ricoh Co. Ltd.

Sirjang Lal (Jugi) **Tandon**
Left Memorex in 1973 to start a floppy disk drive business for Pertec Computer Corp. Founded Tandon Corp. in 1975.

Akio **Tanii**
President, Matsushita Electric Industrial Co. Ltd.

Robert V. **Tarantino**
President and CEO, Dataram Corporation

Blodwen **Tarter**
Director, Marketing, Channelmark Corporation

Patrick H. **Thomas**
Chairman, President & CEO, First Financial Management Corporation

Ronald B. **Thomas**
Chairman, President & CEO, Ciprico Inc.

Rowland H. **Thomas** Jr.
Sr Exec Vice President, National Data Corporation

Frank **Thomason**
Vice President & Treas, Computone Systems, Inc.

James E. **Thornton**
Chairman, Network Systems Corp.

Robert S. **Throop**
Chairman and CEO, Anthem Electronics Inc.

James A. **Thwaits**
President Intl Operations, 3M Company

Darrell **Ticehurst**
Founded the accounting software company Quest Inc., and with George Morrow founded Intelligent Access in 1986.

John Tincler
President and COO, US Design Corporation

Wyman Titwell
President, Setpoint

Randall L. Tobias
Chairman and CEO at AT&T Communications and Information Systems.

Richard Todd
Vice President, Finance, Microprose Software

Robert Todd
President and CEO, Flextronics Inc.

James S. Toreson
Founded Microcomputer Systems Corp. in 1974 to produce a hard disk controller for a minicomputer using a microprocessor. In 1980 bought Xebec Systems, which went public in 1983 as Xebec Corp.

Enzo N. Torresi
Co-founded Businessland with David Norman.

Seiki Tosaki
Chairman, C. Itoh & Co. Ltd.

Jack Tramiel
Founded Commodore International in 1954 and ran it until 1984, when he quit and acquired Atari.

James G. Treybig
President and CEO, Tandem Computers, Inc.

Thi T. Truong
Developed French-built Micral, marketed in 1975 and acknowledged as one of the first successful PCs marketed outside the U.S.

Bernard K. Tse
Chairman and CEO, Wyse Technology

William J. Turner
President, Automatic Data Processing

Mathew E. **Tutino**
President and CEO, Mohawk Data Sciences Corporation

Graham **Tyson**
President, Dataproducts Corporation

Ralph K. **Ungermann**
Chairman, President & CEO, Ungermann-Bass, Inc.

Herman E. **Valentine**
President and CEO, Systems Management American Corporation

Lloyd **Van Horn**
Vice President, Setpoint

H. **Van Riemsdijk**
Chairman, Philips N V

Bart **Van Voorhis**
Exec Vice President, WordTech Systems Inc.

Deryk **Vander Weyer**
Chairman, Mitel Corporation

Thomas A. **Vanderslice**
Chairman, President & CEO, Apollo Computer Inc. Formerly VP at General Electric.

Al **Vezza**
Founded Infocom in 1979 with Joel Berez and several others to produce the Zork trilogy and other games.

D.G. **Vice**
President, Northern Telecom Ltd.

Phil **Villars**
Co-founded Computervision with Martin Allen in 1969. Founded Automatix in 1980 and Cognition in 1985.

Bruno **Visentini**
Chairman, Ing. C. Olivetti & Co. S.P.A.

Raymond P. **Von Culin**
Chairman, Dataram Corporation

William F. **Von Meister**
Founded Source Telecomputing Corp. in 1979.

John C. **Waddell**
Chairman and CEO, Arrow Electronics, Inc.

David S. (Dave) **Wagman**
Co-founder of Softsel Computer Products Inc. in 1980 with Robert Leff.

Gerald **Wagner**
Founded Execucom Systems Corporation and developed both concept and software for decision
support systems.

Stanley A. **Wainer**
Chairman and CEO, Wyle Laboratories

Robert G. **Walden**
Sr Vice President and CFO, Logicon Inc.

Jeffrey L. **Walker**
Chief Financial Officer, Oracle Systems

John **Walker**
Co-founded Autodesk, Inc. with Daniel L. Drake.

Steve **Wallach**
In 1982 co-founded with Robert J. Paluck, Convex Computer Corporation, a manufacturer of
minisupercomputers. Previously, product marketing manager at ROLM Corporation and manager of
advanced development of Eclipse Systems for Data General Corporation.

Richard A. **Walter**
Chairman and CEO, Scientific Computers Inc.

An **Wang**
Inventor of core memory and founder and chairman of Wang Laboratories Inc.

Anthony W. **Wang**
President and COO, Computer Associates International Inc.

Ben Wang
Founded Rexon Inc. in 1978 and tape drive subsidiary Wangtek Inc. in 1982, leaving both in 1986.

Charles B. Wang
Founded Computer Associates Inc.

Fredrick A. Wang
President, Wang Laboratories, Inc.

Earl Wantland
President and CEO, Tektronix, Inc.

Jim Warren
Founding editor of DR. DOBB'S JOURNAL OF COMPUTER CALISTHENTICS AND ORTHODONTIA, INTELLIGENT MACHINES JOURNAL renamed INFOWORLD, and in 1976 the West Coast Computer Faire.

Robert Warren
President, Premier Industrial Corporation

Tom Warren
Sr Vice President, BKW Systems, Inc.

Ken Waters
President and COO, ComputerLand Corporation

Gordon M. Watson
Sr Vice President, Sales, Local Data, Inc.

Ulric Weil
Washington consultant and mainframe computer industry analyst for Gartner Securities Corp.

George Weinberger
Chairman and President, Health Information Systems Inc.

Gershon Weintraub
Vice President, Health Information Systems Inc.

Ira Weise
Founded 800-Software in 1982 for mail-order software distribution.

William L. Weiss
Chairman and CEO, Ameritech

William J. Weisz
Vice Chairman and COO, Motorola Inc.

John F. Welch Jr.
Chairman and CEO, General Electric Company

William F. Welsh II
President and COO, Valmont Industries, Inc.

Alfred P. West Jr.
Chairman, President & CEO, SEI Corporation

Josh S. Weston
Chairman and CEO, Automatic Data Processing

David J. Wheeler
Professor of computer science at Cambridge University. Created first wired-in assembler and concept of closed subroutines.

Eugene R. (Gene) White
Chairman, Amdahl Corporation and System Industries Inc.

Philip E. White
President and COO, Wyse Technology

Robie White
Chief Financial Officer, Alpha Software Corporation

Kay R. Whitmore
President, Eastman Kodak Company

L.C. Whitney
Chairman, President & CEO, National Data Corporation

Anthony J. Whitton
President, Lex Electronics Inc.

Robert S. Wiggins
Chairman, President & CEO, Paradyne Corporation

Albert B. Wight
President and COO, Sanders Associates, Inc.

Richard C. **Wilcox**
Chairman, Alpha Microsystems

Q.T. **Wiles**
 Chairman of Hambrecht & Quist Inc. and of seven high-tech companies including Rexon Inc. and MiniScribe Corp. Past turn-arounds include Good-All Electric and Granger Associates.

Dan H. **Wilkie**
President and COO, Tandon Corporation

Jeffrey **Wilkins**
 Founded Meisner-Wilkins in 1967 and CompuServe in 1970.

Sir Graham **Wilkins**
Chairman and CEO, Thorn-EMI plc

Sterling **William**
President and CEO, Sterling Software, Inc.

Leon **Williams**
 President & CEO of MicroPro (1986). Previously, 12 years with Monchik-Weber before negotiating its sale to McGraw-Hill in 1984.

Theodore **Williams**
Chairman, President & CEO, Bell Industries Inc.

Camilo **Wilson**
 Founded Lifetree Software Inc. in 1982 to sell the word processor Volkswriter.

Edward T. **Wilson**
Chairman, Micros Systems, Inc.

G. Larry **Wilson**
Chairman and President, Policy Management Systems Corporation

J. Peter **Wilson**
President and COO, Archive Corporation

T.A. **Wilson**
Chairman and CEO Boeing Company

Warren Winger
Founder of CompuShop Inc., which he sold to Bell Atlantic in 1985.

Francis Winn
Chairman, Computer Language Research

Steve Winn
President and CEO, Computer Language Research

Walter Winnitzki
Computer industry analyst for L.F. Rothschild, Unterberg, Towbin.

Ted Withington
Computer industry analyst with A.D. Little.

Amy D. Wohl
Office automation analyst, principal of Amy D. Wohl & Associates Inc. and editor of THE WOHL REPORT ON END-USER COMPUTING newsletter.

Charles Wohlstetter
Chairman, Continental Telecom, Inc.

Albert C. Wong
Co-founder of and the "A" in AST Research.

John R. Woodhull
President and CEO, Logicon Inc.

J. Mark Woods
Exec Vice President & COO, Anacomp, Inc.

Steve Wozniak
Co-founder with Steve Jobs of Apple Computer in 1976 and designer of the original Apple computer. Founded CL-9.

Sam Wyly
In 1963 founded University Computing Co., which became Uccel. Also founded Datran.

Takuma Yamamoto
President, Fujitsu Ltd.

Frank **Yanda**
Regional President, Teleconnect

Jean **Yates**
Founded Yates Associates to research UNIX market and sold it in 1984 to International Data Corporation, where she is a VP.

Jose **Yglesias**
Chairman and CEO, Syscon Corporation

William T. **Ylvisaker**
Chairman and CEO, Gould Inc.

Delbert W. **Yocam**
Exec Vice President & COO, Apple Computer

Leo W. **Yochum**
Sr Vice President, Finance, Westinghouse Electric Corporation

David C. **Yoder**
Chairman, President, & CEO, Computer Products Inc.

Isao **Yonekura**
President, C. Itoh & Co. Ltd.

Hirokichi **Yoshiyama**
Chairman, Hitachi Ltd.

John A. **Young**
President and CEO, Hewlett-Packard Company

Ed **Yourdon**
President of Yourdon Inc. and an authority on structured programming.

Tom **Yuen**
Co-founder of and the "T" in AST Research.

David **Zacarias**
Chief Operating Officer, Altos Computer Systems

Norman **Zachary**
President and COO, Data Architects, Inc.

William F. Zachmann
Vice President and computer analyst for International Data Corporation.

David O. Zertuche
VP Finance and CFO, Marshall Industries

Daniel W. Zipkin
President and COO, Personal Computer Products, Inc.

Lewis G. Zirkle
Chairman, President & CEO, Key Tronic Corporation

Thomas B. Zmach
Vice President, Marketing, Anderson Jacobson Inc.

George A. Zugmier
Chairman and President, Lodgistix, Inc.

5 INTERNATIONAL MARKETPLACE

DATAMATION
EUROPEAN 25
August 1, 1986

"Economic conditions on the Continent beefed up the 1985 revenues of Europe's leading data processing companies; the top 25 companies in the European market last year had revenues totaling $34.5 billion. All revenue figures have been adjusted to calendar year calculations. All European company figures were converted to U.S. dollars, using OECD exchange rates."--DATAMATION.

1985 Rank	1984 Rank	Company	Head-quarters	1985 Eur DP Rev ($M)	Total DP Rev ($M)
1	1	International Business Machines	U.S.	13,440.2	48,554.0
2	2	Siemens AG	W. Germany	2,775.2	3,265.0
3	4	Digital Equipment Corp.	U.S.	2,179.1	7,029.4
4	3	Ing. C. Olivetti & Co. S.P.A.	Italy	1,862.8	2,637.7
5	5	Groupe Bull	France	1,668.8	1,794.5
6	8	Nixdorf Computer AG	W. Germany	1,192.5	1,339.9
7	9	Burroughs Corp.	U.S.	1,124.4	4,685.3
8	6	L.M. Ericsson	Sweden	1,097.1	1,232.8
9	11	N.V. Philips Gloeilampenfabrieken	Netherlands	1,078.2	1,365.6
10	10	STC plc	U.K.	1,038.0	1,330.8
11	12	Sperry Corp.	U.S.	1,020.0	4,755.1
12	7	Hewlett-Packard Co.	U.S.	992.2	3,675.0
13	13	NCR Corp.	U.S.	932.5	3,885.5
14	19	Honeywell Inc.	U.S.	487.9	1,951.9
15	--	British Telecom	U.K.	455.1	455.1
16	14	Wang Laboratories Inc.	U.S.	437.0	2,428.3
17	--	Compagnie Generale d'Electricite	France	431.1	479.0
18	16	Control Data Corp.	U.S.	423.0	3,679.7
19	15	Commodore International Ltd.	U.S.	397.5	750.0
20	17	Mannesmann AG	W. Germany	320.1	355.7
21	23	BASF	W. Germany	282.1	357.1
22	--	Prime Computer Inc.	U.S.	238.6	769.7
23	18	Apple Computer Corp.	U.S.	227.9	1,753.8
24	20	Plessey Co. plc	U.K.	225.0	250.0
25	--	Atlantic Computers plc	U.K.	219.5	224.4

DATAMATION
JAPAN 10
September 1, 1986

This list ranks the 10 leading data processing companies in Japan. According to DATAMATION, Japan is the world's second largest data processing market. "The 1985 Japan top 10 survey was compiled exclusively by DATAMATION from information culled from our in-house database, which tracks the dp results of over 200 companies worldwide. The fiscal year of most Japanese companies ends March 31 and consolidated results are usually not announced until three to four months later. Therefore, DATAMATION has revised some of the figures in its database to reflect this more recent information. All revenue and earnings figures have also been adjusted to calendar year calculations and converted to U.S. dollars, using OECD exchange rates for the appropriate period."--DATAMATION.

1985 Rank	1984 Rank	Company	1985 Japan DP Rev ($MIL)	1985 Total DP Rev ($MIL)	1985 Total Rev ($MIL)
1	1	Fujitsu Ltd.	$3,528.6	$4,303.5	$6,550.2
2	2	NEC Corp.	2,965.3	3,753.5	9,704.8
3	3	IBM Japan Ltd.	2,677.5	48,554.0*	50,056.0*
4	4	Hitachi Ltd.	2,346.8	2,879.1	20,995.7
5	--	Matsushita Electric Industry	1,154.0	1,444.1	21,174.7
6	5	Toshiba Corp.	1,105.6	1,382.0	14,101.9
7	--	Nippon Telegraph & Telephone	762.3	762.3	20,606.0
8	6	Mitsubishi Electric Corp.	719.1	887.8	8,762.0
9	7	Oki Electric Industry Co. Ltd.	621.9	888.4	1,676.3
10	8	Nippon Univac Kaisha Ltd.	552.2	552.2	552.2

* Includes parent company revenues.

ELECTRONIC NEWS
LOOKING AT THE LEADERS 1986
August 25, 1986

This list ranks the leading foreign manufacturers in the electronics industry by each company's
electronics sales.--COMPUTER INDUSTRY ALMANAC.

Reprinted with permission from ELECTRONIC NEWS, August 25, 1986. Copyright 1986 by
Fairchild Publications, New York, NY.

	Foreign Companies	Electronic Sales	Percent of Electronic Sales	Latest Available Four Quarters
1	N.V. Philips	$19,071,744,000	75.0%	$25,428,992,000
2	Matsushita	16,553,000,000	70.0	23,647,000,000
3	Hitachi Ltd.	16,505,000,000	56.0	29,473,000,000
4	Siemens	12,701,400,000	50.0	25,403,790,000
5	NEC	10,900,000,000	100.0	10,900,000,000
6	Toshiba	10,113,266,000	54.0	18,738,638,000
7	Fujitsu Ltd.	7,942,000,000	100.0	7,942,000,000
8	Northern Telecom Ltd.	5,436,400,000	93.4	5,814,300,000
9	General Electric Co. plc	4,975,641,000	64.0	7,774,440,000
10	Thomson-CSF	3,622,000,000	100.0	3,622,000,000
11	Mitsubishi	3,015,300,000	24.3	12,408,700,000
12	LM Ericsson	2,911,000,000	62.7	4,642,000,000
13	Plessey Co. plc	2,054,306,000	95.0	2,162,428,000
14	Nixdorf Computer AG	1,725,000,000	100.0	1,725,000,000
15	Racal Electronics plc	1,686,753,000	90.0	1,874,170,000
16	Oki Electric	1,632,080,000	100.0	1,632,080,000
17	Thorn EMI	1,260,812,000	25.7	4,908,420,000
18	Sharp Corp.	1,069,200,000	81.0	1,320,000,000

*Estimated by Electronic News

FORBES

THE 500 LARGEST FOREIGN COMPANIES: COMMUNICATIONS, ELECTRICAL
EQUIPMENT AND OFFICE EQUIPMENT
April 18, 1986

This list ranks the top 500 foreign companies by revenue, organizes them by industry and positions
them by company sales. The current and previous year's ranks in the top 500 are also shown.--
COMPUTER INDUSTRY ALMANAC.

From this list COMPUTER INDUSTRY ALMANAC has selected only industry-related companies.

1985 Rank	1984 Rank	Company	Country	Fiscal year-end	Revenue (millions)	Employees (thousands)
Communications						
12	18	Nippon Telegraph & Telephone Corp	Japan	Mar	$23,029	300.0
27	22	Deutsche Bundespost	Germany	Dec	17,227	488.1
41	32	PTT-Postes et Telecommunications	France	Dec	14,256	499.0
56	68	British Telecom	UK	Mar	11,554	236.0
74	84	Bell Canada Enterprises	Canada	Dec	9,708	108.3
230	207	British Post Office	UK	Mar	4,036	182.4
258	267	Telefonaktiebolaget LM Ericsson	Sweden	Dec	3,776	74.7
298	297	Schweizerische PTT	Switzerland	Dec	3,383	57.0
328	326	Netherlands PTT	Netherlands	Dec	3,186	90.6
391	388	STC Group Plc	UK	Dec	2,589	48.0
420	440	Telefonica	Spain	Dec	2,421	62.8

(Continued next page)

FORBES

THE 500 LARGEST FOREIGN COMPANIES: COMMUNICATIONS, ELECTRICAL
EQUIPMENT AND OFFICE EQUIPMENT (Continued)

1985 Rank	1984 Rank	Company	Country	Fiscal year-end	Revenue (millions)	Employees (thousands)
Electrical Equipment						
22	25	Philips Group	Netherlands	Dec	$18,078	347.2
24	26	Siemens Group	Germany	Sept	17,841	348.0
87	80	Cie Generale d'Electricite	France	Dec	8,741	153.8
120	114	Le Groupe Thomson	France	Dec	6,588	107.0
149	176	BBC-Brown Boveri Group	Switzerland	Dec	5,647	97.8
188	195	ASEA Group	Sweden	Dec	4,672	61.0
263	238	AEG Group	Germany	Dec	3,683	73.8
373	406	Sumitomo Electric Industries Ltd	Japan	Mar	2,756	12.8
377	360	BICC Plc Group	UK	Dec	2,733	46.4
409	415	Furukawa Electric Co Ltd	Japan	Mar	2,486	7.7
413	419	Matsushita Electric Works	Japan	Nov	2,464	16.2
80	95	NEC Corp	Japan	Mar	9,248	90.1
Office Equipment						
124	157	Fujitsu Ltd	Japan	Mar	6,397	74.2
236	272	Canon Inc	Japan	Dec	4,006	34.1
317	394	Olivetti Group	Italy	Dec	3,215	48.9
464	*	Ricoh Co Ltd	Japan	Mar	2,234	25.0

*Not ranked last year.

FORTUNE

THE FORTUNE INTERNATIONAL 500: THE 500 LARGEST INDUSTRIAL CORPORATIONS OUTSIDE THE U.S.
August 4, 1986

"The International 500 is the FORTUNE directory of the largest industrial corporations outside the U.S. The revenues of computer companies rose faster than any other industry's group. All companies on the list have derived more than 50% of their sales from manufacturing/mining. Net income is shown after taxes, minority interests and extraordinary items. Figures have been converted to U.S. dollars. Employee figure shown is year-end."--FORTUNE.
From this list COMPUTER INDUSTRY ALMANAC has selected ony the industry-related companies.

Rank	Company	Country	Sales ($000)	Net Income ($000)	Employees
7	Matsushita Electric Industrial	Japan	$20,749,191	$1,012,044	133,963
8	Hitachi (2)	Japan	20,525,413	860,448	164,951
13	Philips' Gloeilampenfabrieken	Netherlands	18,079,488	276,710	345,600
14	Siemens (3)	W. Germany	17,833,563	490,555	348,000
23	Samsung	South Korea	14,193,095	113,258	129,039
25	Hyundai	South Korea	14,024,594	79,601	156,000
31	Toshiba (2)	Japan	13,502,659	352,588	114,000
43	Lucky-Goldstar	South Korea	9,859,920	78,501	62,500
47	NEC (2)	Japan	9,246,225	274,872	90,102
48	CGE(Cie.Generale d'Electricite)	France	8,741,903	84,752	153,800
49	Daewoo	South Korea	8,698,021	53,587	92,745
64	General Electric	Britain	6,556,571	520,809	165,593
68	Fujitsu (2)	Japan	6,396,195	364,498	74,187
73	Sanyo Electric (5)	Japan	6,227,998	149,342	25,429
74	Mannesmann	W. Germany	6,171,069	77,700	107,804
75	Schlumberger	Neth. Antilles	6,119,447	351,036	72,810
80	Sony (6,7)	Japan	5,776,507	297,409	44,908
106	Sharp (2)	Japan	4,671,672	162,703	28,221

(Continued next page)

(2) Figures are for fiscal year ended March 31, 1985
(3) Figures are for fiscal year ended September 30, 1985
(5) Figures are for fiscal year ended November 30, 1985
(6) Figures are for fiscal year ended October 31, 1985
(7) Includes only wholly owned subsidiaries

THE FORTUNE INTERNATIONAL 500: THE 500 LARGEST INDUSTRIAL CORPORATIONS OUTSIDE THE U.S. (Continued)

Rank	Company	Country	Sales ($000)	Net Income ($000)	Employees
111	IBM Deutschland	W. Germany	$4,493,532	$289,383	28,172
117	Northern Telecom	Canada	4,259,776	301,190	46,549
118	IBM France	France	4,181,080	319,978	22,452
124	Thorn EMI (2)	Britain	4,023,339	47,460	89,354
125	Canon	Japan	4,008,023	155,393	34,129
127	IBM United Kingdom Holdings	Britain	3,941,459	399,040	18,798
130	IBM Japan	Japan	3,835,081	306,101	16,775
132	L.M. Ericsson Telephone	Sweden	3,817,493	85,452	78,159
138	AEG Aktiengesellschaft (8)	W. Germany	3,682,628	--	73,760
158	Olivetti	Italy	3,215,744	263,771	48,944
190	STC (9)	Britain	2,587,538	(69,702)	43,200
220	Ricoh (2)	Japan	2,231,139	68,619	25,000
243	Hattori Seiko(2)	Japan	2,051,953	10,846	7,701
278	Bull (4)	France	1,792,885	12,267	26,403
281	Plessey (2)	Britain	1,777,558	113,727	37,533
286	TDK (5)	Japan	1,762,647	24,390	14,661
297	Oki Electric Industry (2)	Japan	1,709,404	37,118	18,134
318	East Asiatic	Denmark	1,573,907	18,948	15,969
326	Alps Electric (2)	Japan	1,541,120	74,735	11,392
357	Racal Electronics (2)	Britain	1,389,876	96,257	33,167
358	Pioneer Electronic (3)	Japan	1,374,242	(9,883)	12,522
364	Nixdorf Computer	W. Germany	1,333,442	57,031	23,290
365	Kyocera (2)	Japan	1,329,679	155,873	17,133
403	Esselte	Sweden	1,187,661	21,134	17,177
448	Citizen Watch (2)	Japan	1,052,904	27,083	10,955
477	Casio Computer (10)	Japan	961,201	37,339	6,770

(2) Figures are for fiscal year ended March 31, 1985
(3) Figures are for fiscal year ended September 30, 1985
(4) Government owned
(5) Figures are for fiscal year ended November 30, 1985
(8) Name changed from AEG-Telefunken on June 27, 1985
(9) Name changed from Standard Telephones & Cables on June 17, 1985
(10) Figures are for fiscal year ended March 20, 1985

INTERNATIONAL STATISTICS
1986

In this section COMPUTER INDUSTRY ALMANAC presents key industry statistics estimated by country for 1986. In addition to comparing computers in use with telephones and televisions, the data includes computer power in MIPS (million instructions per second) with each country's share of worldwide MIPS. Also shown are MIPS per thousand people and computing power per person indexed against the United States, with the U.S. equal to 100.

Australia

Size in square miles:	#K	2968	Population:	#M	15.6
Gross National Product:	$B	160	Computers in use:	#M	.60
GNP/capita:	$	10237	Computers/person:	#	.038
Phones in use:	#M	9.7	Computer power-MIPS:	#K	206
Phones/person:	#	.621	Computing power share:	%	0.87
TVs in use:	#M	7.3	MIPS/1000 people:	#	13.17
TVs/person:	#	.465	Index versus USA:	#	24.7

Austria

Size in square miles:	#K	32	Population:	#M	7.6
Gross National Product:	$B	75	Computers in use:	#M	.12
GNP/capita:	$	9934	Computers/person:	#	.016
Phones in use:	#M	4.1	Computer power-MIPS:	#K	41
Phones/person:	#	.543	Computing power share:	%	0.17
TVs in use:	#M	2.6	MIPS/1000 people:	#	5.43
TVs/person:	#	.348	Index versus USA:	#	10.2

Belgium

Size in square miles:	#K	12	Population:	#M	9.9
Gross National Product:	$B	95	Computers in use:	#M	.29
GNP/capita:	$	9635	Computers/person:	#	.030
Phones in use:	#M	4.7	Computer power-MIPS:	#K	101
Phones/person:	#	.475	Computing power share:	%	0.43
TVs in use:	#M	3.3	MIPS/1000 people:	#	10.20
TVs/person:	#	.333	Index versus USA:	#	19.1

(Continued next page)

INTERNATIONAL STATISTICS (Continued)

Brazil

Size in square miles:	#K	3286	Population:	#M	140
Gross National Product:	$B	290	Computers in use:	#M	.39
GNP/capita:	$	2071	Computers/person:	#	.003
Phones in use:	#M	14.0	Computer power-MIPS:	#K	138
Phones/person:	#	.100	Computing power share:	%	0.58
TVs in use:	#M	20.1	MIPS/1000 people:	#	.99
TVs/person:	#	'.144	Index versus USA:	#	1.9

Canada

Size in square miles:	#K	3852	Population:	#M	25
Gross National Product:	$B	325	Computers in use:	#M	1.80
GNP/capita:	$	12795	Computers/person:	#	.071
Phones in use:	#M	17.5	Computer power-MIPS:	#K	600
Phones/person:	#	.691	Computing power share:	%	2.54
TVs in use:	#M	12.9	MIPS/1000 people:	#	23.62
TVs/person:	#	.509	Index versus USA:	#	44.3

China

Size in square miles:	#K	3705	Population:	#M	1038
Gross National Product:	$B	480	Computers in use:	#M	.29
GNP/capita:	$	462	Computers/person:	#	0.0003
Phones in use:	#M	7.3	Computer power-MIPS:	#K	88
Phones/person:	#	.007	Computing power share:	%	0.37
TVs in use:	#M	9.4	MIPS/1000 people:	#	.08
TVs/person:	#	.009	Index versus USA:	#	.2

Denmark

Size in square miles:	#K	17	Population:	#M	5.1
Gross National Product:	$B	57	Computers in use:	#M	.23
GNP/capita:	$	11176	Computers/person:	#	.045
Phones in use:	#M	3.7	Computer power-MIPS:	#K	78
Phones/person:	#	.734	Computing power share:	%	0.33
TVs in use:	#M	2.1	MIPS/1000 people:	#	15.34
TVs/person:	#	.406	Index versus USA:	#	28.8

(Continued next page)

INTERNATIONAL STATISTICS (Continued)

Europe

Size in square miles:	#K	1307	Population:	#M		343
Gross National Product:	$B	3288	Computers in use:	#M		14.45
GNP/capita:	$	9600	Computers/person:	#		0.042
Phones in use:	#M	202.8	Computer power-MIPS:	#K		4778
Phones/person:	#	.590	Computing power share:	%		20.20
TVs in use:	#M	136.4	MIPS/1000 people:	#		13.95
TVs/person:	#	.400	Index versus USA:	#		26.2

Finland

Size in square miles:	#K	130	Population:	#M		4.9
Gross National Product:	$B	49	Computers in use:	#M		.16
GNP/capita:	$	10000	Computers/person:	#		.033
Phones in use:	#M	3.2	Computer power-MIPS:	#K		56
Phones/person:	#	.656	Computing power share:	%		0.24
TVs in use:	#M	1.9	MIPS/1000 people:	#		11.41
TVs/person:	#	.393	Index versus USA:	#		21.4

France

Size in square miles:	#K	221	Population:	#M		55
Gross National Product:	$B	615	Computers in use:	#M		2.21
GNP/capita:	$	11182	Computers/person:	#		.040
Phones in use:	#M	37.2	Computer power-MIPS:	#K		736
Phones/person:	#	.676	Computing power share:	%		3.11
TVs in use:	#M	23.5	MIPS/1000 people:	#		13.37
TVs/person:	#	.428	Index versus USA:	#		25.1

Greece

Size in square miles:	#K	51	Population:	#M		9.9
Gross National Product:	$B	45	Computers in use:	#M		.10
GNP/capita:	$	4545	Computers/person:	#		.010
Phones in use:	#M	3.9	Computer power-MIPS:	#K		33
Phones/person:	#	.390	Computing power share:	%		0.14
TVs in use:	#M	2.0	MIPS/1000 people:	#		3.31
TVs/person:	#	.197	Index versus USA:	#		6.2

(Continued next page)

INTERNATIONAL STATISTICS (Continued)

India

Size in square miles:	#K	1267	Population:	#M	768
Gross National Product:	$B	230	Computers in use:	#M	.15
GNP/capita:	$	299	Computers/person:	#	0.0002
Phones in use:	#M	5.0	Computer power-MIPS:	#K	43
Phones/person:	#	.006	Computing power share:	%	0.18
TVs in use:	#M	3.7	MIPS/1000 people:	#	.06
TVs/person:	#	.005	Index versus USA:	#	.1

Indonesia

Size in square miles:	#K	735	Population:	#M	173
Gross National Product:	$B	105	Computers in use:	#M	.04
GNP/capita:	$	607	Computers/person:	#	0.0003
Phones in use:	#M	4.8	Computer power-MIPS:	#K	15
Phones/person:	#	.028	Computing power share:	%	0.06
TVs in use:	#M	8.0	MIPS/1000 people:	#	.08
TVs/person:	#	.046	Index versus USA:	#	.2

Ireland

Size in square miles:	#K	27	Population:	#M	3.6
Gross National Product:	$B	18	Computers in use:	#M	.19
GNP/capita:	$	5000	Computers/person:	#	.053
Phones in use:	#M	1.0	Computer power-MIPS:	#K	65
Phones/person:	#	.282	Computing power share:	%	0.28
TVs in use:	#M	.9	MIPS/1000 people:	#	18.12
TVs/person:	#	.263	Index versus USA:	#	34.0

Israel

Size in square miles:	#K	8	Population:	#M	4.1
Gross National Product:	$B	25	Computers in use:	#M	.13
GNP/capita:	$	6098	Computers/person:	#	.032
Phones in use:	#M	1.6	Computer power-MIPS:	#K	45
Phones/person:	#	.392	Computing power share:	%	0.19
TVs in use:	#M	1.4	MIPS/1000 people:	#	10.19
TVs/person:	#	.333	Index versus USA:	#	20.5

(Continued next page)

INTERNATIONAL STATISTICS (Continued)

Italy

Size in square miles:	#K	116	Population:	#M	57
Gross National Product:	$B	370	Computers in use:	#M	1.52
GNP/capita:	$	6491	Computers/person:	#	.027
Phones in use:	#M	27.4	Computer power-MIPS:	#K	522
Phones/person:	#	.481	Computing power share:	%	2.21
TVs in use:	#M	15.2	MIPS/1000 people:	#	9.16
TVs/person:	#	.267	Index versus USA:	#	17.2

Japan

Size in square miles:	#K	144	Population:	#M	121
Gross National Product:	$B	1250	Computers in use:	#M	6.94
GNP/capita:	$	10331	Computers/person:	#	0.057
Phones in use:	#M	69.8	Computer power-MIPS:	#K	2463
Phones/person:	#	.580	Computing power share:	%	10.41
TVs in use:	#M	94.2	MIPS/1000 people:	#	20.35
TVs/person:	#	.780	Index versus USA:	#	38.2

Mexico

Size in square miles:	#K	762	Population:	#M	80
Gross National Product:	$B	170	Computers in use:	#M	.21
GNP/capita:	$	2125	Computers/person:	#	0.003
Phones in use:	#M	8.5	Computer power-MIPS:	#K	69
Phones/person:	#	.107	Computing power share:	%	0.29
TVs in use:	#M	9.9	MIPS/1000 people:	#	.87
TVs/person:	#	.124	Index versus USA:	#	1.6

Netherlands

Size in square miles:	#K	16	Population:	#M	14.5
Gross National Product:	$B	155	Computers in use:	#M	.48
GNP/capita:	$	10690	Computers/person:	#	.033
Phones in use:	#M	9.7	Computer power-MIPS:	#K	164
Phones/person:	#	.667	Computing power share:	%	0.69
TVs in use:	#M	7.8	MIPS/1000 people:	#	11.31
TVs/person:	#	.540	Index versus USA:	#	21.2

(Continued next page)

INTERNATIONAL STATISTICS (Continued)

New Zealand

Size in square miles:	#K	104	Population:	#M	3.3
Gross National Product:	$B	23	Computers in use:	#M	.14
GNP/capita:	$	6970	Computers/person:	#	.043
Phones in use:	#M	2.2	Computer power-MIPS:	#K	49
Phones/person:	#	.657	Computing power share:	%	0.20
TVs in use:	#M	1.0	MIPS/1000 people:	#	14.69
TVs/person:	#	.317	Index versus USA:	#	27.6

Norway

Size in square miles:	#K	125	Population:	#M	4.2
Gross National Product:	$B	57	Computers in use:	#M	.22
GNP/capita:	$	13735	Computers/person:	#	.054
Phones in use:	#M	2.9	Computer power-MIPS:	#K	76
Phones/person:	#	.695	Computing power share:	%	0.32
TVs in use:	#M	1.5	MIPS/1000 people:	#	18.41
TVs/person:	#	.350	Index versus USA:	#	34.5

Philippines

Size in square miles:	#K	116	Population:	#M	57
Gross National Product:	$B	45	Computers in use:	#M	.11
GNP/capita:	$	789	Computers/person:	#	.002
Phones in use:	#M	1.0	Computer power-MIPS:	#K	37
Phones/person:	#	.017	Computing power share:	%	0.15
TVs in use:	#M	1.8	MIPS/1000 people:	#	.64
TVs/person:	#	.031	Index versus USA:	#	1.2

Portugal

Size in square miles:	#K	36	Population:	#M	10
Gross National Product:	$B	25	Computers in use:	#M	.15
GNP/capita:	$	2500	Computers/person:	#	.015
Phones in use:	#M	2.0	Computer power-MIPS:	#K	50
Phones/person:	#	.199	Computing power share:	%	0.21
TVs in use:	#M	2.0	MIPS/1000 people:	#	4.95
TVs/person:	#	.196	Index versus USA:	#	9.3

(Continued next page)

INTERNATIONAL STATISTICS (Continued)

Saudia Arabia

Size in square miles:	#K	830	Population:	#M	11.2
Gross National Product:	$B	115	Computers in use:	#M	.11
GNP/capita:	$	10268	Computers/person:	#	.010
Phones in use:	#M	3.3	Computer power-MIPS:	#K	36
Phones/person:	#	.292	Computing power share:	%	0.15
TVs in use:	#M	3.8	MIPS/1000 people:	#	3.23
TVs/person:	#	.343	Index versus USA:	#	6.1

Singapore

Size in square miles:	#K	0.22	Population:	#M	2.6
Gross National Product:	$B	19	Computers in use:	#M	.14
GNP/capita:	$	7308	Computers/person:	#	.052
Phones in use:	#M	1.3	Computer power-MIPS:	#K	43
Phones/person:	#	.514	Computing power share:	%	0.18
TVs in use:	#M	.6	MIPS/1000 people:	#	16.57
TVs/person:	#	.226	Index versus USA:	#	31.1

South Africa

Size in square miles:	#K	471	Population:	#M	33
Gross National Product:	$B	75	Computers in use:	#M	.16
GNP/capita:	$	2308	Computers/person:	#	.005
Phones in use:	#M	5.2	Computer power-MIPS:	#K	53
Phones/person:	#	.161	Computing power share:	%	0.22
TVs in use:	#M	.5	MIPS/1000 people:	#	1.63
TVs/person:	#	.014	Index versus USA:	#	3.1

South Korea

Size in square miles:	#K	38	Population:	#M	43
Gross National Product:	$B	100	Computers in use:	#M	.39
GNP/capita:	$	2326	Computers/person:	#	.009
Phones in use:	#M	10.3	Computer power-MIPS:	#K	124
Phones/person:	#	.238	Computing power share:	%	0.52
TVs in use:	#M	11.3	MIPS/1000 people:	#	2.89
TVs/person:	#	.262	Index versus USA:	#	5.4

(Continued next page)

INTERNATIONAL STATISTICS (Continued)

Spain

Size in square miles:	#K	195	Population:	#M	39
Gross National Product:	$B	210	Computers in use:	#M	.32
GNP/capita:	$	5385	Computers/person:	#	.008
Phones in use:	#M	15.5	Computer power-MIPS:	#K	102
Phones/person:	#	.397	Computing power share:	%	0.43
TVs in use:	#M	11.6	MIPS/1000 people:	#	2.60
TVs/person:	#	.297	Index versus USA:	#	4.9

Sweden

Size in square miles:	#K	174	Population:	#M	8.4
Gross National Product:	$B	110	Computers in use:	#M	.36
GNP/capita:	$	13174	Computers/person:	#	.043
Phones in use:	#M	8.0	Computer power-MIPS:	#K	123
Phones/person:	#	.961	Computing power share:	%	0.52
TVs in use:	#M	3.5	MIPS/1000 people:	#	14.73
TVs/person:	#	.421	Index versus USA:	#	27.6

Switzerland

Size in square miles:	#K	16	Population:	#M	6.50
Gross National Product:	$B	112	Computers in use:	#M	.30
GNP/capita:	$	17231	Computers/person:	#	.047
Phones in use:	#M	5.5	Computer power-MIPS:	#K	104
Phones/person:	#	.852	Computing power share:	%	0.44
TVs in use:	#M	2.8	MIPS/1000 people:	#	16.06
TVs/person:	#	.423	Index versus USA:	#	30.1

Taiwan

Size in square miles:	#K	14	Population:	#M	19
Gross National Product:	$B	65	Computers in use:	#M	.16
GNP/capita:	$	3368	Computers/person:	#	.008
Phones in use:	#M	7.5	Computer power-MIPS:	#K	58
Phones/person:	#	.387	Computing power share:	%	0.24
TVs in use:	#M	4.1	MIPS/1000 people:	#	2.98
TVs/person:	#	.210	Index versus USA:	#	5.6

(Continued next page)

INTERNATIONAL STATISTICS (Continued)

United Kingdom

Size in square miles:	#K	94	Population:	#M	56
Gross National Product:	$B	570	Computers in use:	#M	4.88
GNP/capita:	$	10179	Computers/person:	#	.087
Phones in use:	#M	32.1	Computer power-MIPS:	#K	1650
Phones/person:	#	.574	Computing power share:	%	6.97
TVs in use:	#M	30.8	MIPS/1000 people:	#	29.46
TVs/person:	#	.551	Index versus USA:	#	55.3

USA

Size in square miles:	#K	3623	Population:	#M	239
Gross National Product:	$B	3850	Computers in use:	#M	35
GNP/capita:	$	16109	Computers/person:	#	0.146
Phones in use:	#M	222	Computer power-MIPS:	#K	12739
Phones/person:	#	.929	Computing power share:	%	53.85
TVs in use:	#M	208	MIPS/1000 people:	#	53.30
TVs/person:	#	.871	Index versus USA:	#	100.0

USSR

Size in square miles:	#K	8649	Population:	#M	277
Gross National Product:	$B	2070	Computers in use:	#M	.28
GNP/capita:	$	7473	Computers/person:	#	.001
Phones in use:	#M	30.9	Computer power-MIPS:	#K	87
Phones/person:	#	.112	Computing power share:	%	0.37
TVs in use:	#M	98.1	MIPS/1000 people:	#	.31
TVs/person:	#	.354	Index versus USA:	#	0.6

West Germany

Size in square miles:	#K	96	Population:	#M	61
Gross National Product:	$B	770	Computers in use:	#M	2.73
GNP/capita:	$	12623	Computers/person:	#	.045
Phones in use:	#M	41.8	Computer power-MIPS:	#K	911
Phones/person:	#	.685	Computing power share:	%	3.85
TVs in use:	#M	24.2	MIPS/1000 people:	#	14.94
TVs/person:	#	.396	Index versus USA:	#	28.0

(Continued next page)

INTERNATIONAL STATISTICS (Continued)

Worldwide

Size in square miles:	#K	52426	Population:	#M	4865
Gross National Product:	$B	14640	Computers in use:	#M	67
GNP/capita:	$	3009	Computers/person:	#	0.014
Phones in use:	#M	687	Computer power-MIPS:	#K	23655
Phones/person:	#	.141	Computing power share:	%	100.00
TVs in use:	#M	708	MIPS/1000 people:	#	4.86
TVs/person:	#	.145	Index versus USA:	#	9.1

6 ADVERTISING AND MARKETING

AMERICAN MARKETING ASSOCIATION
EFFIE AWARDS

"EFFIE is presented each year by the American Marketing Association/New York to advertising agencies and their clients in recognition of those advertising campaigns judged most effective. EFFIE is the most important advertising award in the United States because it recognizes the highest achievement in advertising: superior results in meeting objectives."--American Marketing Association.

From this list COMPUTER INDUSTRY ALMANAC has selected only the industry-related companies.

Reprinted with permission from American Marketing Association, 1986. Copyright 1985, 1986 by American Marketing Association, New York, NY.

1986 EFFIE AWARDS

BUSINESS TO BUSINESS EQUIPMENT

GOLD EFFIE

NCR CORPORATION (Advertiser)
Vernon Yates - VP, Genl Mgr, PC Division. Lew Van Antwerp - Asst Vice President.
Jeffrey Wise - Dealer/Marketing Manager. Craig Jensen - Dealer/Marketing Specialist.

BACKER & SPIELVOGEL (Agency)
Charles L. Decker - Sr VP, Mgmt Supervisor. J. Edmund Keating - VP, Mgmt Supervisor.
Deborah Pawlik - Account Supervisor. Thomas Nathan - Sr VP, Grp Creative Dir. Gerald Pfiffner - Sr VP, Grp Creative Dir. Alain Zutter - VP, Media Director. Cathy Sagansky - Assoc Research Director.

The purpose of the campaign was to demonstrate NCR's credibility as a major factor in the personal computer category by creating instant brand recognition and quickly building a national dealer network. To this end, advertising was needed to communicate that this product was compatible with standard software, included many superior features, and was backed by a company with a history of reliability and business expertise. Finally, humor was used to offset the company's conservative image and make the product less threatening.

AMERICAN MARKETING ASSOCIATION
EFFIE AWARDS (Continued)

BUSINESS TO BUSINESS EQUIPMENT

SILVER EFFIE

NCR CORPORATION
John M. Walsh - Asst VP, Product Marketing. Bill LeMaster - Director, Product Promotions. Edward J. Feltz - Manager, Advertising. William Saylor - Supervisor, Advertising.

BACKER & SPIELVOGEL
Charles L. Decker - Sr VP, Mgmt Supervisor. Thomas C. Cotton - VP, Account Director. Matthew L. Sawyer - Account Executive. Richard K. Mahan - VP, Assoc Dir, Art. Philip A. Guthrie - VP, Assoc Dir, Copy. Alain S. Zutter - VP, Media Director. William Harris - Media Supervisor. Marylin Silverman, Cathy Sagansky - Associate Research Directors

The campaign was designed to expand the market for the NCR Tower Computer and to greatly increase brand awareness. It also sought to quickly generate high-quality sales leads and spur a significant increase in sales.

BUSINESS TO BUSINESS SERVICES

BRONZE EFFIE

AT&T INFORMATION SERVICES
Robert Casale - Executive Vice President. Hal Burlingame - Vice President. Dick Draper - Director. Karen Vereb - Division Manager. Maryann Seduski - District Manager.

OGILVY & MATHER
Kelly O'Dea - Group Director. Irene Frary - Management Supervisor. Kathy Moriarty, Marjorie Kaplan - Account Supervisors. Jay Jasper - Creative Director. Chris Moore - Writer. Greg Campbell - Art Director. Bernie Wesson - Producer. Patricia Doyle - Planning & Research. Wilma Epstein - Media.

The IMM campaign was developed to establish AT&T as a leader in the field of Information Movement and Management and as a source of valuable information for potential customers. To do this, the role of advertising was to leverage AT&T's communications strengths and to establish the validity of the company's unique approach to office automation.

AMERICAN MARKETING ASSOCIATION
EFFIE AWARDS (Continued)

1985 EFFIE AWARDS

GRAND EFFIE WINNER

APPLE COMPUTER (Advertiser)
CHIAT/DAY (Agency)

BUSINESS TO BUSINESS: COMPUTERS/SOFTWARE

GOLD EFFIE

APPLE COMPUTER (Advertiser)
Del Yocam - Vice President, General Manager, Marketing. Dave Larson - Marketing
Director. Bill Cleary - Product Manager. Bruce Mowery - Advertising Director.

CHIAT/DAY (Agency)
Robert Pinzler - Management Supervisor. Caroline Beck - Account Executive. Lee Clow,
Steve Hayden, Laurie Brandalise, Gary Johnston - Creative. Camille Johnson, Steve
Davison, Debbie Kelly - Media.

This campaign had just three goals. Within 100 days of introduction: (1) create
sufficient excitement about Macintosh to produce significant in-store traffic, (2) generate
immediate sales momentum to keep Macintosh back-ordered through at least the first half
of 1984, and (3) establish Macintosh as the third industry standard in the PC category.

AMERICAN MARKETING ASSOCIATION
EFFIE AWARDS (Continued)

BUSINESS TO BUSINESS: COMPUTERS/SOFTWARE

SILVER EFFIE

COMPAQ COMPUTER CORPORATION (Advertiser)
Bill Murto - Vice President, Marketing. James D'Arezzo - VP, Corporate Communications. Diana Cox - Advertising & Sales Promotion. Brant Wilson - Market Research Manager.

OGILVY & MATHER - HOUSTON (Agency)
Kirk Walden - VP, Management Supervisor. Lisa Fugitt, Iris Karsenty, Gregory Gaston - Account Supervisors. Peter Martin - Account Executive. Joe Kilgore - Sr.VP, Exec. Creative Dir. Pam Warren - VP, Assoc. Media Director. Laura Metzger - VP, Research Director.

The "Right Decision" campaign had to establish relatively unknown Compaq Computers above 100 competitors and alongside the leaders, IBM and Apple, without a significant increase in share of voice. It had to convince prospects that not considering Compaq before making a purchase would be the "wrong decision."

BRONZE EFFIE

IBM CORPORATION - ISG HEADQUARTERS (Advertiser)
Byron G. Quann - Group Dir., Communications. Antoinette A. Emerson - Advertising Director. William H. Harrison - Advertising Manager. Steve B. Carpender - Program Manager.

DOYLE DALE BERNBACH (Agency)
Joseph Dell'Aquila - Sr. VP, Mgmt Supervisor. Paul R. Katzka - VP, Account Supervisor. Maria Castells - Account Executive. Irwin Warren - SR VP, Creative Director. Rich Middendorf - Copywriter. Amy Levitan - Art Director. Conant Sawyer - VP, Media Director. Pat Alexander - Media Planner. Stan Schumsky, Peter Justinius, Shelly Hershaff - Research.

The primary objective of the IBM Business Computer Systems campaign was to maintain awareness among its target that IBM is in the Business Computer Systems category. It was also designed to communicate in a unique and obtrusive manner the key message that IBM's Systems offer a "wide range of solutions and benefits."

AMERICAN MARKETING ASSOCIATION
EFFIE AWARDS (Continued)

CORPORATE IMAGE

BRONZE EFFIE

AT&T (Advertiser)
Edward M. Block - Senior Vice President. James L. Brunson - Corporate Vice President. David J. Shaver - Division Manager. Linda B. Urben, Alvin M. Winters - District Mgrs. Gary L. Schmermund - Division Manager, Research.

N W AYER INC (Agency)
Howard Stoner - Management Supervisor. John Quigley - Account Supervisor. Nancy Ryan, Ted Kolota, Austin Patrick - Account Executives. John Walsh, Jim Murphy - Creative. Suzanne Kaufman - Media.--Lew Mottley - Research.

The AT&T "New Directions" campaign has been described as the largest corporate explanatory job in history. In complexity and scope "New Directions" has successfully redefined the new AT&T and created an umbrella brand image of quality, value, technology and reliability for all AT&T products and services. "AT&T, We're Reaching Out In New Directions" summarized the new spirit of a corporation eager to serve and compete on a global basis.

AMERICAN MARKETING ASSOCIATION
EFFIE AWARDS (Continued)

RETAIL: NATIONAL

SILVER EFFIE

COMPUTERLAND (Advertiser)
Roger Lewis - Vice President, Marketing. David Spencer - Marketing Director. Fred Whelan - Advertising Director. Dana McCready - Advertising Manager. Kathie Pasters - Market Research.

J. WALTER THOMPSON - SAN FRANCISCO (Agency)
Arnold Berger - Management Supervisor. Cheryl French - Account Supervisor. Kim Worman - Account Executive. Jim Sanderson - Creative. Sydney Randazzo - Media. Jesse Bedi - Research.

The objectives of this campaign were to increase ComputerLand awareness and increase preference to shop at ComputerLand stores. This was achieved by convincing the target that ComputerLand is dedicated to helping customers learn about computer systems and accurately select the best system for their businesses.

AMERICAN MARKETING ASSOCIATION
EFFIE AWARDS (Continued)

RETAIL: REGIONAL/LOCAL

GOLD EFFIE

COMPCO COMPUTER CENTER (Advertiser)
Bill Voss - Vice President, Merchandising.

BOZELL & JACOBS (Agency)
Jim Gibbon - Management Supervisor. Mike Spence - Account Supervisor. Michael Millikan - Account Executive. Ron Fisher, Michael Baumayr, Liza Orchard, Donna Jackson - Creative. Larry Kelley, Mary Burke-Kelly, Eric Snyder - Media.

This campaign was developed to increase sales by 25%. It achieved this goal by convincing consumers, who are unfamiliar with computers, that Compco Computer Centers can help them choose the right computers at the right price.

CLIO MAGAZINE
CLIO '86 AWARDS
1986

"Since 1959, the CLIO Awards have represented the standard of creative excellence in advertising. In 1986, nearly 22,000 entries from 53 countries competed in the 17th Annual CLIO Awards. The entries are judged by more than 1,000 advertising creatives over a three-month period."--CLIO MAGAZINE.

From this list COMPUTER INDUSTRY ALMANAC has selected only industry-related companies.

Reprinted with permission from CLIO MAGAZINE, 1986. Copyright 1986 by CLIO Enterprises, Inc., New York, NY.

U.S. TELEVISION

NATIONAL CAMPAIGN

Company:	AT&T Information Systems
Title:	"Slinky", "Trays", "Tangram"
Agency:	Ogilvy & Mather, New York
Details:	TV, 60 Seconds Each, Color

Company:	Apple Computer
Title:	"Snowed-In", "Teacher","Astronaut"
Agency:	Chiat/Day, Los Angeles
Details:	TV, 30 Seconds Each, Color
First Appearance:	February 28, 1985

Company:	Hewlett-Packard
Title:	"Shower", "Busy Signal", "Desert"
Agency:	Leo Burnett, Chicago
Details:	TV, 30 Seconds Each, Color
First Appearance:	November 1985

(Continued next page)

CLIO AWARDS
1986 (Continued)

CORPORATE

Company:	AT&T
Title:	"Live Aid"
Agency:	NW Ayer, New York
Details:	TV, 60 Seconds, Color
First Appearance:	July 1985

Company:	IBM
Title:	"Here I Am"
Agency:	Lord, Geller, Frederico & Einstein, New York
Details:	TV, 60 Seconds, Color
First Appearance:	January 1985

Company:	ITT
Title:	"Talking XTRA"
Agency:	Biederman, New York
Details:	TV, 60 Seconds, Color
First Appearance:	May 13, 1985

HOME ENTERTAINMENT EQUIPMENT

Company:	Apple Computer
Title:	"Christmas"
Agency	Chiat/Day, Los Angeles
Details	TV, 60 Seconds, Color
First Appearance:	November 15, 1985

Company:	Apple Computer
Title:	"Skateboard"
Agency:	Chiat/Day, Los Angeles
Details:	TV, 60 Seconds,Color
First Appearance:	September 15, 1985

(Continued next page)

CLIO AWARDS
1986 (Continued)

OFFICE EQUIPMENT/SUPPLIES

Company:	AT&T*
Title:	"Slinky"
Agency:	Ogilvy & Mather, New York
Details:	TV, 60 Seconds, Color

Company:	AT&T
Title:	"Tangram"
Agency:	Ogilvy & Mather, New York
Details:	TV, 60 Seconds, Color

Company:	Apple Computer
Title:	"Do-It-Yourself"
Agency:	Chiat/Day, Los Angeles
Details:	TV, 30 Seconds, Color
First Appearance:	March 26, 1985

Company:	Apple Computer
Title:	"Understood"
Agency:	Chiat/Day, Los Angeles
Details:	TV, 60 Seconds, Color
First Appearance:	April 16, 1985

Company:	Hewlett-Packard
Title:	"Shower"
Agency:	Leo Burnett, Chicago
Details:	TV, 30 Seconds, Color
First Appearance:	November 1985

Company:	IBM Personal Computer
Title:	"Crosswalk"
Agency:	Lord, Geller, Federico, Einstein, New York
Details:	TV, 60 Seconds, Color
First Appearance:	August 31, 1985

(Continued next page)

* CLIO Award Winner in This Category

CLIO AWARDS
1986 (Continued)

OFFICE EQUIPMENT/SUPPLIES (Continued)

Company:	IBM Personal Computer
Title:	"High Performance"
Agency:	Lord, Geller, Federico, Einstein, New York
Details:	TV, 60 Seconds, Color
First Appearance:	December 5, 1985

U. S. RADIO

NATIONAL CAMPAIGN

Company:	Apple Computer, Inc.
Title:	"Space Monster", "Christmas Presents", "New Underwear"
Agency:	Chiat/Day, Los Angeles
Details:	60 Seconds Each
First Air Date:	November 15, 1985

Company:	Automatic Data Processing
Title:	"Smiley Faces", "A Little Boo Boo"
Agency:	Schaefer Adv. Inc., Wayne
Details:	60 Seconds Each
First Air Date :	September 1985

LOCAL SMALL MARKET

Company:	The Office Works/Computers
Title:	"Friends"
Details:	60 Seconds Each
First Appearance:	October 15, 1985

HOME FURNISHINGS

Company:	Apple Computer*
Title:	"Hi, Dad"
Agency:	Chiat/Day, Los Angeles
Details:	60 Seconds
First Air Date:	August 19, 1985

* CLIO Award Winner in This Category

CLIO MAGAZINE
CLIO '85 AWARDS
1985

"The CLIO Award is the world's most recognized and coveted advertising accolade. For 26 years, it has become the standard setter for excellence in advertising around the world. In 1985, 19,506 entries were received from 40 countries."--CLIO MAGAZINE.

From this list COMPUTER INDUSTRY ALMANAC has selected only finalists from industry-related companies.

Reprinted with permission from CLIO MAGAZINE, 1985. Copyright 1985 by CLIO Enterprises, Inc., New York, NY.

U.S. TELEVISION/CINEMA

NATIONAL CAMPAIGN

Company:	Apple Computer
Title:	"Factory", "Building"
Agency:	Chiat/Day Advertising, Los Angeles
Details	TV, 60 Seconds, 30 Seconds, Color
First Appearance:	November 1, 1984

Company:	Apple Computer
Title:	"Manuals", "Screens", "Plug Rev"
Agency:	Chiat/Day Advertising, Los Angeles
Details:	TV, 10 Seconds Each, Color
First Appearance:	May 28, 1984

Company	IBM Personal Computers
Title:	"Skates", "Home Demonstration"
Agency:	Lord, Geller, Federico, Einstein, New York
Details:	TV, 60 Seconds Each, Color

(Continued next page)

CLIO AWARDS
1985 (Continued)

REGIONAL CAMPAIGN

Company:	Businessland
Title:	"Dummy", "Parrot"
Agency:	Chiat/Day Advertising, Los Angeles
Details:	TV, 60 Second, 30 Seconds, Color

Company:	Nynex
Title:	"Store Fronts", "Pizza", "Restaurant"
Agency:	Cabot Advertising, Boston
Details:	TV, 30 Seconds Each, Color
First Appearance:	May 1984

CORPORATE

Company:	AT&T
Title:	"Connections"
Agency:	Young & Rubicam, New York
Details:	TV, 30 Seconds, Color
First Appearance:	June 1984

Company:	AT&T
Title:	"Take For Granted"
Agency:	NW Ayer Inc., New York
Details:	TV, 30 Seconds, Color
First Appearance:	July 1984

Company:	Wang
Title:	"Choir"
Agency:	HHCC, Boston
Details:	TV, 60 Seconds, Color

Company:	Wang
Title:	"Power and Glory"
Agency:	HHCC, Boston
Details:	TV, 90 Seconds, Color
First Appearance:	September 1984

(Continued next page)

CLIO AWARDS
1985 (Continued)

HOME ENTERTAINMENT EQUIPMENT

Company:	Apple Computer
Title:	"Building"
Agency:	Chiat/Day Advertising, Los Angeles
Details:	TV, 30 Seconds, Color
First Appearance:	November 1, 1984

Company:	Apple Computer
Title:	"Factory"
Agency:	Chiat/Day Advertising, Los Angeles
Details:	TV, 60 Seconds, Color
First Appearance:	November 1, 1984

Company:	Apple Computer
Title:	"Proportions"
Agency:	Chiat/Day Advertising, Los Angeles
Details:	TV, 30 Seconds, Color
First Appearance:	May 22, 1984

Company:	Columbia Data Computers
Title:	"Combination Day 2"
Agency:	Kenyon & Eckhardt, New York
Details:	TV, 30 Seconds, Color
First Appearance:	May 22, 1984

Company:	Data General
Title:	"Escape"
Agency:	Foote, Cone & Belding, New York
Details:	TV, 60 Seconds, Color
First Appearance:	January 6, 1985

Company:	IBM Computers
Title:	"Home Demonstration"
Agency:	Lord, Geller, Federico, Einstein, New York
Details:	TV, 60 Seconds, Color

(Continued next page)

CLIO AWARDS
1985 (Continued)

HOME ENTERTAINMENT EQUIPMENT (Continued)
Company:	NCR
Title:	"Showroom"
Agency:	Backer & Spielvogel, New York
Details:	TV, 60 Seconds, Color
First Appearance:	September 9, 1984

OFFICE EQUIPMENT/SUPPLIES
Company:	IBM Personal Computer*
Title:	"Skates"
Agency:	Lord, Geller, Federico, Einstein, New York
Details:	TV, 60 Seconds, Color
First Appearance:	April 15, 1984

Company:	Apple Computer
Title:	"Glove"
Agency:	Chiat/Day Advertising, Los Angeles
Details:	TV, 30 Seconds, Color
First Appearance:	November 1, 1984

Company:	Apple Computer
Title:	"Hands"
Agency:	Chiat/Day Advertising, Los Angeles
Details:	TV, 30 Seconds, Color
First Appearance:	February 7, 1984

Company:	Apple Computer
Title:	"Lemmings"
Agency:	Chiat/Day Advertising, Los Angeles
Details:	TV, 60 Seconds, Color
First Appearance:	January 20, 1985

Company:	Apple Computer
Title:	"Manuals"
Agency:	Chiat/Day Advertising, Los Angeles
Details:	TV, 10 Seconds, Color
First Appearance:	May 28, 1984

(Continued next page)

* CLIO Award Winner in this Category

CLIO AWARDS
1985 (Continued)

OFFICE EQUIPMENT/SUPPLIES (Continued)

Company:	Apple Computer
Title:	"Manuals"
Agency:	Chiat/Day Advertising, Los Angeles
Details:	TV, 30 Seconds, Color
First Appearance:	May 28, 1984

Company:	Apple Computer
Title:	"Screens"
Agency:	Chiat/Day Advertising, Los Angeles
Details:	TV, 10 Seconds, Color
First Appearance:	May 28, 1984

Company:	Apple Computer
Title:	"Screens"
Agency:	Chiat/Day Advertising, Los Angeles
Details:	TV, 30 Seconds, Color
First Appearance:	May 28, 1984

Company:	COMPAQ Computer
Title:	"Well-Known"
Agency:	Ogilvy & Mather, Houston
Details:	TV, 30 Seconds, Color
First Appearance:	August 28, 1984

Company:	Data General
Title:	"Catapult"
Agency:	Foote, Cone & Belding, New York
Details:	TV, 60 Seconds, Color
First Appearance:	November 4, 1984

Company:	IBM Copiers
Title:	"Invisible Copiers"
Agency:	Doyle Dane Bernbach, New York
Details:	TV, 30 Seconds, Color
First Appearance:	May 1984

(Continued next page)

CLIO AWARDS
1985 (Continued)

OFFICE EQUIPMENT/SUPPLIES (Continued)

Company:	IBM Personal Computer Software
Title:	"Ducks"
Agency:	Lord, Geller, Federico, Einstein, New York
Details:	TV, 30 Seconds, Color
First Appearance:	December 17, 1984

Company:	3M Diskettes
Title:	"Businesswoman"
Agency:	Chiat/Day Advertising, San Francisco
Details:	TV, 30 Seconds, Color
First Appearance:	September 16, 1984

Company:	Wang
Title:	"Power and Glory"
Agency:	HHCC, Boston
Details:	TV, 90 Seconds, Color
First Appearance:	September 1984

OLYMPICS

Company:	AT&T
Title:	"Connection"
Agency:	Young Rubicam, New York
Details:	TV, 60 Seconds, Color
First Appearance:	April 1984

(Continued next page)

CLIO AWARDS
1985 (Continued)

U.S. RADIO

NATIONAL CAMPAIGN

Company:	Apple Computer
Title:	"CSS Hotline No. 1", "CSS Hotline No. 2", "CSS Potpourri"
Agency:	Chiat/Day Advertising, Los Angeles
Details:	60 Seconds Each
First Air Date:	November 19, 1984

Company:	AT&T Information Systems
Title	"One Potato", "Grand Opening", "The Promotion"
Agency:	Ogilvy & Mather, New York
Details:	60 Seconds Each
First Air Date:	September 1984

Company:	Automatic Data Processing
Title:	"Sings", "Cat's Meow", "Paper Clip"
Agency:	Schaefer Advertising, Valley Forge
Details:	60 Seconds Each
First Air Date:	September 1984

(Continued next page)

CLIO AWARDS
1985 (Continued)

HOME FURNISHINGS

Company:	Apple Computer*
Title:	"Little Albert"
Agency:	Chiat/Day Advertising, Los Angeles
Details:	60 Seconds
First Air Date:	August 20, 1984

Company:	Apple Computer
Title:	"Left Behind"
Agency:	Chiat/Day Advertising, Los Angeles
Details:	60 Seconds
First Air Date:	November 1, 1984

Company:	Apple Computer
Title:	"Little Suzy"
Agency:	Chiat/Day Advertising, Los Angeles
Details:	60 Seconds
First Air Date:	August 20, 1984

* CLIO Award Winner in this Category

CLIO MAGAZINE
CLIO '84 AWARDS
1984

"The 1984 award year marks CLIO's 25th year of honoring advertising excellence. In 1984, 17,669 entries were received from 44 countries."--CLIO MAGAZINE.

From this list, COMPUTER INDUSTRY ALMANAC has selected only finalists from the industry-related companies.

Reprinted with permission from CLIO MAGAZINE, 1984. Copyright 1984 by CLIO Enterprises, Inc., New York, NyY.

U.S. TELEVISION/CINEMA

NATIONAL CAMPAIGN

Company: Apple Computers
Title: "Soloist"," Basketball","Breakfast"
Agency: Chiat/Day, Los Angeles
Details: TV, 60 Seconds Each, Color
First Appearance:October 1, 1983

Company: Kaypro Computers
Title: "Complete Computer", "Options"
Agency: Della Femina, Travisano & Prtnrs, Los Angeles
Details: TV, 30 Seconds Each, Color
First Appearance:October 1983

CINEMA

Company: Apple Computer*
Title: "1984"
Agency: Chiat/Day, Los Angeles
Details: Cinema, 60 Seconds, Color
First Appearance:December 15, 1983

Company: Atari
Title: "The Jerks"
Agency: Doyle Dane Bernbach, New York
Details: Cinema, 90 Seconds, Color
First Appearance:August 1, 1983
(Continued next page)

CLIO AWARDS
1984 (Continued)

CORPORATE

Company: Burroughs
Title: "Conference Room"
Agency: Penchina, Selkowitz, New York
Details: TV, 30 Seconds, Color
First Appearance: August 26, 1983

Company: Burroughs
Title: "Dining Room"
Agency: Penchina, Selkowitz, New York
Details: TV, 30 Seconds, Color
First Appearance: August 22, 1983

Company: IBM
Title: "Brothers"
Agency: Doyle Dane Bernbach, New York
Details: TV, 60 Seconds

Company: IBM
Title: "Town Square"
Agency: Doyle Dane Bernbach, New York
Details: TV, 60 Seconds, Color
(Continued next page)

CLIO AWARDS
1984 (Continued)

HOME ENTERTAINMENT EQUIPMENT
        Company: Kaypro Computer*
        Title: "Complete Computer"
        Agency: Della Femina, Travisano & Prtnrs, Los Angeles
        Details: TV, 30 Seconds, Color
        First Appearance:September 14, 1983

        Company: Actrix Computer
        Title: "Personal Problems"
        Agency: Cunningham & Walsh
        Details: TV, 30 Seconds, Color
        First Appearance:October 1983

        Company: Apple Computer
        Title: "Alone Again"
        Agency: Chiat/Day, Los Angeles
        Details: TV, 60 Seconds, Color
        First Appearance:August 15, 1983

        Company: Apple Computer
        Title: "Basketball"
        Agency: Chiat/Day, Los Angeles
        Details: TV, 60 Seconds, Color
        First Appearance:October 1, 1983

        Company: Apple Computer
        Title: "Breakfast"
        Agency: Chiat/Day, Los Angeles
        Details: TV, 60 Seconds, Color
        First Appearance:October 1, 1983

        Company: Apple Computer
        Title: "1984"
        Agency: Chiat/Day, Los Angeles
        Details: TV, 60 Seconds, Color
        First Appearance:December 15, 1983
        (Continued next page)

CLIO AWARDS
1984 (Continued)

HOME ENTERTAINMENT EQUIPMENT (Continued)

Company: Apple Computer
Title: "Soloist"
Agency: Chiat/Day, Los Angeles
Details: TV, 60 Seconds, Color
First Appearance:October 1, 1983

Company: Commodore Computers
Title: "Update Rev."
Agency: Ally & Gargano, New York
Details: TV, 30 Seconds, Color
First Appearance:May 27, 1983

Company: Hewlett-Packard Personal Computer
Title: "Setting You Free"
Agency: J. Walter Thompson, San Francisco
Details: TV, 60 Seconds, Color
First Appearance:November 1983

Company: IBM
Title: "Town Square"
Agency: Doyle Dane Bernbach, New York
Details: TV, 60 Seconds, Color

Company: Kaypro Computer
Title: "Options"
Agency: Della Femina, Travisano & Prtnrs, Los Angeles
Details: TV, 30 Seconds, Color
First Appearance:September 14, 1983

Company: Timex Computers
Title: "Love It - Hate It"
Agency: J. Walter Thompson, San Francisco
Details: TV, 30 Seconds, Color
First Appearance:May 1983
(Continued next page)

CLIO AWARDS
1984 (Continued)

OFFICE EQUIPMENT/SUPPLIES
Company: IBM Personal Computer*
Title: "Hats"
Agency: Lord, Geller, Federico, Einstein, New York
Details: TV, 60 Seconds, Color
First Appearance:February 6, 1983

Company: IBM
Title: "Brothers"
Agency: Doyle Dane Bernbach, New York
Details: TV, 60 Seconds, Color

Company: IBM Displaywriter
Title: "Demo"
Agency: Doyle Dane Bernbach, New York
Details: TV, 30 Seconds, Color
First Appearance:January 1983

Company: IBM Personal Computer
Title: "Hats"
Agency: Lord, Geller, Federico, Einstein, New York
Details: TV, 30 Seconds, Color
First Appearance:February 8, 1983

Company: IBM Personal Computer Software
Title: "Stack"
Agency: Lord, Geller, Federico, Einstein, New York
Details: TV, 30 Seconds, Color
First Appearance:October 14, 1983

Company: NEC Portable Computer
Title: "Phone Booth/USA"
Agency: Clinton E. Frank Adv., Chicago
Details: TV, 30 Seconds, Color
First Appearance:October 15, 1983

INFORMATION INDUSTRY ASSOCIATION
IMMY AWARDS
November 12, 1986

"The Information Industry Association sponsors an annual competition to honor outstanding industry marketing achievements. The IMMY awards showcase the information industry's creative work and recognize excellence in marketing achievements. Entries are judged on concept, copy, and design in eight categories. The winners are prominently displayed during the IIA Annual Convention & Exhibition."--Information Industry Association.

Reprinted with permission from Information Industry Association 1986. Copyright 1986 by Information Industry Association, Washington, D.C.

Direct Mail, 4-Color Category
IMMY: BYTE Magazine (Legasse Associates Advertising);
2nd Place: Pacific Bell Directory (Ogilvy & Mather Direct);
3rd Place: West Publishing Company (No agency).

Direct Mail, Less Than 4-Color Category
IMMY: University Microfilms (Gene Jones Studio);
2nd Place: DIALOG Info Services (Harris INK);
3rd Place: Dow Jones & Co. (Gillespie Adv. Inc.);
(tie) COVIDEA (Ogilvy & Mather Direct).

Space Advertising, 4-Color Category
IMMY: West Publishing Co. (No agency);
2nd Place: Alpert & Alpert Inc. (for Mgmt Logistics Intl);
3rd Place: AT&T (Ogilvy & Mather).

Space Advertising, Less Than 4-Color Category
IMMY: Dow Jones & Co., Inc. (Gillespie Adv. Inc.);
2nd Place: NewsNet, Inc. (Halcyon Associates);
3rd Place: ProNet/Div. Vance Publ. Co. (No agency).

Sales Literature/Collateral Material Category
IMMY: WANG Fin. Info. Svcs. (Slater Hanft Martin);
2nd Place: Data Retrieval (ADS INC.);
3rd Place: Sweet's Div. McGraw-Hill (St. Vincent, Milone, & McConnells).

(Continued next page)

INFORMATION INDUSTRY ASSOCIATION IMMY AWARDS (Continued)

User Newsletters Category
IMMY: Dow Jones & Co., Inc. (LGI Publications);
2nd Place: NewsNet (TYL Assoc./The Kingswood Group);
3rd Place: COVIDEA (Harmon Kemp Inc./Ogilvy & Mather Direct).

User Aids Category
IMMY: Mead Data Central, Inc. (No agency);
2nd Place: COVIDEA (Harmon Kemp, Inc.);
3rd Place: Official Airline Guides, Inc. (No agency).

Campaign Category
IMMY: Dialog Info Svcs. (Humpal, Leftwich, Lauck & Sinn);
2nd Place: Pacific Bell Directory (Ogilvy & Mather Direct; Torme & Co.;
   Foote, Cone & Belding);
3rd Place: Western Union (DFS Direct).

Best In Show Exhibit Category
IMMY: TRW Information Systems Group
(tie)WANG Financial Information Services

C SYSTEMS, LTD.
COMPANIES RANKED BY ADVERTISING PAGES AND DOLLARS
Based on January-September, 1986

"These rankings are based on a survey of 178 trade and business publications. The expenditures are estimates based on the rate cards of the publications and do not reflect any discount rates individual companies may have received."--C Systems, Ltd.

Reprinted with permission from C Systems, Ltd., 1986. Copyright 1986 by C Systems, Ltd., Ridgefield, CT.

ADVERTISING OF DATA PROCESSING PRODUCTS
(Excluding Software)

Ranked by Advertising Pages

IBM	1,100
Digital Equipment Corp.	482
Compaq Computer Corp.	466
AST Research, Inc.	432
PC's Limited	427
Toshiba America	412
Hewlett-Packard	406
NEC Information Systems	378
Xerox Corp.	375
PC Network	347
Televideo Systems, Inc.	346
Intel Corp.	328
Tandy/Radio Shack Div.	304
N.C.R.	289
Northeastern Software, Inc.	285
AT&T	283
Wyse Technology	277
Protecto Enterprises	237
PC Connection	234
Cauzin Systems, Inc.	223
Alps	222
Logicsoft	215
Cordata, Inc.	202
Fujitsu America	199
Paradise Systems, Inc.	191
(Continued next page)	

C SYSTEMS, LTD.
COMPANIES RANKED BY ADVERTISING PAGES AND DOLLARS (Continued)

ADVERTISING OF DATA PROCESSING PRODUCTS
    (Excluding Software)

Ranked by Advertising Expenditure ($ millions)

IBM	$21.7
Compaq Computer Corp.	5.7
N.C.R.	5.1
AT&T	5.0
Tandy/Radio Shack Div.	4.8
Hewlett-Packard	4.1
Epson	4.1
Xerox Corp.	4.0
NEC Information Systems	3.9
Digital Equipment Corp.	3.8
PC's Limited	3.6
Televideo Systems, Inc.	3.6
AST Research, Inc.	3.2
Toshiba America	3.1
PC Network	3.0
ITT	2.9
Commodore Electronics Ltd.	2.8
Texas Instruments	2.3
Intel Corp.	2.2
Alps	2.1
Northeastern Software, Inc.	2.1
Logicsoft	2.0
Wyse Technology	2.0
PC Connection	2.0
3M Corp.	1.7

(Continued next page)

C SYSTEMS, LTD.
COMPANIES RANKED BY ADVERTISING PAGES AND DOLLARS (Continued)

ADVERTISING OF ELECTRONICS PRODUCTS

Ranked by Advertising Pages

Mini-Circuits Labs	575
Texas Instruments	378
Amp, Inc.	373
Tektronics	347
Fairchild	335
AT&T Technologies	333
LH Research	325
Hewlett-Packard	313
RCA Solid State	306
National Semiconductor	301
General Electric	269
Hitachi America	258
Honeywell	252
3M Corp.	242
Advanced Micro Devices	238
Gould	236
Toshiba America	225
Inmos	215
Lambda Electronics	213
Dupont	202
Fluke Manufacturing	180
Siemens Components	170
Motorola	163
Allen-Bradley	162
Kepco	159

(Continued next page)

C SYSTEMS, LTD.
COMPANIES RANKED BY ADVERTISING PAGES AND DOLLARS (Continued)

ADVERTISING OF ELECTRONICS PRODUCTS

Ranked by Advertising Expenditures ($ millions)

Mini-Circuits Labs	$2.4
Texas Instruments	2.2
Amp, Inc.	2.1
Tektronics	2.0
Fairchild	2.0
AT&T Technologies	1.9
LH Research	1.9
RCA Solid State	1.8
National Semiconductor	1.8
Motorola	1.8
Hewlett-Packard	1.6
Honeywell	1.6
General Electric	1.6
Hitachi America	1.4
Advanced Micro Devices	1.4
Gould	1.3
Toshiba America	1.3
Lambda Electronics	1.3
Inmos	1.2
Allen-Bradley	1.2
Dupont	1.2
Siemens Components	1.1
3M Corp.	1.1
Square D Company	1.0
Fluke Manufacturing	.9
Sprague Electric Co.	.9

(Continued next page)

C SYSTEMS, LTD.
COMPANIES RANKED BY ADVERTISING PAGES AND DOLLARS (Continued)

ADVERTISING OF SOFTWARE PRODUCTS

Ranked by Advertising Pages

Borland International	356
Microsoft	336
Ashton-Tate	261
SAS Institute	239
IBM	193
Cullinet Software	192
Microrim	182
MicroPro International	165
Management Science of America	147
Computer Associates	143
Microstuf	143
Software Publishing	123
Applied Data Research	119
Relational Database Systems	114
Software Link	108
Sublogic Corp.	108
SPSS, Inc.	103
General Electric	99
Software AG of North America	99
Cincom Systems	98
Novell Data Systems	94
3Com	94
Computronics/H&E	93
Barrington Systems	88
Information Builders	88

(Continued next page)

C SYSTEMS, LTD.
COMPANIES RANKED BY ADVERTISING PAGES AND DOLLARS (Continued)

ADVERTISING OF SOFTWARE PRODUCTS

Ranked by Advertising Expenditure ($ millions)

IBM	$3.66
Microsoft	3.25
Borland International	2.74
Ashton-Tate	2.59
SAS Institute	2.37
Cullinet Software	1.99
Management Science of America	1.68
Apple Computer	1.62
Applied Data Research	1.44
Computer Associates	1.39
MicroPro International	1.28
Microrim	1.23
Microstuf	1.20
Software Publishing	1.14
McCormick & Dodge	1.05
Cincom Systems	1.00
Software Link	.97
SPSS, Inc.	.91
Software AG of North America	.85
Syncsort, Inc.	.81
Computer Corporation of America	.77
Relational Database Systemsd	.77
Novel Data Systems	.75
Barrington Systems	.73
Information Builders	.73
Lotus	.73
Sublogic Corp.	.73

(Continued next page)

C SYSTEMS, LTD.
COMPANIES RANKED BY ADVERTISING PAGES AND DOLLARS (Continued)

ADVERTISING OF TELECOMMUNICATIONS PRODUCTS

Ranked by Advertising Pages

AT&T Technologies	587
AT&T	503
Northern Telecom, Inc.	462
AT&T Information Systems	402
NEC America	290
GTE	275
ITT	247
AT&T Communications	241
U.S. Sprint	230
Siemens Corp.	203
Bell Atlantic	167
Rockwell International	142
MCI	137
Codex	135
Universal Data Systems	132
Digital Communications	124
Ventel Corp.	124
Digital Equipment Corp.	123
Honeywell	120
CIT-Alcatel, Inc.	113
Cannon U.S.A.	98
IBM	87
NEC Radio & Transmission	86
Infotron	85
Allnet Business Long Distance	84
Equinox Systems, Inc.	84

(Continued next page)

C SYSTEMS, LTD.
COMPANIES RANKED BY ADVERTISING PAGES AND DOLLARS (Continued)

ADVERTISING OF TELECOMMUNICATIONS PRODUCTS

Ranked by Advertising Expenditure ($ millions)

AT&T	$16.0
AT&T Communications	5.7
U.S. Sprint	5.5
AT&T Information Systems	5.2
Northern Telecom, Inc.	5.1
NEC America	3.1
GTE	3.1
AT&T Technologies	2.7
Bell Atlantic	2.7
MCI	2.5
Honeywell	2.4
Southern New England Telephone	2.3
Digital Equipment Corp.	2.2
New York Telephone	2.0
Bell South	1.9
Cannon U.S.A.	1.8
Motorola	1.7
Siemens Corp	1.7
ITT	1.4
NYNEX Business Information Systems	1.3
Contel	1.2
IBM	1.2
Allnet Business Long Distance	1.1
Codex	1.1
Universal Data Systems	1.0
Digital Communications	1.0

C SYSTEMS, LTD.

PUBLICATIONS RANKED BY ADVERTISING PAGES AND DOLLARS

Based on January - September, 1986

"These rankings are based on a survey of 178 trade and business publications. The revenues are estimates based on the rate cards of the publications and do not reflect any discount rates individual companies may have received."--C Systems, Ltd.

Reprinted with permission from C Systems, Ltd., 1986 Copyright 1986 by C Systems, Ltd., Ridgefield, CT.

ADVERTISING OF DATA PROCESSING PRODUCTS
(Excluding Software)

Ranked by Advertising Pages

Publication	Pages
PC Week	2,912
PC	1,862
Computer Reseller News	1,834
Computer Systems News	1,534
Byte	1,445
Computerworld	1,139
PC World	1,052
Computer+ Software News	963
Mini-Micro Systems	694
Datamation	643
Infoworld	635
Personal Computing	633
EDN	568
Digital Review	533
Wall Street Journal	492
Computer Decisions	485
Micro Market World	476
Hardcopy	469
Rainbow	436
Information Week	431
A+	409
Electronic Design	408
Government Computer News	403
Computer Design	400
80 Micro	400
(Continued next page)	

C SYSTEMS, LTD.
PUBLICATIONS RANKED BY ADVERTISING PAGES AND DOLLARS (Continued)

ADVERTISING OF DATA PROCESSING PRODUCTS
(Excluding Software)

Ranked by Advertising Revenue ($ millions)

Publication	Revenue
PC Week	$24.8
PC	17.9
Wall Street Journal	16.6
Byte	14.3
Computerworld	14.0
Business Week	12.8
PC World	10.2
Computer Systems News	9.1
Computer Reseller News	7.3
Fortune	7.0
Time	6.6
Forbes	6.5
Datamation	6.4
Personal Computing	6.2
Infoworld	5.4
Computer Decisions	4.9
Mini-Micro Systems	4.8
Newsweek	4.6
US News & World Report	4.5
Information Week	3.9
Inc.	3.7
EDN	3.2
Computer+ Software News	3.0
A+	3.0
Sports Illustrated	3.0

(Continued next page)

C SYSTEMS, LTD.

PUBLICATIONS RANKED BY ADVERTISING PAGES AND DOLLARS (Continued)

ADVERTISING OF ELECTRONICS PRODUCTS

Ranked by Advertising Pages

Publication	Pages
EDN	2,764
Electronic Design	2,608
Electronic Engineering Times	2,006
Electronic Buyers News	1,987
Design News	1,844
Machine Design	1,649
Electronic News	1,200
Electronic Products Magazine	1,180
Microwave Journal	1,079
Microwaves & RF	1,056
Semiconductor International	987
Electronic Business	915
Electronic Pkg & Prod	861
Electronics	788
Solid State Technology	770
MSN	723
Control Engineering	716
Plant Engineering	610
Test & Measurement World	541
Electronic Component News	531
Evaluation Engineering-EE	492
Electronics Test	479
EE Electronic/Electrical	475
R.F. Design	411
I & CS	401

(Continued next page

C SYSTEMS, LTD.

PUBLICATIONS RANKED BY ADVERTISING PAGES AND DOLLARS (Continued)

ADVERTISING OF ELECTRONICS PRODUCTS

Ranked by Advertising Revenue ($ millions)

Publication	Revenue
EDN	$16.0
Electronic Design	15.6
Electronic Engineering Times	13.6
Design News	11.3
Electronic Buyers News	10.1
Machine Design	9.8
Electronic News	8.0
Plant Engineering	7.4
Electronic Products Magazine	6.5
Electronic Business	4.6
Electronics	4.2
Electronic Component News	4.2
Control Engineering	3.9
Microwave Journal	3.9
Microwaves & RF	3.6
EE Electronic/Electrical	3.3
Semiconductor International	3.0
Electronic Packaging & Production	2.9
Purchasing	2.5
MSN	2.4
Solid State Technology	2.2
Computer Design	2.2
Electronics Test	2.0
I & CS	2.0
Test & Measurement World	1.7

(Continued next page)

C SYSTEMS, LTD.
PUBLICATIONS RANKED BY ADVERTISING PAGES AND DOLLARS (Continued)

ADVERTISING OF SOFTWARE PRODUCTS

Ranked by Advertising Pages

Publication	Pages
Computerworld	1,181
PC Week	1,056
PC	1,020
PC World	756
BYTE	678
Computer Reseller News	617
PC Tech Journal	574
InfoWorld	512
Computer+ Software News	450
Datamation	423
MacWorld	420
Digital Review	386
ICP Business Software Review	357
Information Week	316
Rainbow	314
Personal Computing	303
A+	297
Lotus	279
Software News	271
MacUser	263
Government Computer News	259
DEC Professional	256
80 Micro	243
Hardcopy	237
Run	231

(Continued next page)

C SYSTEMS, LTD.
PUBLICATIONS RANKED BY ADVERTISING PAGES AND DOLLARS (Continued)

ADVERTISING OF SOFTWARE PRODUCTS

Ranked by Advertising Revenue ($ millions)

Publication	Revenue
Computerworld	$14.0
PC	9.8
PC Week	9.2
PC World	7.3
BYTE	6.8
InfoWorld	4.5
Datamation	4.2
PC Tech Journal	3.4
Wall Street Journal	3.3
MacWorld	3.1
Personal Computing	3.0
Lotus	2.9
Information Week	2.8
Business Week	2.7
Computer Reseller News	2.4
A+	2.3
ICP Business Software Review	2.0
Computer Decisions	1.9
Digital Review	1.8
Fortune	1.7
Software News	1.5
Computer+ Software News	1.4
MacUser	1.3
Government Computer News	1.3
Run	1.3

(Continued next page)

C SYSTEMS, LTD.
PUBLICATIONS RANKED BY ADVERTISING PAGES AND DOLLARS (Continued)

ADVERTISING OF TELECOMMUNICATIONS PRODUCTS

Ranked by Advertising Pages

Publication	Pages
Telephony	1,535
Data Communications	1,152
Communications Week	1,143
Telephone Engineer & Management	1,060
Teleconnect	711
Telecommunications	569
Computerworld	496
Communications News	376
MIS Week	333
Network World	312
Telecommunication Products + Technology	290
Datamation	271
Wall Street Journal	249
Business Week	239
Communications Consultant	214
Information Week	211
Forbes	188
PC Week	187
Fortune	182
Computer Decisions	158

(Continued next page)

C SYSTEMS, LTD.
PUBLICATIONS RANKED BY ADVERTISING PAGES AND DOLLARS (Continued)

ADVERTISING OF TELECOMMUNICATIONS PRODUCTS

Ranked by Advertising Revenue ($ millions)

Publication	Revenue
Time	$9.0
Business Week	8.9
Wall Street Journal	8.4
Communications Week	8.3
Newsweek	6.2
Forbes	6.2
Computerworld	6.1
Data Communications	5.9
Fortune	5.8
US News & World Report	5.3
Sports Illustrated	4.7
Telephony	4.4
Telecommunications	3.3
MIS Week	3.2
Telephone Engineer & Management	2.9
Communications News	2.7
Datamation	2.7
Network World	2.3
Inc.	2.0
Information Week	1.9

COMPUTER MARTS

In this section COMPUTER INDUSTRY ALMANAC provides name and address information for all U.S. computer marts. The marts are listed alphabetically by name and include such information as unique features, services, size, date opened, contact and a brief description.

Infomart
1950 Stemmons Freeway
Dallas, TX 75207
Phone: 214/746-3500   Telex: 4943073 INFO
Description: Offers permanent product showroom and demonstration areas for over 225 computer hardware, software, telecommunications, peripherals, education, and service firms.
Date Open: Jan 1985
Size (Square feet): 1.5 M
Developer: Trammel Crow
Contact: Bill Winsor, President and General Manager; Lynda Rosenthal, Vice President, Marketing Services
Unique Features: Architectural inspiration from the legendary Victorian predecessor London Crystal Palace built in 1851.

On-site computer retail sales? No	Tours? Yes
Trade shows/conventions? Yes	Library? Yes
Conferences/forums/seminars? Yes	Bookstore? Yes
On-site classes/training? Yes	Restaurants/shops? Yes
User group meetings? Yes	Mail center? Yes
On-site museum? No	

COMPUTER MARTS (Continued)

Inforum
240 Peachtree St. NW, Ste 2200
Atlanta, GA 30043
Phone: 404/584-8593   Telex: 4611135
Description: Dedicated to the marketing of information processing and telecommunications products by providing a high profile, prominent southeastern location for the industry to market products and services to qualified end users and resellers.
Date Open: Fall 1988
Size (Square feet): 1.5 M
Developer: John C. Portman, Jr., General Partner
Contact: Jim Kranzusch, Executive Vice President; Rich Mauro, Vice President, Marketing & Sales; Bill Bryant, Communications Manager
Unique Features: Nine story, 1.5 M s.f. building with more than 100 showrooms

On-site computer retail sales? No	Tours? Yes
Trade shows/conventions? Yes	Library? Yes
Conferences/forums/seminars? Yes	Bookstore? Yes
On-site classes/training? Yes	Restaurants/shops? Yes
User group meetings? Yes	Mail center? Yes
On-site museum? No	

Techmart
5201 Great America Pkw, Ste 532
Santa Clara, CA 95054
Phone: 408/998-1411
Description: Master-planned environment for marketers of computer hardware, software, peripherals, telecom, automated office systems, and data communications products. Membership consists of buyers of high technology equipment.
Date Open: Spring 1987
Size (Square feet): 320,000
Developer: Kimball Small Properties
Contact: Harvey Hartman, Executive Director; Mary Benek, Director of Marketing
Unique Features: Part of an integrated complex also housing the Santa Clara Convention Center and Doubletree Hotel. Strong focus on education (U of CA uses Techmart for extension classes, many of which are on high-tech mktg and mgmt)

On-site computer retail sales? Yes	Tours? Yes
Trade shows/conventions? Yes	Library? Yes
Conferences/forums/seminars? Yes	Bookstore? Yes
On-site classes/training? Yes	Restaurants/shops? Yes
User group meetings? Yes	Mail center? Yes
On-site museum? No	

COMPUTER MARTS (Continued)

Techworld
901 Eighth St., NW
Washington, DC 20001
Phone: 202/682-2190
Description: Provides integrated showroom and office space for telecommunications, computer systems, office automation equipment, information services, graphic and reprographic, peripherals, and related professional companies and services.
Date Open: 4Q 1988
Size (Square feet): 1 M
Developer: Guiseppi Cecchi, President
Managing Firm: International Developers, Inc.
Contact: Alan Bogatay, Sr. Vice President; Howard Steinhardt, Vice President
Unique Features: Spans two city blocks and is a fully enhanced, world-class market facility for buyers and sellers of information technologies.

On-site computer retail sales? No	Tours? No
Trade shows/conventions? Yes	Library? Yes
Conferences/forums/seminars? Yes	Bookstore? Yes
On-site classes/training? Yes	Restaurants/shops? Yes
User group meetings? Yes	Mail center? No
On-site museum? Yes	

7 EDUCATION

COMPUTER INDUSTRY ALMANAC
TOP UNIVERSITIES IN COMPUTER SCIENCE
1986

These universities have been selected by COMPUTER INDUSTRY ALMANAC and are arranged in alphabetical order.--COMPUTER INDUSTRY ALMANAC.

University of California/Berkeley
University of California/San Diego
California Institute of Technology
Carnegie-Mellon University
Cornell University
Georgia Institute of Technology
University of Illinois/Champaign-Urbana
Massachusetts Institute of Technology
Princeton University
Purdue University
Rensselaer Polytechnic Institute
Rice University
Stanford University
University of Texas
University of Utah

COMPUTING SCIENCES ACCREDITATION BOARD, INC.
COMPUTER SCIENCE PROGRAMS ACCREDITED BY CSAB
1986

The Computing Sciences Accreditation Board, Inc. (CSAB) is an accrediting organization established in 1984 by the Association for Computing Machinery (ACM) and the Computer Society of the Institute of Electrical and Electronic Engineers (IEEE-CS). Of 125 institutions applying to CSAB for accreditation, only 31 were evaluated because of the limited number of volunteer evaluators. Of the 31 chosen by CSAB for its first accreditation evaluations, nine failed and the following 22 (listed below alphabetically by state) have had accreditation granted to their 4-year computer science programs.--COMPUTER INDUSTRY ALMANAC.

CALIFORNIA
> California State University, Sacramento
> California State Polytechnic University, San Luis Obispo
> University of California, San Diego
> University of California, Santa Barbara

COLORADO
> U.S. Air Force Academy

GEORGIA
> Georgia Institute of Technology

IOWA
> Iowa State University

MASSACHUSETTS
> Brandeis University
> Northeastern University
> Worchester Polytechnic University

MICHIGAN
> Western Michigan University

MISSISSIPPI
> Mississippi State University

MISSOURI
> University of Missouri, Rolla
> (Continued next page)

COMPUTING SCIENCES ACCREDITATION BOARD, INC.
COMPUTER SCIENCE PROGRAMS ACCREDITED BY CSAB
1986 (Continued)

NEW JERSEY

New Jersey Institute of Technology

Stevens Institute of Technology

NEW YORK

Pace University

NORTH DAKOTA

North Dakota State University

PENNSYLVANIA

Allegheny College

Drexel University

SOUTH CAROLINA

Clemson University

TEXAS

North Texas State University

UTAH

University of Utah

U.S. NATIONAL CENTER FOR EDUCATION STATISTICS
NUMBER OF EARNED DEGREES CONFERRED
1986

In the DIGEST OF EDUCATION STATISTICS (1986), the U.S. National Center for Education Statistics lists fields of study, levels of degrees, and number of earned degrees.--COMPUTER INDUSTRY ALMANAC.

Level and Field	1975	1980	1983
Bachelor's Degrees: Total	922,933	929,417	969,504
Computer and information sciences	5,033	11,154	24,506
Engineering	46,852	68,893	89,270
Master's Degrees: Total	292,450	298,081	289,921
Computer and information sciences	2,299	3,647	5,321
Engineering	15,348	16,243	19,350
Doctor's Degree	34,083	32,615	33,088
Computer and Information Sciences	213	240	262
Engineering	3,108	2,507	2,831

U.S. NATIONAL SCIENCE FOUNDATION
RESEARCH AND DEVELOPMENT EXPENDITURES IN SCIENCE AND ENGINEERING AT
UNIVERSITIES AND COLLEGES

In the SURVEY OF SCIENTIFIC AND ENGINEERING EXPENDITURES AT UNIVERSITIES
AND COLLEGES (annual), the U.S. National Science Foundation lists research and development
(R&D) expenditures in the fields of science and engineering at universities and colleges. Figures
given are in millions of dollars.--COMPUTER INDUSTRY ALMANAC.

Year	1980	1983
Total	$6,060	$7,745
Engineering	864	1,101
Mathematics and computer sciences	193	278

8 EMPLOYMENT

AMERICAN ELECTRONICS ASSOCIATION
ELECTRONICS INDUSTRY EMPLOYS MOST WORKERS
1986

The following data is compiled by the American Electronics Association, a Palo Alto, CA trade group.--COMPUTER INDUSTRY ALMANAC.

Reprinted with permission from American Electronics Association, 1986. Copyright 1986 by American electronics Association, Palo Alto, CA.

The U.S. electronics industry employed 2.52 million workers in September 1986. This was 40,000 fewer than a year earlier, but still well ahead of the transportation industry which employed 2 million workers. Electronics has been the leader in manufacturing employment since 1980.

AMERICAN ELECTRONICS ASSOCIATION
TOP STATES FOR ELECTRONICS EMPLOYMENT
1986

These charts show for 1985 the top ten states in electronics employment and the top ten states in electronics employment as a percent of total work force.--COMPUTER INDUSTRY ALMANAC.

Reprinted with permission from American Electronics Association, 1986. Copyright 1986 by American Electronics Association, Palo Alto, CA.

TOP STATES IN ELECTRONICS EMPLOYMENT

1. California   (586,000)
2. New York   (222,000)
3. Massachusetts   (207,000)
4. Texas   (152,000)
5. New Jersey   (107,000)
6. Florida   (104,000)
7. Illinois   (101,000)
8. Pennsylvania   (87,000)
9. Minnesota   (78,000)
10. Arizona   (61,000)
10. North Carolina   (61,000)

TOP STATES IN ELECTRONICS EMPLOYMENT AS PERCENT OF TOTAL WORK FORCE

1. New Hampshire   (4%)
2. Massachusetts   (3.7%)
3. California   (2.3%)
3. Vermont   (2.3%)
5. Arizona   (2.1%)
6. Minnesota   (1.9%)
7. Connecticut   (1.7%)
8. Colorado   (1.6%)
9. New Jersey   (1.5%)
10. Maryland   (1.4%)

U.S. BUREAU OF LABOR STATISTICS
EMPLOYMENT PROJECTIONS

The U.S. Bureau of Labor Statistics lists actual employment figures (in thousands) for 1970 and 1980 and projected figures based on assumptions of moderate growth for 1990 and 1995.-- COMPUTER INDUSTRY ALMANAC.

From this list COMPUTER INDUSTRY ALMANAC has selected only industry-related categories.

Industry	1970	1980	1990	1995
Manufacturing				
Computers, peripheral equipment	236	376	586	694
Radio, communications equipment	362	378	433	460
Electronic components	367	554	745	850
Business services[1]	1,756	3,404	5,172	6,183

[1]Includes computer programming and data processing services.

U.S. BUREAU OF LABOR STATISTICS
CHARACTERISTICS OF EMPLOYED SCIENTISTS AND ENGINEERS

The U.S. Bureau of Labor Statistics lists characteristics of employed scientists and engineers using U.S. National Foundation data and unpublished data. Percent distribution, except as indicated, represents the total science and engineering employment in the U.S. The total also includes life and physical scientists, which are not shown here.--COMPUTER INDUSTRY ALMANAC.

From this list COMPUTER INDUSTRY ALMANAC has selected only industry-related categories.

Characteristic	Total	Engineers	Computer specialists
Total: (1,000)	3,466	1,940	349
Male	87.3%	96.7%	72.1%
Female	12.7%	3.3%	27.9%
Highest degree:			
Doctorate	10.5%	3.2%	3.0%
Master's	26.3%	21.0%	27.7%
Bachelor's	52.7%	58.1%	68.5%
Other	10.5%	17.7%	0.8%
Type of employer:			
Business	67.2%	79.8%	79.2%
Education	12.0%	2.7%	5.6%
Nonprofit	3.4%	1.3%	2.8%
Federal	8.8%	7.1%	7.0%
Military	0.5%	0.6%	0.5%
Other government	5.4%	4.8%	3.7%
Other	2.6%	3.6%	1.1%

9 FINANCIAL FACTS

INITIAL PUBLIC OFFERINGS -- 1986

In this section COMPUTER INDUSTRY ALMANAC lists in alphabetical order the Initial Public Offerings (IPOs) for 1986 along with the date, size of offering, and underwriters.

Company/Business	Offered	Shares	Price	Underwriters
Adaptec, Inc.	6/11/86	1.3M	$9.50	Shearson Lehman Brothers and
Produces computer input/output components.				Robertson Colman & Stephens
Adobe Systems	8/13/86	0.5M	$11.00	Hambrecht & Quist
Systems software for publishing.				
Alliant Computer Systems Corp.	12/17/86	2M	$15.00	Morgan Stanley & Co. and
High-performance computers for eng. applications.				Hambrecht & Quist Inc.
Alloy Computer Products	6/26/86	1.2M	$10.00	Drexel Burnham Lambert
Peripherals to improve microcomputer performance.				
Applied Control Systems Inc.	11/13/86	0.7M	$5.00	D.H. Blair & Co.
Software for the food and beverage industry.				
Atari Corp.	11/07/86	4.5M	$11.50	PaineWebber Inc.
Microcomputer systems and video games.				
AutoInfo, Inc.	5/20/86	0.63M	$6.00	Starr Securities
Computerized products for sale of used auto parts.				
Axlong, Inc.	8/21/86	1.2M	$9.00	Steinberg & Lyman
Electronic toys.				
California Micro Devices Corp.	10/24/86	1.2M	$6.00	Swergold, Chefitz &
Electronic components.				Sinsabaugh Inc.
Chips & Technologies	8/14/86	2.0M	$5.00	Shearson Lehman Brothers Inc.
Proprietary VLSI circuits/microcomputer systems.				and E.F. Hutton & Co.
Cluster Technology Corp.	1/02/86	1.2M	$1.00	Covey & Co., Inc.
Processors to enhance minicomputers.				
Cognitive Systems	5/16/86	1.0M	$6.50	Ladenburg, Thalmann & Co.
Applications software.				
Concurrent Computer Corp.	1/24/86	2.0M	$20.00	First Boston Corp.
32-bit superminicomputers.				
Convex Computer	7/09/86	3.135M	$7.50	Goldman, Sachs & Co. and
High-performance computer systems.				Robertson, Colman & Stephens
Cypress Semiconductor	5/29/86	7.5M	$9.00	Morgan Stanley & Co. and
High-performance digital integrated circuits.				Robertson, Colman & Stephens
Datarex Systems	10/03/86	0.6M	$7.25	Josephthal & Co.
Distributes computer supplies.				
Dense-Pac Microsystems, Inc.	1/22/86	0.6M	$4.50	Rooney, Pace Inc.
Memory modules.				
(Continued next page)				

INITIAL PUBLIC OFFERINGS -- 1986 (Continued)

Company/Business	Offered	Shares	Price	Underwriters
Elcotel Inc.	11/21/86	1.0M	$6.00	F.N. Wolf & Co.
Privately owned pay telephones.				
EMC Corp.	4/01/86	2.2M	$15.00	Salomon Brothers, and
Add-on memory & enhancement products.				Merrill Lynch
FIserv	9/25/86	1.5M	$12.50	Merrill Lynch Capital Markets &
On-line data processing services.				Robertson, Colman & Stephens
Gartner Group	7/17/86	1.1M	$10.50	Shearson Lehman Brothers and
Markets research products relating to info.tech.				Robertson Colman & Stephens
General Computer	3/31/86	0.9M	$13.00	McDonald
Markets computer systems.				
General Parametrics	7/30/86	1.25M	$13.00	Morgan Stanley & Co. and
Desktop presentation graphics products.				Montgomery Securities
Genicom Corp.	6/25/86	2.2M	$9.00	First Boston Corp. and L.F.
Computer printers.				Rothschild, Unterberg, Towbin
Image Management Systems Inc.	5/07/86	0.65M	$6.00	D. H. Blair Inc.
Informix	8/14/86	1.4M	$7.50	Hambrecht & Quist Inc. and
Relational database mgmt software products.				Smith Barney & Co.
Interleaf Inc.	6/27/86	3M	$10.00	Alex. Brown & Sons Inc., Lazard
Turnkey systems for computer-aided publishing.				Freres, and Hambrecht & Quist
Irwin Magnetic Systems, Inc.	11/20/86	2.4M	$8.00	Drexel Burnham Lambert, Inc.
Low cost minicartridge tape drives.				
MAI Basic Four	6/24/86	4M	$15.00	Drexel Burnham Lambert Inc.
Superminicomputers & systems.				and Wertheim & Co. Inc.
Microsoft Inc.	3/13/86	2.8M	$21.00	Goldman, Sachs
Develops/markets computer software.				
MTech Corp.	12/19/86	2.25M	$17.00	Alex. Brown & Sons Inc.
Bank data processing services.				
Neeco Inc.	6/18/86	1.5M	$6.00	Mosley Securities Corp.
Markets microcomputer systems.				
Network Control Corp.	8/06/86	0.7M	$6.00	Whale Securities Corp.
Telecommunications test equipment & software.				
Oracle Systems Corp.	3/12/86	2.1M	$15.00	Alex. Brown & Sons Inc.
Software development.				
PCS Inc.	11/25/86	2M	$13.50	Morgan Stanley & Co. and
Computer-based prescription drug claim processing.				Goldman, Sachs & Co.
Perception Technology	6/04/86	1.2M	$18.00	Kidder, Peabody & Co.
Voice response systems to interface w/computers.				

(Continued next page)

INITIAL PUBLIC OFFERINGS -- 1986 (Continued)

Company/Business	Offered	Shares	Price	Underwriters
Rubicon	3/31/86	0.4M	$10.00	Rotan Mosle
Develops/sells computer systems.				
SCS-Compute Inc.	9/03/86	1M	$8.75	Wedbush, Noble, Cooke Inc.
Income tax return processing services.				
Sage Software Inc.	12/17/86	1.8M	$12.50	Alex. Brown & Sons Inc. and
Software engineering tools for IBM mainframes.				Hambrecht & Quist Inc.
Scientific Systems Inc.	10/10/86	0.7M	$5.00	K. A. Knapp & Co.
Software training products.				
Sigma Designs Inc.	5/31/86	1M	$5.75	Laidlaw, Adams and Peck Inc.
Personal computer enhancements.				
Silicon Graphics Inc.	10/29/86	1.8M	$11.25	Morgan Stanley & Co. and
Superworkstations.				Alex. Brown & Sons Inc.
Southern Electronics	10/21/86	0.9M	$6.00	Drexel Burnham Lambert Inc.
Wholesale distr. of consumer electronic products.				
Sun Microsystems	3/04/86	4M	$16.00	Robertson, Colman
Markets 32-bit workstations.				
Sungard Data Systems	3/31/86	2.3M	$11.00	Alex. Brown & Sons Inc.
Provides data-processing service.				
Synercom Technology	3/31/86	2M	$15.00	Morgan Stanley & Co.
Designs/markets mapping database.				
Tech Data Corp.	4/22/86	1M	$9.75	Robinson-Humphrey Co.
Hardware distributor.				
Teknowledge Inc.	3/31/86	2.2M	$13.00	Shearson Lehman
Developer of artificial intelligence software.				
Telesis Systems	5/07/86	1.1M	$7.50	PaineWebber Inc. and
Manufactures CAD/CAM, CAE systems.				Cowen & Co.
Verticom, Inc.	5/14/86	0.9M	$5.00	Baer & Company
Develops high performance color graphics systems.				
Worldwide Computer Services Inc.	5/29/86	1.2M	$3.75	Hickey Kober Inc.
Unit of General Devices.				
Xiox Corp.	2/28/86	0.6M	$5.00	D.H. Blair & Co. Inc.
Telephone call accounting & management systems.				
Xyvision, Inc.	7/02/86	1.1M	$13.50	First Boston Corp., and
Computer-integrated publishing systems.				Montgomery Securities

MERGERS AND ACQUISITIONS - 1986

In this section COMPUTER INDUSTRY ALMANAC lists the industry mergers and acquisitions for 1986 in alphabetical order by acquiring company. While terms are frequently undisclosed, amounts in cash, stock, and debt are listed when known along with a brief description of the acquired business.

Acquiring Company/Date	Acquired Company/Comments
3Com 2/86	DynaMicro Software Cash undisclosed amount.
800-Software 2/86	Smartware Inc. Cash undisclosed amount.
AEG Aktiengesellschaft 7/86	Modular Computer Sys. $41.3M cash for 81%, $51M total value.
AIFS Inc. 7/86	Computer Curriculum Corp. Terms not disclosed. Computer aided instruction system.
AM International Inc. 7/86	Nicolet Zeta Corp. From Nicolet Instrument Corp. for cash. Pen plotters.
AST Research Inc. 2/86	Camintonn Corp. Undisclosed stock & cash. $6M sales.
Activision Inc. 5/86	Infocom Inc. 2M shares valued at $7.5M. Completed 6/13/86.
Alpha Electronics 4/86	Quantech Distribution Div. For book value of $1.2M
Alpha Microsystems 10/86	Fasuma plc and Jewelsea plc To operate under the name Alpha Micro Australia Ltd.
Altos Computer Systems 7/86	Communications Solutions Inc. From Control Data Corp. Communication software.
American Management Sys. 7/86	Bankserve product line From Anacomp Inc. for undisclosed cash & royalties.
American Management Sys. 12/86	Data Base Management Inc. And affiliated Courseware Developers Inc. for $5M.
Ameritrust Corp. 11/86	Network Concepts Inc. Undiscl. terms. Equipment & services through telemarketing.
Anthem Electronics, Inc. 8/86	Lionex Corp. $17M cash for private Lionex, northeastern US electron. distr.
Applied Magnetics Corp. 7/86	Wilson Laboratories Inc. Stock pooling. Test equipment for computer peripherals.
Ashton-Tate 9/86	Decision Resources Inc. $12.9M in cash. Business graphics software packages.

(Continued next page)

MERGERS AND ACQUISITIONS - 1986 (Continued)

Acquiring Company/Date	Acquired Company/Comments
Automated Industrial Systems 4/86	Computer Integrated Mfg. From UCCEL for "modest gain."
BaronData Systems 7/86	Legal Systems Division From Sterling Software, was Informatics Legal Division.
Bell & Howell Co. 5/86	Data Courier Inc. Electronic business information databases.
Bell Atlantic 9/86	Greyhound Capital Corp. $140M. Provides direct finance for leasing of computers.
Bell Canada International 12/86	Dataway GmbH Terms not disclosed. Computer maintenance in Germany.
British Telecom 4/86	IAL Plc. From STC Plc for 22M pounds ($34M).
British Telecom 5/86	ITT Corp.'s Dialcom Cash, amount not disclosed.
British Telecom 3/86	Mitel Ltd. 51% for $320M.
Burroughs Corp. 5/86	Sperry Corp. $4.78B incl. about half in cash, bal. in preferred & debentures.
Businessland Inc. 6/86	Amerisource Acquisition announced April 1, completed 6/86.
Businessland Inc. 9/86	Morris Decision Systems Inc. For cash and assumption of liabilities.
Carlisle Co. 8/86	Data Electronics Inc. $24M. Magnetic tape, data cartridges and data comm. products.
CCX Network 12/86	Southwark Computer Serv. Ltd. $3.9M in stock. London-based computer service company.
Centel Corp 9/86	Perry Cable Mgt. Serv. Inc. Cash. Software and systems development company.
Centel Corp. 9/86	Information systems unit From M/A-COM for undisclosed cash. System integrator.
Centronics Data Computer 6/86	BDS Computer Australia Pty Ltd From BDS Corp. Interfaces for plug-compatible mainframes.
Cincinnati Bell Inc. 9/86	Abacus Computer Stores Terms undisclosed.
Cincinnati Bell Inc. 6/86	Cellular Business Systems Inc. Billing services in most of the nation's 30 largest markets.

(Continued next page)

MERGERS AND ACQUISITIONS - 1986 (Continued)

Acquiring Company/Date	Acquired Company/Comments
Cipher Data Products Inc. 6/86	Optimem Inc. $6.3M cash plus $3M note and royalties for 90% from Xerox.
Citicorp 5/86	Quotron Systems Inc. Tender offer at $19/share.
Cmptr. Entry Sys. 4/86	Laser Data Sys. assets To service Laser Data's TRP 700, undisclosed cash.
Comarco Inc. 11/86	Automated Design Centers Inc. Engr. support services through CAD/CAM workstations.
Comp-U-Card Intl. Inc. 10/86	Certified Collateral Corp. Shares valued at $83.5M.
Comp-U-Card Intl. Inc. 6/86	Madison Financial Corp. $33.3M incl. $15.3M cash, $12M debentures, and $6M stock.
Computer Horizons Corp. 12/86	Data processing consulting Business of Infogroup. Agreement in principle.
Computer Identics 6/86	Spectra-Physics' scanner line Cash & royalties.
Computer Innovations 4/86	ComputerLand Canada $58M Canadian incl. $14M cash + 2.5M shrs + 10M earnout.
Computer Sciences Corp. 7/86	Computer Partners Inc. Cash purchase. Consulting servs. in computer-based info. syst.
Computer Task Group Inc. 9/86	Maxima Comp. Mgmt. Cnslts. Ltd Terms not disclosed. Serves the federal govt. in Ottawa.
Computer Task Group Inc. 5/86	Quadra Systems' DP Service Bus San Antonio clients. Terms not disclosed.
Computer Task Group Inc. 7/86	Shubrooks International Ltd. Terms not disclosed. Software consulting firm.
ComputerWorks 11/85	Morris Decision Systems Merger.
Contel Corp. 5/86	Western Union Govt. Sys. Div. $155M.
Convergent Technologies Inc. 8/86	Digital Syst.& Open Syst.units From UCCEL for $28.5M cash. Turnkey syst.& microsoftware.
Convergent Technologies Inc. 10/86	Display Data Corp. $56M in stock. Systems for auto, beverage, and lumber dealers.
Cullinet Software Inc. 7/86	Esvel Inc. $8.4M cash. Software for minicomputers & personal computers.

(Continued next page)

MERGERS AND ACQUISITIONS - 1986 (Continued)

Acquiring Company/Date	Acquired Company/Comments
Cybernex Corp.	Century Data Systems
7/86	From Xerox Corp. for undisclosed terms. Rigid disk drives.
Daewoo Corp. (Korea)	Zymos Corp.
4/86	Controlling interest in multimillion dollar deal.
Data Card Corp.	Addressograph Farrington Inc.
8/86	$52M cash. Electronic point-of-sale terminals for plastic cards.
Data General Corp.	Dama Telecommunications Corp.
5/86	Minority interest, undisclosed stake and price.
Data Packaging Intl. Inc.	Domestic OEM Cmptr.Prods. business.
11/86	From Costar Corp., for $5.15M in cash and notes.
Datametrics Corp.	Magnetic Storage Corp.
7/86	Militarized magnetic tape cartridge systems.
Datum Inc.	Spectrum Technology
4/86	Undisclosed cash. Completed 6/30/86.
Decision Data Computer	Panatec Inc.
4/86	Terms not disclosed.
Digital Communications	Cohesive Network Corp.
9/86	1.65M shrs new stock worth $28M. R&D of T1 products.
Digital Equipment	Trilogy Ltd.'s packaging business.
6/86	$10M cash.
Docugraphix Inc.	Micad Systems Inc.
7/86	$1M in stock. Computer-aided design and data management.
Dotronix Inc.	Electronics Sys. Div.
4/86	From Audiotronics Corp. for $1.8M cash and notes.
ERC International Inc.	Appalachian Cmptr. Servs. Inc.
7/86	$22.6M in stock. Data processing services.
Endata Inc.	COM (Micrographics) operations
9/86	From Micro Graphic Reproduction Inc. Terms not disclosed.
Euro-Magnetic Products Ltd.	Computer Resources Inc.
10/86	$0.75 share. Euro-Magnetic mfrs. magnetic media products.
Formaster Corp.	Magnetic Designs Corp.
7/86	Merger to form Formaster Magnetic Designs Inc. Data duping.
GEAC Computer Corp.	Citicorp Information Resources
9/86	Terms undisclosed. In-house DP services to credit unions.
GTE Telenet	Consortium Comm. Intl. Inc.
6/86	60% stake w/option on other 40%.

(Continued next page)

MERGERS AND ACQUISITIONS - 1986 (Continued)

Acquiring Company/Date	Acquired Company/Comments
Gartmore & Lazard 4/86	Scott Instruments 17.1% for $2M by two London institutions.
General Electric Company 6/86	RCA Corp. Completed merger for $6.4B in cash.
General Instrument Corp. 9/86	Cable-home comm. business From M/A-COM for $220M. Scrambling of satellite TV.
Grumman Corp. 3/86	Arrow Elec Field Svce Div. w/2500 computer maintenance customers.
Hammer Computer Systems 4/86	Certified Software Systems Inc Portland, OR software developer.
Harris Corp. 8/86	Scientific Calculations Inc. Terms not disclosed. Software development firm.
Hewlett-Packard Co. 11/86	MCC share From BMC Industries Inc., for undisclosed terms.
Hewlett-Packard Co. 7/86	Natural Microsystems interest Minority interest. Terms not discl. Voice-processing devel.
Icot Corp. 12/86	Point-of-sale division Of Lexicon Corp. for $6M cash and 200,000 shares.
Information Resources Inc. 4/86	Data Group Inc. For 40,000 common shares.
Ingram Distribution Group 12/85	Micro D 50% from Lorraine Mecca.
Ingram Industries Inc. 6/86	Micro D Inc. option on 10.4% To bring total stake in Micro D to 60.7%.
Ingram Software 12/85	Softeam To form Ingram Distribution.
Inspectorate Intl. SA 3/86	Automation Cntr International From Uccel.
Inspectorate Intl. SA 3/86	University Computing Co. Ltd. From Uccel.
Integrated Software Systems 6/86	Mimer Information Systems AB $4.7M for 60% with option on addnl. 31% for $4.5M + 6% int.
Interdyne Co. 9/86	Anthem Systems Pooling of interests. VAD of computer peripheral equipment.
Interdyne Co. 7/86	Peachtree Technology Inc. Terms not disclosed. Markets computer memory devices.

(Continued next page)

MERGERS AND ACQUISITIONS - 1986 (Continued)

Acquiring Company/Date	Acquired Company/Comments
Intergraph	Optronics Int'l
2/86	$3M in stock.
International Thomson Org.	Cordura Corp.
5/86	$35/share or about $203M. Employee benefit svces & dbases.
Jefferson-Pilot Data Systems	Data Communications Corp.
11/86	Terms not disclosed. Software to television and radio stations.
Steve Jobs	Pixar
2/86	From Lucasfilm Ltd. for "millions."
Charles C. Johnston	ISI Systems Inc.
4/86	From Grumman for $14M cash and $6M notes.
Kalvar Corp.	Micrographics & printing units
11/86	Of Seafirst Computer Services Corp. Terms not disclosed.
Keane Inc.	Reden Consultants Corp.
6/86	Cash for customized software services firm.
Lockheed Corp.	Sanders Associates Inc.
8/86	$1.18B at $60/share for defense electronics firm. Loral bid $50.
Logicon Inc.	Control Dynamics
3/86	Completed acq. for stock.
Lotus Development Corp.	GNP Development
2/86	Not disclosed.
Lotus Development Corp.	Graphic Communications Inc.
6/86	Undisclosed terms. Graphic software packages.
Lotus Development Corp.	ISYS Corp.
2/86	Not disclosed.
MBI Business Centers Inc.	Micro-South Corp
4/86	For 152,280 shrs. worth $1.94M.
MBI Business Centers Inc.	Prodigy Systems Inc.
9/86	$1.4M. Prodigy operates four computer stores in NJ.
Management Science America	Information Associates Inc.
5/86	$15M cash for college software vendor.
McGraw-Hill	Coade
4/86	Sim. & design SW for process engs., from Intl. Thomson.
McGraw-Hill	Numerax
4/86	$44M in cash.
Mgt. Science America	RTS Ltd.
4/86	Mfg. & fin. SW. $5.5M '85 rev. Dublin, Ireland firm.

(Continued next page)

MERGERS AND ACQUISITIONS - 1986 (Continued)

Acquiring Company/Date	Acquired Company/Comments
Microphonics Technology 4/86	Data Terminal Mart Stock in Canadian company.
Microsemi Corp. 7/86	Bikor Corp. Undisclosed stock and cash. Makes power supplies.
Microsoft Corp. 6/86	Dynamical Systems Research Inc. Terms not disclosed.
Millipore Corp. 8/86	Dynamic Solutions Corp. Common stock worth $4.5M. SW for lab. anal. instr. systs.
Minnesota Mining & Mfg. Co. 9/86	Optimem Minority share of stock. Mfrs. optical-disk drives.
Mohawk Acquisition 4/86	5 Operations of MDS $80M cash plus service commissions & fees.
Moore Bus. Forms 4/86	KCR Technology Inc. 30% for $5M w/ options to 51% for R&D of printers.
NYNEX 7/86	IBM Product Centers 81 stores for undisclosed amount.
NYNEX 4/86	Telco Research Undisclosed terms.
Nashua Corp. 6/86	Disk-Tec Inc. Machined substrates used in making rigid memory disks.
National Business Systems Inc. 9/86	Southern Systems Inc. $7.9M in cash & shares. Non-impact printers & elec. processors.
National Computer Systems 4/86	Key Financial Systems From Ziff Communications Co.
National Computer Systems 5/86	Kaiser Datentechnik GmbH Nurnberg-based optical mark reader.
Norcom Electronics Corp. 11/86	AFI 1500-1600 product line From Data Card Corp. Terms were not disclosed.
Nu-Kote International 11/86	Intl. bus.forms & supplies operations From Unisys Corp. $50M cash plus notes by LBO mgt. group.
Olivetti 4/86	Bunker Ramo Information Syst. From ADP for cash.
Omnibus Computer Graphics 7/86	Digital Productions unit From Ramtek Corp. along with a Cray-XMP.
On-Line Software Intl. Inc. 10/86	Data syst. pkg. software business. From Martin Marietta for $35M. Ramis, UFO,Unison products.

(Continued next page)

MERGERS AND ACQUISITIONS - 1986 (Continued)

Acquiring Company/Date	Acquired Company/Comments
Pacific Telesis Group 6/86	Communications Industries $431M. Competing acquisition agreed to one year before.
Pansophic Systems Inc. 8/86	Fusion Products Intl. Inc. $7.2M in stock. Info. retrieval & report writing systems.
Paychex Inc. 11/86	Payroll General Corp. Terms not disclosed.
Philips International 4/86	Bunker Ramo Bank Subsidiary From ADP for cash.
Policy Management Systems 2/86	Insurance Systems Division From Sterling Software.
Policy Management Systems 5/86	Standard Service Bureau Inc. Terms not disclosed.
Primages Inc. 6/86	Cabletech Inc. Completed acquisition for undisclosed terms.
Proctor & Gamble Co. 9/86	Metaphor Computer Systems interest $10M for minority stake; percentage of stock not disclosed.
Quotron Systems Inc. 6/86	Securities Industry SW Corp. Transaction-oriented software for financial firms.
Rexon Inc. 10/86	Tecmar Inc. For 261,829 shares & $314,194 cash; $314,194 notes.
Rotan Mosle Tech. Prtnrs Ltd 9/86	Digicon Inc. $12.5M. Hardware and software to the geophysical industry.
Sandsport Data Services Inc. 11/86	Madison Data Systems Inc. Undiscl. cash & stock. Turnkey real-estate mgmt. servs.
Sci Systems Inc. 6/86	AWI Services & products for surface mount technology.
Scientific Micro Systems Inc 6/86	Sigen Corp. Tape controllers and disk-tape storage systems.
Scientific Technology 2/86	Zaisan, Inc. $800K.
Shape Inc. 6/86	Wabash Datatech Inc. From Kearny-National Inc. for cash. Memory products.
Siemens AG 9/86	GTE's US & intl. trans. systems For cash payment & 20% of new company.
Simon & Schuster 4/86	Management Control Systems Completed acq. from Sterling Software.

(Continued next page)

MERGERS AND ACQUISITIONS - 1986 (Continued)

Acquiring Company/Date	Acquired Company/Comments
SofTech Inc.	AMG Associates
4/86	Undisclosed terms.
Sperry Corp.	Foundation Computer Systems
4/86	From Encore Computer Corp.
Sungard Data Systems Inc.	HSH National Management Inc.
10/86	Undisclosed terms. Planning for computer center disasters.
Sungard Data Systems Inc.	Peachtree Financial Systems
5/86	Loan origination systems for community banks.
Sungard Data Systems Inc.	Wismer Associates Inc.
10/86	In excess of $10M. Computer services firm.
Tab Products Co.	Acctex Information Systems
3/86	20% int. w/option for all. $1.5M rev. in computer software.
Telematics International Inc.	Protocol Computers Inc.
8/86	$1.02/share to R.L. Swarz founder, $1.40/share to others.
Telequest Inc.	Zelex Corp. assets
12/86	Undisclosed sum. Manufacturer of Telephone dialers.
Tera Corp.	Balance of Tenera Corp.
7/86	For 1.42M additional shares of Tera worth $7M at market.
Texas Instruments	ETI Micro
4/86	Terms not disclosed.
Triad Systems Corp.	Mainstreet Systems Corp.
5/86	Terms not disclosed.
U.S. Trust Corp	Advanced Information Managmnt.
4/86	Controlling interest.
U.S. West Information Syst.	Applied Communications Inc.
5/86	$120M for 96.5%.
Universal Tech Systems	TK!Solver
1/86	From Lotus Development.
VLSI Technology	VISIC Inc.
10/86	Majority ownership.
Votrax International Inc.	Data Voice Solutions Corp.
12/86	Undisclosed terms. Multi-user computer systems.
Wang Laboratories Inc.	Custom Software Services interest
8/86	21% of stock by 1989. Software for the legal industry.
Wang Laboratories Inc.	Intecom Inc.
9/86	80% not already owned for $157M in stock.

(Continued next page)

MERGERS AND ACQUISITIONS - 1986 (Continued)

Acquiring Company/Date	Acquired Company/Comments
Western Digital Corp.	Adaptive Data Systems, Inc.
7/86	Terms not disclosed. High-end disk & tape controllers.
Wyse Technology	Amdek Corp.
2/86	$8.4M in stock +3yr employment contract & options.
Xidex Corp.	Charlton Associates
4/86	2.4M Xidex shares ($19) plus options.
York Research	Phoenix Computer Tech
4/86	72% for undisclosed price.
Zentec Corp.	Data Products Division
8/86	From Lear Siegler for cash & notes. Display terminals.

STOCK TRENDS - 1986

In this section COMPUTER INDUSTRY ALMANAC identifies the winners and losers in the U.S. stock markets and ranks them by the percent of change in price per share for the calendar year 1986.--COMPUTER INDUSTRY ALMANAC.

Company	12/31/86 Close	Market Value ($M)	Price/ Earnings	Price/ Revenues	12 Month Change %
Systems					
IPL Systems	2.12	10.6	10.6	5.31	88.9
Apple	40.50	2578	16.7	1.35	84.1
Amdahl Corp	23.38	1110	51.4	1.25	59.8
Digital Equipment	104.75	13470	18.5	1.68	58.1
Tandem Computers	34.25	1487	23.3	1.93	54.8
COMPAQ	19.25	516.0	14.1	0.86	45.3
C 3 Inc.	12.38	119.9	NMF	2.06	39.4
Wyse Technology	17.25	204.2	13.9	1.04	29.0
Control Data	26.38	1085	NE	0.30	27.1
Unisys	80.00	3664	14.1	0.55	26.2
Cray Research	80.88	2431	21.4	4.47	23.5
Computer Automation	3.50	7.2	NMF	0.36	21.7
Datapoint	6.38	113.8	NE	0.35	21.4
Rexon	6.50	21.5	10.7	0.39	20.9
Apollo Computer	16.12	558.5	NMF	1.63	17.3
Sci Systems Inc.	17.62	243.0	17.1	0.53	16.5
Mohawk Data	2.88	43.2	NE	0.22	15.0
Hewlett-Packard	41.88	10742	20.8	1.51	13.9
Computer Consoles	8.25	100.1	NE	0.88	11.9
Electronic Associates	4.75	13.5	33.9	0.46	11.8
NCR	44.12	4316	13.7	0.91	9.6
Zenith	21.88	508.1	NE	0.28	6.7
Computervision	13.38	384.2	NE	0.80	5.9
Tandy	42.50	3811	19.1	1.23	4.3
Kaypro	1.38	49.7	NMF	0.64	-4.3
Altos Cptr Syst	11.25	150.5	7.8	1.11	-10.9
Stratus Computer	21.12	391.4	30.8	3.43	-11.1
Commodore Int'l	8.88	277.3	NE	0.30	-16.5
ASK Computer Systems	10.50	135.5	19.4	1.63	-19.2
Honeywell	59.12	2652	12.3	0.42	-20.2
IBM	120.00	73872	12.2	1.43	-22.8

(Continued next page)

STOCK TRENDS - 1986 (Continued)

Company	12/31/86 Close	Market Value ($M)	Price/ Earnings	Price/ Revenues	12 Month Change %
Prime Computer	16.38	788.7	15.7	0.94	-24.3
Alpha Microsystems	4.62	14.7	NE	0.32	-26.0
Fortune Systems	1.25	26.3	NE	0.64	-31.0
TeleVideo Systems	2.00	84.3	NMF	0.90	-33.3
Data General	29.62	778.8	NMF	0.61	-34.7
Wicat Systems	2.62	55.9	NE	1.64	-38.2
Wang	11.62	1742	34.2	0.65	-40.8
Valid Logic	4.88	66.0	NMF	1.11	-46.6
Convergent Technologies	6.00	221.8	NE	0.67	-49.5
CSP Inc.	5.75	16.2	9.6	1.16	-50.0
Intergraph	17.00	948.8	13.7	1.57	-53.4
Verdix Corp	1.81	14.0	NE	3.50	-64.6
Floating Point Systems	11.25	96.7	12.2	0.81	-68.3
Daisy Systems	8.38	147.4	NE	1.37	-71.4
Trilogy Ltd	0.31	24.2	NE	0.57	-79.2
Totals - Hardware	55.21	130091	16.1	1.21	

Peripherals - Communications

Company	12/31/86 Close	Market Value ($M)	Price/ Earnings	Price/ Revenues	12 Month Change %
Computer Network	8.00	18.5	NE	0.48	45.4
3COM	16.12	222.5	30.9	3.17	43.3
Novell	25.75	289.4	34.4	4.45	35.5
Gandalf Technology	7.12	71.4	21.5	0.66	-1.7
Data Switch Corp	5.38	51.1	NMF	1.27	-14.0
Anderson Jacobson	1.88	5.1	NE	0.13	-25.0
Network Systems	13.88	401.8	27.5	4.14	-31.5
General Datacomm	8.00	120.9	31.0	0.67	-31.9
Micom Systems	13.50	233.9	22.7	1.23	-38.6
Astrocom Corp	2.00	5.1	17.1	0.42	-40.7
Ungermann Bass	9.25	159.5	NE	1.57	-42.2
Corvus Systems	0.94	26.2	NE	0.67	-42.3
Totals - Communications	10.11	1605	203.	1.64	

(Continued next page)

STOCK TRENDS - 1986 (Continued)

Company	12/31/86 Close	Market Value ($M)	Price/ Earnings	Price/ Revenues	12 Month Change %
Peripherals - Input/Output					
Zentec	3.88	13.4	8.9	0.60	181.8
Digilog Inc	7.12	11.5	NE	0.88	78.1
QMS Inc	14.50	130.5	17.4	1.78	61.1
Intelligent Systems	7.12	77.3	19.8	0.51	54.1
Personal Computer	10.00	17.0	NE	8.51	50.9
Telxon Corp	20.50	262.0	24.5	3.27	33.7
Syntech Intl	8.62	38.9	NE	2.59	25.4
Esprit Systems	1.38	10.5	NE	0.47	22.2
Recognition Equipment	15.50	150.6	27.9	0.69	14.8
Telex	67.00	978.3	13.5	1.24	12.4
Tab Products	13.38	88.8	15.1	0.73	12.2
Lee Data	6.62	93.4	37.4	0.91	10.4
Micros Systems	2.25	10.8	NE	0.59	0.0
American Magnetics	5.25	25.5	NMF	2.54	-4.5
Interface Systems	7.12	27.6	10.2	1.72	-7.5
Datasouth Computer	2.75	16.1	17.8	0.89	-10.2
Centronics Data	4.38	109.4	NMF	0.60	-12.5
Datacopy	5.88	28.0	NMF	4.67	-19.0
Wespercorp	0.69	1.4	NE	0.10	-21.4
Copytele Inc	11.50	98.7	NE	NMF	-22.0
Printronix	10.00	50.0	NE	0.39	-23.1
Genisco Technology	4.25	11.3	16.2	0.29	-26.1
Emulex Corp	8.25	107.2	13.9	1.02	-27.5
Analogic Corp	10.75	202.9	20.1	1.49	-28.3
Par Technology Corp	12.50	96.5	13.4	1.30	-29.6
Dataproducts	11.50	240.7	20.6	0.67	-29.8
Decision Industries	8.75	82.0	35.6	0.44	-34.0
ISC Systems	9.25	147.9	10.5	0.88	-36.8
Terminal Data	2.00	9.0	NE	0.29	-38.5
Ziyad Inc	3.38	18.8	NE	0.72	-40.0
Delta Data	0.38	2.6	NE	0.12	-40.0
Dicomed	2.25	8.9	NE	0.44	-51.4
TEC Inc	3.38	2.9	NE	0.26	-52.6
Chancellor Computer	0.31	3.1	NE	NMF	-54.5
AST Research	12.88	147.0	6.6	0.87	-58.0
Totals - Input/Output	11.33	3320	24.9	0.99	

(Continued next page)

FINANCIAL - Copyright 1987 Computer Industry Almanac

STOCK TRENDS - 1986 (Continued)

Company	12/31/86 Close	Market Value ($M)	Price/ Earnings	Price/ Revenues	12 Month Change %
Peripherals - Memory					
Seagate	19.00	897.6	15.7	1.60	162.1
Miniscribe	8.75	177.5	9.4	1.06	154.6
Micropolis	18.75	210.0	13.6	1.06	114.3
Storage Technology	3.50	121.7	7.8	0.17	100.0
Masstor	3.12	50.0	NE	1.78	85.2
Vermont Research	5.75	11.2	NE	2.80	27.8
Ciprico Inc	6.25	13.7	15.2	1.37	10.0
Computer Memories	2.44	27.1	NE	0.87	2.6
Scientific Micro	4.62	33.7	19.8	0.56	0.0
Applied Magnetics	14.88	94.0	39.1	0.76	0.0
US Design Corp	2.38	12.0	NE	1.70	-5.0
System Industries	5.88	25.0	6.8	0.22	-19.0
Quantum	20.75	196.4	11.4	1.73	-22.4
Dataram Corp	6.62	13.0	4.2	0.76	-25.4
Distributed Logic	4.62	11.5	9.6	0.82	-30.2
Xebec	1.56	20.6	NE	0.17	-34.2
Cipher Data	11.12	159.0	21.2	0.92	-36.0
Archive Corp	5.00	52.3	26.1	0.67	-41.2
National Micronetics	1.94	17.8	NE	0.45	-44.6
Zitel Corp	1.62	7.7	NMF	0.42	-48.0
Computer & Com.	3.50	27.0	NE	0.42	-49.1
Tandon	2.31	118.7	NE	0.55	-51.3
Iomega	5.75	87.3	21.8	0.68	-52.1
Computer Resources	0.75	1.6	NE	0.08	-53.8
Rodime PLC	4.75	37.3	NE	NE	-57.8
Priam	2.38	56.2	NE	0.44	-60.4
Totals - Memory	7.27	2480	NE	0.77	

(Continued next page)

STOCK TRENDS - 1986 (Continued)

Company	12/31/86 Close	Market Value ($M)	Price/ Earnings	Price/ Revenues	12 Month Change %
Software					
Ashton-Tate	44.50	524.5	20.6	2.77	143.8
Microsoft*	48.25	1193	25.7	5.39	129.8
Lotus Development Corp.	51.75	793.3	17.9	2.91	107.0
Innovative Software	13.88	33.7	22.5	2.41	98.2
Autodesk	38.50	262.3	25.2	5.70	55.6
Hogan Systems	10.62	144.2	NE	3.89	51.8
Syscon Corp	19.88	92.7	18.5	0.71	47.2
Boole & Babbage	5.75	18.2	15.2	0.53	43.8
MPSI Systems	6.00	49.8	19.2	2.16	37.1
On Line Software	14.25	56.0	19.3	1.47	35.7
American Software	16.38	112.6	17.9	2.88	33.7
NCA Corp	4.50	12.5	NE	0.65	28.6
MacNeal Schwendler	25.88	157.6	24.6	6.30	23.2
Management Science Amer	12.75	219.2	13.8	1.26	15.9
Pansophic Systems	25.88	220.8	14.9	2.42	5.6
Micropro International	2.56	32.2	NE	0.84	0.0
Policy Management	23.00	373.4	28.9	2.80	0.0
Sterling Software	11.25	102.0	12.4	0.43	-7.2
BaronData	9.25	32.3	23.0	1.11	-14.0
Software Publishing	7.00	50.4	71.9	2.18	-15.2
Mentor Graphics	15.25	243.3	27.6	1.52	-20.8
Integrated Software	11.50	63.7	19.9	1.59	-29.2
Stockholders Systems	6.50	22.4	11.2	1.86	-29.7
Softech Inc	7.00	25.3	11.0	0.55	-31.7
Intermetrics	3.88	13.2	NE	0.30	-46.6
BPI Systems Inc.	1.62	9.2	NMF	0.83	-48.0
FDP Corp.	3.75	15.6	22.3	1.11	-50.0
Cullinet	6.88	208.1	NE	1.26	-63.8
Intellicorp	5.00	34.6	16.5	1.82	-68.3
Totals- Software	19.40	5116	24.7	2.20	

*1986 new issue.

(Continued next page)

STOCK TRENDS - 1986 (Continued)

Company	12/31/86 Close	Market Value ($M)	Price/ Earnings	Price/ Revenues	12 Month Change %
Services					
DST Systems	26.00	252.2	28.0	3.11	131.1
Endata Inc.	6.75	26.4	NE	1.01	63.6
American Management	19.25	92.4	18.8	0.71	55.6
Auxton Computer Ent.	11.25	56.9	21.1	1.89	50.0
UCCEL Corp	24.62	406.4	58.9	2.57	41.7
Computer Sciences	42.25	643.8	23.3	0.69	26.1
Hadron Inc	0.94	12.8	16.0	1.82	25.0
Quality Systems	2.12	9.3	15.6	0.93	21.4
AGS Computer	28.00	142.0	17.7	0.41	21.1
Analysts International	9.00	24.5	NE	0.53	20.0
Automatic Data Process.	35.25	2579	23.4	2.05	19.5
Comshare Inc.	12.50	33.3	20.8	0.48	19.0
National Data Corp	21.25	238.0	32.2	1.67	16.4
Shared Medical Systems	40.50	1025	35.2	2.86	15.3
First Financial Mgmt	23.75	124.9	28.4	2.11	14.5
Systems Assoc	12.25	31.3	39.1	0.94	14.0
Dyatron	5.12	24.0	NMF	0.66	13.9
Gtech Corp	21.00	196.5	NMF	2.02	13.5
Anacomp	3.75	112.6	NE	1.02	11.1
Advanced Computer Tech	4.00	6.9	9.8	0.45	6.7
Computer Horizons	10.50	26.4	13.2	0.49	-3.4
Data Architects	8.25	17.8	12.7	0.71	-12.0
CCX Network	14.75	56.8	31.6	NC	-15.7
Epsilon Data	8.88	24.6	NE	0.46	-19.3
Scientific Computers	4.44	4.8	47.7	0.34	-19.3
Datatab Inc.	0.50	0.4	NE	0.11	-20.0
SEI Corp	18.50	108.8	NE	0.96	-21.3
Computer Data Systems	6.88	20.3	9.7	0.39	-21.4
Tera Corp (LP)	3.00	21.9	NMF	NMF	-22.6
Avante Garde	4.00	14.7	NE	0.98	-23.8
Selecterm Inc	5.25	13.7	9.8	0.54	-25.0

(Continued next page)

STOCK TRENDS - 1986 (Continued)

Company	12/31/86 Close	Market Value ($M)	Price/ Earnings	Price/ Revenues	12 Month Change %
Cycare Systems	7.38	38.6	11.0	0.68	-29.8
Technalysis Corp	8.00	12.8	12.8	1.07	-30.4
Software AG Systems Gp	11.75	68.2	10.2	1.15	-31.4
Computer Language Rsh	5.25	71.5	NMF	0.77	-33.3
Continuum	9.00	38.9	NE	0.74	-33.3
Logicon	24.12	113.4	11.8	0.55	-41.2
Lodgistix	2.69	15.2	NMF	0.63	-41.9
Decision Systems	1.25	2.9	NE	0.12	-44.4
Keane Inc.	5.25	7.1	23.8	0.18	-47.5
Scientific Software	3.75	13.2	NE	0.50	-51.6
Totals- Services	20.36	6730	32.7	1.37	

Distribution

Company	12/31/86 Close	Market Value ($M)	Price/ Earnings	Price/ Revenues	12 Month Change %
Computer Factory	17.50	71.6	34.1	0.79	119.6
Businessland	11.25	267.2	74.2	0.59	50.0
Neeco*	6.75	16.4	16.4	0.45	12.5
Valmont	15.00	39.0	NE	0.12	-6.3
Inacomp	3.75	19.3	19.3	0.12	-26.8
MBI Business Ctr	5.25	25.3	11.5	0.22	-32.3
Entre	2.56	24.1	NE	0.36	-62.0
Computone Systems	0.22	0.8	NE	0.01	-94.9
Totals - Distribution	8.31	463.6	NE	0.35	

*1986 new issue.

(Continued next page)

STOCK TRENDS - 1986 (Continued)

Company	12/31/86 Close	Market Value ($M)	Price/ Earnings	Price/ Revenues	12 Month Change %
Telecommunications					
Cincinnati Bell	41.00	671.5	11.9	1.39	48.4
Alltel Corp	39.38	821.6	10.6	1.18	33.5
Southwestern Bell	112.25	11182	11.5	1.41	31.3
NYNEX	64.12	12982	10.8	1.18	31.2
Graphic Scanning	9.50	378.2	NE	3.12	28.8
GTE	58.38	12523	NE	0.81	26.9
Bell Atlantic	67.50	13455	11.6	1.39	26.8
Pac Telesis	53.25	11458	10.9	1.27	25.8
Ameritech	132.50	12899	11.6	1.39	24.4
US West	54.00	10256	10.8	1.24	21.3
So. New England Tel	53.88	1636	12.3	1.21	19.7
Century Telephone Ent.	16.12	178.4	10.6	1.14	19.4
Bell South	57.75	18261	11.7	1.66	17.9
Centel Corp	55.38	1533	11.4	1.15	17.2
Rochester Telephone	44.75	456.8	12.0	1.14	15.5
Continental Telecom	28.38	2172	9.4	0.70	10.7
United Telecom	25.50	2463	NMF	0.78	7.4
AT&T	25.00	26738	14.5	0.77	0.0
Northern Telecom	31.62	3703	12.1	0.75	-9.6
M/A-COM	12.62	552.3	NE	0.63	-15.8
Comm Satellite	28.12	513.3	NE	1.10	-20.8
Mitel	4.38	345.4	NE	0.75	-30.0
DSC Communications	5.75	243.4	13.9	0.81	-35.2
MCI Communications	6.25	1766	16.7	0.52	-44.4
Western Union	4.00	97.6	NE	0.10	-67.7
Totals - Telecomm	41.59	147285	14.4	1.06	

(Continued next page)

STOCK TRENDS - 1986 (Continued)

Company	12/31/86 Close	Market Value ($M)	Price/ Earnings	Price/ Revenues	12 Month Change %
Summary					
Systems Companies	55.21	130091	16.1	1.21	-8.0
Peripherals--Commun	10.11	1605	NMF	1.64	1.1
Peripherals--I/O	11.33	3320	24.9	0.99	-16.0
Peripherals--Memory	7.27	2480	NE	0.77	-14.5
Software Companies	19.40	5116	24.7	2.20	46.4
Services Companies	20.36	6730	32.7	1.37	-9.5
Distribution Cos.	8.31	463.6	NE	0.35	-7.6
Telecommunication Cos.	41.59	147285	14.4	1.06	-16.8
INDUSTRY INDEX	40.47	297091	15.8	1.13	

ELECTRONIC BUSINESS
VENTURE CAPITALISTS
June 15, 1986

This list includes Venture Capitalists having total investments of $10 million and over.--
COMPUTER INDUSTRY ALMANAC.
Reprinted with permission from ELECTRONIC BUSINESS, June 15, 1986. Copyright 1986 by
Reed Publishing USA, a division of Reed Holdings, Inc., Newton, MA.

Name	Total investments ($ millions)	Investment in electronics companies ($ millions)	Total number of deals in electronics companies	Average per electronics deal ($ millions)
Adler	$26.	$22.	18	$1.2
Alan Patricof Associates	27.	22.	28	0.8
Arscott, Norton & Associates	10.	10.	6	1.7
Asset Management	11.	8.	10	0.8
Bessemer Venture Partners	100.	75.	18	4.2
Brentwood Associates	55.7	48.	35	1.4
Burr, Egan, Deleage	25.	18.	7	2.6
Business Resource Investors	N/A	N/A	N/A	N/A
Charles River Partnerships	10.	7.	6	1.2
Continental Illinois Ventures	N/A	N/A	11	N/A
Crosspoint Venture Partners	14.	14.	20	0.7
Dougery, Jones & Wilder	43.	19.	7	2.7
Fairfield Venture Partners	12.	7.	11	0.6
General Electric Venture Capital	31.2	24.0	18	1.3
General Instrument	30.	30.	3	10.0
Greylock Management	20.	18.	13	1.4
Hembrecht & Quist	97.	76.7	84	0.9
Hutton Venture Investment Partners	10.	8.	7	1.1
Institutional Venture Partners	19.3	19.2	24	0.8
Investech L.P.	N/A	N/A	N/A	N/A
Lawrence Venture Associates	N/A	N/A	N/A	N/A
Melchor Venture Management	30.	30.	2	15.0
Menlo Ventures	16.0	15.0	17	0.9
Merrill, Pickard, Anderson & Eyre	12.	12.	16	0.8
Montgomery Securities	25.7	7.5	23	0.3

(Continued next page)

ELECTRONIC BUSINESS
VENTURE CAPITALISTS (Continued)

Name	Total investments ($ millions)	Investment in electronics companies ($ millions)	Total number of deals in electronics companies	Average per electronics deal ($ millions)
Morgan Stanley Ventures	$10.	$6.5	2	$3.3
Nautilus Fund	N/A	N/A	N/A	N/A
Norwest Venture Capital	27.2	15.9	30	0.5
Orange Nassau	15.	8.	3	2.7
Pittsford Group	12.	1.	N/A	N/A
Regional Financial Enterprises	24.5	7.0	10	0.7
Robertson Colman & Stephens Venture Fund	20.	14.	35	0.4
Schroder Venture Managers	13.	6.	11	0.5
Scientific Advances	N/A	N/A	3	N/A
Sevin Rosen Management	15.	15.	25	0.6
Sprout Group	17.	3.7	6	0.6
Summit Ventures	20.	20.	9	2.2
T.A. Associates	104.2	41.1	28	1.5
U.S.Venture Partners	20.	11.	7	1.6
Vista Ventures	10.5	7.5	14	0.5
Warburg, Pincus Ventures	95.	8.5	7	1.2
Welsh, Carson, Anderson & Stowe	N/A	18.	N/A	N/A

ELECTRONIC BUSINESS
VENTURE CAPITALISTS: TOP 10 IN ELECTRONICS
June 15, 1986

From the ELECTRONIC BUSINESS Venture Capitalists (companies having total investments of
$10 million and over), this list ranks the top ten companies by venture capital investments in
electronics.--COMPUTER INDUSTRY ALMANAC.
Reprinted with permission from ELECTRONIC BUSINESS, June 15, 1986. Copyright 1986 by
Reed Publishing USA, a division of Reed Holdings, Inc., Newton, MA.

		Total investments ($ millions)
1	Hambrecht & Quist	$76.7
2	Bessemer Venture Partners	75
3	Brentwood Associates	48
4	T.A. Associates	41.1
5	General Instrument	30
6	Melchor Venture Management	30
7	GE Venture Capital	24.0
8	Adler	22
9	Alan Patricof Associates	22
10	Summit Ventures	20

VENTURE MAGAZINE
THE VENTURE CAPITAL 100: 1985 INVESTMENTS
August 1986

"VENTURE prepared the Venture Capital 100 from information provided by more than 200 venture capital firms. The firms on the Venture Capital 100 invested $2.29 billion in 1985, essentially the same as 1984's $2.28 billion."--VENTURE.

Reprinted with permission from VENTURE Magazine, August 1986. Copyright 1986 by Venture Magazine Inc.

	Total 1985 Investments			Paid-in Capital
Rank	$ Mil.	Deals	Firm/Location	$ Mil.
1	119.23	59	First Chicago Venture Capital/First Capital Corp. of Chicago (SBIC)* Chicago, IL	264.00
2	109.51	53	TA Associates Boston, MA	403.54
3	101.31	67	Citicorp Capital Investors Ltd./Citicorp Venture Capital Ltd. (SBIC) New York, NY	210.00
4	96.58	128	Hambrecht & Quist Venture Partners San Francisco, CA	N.A.
5	92.06	20	Warburg, Pincus Ventures New York, NY	440.00
6	67.24	44	Security Pacific Capital Corp./First SBIC of California* Costa Mesa CA	N.A.
7	55.66	41	Brentwood Associates/Brentwood Capital Corp. (SBIC) Los Angeles, CA	210.71
8	51.26	51	Hillman Ventures Inc. Pittsburgh, PA	N.A.
9	45.50	13	Narragansett Capital Corp. Providence, RI	N.A.
10	44.50	34	Harvard Management Co. Inc./Aeneas Venture Corp.[1] Boston, MA	396.00
11	44.05	45	Welsh, Carson, Anderson & Stowe New York, NY	330.00
12	43.91	72	Investors in Industry[2] Boston, MA	60.00
13	39.16	279	Clinton Capital Corp. (SBIC) New York, NY	11.15

(Continued next page)

* Bank-affiliated.   N.A. Not Available/Not Applicable.

1. Subsidiary of Harvard University.

2. Figures represent fiscal year ended March 31, 1986.

VENTURE MAGAZINE: THE VENTURE CAPITAL 100 (Continued)

	Total 1985 Investments			Paid-in Capital
Rank	$ Mil.	Deals	Firm/Location	$ Mil.
14	36.98	10	Palms & Co. Inc. Seattle, WA	N.A.
15	35.87	73	New Enterprise Associates Baltimore, MD	124.77
16	33.48	40	Rothschild Ventures Inc. New York	N.A.
17	33.41	49	Oak Investment Partners Westport, CT	160.54
18	31.18	34	General Electric Venture Capital Corp. Fairfield, CT	200.00
19	30.70	10	Summit Ventures L.P. Boston, MA	159.70
20	28.85	43	Kleiner Perkins Caufield & Byers San Francisco, CA	238.00
21	28.68	49	Norwest Venture Capital Management Inc.* Minneapolis, MN	98.76
22	28.22	12	BT Capital Corp. (SBIC) New York, NY	35.01
23	27.43	39	J.H. Whitney & Co. New York, NY	N.A.
24	24.71	22	Adler & Co. New York, NY	236.00
25	24.53	24	Regional Financial Enterprises/Regional Financial Ent. L.P.(SBIC) New Canaan, CT	142.00
26	24.06	66	Alan Patricot Associates Inc. New York, NY	114.15
27	23.80	26	T. Rowe Price Threshold Fund, L/P. Baltimore, MD	74.00
28	23.70	11	Lubrizol Enterprises Inc.3 Wickliffe, OH	75.91
29	23.20	62	RIHT Capital Corp. (SBIC)* Providence, RI	5.50

(Continued next page)

* Bank-affiliated.   N.A. Not Available/Not Applicable.

3. Includes SBIC.

VENTURE MAGAZINE: THE VENTURE CAPITAL 100 (Continued)

Rank	Total 1985 Investments $ Mil.	Deals	Firm/Location	Paid-in Capital $ Mil.
30	23.13	39	Allstate Insurance Co. Northbrook, IL	N.A.
31	21.08	35	Montgomery Securities San Francisco, CA	88.63
32	20.52	31	U.S.Venture Partners Menlo Park, CA	109.80
33	20.20	49	Robertson, Colman & Stephens San Francisco, CA	117.00
34	19.83	20	Institutional Venture Partners Menlo Park, CA	77.60
35	19.31	21	Michigan Venture Capital Fund Lansing, MI	55.00
36	19.20	2	Founders Equity Inc. New York, NY	N.A.
37	19.00	12	Bridge Capital Advisors Inc. New York, NY	50.00
38	18.87	22	Golder, Thoma & Cressey Chicago, IL	113.66
39	18.67	8	Prudential Venture Capital New York, NY	N.A.
40	18.15	21	Sprout Group New York, NY	N.A.
41	17.75	363	Edwards Capital Co. (SBIC) New York, NY	4.20
42	17.60	38	John Hancock Venture Capital Management Inc. Boston, MA	283.00
43	17.32	89	Allied Capital Corp.[4] Washington, DC	14.21
44	17.18	23	Greylock Management Corp. Boston, MA	73.67
45	17.07	35	Cable, Howse & Cozadd, Inc. Seattle, WA	125.72

(Continued next page)

N.A. Not Available/Not Applicable.

4. Includes SBIC and MESBIC.

VENTURE MAGAZINE: THE VENTURE CAPITAL 100 (Continued)

Rank	Total 1985 Investments $ Mil.	Deals	Firm/Location	Paid-in Capital $ Mil.
46	17.05	21	Crosspoint Venture Partners	65.00
			Mountain View, CA	
47	16.52	132	Pierre Funding Corp. (MESBIC)	1.77
			New York, NY	
48	16.23	35	Burr, Egan, Deleage & Co.	N.A.
			Boston, MA	
49	15.60	186	Transportation Capital Corp (MESBIC)	7.86
			New York, NY	
50	15.57	16	Manufacturers Hanover Venture Capital Corp.*	N.A.
			New York, NY	
51	15.11	7	Mesirow Venture Capital[3]	43.77
			Chicago, IL	
52	15.00	15	Hutton Venture Investment Partners Inc.	N.A.
			New York, NY	
53	14.83	24	BancBoston Capital Inc./BancBoston Ventures Inc. (SBIC)*	N.A.
			Boston, MA	
54	14.78	52	ABS Ventures Limited Partnerships	80.41
			Baltimore, MD	
55	14.74	164	Medallion Funding Corp. (MESBIC)	5.27
			New York, NY	
56	14.42	5	Wheat First Securities[2]	N.A.
			Richmond, VA	
57	14.37	33	Mayfield Fund	136.25
			Menlo Park, CA	
58	13.99	3	Bradford Associates	70.45
			Princeton, NJ	
59	13.71	24	Sequoia Capital	104.00
			Menlo Park, CA	
60	13.65	19	Rainier Venture Partners	19.24
			Mercer Island, WA	
61	13.51	17	Concord Partners	114.55
			New York, NY	
			(Continued next page)	

* Bank-affiliated.   N.A. Not Available/Not Applicable.

2. Figures represent fiscal year ended March 31, 1986.

3. Includes SBIC.

VENTURE MAGAZINE: THE VENTURE CAPITAL 100 (Continued)

Rank	Total 1985 Investments $ Mil.	Deals	Firm/Location	Paid-in Capital $ Mil.
62	13.49	23	Menlo Ventures Menlo Park, CA	90.70
63	13.00	21	Merrill, Pickard, Anderson & Eyre Palo Alto, CA	85.00
64	12.90	16	R.H. Chappell Co.5 San Francisco, CA	N.A.
65	12.64	18	Fairfield Venture Partners Stamford, CT	65.25
66	12.50	12	Eberstadt Fleming Inc.6 New York, NY	55.00
67	12.47	16	Sevin Rosen Management Co. Dallas, TX	85.00
68	12.37	28	Charles River Ventures Boston, MA	108.10
69	12.10	25	MVenture Corp. (SBIC) Dallas, TX	16.25
70	12.00	25	The Southwest Venture Partnerships San Antonio, TX	58.41
71	11.80	16	Chemical Equity Inc./Chemical Venture Capital Corp. (SBIC)* New York, NY	100.00
72	11.74	31	InterWest Partners Menlo Park, CA	103.07
73	11.45	6	Interscope Investments Inc. Los Angeles, CA	N.A.
74	11.05	28	Enterprise Capital Corp. (SBIC)* Houston, TX	5.00
75	11.00	2	Philadelphia Industries Inc. Philadelphia, PA	29.95
76	10.70	26	Vista Ventures New Canaan, CT	104.68
77	10.52	23	DSV Partners Princeton, NJ	57.00

(Continued next page)

* Bank-affiliated. N.A. Not Available/Not Applicable.

5. Figures cover May, 1985 through Dec., 1985.

6. F. Eberstadt & Co. Inc. merged with Robert Fleming Inc.

VENTURE MAGAZINE: THE VENTURE CAPITAL 100 (Continued)

	Total 1985 Investments			Paid-in Capital
Rank	$ Mil.	Deals	Firm/Location	$ Mil.
78	10.35	19	Oxford Partners	67.17
			Stamford, CT	
79	10.25	13	Analog Devices Enterprises[7]	36.85
			Norwood, MA	
80	10.20	15	Edelson Technology Partners	36.00
			Saddle Brook, NJ	
81	10.00	10	The Pittsford Group Inc.	74.50
			Pittsford, NY	
82	9.90	7	Revere AE Capital Fund Inc.	47.70
			New York, NY	
83	9.52	10	MarketCorp Ventures	32.83
			Westport, SCT	
84	9.29	21	Larimer & Co.[8]	80.89
			Denver, CO	
85	9.25	12	Sierra Ventures/Wood River Capital (SBIC)	80.00
			Menlo Park, CA	
86	9.18	15	ML Venture Partners IL.P.	60.60
			New York, NY	
87	9.17	13	Euclid Partners Corp.	22.80
			New York, NY	
88	9.16	15	InterFirst Venture Corp. (SBIC)*	24.99
			Dallas, TX	
89	8.80	16	Matrix Partners	114.00
			Boston, MA	
90	8.80	4	McGowan Leckinger Berg	N.A.
			Braintree, MA	
91	8.69	25	Venrock Associates[7]	90.00
			New York, NY	
92	8.57	23	InnoVen Group	70.00
			Saddle Brook, NJ	
93	8.50	4	Caterpillar Venture Capital Inc	N.A.
			Peoria, IL	
			(Continued next page)	

* Bank-affiliated.   N.A. Not Available/Not Applicable.

7. Figures represent fiscal year ended Oct. 31, 1985.

8. Formerly The Centennial Funds.

VENTURE MAGAZINE: THE VENTURE CAPITAL 100 (Continued)

Rank	Total 1985 Investments $ Mil.	Deals	Firm/Location	Paid-in Capital $ Mil.
94	8.11	30	Inco Venture Capital Management[2] New York, NY	66.34
95	8.10	30	Venture Founders Corp. Lexington, MA	55.70
96	8.10	14	Dougery, Jones & Wilder Mountain View, CA	100.00
97	8.09	11	Bessemer Venture Partners New York, NY	65.00
98	8.05	20	Asset Management Co. Palo Alto, CA	N.A.
99	8.00	19	Harvest Ventures Inc. New York, NY	63.75
100	8.00	7	Julian, Cole & Stein Los Angeles	15.31

2. Figures represent fiscal year ended March 31, 1986.

10 FORECASTS

COMPUTER INDUSTRY ALMANAC
WORLDWIDE MAINFRAME COMPUTER MARKET FORECAST
January 1987

This mainframe computer forecast includes supercomputers and traditional mainframe computers such as IBM's 3090 series, IBM 303X, IBM 308X and similar computers. It is a worldwide forecast including U.S. and foreign vendors. The forecast uses a variety of sources such as government forecasts and Wall Street forecasts. Both worldwide units and revenue forecasts are listed below. Only hardware (processors and peripherals) is included.

	Mainframe Unit Sales (thousands)	Mainframe Value ($B)
1985	4.8	$22.6
1986	5.4	25.4
1987	5.9	27.4
1988	5.9	29.0
1989	6.3	31.8
1990	7.0	34.6

The compound annual growth rate between 1985 and 1990 is 7.8% in units and 8.9% in dollars.

COMPUTER INDUSTRY ALMANAC
WORLDWIDE MINICOMPUTER MARKET FORECAST
January 1987

This minicomputer forecast includes traditional minicomputers, superminicomputers and minisupercomputers. Example products are DEC's PDP-11 and VAX family, IBM's 4300 series and System 36, and minicomputers from Data General, HP, Tandem and other vendors. Both U.S. and foreign vendors' sales are included. The forecast uses information such as government data and Wall Street's market forecasts. Worldwide units sales and revenues are listed below. Only hardware (processors and peripherals) is included.

	Minicomputer Unit Sales (thousands)	Minicomputer Value ($B)
1985	580	$37.4
1986	646	41.7
1987	734	47.7
1988	850	54.3
1989	979	61.6
1990	1118	68.7

The compound annual growth rate between 1985 and 1990 is 14.0% in units and 12.9% in dollars.

COMPUTER INDUSTRY ALMANAC
WORLDWIDE MICROCOMPUTER MARKET FORECAST
January 1987

This microcomputer forecast includes personal computers, workstations, multiuser microcomputers and supermicrocomputers. Example products included are Apple, Commodore, and Tandy computers, IBM's PC family, and Sun and Apollo workstations. Both U.S. and foreign vendors' sales are included in the forecast. The forecast uses information sources from government data and Wall Street projections. Worldwide unit sales and revenues are listed below. Only hardware (processors and peripherals) is included.

	Microcomputer Unit Sales (millions)	Microcomputer Value ($B)
1985	13.5	$32.5
1986	15.4	40.5
1987	17.9	50.9
1988	20.8	62.0
1989	24.0	73.6
1990	27.4	86.0

Compound annual growth rate between 1985 and 1990 is 15.2% in units and 21.5% in dollars.

FUTURE COMPUTING INCORPORATED
FORECAST FOR PERSONAL COMPUTER MARKETPLACE
January 1987

This forecast for the U.S. personal computer marketplace shows hardware and software estimates for both units sold (shown in thousands of units) and revenue earned (shown in millions of dollars). It includes personal computers from such companies as IBM, Compaq, Apple, and Tandy.-- COMPUTER INDUSTRY ALMANAC.

Reprinted with permission from Future Computing Incorporated, January 1987. Copyright 1987 by Future Computing Incorporated, Dallas, TX.

Personal Computers

	1986	1987	1988	1989	1990
Hardware*					
Revenue U.S. ($M)	22,455	27,978	34,139	40,536	47,338
Units U.S. (#K)	8,284	9,956	11,694	13,475	15,328
Software					
Revenue U.S. ($M)	6,480	7,891	9,331	10,667	12,054
Units U.S. (#K)	56,608	69,912	83,551	97,737	112,288

*Does not include peripherals

COMPUTER INDUSTRY ALMANAC
TOTAL WORLDWIDE COMPUTER HARDWARE FORECAST
January 1987

This total worldwide computer hardware forecast is the sum of COMPUTER INDUSTRY
ALMANAC's five-year projected forecasts for mainframes, minicomputers and microcomputers.

	Computer Unit Sales (millions)	Computer Value ($B)
1985	14.1	$92.5
1986	16.1	107.6
1987	18.6	126.0
1988	21.6	145.4
1989	25.0	167.1
1990	28.6	189.2

The compound annual growth rate between 1985 and 1990 is 15% in units and 15% in revenue.

IN-STAT, INC.
INTEGRATED CIRCUITS WORLDWIDE CONSUMPTION FORECAST
October 1986

This forecast shows worldwide integrated circuits consumption in terms of dollars, units, and average selling price. Each category is broken out to show separately the United States, Japan, Europe, and the rest of the world (R.O.W.).--COMPUTER INDUSTRY ALMANAC.
Reprinted with permission from In-Stat, Inc., October 1986. Copyright 1986 by In-Stat, Inc., Scottsdale, AZ.

TOTAL I.C. - WORLDWIDE CONSUMPTION
DOLLARS (MILLIONS)

	1986	1987	1988	1989	1990
U.S.A.	$6,849	$7,245	$7,078	$8,423	$9,602
Japan	7,320	7,796	7,757	9,308	10,611
Europe	3,885	4,122	4,122	4,699	5,239
R.O.W.	1,230	1,451	1,691	2,080	2,475
Total World	$19,284	$20,614	$20,648	$24,510	$27,928
% Growth	17%	6.9%	0.2%	18.7%	13.9%

TOTAL I.C. - WORLDWIDE CONSUMPTION
UNITS (MILLIONS)

	1986	1987	1988	1989	1990
U.S.A.	5,201	5,534	5,473	6,624	7,179
Japan	9,224	10,028	9,906	11,758	12,294
Europe	2,834	2,954	2,929	3,288	3,552
R.O.W.	2,088	2,509	2,950	3,673	4,722
Total World	19,347	21,025	21,257	25,343	27,746
% Growth	12.6%	8.7%	1.1%	19.2%	9.5%

TOTAL I.C. - WORLDWIDE CONSUMPTION
AVERAGE SELLING PRICE (DOLLARS)

	1986	1987	1988	1989	1990
U.S.A.	$1.317	$1.309	$1.293	$1.272	$1.338
Japan	0.794	0.777	0.783	0.792	0.863
Europe	1.371	1.396	1.407	1.429	1.475
R.O.W.	0.589	0.579	0.573	0.566	0.524
Total World	$0.997	$0.980	$0.971	$0.967	$1.007

INTEGRATED CIRCUIT ENGINEERING CORPORATION
WORLDWIDE MERCHANT SEMICONDUCTOR PRODUCTION FORECAST
November 1986

This forecast shows estimates for worldwide merchant semiconductor production in millions of dollars for three categories: integrated circuit merchant, discrete semiconductor merchant, and total merchant semiconductor.--COMPUTER INDUSTRY ALMANAC.

Reprinted with permission from Integrated Circuit Engineering Corporation, November 1986. Copyright 1986 by Integrated Circuit Engineering Corporation, Scottsdale, AZ.

Year	IC Merchant ($M)	% Growth Over Prior Year	Discrete Merchant ($M)	% Growth Over Prior Year	Total Merchant Semi($M)	% Growth Over Prior Year
1987	24,325	12	7,075	5	31,400	+10
1988	30,200	24	7,800	10	38,000	+21
1989	32,200	7	8,100	4	40,300	+6
1990	37,200	16	8,600	6	45,800	+14
1991	42,400	14	9,300	8	51,700	+13

NORTHERN BUSINESS INFORMATION
FORECAST FOR WORLD TELECOMMUNICATIONS MARKET
November 1986

This forecast for the worldwide telecommunications market is shown in millions of dollars and is divided into five marketplaces: public switching, transmission, customer premise equipment, total equipment, and services.--COMPUTER INDUSTRY ALMANAC.

Reprinted with permission from Northern Business Information, Inc., November 1986. Copyright 1986 by Northern Business Information, Inc., New York, NY.

	1985	1986	1987
Public Switching	14158	13643	14436
Transmission	21796	21197	23600
Customer Premise Equipment	13101	13868	14658
Total Equipment	51632	50892	55404
Services	227931	239328	253687
Total Telecom	279563	290219	309091

	1988	1989	1990	CAGR85-90
Public switching	14909	16236	17560	3%
Transmission	24668	26545	28246	5%
Customer Premise Equipment	15943	17058	18343	7%
Total Equipment	58064	61999	65674	5%
Services	279509	293161	316614	7%
Total Telecom	329509	355160	382288	6%

(Market figures are in millions of dollars.)

11 HISTORY OF THE COMPUTER INDUSTRY

COMPUTER INDUSTRY ALMANAC has derived the following historical milestones from a wide variety of sources to show the evolution of the computer industry.

3000 BC- Dust abacus is invented, probably in Babylonia.

1800 BC- Babylonian mathematician develops algorithms to resolve numerical problems.

500 BC- Bead and wire abacus originates in Egypt.

200 AD- Saun-pan computing tray is used in China; soroban computing tray is used in Japan.

1617 - Scottish inventor John Napier uses "bones" to demonstrate division by subtraction and multiplication by addition.

1622 - William Oughtred develops the slide rule in England.

1624 - Wilhelm Schickard builds first four-function "calculator-clock" at the University of Heidelberg.

1642 - Blaise Pascal builds the first numerical calculating machine in Paris.

1673 - Gottfried Leibniz builds a mechanical calculating machine that can multiply and divide as well as add and subtract.

1780 - American Benjamin Franklin discovers electricity.

1805 - Joseph-Marie Jacquard invents perforated card for use on his loom.

1833 - In England Charles Babbage designs an analytical machine that follows instructions from perforated tape.

1842 - Lady Ada Byron, Countess of Lovelace and daughter of Lord Byron, the poet, writes programs for Babbage.

1847 - Irishman George Boole publishes "The Mathematical Analysis of Logic" using the binary system now known as Boolean algebra.

1855 - George and Edvard Scheutz of Stockholm build the first practical mechanical computer based on Babbage's work.

1876 - Telephone is invented by Alexander Graham Bell.

1884 - Herman Hollerith applies for patents for automatic punch-card tabulating machine.

1884 - Institute of Electrical Engineers (IEE) is founded.

1886 - William Burroughs develops the first commercially successful mechanical adding machine.

1889 - Patent is issued for Hollerith tabulating machine.

1890 - Dr. Herman Hollerith constructs an electromechanical machine using perforated cards for use in the U.S. census.

1896 - Hollerith founds the Tabulating Machine Co.

1903 - Nikola Tesla, a Yugoslavian who worked for Thomas Edison, patents electrical logic circuits called gates or switches.

1911 - Computer-Tabulating-Recording Company is formed through a merger of the Tabulating Company (founded by Hollerith), the Computing Scale Company, and the International Time Recording Company.

(Continued next page)

1912 - Institute of Radio Engineers (IRE) is formed.

1914 - Thomas J. Watson becomes president of Computing-Tabulating-Recording Company.

1921 - Czech word "robot" is used to describe mechanical workers in the play "R.U.R." by Karel Capek.

1924 - Computing-Tabulating-Recording Company changes its name to International Business Machines.

1925 - Vannevar Bush builds a large scale analog calculator, the differential analyzer, at MIT.

1927 - First public demonstration of television. Radio-telephone becomes operational between London and New York.

1927 - Powers Accounting Machine Company becomes the Tabulating Machines Division of Remington-Rand Corp.

1931 - First calculator, the Z1, is built in Germany by Konrad Zuse.

1933 - First electronic talking machine, the Voder, is built by Dudley, who follows in 1939 with the Vocoder (Voice coder).

1936 - Hungarian Alan M. Turing while at Princeton University formalizes the notion of calculableness and adapts the notion of algorithm to the computation of functions. "Turing's machine" is defined to be capable of computing any calculable function.

1937 - George Stibitz builds the first binary calculator at Bell Telephone Laboratories.

1938 - Hewlett-Packard Co. is founded to make electronic equipment.

1939 - First Radio Shack catalog is published.

1939 - John J. Atanasoff designs a prototype for the ABC (Atanasoff-Berry Computer) with the help of graduate student Clifford Berry at Iowa State College. It is said to be the first working model of the electronic digital computer.

1940 - At Bell Labs, George Stibitz demonstrates the Complex Number Calculator, which some say is the first digital computer.

1940 - First color TV broadcast.

1940 - Remote processing experiments, conducted by Bell Laboratories, create the first terminal.

1941 - Colossus computer is designed by Alan M. Turing and built by M.H.A. Neuman at the University of Manchester, England.

1941 - Konrad Zuse builds the Z3 computer in Germany, the first calculating machine with automatic control of its operations.

1944 - Colossus Mark II is built in England.

1944 - Mark I (IBM ASCC) is completed, based on the work of Professor Howard H. Aiken at Harvard and IBM.

1945 - John von Neumann paper describes stored-program concept for EDVAC.
(Continued next page)

1946 - Binac (Binary Automatic Computer), the first computer to operate in real time, is started by Eckert and Mauchly; it is completed in 1949.

1946 - ENIAC (Electronic Numerical Integrator and Computer), with 18,000 vacuum tubes, is dedicated at the University of Pennsylvania.

1946 - Eckert-Mauchly Computer Corporation is formed as the Electronic Control Co. to design a Universal Automatic Computer (Univac).

1946 - Term "bit" for binary digit is used for first time by John Tukey.

1947 - Alan M. Turing publishes an article on "Intelligent Machinery" which launches artificial intelligence.

1947 - Association for Computing Machinery (ACM) is formed.

1947 - Transistor is demonstrated by Bell Telephone Laboratories.

1948 - EDSAC (Electronic Delay Storage Automatic Calculator) is developed at the University of Cambridge by Maurice V. Wilkes.

1948 - IBM introduces the 604 electronic calculator.

1948 - John von Neumann builds the first stored-program ("true") computer, the IBM SSEC (Selective Sequence Electronic Calculator) under the direction of Frank Hamilton. The stored program was conceived by von Neumann, Mauchly, Eckert, and H.H. Goldstine.

1948 - Transistor is invented by William Bradford Shockley with John Bardeen and Walter H. Brattain.

1949 - EDVAC (Electronic Discrete Variable Automatic Computer) supports the first tests of magnetic disks.

1949 - Jay Forrester uses iron cores as main memory in Whirlwind. Forrester patent is issued in 1956.

1950 - Maurice V. Wilkes at Cambridge University uses assembler (symbolic assembly language) on EDSAC.

1950 - Remington-Rand acquires Eckert-Mauchly Computer Corp.

1950 - SEAC (Standards Eastern Automatic Computer) is delivered to the National Bureau of Standards.

1951 - First Joint Computer Conference is held.

1951 - Maurice V. Wilkes introduces the concept of microprogramming.

1951 - IEEE Computer Society is formed.

1951 - UNIVAC I is installed at the Bureau of Census using a magnetic tape unit as a buffer memory.

1951 - Wang Laboratories, Inc. is founded by An Wang in Boston.

(Continued next page)

1952 -   First computer manual is written by Fred Gruenberger.

1952 -   IBM introduces the 701, its first electronic stored-program computer.

1952 -   Nixdorf Computer is founded in Germany.

1952 -   Remington-Rand acquires Engineering Research Associates (ERA).

1952 -   RCA develops Bizmac with iron-core memory and a magnetic drum supporting the first data base.

1952 -   UNIVAC I predicts an Eisenhower landslide with 7% of the votes, just one hour after the polls close.

1952 -   U.S. Department of Justice sues IBM for monopolizing the punched-card accounting machine industry.

1953 -   Burroughs Corp. installs the Universal Digital Electronic Computer (UDEC) at Wayne State University.

1953 -   First high-speed printer is developed by Remington-Rand for use on the Univac.

1953 -   First magnetic tape device, the IBM 726, is introduced with 100 character-per-inch density and 75 inches-per-second speed.

1953 -   IBM ships its first stored-program computer, the 701. It is a vacuum tube, or "first generation," computer.

1954 -   FORTRAN is created by John Backus at IBM following his 1953 SPEEDCO program. Harlan Herrick runs the first successful FORTRAN program.

1954 -   Gene Amdahl develops the first operating system, used on IBM 704.

1955 -   First SHARE users group meeting is held.

1955 -   Remington-Rand merges with Sperry Gyroscope to form Sperry-Rand.

1955 -   Whirlwind computer becomes operational at MIT. It has been under development since 1944 and remains operational until 1959.

1956 -   APT (Automatic Programmed Tool) is developed by D.T. Ross.

1956 -   Burroughs acquires Electrodata and the Datatron computer, which becomes the Burroughs 205.

1956 -   Government antitrust suit against IBM is settled; consent decree requires IBM to sell as well as lease machines.

1956 -   IPL (Information Processing Language) is invented by A. Newell, D. Shaw, and F. Simon.

1956 -   RCA ships the Bizmac.

1956 -   T.J. Watson, Jr. assumes presidency of IBM.

1957 -   Control Data Corporation is formed by William C. Norris and a group of engineers from Sperry-Rand.

1957 -   Digital Equipment Corporation is founded.

1957 -   First issue of Datamation is released.

1957 -   Honeywell joins with Raytheon to ship the Datamatic 1000.
         (Continued next page)

1958 - ALGOL, first called IAL (International Algebraic Language), is presented in Zurich.

1958 - First virtual memory machine, Atlas, is installed in England by Feranti. It was developed at the University of Manchester by R.M. Kilburn.

1958 - First electronic computers are built in Japan by NEC: the NEAC-1101 and -1102.

1958 - Frank Rosenblatt builds the Perceptron Mark I using a CRT as an output device.

1958 - LISP is developed on IBM 704 at MIT under John McCarthy.

1958 - Seymour Cray builds the first fully transistorized supercomputer for Control Data Corp., the CDC 1604.

1959 - COBOL is defined by the Conference on Data System Languages (Codasyl), based on Grace Hopper's Flow-Matic.

1959 - First packaged program is sold by Computer Science Corporation.

1959 - IBM introduces the 1401. Over 10,000 units will be delivered during its lifetime.

1959 - IBM ships its first transistorized, or "second generation," computers, the 1620 and 1790.

1959 - Jack S. Kilby at Texas Instruments files a patent for the first integrated circuit.

1959 - Robert Noyce of Fairchild Semiconductor develops "the monolithic idea" for integrated circuits.

1960 - Benjamin Curley develops the first minicomputer, the PDP-1, at Digital Equipment Corporation.

1960 - COBOL runs on UNIVAC II and RCA 501.

1960 - Control Data Corporation delivers its first product, a large scientific computer named the CDC 1604.

1960 - DEC ships the first small computer, the PDP-1.

1960 - First electronic switching central office becomes operational in Chicago.

1960 - Removeable disks first appear.

1961 - AFIPS (American Federation of Information Processing Societies) forms.

1961 - Multiprogramming runs on Stretch computer. Time-sharing runs at MIT on IBM 709 and 7090 computers by F. Corbato.

1961 - IBM delivers the Stretch computer to Los Alamos. This transistorized computer with 64-bit data paths is the first to use eight-bit bytes; it remains operational until 1971.

1962 - APL (A Programming Language) is developed by Ken Iverson, Harvard University and IBM.

1962 - First general-purpose simulation languages are proposed: (1) SIMSCRIPT by the Rand Corporation, and (2) GPSS by IBM.

1962 - IBM markets 1311 using removeable disks.

1962 - IBM's U.S.-based annual revenues from computer products reaches $1 billion and for the first time surpasses its other revenue.

1962 - H. Ross Perot founds EDS (Electronic Data Systems, Inc.) in Dallas, TX.
(Continued next page)

1963 -   Control Data acquires Bendix Corp. computer division.

1963 -   Conversational graphics consoles are developed by General Motors (DAC-1) and MIT Lincoln Laboratories (Sketchpad), resulting in computer-aided design (CAD). Sketchpad uses the first light-pen, developed by I.E. Sutherland.

1963 -   DEC ships the first minicomputer, the PDP-5.

1963 -   Tandy acquires Radio Shack (9 stores).

1964 -   Control Data Corporation introduces the CDC 6000, which uses 60-bit words and parallel processing. CDC ships the 6600, the most powerful computer for several years.

1964 -   BASIC (Beginner's All-purpose Symbolic Instruction Language) is created by Tom Kurtz and John Kemeny of Dartmouth. First time-sharing BASIC program runs.

1964 -   Graphic tablet is developed by M.R. Davis and T.D. Ellis at Rand Corporation.

1964 -   Honeywell introduces the H-200 attacking IBM's installed base of 1400 systems.

1964 -   NCR introduces the 315/100.

1965 -   CDC founds the Control Data Institute to provide computer-related education.

1965 -   Digital Equipment ships the first PDP-8 minicomputer.

1965 -   First computer science PhD is granted to Richard L. Wexelblat at the University of Pennsylvania.

1965 -   IBM ships the first System 360, its first integrated circuit-based, or "third generation," computer.

1966 -   Honeywell acquires Computer Control Company, a minicomputer manufacturer.

1966 -   Scientific Data Systems (SDS) introduces Sigma 7.

1966 -   Texas Instruments offers the first solid-state hand-held calculator.

1967 -   A.H. Bobeck at Bell Laboratories develops bubble memory.

1967 -   Burroughs ships the B3200.

1967 -   First issue of ComputerWorld is released.

1968 -   Dendral, the first medical diagnostic medical program, is created by Joshua Lederberg at Stanford University.

1968 -   Integrated Electronics (Intel) Corp. is founded by Gordon Moore and Robert Noyce.

1969 -   Edson deCastro leaves DEC to start Data General Corp. and introduces the Nova, the first 16-bit minicomputer.

1969 -   First International Joint Conference on Artificial Intelligence is held.

1969 -   IBM "unbundles" hardware and software and introduces minicomputer line, System 3.

1969 -   Lockheed Electronics ships the MAC-16.

1969 -   PASCAL compiler is written by Niklaus Wirth and installed on the CDC 6400.

(Continued next page)

1970 -   Computer Logic Systems ships SLS-18.

1970 -   DEC ships its first 16-bit minicomputer, the PDP-11/20.

1970 -   Data General ships SuperNova.

1970 -   First ACM Computer Chess tournament is held.

1970 -   Honeywell acquires General Electric's computer operations.

1970 -   IBM ships its first System 370, a "fourth generation," computer.

1970 -   Xerox Data Systems introduces the CF-16A.

1971 -   Computer Automation introduces the Alpha-16.

1971 -   Floppy disks are introduced to feed the IBM 370.

1971 -   Intel Corporation announces the first microprocessor, the Intel 4004, developed by a team headed by Marcian E. Hoff.

1971 -   John Blankenbaker builds the first personal computer, the Kenbak I.

1971 -   NCR introduces Century 50.

1971 -   Sperry-Rand takes over the RCA computer product line.

1972 -   Cray Research is founded.

1972 -   First electronic pocket calculator is developed by J.S. Kilby, J.D. Merryman, and J.H. VanTassel of Texas Instruments.

1972 -   Gary Kildall at Naval Postgraduate School writes PL/1, the first programming language for the Intel 4004 microprocessor.

1972 -   Prime Computer is founded.

1973 -   First National Computer Conference (NCC) is held in New York City.

1973 -   IBM settles a lawsuit by Control Data, selling Service Bureau Corporation (SBC) to Control Data.

1973 -   PROLOG language is developed by Alain Comerauer at the University of Marseilles-Luminy, France.

1973 -   R2E markets the MICRAL, the first microcomputer in France.

1973 -   "Winchester" disk drives are first introduced by IBM, who uses the term as a code name for its Model 3340 direct-access storage device (DASD).

1974 -   Digital Equipment enters the Fortune 500.

1974 -   Zilog, Inc. is formed.

1975 -   Cray-1 supercomputer is introduced.

1975 -   Homebrew Computer Club, considered the first personal computer users group, is formed.

1975 -   MITS introduces the Altair personal computer, named after a Star Trek episode, "A Voyage to Altair."

1975 -   Microsoft is founded after Bill Gates and Paul Allen adapt and sell BASIC to MITS for the Altair PC.

          (Continued next page)

1976 -   First fault-tolerant computer, the T/16, is introduced by Tandem.

1976 -   MYCIN, an expert system to diagnose and treat infectious blood diseases, is developed at Stanford University by E. Shortliffe.

1976 -   NEC System 800 and 900 general-purpose mainframes are introduced.

1976 -   Seymour Cray engineers and delivers Cray 1 with 200,000 freon-cooled ICs and 100 million floating point operations per second (MFLOP) performance.

1976 -   Superminicomputers are introduced by Perkin-Elmer and Gould SEL.

1976 -   Zilog Z-80 chip is introduced.

1977 -   Apple Computer is founded and introduces the Apple II personal computer.

1977 -   Apple, Commodore, and Tandy begin selling personal computers.

1977 -   DEC introduces its first 32-bit superminicomputer, the VAX-11/780.

1977 -   Datapoint introduces ARC system, the first local area network.

1977 -   First ComputerLand franchise store opens in Morristown, NJ under the name Computershack.

1977 -   First NCC to exhibit personal computers.

1978 -   SPRINT business service is inaugerated.

1978 -   Texas Instruments introduces the Speak-and-Spell toy featuring digital speech.

1978 -   Total computers in use in the U.S. exceed a half million units.

1979 -   Ada language is developed by a team at CII-Honeywell Bull (France) directed by Jean Ichbiah.

1979 -   The Source and CompuServe Information Services go online.

1979 -   VisiCalc, the first electronic spreadsheet software, is shown at West Coast Computer Faire.

1979 -   Wordstar, one of the best-selling word processing programs for personal computers, is released by Micropro International.

1980 -   Control Data Corporation introduces the Cyber 205 supercomputer.

1980 -   First issue of InfoWorld is released.

1980 -   Microsoft licences UNIX operating system from Bell Laboratories and introduces Xenix adaptation.

1980 -   Total computers in use in the U.S. exceed one million units.

1981 -   Commodore introduces the VIC-20 home computer, which sells more than one million units.

1981 -   IBM enters the personal computer market, creating a "de facto" standard.

1981 -   Osborne Computer introduces the Osborne 1, the first portable computer.
         (Continued next page)

1982 - AT&T agrees to give up 22 Bell System companies in settling a 13-year-old lawsuit brought by the Justice Department.

1982 - Compaq Computer incorporates.

1982 - Microsoft licences MS-DOS to 50 microcomputer manufacturers in the first 16 months of availability.

1982 - Time Magazine names the computer its "Man of the Year."

1982 - U.S. drops IBM antitrust suit begun in 1969.

1983 - Compaq ships its first computer in January and sells $111M, the greatest first-year sales in the history of American business.

1983 - Cray 2 computer introduced with one billion FLOPs (floating point operations per second) performance rating.

1983 - Lotus 1-2-3 replaces VisiCalc as the spreadsheet software of choice for microcomputers.

1983 - NEC announces the SX-1 and SX-2 supercomputers.

1983 - Total computers in use in the U.S. exceed ten million units.

1984 - Apple introduces the Macintosh computer.

1984 - IBM introduces the PC AT (Advanced Technology). IBM merges with Rolm Corp., which becomes a telecommunications subsidiary.

1984 - The Tandy 1000 personal computer becomes the #1 selling IBM PC-compatible in its first year.

1985 - IBM delivers the new 3090 "Sierra" systems.

1986 - Burroughs merges with Sperry to form Unisys Corporation, second only to IBM in computer revenues.

1986 - Compaq makes the Fortune 500. Introduces its first Intel 80386-based PC.

1986 - Computerworld publishes its 1,000th issue on November 3.

1986 - Hewlett Packard introduces Spectrum line of reduced instruction set computers (RISC).

1986 - Tandy has over 7300 retail outlets including more than 4800 company-owned Radio Shack stores in the U.S.

1989 - Cray 3 computer expected with 10 billion FLOPs performance level.

1990 - IBM expects to reach $100 billion in revenue.

2000 - The electronics industry is expected to be a $900 billion-a-year business, second only to agriculture in the world economy.

12 NEWS ITEMS AND EVENTS

CONFERENCES

In this section COMPUTER INDUSTRY ALMANAC lists over 90 major, industry-related conferences arranged alphabetically by conference name. Each listing includes the date, location, and sponsoring group of the conference and a phone number to obtain additional information.

August 19, 1987 to August 21, 1987	**COMDEX/Australia**, Sydney, Australia Sponsor: Interface Group Inc., 617/449-6600
November 2, 1987 to November 6, 1987	**COMDEX/Fall 87**, Las Vegas, NV Sponsor: Interface Group Inc., 617/449-6600
May 19, 1987 to May 21, 1987	**COMDEX/International Europe**, Nice, France Sponsor: Interface Group Inc., 617/449-6600
March 3, 1987 to March 5, 1987	**COMDEX/Japan**, Tokyo, Japan Sponsor: Interface Group Inc., 617/449-6600
June 1, 1987 to June 4, 1987	**COMDEX/Spring 87**, Atlanta, GA Sponsor: Interface Group Inc., 617/449-6600
February 29, 1988 to March 3, 1988	**COMPCON Spring 88**, San Francisco, CA Sponsor: IEEE Computer Society (Inst of Electrical & Electronics Eng), 202/371-0101
May 11, 1987 to May 15, 1987	**COMPEURO 87**, Hamburg, Germany Sponsor: IEEE Computer Society (Inst of Electrical & Electronics Eng), 202/371-0101
April 11, 1988 to April 15, 1988	**COMPEURO 88**, Brussels, Belgium Sponsor: IEEE Computer Society (Inst of Electrical & Electronics Eng), 202/371-0101
February 17, 1987 to February 19, 1987	**CSC 87** (Computer Science Conference), St. Louis, MO Sponsor: ACM (Association for Computing Machinery), 212/869-7440
February 23, 1988 to February 25, 1988 (Continued next page)	**CSC 88** (Computer Science Conference), Atlanta, GA Sponsor: ACM (Association for Computing Machinery), 212/869-7440

CONFERENCES (Continued)

February 21, 1989 to February 24, 1989	**CSC 89** (Computer Science Conference), Louisville, KY Sponsor: ACM (Association for Computing Machinery), 212/869-7440
January 25, 1988 to January 28, 1988	**Communication Networks Conference & Exposition**, Washington, DC Sponsor: Conference Management Group (CW Communications), 617/879-0700
February 6, 1989 to February 9, 1989	**Communication Networks Conference & Exposition**, Washington, DC Sponsor: Conference Management Group (CW Communications), 617/879-0700
February 5, 1990 to February 8, 1990	**Communication Networks Conference & Exposition**, Washington, DC Sponsor: Conference Management Group (CW Communications), 617/879-0700
January 28, 1991 to January 31, 1991	**Communication Networks Conference & Exposition**, Washington, DC Sponsor: Conference Management Group (CW Communications), 617/879-0700
January 27, 1992 to January 30, 1992	**Communication Networks Conference & Exposition**, Washington, DC Sponsor: Conference Management Group (CW Communications), 617/879-070
February 1, 1993 to February 4, 1993	**Communication Networks Conference & Exposition**, Washington, DC Sponsor: Conference Management Group (CW Communications), 617/879-0700
January 24, 1994 to January 27, 1994	**Communication Networks Conference & Exposition**, Washington, DC Sponsor: Conference Management Group (CW Communications), 617/879-0700
January 23, 1995 to January 26, 1995	**Communication Networks Conference & Exposition**, Washington, DC Sponsor: Conference Management Group (CW Communications), 617/879-0700
October 14, 1987 to October 16, 1987 (Continued next page)	**EASTCON (Electronics & Aerospace Systems Conference)**, Wash. DC Sponsor: IEEE, 212/705-7900

CONFERENCES (Continued)

April 7, 1987 to April 9, 1987	**ELECTRO 87**, New York, NY Sponsor: IEEE, 212/705-7900
May 17, 1988 to May 19, 1988	**ELECTRO 88**, Boston, MA Sponsor: IEEE, 212/705-7900
April 18, 1989 to April 20, 1989	**ELECTRO 89**, New York, NY Sponsor: IEEE, 212/705-7900
March 13, 1988 to March 16, 1988	**ENTELEC**, Dallas, TX Sponsor: Energy Telecommunications & Electrical Assn., 214/578-1900
March 12, 1989 to March 15, 1989	**ENTELEC**, Houston, TX Sponsor: Energy Telecommunications & Electrical Assn., 214/578-1900
March 10, 1990 to March 14, 1990	**ENTELEC**, San Antonio, TX Sponsor: Energy Telecommunications & Electrical Assn., 214/578-1900
March 17, 1991 to March 22, 1991	**ENTELEC**, New Orleans, LA Sponsor: Energy Telecommunications & Electrical Assn., 214/578-1900
October 25, 1987 to October 29, 1987	**Fall Joint Computer Conference** (FJCC), Dallas, TX Sponsor: ACM (212/869-7440) & IEEECS, 202/371-0101
April 27, 1987 to April 29, 1987	**Federal DP & Communications Conference & Expo 87**, Wash. D.C. Sponsor: Interface Group Inc., 617/449-6600
March 4, 1987 to March 11, 1987	**Hannover Fair CeBIT**, Hannover, West Germany Sponsor: Hannover Fair, 609/987-1202
April 1, 1987 to April 8, 1987	**Hannover Fair INDUSTRY**, Hannover, West Germany Sponsor: Hannover Fair, 609/987-1202
May 17, 1987 to May 22, 1987	**ICA Annual Convention**, New Orleans, LA Sponsor: International Communications Association (ICA), 214/233-3889

(Continued next page)

CONFERENCES (Continued)

May 15, 1988 to May 20, 1988	**ICA Annual Convention**, Anaheim, CA Sponsor: International Communications Association (ICA), 214/233-3889
May 21, 1989 to May 26, 1989	**ICA Annual Convention**, Dallas, TX Sponsor: International Communications Association (ICA), 214/233-3889
May 20, 1990 to May 25, 1990	**ICA Annual Convention**, New Orleans, LA Sponsor: International Communications Association (ICA), 214/233-3889
August 28, 1989 to September 1, 1989	**IFIP 89** - 11th World Computer Congress, San Francisco, CA Sponsor: IFIP (Hosted by Amer. Fed. of Information Processing Soc.), 703/620-8900
September 1, 1987 to September 4, 1987	**INTERACT 87**, Stuttgart, Germany Sponsor: IFIP (Intl Fed of Info Processing), Geneva, Switzerland, 41 22 28 26 49
March 30, 1987 to April 2, 1987	**Interface 87**, Las Vegas, NV Sponsor: Interface Group Inc., 617/449-6600
May 4, 1987 to May 7, 1987	**International Conference on Supercomputing** (2nd annual), San Francisco, CA Sponsor: ACM (Association for Computing Machinery), 212/869-7440
May 30, 1987 to June 2, 1987	**International Summer Consumer Electronics Show** (CES), Chicago, IL Sponsor: Consumer Electronics Shows, 202/457-8700
June 4, 1988 to June 7, 1988	**International Summer Consumer Electronics Show** (CES), Chicago, IL Sponsor: Consumer Electronics Shows, 202/457-8700
January 8, 1987 to January 11, 1987	**International Winter Consumer Electronics Show** (CES), Las Vegas Sponsor: Consumer Electronics Shows, 202/457-8700
January 8, 1988 to January 10, 1988	**International Winter Consumer Electronics Show** (CES), Las Vegas Sponsor: Consumer Electronics Shows, 202/457-8700
September 15 to September 17, 1987	**MIDCON**, Rosemont, IL Sponsor: IEEE, 212/705-7900

(Continued next page)

CONFERENCES (Continued)

August 30, 1988 to September 1, 1988	**MIDCON**, Dallas, TX Sponsor: IEEE, 212/705-7900
September 12 to September 14, 1989	**MIDCON**, Rosemont, IL Sponsor: IEEE, 212/705-7900
June 21, 1987 to June 24, 1987	**NECC 87** (National Education Computing Conference), Philadelphia, PA Sponsor: ACM (Association for Computing Machinery), 212/869-7440
June 12, 1988 to June 15, 1988	**NECC 88** (National Education Computing Conference), Exact location to be announced Sponsor: ACM (Association for Computing Machinery), 212/869-7440
June 15, 1987 to June 18, 1987	**National Computer Conference** (NCC), Chicago, IL Sponsor: American Federation of Info Proc Societies (AFIPS), 703/620-8900
May 31, 1988 to June 3, 1988	**National Computer Conference** (NCC), Los Angeles, CA Sponsor: American Federation of Info Proc Societies (AFIPS), 703/620-8900
April 10, 1989 to April 13, 1989	**National Computer Conference** (NCC), Chicago, IL Sponsor: American Federation of Info Proc Societies (AFIPS), 703/620-8900
April 2, 1990 to April 5, 1990	**National Computer Conference** (NCC), New York, NY Sponsor: American Federation of Info Proc Societies (AFIPS), 703/620-8900
April 15, 1991 to April 18, 1991	**National Computer Conference** (NCC), Anaheim, CA Sponsor: American Federation of Info Proc Societies (AFIPS), 703/620-8900
April 6, 1992 to April 9, 1992	**National Computer Conference** (NCC), Chicago, IL Sponsor: American Federation of Info Proc Societies (AFIPS), 703/620-8900
June 15, 1987 to June 18, 1987	**Network 90's USTSA & Pacific Bell**, San Francisco, CA Sponsor: U.S. Telephone Association (U.S.T.A.), 202/835-3100

(Continued next page)

CONFERENCES (Continued)

June 1, 1987 to June 4, 1987	**Network Management & Technology**, New York, NY Sponsor: Conference Management Group (CW Communications), 617/879-0700
October 19, 1987 to October 22, 1987	**Network Management & Technology**, Chicago, IL Sponsor: Conference Management Group (CW Communications), 617/879-0700
October 15, 1987 to October 17, 1987	**Northeast Computer Faire**, Boston, MA Sponsor: Interface Group Inc., 617/449-6600
March 9, 1987 to March 11, 1987	**OAC 87** (Office Automation Conference), Dallas, TX Sponsor: ACM (Association for Computing Machinery), 212/869-7440
March 6, 1989 to March 8, 1989	**OAC 89** (Office Automation Conference), Atlanta, GA Sponsor: ACM (Association for Computing Machinery), 212/869-7440
February 12, 1990 to February 14, 1990	**OAC 90** (Office Automation Conference), New Orleans, LA Sponsor: ACM (Association for Computing Machinery), 212/869-7440
October 20, 1987 to October 22, 1987	**Online 87**, Anaheim, CA Sponsor: Online Inc., 203/227-8466
October 10, 1988 to October 12, 1988	**Online 88**, New York, NY Sponsor: Online Inc., 203/227-8466
October 18, 1989 to October 20, 1989	**Online 89**, San Francisco, CA Sponsor: Online Inc., 203/227-8466
September 1, 1987 to September 3, 1987	**PC Expo**, New York, NY Sponsor: PC Expo, 201/569-8542
October 13, 1987 to October 15, 1987	**PC Expo**, Chicago, IL Sponsor: PC Expo, 201/569-8542
June 21, 1988 to June 23, 1988	**PC Expo**, New York, NY Sponsor: PC Expo, 201/569-8542
June 14, 1989 to June 16, 1989	**PC Expo**, New York, NY Sponsor: PC Expo, 201/569-8542

(Continued next page)

CONFERENCES (Continued)

June 20, 1990 to June 22, 1990	**PC Expo**, New York, NY Sponsor: PC Expo, 201/569-8542
June 5, 1991 to June 7, 1991	**PC Expo**, New York, NY Sponsor: PC Expo, 201/569-8542
June 23, 1992 to June 25, 1992	**PC Expo**, New York, NY Sponsor: PC Expo, 201/569-8542
September 28 to October 2, 1987	**TCA Annual Conference**, San Diego, CA Sponsor: Tele-Communications Association, 818/960-1838
September 26 to October 1, 1988	**TCA Annual Conference**, San Diego, CA Sponsor: Tele-Communications Association, 818/960-1838
September 25 to September 30, 1989	**TCA Annual Conference**, San Diego, CA Sponsor: Tele-Communications Association, 818/960-1838
October 13, 1987 to October 15, 1987	**USTA National Convention**, Orlando, FL Sponsor: U.S. Telephone Association (U.S.T.A.), 202/835-3100
October 10, 1988 to October 12, 1988	**USTA National Convention**, New York, NY Sponsor: U.S. Telephone Association (U.S.T.A.), 202/835-3100
October 16, 1989 to October 18, 1989	**USTA National Convention**, San Francisco, CA Sponsor: U.S. Telephone Association (U.S.T.A.), 202/835-3100
October 21, 1990 to October 24, 1990	**USTA National Convention**, Las Vegas, NV Sponsor: U.S. Telephone Association (U.S.T.A.), 202/835-3100
October 7, 1991 to October 9, 1991	**USTA National Convention**, Honolulu, HI Sponsor: U.S. Telephone Association (U.S.T.A.), 202/835-3100
October 19, 1992 to October 21, 1992	**USTA National Convention**, Philadelphia, PA Sponsor: U.S. Telephone Association (U.S.T.A.), 202/835-3100
October 4, 1993 to October 6, 1993	**USTA National Convention**, Boston, MA Sponsor: U.S. Telephone Association (U.S.T.A.), 202/835-3100

(Continued next page)

CONFERENCES (Continued)

May 24, 1988 to May 26, 1988	**USTA/USTSA National Showcase**, Atlanta, GA Sponsor: U.S. Telephone Association (U.S.T.A.), 202/835-3100
May 23, 1989 to May 25, 1989	**USTA/USTSA National Showcase**, Anaheim, CA Sponsor: U.S. Telephone Association (U.S.T.A.), 202/835-3100
April 17, 1990 to April 19, 1990	**USTA/USTSA National Showcase**, Atlanta, GA Sponsor: U.S. Telephone Association (U.S.T.A.), 202/835-3100
February 19, 1991 to February 21, 1991	**USTA/USTSA National Showcase**, Las Vegas, NV Sponsor: U.S. Telephone Association (U.S.T.A.), 202/835-3100
January 7, 1992 to January 9, 1992	**USTA/USTSA National Showcase**, Atlanta, GA Sponsor: U.S. Telephone Association (U.S.T.A.), 202/835-3100
February 17, 1987 to February 19, 1987	**USTA/USTSA Telecommunications Showcase**, Indianapolis, IN Sponsor: U.S. Telephone Association (U.S.T.A.), 202/835-3100
April 14, 1987 to April 16, 1987	**USTA/USTSA Telecommunications Showcase**, Las Vegas, NV Sponsor: U.S. Telephone Association (U.S.T.A.), 202/835-3100
November 17, 1987 to November 19, 1987	**WESTCON (Western Electronics Show & Convention)**, San Francisco Sponsor: IEEE, 212/705-7900
November 15, 1988 to November 17, 1988	**WESTCON (Western Electronics Show & Convention)**, Anaheim, CA Sponsor: IEEE, 212/705-7900
November 14, 1989 to November 16, 1989	**WESTCON (Western Electronics Show & Convention)**, San Francisco Sponsor: IEEE, 212/705-7900
March 26, 1987 to March 29, 1987	**West Coast Computer Faire**, San Francisco, CA Sponsor: Interface Group Inc., 617/449-6600

HEADLINES OF THE YEAR: 1986

In this section COMPUTER INDUSTRY ALMANAC highlights industry events in 1986 by featuring headlines compiled from a wide variety of industry-related magazines and newspapers. Events in the computer, electronics, and telecommunications industries are shown throughout the year by month.

January 1986

IBM Introduces 32-bit RISC-Based RT PC Workstation for the Technical Professional

Apple Computer Announces Macintosh Plus and LaserWriter Plus

Lotus Development Corp. Plans to Sell TK!Solver to Universal Technical Systems

Pacific Bell Unveils Technology that Converts a Telephone Line into
    Seven Simultaneous Communications Channels

DEST Corp. Introduces Low-Cost Page Scanner for IBM Personal Computers

Semiconductor Industry Association Says Book-to-Bill Ratio Rose to 1.05 in January--
    Previously at 0.65 in January 1985 and at 1.53 in January 1984

Sun Microsystems Introduces New Workstation

Xerox Corp. Expands Office Systems Product Line

Ashton-Tate Ships dBase III PLUS

IBM Introduces Retail Point-of-Sale System Using IMB PC AT as Controller

Grolier Electronic Publishing Announces Electronic Encyclopedia on CD ROM Disk Drive
    Available Now in Retail Stores

3Com Corp. Announces DiskPlus--High-Performance, High-Capacity Disk Drive
    for Apple's Macintosh Plus

Subscriptions to Online Database Services Increased 22% in 1985

Tolerant Systems Enters the Fault-Tolerant Computer Market

Stratus Computer Introduces MAP Communications Support Software

Pacific Telesis Acquires Teleconsult

Identix Introduces a System to Read Fingerprints Electronically

Digital Equipment Announces Color VAXstation II/GPX

Prime Computer Announces Two Low-End Office Systems

Microsoft Corp. and Lotus Development Corp. Announce that
    Lotus Will Support Microsoft Windows

Sun Microsystems Files Registration Statement for Initial Public Offering
    of 4 Million Shares of Common Stock

Xidex Corp. to Market Iomega Corporation's Bernoulli Disk Cartridges Under the Dysan Label

Software Publishing Corp. Announces Harvard Presentation Graphics

Interface Group Acquires Computer Faire Inc.

BPI Systems Introduces BPI General Accounting for the Macintosh

(Continued next page)

HEADLINES OF THE YEAR: 1986 (Continued)

February 1986

Plus Development Corp. Reduces Price of Hardcard from $1,095 to $895

Tallgrass Technologies Announces New Line of Internal Tape and Disk/Tape Subsystems

Helix Systems and Development Corp. Introduces Bubble Memory
for Nonexpansion-Slot Microcomputer Systems

Apple Computer Names John Sculley Chairman of the Board

Ashton-Tate Ships DBase III PLUS LAN Pack

Digital Equipment Corp. Introduces three New VAX Computer Systems

Wyse Technology Files Registration for Public Offering

Ungermann-Bass Inc. to Acquire Software Vendor Linkware Corp.

Pixar, the Computer Graphics Division of Lucasfilm, Ltd, Acquired by Steve Jobs and
the Employees of Pixar

Fort Worth, Texas Breaks Ground for Construction of the Advanced Robotics Research Institute

Corvus Completes Acquisition of Oemtek, Inc.

Monolithic Memories Announces Plans for 2-Million Share Public Offering

IBM Announces New Release of its DATABASE 2 Relational Database Program

Four-Phase Systems To Change its Name to Motorola Computer Systems

Microsoft Files Proposed Initial Public Offering of 2.5 Million Shares of Common Stock

Floating Point Systems Inc. Announces Additions to its Supercomputing Product Line

Infomart in Dallas Announces February Visit by Prince Charles

Compaq Computer Corp. Introduces the Compaq Portable II: Small, Light, High-Performance,
Full-Function Portable Computer

AST Research Inc. Acquires Camintonn Corp.--Enters DEC Add-On Market

ComputerLand Celebrates Opening of 200th Store Outside the U.S.

Automatic Data Processing Inc. Concludes Acquisition of Bunker Ramo Information Systems

Activision Inc. Will Acquire Infocom Inc., Publisher of Adventure Games

Corvus Systems Inc. Sells Onyx Line of Multiuser Systems to Megalogic Inc.

Apollo Computer Introduces New Line of Workstation Products

Phoenix Software Associates Ltd. is Developing PC AT-Compatible Coprocessor Board
for Apollo's DOMAIN Series 3000 Personal Workstations

ComputerLand Launches National Accounts Program

Wyse Technology Completes Acquisition of Amdek Corp.

Lotus Development Corp. Acquires iLINK from InfoCenter Software

Korean Computer Manufacturer Daewoo Corp. Annual Exports Exceed $3 Billion
for First Time

(Continued next page)

HEADLINES OF THE YEAR: 1986 (Continued)

March 1986

Tandem and Rockwell Sign Agreement for Integrated Telecommunications
and Computer System

Counterpoint Computer Announces System 19 Family of Advanced Computer Systems
for Original Equipment Manufacturer Market

Artificial Intelligence Software Firm Teknowledge Begins Initial Public Offering

Corporation for Open Systems' Membership Increases as More Vendors Join

Vodavi Technology Corp. Announces Letter of Intent to Acquire 51% of GTC Technologies,
Laser Printer Manufacturer

Gallium Arsenide Rapidly Gaining Popularity as an Alternative to Silicon
in Semiconductor Industry

VLSI Technology Announces Proposed Public Offering

IBM Elects John F. Akers Chairman to Succeed John R. Opel

Sperry Introduces Two Optical Disk Subsystems for its Series 1100 Mainframe Family

Half of Microcomputer Models Exceed Radio Interference Standards FCC Tests Show

Zenith Enters Local Area Network Market with Z-LAN

IBM Completes Sale of Satellite Business Systems to MCI--Retains Ownership of Three
SBS Satellites

Hewlett-Packard Launches RISC-Based 32-bit Extensions to its 3000 Line

Burroughs Unveils B27 Intel 80186-Based Microcomputer

IBM Will Sell Micro-to-Mainframe Link Software for Dbase and 1-2-3 Files

Toshiba Machine Sold in Europe Said to be First Laptop to Use 80286 Microprocessor

Commodore Cuts $500 from Price of Amiga with Color Monitor

Desktop Publishing Packages for IBM PC Begin to Cut into Apple Macintosh Domination

Microsoft Readying New Release of MS-DOS Word Processing Program Word 3.0

Zenith Data Systems Receives Largest Microcomputer Government Contract Ever Awarded--
90,000 Microcomputers Over Three-Year Period

Apple Computer to Form Venture Capital Group

Compaq Computer Corp. Becomes the Youngest Company to be Named to the Fortune 500

(Continued next page)

HEADLINES OF THE YEAR: 1986 (Continued)

April 1986

IBM Launches Laptop PC Convertible Computer

Large Corporations Turning Away from Microcomputer-Only Databases in Favor of
Microcomputer Versions of Mainframe Database Managers

IBM Enhances Token-Ring Local Area Network with System/370 and System/36 Links

Apple Announces Enhanced Mac

Commerce Department Rules Four Japanese Firms Dumped 64K DRAMS in the U.S. Market

Users are Forcing an End to Copy Protected Software--Too Hard to Use

IBM Uses its First 1-Megabit Chips in Sierra 3090 Series Mainframes

Nynex Buys IBM's Computer Stores--Creates Potential New Force in the Industry

U.S. Computer Companies Expected to Pay $2B for Ads/Promos in 1986

Generic PCs Gaining Industry Market Share

IBM Announces New Upgrade to TopView but Windows Is Still Strong

Apple Drops Sears Business Systems Centers from its Distribution Network

Wozniak and Bushnell Plan to Tinker Together on Toys

Microsoft Working on 80386 and 80286 DOS Versions

National Semiconductor, Facing Slump, Splits its Chip Business from Computer Business

New York Telephone Announces Switching Net for Large Corporate Users

Apple to Support MS-DOS and UNIX on its Personal Computers

(Continued next page)

HEADLINES OF THE YEAR: 1986 (Continued)

May 1986

Burroughs proposes to Buy Sperry--Create New Number 2 Computer Company

IBM Plans to Open Up SNA to Other Vendors

Genicom Corp. Announces 10-Page-Per-Minute Laser Printer for Under $3000

Floating Point Unveils T Series Supercomputers--Competes with Cray, CDC, and Hitachi

With IBM Using 3.5-inch Floppy, Will Microfloppy Become Industry Standard?

NCR Unveils New Generation of Computers: 9800 Series

80386 Machines Due by End of Year

Mannesmann Tally Introduces 10-Page-Per-Minute Laser Printer Priced at $3695

Half-Card Version of Smartmodem 1200B to Replace Full-Sized Internal Modem

IBM to Phase Out the 8100

Hoping for Signs of Recovery in the Semiconductor Industry

Nebraska Law Deregulating Phone Rates May Spur Some Changes in Other States

IBM to Cease Displaywriter Marketing--Customers Moving to PCs for Word Processing

Software Publishing Announces Plans to Market an IBM PC Desktop Publishing Program

Companies Seek Site-License and Volume-Purchase Agreements with Software Publishers

Datability Software Systems' Communications Link, Remote Access Facility (RAF),
    Links IBM PCs More Easily to DEC Mainframes

Luma Telecom Inc. Offers First "Practical" Video Phone for Home and Business Use

Okidata To Enter Data Communications Market with CLX 96 Modem Line

Corporation for Open Systems Names Faurer President

(Continued next page)

HEADLINES OF THE YEAR: 1986 (Continued)

June 1986

Waldenbooks Opening Software Centers in 540 Stores

Disk Drive Maker Tandon Corp. to Make and Sell PC Clones

ComputerLand and Businessland Dropped from IBM Dealer Advisory Boards

Texas Instruments Unveils 120-Megabyte Business-Pro

Xerox Corp. Announces its 6085 Engineering Workstation

Grid Systems Reduces Prices on its GridCase Laptops between 17% and 28%

ComputerLand Plans to Sell its Own PC Clone

IBM Unveils 8 MHz Desktop Version of its Series 1 Minicomputer

Bill Millard Trying to Sell His 96% of ComputerLand

Data General Forms New Division to Focus on Laptop and Desktop Computers

Expect Microrim to Unveil New Database--Combines Single and Multiuser Capabilities and
Can Be Used on Network File Servers

Polaroid Offers Color Ink-Jet Printer Chromajet 4000

House Passes Stronger Computer Crime/Fraud Act

Tandy Replaces Model 100 Laptop with Model 102--Lighter and Thinner

Ungermann-Bass Ships Net/One Token Ring--Claims First IBM-Compatible Token Ring
Network

AT&T Unveils Release 3.0 of UNIX System V

July 1986

Dealer Prices on IBM PC AT Drop $400--Imports Cutting into Market Share

Microsoft Buys Out TopView Clone Maker Dynamical Systems Research--Product is Mondrian

IBM's 1-Mbit Memory Chips Reach PCs but in Experimental Models Only

Lotus Develops Computer Language Linking PCs Directly to Mainframes

IBM Introduces International Data Service Targeted at Large Multinational Corporations

Bill Gates, Founder and Chairman of Microsoft, Appears on Cover of FORTUNE Magazine--
At Age 30 He's Worth $350 Million

Adapso Abandons Hardware-Based Copy Protection Scheme Proposed Two Years Ago

Voice-Controlled, MS-DOS-based Communications Workstation Introduced
by Microphonics Technology Corp.

Technical Problems with Modems Delay Shipment of IBM Convertible

Lotus and Intel Announce Joint Agreement to Create 80386 Operating Environment

Sun's UNIX Workstations Now Connect to IBM PCs

French Government Okays ITT/CGE (Compagnie Generale d'Electricite) Joint Venture--
Creates No. 2 Telecom Group in World

(Continued next page)

HEADLINES OF THE YEAR: 1986 (Continued)

August 1986

    Japan Temporarily Halts Certain Chip Exports to U.S.: Mostly 256-Kbit DRAMs

    Tandy Introduces Four Low-Priced IBM-Compatible Computers--
        Shakes Up PC-Compatible Marketplace

    IBM Prepares to Drop 500 out of 2,500 Authorized Dealers by 1987

    Burroughs Introduces Software Making Its PCs Run IBM PC Software and
        Communicate with IBM Mainframes

    IBM Reduces IBM PC Prices by Up to 20%--Reflects Impact of Clones

    Japanese Agree to Allow U.S. Chip Manufacturers Double Market Share in Japan by 1991

    Franklin Plans to Market Apple II Clone Through Sears

    PC Clone Manufacturer Leading Edge Cuts Price of its Basic Model D by $200

    Apollo Unveils High-End Color Workstations DN570/80 Turbo

    IBM Ships First 3090-400 Seven Months Ahead of Schedule

    Hyundai Debuts PC XT Clones

    Wordtech Systems DBSQL Merges SQL (Structured Query Language) with QBE
        (Query By Example)

    Data General Abandons DS/7700 High-End Engineering Workstation--
        Software Snags and Bus Bugs

    Siemens and GTE Joint Agreement to Build and Market Switches Fizzles

    Ashton-Tate Removes All Copy Protection Schemes on its Software

    Corvus Unveils 80386-Based Computers--New Computer Generation Hailed

    Microsoft Designing Windows Version for 80386-Based Machines

    Lotus Readies Word Processor for Technical Professional

    Convergent Technology Shifting Away from OEM Business Base--
        Will Introduce IBM-Compatible Machine

    Nynex Settlement Brings End to Eight-Day Strike

    AT&T Consolidated Equipment/Long Distance Service Arms Forcing More Layoffs

(Continued next page)

HEADLINES OF THE YEAR: 1986 (Continued)

September 1986

    IBM Unveils new XT Model-286 in Hopes of Protecting its Large Corporate Accounts

    Price Hikes on Semiconductors May Force Kaypro Overseas for Production

    Mail-Order Company PC Limited Plans to Sell 80386 PC for Under $5,000

    COMPAQ Releases Deskpro 386 Computer--First Major Computer Maker
        to Beat IBM to Market with 80386 Computer

    GTE Laboratories Develops a Division Multiplexer that Doubles Capacity of Fiber-Optic Lines

    Corvus Releases Series 386 Products Based on 80386 State-of-the-Art Chip

    Honeywell Introduces Six New Mainframe Computers in its DPS 88 Line--
        Twice as Powerful as its Other Machines

    Apple Computer Brings Out New Version of its Mainstay Apple II--The Apple IIGS

    IBM Initiates Broad Retirement Incentive Program--Hopes to Reduce U.S. Work Force
        and Maintain No-Layoff Policy

    Counterpoint Unveils UNIX-Based Multiuser System--Expands Workstation-Only Image

    Seven Regional Bell Companies Begin Discussing Opening Local Monopolies to Competition

    Motorola Introduces its Most Advanced 32-bit Chip Yet--MC68030

    Corvus First to Announce Use of 80386 chip in Local Area Network Products

    General-Interest Trade Shows, Comdex and NCC, Losing Attendance to Smaller,
        Application-Specific Shows

    Hewlett-Packard Plans to Delay Shipment of Spectrum Computer

    Sun Systems Remarketing Provides Markets for Discontinued Computers

    On RT PC, IBM Adds Enhancements and Cuts Price by 20% to 30%--
        Hopes to Increase Sales to Technical User

    Memory Board Manufacturer AST Research Sets to Launch its First Microcomputer

    Court Rules that Semiconductor Microcode Can Be Copyrighted

    IRS Plans to Allow Companies to File Income Tax Returns Electronically

    650 Largest Attendance Ever at MAP/TOP Users Meeting

    Atari Files with SEC for Initial Public Offering

    Convergent Technologies Expands MiniFrame and MegaFrame Line with S/Series

    Intel and IBM Announce Plans to Swap Chip Designs for Chips Used in IBM's Products--
        Seen as Launching Intel into Custom Chip Business

    Sperry to Supply Electronic Data Systems with Mainframes for $87 Million
        U.S. Air Force Contract

    Intel Introduces its First True Integrated Services Digital Network (ISDN) Chips

    (Continued next page)

HEADLINES OF THE YEAR: 1986 (Continued)

October 1986

Court Decision Rules in Favor of Broderbund--"Look and Feel" of
Software Package is Copyrightable

Apollo Adds PC-DOS Single-Board Computer to its UNIX-Based
Domain Series 3000 Engineering Workstation Line

IBM Gives RT PC Communication Ability with IBM Mainframe Environments

Realia, Inc. Introduces Product Allowing Applications Developed on Microcomputers
to Run on Both PCs and Mainframes

WordPerfect Corp Plans Version of its Word Processing PC Software for IBM Mainframes and
DEC VAX Machines

Contel and Comsat Merge

Nynex Asks U.S. District Court Judge for Permission to Sell Network Services Through its
Nynex Business Systems Retail Stores

Sytek Debuts Local Area Network Products for IBM Personal Computers

Low Turn Out at Pick Hardware and Software Manufacturers Show

Digital Research Inc. Forms Subsidiary to Develop Micro-to-Mainframe Software and
Operating Systems for 80386 Microprocessor

AT&T Introduces Many New Integrated Services Digital Network-Type Services and Products

ITT Unveils High-End Workstation with Built-In Graphics

IBM Introduces Small Mainframes--9370 Line of System 370 Family--For Use at
Departmental Level

Ashton-Tate Readies New dBASE III Features Allowing Access to Mini and Mainframe Data

IBM Implements Four-Tier Pricing Structure to Reduce Price of Mainframe Software

Burroughs Upgrades its A 10 Mainframe Line with Three New Models

AT&T Considers Offering Optional Industry-Standard Bus for its 3B Line

Concurrent Unveils a Low-End Model to its Series 3200 Supermini Line

Intel and Flexlink Introduce IBM-VAX Channel-Speed Link

Wang, Sun and Apollo Ink Agreement to Offer Integrated Systems to Technical Office and
Engineering Markets

Apple Closes its First Year Under Sculley by Doubling its Earnings

Wang Will Sell Directly its New IBM-Compatible Laptop

TI Meets Request to Shrink Size of Token Ring Chip Set by Using ASIC
(Application Specific Integrated Circuits) Technology

Tektronix Introduces New Line of Color Graphics Terminals Called Series 4200

AT&T Turns Over Production and Development of its PCs to Olivetti

Chips and Technologies Inc. Signs Accord to Have Chips Made by
National Semiconductor

GM, IBM, and Others Plan to Pullout from South Africa

(Continued next page)

HEADLINES OF THE YEAR: 1986 (Continued)

Hewlett-Packard, Microsoft, and Aldus Join to Sell Desktop Publishing System for PCs

Electronic Data Systems Opens Computer Stores as C-Level IBM Dealerships

Lotus Launches 1-2-3 Companion Product, HAL

Kyocera Joins Laser Printer Market with F1010 Compact Laser Printer

Okidata Introduces First Laser Printer and PC Modem

Wang Releases Laptop Computer

SNA Link to non-SNA Devices Announced by Netlink, Inc.

Connection Between IBM PC Local Area Network and IBM System/36 or 38 Minis Announced by Asher Technologies, Inc.

NCR Introduces the Tower 32/400, New 32-bit Supermicro

NEC Brings Out PC-8500 Portable

Schlumberger Ltd. Signs Letter of Intent to Sell 80% of Fairchild Semiconductor to Fujitsu

Texas Instruments Pulls Out of Portable PC Market

(Continued next page)

HEADLINES OF THE YEAR: 1986 (Continued)

November 1986

On January 1, Zenith Plans to Stop Selling Machines to Heath/Zenith Stores at Lower Prices Than Those Offered to Other Authorized Dealers

Fall Comdex Exhibits Industry Optimism According to Long-Time Industry Observers

Ansa Software, Known for Paradox Data Base, Plans to Expand Product Line and Distribution with $2 Million Venture Capital Infusion

Computer Stores Optimistic About Christmas Selling Season but Fear Product Shortages

Rubbermaid, Plastic Housewares Firm, Enters Microcomputer Industry with Purchase of MicroComputer Accessories, an Accessories Manufacturer

National Science Foundation Ranks Parallel Processing as its No. 1 Research Problem and Claims it the Technological Wave of the Future

Uccel Corp. Divests Seven Businesses--Concentrates on Systems and Financial Software

Compaq Deskpro 386 Sales Now Number 10,000--Orders are Backlogged

IBM Plans to Close its Indiana Distribution Center

Plus Development Enhances its Hardcard 20 to Run on 80286-Based Systems

An Wang, Founder, Gives Reigns at Wang to Son, Frederick A. Wang, New President

3Com Corp. to Sell Ethernet Networks at More Than 500 Radio Shack Computer Centers

U.S. Computer Slump Expected to Hit European Computer Companies--Analysts See Signs of Downturn in Growth Overseas

IBM Selects Rabbit Software to Link RT PC with its Mainframes

Chips and Technologies Introduces 7-Chip Setup for 32-bit 80386 PCs

COMPUTER RESELLER NEWS Names Bill Gates, Microsoft Chairman, Most Influential Executive--Propelling Microcomputer Industry's Technological Advances

Apple IIGS in Short Supply for Christmas Season at Computer Stores

Kodak, Philips, and DuPont to Cooperate in Developing Optical Storage Media Standards

IBM Experiences Disappointing Third Quarter

Convergent Technologies Expands its Ngen Workstation Family with 80386-Based System having MS-DOS and Xenix

Epson Joins Laser Printer Marketplace with $2495 Compact Model

Yen's Rise Puts Dent in Japan Inc.'s Profits

Commodore Re-Enters Commercial Semiconductor Market

(Continued next page)

HEADLINES OF THE YEAR: 1986 (Continued)

December 1986

Convex Computer Corp. Announces CSX, Extended Supercomputing Architecture, to
Allow Multiple Convex Supercomputers to Work Simultaneously but
Independently on Multiple Applications

IRS Claims Still Interrupt Storage Technology Emergence from Chapter 11

Hewlett-Packard Readies Spectrum 9000/840s for Shipment

Nynex Enters Commercial Telecommunicatons Software Market

Hewlett-Packard Schedules Workstation to Compete Directly with Sun Microsystems

AT&T Unveils 32200 Chip--Joins Other High-Powered 32-bit Chips

Kaypro To Sell PCs through Amway Corp., International Home Products Distributor

Pentagon Still Split on Implications of Fujitsu Bid for Fairchild Semiconductor--Fear National
Security Implications of Japanese Firm Controlling U.S. Defense Subcontractor

Hitachi and Toshiba Will Begin U.S. Assembly of 1-Megabit Memory Chips--
Manufacturing not Brought to U.S.

IBM's Early Retirement Program Brings 10,000 Signatures--No Real Market Upturn in Sight

Lotus and Microrim Working to Provide Easier PC-to-Mainframe Link for Microrim's
R:base System V Database

Apple's Open-Architecture Macintosh Will Resemble Sun and Apollo Workstations
More Closely Than Upscale PCs

Northern Telecom Announces Sale of its Midwest Integrated Office Systems' Sales and
Service Operations to Centel Business Systems

Lotus and MCI Communications Corp. Announce a Program to Automate Procedures for
Sending and Receiving MCI Electronic Mail

Software Publishing Corp. Working on $249 Professional Plan Spreadsheet that is
Compatible with Lotus 1-2-3

Production of Original IBM PC Is Discontinued After Five Years--Next Generation of PCs,
Expected Next Year, Will Feature Built-In Graphics

13 ORGANIZATIONS AND AGENCIES

ASSOCIATIONS

In this section COMPUTER INDUSTRY ALMANAC lists 59 industry-related associations which are separated according to membership criteria into professional associations (membership comprised of individuals within a specific field) or trade associations (membership comprised of corporate members within a specific industry segment). The entries are arranged alphabetically by name and include address, phone, executive officers, publications, conferences, interest groups and a brief description.

PROFESSIONAL ASSOCIATIONS

Agricultural Computer Association
Acronym: ACA
P.O. Box 253
Elk Grove, CA 95624
Description: Promotes implementation of computers in agriculture and provides information to the industry.
Year Founded: 1981
Individual Members: 95   Corporate Members: 10
Executive Officers: Lyndon S. Hawkins, Acting President
Publications: Newsletter (periodic)

American Association for Artificial Intelligence
Acronym: AAAI
445 Burgess Drive
Menlo Park, CA 94025
Phone: 415/328-3123
Description: Scientific society for the study and application of artificial intelligence science and technology.
Year Founded: 1980
Individual Members: 13000   Corporate Members: 50
Executive Officers: Claudia Mazzetti, Executive Director; Dr. Patrick Winston, President (1985-87)
Publications: AI Magazine (five times a year), Annual Conference Proceedings
Conferences: AAAI-87, Seattle, July 13-17 AAAI-88, St. Paul, August 2

American Association for the Advancement of Science
Acronym: AAAS
1333 H St., NW
Washington, DC 20005
Phone: 202/326-6400
Description: Furthers the work of scientists, facilitates cooperation among them, fosters scientific freedom and responsibility, improves the effectiveness of science in human welfare.
Year Founded: 1848
Individual Members: 150,000
Executive Officers: William D. Carey
Interest Groups: Section T (Information, Computing, Communications)
Publications: Science (weekly), Science 86 (monthly), Science Books & Films (quarterly)
Conferences: Annual meeting (87:Chicago, 88:Boston, 89:San Francisco, 90:New Orleans, 91:Washington, DC.), Annual R&D Symposium.
Awards: Annually 3 prizes, 6 awards, and various research grants

American Society for Information Science
Acronym: ASIS
1424 16th St., NW, Suite 404
Washington, DC 20036
Phone: 202/462-1000
Description: Association of professionals in the information field, provides and improves access to information through policy, technology, applications and research.
Year Founded: 1937
Individual Members: 3700   Corporate Members: 110
Executive Officers: Linda Resnik, Executive Director; Thomas Hogan, President (1987)
Interest Groups: ASIS has 23 Special Interest Groups, each of which is chaired in one-year terms by a member of the SIG
Publications: Bulletin of the Am Society for Info Science (bi-monthly), Journal of the Am Society for Info Science (bimonthly)
Conferences: Annual meeting (87:Boston, Oct 4-8; 88:Atlanta, Oct 23-27; 89: San Diego, Oct 29-Nov 2)
Awards: Several annual awards, scholarships and research grants

Associated Information Managers

Acronym: AIM
1776 E Jefferson St, 4th floor
Rockville, MD 20852
Phone: 301/231-7447
Description: Dedicated to further developing information management as an integral part of an organization by providing forums, publications, and programs.
Year Founded: 1981
Individual Members: 600   Corporate Members: 24
Executive Officers: Sheila Brayman, Executive Director; Dr. Donald Marchand, Chairman (1986-87)
Publications: AIM Network (biweekly), Career Exchange Clearinghouse (biweekly), Who's Who in Info. Mgmt (annually)
Conferences: Annual Conference (87:Washington DC)
Awards: Info Manager, Product, Technology & Pioneer awards annually

Association for Computers and the Humanities

Acronym: ACH
English Dept., Univ. of MN
Minneapolis, MN 55455
Phone: 612/625-2888
Description: Promotes scholarship and applied studies in the use of computers in all humanities disciplines.
Year Founded: 1978
Individual Members: 400
Executive Officers: Donald Ross, Executive Secretary; Nancy Ide, President (1985-87)
Publications: ACH Newsletter (quarterly), Computers and the Humanities (quarterly)
Conferences: Every other year International Conference for Computers and the Humanities (87:Columbia, SC)

Association for Computing Machinery

Acronym: ACM
11 West 42nd St.
New York, NY 10036
Phone: 212/869-7440
Telex: 421686
Description: Dedicated to advancing the science and art of computer use by providing technical and non-technical computing information to its members and the public.
Year Founded: 1947
Individual Members: 75,000
Executive Officers: Richard F. Hespos, Executive Director; Paul W. Abrahams, President (7/1/86-6/30/88)
Interest Groups: ACM has 31 SIGs; each publishes newsletters, organizes tech workshops, and holds computer conferences
Publications: Communications of the ACM (monthly), Journal of the ACM (quarterly), Pubs Catalog; each SIG also publishes
Conferences: Fall Joint Computer Conference (87:Dallas), numerous others (each SIG has conferences)
Awards: Several annual awards
Foreign Offices: Belg., Fr., Gr., It., Nor., Pg., Switz., UK, & W. Ger.

Association of Data Communications Users, Inc.

Acronym: ADCU
P.O. Box 20163
Bloomington, MN 55420
Phone: 612/881-6803
Description: Disseminates information and provides problem solving forums.
Year Founded: 1976
Individual Members: 300   Corporate Members: 225
Executive Officers: August H. Blegen, Executive Director
Publications: Newsletter (bimonthly)
Conferences: National Annual Conference (87:Atlantic City, June 26)

Association of Electronic Cottagers

Acronym: AEC
677 Canyon Crest Dr.
Sierra Madre, CA 91024
Phone: 818/355-0800
Description: Provides services, resources, information, & expertise for people who work at home using a computer.
Year Founded: 1984
Individual Members: 400   Corporate Members: 3
Executive Officers: David May, Executive Director; Paul & Sarah Edwards, Founders
Publications: Electronic Cottage News (monthly), AEC News Report (monthly)
Conferences: Meetings and conferences held on CompuServe, Working from Home Forum (GO WORK)

Association of Independent Microdealers, Inc.

Acronym: AIM
3010 N Sterling Ave.
Peoria, IL 61604
Phone: 309/685-4843
Description: Provides independent computer dealers/music dealers with services and information.
Year Founded: 1984
Individual Members: 180
Executive Officers: Ronald A. Wallace, President
Interest Groups: Computer Musicians Cooperative
Publications: AIM Weekly newsletter (monthly), Minutes (monthly)

Association of Information Managers-Financial Institns

Acronym: AIM
111 E Wacker Dr., Ste 2221
Chicago, IL 60601
Phone: 312/938-2576
Description: Promotes high standards of professionalism in the planning, development, implementation, and operation of automated support systems in financial institutions.
Year Founded: 1973
Individual Members: 705
Executive Officers: Richard A. Yingst, Executive Director; Hosie Maxwell, President
Publications: AIM Newsletter (monthly), Financial Institutions Software Directory (semiannually), Financial Inst. Survey (annually)
Conferences: Annual conference (87:Boston, Oct 4-7; 88:Dallas, Oct 16-19)

Chinese Language Computer Society
Acronym: CLCS
P.O. Box 41
Glencoe, IL 60022
Phone: 312/835-1426
Description: Promotes research and development of Chinese processing computers.
Year Founded: 1972
Individual Members: 250
Executive Officers: Prof. S. F. Chang, Secretary
Publications: Intl Journal of Chinese & Oriental Language Processing (semiannually)
Conferences: Annual August conference

Cognitive Science Society
Acronym: CSS
Carnegie-Mellon University, Dept. of Psy.
Pittsburgh, PA 15213
Phone: 412/268-3790
Description: Promotes scientific interchange among workers in various disciplines that comprise
cognitive science.
Year Founded: 1979
Individual Members: 850
Executive Officers: Edward E. Smith, Chair (1986-87); Kurt VanLehn, Sec/Treas
Publications: Cognitive Science Journal (quarterly)
Conferences: Annual conference

Communications Managers Association
Acronym: CMA
40 Morristown Road
Bernardsville, NJ 07924
Phone: 201/766-3824
Description: Educates members on telecommunications problems, services, and requirements.
Year Founded: 1948
Individual Members: 500   Corporate Members: 206
Executive Officers: Hollis Sobers, President; Patricia Raynes, Executive Assistant
Conferences: Annual Telecom. Conference

Computer Law Association

Acronym: CLA

9520 Lee Highway, Ste A

Fairfax, VA 22031

Phone: 703/591-7014

Description: Informs and educates lawyers about the unique legal issues arising from the evolution, production, marketing, acquisition, and use of computer-communications technology.

Year Founded: 1973

Individual Members: 1,000

Executive Officers: Susan Nycum, President; Daniel Brooks, Sr. Vice President

Interest Groups: Software contracts, litigation, legal education, taxation, and international

Publications: CLA Membership Directory (annually); Computer Law Assoc., newsletter (quarterly); Intl. Update, newsletter (quarterly)

Conferences: Annual Conference (87:Chicago Mar 5-6)

Computer Use in Social Services Network

Acronym: CUSS Network

P.O. Box 19129, Grad. School of Social Wk

Arlington, Tx 76019

Phone: 817/273-3964

Description: Provides professional social service members an opportunity to exchange information and experiences on using computers.

Year Founded: 1981

Individual Members: 800   Corporate Members: 100

Executive Officers: Dr. Dick Schoech, CUSS Network Coordinator

Interest Groups: Educators SIG, Hospital Social Services SIG, various area groups

Publications: Computer Use in Social Service Network Newsletter (quarterly)

Conferences: Conferences and Meetings periodically

Foreign Offices: Australia, Canada, France, Germany, Israel, & UK

Data Entry Management Association
Acronym: DEMA
750 Summer St., Second Floor
Stamford, CT 06901
Phone: 203/967-3500
Description: Provides info to managers involved in both traditional and emerging methods of data entry (key-to-disk, online & distributed processing, voice entry, PCs & word processing).
Year Founded: 1976
Individual Members: 1500
Executive Officers: Norman Bodek, President
Interest Groups: Local chapter activities
Publications: DEMA Newsletter (10 issues annually), The Equipment, VDT, and Statistical Compensation Surveys (yearly)
Conferences: Annual Conference (87:Orlando)

EDP Auditors Association
Acronym: EDPAA
455 E Kehoe Blvd., Ste 106, Box 88180
Carol Stream, IL 60188
Phone: 312/682-1200
Telex: 280-427-EDP-CGO-UD
Description: Contributes to the advancement of the entire EDP audit and control community through educational, research and professional advancement programs.
Year Founded: 1969
Individual Members: 9000
Executive Officers: Gerard Fee, Executive Director; Robert Parker, President
Interest Groups: Various committees and task forces: Education, Publications, Research, Audit Standards Program, and etc.
Publications: EDP Auditors Update (quarterly), EDP Auditors Journal (quarterly), Hotline Newsletter (4-8 issues annually)
Conferences: Annual Conference (87:Seattle, 88:New Orleans, 89:Toronto, 90:New York); CACS (87: Boston)
Foreign Offices: Cen. & So. Am., Europe, UK, Asia, Middle East, Aus. & NZ.

Electronic Representatives Association
Acronym: ERA
20 E Huron St.
Chicago, IL 60611
Phone: 312/649-1333
Description: Provides networking for manufacturers to contact sales representatives for marketing product lines.
Year Founded: 1935
Individual Members: 2200
Executive Officers: Ray Hall, Executive Vice President; Tim Coakley, Chairman of the Board
Publications: Locator Directory (annually), Lines Available Bulletin (monthly), Representor newsletter (bimonthly)
Conferences: Annual Management Conference (87:Palm Desert, CA, April)

Forth Interest Group
Acronym: FIG
P.O. Box 8231
San Jose, CA 95155
Phone: 408/277-0668
Description: Provides resources for Forth computer language implementation materials and publications and promotes use of Forth.
Year Founded: 1978
Individual Members: 5000
Executive Officers: R. Reiling, President; M. Tracy, Vice President
Interest Groups: Local chapters throughout world
Publications: Forth Dimensions magazine (bimonthly), FORML Conference Proceedings (annually)
Conferences: Annual Convention, Annual Conference for Professional Forth Programmers (FORML)
Awards: Annual Outstanding Service to Organization, FIGGY Award

IEEE Computer Society
Acronym: IEEE-CS
1730 Massachusetts Ave., NW
Washington, DC 20036
Phone: 202/371-0101
Telex: 7108250437IEEECOMP
Description: Serves professionals in all aspects of computing. Promotes technical interactions through a variety of programs and activities.
Year Founded: 1951
Individual Members: 87,000
Executive Officers: T. Michael Elliott, Executive Director; Roy L. Russo, President
Interest Groups: Various committees: Scientific, literary, and educational in character.
Publications: Computer magazine (monthly), Computer Graphics and Appl. (monthly); IEEE Micro, Design & Test, Software (bimonthly)
Conferences: Fall Joint Computer Conference (87:Dallas), 100 other type conferences per year
Awards: Several awards and outstanding contribution certificates
Foreign Offices: Ave. de la Tanche, 2, B-1160, Brussels, Belgium

Information Systems Security Association
Acronym: ISSA
P.O. Box 71926
Los Angeles, CA 90071
Phone: 714/863-5583
Description: Association for information security professionals.
Year Founded: 1981
Individual Members: 500   Corporate Members: 200
Executive Officers: Carl B. Jackson, President; Harold F. Tipton, Vice President
Publications: ISSA newsletter (quarterly)
Conferences: Annual ISSA Working Conference (87:Los Angeles Mar 23-25)

International Society of Certified Electronics Techns.
Acronym: ISCET
2708 West Berry St.
Fort Worth, TX 76109
Phone: 817/921-9101
Description: Furthers professionalism in servicing and improves the status of electronics technicians.
Year Founded: 1970
Individual Members: 1239
Executive Officers: Clyde Nabors, Executive Director
Publications: Update newsletter (periodically), Professional Electronics magazine (bimonthly), Technical Notebook, Techni-Tips
Conferences: Conventions (87:Las Vegas Jan 11, 87:Memphis Aug 10, 88:Las Vegas Jan)
Awards: ISCET Certified 20,000 CET, Technicians of the Year

National Alliance for Women in Commmunications Industry
Acronym: THE ALLIANCE
P.O. Box 33984
Washington, DC 20033
Phone: 202/293-1927
Description: Promotes equality of opportunity for women in established and emerging high-technology and computer-related fields.
Year Founded: 1985
Individual Members: 250
Executive Officers: Darlene J. Dolan, Executive Director
Publications: FastForeword newsletter (quarterly), FrontRunners membership directory & resource listing (annually)
Conferences: Annual Spring Leadership Conference, Washington DC

National Computer Graphics Association
Acronym: NCGA
2722 Merrilee Drive, Ste 200
Fairfax, VA 22031
Phone: 703/698-9600
Telex: 510-601-1247NCGA UQ
Description: Develops and promotes the computer graphics industry and graphics applications in business, industry, science, government, and the arts.
Year Founded: 1979
Individual Members: 5500   Corporate Members: 90
Executive Officers: Phillip S. Mittelman, President (1986-87); Robert E. Fulton, President-elect
Publications: Computer Graphics Today magazine (monthly); Corporate Forum newsletter, Graphics Network News newsletter (bimonthly)
Conferences: Computer Graphics (88:Anaheim, CA March 20-24)

National Electronics Sales & Service Dealers Assoc.
Acronym: NESDA
2708 W Berry St.
Fort Worth, TX 76109
Phone: 817/921-9061
Description: Supports and strengthens its members through better business management and technical service knowledge.
Year Founded: 1963
Individual Members: 1904
Executive Officers: Clyde Nabors, Executive Director ; Barbara Rubin, Administrator
Interest Groups: Local chapters, state organizations and national committees.
Publications: Professional Electronics magazine (bimonthly), Professional Electronics Yearbook (annually), newsletters (periodically)
Conferences: National Professional Electronics Conventions (87:Memphis, 87Winter:Las Vegas, 88:Chicago, 88Winter: Las Vegas)
Awards: Hall of Fame Awards and others

Office Automation Society International
Acronym: OASI
15269 Mimosa Trail, Ste B
Dumfries, VA 22026
Phone: 703/690-3880
Description: Promotes quality education & certification of professionals in office automation and office systems.
Year Founded: 1982
Individual Members: 2500   Corporate Members: 10
Executive Officers: Paul D. Oyer, Executive Director & President; Jackie Potts, Executive Vice President
Interest Groups: Professional Certification Council, OA Model Curriculum Council
Publications: Comprehensive Office Automation Glossary (annually), Office Automation News (quarterly)
Conferences: Annual Conference (87:San Fran Sept 8-11, 88:Boston Sept 6-9)

Society for Computer Simulation
Acronym: SCS
P.O. Box 17900
San Diego, CA 92117
Phone: 619/277-3888
Description: Facilitates communications between those in the field of computer simulation via international membership, publications of tech books & journals, & natl. conferences.
Year Founded: 1952
Individual Members: 2302   Corporate Members: 65
Executive Officers: Norbert Pobanz, President; V. Wayne Ingalls, Treasurer
Interest Groups: Simulators Technical Committee
Publications: Simulation technical journal (monthly), Transactions tech. journal (quarterly), also tech reference books periodically
Conferences: SCSC (87:Montreal June, 88:Seattle June), Multiconference (88:San Diego Jan)
Foreign Offices: SCS Europe, Coupure Links 653, B9000, Ghent, Belgium

Society for Information Display
Acronym: SID
8055 W Manchester Ave, Ste 615
Playa del Rey, CA 90293
Phone: 213/305-1502
Description: Serves corporate R&D mgmt, eng, designers, scientists and ergonomists responsible for design and development of I/O display systems in various applications.
Year Founded: 1962
Individual Members: 2000   Corporate Members: 1000
Executive Officers: Bettye Burdett, National Office Manager; John A. van Raalte, President (1987)
Interest Groups: Various committees nationally and locally
Publications: Information Display Journal (monthly), Proc of SID (quarterly), Lecture Notes (semiannually), Digest (annually)
Conferences: Symposium (87:New Orleans May), IDRC (87:London Fall)
Foreign Offices: Canada, Ireland, Great Britian, Japan

Society of Manufacturing Engineers
Acronym: SME
One SME Drive, P.O. Box 930
Dearborn, MI 48121
Phone: 313/271-1500
Telex: 297742 SME UR
Description: Advances scientific knowledge in the field of manufacturing and applies its resources to research, writing, publishing, and disseminating information.
Year Founded: 1932
Individual Members: 80,000
Executive Officers: Kenneth Thorpe, Vice President & General Mgr; Donald Zook, President
Interest Groups: SIGs: MAP/TOP, CASA, RI, AFP, NAMRI, MVA, EM, CoGSME
Publications: Manufacturing Engineering magazine (monthly), Robotics Today (bimonthly), Tool & Mfg Eng Hdbk
Conferences: Annual Conf. (87: Detroit, May 4-7; 88: Cleveland, May)
Awards: Issues 9 annual awards
Foreign Offices: Chapters in 70 countries

Society of Telecommunications Consultants
Acronym: STC
One Rockefeller Plaza, Ste 1410
New York, NY 10020
Phone: 212/582-3909
Description: Serves independent telecommunications consultants.
Year Founded: 1976
Individual Members: 226   Corporate Members: 87
Executive Officers: Bruce Nolin, President; John Barry, Senior Vice President
Interest Groups: Vendor Advisory Council
Publications: STC Lines newsletter (periodically), Membership Directory (quarterly)
Conferences: Conferences (87:New Orleans May 15-18, 88:Anaheim May 13-16, 88:Boston Oct 21-24)
Awards: Telecom Person of the Decade (One time award April 86)

Surface Mount Technology Association

Acronym: SMTA

P.O. Box 1811

Los Gatos, CA 95031

Phone: 408/354-9275

Description: Focuses on issues of importance to users of surface mount technology providing pertinent information to companies and individuals concerned with education and prod. advancement.

Year Founded: 1985

Individual Members: 381   Corporate Members: 280

Executive Officers: Linda West, Executive Director; Norb Socolowski, President

Interest Groups: Various committees and sub-committees

Publications: SMTA newsletter (monthly), SMTA Membership Directory (annually), SMTA Referral Directory (annually)

Conferences: General Meeting, International Meeting

Tele-Communications Association

Acronym: TCA

1515 W Cameron, Ste B140

West Covina, CA 91790

Phone: 818/960-1838

Telex: 818-9607237

Description: Develops a close association with other telecommunication professionals to share common problems, ideas, & solutions through educational programs, committees, & conferences.

Year Founded: 1961

Individual Members: 2500

Publications: Tele-Pro Journal (monthly)

Conferences: Annual conference (87:San Diego Sept 28-Oct 2, 88:San Diego Sept 26-Oct 1, 89:Sept 25-30)

Awards: Prestigious Service Award (annually)

Women in Information Processing
Acronym: WIP
Lock Box 39173
Washington, DC 20016
Phone: 202/328-6161
Description: Provides network for careerists in the fields of information processing, computers, office automation, MIS, telecom, artificial intelligence and all related disciplines.
Year Founded: 1979
Individual Members: 5000   Corporate Members: 2
Interest Groups: Various local chapters
Publications: FORUMNET newsletter (quarterly)
Conferences: Advance Annual Conferences in Washington DC
Awards: Outstanding Women of the Year

TRADE ASSOCIATIONS

ADAPSO (Computer Software and Services Industries Assn)
Acronym: ADAPSO
1300 North 17th St., Ste 300
Arlington, VA 22209
Phone: 703/522-5055
Telex: 4993994
Description: Trade assn for software & services firms providing members with programs in research, statistics, govt relations, joint purchasing, legal support, PR, int'l marketing and mgmt.
Year Founded: 1961
Corporate Members: 828
Executive Officers: George F. Raymond, Chairman; Jerome L. Dreyer, President
Interest Groups: Competitive Practices, Education and Information Services,Government Relations, and Public Communications/Image
Publications: Three monthly newsletters (DATA, UPDATE & Publicity Opp),
Membership Directory (annually) and several survey reports.
Conferences: Management Conference (87:Colorado Springs, Sept 27-30)

American Electronics Association
Acronym: AEA
2670 Hanover St., P.O. Box 10045
Palo Alto, CA 94303
Phone: 415/857-9300
Description: Serves and represents the nation's electronics industry.
AEA is the nation's largest electronics trade group.
Year Founded: 1943
Corporate Members: 2700
Executive Officers: J. Richard Iverson, President & CEO
Publications: UPDATE newspaper (monthly), Membership Directory (annually), Annual Report
Awards: Medal of Achievement, presented annually
Foreign Offices: Nanbu Bldg. 3rd fl, 3-3 Kioicho, Chiyoda-ku, Tokyo 102, JAP

American Federation of Info Processing Societies
Acronym: AFIPS
1899 Preston White Drive
Reston, VA 22091
Phone: 703/620-8900
Telex: 710-833-9037
Description: Acts in behalf of member societies in carrying out programs designed to advance the information processing profession. American rep to Int'l Fed of Info Processing (IFIP).
Year Founded: 1961
Corporate Members: 11 societies
Executive Officers: Egils Milbergs, Executive Director
Publications: Annals of the History of Computing (quarterly), AFIPS Press Pubs Catalog, proceedings, reports
Conferences: Annual NCC (87: Chicago, June 15-18)
Awards: Annually 5 awards

Association of Better Computer Dealers
Acronym: ABCD
8725 W Higgins Rd., Ste 430
Chicago, IL 60631
Phone: 312/693-2223
Description: Promotes and encourages professionalism and business ethics in microcomputer industry.
Year Founded: 1982
Corporate Members: 190
Executive Officers: Bernard F. Whalen, Executive Vice President
Publications: A Better Channel (monthly)
Conferences: Annual Conference
Awards: Annual Advertising and Editorial Achievement Awards

Association of Computer Retailers
Acronym: ACR
107 S Main St., Ste 202
Chelsea, MI 48118
Phone: 313/475-1378
Description: Provides computer & software resellers benefits members could not obtain singly.
Year Founded: 1983
Corporate Members: 200
Executive Officers: Patrice Johnson, President
Publications: Hardcopy (quarterly), Directory of Members (annually)
Conferences: Annual Conference during COMDEX/Fall
Awards: Member of Merit, awarded quarterly

Association of Information and Dissemination Ctrs

Acronym: ASIDIC

P.O. Box 8105

Athens, GA 30603

Phone: 404/542-3106

Description: Fosters, encourages, and improves research, development, production, processing, storage, retrieval, dissemination, and use of machine-readable information and data.

Year Founded: 1968

Corporate Members: 113

Executive Officers: Marjorie Hlava, President

Publications: Newsletter (semi-annually)

Conferences: Member conference twice a year (spring and fall)

Computer Aided Manufacturing-International, Inc.

Acronym: CAM-I, INC

611 Ryan Plaza Dr., Ste 1107

Arlington, TX 76011

Phone: 817/860-1654

Telex: 910-890-5127CAMIARTN

Description: Conducts R&D in areas of computer-aided manufacturing.

Year Founded: 1975

Corporate Members: 78

Executive Officers: William A. Carter, President; James Brimson, Vice President of Business Development

Publications: NewsAlert newsletter (monthly)

Conferences: Annual Meeting and Technical Conference (87: Phoenix, Oct)

Foreign Offices: Newfoundland House, Poole Quay, Poole, Dorset, BH15 1HJ, UK

Computer Dealers and Lessors Associations, Inc.
Acronym: CDLA
1212 Potomac St., NW
Washington, DC 20007
Phone: 202/333-0102
Description: Ethics-oriented trade assn for firms providing savings/service to customers who
lease/purchase dp equipment.
Year Founded: 1981
Corporate Members: 277
Executive Officers: James F. Benton, Executive Director; Harry E. Goetzmann, Jr, President
Interest Groups: Various committees: Industry Practices, IBM Relations, FASB Task Force,
CDLA/NET, etc.
Publications: Printout, newsletter (quarterly), Membership Directory (annually)
Conferences: Two meetings a year (spring and fall), Regional forums (87:Chicago-Jan 22, New
York-Jan 29)
Foreign Offices: Canada, Japan, South Africa, and Switzerland

Computer and Business Equipment Manufacturers Assoc.
Acronym: CBEMA
311 First St., NW, Ste 500
Washington, DC 20001
Phone: 202/737-8888
Telex: 270-0995
Description: Identifies and resolves issues of importance to the industry; supports the development of
industry standards.
Year Founded: 1916
Corporate Members: 35
Executive Officers: Vico E. Henriques, President; Oliver R. Smoot, Executive Vice President
Publications: Industry statistical reports (periodically)
Conferences: Annual meeting

Computer and Communications Industry Association
Acronym: CCIA
1500 Wilson Boulevard, Ste 512
Arlington, VA 22209
Phone: 703/524-1360
Description: Trade assn which participates in national policy debates on issues which determine the
environment in which member companies compete.
Year Founded: 1972
Corporate Members: 60
Executive Officers: A. G. W. Biddle, President
Conferences: Three general board meetings (annually), Workshops and conferences (periodically)

Electronic Industries Association
Acronym: EIA
2001 I St., NW
Washington, DC 20006
Phone: 202/457-4900
Telex: 710-822-0148 EIA WSH
Description: Represents companies involved in manufacturing electronic components, parts, systems, and equipment for communications, industry, government, & consumer end uses.
Year Founded: 1924
Corporate Members: 1000
Executive Officers: Bruce Carswell, Chairman of the Board; Peter F. McCloskey, President
Publications: Executive Report newsletter, Trade Directory and Membership List (annually), Electronic Mkt Trends, Electronic Data Book
Conferences: Spring Conf-Washington, DC (88:Apr, 89:March, 90:March) Oct Conf (87:LA, 88:San Fran, 89:LA, 90:San Diego)
Awards: Annual Medal of Honor, Chairman's Award, & Service Awards

Highway Engineering Exchange Program
Acronym: HEEP
706 S 17th Ave., %Ellwood Neiman
Phoenix, AZ 85007
Phone: 602/255-7300
Description: Promotes exchange of computer systems and concepts among its membership in the fields of civil engineering, transportation and management.
Year Founded: 1956
Corporate Members: 300
Executive Officers: Ellwood C. Neiman, President; Norman H. Baker, Vice President
Interest Groups: Task Groups
Publications: Newsletter (periodically)
Conferences: International Meeting (87:Des Moines, IA, 88:Atlanta, GA) Area Meetings
Awards: Ken Close Memorial Award
Foreign Offices: Canada

Independent Computer Consultants Association
Acronym: ICCA
P.O. Box 27412
St. Louis, MO 63130
Phone: 314/997-4633
Telex: 1-800-GET-ICCA
Description: Establishes a national network of computer consultants who exchange ideas and concepts.
Year Founded: 1976
Corporate Members: 1800
Executive Officers: John M. Christensen, Executive Director; Jeff Sachs, President
Interest Groups: Various Committees: Government Relations, Vendor Advisory Group. Local, regional and national activities
Publications: The Independent newsletter (bimonthly), Position papers (periodically)
Conferences: National Conference (87:San Fran., 88:Cleveland), Regional and local chapter meetings

Information Industry Association
Acronym: IIA
555 New Jersey Ave., NW
Washington, DC 20001
Phone: 202/639-8262
Description: Represents companies which create, store, manage, or distribute information electronically or through traditional publishing means.
Year Founded: 1969
Corporate Members: 450
Executive Officers: Paul Zurkowski, President; Kenneth Allen, Vice President, Government relations
Publications: Information Times newspaper (monthly), Information Times Bulletin (bimonthly), Proceedings and other pubs
Conferences: Fall Annual Convention (87:Chicago, 88:Boston, 89:New York, 90:San Fran), May Midyear (87:Las Vegas, 88:Boston, 89:NY)
Awards: Hall of Fame and IMMYs (IIA Marketing Awards)

International Communications Association

Acronym: ICA

12750 Merit Drive, Ste 710, LB-89

Dallas, Tx 75251

Phone: 214/233-3889

Description: Provides comprehensive, up-to-the-minute source of information and education in fields of voice, data and image communications.

Year Founded: 1948

Corporate Members: 560

Executive Officers: Stephen M. Christie, Executive Director; M. Duane Heidel, President

Interest Groups: Various committees: Public policy, Industry Research and Info., Academic Development, and etc.

Publications: Communique' magazine (monthly), newsletters (monthly), special reports (periodically)

Conferences: Annual Telecom, Annual ICA Conference & Exposition, various seminars throughout the country

Awards: Annual Citation of Merit, other awards, grants & scholarship

International Federation for Information Processing

Acronym: IFIP

3, Rue Du Marche'

CH 1204 Geneva, Switzerland

Phone: 41(22)282649

Telex: 428-472 IFIP CH

Description: Establishes a multinational forum promoting information science and technology through research, development, communication, and dissemination of information.

Year Founded: 1960

Corporate Members: 45

Executive Officers: A. W. Goldsworthy, President; Bl. Sendov, Vice President

Interest Groups: International Medical Informatics Assoc (IMIA), Working groups (WG) and other technical committees

Publications: IFIP Newsletter (quarterly), conference proceedings, journals (periodically)

Conferences: World Computer Congress, World Congress on Medical Informatics, various conferences and seminars

Awards: Silver Core award

North American Telecommunications Association

Acronym: NATA
2000 M St., NW, Ste 550
Washington, DC 20036
Phone: 202/296-9800
Description: Protects and expands competitive markets (domestic/foreign) for telecom equipment companies. Also provides services to members that give a competitive edge in those markets.
Corporate Members: 650
Executive Officers: Edward Spievack, President; Richard Long, Chairman of the Board
Publications: NATA Telecom. Sourcebook directory & buyers guide (annually), Wash. Update & Mkt. Update newsletters (bimonthly), others
Conferences: Annual NATA Conference (87:Dallas Dec 1-4)

Public Interest Computer Association

Acronym: PICA
2001 O Street NW
Washington, DC 20036
Phone: 202/775-1588
Description: Provides technical, educational, and resource assistance to nonprofit firms in the management and use of microcomputers.
Year Founded: 1984
Corporate Members: 150NFP
Executive Officers: Denise A. Vesuvio, Executive Director
Publications: PICA newsletter (monthly), PICA Resource Notebook (bimonthly)

Semiconductor Industry Association

Acronym: SIA
4320 Stevens Creek Blvd., Ste 275
San Jose, CA 95129
Phone: 408/246-1181
Telex: 408-246-3962
Description: Represents U.S.-based semiconductor manufacturers.
Year Founded: 1977
Corporate Members: 45
Executive Officers: Andrew A. Procassini, President; Warren E. Davis, Vice President
Interest Groups: Various committees: Public Policy, Law, Trade Stats., OSHE, OHC, FABS, & Environmental
Publications: SIA Yearbook/Dir. (biannual), SIA Circuit newsletter (quarterly), SIA Stat. Review (quarterly), WSTS, & others
Conferences: Various conferences

Society for Computer Applications in Eng, Plan, & Arch.

Acronym: CEPA

15713 Crabbs Branch Way

Rockville, MD 20855

Phone: 301/926-7070

Description: Furthers the effective use of computers in the fields of engineering, architecture, and planning.

Year Founded: 1965

Corporate Members: 350

Executive Officers: Patricia C. Johnson, Executive Director; Stephen M. Hartley, P.E., President

Interest Groups: Various committees: Architectural, Civil/Survey, Graphics/CAD, Hardware, Mech./Environ, Structural

Publications: CEPA Newsletter (quarterly), Conference proceedings (semiannually)

Conferences: Spring Conference (87:San Francisco), Fall Conference

Software Publishers Association

Acronym: SPA

1111 19th St NW, Ste 1200

Washington, DC 20036

Phone: 203/452-1600

Description: Provides a forum for software publishing firms who produce, release, develop or license microcomputer software for business, home entertainment, ed and vertical markets.

Year Founded: 1984

Corporate Members: 150

Executive Officers: Kenneth A. Wasch, Executive Director; Douglas G. Carlston, President

Interest Groups: Developers SIG, Distributors SIG

Publications: SPA News newsletter (monthly)

Conferences: Annual meeting, Spring Symposium

Awards: Excellence in Software

US Telecommunications Suppliers Association
Acronym: USTSA
333 N Michigan Ave., Ste 1618
Chicago, IL 60601
Phone: 312/782-8597
Telex: 595236USTSACGO
Description: Association for manufacturer and supplier companies that provide materials, products, systems, and distribution services to the telecommunications industry.
Year Founded: 1979
Corporate Members: 600
Executive Officers: Donald R. Pollock, Managing Director; Michael J. Birck, President
Interest Groups: Various committees
Publications: Industry Pulse (monthly), Product Locator (annually)
Conferences: Telecom (87:Geneva Oct 20-27), Showcase (88:Houston Jan 31-Feb 2, 88:Atlanta May 24-26, 89:New Orleans, Anaheim)

USE, Inc
Box 461
Bladensburg, MD 20710
Phone: 301/699-9336
Description: Exchanges technical information with member corporations.
Year Founded: 1956
Corporate Members: 700
Interest Groups: Twenty chapters
Publications: Newsletter (monthly), Conference Proceedings (biannually)
Conferences: Two conferences a year

World Computer Graphics Association
Acronym: WCGA
2033 M. St, NW, Ste 399
Washington, DC 20036
Phone: 202/775-9556
Telex: 361743 WORLDCOMPUTER
Description: Promotes the growth and serves the needs of the global computer graphics community; works with representatives from countries around the world on conf, exhibits, & seminars.
Year Founded: 1981
Corporate Members: 13
Executive Officers: Caby C. Smith, President and Executive Director; Ronald Crellin, Vice President
Publications: UPDATE newsletter (periodically), conference proceedings
Conferences: CAT (87:Stuttgart, Ger June 2-5)
Foreign Offices: WCGA, Europe, Xantener Strasse 22, D-1000 Berlin, Germany

World Teleport Association
Acronym: WTA
One World Trade Center, 63 SW
New York, NY 10048
Phone: 212/466-4758
Telex: 424747PANYNJ
Description: Promotes the development of teleports and the advancement of telecommunications.
Year Founded: 1985
Corporate Members: 65
Executive Officers: Guy F. Tozzoli, President; Tadayoshi Yamada, Vice President
Interest Groups: Various regional and general committees
Publications: General Assembly Procedures (annually), Membership Directory (annually), newsletter (periodically)
Conferences: WTA General Assembly (87:May, 88:Metz, Fr May, 89:Osaka, Japan Oct)
Foreign Offices: Brazil, France, It, Japan, Korea, Nether., Nigeria, Port.,UK

BOOK CLUBS

In this section COMPUTER INDUSTRY ALMANAC lists information on 16 book clubs which focus primarily on computer industry-related selections. The clubs are listed alphabetically by name and describe the types of books offered. Other information included is address, telephone, number of bulletins issued, minimum purchase required, and reply cards.

BYTE Book Club
McGraw-Hill Book Clubs
P.O. Box 582
Hightstown, NJ 08520
Phone: 212/997-4128
Subjects: Books on programming languages, operating systems, software and hardware, systems design, system analysis, data communications.
Bulletins per year: 14 to 16
Reply/Refusal Card: Yes
Minimum Purchase: Three in first year
Returns: Yes within 10 days

Computer Book Club
P.O. Box 80
Blue Ridge Summit, PA 17214
Phone: 800/233-1128
Subjects: Books on programming techniques and languages, hardware, software, peripherals, operating systems, computer games, computer graphics, how-to computer guides.
Bulletins per year: 13
Reply/Refusal Card: Yes
Minimum Purchase: Four in first year
Returns: Yes within 10 days

Data Processing Book Service
Prentice-Hall
P.O. Box 451
West Nyack, NY 10994
Phone: 201/592-2477
Subjects: Books on theoretical, high-end, practical software development & engineering, cutting-edge applications of hw & sw. For computer professionals at the top end of the market.
Bulletins per year: 13
Reply/Refusal Card: Yes
Minimum Purchase: After 1st, 3 bks/yr
Returns: Yes

Electronics and Control Engineers' Book Club
McGraw-Hill Book Clubs, Inc.
P.O. Box 582
Hightstown, NJ 08520
Phone: 212/512-2000
Subjects: Books on electronic circuits, digital/analog design, microprocessors, circuit analysis & design, digital filters, op amp design, AI, control system design, trouble shooting, antennae engineering.
Bulletins per year: 12 to 14
Reply/Refusal Card: Yes
Minimum Purchase: Three in first year
Returns: Yes within 10 days

Electronics Book Club
Prentice-Hall Book Clubs, Inc.
Route 9W
Englewood Cliffs, NJ 07632
Phone: 201/592-2477
Subjects: Books on trouble shooting, repairing of equipment, intro to new electronic technologies, & illustrated guides to building electronic equipment. For the electronic & skilled hobbyist.
Bulletins per year: 15
Reply/Refusal Card: Yes
Minimum Purchase: Four in first year
Returns: Yes within 10 days

Electronics Book Club
TAB Books Inc.
P.O. Box 10
Blue Ridge Summit, PA 17214
Phone: 717/794-2191
Subjects: Books on practical trouble shooting and repair tips, time and money saving advice, state-of-the-art tech, basic electronics, professional reference, build-it-yourself projects. For hobbyists & professionals.
Bulletins per year: 14
Reply/Refusal Card: Yes
Minimum Purchase: Five in first year
Returns: Yes within 10 days

Electronics Engineers and Designers Book Club
Prentice-Hall Book Clubs, Inc.
Route 9W
Englewood Cliffs, NJ 07632
Phone: 201/592-2477
Subjects: Books on devices, systems design, bit-slice microprocessors, circuitry, opto electronics, linear control, feed back, & analog/digital crossovers.
Bulletins per year: 15
Reply/Refusal Card: Yes
Minimum Purchase: Four in first year
Returns: Yes within 10 days

Library of Computer and Information Sciences
Division of MacMillan Book Clubs, Inc.
Front and Brown Streets
Riverside, NJ 08370
Phone: 212/702-2000
Subjects: Books on large computer systems: systems design, software development, assembler programming, 3rd & 4th generation languages, operating systems, data base (mgmt/design), AI/expert sys, computer sci theory, microcomputing.
Bulletins per year: 16
Reply/Refusal Card: Yes
Minimum Purchase: Three in first year
Returns: Yes within 10 days

Personal Computer Book Club
Prentice-Hall Book Clubs
Route 9W
Englewood Cliffs, NJ 07632
Phone: 201/592-2477
Subjects: Books on introduction to PCs, computer languages, computer systems, guides to computer selections, word processing, data bases, spreadsheets and design of the modern computerized office. For the micro user.
Bulletins per year: 15
Reply/Refusal Card: Yes
Minimum Purchase: Four in first year
Returns: Yes within 10 days

Small Computer Book Club
MacMillan Book Clubs, Inc.
Front and Brown Streets
Riverside, NJ 08370
Phone: 212/702-2000
Subjects: Books on microcomputers (IBM PC, Apple, including Macintosh, Commodore 64 & 128, CP/M machines), users guides, programming aids, application-specific handbooks. For the serious micro user.
Bulletins per year: 16
Reply/Refusal Card: Yes
Minimum Purchase: Three in first year
Returns: Yes within 10 days

GOVERNMENT AGENCIES

In this section COMPUTER INDUSTRY ALMANAC lists U.S. government agencies that affect the computer industry. Some of these agencies support and promote research, some monitor and set standards, some publish and distribute government-sponsored research reports, and others advise the President on technological matters. Agencies are listed alphabetically by name and also give address, contact, year founded, and a brief description.

Advanced Research Projects Agency (Darpa)
Department of Defense
1400 Wilson Blvd.
Arlington, VA 22209
Phone: 202/694-3007
Description: Manages high-risk, high-payoff basic research and applied technology programs; pursues revolutionary technology developments that minimize the possibility of technological surprise (e.g. funds AI & computer networking research).
Founded: 1958
Contact: Robert C. Duncan, Director; Dr. James A. Tegnelia, Deputy Director

Federal Communications Commission
1919 M Street N.W.
Washington, DC 20554
Phone: 202/632-7000
Description: Regulates emissions originating from the operation of devices utilizing digital circuitry in order to minimize the potential of interference to television and radio communications.
Founded: 1934
Contact: Mark S. Fowler, Chairman of Commission; Patti Grace Smith, Chief of Consumer Office

National Bureau of Standards
Department of Commerce
Route I-270 & Quince Orchard Rd.
Gaithersburg, MD 20899
Phone: 301/975-2000
Description: Conducts research to provide groundwork for the nation's physical measurement system as well as scientific & technological services for industry & govt; participates in development of voluntary industry standards for computer & network technology.
Founded: 1901
Contact: Ernest Ambler, Director

National Research Council

National Academy of Science

2101 Constitution Ave N.W.

Washington, DC 20148

Phone: 202/334-2000

Description: Studies research & development applications of new technologies (telecommunications, information and computing). Advises govt & industry on how to stop the erosion of U.S. leadership in computer science & technology.

Founded: 1968

Contact: Frank Press, Director; Robert White, President National Academy of Engineering

National Science Foundation

1800 G Street N.W.

Washington, DC 20550

Phone: 202/357-9859

Description: Promotes the progress of science and engineering through the support of research and education programs.

Founded: 1950

Contact: Erich Bloch, Director; Roland W. Schmitt, Chairman; Charles E. Hess, Vice Chairman

National Security Agency/Central Security Service

Department of Defense

Ft. George G. Mead, MD 20755

Phone: 301/688-6311

Description: Coordinates and performs highly specialized technical functions to protect U.S. communications (communications security, computer security).

Founded: 1952

Contact: Lt. Gen. William E. Odum, Director; Charles R. Lord, Deputy Director

National Technical Information Service (NTIS)

Department of Commerce

Springfield, VA 22161

Phone: 202/487-4600

Description: Acts as the central source for the public sale of U.S. govt-sponsored research, development, and engineering reports. Is developing availability of Federal computer software, programs, and data files.

Founded: 1902

Contact: Dr. Joseph F. Caponio, Director; Dr. Joseph E. Park, Deputy Director

National Telecommunications & Info Admn (NTIA)
Department of Commerce
14th & Constitution NW, Rm 4890
Washington, DC 20230
Phone: 202/377-1832
Description: Supports development and growth of telecommunications, information, and related industries.
Founded: 1978
Contact: Alfred Sikes, Assistant Secretary for Communications & Info; Charles Schott, Deputy Asst Secy for Communications & Info

Office of Science & Technology Policy
Exec Office of the President
Washington, DC 20506
Phone: 202/395-4692
Description: Examines the current status of science & technology in U.S.; gives advice to and makes recommendations to the President; works with the Federal Coordination Council on Sci & Eng Tech (studies supercomputers, netwks).
Founded: 1976
Contact: Jerry D. Jennings, Executive Director; Bernadine H. Bulkley, Deputy Director; John P. McTague, Deputy Director

Office of Technology Assessment
Department of Congress
600 Pennsylvania Ave S.E.
Washington, DC 20510
Phone: 202/224-8713
Description: Identifies existing or future impacts of technology or technological problems and ascertains cause & effect relationships.
Founded: 1974
Contact: John H. Gibbons, Director; Sue Bachtel, Executive Assistant to Director

Patent & Trademark Office (PTO)
Department of Commerce
Office of Public Affairs
Washington, DC 20231
Phone: 202/557-3158
Description: Examines and issues patents, registers trademarks, and represents the U.S. in international efforts to cooperate on patent & trademark policy.
Contact: Donald J. Quigg, Commissioner

Small Business Administration (SBA)
1441 L Street N.W., Room 500
Washington, DC 20416
Phone: 202/653-6600
Description: Provides small firms participation in NSF-sponsored research enabling them to propose long-term, high-risk creative ideas and develops working arrangements with large industries, government and educational institutions.
Founded: 1953
Contact: Richard J. Shane, Assistant Administrator; Charles L. Heatherly, Deputy Administrator; Linda Rule, Chief of Staff

STANDARDS ORGANIZATIONS

In this section COMPUTER INDUSTRY ALMANAC lists 27 major worldwide standards organizations that either encourage, foster, and promote standards activities or establish, administrate, and monitor standards. The nature of each organization's standards activity is described. Each entry also gives acronym, address, contact, and year founded.

American National Standards Institute (ANSI)
1430 Broadway St.
New York, NY 10018
Phone: 212/354-3300
Telex: 424296 ANSIUI
Description: Functions as the body that coordinates the activities of the standards-development organizations in the U.S. and approves documents as American National Standards.
Year Founded: 1918
Contact: Donald L. Peyton, President

Canadian Standards Association (CSA)
178 Rexdale Blvd
Rexdale, Ontario, CAN M9W1R9
Phone: 416/747-4363
Description: Consists of two steering committees: telecommunications & information purchasing systems. Focuses on international standards, safety standards & Canadian telecom standards.
Year Founded: 1919
Contact: John Kean, President

Corporation for Open Systems (COS)
8619 Westwood Center Dr, Ste 700
Vienna, VA 22180
Phone: 703/848-2100
Telex: 8484572
Description: Develops/tests industry stnrds for computer communications. Fosters industry acceptance of communications stnrds and develops testing services to assure product performance.
Year Founded: 1986
Contact: Lt. General Lincoln D. Faurer, President and CEO

Deutsche Industrie Normal (DIN)
P. O. Box 1107
D-1000 Berlin 30, GER
Description: Oversees all standardization activity in the Federal Republic of Germany (W. Ger.) thru its 113 tech stnrds committees which have issued over 23,600 DIN Stnrds for the mfg, electrical, electronics, & chemical inds.
Year Founded: 1917

Electronic Industries Association (EIA)
2001 Eye Street NW
Washington, DC 20006
Phone: 202/457-4900
Telex: 710-822-0148 EIAWSH
Description: Fosters standards activities relating to home bus, component parts (both passive & active), consumer products, & telecommunications.
Year Founded: 1924
Contact: Bruce Carswell, Chairman of the Board; Peter F. McCloskey, EIA President

European Committee for Electrotechnical Standardization (CENELEC)
rue de Brederode 2, Bte 5
B-1000 Bruxelles, BELG
Phone: 511 79 32
Telex: 26257 Cenlec b
Description: Harmonizes natl electrotech stnrds of member countries. Removes trade barriers from natl conformity to standards in member countries. Members are natl electrotechnical committees in 16 countries.
Year Founded: 1973
Contact: Hans-Karl Tronnier

European Committee for Standardization (CEN)
rue de Brederode 2, Bte 5
B-1000 Bruxelles, BELG
Phone: 513 55 64
Telex: 26257 Cenlec b
Description: Develops tech, scientific, and economic procedures for European standardization activities by harmonizing natl stnrds of member countries and by implementing intl stnrds. Members are natl standards organizations in 16 countries.
Year Founded: 1961
Contact: M. Vardakas

Federal Communications Commission (FCC)
1919 M Street NW
Washington, DC 20554
Phone: 202/632-7000
Telex: 710-822-0160
Description: Issues technical standards to minimize interference to radio and television communication services from the use of computers and similar electronic devices.
Year Founded: 1934
Contact: Thomas P. Stanley, Chief Engineer; Frank Rose, Chief of Technical Standards Branch

Institute of Electrical & Electronic Engineers (IEEE)
345 East 47th St.
New York, NY 10017
Phone: 212/705-7900
Description: Develops & publishes stnrds in electrical engineering & electronics (measuremt/test methods, safety, temperature limits, definitions/terminology, application guides, recommended practices).
Year Founded: 1884
Contact: Eric Herz, Exec Director & General Manager; Sava Sherr, Staff Director of Standards

International Electrotechnical Commission (IEC)
3, rue de Varembe
CH-1211 Geneva 20, SWI
Phone: 0114122340150
Telex: 28872CEIEC CH
Description: Provides intl stnrds for the world's electrical & electronics industries thru tech committees that promote, e.g., computer equip stnrds (a joint effort with ISO) and computer components. Members are committees in 42 countries.
Year Founded: 1906
Contact: Roy McDowell, President; Clifton J. Stanford, Secy General

International Standards Organization (ISO)
1 rue de Varembe
CH-1211 Geneva 20, SWI
Phone: 01141341240
Description: Acts as the specified intl agency for standardization. Promotes stnrds to facilitate intl exchange of goods/services & to develop coop in intellectual, scientific, tech, & economic activities. Members are natl stnrds bodies in 89 countries.
Year Founded: 1947
Contact: Lawrence D. Eicher, Secretary General; Christian J. Favre, Asst Secretary General

International Telecommunications Union
Place des Nations
CH-1211 Geneva 20, SWI
Phone: 0114122995111
Description: Produces telecommunications standards and works to make telecommunications systems compatible around the world. Is an international telecom organization affiliated with the United Nations.
Year Founded: 1865
Contact: Richard E. Butler, Secretary General; Jean Jipguep, Deputy Secretary General

National Bureau of Standards (NBS)
Route I-290 & Quince Orchard Rd
Gaithersburg, MD 20899
Phone: 301/921-1000
Telex: 197674 NBSUT
Description: Develops the standards, measurement techniques, reference data, test methods, &
calibration services that help ensure national & international measurement capability &
compatibility.
Year Founded: 1901
Contact: Dr. Ernest Ambler, Director; James H. Burrows, Director, Institute for Comptr Sci & Tech

Standards Council of Canada (SCC)
2000 Argentia, Suite 2-401
Mississauga, Ontario, CAN L5N1V8
Phone: 416/826-8110
Telex: 0697719
Description: Works closely with Canadian standards organizations to ensure the availability of
national standards that will respond to the needs of industry. Furthers international standards work.
Year Founded: 1970
Contact: Michael McKerrow, Director; Charles Ender, Manager

Underwriters Laboratories (UL)
333 Pfingsten Road
Northbrook, IL 60062
Phone: 312/272-8800
Telex: 201227
Description: Sets UL requirements for product safety that are harmonized with nationally and
internationally recognized installation codes & standards and that are distributed & reviewed in
accordance with UL & ANSI procedures.
Year Founded: 1894
Contact: Jack Bono, President; Robert J. Hauth, Chairman of the Board

USERS GROUPS

In this section COMPUTER INDUSTRY ALMANAC lists 35 U.S. users groups alphabetically by name providing acronym, address, number of corporate and/or individual members, conferences, executive officers, foreign offices, and a brief description. These organizations are national users groups; the hundreds of local users groups are beyond the scope of this publication.

Accountants Computer Users Technical Exchange
Acronym: ACUTE, INC
6081 East 82nd St., Ste 110
Indianapolis, IN 46250
Phone: 317/845-8702
Description: Provides members with the opportunity to further the development of electronic data processing through mutual education and offers exchange of ideas through pubs & conf.
Year Founded: 1969
Corporate Members: 700
Executive Officers: Robert A. Woods, CPA, Executive Director; Dale A. Cherry, CPA, President
Publications: The Account newsletter (bimonthly)
Conferences: Semiannual Conferences May and October

Amdahl Users Group
Acronym: AUG
P.O. Box 591, %Norm Laefer
Tulsa, OK 74102
Phone: 918/664-9355
Description: Researches, gathers, exchanges, and distributes facts and ideas relating to Amdahl products and services. Focuses only on data processing and use of Andahl products.
Year Founded: 1976
Corporate Members: 400
Executive Officers: Norm Laefer, President; George Frickle, Vice President
Conferences: Spring Conference each June, Fall Conference each December
Foreign Offices: Australia, Europe

Association of Data Communications Users, Inc
Acronym: ADCU
P.O. Box 20163
Bloomington, MN 55420
Phone: 612/881-6803
Description: Disseminates information and provides problem-solving conferences.
Year Founded: 1976
Individual Members: 300   Corporate Members: 225
Executive Officers: August H. Blegen, Executive Director
Publications: newsletter (bimonthly)
Conferences: Conferences (87:Atlantic City, NJ June 29-July 1)

Boston Computer Society
Acronym: BSC
One Center Plaza
Boston, MA 02108
Phone: 617/367-8080
Description: Provides information and educational services to personal computer users in 50 states and 40 countries.
Individual Members: 20,000   Corporate Members: 150
Executive Officers: Mary E. McCann, Executive Director; Jonathan Rotenberg, President
Interest Groups: 40 SIG Groups
Publications: Computer Update magazine (bimonthly), Calendar (monthly), BCS Buying Guide directory (semiannual), and others
Conferences: 1000 meetings, events and educational programs throughout six New England states; Annual Meeting each June

COMMON: An IBM Computer Users Group
Acronym: COMMON
435 N Michigan Ave., Ste 1717
Chicago, Il 60611
Phone: 312/644-0828   Telex: 701633
Description: Provides IBM computer users group members information and educational opportunities through publications, meetings and etc.
Year Founded: 1960
Individual Members: 4009
Executive Officers: David G. Lister, Executive Director; David M. Pomerance, President
Interest Groups: Several Management Division Chairmen
Publications: CAST publication (10 times a year)
Conferences: Biannual Meetings (87:Reno Apr 8-12, 87:Chicago Oct 17-21, 88:Diplomat, FL Apr 24-29, 88:Toronto Oct 23-27, 89:Dallas)

Complete Applied Data Research Environment
Acronym: CADRE
Route 206 and Orchard Rd., CN-8
Princeton, NJ 08540
Phone: 201/874-9000
Description: Provides ADR users group members information exchange, education, and discussion groups through annual meetings and conferences.
Year Founded: 1980
Individual Members: 2000
Executive Officers: Allen Haggar, ADR, Director of Client Relations; Bob Brandt, President (1987)
Interest Groups: Several Product Committee Chairpersons
Conferences: Annual Conferences (87:Las Vegas, 88:Atlanta, 89:Dallas, 90:New Orleans)

Concurrent Users Group
Acronym: CONUG
P.O. Box 734
Marina, CA 93933
Phone: 408/384-5575
Description: Provides news, technical information, and support for users of any of Digital Research's Concurrent DOS products.
Year Founded: 1985
Individual Members: 50   Corporate Members: 5
Executive Officers: Garry M. Silvey, President
Publications: Resource newsletter (monthly), CONG software library
Foreign Offices: Australia, Belgium, UK, Israel, Japan, Malaysia, Nor, Ger

Cooperating Users of Burroughs Equipment
Acronym: CUBE
P.O. Box 33053
Detroit, MI 48232
Phone: 313/972-9260
Description: Provides a forum where users may exchange information among themselves and with the manufacturer relevant to the use of electronics data processing systems mfg by Burroughs Corp.
Year Founded: 1962
Individual Members: 3300
Executive Officers: Thomas S. Grier, Executive Secretary; Julia Branham, President (1986)
Interest Groups: Common Interest Groups (EDP mgmt, financial industry); Systems-related Subgroups (lrg systems, sml bus systems)
Publications: Conference report (semiannually)
Conferences: Semiannual Conferences (87:Anaheim April, 87:New Orleans Nov, 88:San Diego April, 88:Chicago Oct)

Digital Equipment Computer Users Society
Acronym: DECUS
219 Boston Post Road, BP02
Marlboro, MA 01752
Phone: 617/480-3290
Description: Promotes the exchange of information-processing-related information among users of Digital Equipment Corp products.
Year Founded: 1961
Individual Members: 90,000
Executive Officers: Andrew Powderly, Executive Director; C. W. Goldsmith, President
Interest Groups: 24 SIG groups coordinated by a SIG Council
Publications: DECUSCOPE magazine (quarterly), SIGs newsletter (monthly), Membership Handbook (annually), others periodically
Conferences: DECUS Annual Conference (87:Nashville Apr 27-May 1, 87:Anaheim Dec 7-11)
Awards: Seven annual awards each October
Foreign Offices: DECUS Europe, Geneva, Switzerland

Federation of NCR User Groups
Acronym: FNUG
Mail Station USG-1
Dayton, OH 45479
Phone: 513/445-3131   Telex: 469665
Description: Provides education for the NCR computer user.
Year Founded: 1970
Corporate Members: 33
Executive Officers: Rasma Thomas, Chairman; Rod McComas, Vice Chairman
Publications: SITEBYTES newsletter (quarterly)
Conferences: NUCON Conf (87:Chicago Apr 12-15, 88:Nashville Apr 24-27, 89:Orlando Apr 23-26, 90:Reno 91:New Orleans 92:Atlanta)

FOG
Acronym: FOG
P.O. Box 3474
Daly City, CA 94015
Phone: 415/755-2000
Description: Provides exchange of information for users of CP/M and MS-DOS.
Year Founded: 1981
Individual Members: 15,000
Executive Officers: Gales P. Rhoades, Executive Director; Ron Forsythe, President (1986-87)
Publications: FOGHORN CP/M publication (monthly), FOGLIGHT MS-DOS (monthly)

GUIDE International Corporation
Acronym: GUIDE
111 E Wacker Dr., Ste 600
Chicago, IL 60601
Phone: 312/644-6610   Telex: 254-073
Description: Disseminates information for commercial dp computer users running IBM 4300 and larger systems & exchanges dialogue with IBM.
Year Founded: 1956
Corporate Members: 2800
Executive Officers: John E. Nack, President; Ricky A. Barron, Vice President Divisions
Publications: Annual Report (annually), Proceedings & GUIDE Conference Reports (three times a year), 147 pubs periodically
Conferences: Three conferences per year (87:Boston July 19-24, 87:Atlanta Nov 1-6)
Awards: GUIDE President's Award

Honeywell Large Systems Users Association
Acronym: HLSUA
4000 Town Center, 8th Floor
Southfield, MI 48075
Phone: 313/353-7460   Telex: 247331 AEGIS UR
Description: Provides a forum for Honeywell Large Systems Users for information exchange, education & updates through seminars and publications.
Year Founded: 1965
Corporate Members: 550
Executive Officers: Ronald T. Wong, President; Herbert G. Frazier, Vice President
Interest Groups: Health Care SIG, DTSS SIG
Publications: Update newsletter, Proceedings Publication (semiannually)
Conferences: Conferences semiannually (87:New Orleans Oct)
Foreign Offices: France, Australia

ICES Users Group, Inc.
Acronym: IUG
P.O. Box 8243
Cranston, RI 02920
Phone: 401/885-1688
Description: Fosters the development, exchange and dissemination of information and data
pertaining to the ICES family of computer programs.
Year Founded: 1967
Corporate Members: 425
Executive Officers: F. E. Hajjar, Executive Director; Dr. A.W.M. Kok, President
Publications: ICES Journal (March, July, November)
Conferences: Annual International Conference (87:Munich, 88:Tokyo)
Foreign Offices: Japan, England

International Society of Wang Users
Acronym: ISWU
One Industrial Ave.
Lowell, MA 01851
Phone: 617/967-4322
Description: Promotes information sharing and applications worldwide for Wang users.
Individual Members: 8000
Executive Officers: Evelyn McGuire, Manager; Carrie Frontiero, Membership Coordinator
Publications: TechKnowledge (bimonthly)
Conferences: Annual Conference (87:Oct 18-21)

International Tandem Users' Group
Acronym: ITUG
111 E Wacker Drive, Ste 600
Chicago, IL 60601
Phone: 312/644-6610   Telex: SBA 25-40-73
Description: Advances the effective utilization of Tandem Computers by promoting the free
exchange of information concerning the use of such machines.
Year Founded: 1978
Individual Members: 223   Corporate Members: 531
Executive Officers: Ruth A. White, Executive Secretary; Wilbur Highleyman, President
Publications: Tandem Users' Journal (bimonthly), ITUG Newsletter (bimonthly)
Conferences: Conferences (87:Paris May 5-7, 87:New Orleans Oct 18-22, 88:San Diego Oct 16-18)
Foreign Offices: London, Canada

International Telecommunications Users Group
Acronym: INTUG
Xerox Sq., 052A, %B. Overeynder
Rochester, NY 14644
Phone: 716/423-3414   Telex: 646930
Description: Umbrella organization of telecom users organizations in 13 countries. Promotes telecom user interests at regional and international levels.
Year Founded: 1972
Individual Members: 10 (+30 assoc. mbrs.)
Corporate Members: 13 mbr. user org's.
Executive Officers: George McKendric, Chairman; Peter Smith, Vice Chairman Administration
Interest Groups: Regulatory Affairs
Publications: INTUG News newsletter (quarterly)
Conferences: Three plenary meetings a year in varying member countries, (87:Paris June 25-26, Lausanne, Switz Oct 28-28)
Foreign Offices: Austria, Belgium, France, Japan, Nether., Nor, Switz, & UK

Interpress Implementors Group
Acronym: IPSIG
475 Oakmead Parkway, % Bruce Schatzman
Sunnyvale, CA 94086
Phone: 408/737-4653
Description: Supports implementors of Xerox industry-standard Interpress with a wide range of informative presentations & workshops.
Year Founded: 1986
Individual Members: 50   Corporate Members: 18
Executive Officers: Dennis G. Frahmann, Interpress Marketing Manager
Publications: Courier newsletter (quarterly)
Conferences: Twice yearly

IV League, Inc.
P.O. Box 1403
Canoga Park, CA 91304
Phone: 818/716-1616
Description: Fosters the development, free exchange, and communication of research among the users of data processing software products licensed by Sterling Software's Answer System Div.
Year Founded: 1966
Corporate Members: 2000
Executive Officers: E. Woodward, President; C. Young, Vice President
Interest Groups: System Evaluation Committees for all products (Mark V, Mark IV, Answer/DB)
Publications: Proceedings published (annually)
Conferences: Annual conferences (87:Los Angeles Apr, 88:Orlando April)

Manufacturing Automation Protocol/Tech & Office Protocol

Acronym: MAP/TOP SME

One SME Drive, Box 930

Dearborn, MI 48121

Phone: 313/271-1500   Telex: 297742 SMEUR VIA RCA

Description: Focuses activities on existing and emerging international communication standards and accepted industry practices. Addresses comm intergration in multi-vendor environments.

Year Founded: 1984

Individual Members: 1300

Executive Officers: James Doar, MAP Executive Committee Chair; David Judson, TOP Executive Committee Chair

Interest Groups: Various committees

Publications: MAP/TOP INTERFACE TECHNICAL (quarterly), MAP & TOP Specifications, Product Dir., Meeting Summaries, and other

Conferences: MAP/TOP Users Group Meeting (January/May/September)

Foreign Offices: Australia, Canada, Europe, Japan

MTPUG Pascal/MT User Group

Acronym: MTPUG

P.O. Box 192

Westmont, IL 60559

Phone: 312/986-1550

Description: Shares information about Pascal, User Programs, Reviews.

Year Founded: 1981

Individual Members: 500

Executive Officers: Henry Lucas, Editor

Publications: Newsletter (quarterly)

Foreign Offices: Germany

MUMPS Users' Group
Acronym: MUG
4321 Hartwick Rd., #510
College Park, MD 20740
Phone: 301/779-6555
Description: Provides a forum for the exchange of information and knowledge for MUMPS computer lang users from business, medical professions and academic communities.
Year Founded: 1971
Individual Members: 1224   Corporate Members: 147
Executive Officers: Helmuth Orthner, Executive Director; Glen Steinbach, Chairman of the Board
Interest Groups: Various SIGs: M-Users, Tri-state, Costar, Circumpolar MUMPS, DECUS MUMPS.
Publications: MUG, MUMPS Dir, ANSI Lang. Standard, MUMPS News (quarterly), MUMPS Primer, Programmer's Reference Manual, and others
Conferences: Annual Meeting (87:Atlanta June)

National Computer Association
Acronym: NUG
P.O. Box 7796
San Jose, CA 95150
Phone: 408/993-1662
Description: Provides support system to MAXCIM software users. Separate corporation owned by the users, not the company that produces the software.
Year Founded: 1981
Corporate Members: 250
Executive Officers: Charlene Rose, Administrator; Ken Allen, President
Interest Groups: Various SIG groups: MS-Manufacturing, Financial, DBMS VAX, Executive Mgmt, Share, Marketing and Customer Support
Publications: CONCOURSE magazine (quarterly), SIG newsletters
Conferences: Symposium (87:Anaheim March 22-25)

National Epson Users Group
Acronym: NEUG
Box 8088
State College, PA 16803
Phone: 814/237-5511
Description: Provides support system for all Epson computers and IBM compatibles.
Year Founded: 1983
Individual Members: 1743
Executive Officers: Richard Shoemaker, Executive Director
Publications: Epson Lifeboat (6-9 times a year)
Conferences: Epson Interact events

National Online Circuit
Acronym: NOC
P.O. Nox 1019, Public Library
Santa Barbara, CA 93102
Phone: 805/962-7653
Description: Networks online users groups for information exchange of ideas and concerns.
Year Founded: 1978
Corporate Members: 70 groups
Executive Officers: Bill Richardson, Chairperson; Connie Riley, Secretary/Treasurer
Publications: Directory of Online User Groups (periodically)
Conferences: Annual meeting

North American Honeywell
Acronym: NAHU
P.O. Box 2037
Willingboro, NJ 08046
Phone: 215/597-0551
Description: Promotes timely exchange of information by professionals in the data processing
industry using Honeywell Automatic Data Processing Equipment.
Year Founded: 1977
Individual Members: 100   Corporate Members: 436
Executive Officers: Shirley Eick, President; Michael Spire, Vice President
Interest Groups: Various SIG groups
Publications: User Formation Guide (periodically)
Conferences: Semiannual Conferences (Spring and Fall)

Penta Users Group
Acronym: PUG
6711 Dover Road
Glen Burnie, MD 21061
Phone: 301/760-7900
Description: Promotes, assists, supports and conducts cooperative educational activities among Penta
users with a view of developing cooperative spirit & assistance among users.
Year Founded: 1978
Corporate Members: 369
Executive Officers: Jeff Barrie, President; Nancy Dahnke, Vice President
Publications: Newsletter (5 per year)
Conferences: PUG Annual Meeting (87:Baltimore June 5-7, 88:Baltimore)

Recognition Technologies Users Association
Acronym: RTUA
Box 2016, Colburn House, 2 floor
Manchester Center, VT 05255
Phone: 802/362-4151
Description: Advances the knowledge and application of recognition technologies (OCR, OMR, OBR, MICR, Image and Voice) as a means of automated data entry.
Year Founded: 1970
Corporate Members: 500
Executive Officers: Ronald Harris, President; Herbert F. Schantz, Vice President
Publications: Recognition Technologies TODAY magazine (quarterly)
Conferences: Forum (87:San Fran Aug 2-5, 88:Scottsdale Jan 10-13, 88: Philadelphia July 24-27, 89:Ft Lauderdale Jan 15-18)
Awards: Annual O. Edward Stolberg Scholarship

SAS Users Group International
Acronym: SUGI
Box 8000
Cary, NC 27511
Phone: 919/467-8000   Telex: 802505 SASRAL
Description: Provides users of the SAS System the opportunity to meet and discuss their software applications, learn new tech., and hear about R&D of new products at SAS Institute.
Year Founded: 1975
Executive Officers: Andrea U. Littleton, Administrative Assistant
Publications: SAS Communications magazine (quarterly), SUGI Proceedings (annually)
Conferences: Annual SUGI (88:Lake Buena Vista, Fl Mar 27-30)
Awards: Several annual awards
Foreign Offices: Australia, Japan, New Zealand, South America and UK

SHARE Inc.
111 East Wacker Drive
Chicago, IL 60601
Phone: 312/644-6610   Telex: 25-4073
Description: Fosters joint research and development for scientific, engineering, & educational
organizations using IBM computers.
Year Founded: 1955
Corporate Members: 2451
Executive Officers: Michael F. Armstrong, President (1986-88); Cecilia M. Cowles, Vice President
(1986-88)
Interest Groups: Organized into Divisions, Groups and Projects, special Task Forces, and Study
Groups
Publications: Proceedings (following major meetings), SSD's (bimonthly),
CME Compendium (every two years), CME Newsletters (monthly)
Conferences: SHARE (87:Denver May 3-6, 87:Chicago Aug 23-28, 87:Orlando Nov 15-18)

Texas Instruments Mini-MicroComputer Info Exchange
Acronym: TI-MIX
P.O. Box 201897
Austin, TX 78720
Phone: 512/250-7151
Description: Promotes the exchange of information between TI and users of TI computers and
peripherals.
Year Founded: 1973
Individual Members: 18,000
Executive Officers: Larry R. Briggs, Chairman; Robert Teague, Vice Chairman
Publications: DirecTIons magazine (monthly)
Conferences: Annual Convention (87:Orlando Apr 26-29)

USENIX Association
Acronym: USENIX
P.O. Box 7
El Cerrito, CA 94530
Phone: 415/528-8649
Description: Provides services and technical information for users of UNIX.
Year Founded: 1975
Individual Members: 1338   Corporate Members: 552
Executive Officers: Peter H. Salus, Executive Director
Publications: Newsletters (bimonthly), proceedings (semiannually)
Conferences: Two USENIX conferences annually (87:Phoenix June)

XNS Implementors Group
Acronym: XNSIG
475 Oakmead Pkwy, %B. Schatzman
Sunnyvale, CA 94086
Phone: 408/737-4653
Description: Supports implementors of Xerox Network Systems with a range of technical and marketing presentations/workshops.
Year Founded: 1984
Individual Members: 300   Corporate Members: 65
Executive Officers: Bruce D. Schatzman, Network Systems Group Director
Publications: Courier newsletter (quarterly)
Conferences: Conferences twice annually

XPLOR International
Acronym: XPLOR
2550 Via Tejon, Ste 3F
Palos Verdes Estates, CA 90274
Phone: 213/373-3633   Telex: 678017
Description: Provides forums for the development and exchange of info and support among users of advanced electronic printing systems. Acts as a liaison among users/suppliers.
Year Founded: 1980
Corporate Members: 600
Executive Officers: Keith T. Davidson, Executive Director
Interest Groups: Five regions around the United States, Canada, Europe
Publications: News & Views newsletter (bimonthly), proceedings (annually)
Conferences: Fall Annual Conference (87:Dallas Nov 1-6, 88:Los Angeles Nov 6-11), Regional meetings
Foreign Offices: Canada, UK

14 PUBLICATIONS

ASSOCIATION OF BUSINESS PUBLISHERS
JESSE H. NEAL AWARDS
1986

The Association of Business Publishers sponsors the Neal Awards which recognize editorial excellence in individual editors. The thirty-two year competition is held annually to reward editorial excellence in audited, independent business publications. Only articles that appear in ABP publications can qualify for these awards. Entries are classified according to size of publication and judged in 5 categories:
1. Best in-depth analysis article or series of articles.
2. Best staff-written editorial.
3. Best article or series of articles demonstrating excellence in reporting.
4. Best regularly featured department, section or column.
5. Best how-to article or series of articles.
Criteria for judging is based on journalistic enterprise, extent of service to the field and editorial craftsmanship.--COMPUTER INDUSTRY ALMANAC.

From this list COMPUTER INDUSTRY ALMANAC has selected only the industry-related awards.

Reprinted with permission from Association of Business Publishers, 1986. Copyright 1986 by Association of Business Publishers, New York, NY.

THE AWARD WINNERS

CLASSIFICATION C - Gross advertising revenues more than $4,000,000

CATEGORY 1
Best in-depth analysis article or subject-related series
Max Schindler, Bob Milne, Stephan Ohr, Frank Goodenough,
Mitch Beedie, Thomas Phon.
ELECTRONIC DESIGN
1985 Technology Forecast

CATEGORY 5
Best how-to article or subject-related series
Mel Mandell, John Rymer, Bonnie Meyer, E.S. Ely,
Bonnie DeBonis, Dennis Mendyk.
COMPUTER DECISIONS
Coping With Your IBM Rep

(Continued next page)

ASSOCIATION OF BUSINESS PUBLISHERS: JESSE H. NEAL AWARDS (Continued)

THE CERTIFICATES OF MERIT

CLASSIFICATION A - Gross advertising revenues up to $2,000,000

CATEGORY 1
Best in-depth analysis article or subject-related series
> Dan Gutman, John Blackford, David Shadovitz, John McLaughlin.
COMPUTER DEALER
Riding the Light Wave

CATEGORY 3
Best article or subject-related series of articles demonstrating excellence in reporting
> Dan Gutman, John Blackford, David Shadovitz, John McLaughlin.
COMPUTER DEALER
Apple at the Turning Point

CLASSIFICATION B - Gross advertising revenues $2,000,000 to $4,000,000

CATEGORY 4
Best regularly featured department, section or column
> Sandy Austin, Douglas Pryor, Mike Roach.
BUSINESS COMPUTER SYSTEMS
Software Decisions

CLASSIFICATION C - Gross advertising revenues more than $4,000,000

CATEGORY 1
Best in-depth analysis article or subject-related series
> Al Perlman, Ellen Pearlman, Mike Perkowski, Michael Azzara, Laura Allyn Post,
> Susan Mennear-Dubas.
COMPUTER SYSTEMS NEWS
Getting Into Bed With IBM

CATEGORY 4
Best regularly featured department, section or column
> Roger J. Hannan, Timothy J. Grogan, Eric J. Kalkbrenner, Joseph S. Poznanski,
> Steven W. Adams.
ENGINEERING NEWS-RECORD
Cost Reports

B. DALTON
COMPUTER BOOK BESTSELLERS
Week ending September 28, 1986

Based on sales at more than 700 B. Dalton stores for the week ending September 28, 1986.--
COMPUTER INDUSTRY ALMANAC.
Reprinted with permission from B. DALTON, 1986. Copyright 1986 by B. Dalton, Minneapolis,
MN.

1. **Using 1-2-3** 2E
   Que Corp.
2. **Mastering WordPerfect**
   Sybex
3. **Using PC DOS**
   Que Corp.
4. **dBase III Plus Handbook**
   Que Corp.
5. **Advanced MS DOS**
   Microsoft/H&R
6. **Using WordPerfect** 2E
   Que Corp.
7. **Running MS DOS** 2E
   Microsoft/H&R
8. **Understanding dBase III Plus**
   Sybex
9. **P Norton Programmer IBM**
   Microsoft/H&R
10. **Dictionary of Computer Terms**
    Barrons
11. **Inside the IBM Review**
    Brady/Simon
12. **Using Turbo Prolog**
    Osborne/McGraw
13. **C Programming Language**
    Brady/Prentice
14. **Assembly Language Primer IBM PC**
    NAL
15. **Lotus 1-2-3 Simplified** 2E
    Tab Books

PUBLICATIONS DIRECTORY

COMPUTER INDUSTRY ALMANAC lists in this section over 155 of the industry-related magazines, newspapers, and newsletters. The entries are arranged alphabetically by title and include such information as frequency of publication, subscription price, publisher information, and a brief description.

80 Micro
80 Elm Street
Peterborough, NH 03458
Phone: 603/924-9471
Editor: Eric Maloney
Publisher: CW Communications/Peterborough
Circulation: 86,631   Frequency: Monthly
Subscription price: $25   Advertising? Yes
Description: Specializes in business & programming applications for Tandy microcomputer users; includes news, programs, and problem solutions.

80/88 National Newsletter
P.O. Box 28360
Queens Village, NY 11428
Phone: 718/776-2909
Editor: Steve Bender
Publisher: The National Chameleon Users Group
Circulation: 100   Frequency: Semiannual
Subscription price: $15   Advertising? No
Description: Provides information updates and repair information specifically for the National Chameleon Computer.

A+, The Independent Guide for Apple Computing
One Park Avenue
New York, NY 10016
Phone: 212/503-3500
Publisher: Ziff-Davis Publishing Company
Circulation: 175,000   Frequency: Monthly
Subscription price: $24.97   Advertising? Yes
Description: Specializes in new applications, uses, product evaluations for owners/users/buyers of any Apple microcomputer. Subjects for professional and home use, including entertainment.

ADWEEK's Computer & Electronics Marketing
100 Boylston Street
Boston, MA 02116
Phone: 617/482-0876
Editor: Ronald Karjian
Publisher: A/S/M Communications, Inc.
Frequency: Monthly
Subscription price: $25   Advertising? Yes
Description: Contains articles on advertising and marketing strategies used by computer companies.

AI Capsule
14 Franklin St., Ste 920
Rochester, NY 14604
Phone: 716/546-7480
Editor: Joan Creatura
Publisher: Winters Group
Circulation: N/A   Frequency: Monthly
Subscription price: $195   Advertising? No
Description: Presents trade press abstracts, state-of-the-industry notes, development updates, book reviews, product announcements, calendar of events--all for the Artificial Intelligence community.

Ahoy!
45 West 34th Street
New York, NY 10001
Phone: 212/239-0855
Editor: David Allikas
Publisher: Haymarket Group, Ltd.
Circulation: 126,019   Frequency: Monthly
Subscription price: $23   Advertising? Yes
Description: Serves the Commodore market by offering novice & experienced users news, hardware/software applications information, and inner workings of computers.

AmigaWorld
80 Elm Street
Peterborough, NH 03458
Phone: 603/924-9471
Editor: Guy Wright, Editor in Chief
Publisher: CW Communications/Peterborough
Circulation: 70,000   Frequency: Bimonthly
Subscription price: $14.97   Advertising? Yes
Description: Provides Commodore Amiga owners with reviews, features, graphics, entertainment and how-to-achieve-best-use tips.

Analog Computing
565 Main Street
Cherry Valley, MA 01611
Phone: 617/892-3488
Editor: Diane Gaw, Managing Editor
Publisher: A.N.A.L.O.G. Magazine Corporation
Circulation: 98,000   Frequency: Monthly
Subscription price: $28   Advertising? Yes
Description: Serves the Atari user/owner focusing on hardware/software reviews, program listings, & instruction.

Antic: The Atari Resource
524 Second Street
San Francisco, CA 94107
Phone: 415/957-0886
Editor: DeWitt Robbeloth
Publisher: Antic Publishing, Inc.
Circulation: 100,500   Frequency: Monthly
Subscription price: $28   Advertising? Yes
Description: Serves as a resource publication for Atari owners/users. Most of the material instructs and teaches. It lists compatible software for the Atari. Products are described and reviewed.

Apple II Review, The
3381 Ocean Drive
Vero Beach, FL 32963
Phone: 305/231-6904
Editor: Ted Leonsis
Publisher: Redgate Communications Corporation
Circulation: 100,000   Frequency: Quarterly
Subscription price: $14   Advertising? Yes
Description: Informs Apple II users of new products and applications. Products are thoroughly examined by a review board.

Artificial Intelligence Today
104 Frame Road
Elkview, WV 25071
Phone: 304/965-5548
Editor: Roger C. Thibault
Publisher: Artificial Research Labs
Circulation: 5,000   Frequency: Monthly
Subscription price: $395   Advertising? No
Description: Gears information to professionals who are introducing Artificial Intelligence applications into their business and want to stay abreast of applications in other industries.

Audio-Visual Communications
50 West 23rd Street
New York, NY 10010
Phone: 212/645-1000
Editor: Mike Yuhas
Publisher: Media Horizons, Inc.
Frequency: Monthly
Subscription price: $13.50   Advertising? Yes
Description: Specializes in the audiovisual market with some emphasis given to computer graphics
and related hardware/software.

Authorized OA Dealer Report
345 Carrol Road
Fairfield, CT 06430
Phone: 203/255-4100
Editor: Kenneth D. Camarro
Publisher: Camarro Research
Circulation: 200   Frequency: Monthly
Subscription price: $235   Advertising? No
Description: Publishes research findings targeted to office machine and computer specialty outlets,
corporate equipment buyers & mfrs. Features sales trends, sales statistics, product reviews, and
vendor reports.

Business Computer Review
3800 North Central Avenue, #A-5
Phoenix, AZ 85012
Phone: 602/279-3056
Editor: Gene Baird
Publisher: The Micro Times Network
Circulation: 20,000   Frequency: Monthly
Subscription price: $15   Advertising? Yes
Description: Focuses on the Phoenix personal computer market. Includes interviews/profiles in local
scene, special interest topics, new products, & how-to's.

Business Computer Systems
275 Washington Street
Newton, MA 02158
Editor: Terry Catchpole
Publisher: Cahners Publishing, A Division of Reed Publ. USA
Frequency: Monthly
Subscription price: $40   Advertising? Yes
Description: Specializes in computer strategies for FORTUNE 1000 management. Includes news,
features, reviews, and products in hardware and software.

Business Software Review
9100 Keystone Crsng POBox 40946
Indianapolis,IN 46240
Phone: 317/844-7461
Editor: Dennis L. Hamilton
Publisher: International Computer Programs, Inc., L.W. Harm
Circulation: 75,000   Frequency: Monthly
Subscription price: $Free   Advertising? Yes
Description: Supplies information to end users of business software and DP/MIS professionals in
medium to large companies.

Byte
One Phoenix Mill Lane
Peterborough, NH 03458
Phone: 603/924-9281
Editor: Philip Lemmons
Publisher: McGraw-Hill
Circulation: 400,133   Frequency: Monthly
Subscription price: $21   Advertising? Yes
Description: Provides the knowledgeable microcomputer owner/user with product information for
business and home use. Previews new products (hardware, software, & systems).

CAE Computer-Aided Engineering
1100 Superior Avenue
Cleveland, OH 44114
Phone: 216/696-7000
Telex: TWX 810/431-8245
Editor: John K. Krouse
Publisher: Penton Publishing
Frequency: Monthly
Subscription price: $30   Advertising? Yes
Description: Provides data base applications for computer-aided design & manufacturing engineers.

CD-I News, LINK Resources Corporation
79 Fifth Avenue, 12th Floor
New York, NY 10003
Phone: 212/473-5600
Editor: David Rosen, Executive Editor
Publisher: Haines Gaffner
Circulation: 16,000   Frequency: Monthly
Subscription price: $95   Advertising? No
Description: Covers developments in Compact Disk Interactive, a new standard that is an extension
of the Compact Disk Digital Audio standard developed by Sony & Philips.

CD-ROM
80 Elm Street
Peterborough, NH 03458
Phone: 603/924-9471
Editor: Jeff Detray
Publisher: CW Communications
Frequency: Bimonthly
Subscription price: $24.97   Advertising? Yes
Description: Covers CD-ROM technology, which is a new high-tech way of storing and retrieving
data on a computer.

CIME
175 Fifth Avenue
New York, NY 10010
Phone: 212/705-7722
Editor: Ali A. Seireg
Publisher: Springer-Verlag New York, Inc.
Frequency: Bimonthly
Subscription price: $35   Advertising? Yes
Description: Provides in-depth features, editorial, industry news, literature, new products,
conferences, letters, and software info for the American Society of Mechanical Engineers
membership.

Capital Computer Digest
1408 N. Fillmore, Suite 1
Arlington, VA 22201
Editor: Michelle Robbins
Publisher: Peggy Clark
Circulation: 50,000   Frequency: Monthly
Subscription price: $5   Advertising? Yes
Description: Provides end-users of personal computers in the Washington, DC area with in-depth interviews, company profiles, product reviews & information on operating systems and applications.

Classroom Computer Learning
19 Davis Drive
Belmont, CA 94002
Phone: 513/294-5785
Editor: Holly Brady
Publisher: Peter J. Li
Circulation: 83,000   Frequency: 8/Year
Subscription price: $22.50   Advertising? Yes
Description: Provides computer-using educators and administrators, for grades K-12, with feature articles on all aspects of educational computing, software reviews, programs, and products.

Colorado Computing
2006 Broadway, Suite 301
Boulder, CO 80302
Phone: 303/447-1300
Editor: Bob Wells
Publisher: Bob Wells
Circulation: 20,000   Frequency: Bimonthly
Subscription price: $10   Advertising? Yes
Description: Publishes in-depth interviews, company profiles, product reviews, information, & special interest topics for end-users of personal computers in the Denver area.

Communications of the ACM
11 West 42nd Street
New York, NY 10036
Phone: 212/869-7440
Telex: 421686
Editor: Peter J. Denning
Publisher: Association for Computing Machinery
Frequency: Monthly
Subscription price: Assn. Dues   Advertising? Yes
Description: Informs ACM members of current developments in information processing and of the responsible use of computers.

CommunicationsWeek
600 Community Drive
Manhasset, NY 11030
Phone: 516/365-4600
Editor: Al Perlman
Publisher: CMP Publications, Inc.
Frequency: Weekly
Subscription price: $65   Advertising? Yes
Description: Publishes a newspaper for the communications industry management and professional personnel.

Computer
10662 Los Vaqueros Circle
Los Alamitos, CA 90720
Phone: 714/821-8380
Editor: Marilyn Potes, Managing Editor
Publisher: IEEE Computer Society, True Seaborn
Circulation: 89,800   Frequency: Monthly
Subscription price: Assn. Dues   Advertising? Yes
Description: Provides members of IEEE Computer Society with articles and papers on hardware and software design and applications. Contains IEEE Computer Society conference and workshop reports, book and product reviews, and new applications.

Computer Buyer's Guide and Handbook
150 Fifth Avenue
New York, NY 10011
Phone: 212/807-8220
Editor: Ephraim Schwartz
Publisher: Computer Information Publishing
Circulation: 62,995   Frequency: 10/year
Subscription price: $22/6 issue   Advertising? Yes
Description: Publishes intensive microcomputer product review for the business buyer. Features articles on developments and trends of computer systems, peripherals, and software. Many products are evaluated.

Computer Currents
P.O.Box 2339
Berkeley, CA 94702
Phone: 415/547-6800
Editor: Lynne Verbeck
Publisher: Stan Politi
Circulation: 60,000   Frequency: Semimonthly
Subscription price: $18   Advertising? Yes
Description: Provides general information on computer industry, including lists of all user groups.

Computer Dealer
13 Emery Avenue
Randolph, NJ 07869
Phone: 201/361-9060
Editor: Tom Farre
Publisher: Koulbanis
Circulation: 45,000   Frequency: Monthly
Advertising? Yes
Description: Provides timely information to computer resellers and people who market and sell
computer hardware, software, accessories and services to end users in business, government,
education and the home.

Computer Decisions
10 Mulholland Drive
Hasbrouck Heights, NJ 07604
Phone: 201/393-6030
Editor: Mel Mandell
Publisher: Don Huber
Circulation: 175,000   Frequency: Biweekly
Advertising? Yes
Description: Provides Management Information Systems executives timely information on
networking, communications, software, departmental computing and other pertinent information.

Computer Design
119 Russell Street, P.O.Box 417
Littleton, MA 01460
Phone: 617/486-9501
Editor: Sydney F. Shapiro, Managing Editor
Publisher: Michael Elthick, PennWell Publ. Co., Adv Tech Grp
Circulation: 100,000+   Frequency: Semimonthly
Subscription price: $70   Advertising? Yes
Description: Specializes in new design ideas & information in computer technology for system designers & design managers. Comprehensive coverage in many fields of system design applications.

Computer Graphics Today
50 West 23rd Street
New York, NY 10010
Phone: 212/645-1000
Editor: Brad Schultz
Publisher: Randall Stickrod
Circulation: 35,000   Frequency: Monthly
Subscription price: $12   Advertising? Yes
Description: Focuses on the computer graphics industry with news and developments in equipment, systems, programs, and applications.

Computer Industry Report, The
5 Speen Street
Framingham, MA 01701
Phone: 617/872-8200
Editor: Donald Bellamy
Publisher: International Data Corporation
Circulation: Confidential   Frequency: 24/year
Subscription price: $395   Advertising? No
Description: Targets user & vendor execs who need coverage & analysis of current trends in the information industry. Contains graphs, stats, and hard facts including an annual review & forecast issue.

Computer Music Journal
55 Hayward Street
Cambridge, MA 02142
Phone: 617/253-2889
Editor: Curtis Roads
Publisher: MIT Press Journals
Circulation: 3,700   Frequency: Quarterly
Subscription price: $26   Advertising? Yes
Description: Publishes technical and musical information for computer music and digital sound synthesis. Covers composition, performance, sound production, music printing, score analysis & digital audio.

Computer Publishing & Advertising Report
2 East Avenue
Larchmont, NY 10538
Phone: 914/833-0600
Editor: Daniel McCarthy
Publisher: Communications Trends, Inc.
Circulation: Confidential   Frequency: Biweekly
Subscription price: $312   Advertising? No
Description: Focuses on computer applications for publishing and advertising executives and agencies.

Computer Reseller News
600 Community Drive
Manhasset, NY 11030
Phone: 516/365-4600
Editor: Bob Donohue-Evans
Publisher: CMP Publications, Inc.
Frequency: Weekly   Subscription price: $80
Advertising? Yes
Description: Specializes in microcomputers, software, peripherals, and reselling information.

Computer Shopper
407 South Washington Avenue
Titusville, FL 32780
Phone: 305/269-3211
Editor: Stan Veit
Publisher: Patch Publications
Circulation: 108,490   Frequency: Monthly
Subscription price: $18   Advertising? Yes
Description: Focuses on various major computers & software. Includes editorials and display
advertising. Large classified ad section for new/used computers, peripherals, software, and
employment.

Computer Street Journal
325 RR 620 South, #104
Austin, TX 78734
Phone: 512/263-9166
Editor: Lorie Richter
Publisher: Tom Clark
Circulation: 50,000   Frequency: Monthly
Subscription price: $15   Advertising? Yes
Description: Provides Dallas/Ft.Worth, Houston, Austin/San Antonio personal computer end-users
with in-depth interviews, company profiles, product information, and special topics on specific
machines.

Computer Systems News
600 Community Drive
Manhasset, NY 11030
Phone: 516/365-4600
Editor: Al Perlman
Publisher: CMP Publications, Inc.
Frequency: Weekly   Subscription price: $75
Advertising? Yes
Description: Supplies weekly news and views to the Original Equipment Manufacturer (OEM)
professional.

Computer+ Software News
425 Park Avenue
New York, NY 10022
Phone: 212/371-9400
Editor: Charles Humphrey
Publisher: Lebhar-Friedman, Inc.
Frequency: Weekly   Subscription price: $36
Advertising? Yes
Description: Provides current information to computer and software resellers.

Computergram
110 Greene Street
New York, NY 10012
Phone: 212/334-9750
Editor: Vicy Houck
Publisher: Technology News of America Co. Inc.
Circulation: Confidential   Frequency: Daily
Subscription price: $975   Advertising? No
Description: Disseminates computer industry news and information electronically to financial
analysts, vendors and technical tracking staffs in major user organizations.

Computers in Banking
150 Broadway
New York, NY 10038
Phone: 212/227-1200
Editor: John Dickenson
Publisher: Dealer's Digest, Inc.
Circulation: 30,000   Frequency: Monthly
Subscription price: $35   Advertising? Yes
Description: Focuses on hardware & software applications for automation within the banking
industry.

Computerworld
375 Cochituate Road, Box 9171
Framingham, MA 01701
Phone: 617/879-0700
Editor: William Laberis
Publisher: CW Communications, Inc.
Circulation: 125,000   Frequency: Weekly
Subscription price: $44   Advertising? Yes
Description: Provides computer professionals a newsweekly with broad coverage of the computer
industry.

Computerworld Focus
Box 9171, 375 Cochituate Road
Framingham, MA 01701
Phone: 617/879-0700
Editor: Ann Dooley
Publisher: CW Communications, Inc.
Circulation: Confidential   Frequency: Weekly
Advertising? Yes
Description: Includes feature articles, editorials, news, issues & answers, products, and calendars.
Published as a supplement to COMPUTERWORLD.

Computing Today
179 Pebble Place
San Ramon, CA 94583
Phone: 415/828-1528
Editor: Patty Lesser
Publisher: Hartley Lesser
Circulation: 40,000   Frequency: Weekly
Advertising? No
Description: Covers the entire microcomputer field of hardware & software on a weekly basis.
Currently read on Newsnet and General Electric's Genie network.

Data Based Advisor
1975 Fifth Avenue, Suite 105
San Diego, CA 92101
Phone: 619/236-1182
Editor: David Kalman
Publisher: Data Based Solutions
Circulation: 33,000   Frequency: Monthly
Subscription price: $35   Advertising? Yes
Description: Provides data base management systems users with techniques for improving data base
management systems (DBMS) and data base software applications.

Data Communications
1221 Avenue of the Americas
New York, NY 10200
Phone: 212/512-2000
Telex: 12-7960
Editor: Collin B. Ungaro
Publisher: McGraw-Hill, Inc.
Frequency: Monthly   Subscription price: $30
Advertising? Yes
Description: Specializes in data processing and information network fields.

Data Management
505 Busse Highway
Park Ridge, IL 60068
Frequency: Monthly   Subscription price: $16
Advertising? Yes
Description: Focuses on issues pertinent to the information management executive.

Datamation
875 Third Avenue
New York, NY 10022
Phone: 212/605-9400
Editor: Rebecca S. Barna
Publisher: Technical Publishing
Frequency: Semimonthly   Subscription price: $50
Advertising? Yes
Description: Provides the executive, manager, or electronic data processing (EDP) professional with the latest in computing management and technological information.

Digital Design
1050 Commonwealth Ave.
Boston, MA 02215
Phone: 617/277-1120
Editor: David Wilson
Publisher: Digital Design Publishing Corporation
Frequency: 14/year   Subscription price: $50
Advertising? Yes
Description: Serves the manufacturers of computer-related Original Equipment Manufacturer (OEM) products including primary computer and system mfrs., system integrators, components and peripheral mfrs., integrating OEMs & commercial end-users.

Digital Review
800 Boylston Street
Boston, MA 02199
Phone: 617/375-4300
Editor: Johnathan Cohler
Publisher: Ziff-Davis Publishing Company, Inc.
Circulation: 80,000   Frequency: Biweekly
Subscription price: $40   Advertising? Yes
Description: Focuses exclusively on DEC computers, providing in-depth product evaluations and measured result comparisons of hardware/software from DEC and DEC-compatible manufacturers.

Dr. Dobb's Journal of Software Tools
501 Galveston Drive
Redwood City, CA 94063
Phone: 415/366-3600
Editor: Michael Swaine
Publisher: M&T Publishing, Inc.
Circulation: 50,000   Frequency: Monthly
Subscription price: $29.97   Advertising? Yes
Description: Specializes in information for the professional programmer. Features include in-depth articles on programming, programmers' services, reports, and forums.

EDN Product News
275 Washington Street
Newton, MA 02158
Phone: 617/964-3030
Editor: Jonathan Titus
Publisher: Cahners Publishing Company
Circulation: 136,000   Frequency: Monthly
Subscription price: Qual.Rcps.   Advertising? Yes
Description: Concentrates on electronics industry including industry expenditures, special design projects, new technology and new product design.

Electronic Business
Cahners Bldg. 275 Washington St.
Newton, MA 02158
Phone: 617/964-3030
Editor: Eric Lundquist
Publisher: Cahners Publishing, a Div. of Reed Publ. USA
Frequency: Semimonthly   Subscription price: $50
Advertising? Yes
Description: Specializes in information for the electronics industry.

Electronic Design
10 Mulholland Drive
Hasbrouck Heights, NJ 07604
Phone: 201/383-6000
Telex: TWX 710-990-5071
Editor: Lucinda Mattera
Publisher: Hayden Publishing Company, Inc.
Circulation: 142,949   Frequency: Bimonthly
Subscription price: $65   Advertising? Yes
Description: Targets the Original Equipment Manufacturer (OEM) market of qualified engineers and engineering managers.

Electronic News
7 East 12 Street
New York, NY 10003
Phone: 212/741-4203
Editor: James J. Lydon
Publisher: Fairchild Publications
Frequency: Weekly   Subscription price: $40
Advertising? Yes
Description: Concentrates on the electronics industry and market.

Electronics
1221 Ave. of the Americas
New York, NY 10020
Phone: 212/512-2645
Editor: Robert W. Henkel
Publisher: McGraw-Hill, Inc.
Frequency: Biweekly   Subscription price: $32
Advertising? Yes
Description: Provides news, technology, and new product information in the electronics field.

Electronics Test
1050 Commonwealth Avenue
Boston, MA 02215
Phone: 617/232-5470
Editor: Richard Comerford
Publisher: Miller Freeman Publications, Sten Tallarida
Circulation: 50,000   Frequency: Monthly
Subscription price: $100   Advertising? Yes
Description: Provides pertinent information to engineers, engineering managers & supervisory personnel engaged in application, selection and procurement of automatic test equipment (ATE) systems, hardware, software, etc.

Family Computing
730 Broadway
New York, NY 10003
Phone: 212/505-3585
Editor: Claudia Cohl
Publisher: Shirrel Rhoades
Circulation: 420,000   Frequency: Monthly
Subscription price: $19.97   Advertising? Yes
Description: Explains computer applications in plain English. Features nontechnical articles and new product information for business, entertainment, and at-home use.

FutureViews
8111 LBJ Freeway
Dallas, TX 75251
Phone: 214/437-2400
Telex: 804294
Editor: Joe W. Cross
Publisher: Future Computing Incorporated
Circulation: Confidential Frequency: Monthly
Subscription price: $395 Advertising? No
Description: Focuses on emerging issues in the personal computer industry.

Hardcopy
1061 South Melrose, Suite D
Placentia, CA 92670
Phone: 714/632-6924
Editor: Dan Reese
Publisher: Digital Equipment Corporation
Circulation: 85,000 Frequency: Monthly
Advertising? Yes
Description: Focuses on the Digital Equipment market, primarily DEC users, manufacturers, and distributors.

Heinz Dinter on Desktop Publishing
P.O. Box 558250
Miami, FL 33155
Phone: 305/233-4146
Editor: Heinz Dinter, Ph.D.
Publisher: Heinz Dinter, Ph.D.
Circulation: 5,000 Frequency: Monthly
Subscription price: $48 Advertising? No
Description: Covers problem solving and improving productivity and business image in the PC publishing marketplace.

Hewlett-Packard Journal
3000 Hanover Street
Palo Alto, CA 94304
Phone: 415/857-1501
Editor: Richard P. Dolan
Publisher: Hewlett-Packard
Circulation: 300,000   Frequency: Monthly
Advertising? No
Description: Provides technical information on Hewlett-Packard products from the laboratories of
the Hewlett-Packard Company.

High-Tech Marketing
1460 Post Road East
Westport, CT 06880
Phone: 203/255-9997
Editor: Candace Port
Publisher: Robert J. Dowling
Circulation: 10,000   Frequency: Monthly
Subscription price: $42   Advertising? Yes
Description: Serves marketing, advertising and sales management of computers, communications,
electronics and automation fields. Covers advertising, promotion, sales mgmt, and position
strategies.

HighTechnology
38 Commercial Wharf
Boston, MA 02110
Phone: 617/227-4700
Editor: Steven J. Marcus
Publisher: High Technology Publishing Corporation
Frequency: Monthly
Subscription price: $21
Description: Specializes in advanced technology and developments in computers, robotics,
aerospace, telecommunications, and industrial technology.

Home Office Newsletter
4734 E 26th St
Tucson, AZ 85711
Phone: 602/790-6333
Editor: Joseph Rotello
Publisher: Compusystems Management
Circulation: 500   Frequency: Monthly
Subscription price: $21.50   Advertising? Yes
Description: Provides information to individuals who run businesses from their homes.

IEEE Computer Graphics and Applications

10662 Los Vaqueros Circle
Los Alamitos, CA 90720
Phone: 714/821-8380
Editor: Margaret Neal, Managing Editor
Publisher: True Seaborn
Circulation: 15,589   Frequency: Monthly
Subscription price: Assn. Dues   Advertising? Yes
Description: Focuses on computer graphics research, technology, and applications. Includes coverage on microcomputers, computer-aided design, human aspect of system design and business data graphics.

IEEE Micro

10662 Los Vaqueros Circle
Los Alamitos, CA 90720
Phone: 714/821-8380
Editor: Marie English, Managing Editor
Publisher: True Seaborn
Circulation: 21,663   Frequency: Bimonthly
Subscription price: Assn. Dues   Advertising? Yes
Description: Specializes in material for advanced computer users & covers applications, software, hardware design, new technical developments & microcomputer standards.

IEEE Spectrum

345 East 47th St
New York, NY 10017
Phone: 212/705-7900
Telex: 236-411 Intl only
Editor: Donald Christiansen
Publisher: Donald Christiansen
Circulation: 280,000   Frequency: Monthly
Subscription price: Assn. Dues   Advertising? Yes
Description: Provides current information on electrical and electronic fields with updates on what is happening in the industry.

IEEE Transactions on Computers
1730 Massachusetts Ave. N.W.
Washington, DC 20036
Phone: 212/705-7900
Telex: 236-411 Intl only
Editor: Ming T. Lu
Publisher: IEEE Computer Society
Frequency: Monthly
Subscription price: Assn. Dues   Advertising? No
Description: Specializes in papers on fields of computation, processing of information, applications, & computer systems design & research.

IEEE Transactions on Software Engineering
1730 Massachusetts Ave. N.W.
Washington, DC 20036
Phone: 212/705-7900
Telex: 236-411 Intl only
Editor: C.V. Ramamoorthy
Frequency: Monthly
Subscription price: Assn. Dues
Advertising? No
Description: Publishes papers on all aspects of development, specification, test, management, maintenance and documentation of computer software.

II Computing
524 Second Street
San Francisco, CA 94107
Phone: 415/957-0886
Editor: DeWitt Robbeloth
Publisher: Antic Publishing Company
Circulation: 46,666   Frequency: Bimonthly
Subscription price: $11.97   Advertising? Yes
Description: Specializes in supplying Apple II users with information & programs for Apple II computers. Feature articles include integration of computing into everyday activities plus news and reviews.

InCider

Elm Street
Peterborough, NH 03450
Phone: 603/924-7138
Editor: Debbie dePeyster
Publisher: CW Communications/Peterborough

Circulation: 123,773	Frequency: Monthly
Subscription price: $25	Advertising? Yes

Description: Serves the Apple II family users at various levels of expertise. Publishes hardware/software reviews, new products, program listings, technical assistance and special features.

InfoWorld

1060 Marsh Road, Suite C-200
Menlo Park, CA 94025
Phone: 415/328-4602
Telex: 176072
Editor: Johnathan Sacks
Publisher: CW Communications, Inc.

Circulation: 180,000	Frequency: Weekly
Subscription price: $39	Advertising? Yes

Description: Focuses on the microcomputer industry with articles on computer hardware and software, communications, business, and education.

Information Center

38 Chauncy Street
Boston, MA 02111
Phone: 617/542-0146
Editor: Floyd Kemske
Publisher: Weingarten Publications, Inc.
Frequency: Monthly

Subscription price: Free	Advertising? Yes

Description: Provides information on managing the growth of end-user computing.

Information Strategy, The Executive's Journal

210 South Street
Boston MA 02111
Phone: 617/423-2020
Publisher: Auerbach Publishers Inc

Circulation: Confidential	Frequency: Quarterly
Subscription price: $72	Advertising? No

Description: Focuses on issues pertaining to information management for senior executives and their impact on the success of any organization.

Information Week
600 Community Drive
Manhasset, NY 11030
Phone: 516/365-4600
Editor: Michael Karnow
Publisher: CMP Publications, Inc.
Frequency: Weekly   Subscription price: $65
Advertising? Yes
Description: Focuses on information management in a news magazine format.

Inside DPMA
505 Busse Highway
Park Ridge, IL 60068
Phone: 312/825-8124
Editor: Bill Zalud
Publisher: Data Processing Management Assn.
Circulation: 35,000   Frequency: Quarterly
Subscription price: Assn. Dues   Advertising? No
Description: Provides members of the Data Processing Management Association (DPMA) with news items, articles, stories, and suggestions about the data processing industry.

Institute, The
345 East 47th St
New York, NY 10017
Phone: 212/705-7555
Editor: Donald Christiansen
Publisher: The Inst. of Electrical & Electronics Engrs Inc
Circulation: 270,000   Frequency: Monthly
Subscription price: Assn. Dues   Advertising? Yes
Description: Provides IEEE members with news, editorials, viewpoints and special reports within the Institute of Electrical and Electronics Engineers (IEEE) spectrum.

Instructor's Computer Directory for Schools
545 Fifth Avenue
New York, NY 10017
Phone: 212/503-2888
Editor: Leanna Landsmann
Publisher: Harcourt, Brace, Jovanovich
Circulation: 258,000   Frequency: 10/year
Subscription price: $9.95   Advertising? Yes
Description: Provides a buyer's guide to microcomputers, peripherals, courseware, books, resources, magazines & journals.

International Journal of Parallel Programming

233 Spring Street
New York, NY 10013
Phone: 212/620-8000
Editor: Gary Lindstrom
Publisher: Plenum Publishing Corporation
Circulation: Confidential   Frequency: Bimonthly
Subscription price: $195   Advertising? Yes
Description: Specializes in peer-reviewed, high-quality original papers in the computer & information sciences areas, focusing on programming aspects of parallel computing systems.

Journal of Accounting and EDP

210 South Street
Boston, MA 02111
Phone: 617/423-2020
Publisher: Auerbach Publications, Inc.
Circulation: Confidential   Frequency: Quarterly
Subscription price: $64
Description: Provides information to successfully address planning, operational & control issues arising from the impact of data processing on accounting functions.

Journal of Data Processing Management

210 South Street
Boston, MA 02111
Phone: 617/423-2020
Publisher: Auerbach Publications, Inc.
Circulation: Confidential   Frequency: 6/year
Subscription price: $415
Description: Provides data processing management with articles on implementation, office automation control, cost control procedures, and hardware/software issues.

Journal of Information Systems Management

210 South Street
Boston, MA 02111
Phone: 617/423-2020
Publisher: Auerbach Publications, Inc.
Circulation: Confidential   Frequency: Quarterly
Subscription price: $60
Description: Provides in-depth expert advice for solving problems. Offers guidance on the establishment of information systems-related policy and procedures.

Journal of Scientific Computing
233 Spring Street
New York, NY 10013
Phone: 212/620-8000
Editor: Professor Steven A. Orszag, Princeton University
Publisher: Plenum Publishing Corporation
Circulation: Confidential   Frequency: Quarterly
Subscription price: $50   Advertising? Yes
Description: Presents papers on scientific computing and its applications in science & engineering; addresses topics of interest to supercomputer workers.

Knowledge Engineering Newsletter
P.O.Box 366 Village Station
New York, NY 10014
Phone: 212/627-2666
Editor: Louis Giacalone
Publisher: Richmond Publishing Corporation
Circulation: 1,000   Frequency: Monthly
Subscription price: $275   Advertising? Yes
Description: Provides information to corporate managers interested in applying the technology of knowledge-based systems (AI) to a business environment. It is applications-oriented & nontechnical.

LAN TIMES
122 East 1700 South
Provo, UT 84601
Phone: 801/379-5845
Editor: Jennifer J. Johnson
Publisher: Novell, Inc., Judith Clarke
Circulation: 40,000   Frequency: Monthly
Subscription price: Qual.Rcps.   Advertising? Yes
Description: Publishes trade magazine for NetWare affiliates, Novell resellers, Novell employees, and anyone interested in local area network (LAN) industry. Features industry news, new product information, technical articles, and user group information.

LOCALNetter

P.O.Box 24344
Minneapolis, MN 55424
Editor: The LOCALNetter
Publisher: Architecture Technology Corporation
Circulation: Confidential   Frequency: Monthly
Subscription price: $300   Advertising? No
Description: Covers U.S. & Intl. news, new product information, & standards activities. Provides special in-depth reports on specific products for the Local Area Network (LAN) industry.

Library Software Review

11 Ferry Lane West
Westport, CT 06880
Phone: 203/226-6967
Editor: Tony Abbott
Publisher: Alan Neckler
Circulation: 1,800   Frequency: Semimonthly
Subscription price: $75   Advertising? Yes
Description: Provides the library professional with necessary information to make intelligent software decisions. Reviews books/periodicals about software for libraries/information centers.

Link-Up

143 Old Marlton Pike
Medford, NJ 08055
Phone: 609/654-6266
Editor: Loraine Page
Publisher: Learned Information, Inc.
Circulation: 20,000   Frequency: Monthly
Subscription price: $24   Advertising? Yes
Description: Specializes in computer communications for small computer users.

Lotus

P.O.Box 9123
Cambridge, MA 02139
Phone: 617/494-1192
Telex: 948649
Editor: Steven E. Miller
Publisher: Lotus Magazine - James R. Pierce
Circulation: 366,020   Frequency: Monthly
Subscription price: $18   Advertising? Yes
Description: Covers trends and applications, hints and tips, solutions and tutorials for Lotus 1-2-3 and Symphony.

MIS Week

7 East 12th Street

New York, NY 10003

Phone: 212/741-4203

Publisher: Fairchild Publications

Frequency: Weekly

Subscription price: $40   Advertising? Yes

Description: Provides weekly computer news for management information systems workers.

Macintosh Buyer's Guide, The

3381 Ocean Drive

Vero Beach, FL 32963

Phone: 305/231-6904

Editor: Thomas Kempf

Publisher: Redgate Communications Corporation

Circulation: 155,000   Frequency: Quarterly

Subscription price: $14   Advertising? Yes

Description: Focuses on hardware, software and peripheral products available to the Macintosh user.

MacUser

25 West 39th Street #1102

New York, NY 10018

Phone: 212/302-2626

Editor: Steven Bobker

Publisher: MacUser Publications, Inc.

Circulation: 100,000   Frequency: Monthly

Subscription price: $23   Advertising? Yes

Description: Educates Macintosh owners on desktop publishing, business applications, networking, communication graphics, programming, and entertainment.

MacWorld

502 Second Street, Suite 600

San Francisco, CA 94107

Phone: 415/546-7722

Editor: Jerry Borrell

Publisher: PC World Communications, Inc.

Circulation: 156,176   Frequency: Monthly

Subscription price: $24   Advertising? Yes

Description: Informs Macintosh users of new products and applications with specific advice and problem-solving techniques.

Macazine
113 East Tyler, P.O.Box 1936
Athens, TX 75751
Phone: 214/677-2793
Editor: Robert A. LeVitus
Publisher: Icon Concepts Corporation, Charles Abrams
Circulation: 75,000   Frequency: Monthly
Subscription price: $21/yr   Advertising? Yes
Description: Provides Macintosh owners/users with in-depth coverage of their equipment and its applications. Aimed at business, professional and recreational users.

Machine Design
1100 Superior Avenue
Cleveland, OH 44114
Phone: 216/696-7000
Editor: Ronald Khol
Publisher: Robert Chew
Circulation: 170,000   Frequency: Biweekly
Subscription price: $60   Advertising? Yes
Description: Addresses issues for design engineers functioning in the process industry, OEM sites, R&D labs, and SICs 34-39.

MapNetter, The
P.O.Box 24344
Minneapolis, MN 55424
Publisher: Architecture Technology Corporation
Circulation: Confidential   Frequency: Monthly
Advertising? No
Description: Follows developments in factory data communications systems in manufacturing automation protocol (MAP) & technical & office protocol (TOP). Latest news and information on new products.

Marketer, The
3381 Ocean Drive
Vero Beach, FL 32960
Phone: 305/231-6904
Editor: Paul Pinella, Managing Editor
Publisher: Redgate Communications Corporation
Circulation: 3,237   Frequency: Quarterly
Advertising? Yes
Description: Provides Apple Computer dealers with information on marketing tips, sales advice, and product comparison.

Micro Marketworld
375 Cochituate Road Box 9171
Framingham, MA 01701
Phone: 617/879-0700
Telex: 95-1153
Editor: Bill Laberis
Publisher: CW Communications, Inc.
Frequency: Semimonthly
Subscription price: $Free   Advertising? Yes
Description: Focuses on marketing concepts for small computers & software. Features new products, sales trends, and related news items.

Micro-Product Review
600 Community Drive
Manhasset, NY 11030
Phone: 516/365-4600
Editor: Susan Mannear-Irsfeld
Publisher: CMP Publications, Inc.
Frequency: Weekly
Advertising? Yes
Description: Focuses on only one subject per issue and is a supplement to COMPUTER RETAIL NEWS. Specific issues are addressed with feature articles, reviews, market trends, and new products.

Microcomputer Industry Update
960 N. San Antonio Rd., Ste 130
Los Altos, CA 94023
Phone: 415/941-6679
Editor: George Weiser
Publisher: Industry Market Reports, Inc.(IMR)
Frequency: Monthly
Subscription price: $265
Description: Offers abstracts of the microcomputer industry trade press.

MicroTimes

5951 Canning Street
Oakland, CA 94609
Phone: 415/652-3810
Editor: Dennis Erokan
Publisher: Bam Publications
Circulation: 120,000   Frequency: Monthly
Subscription price: $12   Advertising? Yes
Description: Provides broad spectrum articles for the end-user. Contains interviews, company profiles, product information, and topics of special interest.

MicroTimes Midwest

101 West Locust
Fairbury, IL 61739
Phone: 815/692-2366
Editor: Dave Roberts
Publisher: The MicroTimes Network
Circulation: 70,000   Frequency: Monthly
Subscription price: $15   Advertising? Yes
Description: Focuses on Chicago area end-users. Provides in-depth interviews, company profiles, product information, topics of special interest, and operating systems/applications.

Mini-Micro Systems

270 St. Paul St.
Denver, CO. 80206
Phone: 303/388-4511
Editor: George Kotelly
Publisher: Cahners Publishing Company
Circulation: 138,600   Frequency: Monthly
Subscription price: Qual. Rcps   Advertising? Yes
Description: Publishes information on computer systems integration.

NAMUG Newsletter

P.O.Box 151
Oakland Gardens, NY 11364
Phone: 718/776-2909
Editor: Steve Bender
Publisher: National Amiga Users Group
Circulation: 300   Frequency: Bimonthly
Subscription price: Assn. Dues   Advertising? No
Description: Updates and reviews both software and hardware products. Provides a forum for Amiga users.

Network World
Box 9171, 375 Cochituate Road
Framingham, MA 01701
Phone: 617/879-0700
Editor: Bruce Hoard
Publisher: CW Communications, Inc.
Circulation: 60,600   Frequency: Weekly
Subscription price: $95   Advertising? Yes
Description: Presents timely information to leading users of communications products and services.

Nibble
45 Winthrop Street
Concord, MA 01742
Phone: 614/347-8600
Editor: David Szetela
Publisher: The Micro SPARC, Inc., Mike Harvey, Publisher
Circulation: 72,068   Frequency: Monthly
Subscription price: $26.95   Advertising? Yes
Description: Provides personal, educational and small business Apple computer owners with lists of commercial quality software, novice exercises, advanced tips and techniques.

Nibble Mac
45 Winthrop Street
Concord, MA 01742
Phone: 614/371-1660
Editor: David Szetela
Publisher: Mike Harvey
Circulation: 30,000   Frequency: Bimonthly
Subscription price: $20/8 iss.   Advertising? Yes
Description: Provides Macintosh enthusiasts with tips and techniques, new features and applications, and new programs.

OPS: The Data Center Newsletter
210 South Street
Boston, MA 02111
Phone: 614/423-2020
Editor: Layne C. Bradley, Consulting Editor
Publisher: Auerbach Publishers, Inc.
Circulation: Confidential   Frequency: Monthly
Subscription price: $68   Advertising? Yes
Description: Provides ideas, cost-saving procedures and special topics for data center operations.

OSINetter, The
P.O.Box 24344
Minneapolis, MN 55424
Publisher: Architecture Technology Corporation
Circulation: Confidential   Frequency: Monthly
Subscription price: $372   Advertising? No
Description: Covers product and company activity in the area of open systems interconnection.
Special reports provide in-depth look at key OSI-compatible products. U.S. and Intl. news, products,
and standards.

Online Access Guide
53 West Jackson, Suite 1750
Chicago, IL 60604
Phone: 800/922-9232
Editor: Elias Crim
Publisher: Online Access Publishing Group, Inc.
Circulation: 100,000   Frequency: Bimonthly
Subscription price: $24.95   Advertising? Yes
Description: Covers the use of online information services with articles on applications and benefits
of online info for investing, marketing, advertising, current planning, and business communications.

Online Today, The Computer Communications Magazine
5000 Arlington Centre Blvd.
Columbus, OH 43220
Phone: 614/457-8600
Editor: Douglas G.Branstetter
Publisher: Calvin F. Hamrick III
Circulation: 234,241   Frequency: Monthly
Subscription price: $18   Advertising? Yes
Description: Covers the online computer information industry.

Optical Information Systems
11 Ferry Lane West
Westport CT 06880
Phone: 203/226-6967
Editor: Judith Roth
Publisher: Meckler Publishing
Circulation: 1,400   Frequency: Bimonthly
Subscription price: $95   Advertising? Yes
Description: Covers issues for the professional involved in design development and evaluation.

P.C. Letter
113 Somerset Street
Redwood City, CA 94062
Phone: 415/363-8080
Editor: Stewart Alsop
Publisher: Stewart Alsop
Circulation: 600   Frequency: 22/year
Advertising? No
Description: Interprets and analyzes actions taken by IBM, Compaq, Apple, Lotus, and Microsoft in the PC industry. Also covers the home computer market and large data processing business sites.

PC Magazine
One Park Avenue
New York, NY 10016
Phone: 212/503-5255
Editor: Bill Machrone
Publisher: Ziff-Davis Publishing Company
Circulation: 375,000   Frequency: Biweekly
Subscription price: $34.97   Advertising? Yes
Description: Serves as an independent guide to IBM-standard personal computer users.

PC Netline
P.O.Box 662
Andover, MA 01810
Phone: 617/475-4904
Editor: Paula J. Musich
Publisher: Hyatt Research Corporation, Eric H. Killorin
Circulation: Confidential   Frequency: Monthly
Subscription price: $397   Advertising? No
Description: Analyzes personal computer and office system communications.

PC Tech Journal
10480 Little Patuxent Parkway
Columbia, MD 21044
Phone: 301/740-8300
Editor: Will Fastie
Publisher: Newt Barrett
Circulation: 100,000   Frequency: Monthly
Advertising? Yes
Description: Supplies technical information to computer professionals whose daily work focuses on system design, integration, and application development.

PC Week
800 Boylston Street
Boston, MA 02199
Phone: 617/375-4000
Editor: Ernest F. Baxter
Publisher: Ziff-Davis Publishing Company
Frequency: Weekly
Subscription price: $120   Advertising? Yes
Description: Provides a weekly newspaper geared to IBM-standard microcomputing.

PC World
501 Second Street, Suite 600
San Francisco, CA 94107
Phone: 415/546-7722
Editor: Harry Miller
Publisher: James Martin
Circulation: 290,548   Frequency: Monthly
Subscription price: $29.90   Advertising? Yes
Description: Provides computer news, information, hands-on articles for the IBM PC user, with
regular feature columns, questions/answers, product announcements, reviews, and upcoming events.

PCM
P.O. Box 385
Prospect, KY 40059
Phone: 502/228-4492
Editor: Lawrence C. Falk
Publisher: Falsoft, Inc.
Circulation: 19,109   Frequency: Monthly
Subscription price: $28   Advertising? Yes
Description: Serves as the personal computer magazine for Tandy Computer users. Offers programs,
articles, hints, reviews, columns and teaching articles for the Tandy portable & MS-DOS computers.

Personal Computer Technology
P.O. Box 24344
Minneapolis, MN 55424
Phone: 612/935-2035
Frequency: Monthly
Subscription price: $187
Description: Follows major developments in the personal computer industry.

Personal Computing, The Magazine
10 Mulholland Drive
Hasbrouck Heights, NJ 07604
Phone: 201/393-6165
Telex: TWX 7109905071
Editor: Fred Abatermarco
Publisher: The Hayden Publishing Company, Inc., Jeff Weiner
Circulation: 475,000   Frequency: Monthly
Subscription price: $18   Advertising? Yes
Description: Focuses on the personal computer user who wants to expand computer knowledge
without having advanced technical knowledge. Contains articles, columns, features and editorials.

Pico: The Journal of Portable Computing
P.O. Box 481
Peterborough, NH 03458
Phone: 603/924-7859
Editor: Terry Kepner
Publisher: Terry Kepnew & Mark Robinson
Circulation: 5,000   Frequency: Monthly
Subscription price: $29.97   Advertising? Yes
Description: Provides users of lap-top and portable computers with comprehensive application
information.

Profiles
533 Stevens Avenue
Solana Beach, CA 92075
Phone: 619/481-4353
Editor: Diane Ingalls & Terian Tyre, Co-Editors
Publisher: Janet Galison
Circulation: 100,000   Frequency: Monthly
Subscription price: $25   Advertising? Yes
Description: Provides users of CP/M & MS-DOS with articles on software, hardware, technical tips,
and general information.

Publish!
501 Second Street, Suite 600
San Francisco, CA 94107
Phone: 415/546-7722
Editor: David Bunnell
Publisher: PC World Communications, Inc.
Frequency: Monthly
Subscription price: $39.90   Advertising? Yes
Description: Specializes in desktop & personal computer publishing with emphasis on how to use personal computers to integrate text & graphics into printed communication.

Rainbow, The
P.O.Box 385
Prospect, KY 40059
Phone: 502/228-4492
Editor: Lawrence C. Falk
Publisher: Falsoft, Inc.
Circulation: 69,546   Frequency: Monthly
Subscription price: $31   Advertising? Yes
Description: Publishes articles, programs, hints, instructional features, and product reviews for the Tandy Color Computer user.

Ratings Newsletter (Software Digest)
One Winding Drive
Philadelphia, PA 19131
Phone: 215/878-9300
Editor: John R. Bell
Publisher: Michael D. Stern
Circulation: 7,000   Frequency: Monthly
Subscription price: $295/yr   Advertising? No
Description: Provides results of tests & rates PC software to offer comparative information that can help users select software to best fit their needs.

Release 1.0
375 Park Avenue, Suite 2503
New York, NY 10152
Phone: 212/758-3434
Editor: Esther Dyson
Publisher: EDventure Holdings, Inc., Sylvia Franklin, Assoc.
Circulation: Confidential   Frequency: 15/yr
Subscription price: $395   Advertising? No
Description: Publishes newsletters covering personal computers, software, and the transformation of artificial intelligence into a commercial technology. Comprehensive events calendar in every issue.

Run
80 Elm Street
Peterborough, NH 03458
Phone: 603/924-9471
Editor: Dennis Brisson
Publisher: CW Communications/Peterborough
Circulation: 195,288   Frequency: Monthly
Subscription price: $19.97   Advertising? Yes
Description: Serves as a home-user's guide to Commodore Computing, for the C-64 & C-128 computers, which emphasizes the fun of computing along with widening the possibilities of the systems.

Semiconductor Industry Update
960 N. San Antonio Rd., Ste 130
Los Altos, CA 94023
Phone: 415/941-6679
Editor: Yves Blanchard
Publisher: IMR (Industry Market Reports, Inc.)
Frequency: Monthly
Subscription price: $345
Description: Offers abstracts of the semiconductor industry trade press.

Sentinel
P.O.Box 635
Dunlap, CA 93621
Phone: 209/338-2472
Editor: Dick Mitch
Publisher: Datatext Computer Services
Circulation: 1,300   Frequency: Monthly
Subscription price: $16   Advertising? Yes
Description: Provides a newsletter for users of Texas Instruments Professional Computers (TIPC). Features news and reviews of hardware and software.

Sextant

716 E Street, S.E.

Washington, DC 20003

Phone: 202/544-2868

Editor: Charles Sloto, Editor & Publisher

Publisher: Sextant Publishing Company

Circulation: 18,500   Frequency: Bimonthly

Subscription price: $14.97   Advertising? Yes

Description: Provides information on microcomputer products of Zenith Data Systems & Heath Company to the expert, novice, hobbyist, & business person. Feature articles focus on construction, programs, applications, and news.

Signal

1616 Anderson Road

McLean, VA 22102

Phone: 703/734-7500

Editor: Laura Penny

Publisher: The Source Telecomputing Corporation

Circulation: Variable   Frequency: Bimonthly

Subscription price: Assn. Dues   Advertising? No

Description: Publishes newsletter for use by special interest groups (IBM SIG, Law SIG, Apple SIG, Ashton-Tate SIG). Access on-line or in paper form. User tips and public domain programs featured.

Sigsmall/PC

11 West 42nd Street

New York, NY 10036

Phone: 212/869-7440

Telex: 421686

Editor: Dr. G. W. Gorsline, Virginia Polytechnic Institute

Publisher: Association for Computing Machinery

Subscription price: Assn. Dues   Advertising? No

Description: Published by the Special Interest Group on Small Personal Computing Systems and Applications for ACM members.

Silicon Gulch Gazette
345 Swett Road
Woodside, CA 94062
Phone: 415/851-7075
Editor: Jim Warren
Publisher: IEEE Computer Society Compcon'86
Frequency: Round-tuit
Subscription price: Free   Advertising? Yes
Description: Microcomputing's first news(?)paper; it is an experiment in alternative advertising and lies somewhere between a real trade publication and a house organ for IEEE.

Small Computers in Libraries
11 Ferry Lane West
Westport, CT 06880
Phone: 203/226-6967
Editor: Nancy Nelson
Publisher: Meckler Publishing
Circulation: 4,500   Frequency: Monthly
Subscription price: $39.50   Advertising? Yes
Description: Specializes in software and new products for library applications.

Soft Sector
P.O.Box 385
Prospect, KY 40059
Phone: 502/228-4492
Editor: Lawrence C. Falk
Publisher: Falsoft, Inc.
Circulation: 14,002   Frequency: Monthly
Subscription price: $28   Advertising? Yes
Description: Contains computer programs, articles, columns, product reviews and tutorials pertaining to IBM compatibles.

Soft-letter
1679 Massachusetts Avenue
Cambridge, MA 02138
Phone: 617/868-0157
Editor: Jeffrey Tarter
Publisher: Jeffrey Tarter
Circulation: Confidential   Frequency: Biweekly
Subscription price: $135   Advertising? No
Description: Focuses on trends and strategies in software publishing. Also publishes annual industry research called THE SOFT-LETTER 100, ranking top 100 software companies.

Software News
1900 W. Park Dr. Westbgh Of. Pk.
Westborough, MA 01581
Phone: 800/225-9218
Editor: Edward Bride
Publisher: William Gannon
Circulation: 83,000   Frequency: Monthly
Advertising? Yes
Description: Targets the corporate professional software user, specializing in banking, finance,
manufacturing., wholesale/retail, government, education & other business and industry sectors.

Start, The ST Quarterly
524 Second Street
San Francisco, CA 94107
Phone: 415/957-0886
Editor: DeWitt Robbeloth
Publisher: Antic Publishing Company
Circulation: 30,000   Frequency: Quarterly
Subscription price: $59.95   Advertising? Yes
Description: Serves the serious Atari ST user providing comprehensive articles; programs covering
applications, languages, programming theory & techniques; and reviews of products.

Subroutines
555 De Haro Street
San Francisco, CA 94107
Phone: 415/861-3861
Publisher: PC World Communications, Inc.
Frequency: Monthly
Subscription price: $195   Advertising? No
Description: Offers inside views on the personal computer industry. Subtitle is "David Bunnell's
Newsletter for the Personal Computer Industry."

Telecom Strategy Letter, The
157 Chambers Street
New York, NY 10007
Phone: 212/732-0775
Telex: 449-0412
Editor: Glenn Powers
Publisher: Glenn Powers
Circulation: Confidential   Frequency: Monthly
Subscription price: $995   Advertising? No
Description: Analyzes competition and strategic developments in telecommunications.

Telecommunications
610 Washington Street
Dedham, MA 02026
Phone: 617/326-8220
Telex: 951-659
Editor: Charles E White
Publisher: Horizon House-Microwave, Inc.
Frequency: Monthly
Subscription price: $40
Description: Focuses on the worldwide telecommunications industry.

Texas Computer Market
P.O. Box 796102, 17818 Davenport
Dallas, TX 75252
Phone: 214/931-0157
Editor: Robert Martin, Managing Editor
Publisher: Susan Plonka
Circulation: 60,000
Frequency: Monthly
Subscription price: $13.95   Advertising? Yes
Description: Focuses on the PC community providing state and local news of
events/shows/conferences and who's who of news-makers in the industry.

Token Perspectives Newsletter
P.O. Box 24344
Minneapolis, MN 55424
Phone: 612/935-2035
Publisher: Architecture Technology Corporation
Frequency: Monthly
Subscription price: $312
Description: Specializes in IBM product developments in the field of local networks.

Token Perspectives, The
P.O.Box 24344
Minneapolis, MN 55424
Publisher: Architecture Technology Corporation
Circulation: Confidential   Frequency: Monthly
Subscription price: $312   Advertising? No
Description: Concentrates on developments within the IBM token ring arena. Vendor-developed
products based on IBM tech papers on ring technology, compatibility, and cost.

Unix/World
444 Castro Street
Mountain View, CA 94041
Phone: 415/940-1500
Editor: David L. Flack
Publisher: Tech Valley Publishing
Circulation: 32,000   Frequency: Monthly
Subscription price: $18   Advertising? Yes
Description: Specializes in AT&T's UNIX operating system for the multiuser and multitasking
computer systems market. Includes editorials on market trends, hardware and software reviews, and
analyses.

Varbusiness
600 Community Drive
Manhasset, NY 11030
Phone: 516/365-4600
Editor: Ellen Pearlman
Publisher: CMP Publications, Inc.
Advertising? Yes
Description: Provides Value-added Resellers (VARs) with in-depth articles and vendor program
guides.

Video Computing
P.O.Box 3415
Indialantic, FL 32903
Phone: 305/768-2778
Editor: Gwendolyn DeCort
Publisher: Richard Richmond
Subscription price: $130   Advertising? Yes
Description: Provides specific & practical information on all areas which have an effect on the
marketplace and the technology of interactive video & optical systems.

Visual Computer
44 Hartz Way
Secaucus, NJ 07094
Phone: 201/348-4033
Telex: 012-125994
Publisher: Springer-Verlag New York
Frequency: Bimonthly
Subscription price: $167   Advertising? Yes
Description: Provides members of the Computer Graphics Society (CGS) with reports on state-of-
the-art technology in the fields of visual data, computer graphics and imaging.

Wall Street Computer Review
150 Broadway
New York, NY 10038
Phone: 212/227-1200
Editor: Pavan Sahgal
Publisher: Eugene Duncan
Circulation: 30,000   Frequency: Monthly
Subscription price: $39   Advertising? Yes
Description: Focuses on how to use a computer to make and save money in the financial industry.

Wohl Report on End-User Computing, The
555 East City Line Ave., Ste 240
Bala Cynwyd, PA 19004
Phone: 215/667-4842
Editor: Amy D. Wohl
Publisher: Wohl Associates
Circulation: 300   Frequency: Monthly
Subscription price: $250   Advertising? No
Description: Provides the professional & office worker end user with information on products, issues, & events of interest.

Workstation/Server News
P.O. Box 24344
Minneapolis, MN 55424
Phone: 612/935-2035
Publisher: Architecture Technology Corporation
Frequency: Monthly
Subscription price: $275
Description: Focuses on the systems/application level of local networks. Follows developments in workstations and servers.

15 RESEARCH ACTIVITIES

MARKET RESEARCH COMPANIES

In this section COMPUTER INDUSTRY ALMANAC lists 37 market research companies. The entries are arranged alphabetically by name and include complete address, phone, telex, areas of research, 1985 sales, number of employees, key officers and analysts, and type of service provided. Consulting firms who may do market research are outside the scope of this publication.

Adscope, Inc.
P.O.Box 226, 116A W. Main St.
Goldendale, WA 98620
Phone: 509/773-3703
Areas: Computers, telecommunications, electronics.
Employees: 10
Established: 1981
Founders: Art Childs/Sheila Clarke
Chairman & President/CEO: Arthur W. Childs
Vice President(s): Sheila Clarke, Marketing
Top Analysts: Art Childs, Software, hardware, electronics; Sheila Clarke, Publishing, advertising, media buying
Public Relations Contact: Sheila Clarke

In-house online database: Yes	Online access by clients: No
Reports: Yes	Seminars: No
Consulting: Yes	Newsletters: Yes

Titles (frequency): Trendscope (quarterly)

Ampersand Research
P.O. Box 1142
New Canaan, CT 06840
Phone: 203/972-3939   Telex: MCI:SWEISSMAN 277-5476
Areas: Information services (videotex, teletext, online databases), electronic mail, optical memories, personal computers and peripherals, voice processing.
Employees: <10
1985 Sales: $1M
Established: 1985
Founders & President/CEO: Steven B. Weissman
Public Relations Contact: Steven B. Weissman

In-house online database: Yes	Online access by clients: No
Reports: Yes	Seminars: Yes
Consulting: Yes	Newsletters: No

Computer Intelligence
3344 N. Torrey Pines Court, Ste 210
La Jolla, CA 92037
Phone: 619/450-1667
Areas: IBM mainframes, PCs, communications, DEC VAX, mainframe software, PCM, superminis, small business systems dealers.
Employees: 130
Established: 1969
Founders: Hugh Tietjen
President/CEO: Hugh Tietjen
Vice President(s): Mike Hagan, Wally Papciak, Pat McDonald
Public Relations Contact: Paul Hairopoulos, Director of Marketing

In-house online database: Yes	Online access by clients: Yes
Reports: Yes	Seminars: No
Consulting: No	Newsletters: Yes

Titles (frequency): CI Intelligence Report(monthly)

Creative Strategies Research Int.
5300 Stevens Creek Blvd. #400
San Jose, CA 95129
Phone: 408/249-7550
Telex: 5106007545 CSRI
Areas: Computers (hardware, software, peripherals), instrumentation, office automation, factory automation, robotics, healthcare.
Employees: 7
Established: 1984
Founders: E. Poshkus, T. Bajarin
Chairman: E. Poshkus
President/CEO: E. Poshkus
Vice President(s): T. Bajarin, Computers
         C. Dickson, Instrumentation, factory automation, healthcare
Top Analysts: S. Conroy, Healthcare, handheld devices; S. Hess, Software
Public Relations Contact: E. Poshkus

In-house online database: Yes	Online access by clients: No
Reports: Yes	Seminars: Yes
Consulting: Yes	Newsletters: No

Daratech, Inc.
16 Myrtle Avenue
Cambridge, MA 02138
Phone: 617/354-2339
Telex: 509435 DARATECH
Areas: Computer-aided design, manufacturing, & engineering (CAD/CAM, CAE).
Employees: 15
Established: 1978
Founders: Charles M. Foundyller
Chairman: Charles M. Foundyller
President/CEO: Charles M. Foundyller
Top Analysts: Charles M. Foundyller, President, CAD/CAM, CAE; Bruce L. Jenkins, Senior Editor, CAD/CAM, CAE; Karen J. Barss, Editor, CAD/CAM, CAE
Public Relations Contact: C. L. Wade

In-house online database: Yes	Online access by clients: No
Reports: Yes	Seminars: Yes
Consulting: Yes	Newsletters: Yes

Titles (frequency): CAD/CAM, CAE: Survey, Review and Buyers' Guide (bimonthly)

Datapro Research Corporation
1805 Underwood Blvd.
Delran, NJ 08075
Phone: 609/764-0100
Telex: 843392
Areas: EDP systems, microcomputers, communications, online services, information security, industry automation, office automation.
Employees: 425
1985 Sales: $31M-$35M
Established: 1971
Founders: Burt Totaro and others
Chairman: Div. of McGraw-Hill
President/CEO: James P. Murray
Vice President(s): Bruce Hollows, Editorial; Don Welsher, Planning & Development
Top Analysts: Alan Hirsch, Group Managing Editor, Microcomputers; Mary Heminway, Group Managing Editor, Mainframes; Al Salciunas, Group Managing Editor, Communications
Public Relations Contact: Richard Burke, VP, Sales

In-house online database: No	Online access by clients: No
Reports: Yes	Seminars: Yes
Consulting: No	Newsletters: Yes, part of service only

Dataquest
1290 Ridder Park Drive
San Jose, CA 95131
Phone: 408/971-9000
Telex: 171973
Areas: Computer products(personal/bus/tech computers and software), telecom, semiconductors, industrial automation, peripherals, copying & duplicating, office automation.
Employees: 380
1985 Sales: $31M-$35M
Established: 1971
Founders: David A. Norman, William L. Coggshall, Ronald I. Miller
Chairman: Dave Jorgensen
President/CEO: Manny Fernandez
Vice President(s): Fred Zieber, Executive VP; O. Ralph Finley, Executive VP
Top Analysts: Wil Felling, VP & Group Director, Telecommunications; Gwendolyn Peterson, VP & Group Director, Computer products; Howard Bogert, VP & Group Director, Semiconductors
Public Relations Contact: Jewel Peyton, Corp Comm; Cecilia Denny, PR

In-house online database: Yes	Online access by clients: Yes
Reports: Yes	Seminars: Yes
Consulting: Yes	Newsletters: Yes, part of service only

Datek Information Services, Inc.
P.O. Box 68
Newtonville, MA 02160
Phone: 617/893-9130
Telex: 951131 HQ BSN DATEK
Areas: Computer printer industry (related industries including printer supplies, components, & add-ons).
Employees: 8
Established: 1976
Founders: Edward Webster
Chairman: Edward Webster
President/CEO: Jonathan W. Dower
Top Analysts: Jonathan Dower, Printer products, markets, forecasts; Edward Webster, Printer products, markets, supplies, forms; Naomi M. Luft, Res Analyst, Non-impact printing, plotters
Public Relations Contact: Frank A. Stefansson, Director of Marketing

In-house online database: Yes	Online access by clients:
Reports: Yes	Seminars: Yes
Consulting: Yes	Newsletters: Yes

Titles (frequency): The Datek Printer Report (monthly)

Disk/Trend, Inc.
5150 El Camino Real, Suite B-20
Los Altos, CA 94022
Phone: 415/961-6209
Telex: 171-914
Areas: Publishes annual Disk/Trend Rept, covering rigid, flexible, and optical disk drives; co-sponsors data storage and optical storage conferences for industry management.
Employees: 3
1985 Sales: $1M-$5M
Established: 1977
Founders: James N. Porter
President/CEO: James N. Porter
Vice President(s): Robert H. Katzive
Public Relations Contact: James N. Porter

In-house online database: No	Online access by clients: No
Reports: Yes	Seminars: Yes
Consulting: Yes	Newsletters: No

Frost & Sullivan
106 Fulton Street
New York, NY 10038
Phone: 212/233-1080
Areas: Computers, peripherals, software, graphics, telecommunications, videotex, AI, electronic mail, computer security, remote services, VARs, data communications, CAD/CAM.
Employees: 130
1985 Sales: $11M-$15M
Established: 1961
Founders: Daniel M. Sullivan
President/CEO: Daniel M. Sullivan
Vice President(s): Henry M. Berler, Sr. VP, Research
          Donald Borkenstein, Sr. VP, Data processing
Top Analysts: Joe Savino, Dir., Data processing, telecommunications; Harvey Rinn, Dir, Electronic components & instrumentation
Public Relations Contact: Terry McGuire, Managing Dir, PR

In-house online database: No	Online access by clients: No
Reports: Yes	Seminars: Yes
Consulting: Yes	Newsletters: Yes

Future Computing, Inc.
8111 LBJ Freeway
Dallas, TX 75251
Phone: 214/437-2400   Telex: 80-4294
Areas: Microcomputer markets (hardware, software, peripherals), distribution channel tracking and analysis, product testing.
Employees: 30
1985 Sales: $6M-$10M
Established: 1980
Founders: Portia Isaacson, Egil Juliussen
Chairman: Subsid. of McGraw-Hill
Vice President(s): Meg Lewis
Top Analysts: Meg Lewis, Vice President; Tim Williams, Director, Channels & Market Analysis; Lindsay Miller, Director, Testing Operations
Public Relations Contact: Jocelyn Young, Manager, Inquiry Service & Special Projects

In-house online database: Yes	Online access by clients: No
Reports: Yes	Seminars: Yes
Consulting: Yes	Newsletters: Yes

Titles (frequency): FutureViews (monthly), DistributionViews (monthly)

Gartner Group
72 Cummings Point Road
Stamford, CT 06904
Phone: 203/964-0096   Telex: 643528
Areas: Industry services, IBM large computer mkt, telecom, small computer systems, office info systems, PCs, local area communications, sw mgmt strategies, computer integrated mfg, enterprise network strategies, corporate pub strategies.
Employees: 160
1985 Sales: $16M-$20M
Established: 1979
Founder: Gideon I. Gartner
Chairman/President/CEO: Gideon I. Gartner
Vice President(s): Helmut A. Alpers, Executive VP ; Grigsby C. Markham, Executive VP
Top Analysts: Dale Kutnick, Executive VP, Research; Paul Spindel, VP & General Manager, Consulting; Richard Imershein, Sr VP, International marketing
Public Relations Contact: Mimi Ford, Director of Communications

In-house online database: Yes	Online access by clients: Yes
Reports: Yes	Seminars: Yes
Consulting: Yes	Newsletters: Yes, part of service only

Gnostic Concepts, Inc.
951 Mariner's Island Blvd, Suite 300
San Mateo, CA 94404
Phone: 415/345-7400
Areas: Electronic systems, subsystems, electronic components, computer data base service.
Employees: 30
Established: 1973
President/CEO: John O'Boyle
Vice President(s): E. Graham, Passive components
        T. Wong, Active components
Top Analysts: Deborah Thresher, Division Manager, Econometrics; Bob Olton, Computers; Mark Spence, Electronic component pricing
Public Relations Contact: James Chestnut

In-house online database: Yes	Online access by clients: Yes
Reports: Yes	Seminars: No
Consulting: Yes	Newsletters: Yes

Titles (frequency): Part of service only

IMS America Ltd.(Sub of IMS Int'l)
Maple and Butler Avenues
Ambler, PA 19002
Phone: 215/283-8500
Telex: 846396 IMS GLAMBR
Areas: Computer specialty retail chains, value added distribution, computer systems, peripherals, software, supplies.
Employees: 1830
1985 Sales: $100M
Established: 1970
Founders: David Dubow
Chairman: Wholly owned sub IMS Int
President/CEO: Michael J. Pierce
Vice President(s): Ronald Rehling, Computer markets division
        Robert J. Gulick, VP
Top Analysts: Stephen Roberts, Account Executive & Market Analyst; Donald Wright, Sales and marketing
Public Relations Contact: Ronald Rehling

In-house online database: Yes	Online access by clients: Yes
Reports: Yes	Seminars: Yes
Consulting: Yes	Newsletters: Yes

Titles (frequency): National Computer Retail Highlights (monthly)

ITOM International Co.
P.O. Box 1450
Los Altos, CA 94023
Phone: 415/948-4516
Areas: Multiprocessing, parallel processing, fault tolerant systems, advanced architecture computer systems.
Established: 1980
Founders: Omri Serlin
President/CEO: Omri Serlin

In-house online database: No	Online access by clients: No
Reports: Yes	Seminars: Yes
Consulting: Yes	Newsletters: Yes

Titles (frequency): Supermicro Newsletter (monthly); FT Systems Newsletter (monthly)

In-Stat, Inc.
7320 E. 6th Avenue, P.O. Box 8130
Scottsdale, AZ 85252
Phone: 602/994-9560
Areas: Semiconductor industry.
Employees: 12
Established: 1981
Founders: Jack Beedle
President/CEO: Jack Beedle
Vice President(s): Bill Groves, Technology
   Jim Feldhan, Operations
Top Analysts: Bill Groves, Semiconductor technology; Jim Feldhan, Data bases (Semi end-use & mfg locations); Jack Beedle, Semiconductor business
Public Relations Contact: Bill Groves, Jim Feldhan, Jack Beedle

In-house online database: Yes	Online access by clients: No
Reports: Yes	Seminars: Yes
Consulting: Yes	Newsletters: Yes

Titles (frequency): In-Stat Electronics Report (monthly), In-Stat Research Letter (monthly)

InfoCorp
20833 Stevens Creek Blvd.
Cupertino, CA 95014
Phone: 408/973-1010
Telex: 383004
Areas: Microsystems (hardware, software, printers), mass storage, small systems, retail channels (microsystems, software, printers). Purchased by Gartner Group.
Employees: 32
1985 Sales: $1M-$5M
Established: 1982
Founders: R.J. Matlack, Grant Bushee, Ralph Gilman, Wm Frank
Chairman: Richard J. Matlack
President/CEO: Richard J. Matlack
Vice President(s): Grant (Skip) Bushee, Exec VP & Dir of Research
Top Analysts: Ralph A. Gillman, Sr VP, Microsystems; William J. Frank, Sr VP & Director, Mass storage research; Robert M. Lefkowits, VP, Software research
Public Relations Contact: Cornelia Navari, Assistant to the President

In-house online database: Yes	Online access by clients: No
Reports: Yes	Seminars: Yes
Consulting: Yes	Newsletters: Yes

Titles (frequency): Part of service only

Input
1943 Landings Drive
Mountain View, CA 94043
Phone: 415/960-3990
Areas: Computer services industry (processing, software, professional services, turnkey), computer maintenance and telecommunications.
Established: 1975
Founders: Peter Cunningham
President/CEO: Peter Cunningham
Vice President(s): John E. Frank, Michael Dishman, Randi Paul, Don Fostle, Keith Hocking, George Hunter
Top Analysts: Victor Wheatman, Telecommunications; Bonnie Digrius, Software; Rich Brusuelas, Customer service, maintenance
Public Relations Contact: Janet McDaniel

In-house online database: Yes	Online access by clients: No
Reports: Yes	Seminars: Yes
Consulting: Yes	Newsletters: Yes

Integrated Circuit Engineering Corp.
15022 N. 75th Street
Scottsdale, AZ 85260
Phone: 602/998-9780
Areas: All facets of integrated circuits.
Employees: 50
1985 Sales: $1M-$5M
Established: 1965
Founder/Chairman: Glen Madland
President/CEO: Richard Skinner
Vice President(s): George Fry; Jim Griffin
Top Analysts: Bill McClean; Dean Winkelmann; Mary Swanson
Public Relations Contact: Helen Pitcher

In-house online database: No	Online access by clients: Yes
Reports: Yes	Seminars: Yes
Consulting: Yes	Newsletters: Yes

Titles (frequency): ICECAP Report (monthly)

International Data Corporation (IDC)
Five Speen Street
Framingham, MA 01701
Phone: 617/872-8200   Telex: 95-1168
Areas: Information processing industry (computers, communications, software and services, factory automation, leasing).
Employees: 350
1985 Sales: $26M-$30M
Established: 1964
Founder/Chairman: Patrick J. McGovern
President/CEO: Carl Masi
Vice President(s): Joseph L. Levy, Senior Vice President; Thomas Willmott, VP, Research/Analysis
Top Analysts: Molly Upton, VP, Applied technologies; Frank R. Gens, VP, IBM systems advisory; Aaron Goldberg, VP, Microcomputer services
Public Relations Contact: Nina Ricci, Director of Marketing

In-house online database: Yes	Online access by clients: Yes
Reports: Yes	Seminars: Yes
Consulting: Yes	Newsletters: Yes

Titles (frequency): Computer Industry Report, Software Watch, Telecom Insider, OA Reporting Serv, Communications Indus Rept, CIM Report

International Resource Development
6 Prowitt Street
Norwalk, CT 06855
Phone: 203/866-7800   Telex: 643452
Areas: High-tech related topics, including telecommunications, computers, robotics, office
automation, financial services, life sciences, and biotechnology.
Employees: 25
1985 Sales: $6M-$10M
Established: 1971
Founder/President/CEO: Kenneth G. Bosomworth
Top Analysts: Eric Arnum, Senior Analyst, Electronic mail; Leslie Townsend, Senior Analyst,
Satellite communications
Public Relations Contact: Suzanne Bores, Marketing Communications Mgr.

In-house online database: No	Online access by clients: No
Reports: Yes	Seminars: No
Consulting: Yes	Newsletters: Yes

Titles (frequency): EEMS Newsletter, VideoPrint Newsletter (semimonthly); AdaData Newsletter,
Download Newsl., Telecom/IBM (monthly)

Link Resources Corp
215 Park Avenue South
New York, NY 10003
Phone: 212/473-5600   Telex: 429328
Areas: Personal computers, educational computing, new telecommunication services, electronic
information, videotex, telecommuting, computer-based training.
Employees: 40
1985 Sales: $1M-$5M
Established: 1976
Founder: Haines B. Gaffner
Chairman: Wholly owned sub IDC
President/CEO: Haines B. Gaffner
Vice President(s): Diane Gamble, VP and General Manager; Steve Sieck, VP, Electronic services
Top Analysts: Andy Bose, Dir of Microcomputer analysis; Mark Winther, Dir of New
communication services; Corey Bock, Dir of Electronic information
Public Relations Contact: Laura Berland, Director of Marketing

In-house online database: No	Online access by clients: No
Reports: Yes	Seminars: Yes
Consulting: Yes	Newsletters: Yes

Titles (frequency): Electronic Information, Videotex, Thruput, Perspectives in Consumer
Electronics, others, (monthly)

Market Information Center, Inc.
65 Boston Post Road, West
Marlborough, MA 01752
Phone: 617/460-0880
Areas: Communications; vertical markets; end-user, survey-based research.
Employees: 6
1985 Sales: <$1M
Established: 1983
Founders: Harold Henry and Barry Gilbert
President/CEO: Harold Henry
Vice President(s): Barry Gilbert, Executive VP; Bob Paolucci, VP Sales
Public Relations Contact: Barry Gilbert, Executive VP

In-house online database: Yes	Online access by clients: Yes
Reports: Yes	Seminars: No
Consulting: Yes	Newsletters: Yes

Titles (frequency): Comment Newsletter on topics in communications (monthly)

Newton-Evans Research Company, Inc.
3220 Corporate Court, Suite A
Ellicott City, MD 21043
Phone: 301/465-7316
Areas: Computers, communications and controls.
Employees: 8
1985 Sales: <$1M
Established: 1978
Founders: Charles W. Newton
President/CEO: Charles W. Newton
Top Analysts: Loretta M. Smolenski, Supervisory control & data acquisition; Karen P. Dargis, Data communications; Jeanne M. Small, Microcomputers & corporate profiles
Public Relations Contact: Loretta M. Smolenski

In-house online database: No	Online access by clients: No
Reports: Yes	Seminars: Yes
Consulting: Yes	Newsletters: Yes

Titles (frequency): Market Trends Digest (monthly)

Northern Business Information, Inc.

157 Chambers Street
New York, NY 10007
Phone: 212/732-0775
Telex: 499 0412
Areas: Central office (U.S. & worldwide), Centrex, PBX, transmission (digital/fiber optics), strategic analysis of AT&T, IBM, Northern Telecom.
Employees: 20
Established: 1976
Founders: Sean White, Francis McInerney
President/CEO: S. White/F. McInerney
Top Analysts: Glenn Powers, Sr. Anal/Editor, Telecom Strategy Letter; William Rich, Sr. Anal/Editor, Telecom Market Letter; Michael Miller, Sr. Anal, Transmission
Public Relations Contact: Arthur Hill, General Manager

In-house online database: Yes	Online access by clients: No
Reports: Yes	Seminars: Yes
Consulting: No	Newsletters: Yes

Titles (frequency): Telecom Strategy Letter (monthly), Telecom Market Letter (semimonthly)

Novon Research Group

3360 Dwight Way
Berkeley, CA 94704
Phone: 415/641-9800   Telex: 510-601-2977
Areas: "Non Von Neumann" computing (distributed intelligence) including UNIX/DOS systems, supercomputing, AI and human interfaces.
Employees: 14
1985 Sales: $1M-$5M
Established: 1985
Founders: Dr. Brian Boyle, et al.
Chairman: Brian Boyle
Vice President(s): Brian Boyle, Dr. Jay Siegel, Alan Kucheck
Top Analysts: Brian Boyle, Dir of Research, UNIX & Compute-Intensive Mkts; Jay Siegel, Economics research, forecasting & methodologies; Alan Kucheck, Operations, PCs, database & graphic systems
Public Relations Contact: Carol Grant

In-house online database: Yes	Online access by clients: Yes
Reports: Yes	Seminars: Yes
Consulting: Yes	Newsletters: Yes

Titles (frequency): The Next Generation, 8-issue/yr; The Next Generation, videotape, 4 60-min tapes/year

Patricia Seybold Office Computing Group
148 State Street, Suite 612
Boston, MA 02109
Phone: 617/742-5200   Telex: 4945983
Areas: Office information systems, UNIX, networking.
Employees: 12
1985 Sales: $1M-$5M
Established: 1985
Founders/President/CEO: Patricia Seybold
Top Analysts: Patricia Seybold, Integ. office sys, strategic plan'g; Mike Millikin, PCs, networks, communications; Ronni Marshak, Wrd proc sys/integ office sys, user interface
Public Relations Contact: Bruce Polsky, Mktg Dir

In-house online database: No	Online access by clients: No
Reports: Yes	Seminars: Yes
Consulting: Yes	Newsletters: Yes

Titles (frequency): Seybold's Office Systems Report, Seybold's Network Monitor, Seybold's UNIX in the Office (monthly)

Prime Data
2005 Hamilton Avenue, Suite 215
San Jose, Ca 95125
Phone: 408/559-6969
Telex: 17-1618
Areas: Computer-integrated engineering (CAE & CAD), automatic test equipment, & test instruments.
Employees: 8
Established: 1975
Founders: Galen W. Wampler, Kenneth N. Neff
President/CEO: Galen W. Wampler
Vice President(s): Kenneth N. Neff

In-house online database: Yes	Online access by clients: No
Reports: Yes	Seminars: Yes
Consulting: Yes	Newsletters: Yes

SEAI Technical Publications
P.O. Box 590
Madison, GA 30650
Phone: 404/342-9638
Areas: Artificial intelligence, robotics, machine vision, bioengineering, computers.
Employees: 3
Established: 1973
Founders: Richard K. Miller
President/CEO: Marcie Miller
Top Analysts: Richard K. Miller, Terri C. Walker, M. Todd Jarvis
In-house online database: No   Online access by clients: No
Reports: Yes Seminars: No
Consulting: No   Newsletters: No

Seybold Group, Inc., The
20695 Western Ave., Suite 132
Torrance, CA 90501
Phone: 213/320-9151
Areas: Personal computers, desktop publishing, desktop communication, minicomputers, mainframe computers.
Employees: 25
1985 Sales: $1M-$5M
Established: 1984
Founders: Andrew Seybold
Chairman: John Seybold
President/CEO: Andrew Seybold
Vice President(s): Thomas White, Executive VP
Top Analysts: Robert Clark, Connectivity; Michael Weiss, Peripherals; Larry Magid, Software & desktop publishing
Public Relations Contact: Victor Wortman

In-house online database: Yes	Online access by clients: No
Reports: Yes	Seminars: Yes
Consulting: Yes	Newsletters: Yes

Titles (frequency): Seybold Outlook, Seybold Insights (monthly)

StoreBoard Inc.
8111 LBJ Freeway, Suite 1300
Dallas, TX 75251
Phone: 214/231-5964
Areas: Analysis and sales tracking of computer specialty stores in U.S.--Sales data trends (PCs, software, peripherals). Distribution consulting.
Employees: 5
1985 Sales: --
Established: 1986
Founders: Egil Juliussen, Alice Brown, JoeAnn Stahel, Karen Rosinsky
Chairman: Egil Juliussen
President/CEO: Alice Brown
Top Analysts: Egil Juliussen, Industry trends/analysis; Alice Brown, Computer specialty store trends/analysis; JoeAnn Stahel, Computer specialty store sales analysis
Public Relations Contact: Alice Brown

In-house online database: Yes	Online access by clients: No
Reports: Yes	Seminars: No
Consulting: Yes	Newsletters: No

Strategic Incorporated
P.O. Box 3770
Santa Clara, CA 95055
Phone: 408/983-1111
Telex: 427633
Areas: Telecommunications, computers, CAD/CAM, semiconductors.
Employees: 12
1985 Sales: $1M-$5M
Established: 1976
Founders: Michael Killen
President/CEO: Michael Killen
Vice President(s): Ted Wakayama, Research and Development
Top Analysts: Michael Killen, Communications and computers; Ted Wakayama, CAD/CAM and semiconductors

In-house online database: No	Online access by clients: No
Reports: Yes	Seminars: No
Consulting: Yes	Newsletters: No

Technology Research Group
2 Park Plaza, Suite 510
Boston, MA 02116
Phone: 617/482-4200
Areas: Electronic-product development automation, including computer-aided engineering and design, automatic test equipment, software development, custom and semicustom integrated circuits.
Employees: 6   Established: 1984
Founders: Andrew Rappaport, Cindy Thames
Chairman: Andrew Rappaport
President/CEO: Andrew Rappaport
Vice President(s): Cindy Thames
Top Analysts: Andy Rappaport, Electronic-product development automation
Public Relations Contact: Cindy Thames

In-house online database: Yes	Online access by clients: No
Reports: Yes	Seminars: Yes
Consulting: Yes	Newsletters: Yes

Titles (frequency): The Technology Research Letter (monthly)

VLSI Research Inc.
1754 Technology Drive, Suite 117
San Jose, Ca 95110
Phone: 408/289-9983
Telex: 171618 MSG SNDR SNJ
Areas: Specializes in analytic appraisals of VLSI systems. Covers high technology industries, electronics, semiconductors, semiconductor equipment.
1985 Sales: $1M-$5M
Established: 1976
Founders: Jerry Hutcheson
Chairman: Jerry Hutcheson
President/CEO: G. Dan Hutcheson
Top Analysts: J Hutcheson, Corporate strategy, semiconductor equip mfg; G D Hutcheson, Economic analysis, semiconductor equip mfg; Arvind Khilnani, Sr Scientist, Bus and tech plan'g
Public Relations Contact: Debbie Matsuhiro

In-house online database: Yes	Online access by clients: No
Reports: Yes	Seminars: Yes
Consulting: Yes	Newsletters: Yes

Titles (frequency): VLSI Manufacturing Newsletter (monthy); VLSI Manufacturing Outlook

Venture Development Corporation
One Apple Hill
Natick, MA 01760
Phone: 617/653-9000
Telex: 709190 VENTURE
Areas: Communications, computers, instrumentation, components, office equipment, consumer electronics.
Employees: 25
1985 Sales: $1M-$5M
Established: 1971
Founders: Lewis Solomon
President/CEO: Lewis Solomon
Top Analysts: Marc Regberg, Director of Marketing and Sales

In-house online database: Yes	Online access by clients: No
Reports: Yes	Seminars: No
Consulting: Yes	Newsletters: No

Winters Group, The
Temple Bldg., 14 Franklin St,Ste 920
Rochester, NY 14604
Phone: 716/546-7480
Areas: Computers and peripherals, AI, electronic publishing, biotechnology, banking, health care.
Employees: 12
1985 Sales: <$1M
Established: 1984
Founders: Mary-Frances Winters
President/CEO: Mary-Frances Winters
Top Analysts: Joan Creatura, Dir of Pubs, Computers & peripherals, AI; Sandra Atlas, Mktg Analyst, Electronic publishing
Public Relations Contact: Joan Creatura

In-house online database: Yes	Online access by clients: No
Reports: Yes	Seminars: No
Consulting: Yes	Newsletters: Yes

Titles (frequency): AI Capsule, Rpt on Comptrs & Periph, Rpt on Elec Pub'g; Rpt on New Tech (monthly)

Yankee Group
89 Broad Street
Boston, MA 02110
Phone: 617/542-0100
Areas: Communications and computer technologies in business, industry and the home.
Employees: 75
1985 Sales: >$10M
Established: 1970
Founders: Howard Anderson
President/CEO: Howard Anderson
Vice President(s): William F. Rosenberger, Communications/Info Systems; Robert L. Howie, Jr.,
Cons/Tech Div, Mfg automation planning
Top Analysts: David Mack, VP, Consulting Div, Telecom, Fac automation
Public Relations Contact: Rob Howie

In-house online database: No	Online access by clients: Yes
Reports: Yes	Seminars: Yes
Consulting: Yes	Newsletters: Yes

MUSEUMS

In this section COMPUTER INDUSTRY ALMANAC lists 15 museums with industry-related permanent exhibits. The entries are arranged alphabetically by name and include complete address, telephone, type of exhibits, curator, admission, and hours.

Buhl Science Center
Allegheny Square
Pittsburgh, PA 15212
Phone: 412/321-4300
Industry-Related Exhibit: Current model computer exhibits; computer learning lab for school children/adults. Exhibits on sound, image imagination, etc. Hands-on exhibits.
Control: Nonprofit
Museum Opened: 1939   Collection Opened: 1982
Museum Curator: Joshua C. Whetzel, Jr., President
Collection Curator: Ron Baillie, Dir of Computer Education
Hours: Daily, call for information

California Museum of Science and Industry
700 State Drive
Los Angeles, CA 90037
Phone: 213/744-7400
Industry-Related Exhibit: The Creative Computer focuses on computer-generated fine arts; Bicycle Factory focuses on computer-assisted design; ComputerWorks focuses on hardware.
Control: State
Museum Opened: 1912
Museum Curator: Don M. Muchmore, Executive Director
Collection Curator: Dr. J. Rounds, Chief Curator
Hours: Daily 10-5
Admission Fees: No charge

CTS Turner Museum
905 North West Blvd.
Elkhart, IN 46514
Phone: 219/293-7511
Industry-Related Exhibit: Telephones, switchboards from 1896-1940, electronic components from 1926 to present, computer core memories & modums as used 15-20 years ago.
Control: CTS Corporation
Museum Opened: 1979   Collection Opened: 1979
Museum Curator: Basil S. Turner, Director
Collection Curator: Ross Smith, Curator
Hours: Appointment only
Admission Fees: No charge

RESEARCH - Copyright 1987 Computer Industry Almanac

Computer Museum
300 Congress Street
Boston, MA 02210
Phone: 617/426-2800
Industry-Related Exhibit: Collection is all computer related: lab computers, production models, prototype models, classic computers, first/last-in-its class computers; components; computer card evolution; computer artifacts (patents, posters, books, sketches); etc.
Control: Board of Trustees
Museum Opened: 1982   Collection Opened: 1982
Museum Curator: Gwen Bell, Director
Collection Curator: Oliver Strimpel, Curator
Hours: Wed, Sat & Sun 10-6; Th & Fri 10-9
Admission Fees: Adults:$4, Students & Senior Citizens:$2

Discovery Center, Inc.
231 S.W. 2nd Avenue
Fort Lauderdale, FL 33301
Phone: 305/462-4116
Industry-Related Exhibit: Computer Works (computers with programs on video digitizers, arts & graphics, music composition, robotics demonstrations); exhibit on the internal workings of a computer; courses in computer use.
Control: Nonprofit; Board of Trustees
Museum Opened: 1976   Collection Opened: 1976
Museum Curator: Kim L. Maher, Executive Director
Collection Curator: John Ringenberger, Curator of Exhibits
Hours: Tues-Fri 12-5; Sat 10-5; Sun 12-5
Admission Fees: $2; Children under 3: Free; Group rates

Discovery Center of Science and Technology
321 South Clinton Street
Syracuse, NY 13202
Phone: 315/425-9068
Industry-Related Exhibit: Computer Corner (houses logo computers for visitors to learn programming). Display on the "insides" of a computer. Computer components (electronics/microprocessors). Telecom display shows your telephone voice with a voice printout.
Control: Nonprofit
Museum Opened: 1981
Museum Curator: Stephen A. Karon, Executive Director
Hours: Tues-Sat 10-5; Sun 12-5
Admission Fees: Adults:$1; Children:$.50

Discovery Place
301 North Tryon Street
Charlotte, NC 28202
Phone: 704/372-6262
Industry-Related Exhibit: Computers for hands-on learning. Other visitor-interactive exhibits on energy, science, physics, etc.
Control: Nonprofit; Board of Trustees
Museum Opened: 1981   Collection Opened: 1981
Museum Curator: Freda H. Nicholson, CEO and Executive Director
Collection Curator: Jerry Reynolds, Collection Coordinator
Hours: (Sep-May) 9-5 Wkdays; (Jun-Aug) 9-6 Wkdays; Sat 9-6; Sun 1-6
Admission Fees: Adults:$3; Stdnts & Sr. Cit:$2; Mbrs & Child under 3: Free

Exploratorium, The
3601 Lyon Street
San Francisco, CA 94123
Phone: 415/563-7337
Industry-Related Exhibit: Telecom exhibit on speech, collection of old radio tubes & transistors, human perception exhibit uses computers extensively to generate the power & brains of the exhibit.
Control: Nonprofit
Museum Opened: 1969
Museum Curator: Virginia Carollo Rubin, Acting Director
Collection Curator: Rob Semper, Deputy Director
Hours: Winter: Wed 1-9:30; Thu-Fri 1-5; Sat-Sun 10-5
Admission Fees: Adults:$4; Children under 17: Free; Sr. Cit & Groups:$2

Franklin Institute Science Museum & Planetarium
20th & The Benj. Franklin Pkwy
Philadelphia, PA 19103
Phone: 215/448-1200
Industry-Related Exhibit: Permanent exhibit on computer communications. Periodic rotating exhibits on computer chips & electronic devices, AI in robotics, electronic games, history of electricity & old radios, & learning to use a computer.
Control: Nonprofit; Division of Franklin Institute
Museum Opened: 1933
Museum Curator: Joel N. Bloom, President
Collection Curator: Gladys Breuer, Assistant Curator
Hours: M-Sat 10-5; Sun 12-5
Admission Fees: Adults:$3.50; Children 4-12:$2.75; Sr.Cit & Groups:$2.50

Maryland Science Center
601 Light Street
Baltimore, MD 21230
Phone: 301/685-2370
Industry-Related Exhibit: Permanent exhibit on The Computer Company (how to work computers & what they do). Other permanent exhibits: Science Arcade (principles of physics for light, optics, sight, sound, magnetism); Energy; Your World/Maryland (technology in MD).
Control: Private; Not for Profit; Board of Trustees
Museum Opened: 1976
Museum Curator: James R. Backstrom, Exec Director
Collection Curator: Dennis E. Zembawer, Director of Exhibits
Hours: M-Th 10-5; Fri-Sat 10-10; Sun 12-6
Admission Fees: Adults:$5; Family:$18; Child:$4.50; Sr.Cit/Stdnt/Milit:$4.50

MIT Museum, The
265 Massachusetts Avenue
Cambridge, MA 02139
Phone: 617/253-4444
Industry-Related Exhibit: Photograph collection on electronics, computers, and telecom. Old dynamos from early computers developed at MIT.
Control: Affiliated museums & University Branch of MIT
Museum Opened: 1971   Collection Opened: 1971
Museum Curator: Warren A. Seamans, Director
Collection Curator: Michael W. Yeates, Director of Collections
Hours: M-F 9-5, Sat 10-4
Admission Fees: No charge

Museum of History and Science
727 West Main Street
Louisville, KY 40202
Phone: 502/589-4584
Industry-Related Exhibit: Computer workshops for children & adults; CompuServ network for visitors to use. Anticipates a contract with So Central Bell to develop sound & communications exhibit.
Control: Private with Board of Directors
Museum Opened: 1872   Collection Opened: 1985
Museum Curator: Dr. Wm. M. Sudduth, Director
Collection Curator: Donald Binkley, VP History & Collections
Hours: Daily 9:30-5:30
Admission Fees: Adults:$3; Students, Sr. Cit:$2; Children 3-12:$2; Tours:$1

Museum of Science and Industry
57th Street & Lake Shore Drive
Chicago, IL 60637
Phone: 312/684-1414
Industry-Related Exhibit: Exhibits on calculating to computing (traces history of computers, their various applications) and on communications (how scientific principles apply to communications). Others: satellite communication devices & electricity in our future.
Control: Nonprofit
Museum Opened: 1926
Collection Curator: Gregg Loeser, Exhibits Director
Hours: Smr: Daily 9:30-5:30; Wtr: M-F 9:30-4; Sat-Sun-Hol 9:30-5:30
Admission Fees: No charge

Natl Museum of American History, Smithsonian Inst.
14th & Constitution Avenue
Washington, DC 20560
Phone: 202/357-2392
Industry-Related Exhibit: Calculating devices & computing machines from mid ages to now (Eniac computer, Whirlwind computer, IAF computer); documentation manuals; software from cards to disks. Telecom exhibits on electricity, early to 20th century.
Control: Nonprofit; Board of Regents
Museum Opened: 1964   Collection Opened: 1964
Museum Curator: Roger Kennedy, Director
Hours: Daily 10-5:30, except Christmas
Admission Fees: No charge

San Diego Hall of Science
1875 El Prado, Balboa Park
San Diego, CA 92103
Phone: 619/238-1233
Industry-Related Exhibit: "Hands-on" computer exhibits only.
Control: Nonprofit
Museum Opened: 1973
Museum Curator: Jeffrey W. Kirsch, Director
Hours: Smr: Daily 10-10; Wtr: Sun-Fri 10-10:30; Sat 10-11:15
Admission Fees: Adults:$4; Sr.Cit:$2.50; Juniors:$2.25

ONLINE INFORMATION SERVICES

In this section COMPUTER INDUSTRY ALMANAC lists major online information services. The entries are arranged alphabetically by name and include address, telephone, type of service, number of data bases and subscribers, and categories of information.

BRS, BRS Search, BRS/BRKTHRU, BRS/After Dark
Div. of Thyssen Borneszimena
1200 Route 7
Latham, NY 12210
Phone: 518/783-1161
Telex: 7104444965
Description: Provides access to a powerful electronic library with data bases covering virtually every major discipline. System software combines searching, flexibility and speed.
Founded: 1976
No. of Data Bases: 110
No. of Subscribers: Confidential
Categories of Information:
  Medicine & pharmacology
  Business & finance
  Physical & applied sciences
  Life sciences
  Social sciences & humanities
  Education
  Reference & multi-disciplinary
  News & periodicals

CompuServe, Inc.
Box 20212
5000 Arlington Centre Blvd.
Columbus, OH 43220
Phone: 614/457-8600
Description: Provides communication and information services (electronic mail & message systems, value-added network services) to Fortune 500 companies, 1200 other companies, & individuals.
Founded: 1969
No. of Data Bases: 400+
No. of Subscribers: 325,000
Categories of Information:
  News information
  Electronic mail
  Financial products
  Special interest groups
  Home banking & shopping svces

Dialog Information Services Inc.
Subsidiary of Lockheed
3460 Hill View Ave
Palo Alto, CA 94304
Phone: 415/858-3742
Description: Provides retrieval services used for current and retrospective literature searches
covering every major subject field.
Founded: 1978
No. of Data Bases: 260
No. of Subscribers: 80,000+
Categories of Information:
  Business
  Government
  Medical
  Chemistry
  Social science
  Patent trademarks
  Others

Dow Jones News/Retrieval
Dow Jones & Company, Inc.
P. O. Box 300
Princeton, NJ 08543
Phone: 609/452-2000
Description: Provides current business/financial news & information in an interactive information
service (90 sec. to 90 days). General services include electronic mail & shopping.
Founded: 1974
No. of Data Bases: 42
No. of Subscribers: N/A
Categories of Information:
  News information
  Text-search service
  MCI mail
  Stock quotes & mkt averages
  Electronic shopping service

The Source
Source Telecomputing Corporation
1616 Anderson Road
McLean, VA 22102
Phone: 703/734-7500
Telex: 440 486 SOURC UI
Description: Provides the general public access to vast, continually updated information maintained in large data bases and to a variety of electronic communication services.
Founded: 1979
No. of Data Bases: 800+
No. of Subscribers: Confidential
Categories of Information:
  Communications
  News, weather and sports
  Business and investing
  Education, shopping and games
  Travel
  Personal computing
  Special interest groups

RESEARCH CENTERS

In this section COMPUTER INDUSTRY ALMANAC lists 13 U.S. research centers conducting computer-related research. The entries are arranged alphabetically by name and include complete address, areas of research, sources and amounts of funding, year founded, primary sponsors, staff and contact.

Arthur D. Little, Inc.
Acorn Park
Cambridge, MA   02140
Phone: 617/864-5770
Telex: 921436
Areas of Industry-related Research: Information systems, artificial intelligence, and electronics.
Sources of Funding: Contracts derived from all branches of government
Funding/Revenue: $ 232.6M
Nonprofit: No
Year Founded: 1886
Staff: 2600+
  Professional: 1300
  Other Staff: 1300
Contact: John F. Magee, Chairman and CEO
        Dr. Charles LaMontia, President & COO

AT&T Bell Laboratories
Crawfords Corner Road
Holmdel, NJ   07733
Phone: 201/949-3000
Telex: 2019497912
Areas of Industry-related Research: New computer architectures, software, UNIX, fiber optics, microelectronics.
Funding/Revenue: $ 2B
Nonprofit: No
Primary Sponsors: AT&T-owned research center
Year Founded: 1925
Staff: 21,000
Contact: Ian M. Ross, President

Battelle Memorial Institute
505 King Avenue
Columbus, OH   43201
Phone: 614/424-6424
Telex: 245454
Areas of Industry-related Research: Computer-assisted design, computer-integrated mfg, db systems, AI.
Percent Computer Industry-related Research: 20
Sources of Funding: Endowmts, res contracts (govt=70%; states, co's, univ=30%)
Funding/Revenue: $ 200M
Nonprofit: Yes
Year Founded: 1929
Staff: 3000
  Professional: 2000
  Other Staff: 1000
Contact: Dr. Neil Carter, Director of Columbus Division
        Dr. Douglas Alesen, Corporation Operations Officer

Bell Communications Research (Bellcore)
290 West Mt. Pleasant Avenue
Livingston, NJ   07039
Phone: 201/740-3000
Areas of Industry-related Research: Technical research for regional Bell operating companies.
Locations:NJ (4), WA, & IL.
Sources of Funding: Seven regional phone companies
Funding/Revenue: $ 922M
Nonprofit: No
Primary Sponsors: Ameritech, Bell Atlantic, Bellsouth, Nynex, Pacific Telesis, SW Bell, U.S. West
Year Founded: 1984
Staff: 7300
Contact: Rocco Marano, President and CEO
        Ron Riechmann, Public Relations

700 - RESEARCH CENTERS

Charles Babbage Institute
117 Pleasant St.SE, Walter Libry
Minneapolis, MN   55455
Phone: 612/624-5050
Areas of Industry-related Research: Evolution of the computer and scientific/technological history (archives, photo collections, taped interviews).
Sources of Funding: University of Minnesota & various corporations
Primary Sponsors: American Federation of Information Processing Society
Year Founded: 1977
Staff: 7
 Professional: 6
 Other Staff: 1
Contact: Arthur L. Norberg, Director

IBM Almaden Research Center (ARC)
650 Harry Road
San Jose, CA   95120
Phone: 408/927-1846
Areas of Industry-related Research: Computer science, I/O science & technology, storage systems and technology.
Percent Computer Industry-related Research: 100
Sources of Funding: IBM-owned research center
Funding/Revenue: $ 120M est.
Nonprofit: No
Primary Sponsors: IBM-owned research center
Year Founded: 1956
Staff: 800
Contact: Dr. A. Frank Mayadas, Director

IBM Thomas J. Watson Research Center
Route 134, Box 218
Yorktown Heights, NY   10598
Phone: 914/945-3000
Areas of Industry-related Research: Artificial intelligence, computer science.
Percent Computer Industry-related Research: 100
Sources of Funding: IBM-owned research center
Funding/Revenue: $ 320M est.
Nonprofit: No
Primary Sponsors: IBM-owned research center
Year Founded: 1961
Staff: 2200
Contact: John A. Armstrong, Director

Microelectronics & Computer Technology Corp.(MCC)
3500 West Valcones Center Dr.
Austin, TX   78759
Phone: 512/343-0978
Areas of Industry-related Research: Software technology, VLSI/CAD, semiconductor packaging & interconnect, parallel processing, AI, data base, human interface.
Percent Computer Industry-related Research: 100
Sources of Funding: Funded by 21 companies in computer industry
Funding/Revenue: $ 65M
Nonprofit: No
Primary Sponsors: AMD, Allied-Sig, BMC, Bellcore, Boeing, Control Data, DEC, Kodak, Gould, Harris, Honeywell, Lockheed, 3M, Martin Marietta, Motorola, Nat Semi, NCR, RCA, Rockwell, Sperry, Westghse.
Year Founded: 1983
Staff: 460
  Professional: 420
  Other Staff: 40
Contact: Admiral B. R. Inman, Chairman, President, CEO
     Bill Stotesbery, Dir, Govt & Public Affairs

Rand Corporation
1700 Main Street
Santa Monica, CA   90406
Phone: 213/393-0411
Areas of Industry-related Research: Specialized language tools for use in expert systems, microcircuit technology, robotics & artificial intelligence, computer security.
Sources of Funding: Funded by federal, state & local govt; foundations & other private sources; & its own earned fees & endowment income.
Funding/Revenue: $ 60.4M
Nonprofit: Yes
Primary Sponsors: Conrad Hilton, Robert Wood Johnson, Rockefeller and Ford Foundations
Year Founded: 1948
Staff: 1100
 Professional: 550
 Other Staff: 550
Contact: Donald B. Rice, President

Semiconductor Research Corp
4501 Alexander Dr.
Research Triangle Park, NC   27709
Phone: 919/541-9400
Areas of Industry-related Research: Silicon/semiconductor research, chip-making technology, design automation & system simulation tools, chip reliability, 256-Mbit DRAM development.
Percent Computer Industry-related Research: 30
Sources of Funding: Funded by 36 member companies and U.S. government
Funding/Revenue: $ 16.4M
Nonprofit: Yes
Primary Sponsors: 36 major corporations
Year Founded: 1982
Staff: 25
 Professional: 7
 Other Staff: 18
Contact: Larry W. Sumney, President

Software Productivity Consortium
1880 N Campus Commons Dr.
Reston, VA   22091
Phone: 703/648-1880
Areas of Industry-related Research: Advanced software development methods and solutions to
critical software problems for Dept of Defense and other govt agencies.
Percent Computer Industry-related Research: 100
Sources of Funding: Funded by 14 aerospace companies
Nonprofit: Yes
Primary Sponsors: Gen Dynamics, Lockheed, McDonnell Douglas, Boeing, Allied Bendix Aero,
Ford Aero, Grumman, Harris, Martin Marietta, Northrup, SAIC, TRW, United Tech, Vitro
Year Founded: 1985
Staff: 100
Contact: Dr. Howard L. Yudkin, President and CEO
     Bob Cohen, Public Relations

SRI International
333 Ravenswood Ave.
Menlo Park, CA   94025
Phone: 415/326-6200
Areas of Industry-related Research: Computer science, information science, network information &
control, special communication systems, computer security work.
Percent Computer Industry-related Research: 35-40
Sources of Funding: U.S. & foreign government agencies & industrial organizations
Funding/Revenue: $ 211.3M
Nonprofit: Yes
Year Founded: 1946
Staff: 2800
  Professional: 1800
  Other Staff: 1000
Contact: Dr. William F. Miller, President
     Dennis Maxwell, Vice President Corporate Communications

Xerox Palo Alto Research Center (PARC)
3333 Coyote Hill Rd.
Palo Alto, CA   94304
Phone: 415/494-4000
Areas of Industry-related Research: Six labs: Computer Science, Exploratory Development, General
Sciences, Integrated Circuits, Intelligent Systems, & System Concepts.
Percent Computer Industry-related Research: 40
Sources of Funding: Xerox and government contracts
Funding/Revenue: $ 291M
Nonprofit: Yes
Primary Sponsors: Xerox-owned research center
Year Founded: 1970
Staff: 350
  Professional: 280
  Other Staff: 70
Contact: Frank Squires, VP
      Dr. John Seely Brown, VP; Dr. Ron Rider, VP

NSF SUPERCOMPUTER CENTERS

In this section COMPUTER INDUSTRY ALMANAC lists the five National Science Foundation Supercomputer Centers. In 1984, the National Science Foundation established the Office of Advanced Scientific Computing (OASC). The OASC conducted a national competition in 1984-1985 to establish national supercomputer centers dedicated to serving the academic research community. From 22 institutions that responded to the solicitation, the OASC selected, after extensive review, five institutions to become national supercomputer centers. The five centers are listed alphabetically here. Data given includes complete address, telephone, date opened, directors' names, description, funding, and hardware.

Center for Theory & Simulation
Cornell University
265 Olin Hall
Ithaca, NY 14853
Phone: 607/255-2000
Opened: February 1985
Director: Kenneth Wilson, Director
     Ravi Sudan, Deputy Director
     William Schrader, Executive Director
Description: Includes two supercomputing programs: Production Supercomputer Facility (provides supercomputing resources for researchers) and Theory Center (is developing a 1990s-era, highly parallel supercomputer).
Other Funding: State of New York, IBM (equipment), General Electric, Corning Glass, and other corporations
Hardware: IBM 3090-400 with 7 attached Floating Point Sys array scientific processors

John von Neumann Center for Scientific Computing (CSC)
P.O. Box 3717
Princeton, NJ 08543
Phone: 609/520-2000
Opened: December 1985
Director: Dr. Joseph F. Traub, President
Description: Provides state-of-the-art computing and communications to university, government, and industrial researchers. Will acquire the first production ETA-10 Supercomputer in April 1987.
Other Funding: New Jersey Commission on Science & Technology
Hardware: CYBER 205

National Center for Supercomputing Applications (NCSA)
605 East Springfield Ave
154 Computing Applications Bldg
Champaign, IL 61820
Phone: 217/244-0074
Opened: January 1986
Director: Larry L. Smarr, Director
Description: University-based supercomputing and interdisciplinary research community features a comprehensive computer environment with a focus on forefront research programs and user services.
Other Funding: State of Illinois and the University of Illinois at Champaign/Urbana
Hardware: Cray X-MP/48, 120-mega word solid state storage device

Pittsburgh Supercomputer Center
Mellon Institute
4400 5th Avenue
Pittsburgh, PA 15213
Phone: 412/268-4960
Opened: June 1986
Director: Ralph Roskies, Scientific Director & Founder
  Michael Levine, Scientific Director & Founder
  Beverly Clayton, Executive Director
Description: Administrative offices and user services located at Mellon Institute. Supercomputer housed at Westinghouse Energy Systems Computer Center in Monroeville, PA.
Other Funding: State of Pennsylvania and several companies, private and public
Hardware: Cray X-MP/48 with 4 processors; 2 VAX 8650 front-ends

San Diego Supercomputer Center (SDSC)
GA Technologies Inc.
P.O. Box 85608
San Diego, CA 92138
Phone: 619/534-5000
Opened: January 1986
Director: Sidney Karin, Director
Description: Located at UC, San Diego. Has steering committee with one rep from consortium institutions.
Other Funding: Consortium members and industrial participation
Hardware: Cray X-MP/48 with 4 processors

16 SALARIES

COLLEGE PLACEMENT COUNCIL
STARTING SALARIES OF ENGINEERING GRADUATES
1986

"The College Placement Council's SALARY SURVEY reports salary data based on offers, not acceptances, with no limits on the number of offers per student. Data is from 183 placement offices at 161 U.S. colleges and universities. The survey is based on offers reported from September 1, 1985 to June 13, 1986."--College Placement Council.

From this survey COMPUTER INDUSTRY ALMANAC has selected only partial data to list.

Reprinted with permission from College Placement Council, 1986. Copyright 1986 by College Placement Council, Bethlehem, PA.

B.A. Degree	Average Salary	Increase Over 1985
Electrical Engineering	$28,368	3.6%
Computer Science	26,592	6.4%
Economics	22,404	8.0%
Humanities	19,296	10.1%

708 - SALARIES: Engineers

NATIONAL SOCIETY OF PROFESSIONAL ENGINEERS
NSPE PROFESSIONAL ENGINEER INCOME AND SALARY SURVEY
1986

The National Society of Professional Engineers (NSPE) conducted a PROFESSIONAL ENGINEER INCOME AND SALARY SURVEY in 1986. The survey accumulated data from 14,303 non-student association members holding doctorates, master's and bachelor's degrees. Income is defined as an individual's annual base salary from the primary employer as of January 1, 1986. It includes fees, bonuses, and commission during the preceding 12-month period but excludes pay from secondary or part-time employment.--COMPUTER INDUSTRY ALMANAC.

From this survey COMPUTER INDUSTRY ALMANAC has selected partial data.

Reprinted with permission from National Society of Professional Engineers, 1986. Copyright 1986 by National Society of Professional Engineers, Alexandria, VA.

Highest Engineering Degree	Median Annual Income
Doctorate	$58,565
Master's	$49,000
Bachelor's	$45,000
All Engineers	$47,200
All Electrical & Electronic Engineers	$48,691

ELECTRONIC BUSINESS
TOP PAID EXECUTIVES IN THE U.S. ELECTRONICS INDUSTRY
October 15, 1986

"The list of top earners compiled by ELECTRONIC BUSINESS includes cash compensation in the form of salary and bonuses, but does not include stock options or other long-range compensation. Data for the list was gleaned primarily from annual reports and proxy statements. For the entire 100, the average cash compensation last year was $566,350, down from $571,245 in 1984."-- ELECTRONIC BUSINESS.
Reprinted with permission from ELECTRONIC BUSINESS, October 15, 1986. Copyright 1986 by Reed Publishing USA, Newton, MA.

Rank	Executive	1985 Salary	% Change 1985/1984	Company/Position
1	John W. Dixon	$1,703,404	+4.9%	E-Systems Chairman, CEO
2	George L. Bragg	1,298,492	+508.4%	Telex President
3	Paul C. Ely Jr.	1,295,500	N/A	Convergent Technologies President, CEO
4	W.J. Sanders III	1,189,664	+25.5%	Advanced Micro Devices Chairman, president, CEO
5	John Sculley	1,054,396	-51.3%	Apple Computer President, CEO
6	Charles E. Exley Jr.	905,297	+8.9%	NCR Chairman, president, CEO
7	Bernard L. Schwartz	884,160	+0.9%	Loral Chairman, CEO
8	John A. Young	859,590	+7.6%	Hewlett-Packard President, CEO, chairman
9	John R. Opel	847,986	-18.0%	IBM Chairman
10	Cees Bruynes	810,063	+16.1%	N.A. Philips Chairman, president
11	Anthony R. Hamilton	805,811	-23.2%	Avnet Chairman, CEO
12	Leon Machiz	805,811	-5.9%	Avnet President
13	David T. Kearns	798,711	+20.6%	Xerox Chairman, CEO
14	Paul G. Stern	797,172	+13.9%	Burroughs President, CEO

(Continued next page)

N/A: Not Available

ELECTRONIC BUSINESS
TOP PAID EXECUTIVES IN THE U.S. ELECTRONICS INDUSTRY (Continued)

Rank	Executive	1985 Salary	% Change 1985/1984	Company/Position
15	Edson W. Spenser	$789,000	+21.9%	Honeywell Chairman, CEO
16	Kenneth H. Olsen	755,000	+15.3%	Digital Equipment President, CEO
17	John F. Akers	735,715	+6.7%	IBM President, CEO
18	Paul J. Rizzo	721,525	-5.9%	IBM Vice chairman
19	Gerald G. Probst	698,002	+19.2%	Sperry Chairman, CEO
20	William T. Ylvisaker	681,911	+3.0%	Gould Chairman, CEO
21	Joseph A. Boyd	680,764	+1.6%	Harris Chairman, CEO
22	Joe M. Henson	671,528	+66.1%	Prime Computer President, CEO
23	Richard G. Meise	666,154	+2.6%	Convergent Technologies Vice president
24	David R. Tacke	647,392	+42.3%	E-Systems President
25	George B. Harvey	638,489	+4.6%	Pitney-Bowes Chairman, president, CEO
26	John C. Lewis	636,126	+16.6%	Amdahl President, CEO
27	Anthony B. Holbrook	629,256	+44.9%	Advanced Micro Devices Executive VP, COO
28	Ralph H. O'Brien	625,313	N/A	Mohawk Data Sciences Chairman, president
29	Dean P. Phypers	623,782	-5.9%	IBM Senior VP
30	William F. Glavin	620,409	+13.4%	Xerox Vice chairman
31	George B. Beitzel	608,210	-4.0%	IBM Senior VP
32	C. Peter McColough (Continued next page)	560,556	+16.8%	Xerox Chairman, exec committee

N/A: Not Available

ELECTRONIC BUSINESS
TOP PAID EXECUTIVES IN THE U.S. ELECTRONICS INDUSTRY (Continued)

Rank	Executive	1985 Salary	% Change 1985/1984	Company/Position
33	James F. McDonald	$546,763	+89.6%	Gould President, COO
34	James J. Renier	544,333	+23.0%	Honeywell Vice chairman
35	James L. Donald 1	544,231	+20.9%	DSC Communications President, CEO, treasurer
36	Robert W. Galvin	539,687	-1.9%	Motorola Chairman
37	William C. Norris	534,546	-20.8%	Control Data Executive officer
38	Jerome J. Meyer	533,120	N/A	Varian Associates President, COO
39	Dean O. Morton	532,503	+18.0%	Hewlett-Packard Executive VP, COO
40	Eugene R. White	525,376	+12.6%	Amdahl Chairman
41	John T. Hartley	520,389	+0.8%	Harris President, COO
42	Thomas A. Vanderslice	516,545	N/A	Apollo Computer Chairman, president, CEO
43	John A. Rollwagen	507,473	+28.6%	Cray Research Chairman, president, CEO
44	James B. Downey	494,984	+43.1%	Advanced Micro Devices Senior VP
45	Frank C. Lanza	492,486	+0.6%	Loral President, COO
46	Robert M. Price	489,311	-17.7%	Control Data Chairman, president, CEO
47	E. Oran Brigham	489,257	+25.5%	Avantek Chairman, CEO, president
48	Frank W. McBee Jr.	481,191	+6.1%	Tracor President
49	Melvin Howard	480,591	+8.8%	Xerox Executive VP
50	Wallace W. Booth	476,322	-6.9%	Ducommun Chairman, CEO

(Continued next page)

1 Resigned as Treasurer January 13, 1986   N/A: Not Available

ELECTRONIC BUSINESS
TOP PAID EXECUTIVES IN THE U.S. ELECTRONICS INDUSTRY (Continued)

Rank	Executive	1985 Salary	% Change 1985/1984	Company/Position
51	William G. Moore Jr.	$473,889	-25.4%	Recognition Equipment Chairman, president, CEP
52	Joseph J. Kroger	470,470	+22.3%	Sperry Executive VP
53	Stephen J. Jatras	464,553	+15.6%	Telex Chairman, CEO
54	Jack L. Bowers	457,466	-21.7%	Sanders Associates Chairman, CEO
55	Walter F. Raab	457,407	+10.8%	AMP Chairman, CEO
56	William J. Weisz	456,281	-34.0%	Motorola Vice chairman
57	Mark Shepherd Jr.	455,020	-17.3%	Texas Instruments Chairman
58	Vincent R. McLean	450,344	+15.0%	Sperry Executive VP, CFO
59	Stanley A. Wainer	450,000	-12.3%	Wyle Laboratories Chairman, CEO
60	William E. Terry	437,292	+10.4%	Hewlett-Packard Executive VP
61	David A. Bossen	435,000	+6.1%	Measurex President, CEO
62	James M. Nolan 2	422,000	+13.5%	DSC Communications Chairman, consultant
63	Sidney Topol	421,030	+49.2%	Scientific-Atlanta Chairman, CEO
64	Frank J. Pipp	419,924	N/A	Xerox Group VP
65	Rhesa S. Farmer	416,841	N/A	Motorola Executive VP
66	W. Michael Blumenthal	416,250	-56.2%	Burroughs Chairman, CEO
67	John V. Roach	414,368	-25.0%	Tandy Chairman, CEO, president
68	Robert F. Holmes	412,922	+8.7%	Burroughs Senior VP

(Continued next page)

2 Served as CFO from October 17, 1985 to January 13, 1986   N/A: Not Available

ELECTRONIC BUSINESS
TOP PAID EXECUTIVES IN THE U.S. ELECTRONICS INDUSTRY (Continued)

Rank	Executive	1985 Salary	% Change 1985/1984	Company/Position
69	David Simpson	$412,814	+13.0%	Gould Vice chairman
70	John C. Waddell	409,822	-13.7%	Arrow Electronics Chairman, CEO
71	Walter J. Zable	409,698	+10.0%	Cubic Chairman, president, CEO
72	John F. Smith	408,950	+32.4%	Digital Equipment Vice president
73	John J. Shields	408,133	+32.2%	Digital Equipment Vice president, Gen Mgr
74	James S. Toreson	407,010	+38.0%	Xebec Chairman, president, CEO
75	Stephen J. Zelencik	405,976	+38.3%	Advanced Micro Devices Senior VP
76	Frank Hopkins	405,461	+6.9%	N.A. Philips Executive VP
77	An Wang	405,178	-33.1%	Wang Laboratories Chairman, president, CEO
78	Winston R. Hindle Jr.	405,000	-31.2%	Digital Equipment Vice president
79	John F. Cunningham [3]	404,968	-24.1%	Wang Laboratories President, COO
80	E. Gene Keiffer	404,092	+10.2%	E-Systems Senior VP
81	A. Lowell Lawson	399,892	+10.6%	E-Systems Senior VP
82	Norbert R. Berg	396,641	-19.7%	Control Data Deputy chairman
83	Milton Greenberg [4]	393,077	-1.7%	GCA Chairman, CEO
84	Frank G. Hickey	390,167	-29.0%	General Instrument Chairman, CEO
85	E.T. Bahre (Continued next page)	387,620	-1.2%	Computer & Communications Chairman, president, CEO

[3] Resigned July 18, 1985
[4] Resigned during first quarter 1986

ELECTRONIC BUSINESS
TOP PAID EXECUTIVES IN THE U.S. ELECTRONICS INDUSTRY (Continued)

Rank	Executive	1985 Salary	% Change 1985/1984	Company/Position
86	John F. Mitchell	$382,687	-33.0%	Motorola President
87	Winston R. Wallin	378,750	N/A	Medtronic Chairman, president, CEO
88	Manuel Garcia	377,853	+2.8%	NCR Executive VP
89	Jerry R. Junkins	377,390	+16.7%	Texas Instruments President, CEO
90	Edson D. de Castro	375,000	-14.0	Data General President
91	Richard C. Alberding	374,444	N/A	Hewlett-Packard Executive VP
92	John L. Doyle	373,552	N/A	Hewlett-Packard Executive VP
93	J.P. Barger	371,108	+44.5%	Dynatech President
94	Jerry K. Pearlman	367,708	-20.3%	Zenith Electronics Chairman, president, CEO
95	Joseph R. Canion	367,263	+74.6%	COMPAQ President, CEO
96	Dean A. Watkins	366,499	+4.0%	Watkins-Johnson Chairman
97	William F. O'Connell Jr.	362,333	+16.0%	Amdahl Senior VP
98	Charles E. Sporck	361,951	-8.9%	National Semiconductor President
99	James R. Berrett	360,000	-20.0%	Computervision President, CEO
100	George M. Scalise	358,655	+30.7%	Advanced Micro Devices Senior VP, CAO

N/A: Not Available

FORBES
WHO GETS THE MOST PAY
June 2, 1986

"Forbes ranks the chief executives of the 793 largest companies in the U.S. The rankings are based on total compensation." The salary figure includes all "salary and bonus payments in 1985, whether paid in cash or deferred, as well as directors' fees and commissions." The total figure represents the total of salary and bonus plus "payments made under long-term compensation plans, restricted stock awards vested or released from restrictions in 1985, thrift plan contributions, and other benefits," and stock gains including "net value realized in shares or cash from the exercise of stock options and/or stock appreciation rights granted in prior years."--FORBES.

From this list COMPUTER INDUSTRY ALMANAC has selected only the companies coded by FORBES as computer and electronic companies.

Excerpted by permission of FORBES Magazine, June 2, 1986. Copyright Forbes Inc., 1986.

Rank	Chief Executive/Company	1985 Salary ($000)	Total Compensation ($000)	Background
1	E Mandell de Windt Eaton	$1,147	$2,626	Operations
2	Anthony R Hamilton Avnet	806	1,701	Marketing
3	Edson D de Castro Data General	375	1,680	Founder
4	Charles E Sporck National Semiconductor	362	1,542	Production
5	John A Young Hewlett-Packard	860	1,241	Technical
6	Walter J Sanders III Advanced Micro	1,190	1,190	Founder
7	John A Rollwagen Cray Research	497	1,188	Marketing
8	George B Harvey Pitney Bowes	638	1,166	Finance
9	Stephen J Jatras Telex	402	1,059	Technical
10	John Sculley Apple Computer (Continued next page)	1,054	1,054	Marketing

FORBES

WHO GETS THE MOST PAY (Continued)

Rank	Chief Executive/Company	1985 Salary ($000)	Total Compensation ($000)	Background
11	David T Kearns Xerox	799	1,053	Sales
12	W Michael Blumenthal Burroughs	925	1,042	Administration
13	Joe M Henson Prime Computer	$672	$970	Marketing
14	Walter F Rabb AMP	457	956	Finance
15	Charles E Exley NCR	905	915	Finance
16	Joseph A Boyd [3] Harris Corp	862	862	Technical
17	Edson W Spencer Honeywell	789	789	Sales
18	Gerald G Probst Sperry	698	781	Technical
19	Kenneth H. Olsen Digital Equipment	755	755	Founder
20	John F Akers IBM	736	736	Marketing
21	William T Ylvisaker [2] Gould	682	689	Administration
22	David T Kimball General Signal	601	608	Administration
23	Horace G McDonell Jr. Perkin-Elmer	507	569	Technical
24	William C Norris [1] Control Data	535	535	Founder
25	James G Treybig Tandem Computers	320	454	Founder

(Continued next page)

1 Succeeded by Robert M. Price, 1/10/86
2 Succeeded by James F. McDonald, 4/29/86
3 Succeeded by John T. Hartley, 4/1/86

FORBES
WHO GETS THE MOST PAY (Continued)

Rank	Chief Executive/Company	1985 Salary ($000)	Total Compensation ($000)	Background
26	An Wang Wang Laboratories	405	405	Founder
27	Jerry R Junkins Texas Instruments	377	378	Operations
28	Ray Stata Analog Devices	$358	$358	Founder
29	Gordon E Moore Intel	355	356	Founder
30	Earl Wantland Tektronix	296	311	Operations
31	Morton L Mandel Premier Industrial	285	285	Founder
32	James W Meadlock Integraph	175	175	Founder

718 - SALARIES: Information System Workers

A.S. HANSEN, INC.
AVERAGE SALARIES OF INFORMATION SYSTEM WORKERS
1986

Information system workers' average salaries have been compiled for 21 years by A.S. Hansen, Inc.
The data reports survey responses of more than 1,700 organizations and breaks down average
salaries for 100 jobs by industry, location, and type of installation.--COMPUTER INDUSTRY
ALMANAC.

From this survey COMPUTER INDUSTRY ALMANAC has selected only partial data to list.

Reprinted with permission from A.S. Hansen, Inc., 1986. Copyright 1986 by A.S. Hansen, Inc.,
Deerfield, IL.

Position	Avg.Base Salary	Percent Increase
Top corporate data processing executive	$78,200	6.3%
Data processing operations manager	53,300	5.5
Telecommunications manager	48,000	4.8
Computer operations manager	37,100	2.8
Data entry operator	14,400	2.9

17 BITS AND MIPS

ASSOCIATION FOR COMPUTING MACHINERY (ACM)
NORTH AMERICAN COMPUTER CHESS CHAMPIONSHIPS

The Computer Chess Committee is a Committee within the Association for Computing Machinery (ACM). The main function of the committee is to organize annual chess tournaments in North America.--COMPUTER INDUSTRY ALMANAC.

1985 Denver
> Winner: HITECH--Ebeling, Berliner, Goetsch, Palay, Campbell, Slomer--SUN with chess hardware
> Runner-up: BEBE--Scherzer--Chess Engine

1984 San Francisco
> Winner: CRAY BLITZ--Hyatt, Gower, Nelson--Cray XMP/4
> Runner-up: BEBE--Scherzer--Chess Engine, and FIDELITY EXPERIMENTAL--Sparcklen, Spracklen, Fidelity machine

1983 Not held as the ACM's North American Computer Chess Championship that year but as the Fourth World Championship.

1982 Dallas
> Winner: BELLE--Thompson, Condon--PDP 11/23 with chess hardware
> Runner-up: CRAY BLITZ--Hyatt, Gower, Nelson--Cray 1

1981 Los Angeles
> Winner: BELLE--Thompson, Condon--PDP 11/23 with chess hardware
> Runner-up: NUCHESS--Blanchard, Slate--CDC Cyber 17

1980 Nashville
> Winner: BELLE--Thompson, Condon--PDP 11/70 with chess hardware
> Runner-up: CHAOS--Alexander, O'Keefe, Swartz, Berman--Amdahl 470

1979 Detroit
> Winner: CHESS 4.9--Slate, Atkin-CDC Cyber 176
> Runner-up: BELLE--Thompson, Condon--PDP 11/70 with chess hardware

1978 Washington
> Winner: BELLE--Thompson, Condon--PDP 11/70 with chess hardware
> Runner-up: CHESS 4.7--Slate, Atkin--CDC Cyber 176

(Continued next page)

NORTH AMERICAN COMPUTER CHESS CHAMPIONSHIPS - (Continued)

1977 Seattle
   Winner: CHESS 4.6--Slate, Atkin--CDC Cyber 176
   Runner-up: DUCHESS--Truscott, Wright, Jensen--IBM 370/168

1976 Houston
   Winner: CHESS 4.5--Slate, Atkin--CDC Cyber 176
   Runner-up: CHAOS--Swartz, Ruben, Winograd, Berman, Toikka, Alexander--Amdahl 470

1975 Minneapolis
   Winner: CHESS 4.4--Slate, Atkin--CDC Cyber 175
   Runner-up: TREEFROG--Hansen, Calnek, Crook--Honeywell 6080

1974 San Diego
   Winner: RIBBIT--Hansen, Crook, Parry--Honeywell 6050
   Runner-up: CHESS 4.0--Slate, Atkin--CDC 6400

1973 Atlanta
   Winner: CHESS 4.0--Slate, Atkin, Gorlen--CDC 6400
   Runner-up: TECH II--Baisley--PDP 10

1972 Boston
   Winner: CHESS 3.6--Slate, Atkin, Gorlen--CDC 6400
   Runner-up: OSTRICH--Arnold, Newborn--DG Supernova

1971 Chicago
   Winner: CHESS 3.5--Slate, Atkin, Gorlen--CDC 6400
   Runner-up: TECH--Gillogly--PDP 10

1970 New York
   Winner: CHESS 3.0--Slate, Atkin, Gorlen--CDC 6400
   Runner-up: DALY CHESS PROGRAM--Daly, King--Varian 620/i

ASSOCIATION FOR COMPUTING MACHINERY (ACM)
WORLD MICROCOMPUTING CHESS CHAMPIONSHIPS

The Association for Computing Machinery (ACM) sponsors and organizes the World
Microcomputer Chess Tournaments.--COMPUTER INDUSTRY ALMANAC.

1985 Amsterdam
  Winner: MEPHISTO AMSTERDAM I
  Runner-up: MEPHISTO AMSTERDAM II

1984 Glasgow
  Winner: Four way tie: ELITE X, MEPHISTO S/X, PRINCHESS, PSION CHESS

1983 Budapest
  Winner: ELITE A/S
  Runner-up: MEPHISTO X

1981 Travemende
  Winner: FIDELITY X
  Runner-up: CHESS CHAMPION MART V

1980 San Jose
  Winner: CHALLENGER
  Runner-up: MYCHESS B

INTERNATIONAL COMPUTER CHESS ASSOCIATION
WORLD COMPUTER CHESS CHAMPIONSHIP

The International Computer Chess Association was formed in 1977 by the programmers of leading computer chess programs. The association is responsible for organizing World Computer Chess activities. The 700 member worldwide organization also publishes THE ICCA JOURNAL on Computer Chess.--COMPUTER INDUSTRY ALMANAC.

1986   Cologne
Winner: CRAY BLITZ--Hyatt, Gower, Nelson--Cray XMP
Runner-up: HITECH--Berliner, et al.--SUN workstation with chess circuitry

1983   New York
Winner: CRAY BLITZ--Hyatt, Gower, Nelson--Cray XMP 48
Runner-up: BEBE--Scherzer--Chess engine

1980   Linz
Winner: BELLE--Thompson, Condon--PDP 11/23 with chess country
Runner-up: CHAOS--Alexander, Swartz, Berman O'Keefe--Amdahl 470/V8

1977   Toronto
Winner: CHESS 4.6--Slate, Atkin--CDC Cyber 176
Runner-up: DUCHESS--Truscott, Wright, Jensen--IBM 370/165

1974   Stockholm
Winner: KAISSA--Donskoy, Arlazarov--ICL 4/70
Runner-up: CHESS 4.0--Slate, Atkin--CDC 6600

WORKSTATION LABORATORIES
COMPUTER PERFORMANCE
1986

"Which computers are fastest? To determine the speed of computers fairly is impossible. The reason is that the speed of any computer varies and depends on so many factors--factors such as the application software, the compiler or assembler used to generate the code, and the operating system version used while the computer is running. It is possible to construct benchmark programs that show that any computer is faster than any other computer in the same class. Thus, there is caution concerning benchmarks that measure speed--especially if they come from a computer manufacturer. There is an old saying in the computer industry: 'There are lies, damn' lies, and then there are benchmarks.'

However, from third parties it is possible to find benchmark results that are not biased toward any manufacturer. Any benchmark results, though, are limited to the specific aspect of computer performance that the tests are intended to cover. The following speed benchmark results are from two independent sources. Workstation Laboratories, which measures the speed of workstation computers, multiuser microcomputers, and some personal computers, conducted its benchmarks in late 1986. The other benchmarks shown are public domain Dhrystone results, and most are prior to 1986.

The benchmark results shown below are intended to measure the computer processing speed, except floating point arithmetic. The same program written in C has been run on all of the computers. The unit of measurement is called 'Dhrystone.' The larger the Dhrystone number, the faster the computer speed. There are numerous details about the operating system version and compiler version that are not included in the list."--Workstation Laboratories, Inc.

Reprinted with permission from Workstation Laboratories, 1986. Copyright 1986 by Workstation Laboratories, Humboldt, AZ.

Computer	Microprocessor	Processor Clockrate	Dhrystones Per Second
Commodore 64	6510	1MHz	36
IBM PC/XT	8088	4.77MHz	427
IBM PC	8088	4.77MHz	454
Tandy 1000	V20	4.77MHz	458
Onyx C8002	Z8000	4MHz	511
Tandy 6000	68000	8MHz	694
Burroughs XE550	68010	10MHz	769
Altos 586	8086	10MHz	793
AT&T 3B2/300	WE32000	?MHz	806
Apollo DN320	68010	?MHz	806

(Continued next page)

WORKSTATION LABORATORIES
COMPUTER PERFORMANCE (Continued)

Computer	Microprocessor	Processor Clockrate	Dhrystones Per Second
Apple Macintosh Plus*	68000	7.83MHz	850
AT&T 6300	8086	8MHz	943
Plexus P35	68000	10MHz	980
DEC PDP-11/73	KDJ11-AA	15MHz	981
Zilog S8000/11	Z8001	5.5MHz	1084
Natl Semiconductor ICM-3216	NSC 32016	10MHz	1084
DEC VAX 11/750	w/FPA		1091
Commodore Amiga 1000*	68000	7.18MHz	1100
AT&T PC7300	68010	10MHz	1111
Perkin-Elmer 3230			1126
Stride	68000	12MHz	1136
Atari 520 ST*	68000	8MHz	1200
MASSCOMP 500	68010	10MHz	1238
DEC PDP 11/70			1250
AT&T 3B2/400	WE32100	?MHz	1315
Intel 380	80286	8MHz	1315
Sun 2/120	68010	10MHz	1315
Perkin-Elmer 3250XP			1318
Data General MV4000			1333
IBM PC/AT	80286	8MHz	1380
IBM PC/AT	80286	6MHz	1388
AT&T PC6300+	80286	6MHz	1428
COMPAQ/286	80286	8MHz	1443
Cyb DataMate	68010	12.5MHz	1562
DEC MicroVAX-II			1612
DEC VAX 11/780			1662
Apollo DN660			1666
AT&T 3B20			1724
HP 9000-500	B series CPU		1724
NEC PC-98XA	80286	8MHz	1724
Apollo DN460*	TTL 68010 (Custom)		1800
DEC 2065	KL10-Model B		1946
Apollo DN330*	68020	12MHz	1950
Gould PN6005			1964

(Continued next page)

* Indicates Workstation Laboratories Dhrystone results. All others are public domain Dhrystone results.

WORKSTATION LABORATORIES
COMPUTER PERFORMANCE (Continued)

Computer	Microprocessor	Processor Clockrate	Dhrystones Per Second
DEC 2060	KL-10		2000
DEC VAX 11/785			2136
Apollo DN 3000*	68020	12MHz	2300
Sun 3/50*	68020	15 MHz	2500
Sun 3/160*	68020	16.67MHz	3300
IBM 4341-II			3333
Pyramid 90x	w/cache		3333
Silicon Graphics IRIS 2400T	68020	16.67MHz	3401
Sun 3/75	68020	16.67MHz	3571
IBM 4341	Model 12		3685
Sun 3/180	68020	16.67MHz	3846
IBM 4341	Model 12		3910
NCR Tower 32*	68020	16.67MHz	4000
MASSCOMP MC5400	68020	16.67MHz	4054
COMPAQ Deskpro 386*	80386	16MHz	4100
Alliant FX/8	CE		4347
Gould PN9080			4629
MASSCOMP MC5600/5700	68020	16.67MHz	4746
IBM RT PC Model 115*	IBM Custom ROMP		5100
Gould 1460-342	ECL proc.		5677
Sun 3/260*	68020	25MHz	6200
DEC VAX 8600			7142
Sperry (CCI Power 6)			10000
CRAY X-MP/12		105MHz	10204
IBM 3083			12500
CRAY IA		80MHz	13888
IBM 3083			13889
Amdahl 470 V/8			15560
CRAY X-MP/48		105MHz	17857
Amdahl 580			23076
Amdahl 5860			28970

* Indicates Workstation Laboratories Dhrystone results. All others are public domain Dhrystone results.

COMPUTER INDUSTRY ALMANAC
WHO HAS THE POWER? TOP COUNTRIES BY COMPUTING POWER
January 1987

COMPUTER INDUSTRY ALMANAC has calculated the computing power of 34 individual
countries and the total computing power in the world. The calculations are based on the estimated
number of computers (mainframes, minicomputers and microcomputers) in use in each country and
the estimated average processing power per computer in MIPS (million instructions per second).
The following table shows the top 10 countries ranked by computer processing power.

Rank	Country	Estimated MIPS (thousands)	Share of Total MIPS (%)
1	U.S.A.	12,739	53.85
2	Japan	2,463	10.41
3	United Kingdom	1,650	6.97
4	West Germany	911	3.85
5	France	736	3.11
6	Canada	600	2.54
7	Italy	522	2.21
8	Australia	206	0.87
9	Netherlands	164	0.69
10	Brazil	138	0.58

COMPUTER INDUSTRY ALMANAC
WHICH COUNTRIES HAVE THE MOST COMPUTING POWER PER CAPITA?
January 1987

COMPUTER INDUSTRY ALMANAC has estimated the number of computers in use per person
and the amount of computing power in MIPS (million instructions per second) per person. The
following table shows the top 10 countries ranked by computing power per capita.

Rank	Country	Computers in Use Per 1000 People	Computing Power MIPS/1000 People
1	U.S.A.	146	53.3
2	United Kingdom	87	29.5
3	Canada	71	23.6
4	Japan	57	20.4
5	Norway	54	18.4
6	Ireland	53	18.1
7	Singapore	52	16.6
8	Switzerland	47	16.1
9	Denmark	45	15.3
10	W. Germany	45	14.9

The worldwide average number of computers in use per 1000 people is 14. The worldwide average
computer power (in MIPS) per 1000 people is 4.9.

COMPUTER INDUSTRY TRIVIA

The staff of COMPUTER INDUSTRY ALMANAC has compiled the following facts and figures from various industry publications. The COMPUTER INDUSTRY ALMANAC makes no representation or warranties with regard to the accuracy of the contents and disclaims liability to any party for loss or damage caused by error or omissions.

Companies

A survey of 250 senior executives in financial services finds that only one-third of the executives who responded had tried to use information technology to gain a strategic edge.

Apollo Computer Inc. shipped its 20,000th workstation in 1986. The company has sold more than $700 million worth of workstations to over 1,200 corporate customers around the globe.

IBM delivered its 100,000th System/36 microcomputer in 1986.

IBM has registered the design of its PC AT system box, gaining 25 years of protection against copying by other manufacturers and suppliers, closing any loopholes that may have enabled others to sell PC AT look-alikes.

Lotus Development Corp. raised $32,000 for two charities--Oxfam Amerika and Project Bread. All employee donations were matched by the company on a two-to-one basis.

More than half of the states in the U.S. have some form of computer-literacy requirements and 36 states in the U.S. have designated a full-time state computer coordinator to promote computer education.

Name the companies that comprise the "BUNCH" in the mainframe world of IBM and the BUNCH. Answer: Burroughs, Univac (Sperry), NCR, Control Data, Honeywell. (Burroughs and Sperry are now Unisys. Needed: a new "B.")

Ryal R. Poppa brought about the biggest and fastest exit from Chapter 11: Storage Technology Corp. went from a $406 million loss in 1984 to a $2.22 million profit in 1985. The secret was making the company bigger by first making it smaller.

The largest private employer in New York state is International Business Machines Corp. with about 12,500 company employees in the Poughkeepsie area alone.

COMPUTER INDUSTRY TRIVIA (Continued)

Companies (Continued)

What company hired a private-investigating firm to ensure the security of new-product information among third-party developers?
Answer: Apple Computer Inc., Cupertino, CA

What company made the Fortune 500 faster than any other in U.S. history?
Answer: COMPAQ Computer Corporation in four years.

What corporation gives its employees a day off on February 11th in hopes that celebrating the birthday of Thomas A. Edison, the "father of research & development," will remind them of the importance of innovation in solving problems?
Answer: Cadnetix Corporation, Bolder, CO

What corporation is believed to have been the industry's largest buyer of business computers in 1986?
Answer: AT&T

What major cultural event cosponsored by Gould, Hewlett-Packard, and McDonnell Douglas was viewed by over 330 million people on Chinese television?
Answer: 1986 Super Bowl with the Bears and the Patriots.

Who are the "BIG THREE" in the PC software industry?
Answer: Lotus Development Corp., Microsoft Corp. and Ashton-Tate.

Who invented the "mouse" computer control made famous by Apple Corp., and also gave birth to Shakey, one of the world's first robots?
Answer: Stanford Research Institute (SRI), the world's second-largest non-profit research organization, of Menlo Park, CA.

Who sells the most computers to the government?
Answer: Sperry Corporation.

COMPUTER INDUSTRY TRIVIA (Continued)

Facts

A vintage 1971 Kenbak-1 personal computer with 256 bytes of memory won the Early Model Personal Computer Contest held at The Computer Museum in Boston on May 10, 1986.

AT&T has banned pregnant women from working on semiconductor production lines in response to a study finding high miscarriage rates in certain chip-making jobs where toxic substances are used to etch microscopic circuits onto silicon wafers.

According to a 1985 survey of 821 corporate chiefs, 64% thought computers helped managers, 27% kept a terminal within reach, 52% never used one, 18.5% used one often, and 27% used one "sometimes."

According to Congress' Office of Technology Assessment, the federal government maintains 3.5 billion records in computerized record systems creating a de facto national database containing personal information on most Americans.

At the end of 1985 the U.S. State Department had 16,527 employees overseas, including foreign nationals, and IBM had 163,294.

Can you name the world's first electronic computer?
Answer: Colossus, developed by Alan Turing in England. But others say it is the Z3 built by Konrad Zuse in Germany.

IBM's world-wide tax provision in 1984 was $5.04 billion. It would take 1.2 million Americans paying average taxes to equal those revenues.

Information resources represents 1.6% of the U.S. Federal government budget. Software represents 80% of the information budget.

It takes 20% to 30% longer to read the same material from computer screens than it does from paper.

Name the nation's three largest industries.
Answer: (1) Transportation equipment, 7.8% of the GNP, (2) food-related items, 7.4% of the GNP, and (3) electronics, 5.7% of the GNP.

Name the world's first computer market center?
Answer: The Infomart, located in Dallas, Texas. Its architectural inspiration is the Crystal Palace in London, England.

COMPUTER INDUSTRY TRIVIA (Continued)

Facts (Continued)

Scientists at the University of Illinois and General Electric Co. claim to have developed the world's fastest transistor; it switches 230 billion times-per-second (230GHz).

Some artists are now able to take a missing child's picture and change it into what the child might look like in the present through the use of computer programs.

Texan Mark Tracy, while using CompuServe's CB Simulator, met his wife-to-be over the network. They courted over the electronic airwaves for six months before meeting in person. May Mr. & Mrs. Tracy live happily ever after.

The Chocolate Software Co. of Los Angeles has Chocolate Bytes for sale. The Original Chocolate Byte was created as a publicity ploy to sell a cookbook on a floppy disk. The 4.8 ounce milk chocolate replica of a disk is available, but not the cookbook.

The House approved legislation in 1986 that would expand the collection and translation of Japanese scientific discoveries and technological advances for use by U.S. firms.

The Japan Electronic Dictionary Research Institute has a budget of 20 billion Yen for R&D on an electronic dictionary for the fifth-generation computer in four subjects: basic terms, technical terms, conceptual systems, and descriptive terms.

The Statue of Liberty's 100th birthday party, Liberty Weekend, was coordinated by a sophisticated data processing department. This department was responsible for ticketing and accreditation services for five shows over the four-day period.

The U.S. Information Agency will be taking an information technology show, Information U.S.A., on the road to Russia in 1987 as part of the cultural exchange pact signed in 1985 by President Reagan and Soviet Premier Mikhail Gorbachev.

The federal government estimates that if all of its documents were filed in filing cabinets placed side by side, the cabinets would extend more than 1,000 miles. Send in the computers!

The library of Congress is trying to determine if it is feasible to use optical disks both to preserve the library's vast collections and to make its materials more accessible to researchers and the general public.

The majority of cars are expected to have electronic dashboards in the next decade. The displays promise to offer a range of information not possible with traditional analog gauges.

COMPUTER INDUSTRY TRIVIA (Continued)

Facts (Continued)

There are 17,000 mainframes and minis and 100,000 micros in use by the federal government in 1986.

Today's personal computer user has equipment that costs less than $5,000 and has more power available than the machines used by the operator of a million-dollar mainframe of the late 1960s.

Visitors to the Massachusetts Institute of Technology on July 22, 1986, got a look at one of the first 3D images from a computer, a 9-in.-long car that appeared to float in space.

What are Japanese high-technology researchers studying in a quest to create smarter computers that think like humans?
Answer: Leeches, bugs, squids and slugs.

What does ENIAC mean?
Answer: ENIAC (Electronic Numeric Integrator and Calculator) is considered to be the first electronic computer in the U.S. Conceived by John W. Mauchly and J. Prespert Eckert, ENIAC's first calculation took two days to program and 20 seconds to run.

What state is vying for the title of "Software Capital"?
Answer: The Commonwealth of Massachusettes has donated $80,000 to the Massachusetts Software Council to fund a marketing campaign that is designed to make software as synonymous with Massachusetts as oranges are with Florida and potatoes with Idaho.

Figures

According to a survey done by the Association of Better Computer Dealers, (ABCD), the average computer-store salesperson sells over $372,000 worth of computer products annually.

The new title for the merged Burroughs and Sperry companies was chosen from 31,000 suggestions. The winner of the company-wide contest was Lee Machen of Atlanta, who received $5,000 for the suggestion. The winning title is Unisys Corporation.

COMPUTER INDUSTRY TRIVIA (Continued)

Miscellaneous

A best seller book in 1995 will probably be called, "Why Johnny and Lisa can't program."

Brooks' Law: Adding manpower to a late software project makes it later.

By the year 2000, personal computers will be as common as TVs, telephones and automobiles of the 80s.

Hoare's Law of Large Programs: Inside every large program is a small program struggling to get out.

It has been predicted that by the year 2000, high school students will not only pass the 3 "R" tests, but will also have to complete their computer literacy tests.

The computer project cycle: Wild enthusiasm, disillusionment, total confusion, search for the guilty, punishment of the innocent, and promotion of non-participants.

People

According to a recent report issued by the National Center for Computer Crime Data, the age of the greatest number of computer crime defendants is 22.

Prior to founding Lotus, Mitchell Kapor was interviewed for a position by Donald McLagan of Data Resources. Kapor did not get the job because McLagan thought he had too many ideas. Later, Kapor hired McLagan to come to work for him at Lotus.

Rear Admiral Grace Hopper's greatest contribution to data processing was her early recognition of the commercial applications of computers and her ability to attract the interest of business such as insurance companies and aerospace industry.

Steve Wozniak, a designer of the Apple II microcomputer, finally got his bachelor's degree in computer science from the University of California at Berkeley--10 years after creating the computer. He graduated as "Rocky Raccoon Clark."

Who built the first PC?
Answer: John Blankenbaker in 1971, 5 years before the first Apple. His computer was called the Kenbak-I PC.

COMPUTER INDUSTRY TRIVIA (Continued)

People (Continued)

Who coined the phrase "Silicon Valley"?
Answer: A journalist named Don C. Hoefler, who published a weekly newsletter called
Microelectronic News.

Who coined the term "artificial intelligence"?
Answer: John McCarthy, director of the Artificial Intelligence Laboratory at Stanford University,
while working on a research project at Dartmouth College in 1956.

Who is considered by some industry veterans to be the Father of the Mark I, the first real digital
computer?
Answer: Howard Aiken.

Who said, "Products don't have to be good--just adequate--to become industry standards"?
Answer: Adam Osborne.

Products

A Dutch flower farmer has almost doubled his profits by using a computer that tells him what to do
every day. It also waters the flowers, opens windows when needed and feeds the plants. The
greenhouse is kept at an even humidity and at 68ºF all year long.

A Holiday Inn in St. Petersburg-Clearwater, FL has equipped all its rooms with computer terminal
hook-ups and teleconferencing capabilities. How is that for "room-service"?

A Shakespearean data bank is being compiled using the Rev. Donald D. Lynch's computer program
that catalogs, sorts and outlines plots and characters in nearly all of Shakespeare's plays. Rev. Lynch
is an assoc. professor of English at Fairfield Univ.

A program, called Universe, is designed to generate plot outlines for soap operas for use as a
scriptwriter's assistant.

A researcher can enter a word into a personal computer and in seconds find every reference to it in a
20-volume encyclopedia. The volumes are stored digitally on a compact disk, the same kind of
silvery platter that plays music when read by a laser beam.

COMPUTER INDUSTRY TRIVIA (Continued)

Products (Continued)

Apple Computer Inc., National Geographic, and movie maker George Lucas have entered into a joint research arrangement to study the potential uses of compact disks, videodisks and other similar recording devices for new disk-storage technology.

Carnegie-Mellon University scientists developed a computer nicknamed "The Warp" that can drive a cart at less than 1 mile per hour. It uses a television camera to see the road.

Computers are now also being used for dogsled races to help calculate running times instantaneously during different heats and to produce hard copies of the results within minutes after the race is over.

Decisionware, Inc., is producing a program which analyzes grammar and writing style and suggests ways to improve them. The output file contains a marked-up copy of the input text and a summary with a grade level.

Do you know how long it took IBM to develop the Proprinter?
Answer: 2 1/2 years, rather than the usual 4 years by IBM past standards.

Dr. Ralph A. Korpman has developed a patient-care information system that will transfer patient record-keeping from hospital nursing stations to a computer along side the patient's bed. This is called the Ulticare system and costs about $10,000 per bed.

Federal war games staged at the Georgetown University Center for Strategic and International Studies use advanced computers to predict the performance of weapons systems. The war games examine response of U.S. leaders in simulated crisis activity.

Greeting-card software packages provide PC users with animated birthday greeting and all-occasion card maker packages including designer computer paper, envelopes and labels that jazz up all your computer sentiments.

Hitachi Ltd. sells a chip that tells how heavy the fish on the end of a line is--in case the fish gets away.

How many executives did IBM let talk to the press at its landmark Personal Computer introduction in 1981?
Answer: Two.

If you need to call home from 30,000 feet in the air, Airfone Inc. in Oak Brook, Illinois will provide the link from a pay telephone on some of the major airlines.

COMPUTER INDUSTRY TRIVIA (Continued)

Products (Continued)

International Geosystems Corp, a Canadian company, will mass produce a system that creates Chinese characters on a computer much more rapidly than previously devised systems.

K mart Corp. will link its stores with a state-of-the-art satellite network from GTE. GTE will create a private data and telecommunications network for K mart's point-of-sale systems.

Microcomputer mapping is a potent new tool for anybody who needs to understand and make decisions based on geographically oriented data.

Micrologic Inc. of Watertown, MA offers a homing device that can be activated by police tracking units to locate a stolen car.

Nolo Press in Berkeley, California offers a new software package, Willwriter, which makes writing your own will more palatable.

One giant to another--IBM is into communicating with whales. IBM donated a PC XT system to Marineland to establish communications with killer whales Corky and Orky.

Plastic surgeons can now use computer video equipment to show patients what their faces might look like with new features.

Scientists and historians in Southern California are using Imaging Technology's ITEX/PC to decipher an ancient manuscript that may be "the most significant Gospel text ever found."

Seattle is the first of 20 regional FAA centers to replace its 20-year-old computer system with a new $20 million host computer. It is designed to provide quicker and more comprehensive information to air traffic controllers.

South Korean semiconductor makers are banding together to invest close to $80 million to develop 4-MB dynamic random-access memories for mass production within three years.

The MicroAge franchise in Chicago has started a "computer ambulance" service to heal sick PCs. Sometimes problems can be solved over the phone, but if more care is needed, the "ambulance" will transport the computer to the "hospital."

The U.S. Olympic bobsled team is using state-of-the-art equipment and latest CAD techniques to create a fast aerodynamic bobsled. Designers are now able to analyze vibration, distortion under load, and stress data compiling information into graphics.

BITS AND MIPS - Copyright 1987 Computer Industry Almanac

COMPUTER INDUSTRY TRIVIA (Continued)

Products (Continued)

The Whetstone benchmark, used in comparing computer speeds, is named for the English locale where it was invented in the 1960s.

The history of the Statue of Liberty Restoration is recorded on an elaborate computer-aided design system. A series of two-dimensional designs that mark each step of the restoration and a three-dimensional graphic image of the statue are preserved.

The wine exchange links more than 125 wine and brandy producing, selling, buying, and shipping companies in 56 countries and handles thousands of transactions a day on a computerized system headquartered in Philadelphia.

What has become of the million-dollar computer, the Mark III, featured in Time Magazine in January 1950?
Answer: In 1956 it was dumped from a second-floor window at the Naval Proving Ground and sold as scrap for $60.

What is a "boss" button?
Answer: Some computer games are now equiped with a "boss button" you can hit and a dummy financial screen will appear. If you use the fake screen on your boss, you'd better have a good story too, as the same numbers always appear on the spreadsheet.

What is gallium arsenide used for?
Answer: Devotees predict it will surpass silicon as the material used for very high-speed circuits.

What is the "Wizard of Wall Street?"
Answer: A simulation computer game that can teach you the ins and outs of the stock market without "losing your shirt," so to speak.

You can now find a computer-learning program in the market geared to illiterate adults who read below the fourth-grade level or not at all. The computer talks to students, teaching them the basics without making them feel ashamed about mistakes.

COMPUTER INDUSTRY TRIVIA (Continued)

Words

According to David Ritchie, author of "The Computer Pioneers," the earliest mention of the word "computer" dates back to 1646. "Computers" were people who calculated the passage of time and drew up calendars.

Austin, Texas prefers Silicon Hills to Silicon Gulch for its high-tech nickname.

Can you name the two real high-technology centers in the U.S.?
Answer: Silicon Valley in California and Route 128 in Boston.

What does the term "SneakerNet" mean?
Answer: Taking the floppy disk from one computer network and dashing with it, in hand, over to another. This LAN is always up and running.

P. C. LETTER
THE OFFICIAL P.C. LETTER VAPORLIST
November 19, 1986

This table lists wares that have been announced but have never been released and therefore exist only in the vapor of announcement. Months in vapor is the time from the announcement date to the present.--COMPUTER INDUSTRY ALMANAC.

Reprinted with permission from Stewart Alsop's P.C. LETTER: THE INSIDER'S GUIDE TO THE PERSONAL COMPUTER INDUSTRY, November 19, 1986. Copyright 1986 by P.C. Letter Associates, Redwood City, CA.

Product	Company	Announced	Original date	Revised date	Months in vapor
File Server	Apple	01-85	09-85	?????	21
Crosstalk Mk.IV	Microstuff	04-85	06-85	11-86	18
Optical drive	Verbatim	07-85	12-87	NA	16
Hal	Lotus	11-85	12-86	NA	10
ADOS	IBM/Microsoft	02-86	03-87	NA	10
PC Pagemaker	Aldus Corp.	03-86	12-86	NA	8
Dbase Mac	Ashton-Tate	08-86	12-86	NA	4
Pageperfect	Beyond Words/Imsi	09-86	12-86	NA	2
QuadHPG	Quadram	09-86	02-87	NA	1
Manuscript	Lotus	10-86	12-86	NA	*
Mac Word 3.0	Microsoft	10-86	01-87	NA	*
Inboard/386	Intel	10-86	01-87	NA	*

INDEX

A

B

C

E

F

G

H

I

J

K

L

M

P

ABOUT THE EDITORS

Dr. Egil Juliussen is chairman and CEO of StoreBoard Inc., Intellisys, and Computer Industry Almanac, all of Dallas, TX. A native of Norway, Dr. Juliussen received B.S., M.S., and Ph.D. degrees in electrical engineering from Purdue University. He co-founded Dallas-based Future Computing Incorporated in 1980. Prior to that, Dr. Juliussen was with Texas Instruments Incorporated in Dallas.

Dr. Portia Isaacson co-founded Future Computing in 1980, Intellisys in 1985, and Computer Industry Almanac in 1986. She serves on the board of directors of Microsoft Corporation. Dr. Isaacson has been recognized as a visionary leader of the personal computer industry. She holds a Ph.D. in computer science from Southern Methodist University. Her other degrees include computer science, physics, and mathematics.

Luanne Kruse holds a bachelor of arts and master of arts in English from the University of Nebraska and a master of science in library science from the University of Illinois. Ms. Kruse pursued a career in college teaching and as a public librarian and special librarian for IBM and other companies. She was an analyst with Future Computing before joining Computer Industry Almanac as managing editor.

Dale N. Dukes has over 20 years' experience in sales and marketing in the electronics and graphic arts industries. He holds bachelor of science and master of science degrees in electrical engineering and a master of business administration degree from Harvard University. Mr. Dukes previously served as a vice president of Future Computing.

Please send me _____ copies of Computer Industry Almanac at $29.95 each (soft-cover) and _____ copies at $49.95 each (hard-cover).

Name _____

Company _____

Address _____

City, State, Zip _____

Signature _____

Charge my credit card (type) _____

Account No. _____

Expiration Date _____ Interbank No. _____

Please add $2.00 for the first copy and $.50 for each additional copy to cover postage and handling. (Texas residents please include 7.25% sales tax).

Dear Computer Industry Almanac Editors:
In the next edition of Computer Industry Almanac, I would like for you to include _____

_____

_____

_____

_____

_____

_____

You may call me for more information:

Name _____

Phone _____

Computer Industry Almanac
8111 LBJ Freeway
Dallas, TX 75251-1313

Computer Industry Almanac
8111 LBJ Freeway
Dallas, TX 75251-1313